A Natural History of the Chicago Region

A Natural History
of the Chicago Region

JOEL GREENBERG

The University of Chicago Press
Chicago and London

PUBLISHER'S NOTE:
A Natural History of the Chicago Region is the second volume in a new series titled Center Books on Chicago and Environs, created and directed by the Center for American Places. The series, and therefore this book, is supported in part by a grant from the Graham Foundation for Advanced Studies in the Fine Arts. The inaugural volume, *The City in a Garden: A Photographic History of Chicago's Parks*, is also available from the University of Chicago Press.

The University of Chicago Press, Chicago 60637
The University of Chicago Press, Ltd., London
© 2002 by The University of Chicago
All rights reserved. Published 2002
Paperback edition 2004
Printed in the United States of America

11 10 09 08 07 06 05 04   2 3 4 5

ISBN: 0-226-30648-8 (cloth)

ISBN: 0-226-30649-6 (paperback)

Library of Congress Cataloging-in-Publication Data

Greenberg, Joel (Joel R.)
   A natural history of the Chicago Region / Joel Greenberg.
      p.   cm. — (Center books on Chicago and environs)
Includes bibliographical references (p.).
   ISBN 0-226-30648-8 (cloth : alk. paper)
      1. Natural history—Illinois—Chicago Region.   2. Nature—Effect of human beings on —Illinois—Chicago Region.   I. Title.   II. Series.
QH105.13 G74 2002
508.773'11—dc21

2002000244

♾ The paper used in this publication meets the minimum requirements of the American National Standard for Information Sciences—Permanence of Paper for Printed Library Materials, ANSI Z39.48-1992.

To my parents—Sam (1909–91) and Miriam—to whom I owe everything. No parents could have been more supportive.

And I should see you again as I saw you, and I should love you again as I loved you. . . . My thoughts are all filled with you — you who brighten my past when I look back, a past which is bright because of you and which would be dark without you — you who appear to me still young and beautiful and charming as in other days.

Philippe Regis de Trobriand, *Military Life in Dakota* (1951)

Contents

This project began in the fall of 1983 with my mother and me spending our Saturdays combing the holdings of the Chicago Historical Society. Later, I shared my idea with Phil Hanson of the Field Museum, who had done extensive historical natural history research himself (and who, by the way, sent me off on a great beginning by sharing his wonderful files with me). He said that what I wanted to do should take about ten years.

Seventeen years have now elapsed. Although there were periods of relative inactivity, I was always collecting relevant items. That part was fun. Sitting down to write proved to be more difficult. But like the inevitable birth after a long gestation, I began the manuscript in the fall of 1993. From July 1994 to November 1996, I worked on it full time, preparing most of the text. Living on savings and not knowing much about publishing, those were lonely and scary days. Since then, I have devoted most of my spare time to completing the text, finding illustrations, making revisions, and handling other matters related to finishing the book.

In that same seventeen-year period, I have become middle-aged, loved ones have died, and others have moved far away. At least three people who spent time talking into my tape recorder are now deceased. Apropos of this theme, the first time I attempted to interview someone for the book was in September 1983. I contacted the person, a leader among local naturalists and conservationists, and was admonished that I couldn't "just call someone up to pick their brain." He then suggested one or two titles from which I could get everything I needed. A decade passed before I would interview anyone else, but the positive responses and the valuable information I gathered from those later interviews encouraged me to call that first person again. He told me that he had suffered a stroke and most of his memory was gone.

Also during those years, natural history and conservation have moved into the realm of the mainstream. There are growing numbers of birders, stewards, and others who spend large portions of their spare time pursuing natural history goals. Newspapers devote extensive space to these subjects. In many of the collar counties, open space preservation is the cutting-edge issue that dominates political discourse. Federal, state, and local governments have dramatically increased the land they hold and manage for conservation purposes, and they sponsor extensive programming designed to educate the citizenry on the joys and importance of natural history. (Nature centers are everywhere.) Chicago Wilderness (a broad coalition of conservation organizations and agencies) and the various efforts to implement smart growth have also raised the profile of biodiversity and the need for careful land use.

By increasing understanding of local ecosystems and their history, this book will, I hope, contribute, to this growing appreciation of the region's natural history. I document some of the major changes that have occurred in the flora and fauna of the Chicago region since the beginning of European settlement. By examining the early accounts and then moving forward in time, I hope to create a prose version of a time-lapse movie. At the end, the reader will have a good sense of which biota were here, how distribution and abundance have changed, and what remains. While only a tiny fraction of the land surface is still in a state that even approaches its original character, it is surprising how many plants and animals have managed to survive.

Another way to describe this effort is to compare it with William Cronon's highly regarded *Nature's Metropolis*, which chronicles the economic growth of Chicago through the process of what he calls "nature to market." My book could be seen as a flipside of his: rather than looking at the market, I will be looking at nature.

These seventeen years have also seen an expansion in land management on the part of agencies and others. I have tried to emphasize nature's complexities, for I think people need to be reminded that there is much that we still don't know, and that for every action we take (or not take) there are a host of "side-effects." (People tend to see things in black and white, while the truth is often gray.) Ideally, land managers should see their work as experimental and needing to be adaptive. But so much is invested in these activities, there is often little opportunity for reflection or alteration of practices.

It is not my goal, nor would it even be possible, to discuss every species known to inhabit the region. This is not meant to be an encyclopedia. Excellent books have been written presenting identification keys and annotated checklists cataloguing the occurrence and distribution of local vascular plants, birds, mammals, thrips, lichens, etc. (The bibliography identifies many of these treatises so that the interested reader can pursue the subject further.)

I will focus on organisms that characterize their habitat, illustrate ecological processes and principles, are rare because they are habitat dependent or intolerant of human disturbance (the absence or presence of such organisms often tells more about the land than does the status of common species which are capable of thriving in a broad range of conditions), have become extirpated, are spectacular, have been introduced by people and threaten native ecosystems, and/or have become part of a relationship with people due to hunting, harvesting, forensics, or other human activities. And some are probably included because I know them and like them.

Coverage is often limited by the simple fact that very little has been written about the species or its group. This is the case with arthropods; while the overwhelming number of animals are in this phylum, a limited amount of material is available of the type I was seeking. Beetle movements did not grab the attention of the pioneers like those of passenger pigeons. (I have mused that it would be an interesting exercise to get, say, five people all with different emphases to write a natural history of the region. No doubt, five very different books would be produced.)

The Chicago region as defined in this book encompasses the following nineteen counties: Cook, DuPage, Grundy, Kane, Kankakee, Kendall, Lake, McHenry, and Will in Illinois; Jasper, Lake, La Porte, Newton, Porter, and Starke in Indiana; Kenosha, Racine, and Walworth in Wisconsin; and Berrien in Michigan. (Maps are in the appendix.) This is consistent with most recent works on the region's natural history. Swink and Wilhelm (*Plants of the Chicago Region*) deviate by adding to their coverage DeKalb and Boone Counties in Illinois and St. Joseph County in Indiana. Their increase in area does not significantly add to the diversity of the region. Occasionally, accounts from outside the nineteen counties are included because they are extremely close to the edge of the region (Dwight, Illinois, the site of some superb descriptions, is two miles south of the Kankakee County line), or cover a subject much better than any originating within this region's borders.

While exact locations of rare plants and insects are usually not given, the reader will become familiar with many of the best places to enjoy local natural history. (*A Birder's Guide to the Chicago Region* by Lynne Carpenter and me, published by Northern Illinois University Press, provides detailed maps and directions to most of these sites.) These are discussed throughout the text, along with their preservation histories. Within these pages is by far the most extensive treatment yet attempted of the region's conservation battles.

Given how long I have been wed to this undertaking, I realize that the number of people who have contributed either directly or indirectly are legion. In a way, everyone I have ever been in the field with, or otherwise learned something from, added to the final product. This list, as extensive as it is, is therefore only partial. To those who aren't named, you have my deepest appreciation.

My appreciation also goes to the individuals and institutions (roughly forty in all) who provided the illustrations that add so much to this project; acknowledgements appear by the pictures.

This book is immeasurably richer because of the generous souls who either shared information through the mail or over the telephone or graciously spent varying lengths of time talking into my tape recorder. (These interviews spanned a period from the fall of 1993 to the fall of 1996.) I now list those whom I interviewed in person: Tom Anton (herpetofauna), Bert Atkinson (Lake Michigan fish), Dr. William Beecher (birds and prairies), Dr. Robert Betz (prairie ecology and conservation), Dr. Laurence Binford (birds), Dr. Gary Casper (Wisconsin herpetofauna), Ed Collins (mussels and pre-settlement landscape), Kevin Cummings (mussels and other riverine biota), Dr. Gerard Donnelly (forests, particularly Warren Woods), Peter Dring (salamanders and other topics), Alen Feldman (biota of Lake Michigan), Joe Ferencak (fish of rivers and small glacial lakes), Garyn Fyffe ("nuisance" wildlife), the late Gordon Graves (Kankakee River), Dr. Bernard Greenberg (flies and forensic entomology), Dr. Ralph Grundel (Karner blue butterfly), Lynn Hepler (forests and other topics), Rich Hess (Lake Michigan fisheries), Ken Klick (vegetation of Lake Michigan rim), Ed Lace (herpetofauna), Dr. Lawrence Leitner (forests, savannas, and restoration), Irwin Leeuw (butterflies), Dr. J. Ellen Marsden (Lake Michigan biota), Dave Mauger (Will County herpetofauna), Jody Melton (Kankakee River), Dr. Jon Mendelson (forests, savannas and other topics), Judy Mendelson (forests and other topics), Robert Morris (prairie chickens), Dr. Alfred Newton (insects), Dr. Lawrence Page (fish and other aquatic biota), Dr. Ron Panzer (many topics particularly *Papapeima* moths, Hine's emerald dragonfly, and other prairie insects), Dr. Noel Pavlovic (Indiana Dunes and other topics), Irwin Polls (aquatic invertebrates and other topics), Dr. Tom Poulson (Warren Woods, Indiana Dunes, and other topics), Al Puplis (Mitchell's satyr), Charlotte Read (Indiana Dunes), Herbert Read (Indiana Dunes), Michael Redmer (herpetofauna), Alan Resetar (Indiana herpetofauna), Dr. Wayne Schennum (many topics), Greg Seegert (fish), Charles and Judy Sirk (Mitchell's satyr), Paul Strand (prairies and sand savannas), Steve Swanson (herpetofauna), the late Floyd Swink (Illinois Beach, Indiana Dunes, and other topics), Chris Taylor (crayfish), Dr. Nancy Tuchman (Lake Michigan biota, particularly algae and zebra mussels), Dr. Donald Webb (aquatic insects, particularly winter stoneflies), Charles Westcott (birds and particularly prairie chicken reintroduction), Al Westerman (forests, particularly those in Lake

County, IL), Dr. Gerould Wilhelm (rediscovery of leafy prairie clover and other topics), Andrew Williams (insects), the late Bill Wingate (many topics concerning McHenry County), Brad Woodson (river biota), and Dr. Daniel Young (American burying beetles and other insects).

Many of these people also reviewed portions of the manuscript. In that task they were joined by David Aftandilian, Karen Anderson, Dr. Val Beasley, Dr. Richard Brewer, Dan Brouilliard, Dr. James Chapman, Dr. Kenneth Brock, Mike Carpenter, Dr. Mike Chrzastowski, Dr. Don Fago, James Francis, Bill Glass, Dr. Robert Grese, Dr. Ardith Hansel, Philip Hanson, Christie Henry, Dr. Jim Herkert, Dr. Scott Hickman, Janine Kostecki, Dr. James Lloyd, Dr. John Losey, Dr. Dan Ludwig, Dr. Hiltje Maas, Dr. Betsy Mendelsohn, Dr. William Moskoff, Paul Petraitus, Robert Russell, Dr. Jennifer Shopland, Mary Kay Solecki, Dr. Michael Stewart, Dr. Robert Todd, Dr. John Whitaker, Ray Wiggers, Adrian Wydeven, and Yvonne Zipter.

In a category by himself, Floyd Swink applied his remarkable knowledge of the region's natural history and his brilliance as a copy editor to most of the manuscript. (Who else would have caught my misspelling of Henry Eenigenburg?) I cringe at the thought of the errors that might have survived had it not been for this kind gentleman.

Tragically, Floyd died in August of 2000. Everyone who cares about conservation and the natural history of this region mourned this great loss. His passing marks the end of an era.

Ariel Rogers kindly granted permission to use lines from Stan Rogers's beautiful song "White Squall" (© 1984).

Another group has helped me with research, manuscript review, and in other important ways: John Alesandrini, Dr. Brian Anderson, Steve Apfelbaum, Renee Baade, Dr. Sot Barber, Richard Barloga, Phil Bernstein, John Bielefeldt, Marlin Bowles, Glenda Brown, Allen Bruner, Georgina Collins, Grace Dickler, Philip Hanson, Dr. Donald Hey, Libby Hill, interlibrary loan staff of the Glenview Public Library, Dr. John Koprowski, Ron Kurowski, Steve McShane, Margo Milde, Kip Miller, Mike Penskar, Rita Renwick, Robert Russell, Rita Rutledge, Keith Ryder, Caroline Schoenberger, John Shuey, Tom Skilling, Andy Sigler, Kevin Stanziel, Alan Stokie, Ron Vasile, Dr. Jane Walsh-Brown, and Charlie Warrick.

Then there was another small group who provided the support (on many levels) that made the completion of this task eminently more endurable, if not possible. (There were others who made the task more difficult, but of course they must remain nameless.) This assistance was particularly critical during and just after the 3.5 years when I devoted myself almost entirely to the writing of the manuscript. To all of you, I am so very grateful: Renee and David

Baade, John Ball, David Beilenberg, Fairbank and Lynne Carpenter, Dr. Ken Derickson, Danny Diaz, Bill Eyring, Carolyn Fields, Dan Gooch, Miriam and the late Sam Greenberg, Robin Greenberg, Travis Greenberg, Lynn Hepler, Libby and Dr. Win Hill, Dave Johnson, Cindy Kerchmar (who truly endured a lot—may it all have been worthwhile), Ruth Levin, Bob Levin, Tina Osborne, and Celeste A. Thorne.

The Great Forces

Scenery graces the American land in a way that seems haphazard. But that is not really true. . . . Each landscape is the result of the complex interplay of many forces throughout the long history of the continent. The true impact of landscape upon the beholder is not the present scene alone. Rather, understanding lies in knowledge of the many forces— climate, vegetation, soil, geologic change— that have molded the scene. —Peter Farb (1963)

Sometime during July 1673, seven men exploring on behalf of New France and Catholicism left the Mississippi River and proceeded up the Illinois River. They reached the Des Plaines River, which they ascended to the portage that would lead them to the Chicago River and Lake Michigan. Commanded by Father Jacques Marquette and Louis Joliet, this party of Frenchmen became the first Europeans known to have entered the Chicago region. Marquette described his impressions: "We have seen nothing like this river that we enter, as regards its fertility of soil, its prairies and woods; its cattle, elk, deer, wildcats, bustards, swans, ducks, parroquets, and even beaver. There are many small lakes and rivers. That on which we sailed is wide, deep, and still, for 65 leagues. In the spring and during part of the summer there is only one portage of half a league."[1]

Joliet echoed the sentiments of the priest in even more glowing terms: "The river which we named for Saint Louis [Illinois River] which rises near the lower end of lake of the Illinois [Lake Michigan], seemed to me the most beautiful, and most suitable for settlement. . . . The river is wide and deep, abounding in catfish and sturgeon. Game is abundant there; oxen, cows, stags, does, and turkeys are found there in greater numbers than elsewhere. For a distance of eighty leagues, I did not pass a quarter of an hour without seeing some."[2]

The land they had reached lies within a great ecotone—a zone of

1

ecological transition where hardwood forests meet tallgrass prairies. It is contested ground where trees compete with grass for dominance. Fires were frequent and tipped the balance in favor of prairie, which, along with the transitional shrubland and savanna, covered most of the region. Where ravines, water, or other barriers blocked the advancing flames, forests took hold.

As the great glacier that had covered the area for thousands of years melted and receded northward, vast quantities of water were left behind to create and nourish the lakes, rivers, and wetlands that adorned the landscape. These included Lake Michigan (the third largest of the Great Lakes) and some of the grandest marshes in inland North America. The force of the glacier also ordained that the Chicago region would straddle the eastern Continental Divide, separating the drainage area of the Atlantic Ocean from that of the Gulf of Mexico. The rivers Des Plaines, Fox, Kankakee, and their tributaries were in the Illinois and Mississippi watershed, while the Chicago, Calumet, Pike, Root, and St. Joseph fed the Great Lakes. (The Kishwaukee River, draining portions of McHenry, Kane, and Walworth counties, is in the Rock River watershed, and the Tippecanoe River, draining small parts of Starke and Jasper Counties, is in the Ohio River watershed.)

We will never know exactly how this region looked three hundred years ago. Attempts to decipher its original appearance have relied heavily on the data generated by the U.S. Public Land Surveys conducted in the region from 1821 (when Cook County's surveys began) to 1841 (when surveys in Kane and Lake Counties in Illinois were completed). These surveys created a national grid whereby property could be located with ease and precision. In the process, the surveyors noted tree species and size, prairies, location of water bodies, and other landscape features. Their work is the closest thing that scientists have to a systematic inventory of early nineteenth-century plant cover.

A number of ecologists have combined these data with soil distribution, travelers' descriptions, geologic features, and other information to create maps depicting vegetation at the time of the surveys. (For examples, see figs. 1–5.) As you can see, the maps are not uniform in the number and types of plant communities portrayed. This reflects differences not only among authors but also in the plant community classifications in vogue at the time of map preparation and the detail and accuracy of the surveyors' work. Despite their limitations, however, these maps are valuable as another source for illustrating the diversity that once defined this region.

That diversity brought to the land an almost unimaginable fertility and an abundance of life that in some manifestations was unrivaled by any other terrestrial environment on earth. To understand and appreciate this remarkable bounty, one must look at how it came to be.

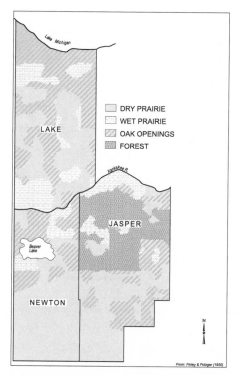

1. Four major vegetation types in Lake, Newton, and Jasper Counties, Indiana, at time of settlement; from Finley and Potzger (1952). (Courtesy Butler University, Indianapolis.)

Ice Sculptor: Glaciation

Part of a huge sheet of ice born in the Laurentide Mountains of Quebec, the Lake Michigan lobe of the Wisconsin Glacial Episode covered the Chicago region until about 13,800 years ago. The Wisconsin was the most recent of a series of glacial episodes over 2 million years, and it obliterated most of the topographic barriers left by its predecessors. The flowing ice, augmented by rocks that adhered to it, leveled the unconsolidated sediments in its path and filled vast areas with the crushed earth it had picked up along the way.

Because the underlying land was not uniform, neither was the glacial advance. The ice mass cut deeper and traveled farther in valleys where the substrate was softer. These advances, or lobes, gouged out tremendous amounts of earth, enough to create their masterpieces: the five Great Lakes holding more than 25 percent of the planet's unfrozen fresh water. The valley that was to hold Lake Michigan was deepened five hundred to nine hundred feet.

Just as a turn of the climatic cycle launched the glacier southward from

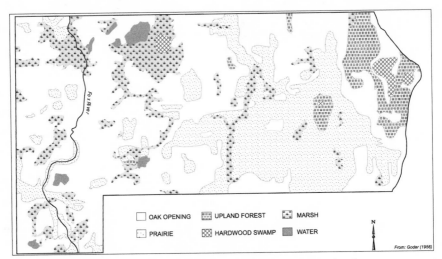

2. Vegetation of Racine County at time of settlement; from H. Goder (1956).

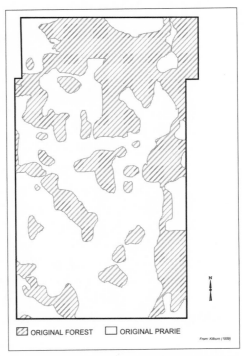

3. Forest and prairie cover in Kane County, Illinois, at time of
settlement; from P. Kilburn (1959). (Courtesy American
Midland Naturalist.)

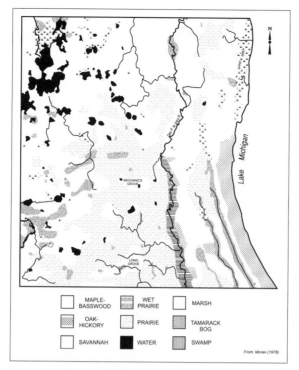

4. Vegetation of Lake County, Illinois, at time of settlement; from
R. Moran (1978a). (Courtesy Iowa State University, Ames.)

its Canadian mooring, a warming trend halted its advance. As temperatures
gradually increased, the ice began to melt, leaving water and pulverized earth
in its wake. These remains formed the plains, uplands, rivers, and lakes that essentially make up the landscape of the Chicago Region. (Depositions by winds
and tides, erosion, and beaver activity have wrought more recent changes.)
Based on these glacial features, geographers have divided the Chicago region
into seven natural divisions.[3] (See fig. A1.)

Where the ice receded without interruption, the material left behind became ground moraines (also known as till plains), marked by flat or gently
rolling surfaces. But the glacial retreat, like its advance, was uneven and halt-
ing. Where it stalled, the crushed earth and rock accumulated and became terminal moraines. A series of these moraines parallels and encircles the southern
portion of Lake Michigan to form three concentric U-shaped uplands. The
morainal system farthest from the lake is the Outer Uplands and includes Kane
County, much of western McHenry County, and the southern portions of
Jasper and Starke Counties but otherwise lies beyond the Chicago region.

Located in the middle, the Valparaiso Upland is the highest of the morainal systems, reaching 1,140 feet above sea level near Lake Geneva, Walworth

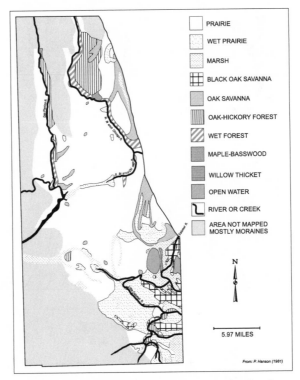

☐	PRAIRIE
⬚	WET PRAIRIE
⬚	MARSH
⊞	BLACK OAK SAVANNA
▦	OAK SAVANNA
▥	OAK-HICKORY FOREST
▨	WET FOREST
▦	MAPLE-BASSWOOD
▩	WILLOW THICKET
▣	OPEN WATER
⌐	RIVER OR CREEK
▨	AREA NOT MAPPED MOSTLY MORAINES

5.97 MILES

From: P. Hanson (1981)

5. Vegetation of the Chicago Lake Plain (Cook County) at time of settlement; from P. Hanson (1981). (Courtesy Philip Hanson.)

County. Its northern sector, principally Walworth, McHenry, Kane, and Lake Counties in Illinois, exhibits some of the most picturesque scenery in the region: where earthen debris accumulated in cavities and channels of the thinning glacier, cone-shaped kames and the serpentiform ridges of eskers rise up from the flat countryside. The ebbing ice also endowed this portion of the upland with numerous lakes, including Lake Geneva, the Chain O' Lakes complex, Lake Elizabeth, Lake Zurich, and Lake Delevan.

Farther south, the Valparaiso Upland becomes less pronounced. Its relative flatness is seen to good advantage from a plane landing at Chicago's O'Hare Airport. As the moraine sweeps around the end of Lake Michigan into Indiana, it becomes three gently rolling ridges roughly coincident with U.S. Route 6 in Lake County and U.S. Route 30 in La Porte County. Cedar Lake is the only water body of any size.

The third morainal complex, and the youngest, is the Lake Border Upland. Its name is derived from the discontinuous bluff, in places reaching an elevation of 140 feet above the lake, that rims the Lake Michigan shoreline in northern Racine County and then from Waukegan southward to Winnetka. Numerous ravines, over thirty of them in the Illinois portion, cut the bluff

6. Knob and swale topography of Kettle Moraine State Forest. (Courtesy
Kettle Moraine State Forest Archives, Eagle, Wis.)

perpendicular to the lake and provide a microclimate suitable for certain
northern plants not otherwise found here. These picturesque landscapes also
provide the location for many of the region's aristocracy, whose estates have often afforded protection to these rare natural communities. Two of the area's
principal military installations are located here as well: Fort Sheridan, now de-
activated, was established as Camp Highwood in 1887 to protect those same
rich families should Chicago's social unrest threaten their baronial home-
steads, and the Great Lakes Naval Training Center, in North Chicago,
through which all of the nation's naval recruits must pass.

The Lake Border Upland was poorly drained by the shallow and slow-
moving Des Plaines, Skokie, north branch of the Chicago, Root, and Pike
rivers. As a result, extensive wetlands developed between the moraines. The
largest was the Skokie Marsh, converted into the Skokie Lagoons by the Civil-
ian Conservation Corps in the 1930s.

As the shrinking glacier retreated northward, the furrow enlarged by the
Lake Michigan lobe filled with water. Hemmed in by the glacial edge and the
Valparaiso Moraine, this meltwater ponded and formed Lake Chicago, an early
stage of ancestral Lake Michigan. (Geologists consider Lake Chicago to have
ended when its icy margin melted about eleven thousand years ago.) Expanding waters of the lake eventually cut through the morainal dike at two points
near Willow Springs in southern Cook County and flowed southwest toward

the Illinois River. The northern or Des Plaines channel provided the main outflow and the southern, known as the Sag, was a tributary that joined it about two miles downstream. Geologists refer to the stream formed by the convergence as the Chicago Outlet. The roughhewn piece of land turned into an island by the outlets became known as Mount Forest Island, now a part of the Palos Forest Preserve complex.

The swollen stream leaving Lake Chicago tore at its banks, creating a bluff-lined channel that was to become the lower Des Plaines River Valley. For twenty miles, from Willow Springs to Joliet, this segment of the Des Plaines provides locally unique habitat for such rare organisms as leafy prairie clover and Hine's emerald dragonfly. With the completion in 1848 of the Illinois and Michigan Canal, which linked the Illinois River and Lake Michigan, and in 1900 of the Chicago Sanitary and Ship Canal, the valley also became a major transportation route between the Mississippi and Great Lakes watersheds. In 1984, the National Park Service designated the Illinois and Michigan Canal as the country's first National Heritage Corridor. The corridor now draws over 1.3 million people a year.

The Chicago area's first tourist attraction, and one of its most notable geologic features, once stood near the edge of the Des Plaines River near Joliet, a creation of the same waters that raged out of Lake Chicago. Known as Mount Joliet, it was a gravel mound shaped in the figure of a cone except that it had a perfectly flat top. Unfortunately, people of the twentieth century know it only from the accounts of early travelers, for over 130 years have passed since the majority of it was hauled away to become city streets and ballast for railroad beds. But starting as early as the 1690s, visitors went out of their way to view it, and, curiously, estimates of its height increased over the years from sixty to one hundred feet. By the time James Paulding saw Mount Joliet in 1848, part of it had been removed during construction of the Illinois and Michigan Canal. Despite the marring, he could still write: "This mound is one of the most remarkable, as well as beautiful objects in nature. . . . It is as regular and perfect in construction, form, and outline as any work of art I ever saw. . . . It is, however, . . . a production of the cunning hand of Nature, who sometimes it would seem, amuses herself by showing how much she can excel her illegitimate sister, Art, even in her most successful attempts at imitation."[4]

Over the thousands of years of its existence, Lake Chicago shrank in a series of successively lower lake phases. (See chap. 10.) When the ice eventually melted throughout the Great Lakes basin, changing elevation and drainage produced the modern configuration of Lake Michigan.

The receding of Lake Chicago's frigid waters exposed previously submerged land that became known as the Chicago Lake Plain. (In Indiana, some people now refer to it as the Calumet Lake Plain.) Millennia of inundation left this land extremely flat, leveled by waves and the still-water deposition of clays. Lake Michigan received the waters of the lake plain via the Root, Pike, Chicago, and Calumet Rivers, the latter two of which now flow toward the Mississippi because of canal construction and other engineering projects.

Most of the relief is provided by three elongated ridges, each of which corresponds to the shoreline of a particular stage of Lake Chicago. But the most massive lake relic of all is six-mile long Blue Island, Cook County, a detached extension of the Lake Border Upland that rises eighty feet above the plain. According to an old newspaper article quoted by historian Ferdinand Schapper, Blue Island, "when viewed from a distance, appears standing in an azure mist or vapor." As for the other part of its name, it was: actually an island, poking above the icy waters of Lake Chicago; practically an island, surrounded by marsh and streams; and metaphorically an island as its timbered slopes rose above the prairie.[5]

Certainly, it would have been hard to imagine that such a landscape as the Chicago Lake Plain, with its marshes, timbered slopes, and prairies, would eventually become the setting for the people, commerce, and industry that have helped define the nation's heartland. The cities of Racine, Kenosha, Waukegan, Michigan City, and St. Joseph are here. So are the Bahai Temple (Wilmette, Cook County), Northwestern University (Evanston, Cook County), Oak Park's (Cook County) concentration of homes designed by Frank Lloyd Wright, and the steel mills of Gary. But the anchor for the region is, of course, Chicago. Home to 2.8 million people, the city draws millions each year as visitors to the Lincoln Park Zoo, Field Museum, Art Institute, McCormick Place, and Shedd Aquarium. Wrigley Field, Comiskey Park, Soldier Field, and the United Center provide examples of both the oldest and newest of professional sports venues. Rooted in the dolomite bedrock, the John Hancock Building, Sears Tower, and other architectural wonders that distinguish Chicago's skyline stand high above the ancient lakebed.[6] Farther south, cultural features include Jackson Park, the University of Chicago, Museum of Science and Industry, and historic Pullman, America's first planned industrial city.

Not only was the Lake Plain attractive to the masses who settled there, it also held some of the region's most significant natural areas. Three are of such importance they warrant mention here. Although constantly augmented by wind and lake currents, the Indiana Dunes were originally the creation of wind-borne sand uncovered by the waning Lake Chicago. The pioneering ecologist Henry Cowles called these dunes "the grandest in the entire world," and most of what is left of them is now under state or federal protection.[7] The Calumet region, on the Illinois-Indiana border, held marshes that were equally grand. Today, we can barely comprehend the abundance of wildlife that once inhabited them. Unfortunately, that area is where Chicago in effect decided to defecate, and most of the former wetlands are now buried under waste. Although perhaps lacking the historical or national significance of the other two sites, Illinois Beach State Park, Zion (Lake County, Ill.), encompasses more relatively undisturbed natural communities than any other place in Illinois.

Sandwiched between the Outer Upland and the Valparaiso Upland are two lowlands considered distinct physiographic provinces. The smaller is known as the Manteno Plain, a wedge-shaped region of ground moraines. The larger Morris-Kankakee Basin combines the Morris Basin, a former glacial lake, and the Kankakee Basin, a valley covered with sand by glacial meltwater and through which the Kankakee River flows. Within its borders are the "swamp and dunes" near Braidwood, Will County, which the botanist Willard Clute studied so carefully, and the once huge Kankakee marshes that rivaled Calumet in their marvelous richness.[8]

Fertility Underfoot: Soils

In its slow and grinding march of expansion and contraction, the ice sheet left behind not only the conspicuous landforms just described but also the more evenly distributed deposits of granulated rock and earth. These deposits are categorized by the size of their particles. The most common of these in this area are clay (the finest grained), silt (less finely grained), sand (coarse), loam (a combination of the previous three and often organic material), and gravel (most coarse).

Although there are a few places where the underlying bedrock is exposed (particularly along the lower Des Plaines, Fox, and Kankakee River valleys), these deposits cover most of the region at depths of seventy-five feet or more. They are the precursors of soil, that layer of varying thickness and character that anchors terrestrial life and reflects the history of the land.

Soils develop from a base known as "soil parent materials." The manner of deposition determines the classification of these materials. In the Chicago region, the most frequently occurring soil parent materials are till (deposited by glacial ice), outwash (deposited by glacial meltwater), alluvium (deposited by rivers and streams), loess (silt deposited by wind), and eolian sand (deposited by wind).

The parent materials and the size of the particles determine the distribution of soils across the landscape. Gravel, for example, being large and heavy was moved by ice (till) and, for shorter distances, by meltwater (outwash); concentrations of it occur in morainal areas. Sand and silt took longer to settle out of water and are common in areas that were formerly submerged such as the Chicago Lake Plain and the Morris-Kankakee Basin. Clay, which took a very long time to settle, is thickest on lands once covered by sheltered ponds and bays. The silt exposed by receding rivers was often deposited as loess, most heavily on the east sides of valleys.

Parent materials became soils through the many agents of change to which they were subjected. Chemical and mechanical forces break down the particle sizes even further and facilitate the downward percolation of clay. Age, slope, and climate are other critical factors in the formation of the more than two hundred soil series that occur in the Chicago region. (Series are to soils as species are to plants and animals.)

Biotic factors are among the most important in determining soil character. Soils that developed under prairies (mollisols) have substantially more organic material than those that formed under forests (alfisols). The quantity of vegetative biomass produced in a prairie is similar to that of an oak woods, but the location of that material is different. Prairie grasses and forbs (herbaceous plants) send their roots deep into the earth to form dense tangles, the first three and a half feet of which can weigh more than 150 tons an acre. The same distance below the surface of an oak woods, however, yields only eighty tons of organic matter per acre; ninety tons are in trunks, limbs, and leaves.

The subterranean mats of woven roots further enrich the mollisols by providing habitat for numerous organisms, from moles to earthworms to bacteria. These inhabitants of the nether zones facilitate the decomposition of surface and subsurface plant matter, keep the soil loose and aerated, and replenish the nitrogen that is so critical to soil fertility. From an agricultural perspective, the deep and black mollisols are among the best soils in the world, a fact that goes a long way to explaining why the tallgrass prairie is virtually extinct.[9]

Atmospheric Impacts: Climate and Weather

Solving the puzzle of the ecotonal landscape was an exercise that took over 150 years. By the end of the nineteenth century, at least ten different theories attempted to explain why some land supported prairie at the expense of forest. Among the factors thought to cause prairies were soil origin, soil composition, bison, a combination of fire and drought, and fire alone.[10] While fire was the most often cited cause during that period, the scientists who worked at the beginning of the twentieth century largely rejected it in favor of climate. Botanists determined that the formation of prairie occurs where the ratio of precipitation to evaporation falls between 60 and 80 percent and is promoted by extreme droughts.[11] In rebutting the fire camp, Henry Gleason noted that "in order to have a prairie fire, you first must have a prairie."[12]

Biologists eventually reached the consensus that climate and fire are the keys to deciphering the complicated vegetation patterns that enrobed the land. Distilled to its essence, the accepted scenario says that the climate of eight thousand years ago was warm and dry enough for prairie species from the west and south to spread eastward through this region into eastern Indiana and Ohio. This projection became known as the prairie peninsula. Starting about five thousand years ago, however, the climate shifted in the other direction, producing wetter and cooler conditions that enabled the forests to regain some of the ground they had lost. Periods of drought hindered the arboreal advance, but it was fire that perpetuated the prairie dominance of the Chicago region. Climate allowed the prairie to develop; fire maintained prairie when the climate changed. In the words of plant ecologist Roger Anderson, "the vegetation of the prairie peninsula was most likely a shifting mosaic of grassland, forest, and savannah that was determined by fire frequency under a climatic regime capable of supporting any of these vegetation types."[13]

Climate determines the vegetation of a region more than any other single factor.[14] In this region three air masses most influence the climate. The dominant mass originates as humid air off the Pacific Coast but sheds its moisture as it rises to clear the Rocky Mountains. This dry rain shadow sweeps east on the same thousand-mile course that enabled it to create the prairie peninsula. Its effects on this region are tempered, however, by the other two air masses—humid air from the Gulf of Mexico meets dry cold air of the Canadian Arctic and produces most of the region's precipitation. The interplay of these air systems translates into the climatic changes that influence the evolving face of the landscape.

Climate manifests itself most noticeably in the day-to-day atmospheric events known as weather. In this region, the weather is marked by great variations in temperature, precipitation, and wind. Chicago has temperatures that average 75°F in July and 26°F in January. Highs and lows at O'Hare Airport have ranged from 104°F on June 20, 1988, to −27°F on January 20, 1985.

The region receives an average of about thirty-four inches of precipitation a year, most of it during the summer. Both prolonged droughts and deluges are uncommon. The wettest month on record, August 1987, produced 17.10 inches of rainfall, 9.35 inches of which fell within one twenty-four-hour period. August 1979 was the driest month ever, when a paltry .02 inches of precipitation fell.

Severe snowstorms occur from time to time, causing an array of serious consequences. Hard snows during the winter of 1842–43 are said to have killed thousands of prairie chickens (*Tympanuchus cupido*) and bobwhite (*Colinus virginianus*) throughout Lake County, Illinois.[15] The storm of January 1979 was memorable in changing the political landscape: challenger Jane Byrne used the snow, and its clean-up, as an issue over which she defeated incumbent Michael Bilandic to become mayor of Chicago.

Winds in the area are predominantly from the west, although there is variation from month to month. They average 10.3 miles per hour, which would give Chicago the title of "eighty-first windiest city," at least among the 270 United States cities looked at as part of a major study of urban climate.[16] Chicago's sobriquet "the windy city" actually came not from its climatic conditions but, rather, from the perceived boastfulness of its citizens during the planning and construction of the 1893 Columbian Exposition.[17] But genuine gusts have exceeded eighty miles per hour, including the record one of eighty-seven miles per hour that came out of the northeast in February 1894.

The region's most spectacular weather arrives as storms, some of which lash the area with deadly fury. The most notorious was the Veteran's Day Storm of 1940. In the three-state area of Illinois, Michigan, and Minnesota, freezing temperatures and high winds killed sixty-six people, caused millions of dollars of property damage, and destroyed large tracts of forest. Fifty-nine more lives were claimed when the storm sank three ships off Pentwater, Michigan.[18]

There are also the short-lived but potentially devastating tornados that occur more commonly on the central grasslands of the United States than anywhere else in the world. On August 28, 1990, a tornado ravaged parts of Will and Kendall Counties, killing twenty-nine, injuring 350, and destroying $115 million worth of property. It was the most destructive of any reported in the country that year.[19]

Local weather conditions affect animal and plant populations in numerous ways. Moisture levels, wind speed, and wind direction at time of seed ripening help determine which plants will successfully colonize a new site. The absence of an insulating snow cover can increase winter plant mortality, especially for seedlings. Temperature and wind strongly influence phenological occurrences, defined by botanist John Curtis as "the seasonal march of observable biological events."[20] Spring flowers bloom along the Des Plaines River two weeks earlier than at cooler sites near Lake Michigan. Major flights of migrating birds can be correlated to the passage of cold and warm fronts, and salamanders emerge in the spring to breed as higher temperatures thaw their winter quarters.

Aquatic ecosystems, particularly small lakes, are even more profoundly affected by weather conditions. Wind and the cycle of water warming and cooling ensure that essential nutrients disperse throughout the community. But during the winter a layer of ice covered by deep snow can prevent light from penetrating the water. Photosynthesis stops, along with the associated production of oxygen; meanwhile, decaying vegetation depletes the oxygen that is present. The devastating oxygen deficiency becomes apparent when the spring thaw reveals a lake surface littered with bloated fish.[21]

Burned to Life: Fire

Perhaps because it was new to their experience, the early commentators were awestruck by the raging conflagrations they came to know on their travels through the Midwest. Many of those who witnessed these displays of heat and color found them exquisite, as glorious as the land itself:

> For a mile and more before you reached the edge of the fire you were in its bright orange light, which made everything as visible as if it were noon day, and the sun was shining fiercely through a blood colored haze. . . . At last you gain a little rise and look beyond into such a scene as nothing but a prairie fire can show. It spreads out a sea of red smoldering ashes, glowing for miles in all directions, while the deep white ridge of flames ahead mount the slopes with awful rapidity, and flap their heavy tongues up into the air with a hoarse roaring noise that fills you with astonishment and almost terror. Hour after hour you may stand, fascinated with the terrible beauties of the scene, as the mass of red sultry ruins grows and grows each minute, till your eyes are pained and heated with its angry glare, and you almost dread the grand, fierce sheet of fire, which has swept all trace of vegetation from the surface of the prairie. . . . On Monday night . . . the wind changed . . . and turned the flames nearly back upon the ground they had already devastated. . . . On the next day, however, they sprang up fresh and raged faster and faster than before. . . . And on the last night the glare was tremendous—as if the world itself was burning. (Near Dwight, Illinois, 1861)[22]

The historical record demonstrates how common a phenomenon fire was on the open prairie. In the fall of 1837, a Chicago resident wrote to relatives in New England that "the prairie takes fire every day that we have, and in the evening burns beautifully and takes up the whole sky."[23] A year later, a traveler entering Chicago by boat from Milwaukee noted "large clouds of smoke that could be seen in various directions," smoke that he was told originated from the prairie burns that occurred every spring and fall.[24] One night in 1858, yet another visitor saw five different fires within a twenty- or thirty-mile stretch as she approached Chicago from Indiana.[25]

There is disagreement among scientists as to whether prairie fires were primarily meteorological or cultural in origin. Those who take the former view argue that the Midwest is a region of unstable weather producing storms frequently punctuated by flashes of lightning. Ecologist Paul Sears points to this as "evidence that, however enthusiastic a pyromaniac man may be, lightning is a far more common and efficient igniter."[26] Opponents counter that substantial quantities of rain accompany most lightning storms, a situation hardly conducive for sustained combustion. They attribute the fires to the human beings who arrived in the region roughly twelve thousand years ago. Burning was used for several purposes, most particularly as an aid to hunting.[27] A fair conclusion is that both causes contributed to the fires, fires that through their power and frequency etched the shifting lines of grass, shrubs, and trees onto a background fixed by climate and topography.

With broad strokes, the relationship between topography, fire, and terrestrial vegetation can be easily outlined. On the level lake plains and ground moraines where the westerly winds could drive the flames unhindered, the prairies flourished. They are composed of perennial grasses and forbs that die back every year. The growing parts of these plants are beneath the soil and thus are unscathed by fire. (Although temperatures at the soil surface during burns can range from $175°$ to $1,300°$F, little increase in temperature has been noted at depths of as little as less than an inch below the surface.)[28] And as fire consumes the thick litter that develops over time, prairie vitality is renewed: light reaches young plants and nutrients are made available for soil enrichment. For some species, scorching heat actually facilitates seed germination.

Lands that were sheltered from the full brunt of the conflagrations by watercourses or morainal ridges supported shrublands and savannas. One of the dominant trees of the open savanna is bur oak, a species endowed with a thick corky bark that enables it to survive repeated fire exposure. And where fires were most infrequent—such as the east side of rivers, north and east faces of morainic slopes, and in ravines—forests were able to develop.

A New Force

Over thousands of years, the great forces of glaciation, climate, and fire had created a seamless mosaic of waters, wetlands, prairies, shrublands, and woods. But the arrival of the Europeans set in motion a new force, one with the power and will to impose upon the landscape a uniformity that is now virtually complete. While this process has diminished our natural heritage to a sorrowful extent, it is a tribute to the resiliency of nature and the efforts of a few farsighted people that so many native plants and animals have managed to survive, albeit in ever shrinking refuges.

In Quality Unexcelled:
Prairie Types and Composition

The prairies have already been described as well perhaps as they ever will be. . . . And there is nothing with which to compare them. To tell of what ingredients they are composed is easy enough, but to give a just idea of the effects of their combination, requires analogies not to be found in the other productions of nature; nor in the imagery of the mind. . . . I believe it is beyond the power of language, almost imagination, to exaggerate the strange and beautiful combination of what is sporting together in perfect harmony on these boundless plains.
— James Paulding (St. Louis to Chicago via the Illinois River in 1848)

Although Americans of our day enjoy a material wealth unknown in human history, we sacrificed certain valuable things to attain that distinction. One of these was the unbroken prairie. Prairie lands were among the most beautiful of all, an opinion shared by many of the early visitors who were privileged to experience them. An 1837 description of the land between Galena (northwestern Illinois) and Chicago provides a glimpse:

> No one can conceive the emotion that rises up in the bosom of the traveller as he stands on the broad prairie, and sees the horizon settling down upon one wide sea of waving grass and can behold around him neither stone, nor stump, nor bush, nor tree, nor hill, nor house. These vast prairies, though bearing a luxuriant growth of grass, would impress one with a sense of desolateness, were they not beautified with flowers, and animated with the songs and the sight of the feathered tribes. The view of the prairie, as it stretches before you, often appears like a perfect flower garden. Though we were too late to see these productions in their rich vernal beauty, yet often they stood strewn around us on every side as far as the eye could reach, spreading out their rich and brilliant petals of every color and hue.[1]

It is a sad and unfortunate fact that by the time these lands became the subject of serious scientific scrutiny, most of the native vegetation was gone. But by seeking out the scraps of prairie that had survived, dedicated biologists across the Midwest began to make sense of the prairie ecosystems. (This evidently irked one Ivy League faculty member who, according to Paul Sears, groused that the "center of botanical influence had shifted from Harvard to the barbarian schools of the Middle West.")[2] But even in 2001, after nearly a century of systematic work, there is need for more research before we can be certain that our stewardship of this imperiled biome is preserving the full measure of its complex diversity.

Of Breezes and Braided Roots: The Grasses

Prairie definitions are as varied as their authors. Everyone does agree, however, that the single most important characteristic of prairie is the prevalence of grass. Two species of grass alone, big bluestem (*Andropogon gerardii*) and little bluestem (*A. scoparius*), can constitute over 75 percent of the vegetation in many prairies.[3] Grasses lack the colorful and fragrant blossoms that many other plants use to attract pollinators, but the wind needs no such cues as it carries the grains of pollen from one tiny grass flower to the other. These individual blooms are part of a larger spikelet that often forms clusters. Like the bird toes of the big bluestem and the dangling florets of the Indian grass (*Sorghastrum nutans*), many of these are finely cut, "an invitation to ministering breezes."[4]

Despite their shrunken flowers, grasses are amply imbued with beauty and color. Donald Culross Peattie wrote that "grass is generous, swift-springing, candid-growing, full of motion and sound and light."[5] May T. Watts described her final visit to a narrow strip of prairie in Kendall County just before it was to be plowed: "The little bluestem was exquisite with turquoise and garnet and chartreuse; and the big bluestem waved its turkey feet of deep purple against the October sky, past the warm russet of the Indian grass."[6]

Every species possesses a unique set of characteristics that enables it to survive the vicissitudes of its particular environment.[7] Little bluestem, best adapted to the droughty conditions of upland prairie, is short and has narrow leaves to minimize water loss through evaporation. Equally revealing is the structure of its finely shaped roots. Some are shallow and parallel to the surface while others grow laterally before dropping twelve to eighteen inches. Most, however, plunge straight down to depths of $5\frac{1}{2}$ feet. The result is a solid tangle of wirelike fibers that prevents the escape of precipitation.

Prairie cordgrass (*Spartina pectinata*) inhabits the wet and poorly aerated

Table 1. Occurrence of Prairie Grasses along Moisture Gradient

	Dry	Dry-Mesic	Mesic	Wet-Mesic	Wet
Side oats grama (*Bouteloua curtipendula*)	A	X	...	...	...
Porcupine grass (*Stipa spartea*)	X	A	X	...	...
Little bluestem (*Andropogon scoparius*)	A	X	X	X	...
Big bluestem (*Andropogon gerardii*)	X	X	A	X	X
Prairie dropseed (*Sporobolus heterolepis*)	X	A	X	X	...
Indian grass (*Sorghastrum nutens*)	...	A	X	X	...
Switch grass (*Panicum virgatum*)	...	...	X	X	...
Scribner's panic grass (*Panicum oligosanthes scribnerianum*)	...	A	X	...	...
Prairie cordgrass (*Spartina pectinata*)	...	...	...	X	A
Bluejoint grass (*Calamagrostis canadensis*)	...	...	...	X	A

Source. After Rock (1981).

Note. A = Where species is most abundant; X = Where species is prevalent; ellipses dots indicate where species is uncommon to absent.

soils at the other end of the moisture spectrum. It has rather broad leaves that maximize its photosynthetic potential and, thus, capacity to grow. And grow it does: by late summer, the leaves can be seven feet high and the flower stalks ten. In common with many other plants inhabiting hydric soils, cordgrass possesses roots that are thick and largely unbranched. They grow virtually straight down, as deep as thirteen feet.

Claiming ground between these two extremes is the big bluestem. Its long intermediate-width leaves spread outward and ultimately encompass an area that may be twice that of the base. This arrangement enables it to both conserve water when it needs to and increase the leaf surface exposed to the sun for photosynthesis. Big bluestem grows fast, up to eight feet or more by the time it blooms in late summer, and is extremely tolerant of shade. Roots form a dense mass in the top several feet of soil before thinning out as they penetrate to depths in excess of seven feet.

Where Spring Begins: The Gravel Prairies

One line of ecological investigation has categorized prairies (and all other ecosystems) by community type, each possessing a characteristic assemblage of plants and animals, although few species are restricted to a single community. Ecologists generally distinguish these types on the basis of two factors. The first of these focuses on substrate or soil texture: gravel, silt loams (particularly the black mollisol soils), sand, and dolomite bedrock. The second factor addresses where a prairie lies along a moisture gradient: dry, dry-mesic, mesic (moist), wet-mesic, and wet.[8]

Gravel prairies are highly localized in the Chicago area, largely confined to northeastern Kane, northwestern Cook, McHenry, and Walworth counties.[9] Because these prairies are situated on morainal ridges underlain by coarsely textured soils, they hold little moisture. Consequently, they are classified as dry or dry-mesic and resemble the more arid grasslands of the west. Although these gravel prairies contain fewer species than the more lush sites generally associated with this region, they provide refugia for many locally rare forms that represent western elements of our biota (animals and plants).

If grasses provide the prairie background, the forbs provide the script and color. Characteristic species of gravel prairies include fringed puccoon (*Lithospermum incisum*), silky aster (*Aster sericeus*), kitten tails (*Wulfenia bullii*) (restricted to the Kettle Moraine country), small skullcap (*Scutellaria parvula*), grooved yellow flax (*Linum sulcatum*), and stiff sandwort (*Arenaria stricta*). These last two prefer the driest and most exposed portion of the prairie, where there is minimal competition with other plants.[10]

Two of the rarer plants in the Chicago region are endemic to dry gravel prairies. The prairie bush clover (*Lespedeza leptostachya*), with small inconspicuous flowers, is known from a handful of sites in the northwestern counties. Its entire range is limited to the upper Midwest, where it is generally rare throughout, and thus the federal government has listed it as a threatened species.[11] Woolly milkweed (*Asclepias lanuginosa*) has a wider distribution nationally but is imperiled locally due to gravel mining, grazing, and the fact that it occurs in small populations that produce few if any seeds.[12]

Because these prairies are more exposed and are often on surfaces facing south and west, they warm sooner in the spring and receive an early dose of

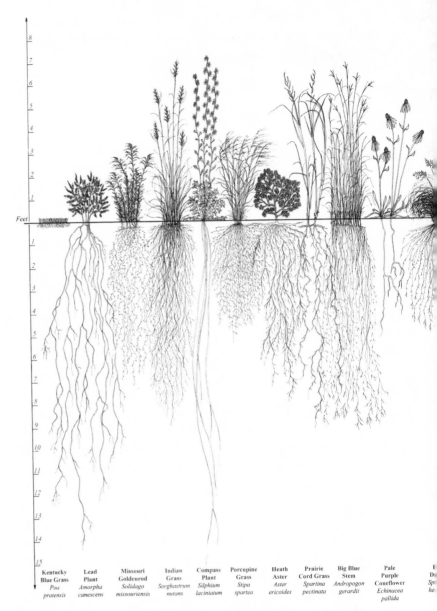

7. Variations in the root structures of prairie plants. (Created by Heidi Natura for use and distribution by Conservation Research Institute.)

water from rapid snowmelt. The pasque flower (*Anemone patens*), a western species restricted to gravel prairies in our region, begins to flower when the winds of early spring are still raw. Resembling a blue-headed mushroom as it emerges from grass singed by an early fire, the pasque flower is the first of all prairie plants to blossom. By the time other members of the flora begin to put forth their own blooms, it has already started to fade. Although once found as

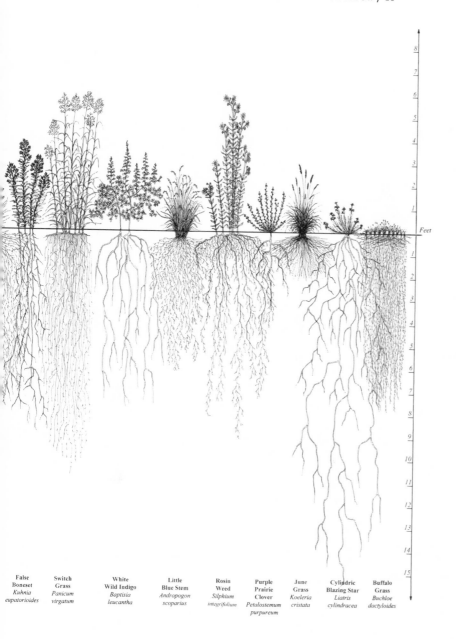

False Boneset	Switch Grass	White Wild Indigo	Little Blue Stem	Rosin Weed	Purple Prairie Clover	June Grass	Cylindric Blazing Star	Buffalo Grass
Kuhnia eupatorioides	*Panicum virgatum*	*Baptisia leucantha*	*Andropogon scoparius*	*Silphium integrifolium*	*Petalostemum purpureum*	*Koeleria cristata*	*Liatris cylindracea*	*Buchloe dactyloides*

close to Chicago as Palatine, pasque flowers are still present in the Kettle Moraine State Forest of Walworth County.

Two other species share the same gritty ground with the pasque flower but are more widespread in this region. The rarer of the two, the prairie buttercup (*Ranunculus rhomboideus*), can bloom almost as early as the pasque flower. The prairie smoke (*Geum triflorum*) flowers later and can be spectacular to behold.

A large population of prairie smoke bedecks the kame at Glacial Park in Ringwood, McHenry County. In May, during late afternoon, the hillside looks to be in flame as the low-hanging sun accentuates the rosy glow of the flowers. Later in the season, the flames become smoke when long grayish fibers project from the fruiting head.[13]

Clearly one reason people find prairies so enchanting is the succession of colors as one plant after another reaches anthesis (time of flowering). The gravel prairies have fewer species than the lowland prairies and thus may be less showy, but because the grasses of the gravel hill prairies are short and sparse, the bursts of flowers throughout the growing season can be enjoyed without obstruction.

In late spring, bird's-foot violet (*Viola pedata*) can carpet acres of the gravel rises, as it does at Ski Hill Prairie in Algonquin, McHenry County. While more common in other types of prairie, the downy phlox (*Phlox pilosa*) and shooting star (*Dodecatheon meadia*) "never appear to such good advantage as when they stud the steep hillsides with a cloud of pink and white."[14] Later, with the onset of summer, purple coneflower (*Echinacea pallida*), cylindric blazing star (*Liatris cylindracea*), and two kinds of prairie clover provide brilliant accents to the green backdrop. And the striking asters, goldenrods, and gentians of autumn may surpass the colors on display at moister sites.

One of the last gravel hill prairies in Cook County was destroyed in 1990 for the value of its minerals. Serious attempts to preserve the property failed because the price of gravel made any purchase prohibitive. The wife of the owner was taking tennis lessons from a conservationist and was said to be sympathetic to preservation, but she seemed to have little influence on the result. In the end, conservationists were allowed to relocate many of the plants to a protected site.

The desecration of the gravel hills is not new. Over sixty years ago, Herman Pepoon, in his great work on the flora of the Chicago area, wrote of the gravel prairies he knew: "Some of the bare and barren, gravelly, sandy or clay knolls of the morainal hills are interesting places and the prairie forms here, making their last stand, are a pathetic reminder of the bitter struggle plants are subjected to in order to maintain a hold on the land, against the combined attack of cow and sheep, hog and man."[15]

The Richest of All: The Black-Soil Prairies

The black-soil prairies formed primarily on silt loam and clay loam and were the most common type in the prairie peninsula. Because so much of the land in this area is poorly drained, these prairies are usually mesic to wet. The mesic

8. Mesic prairie (with switchgrass, blazing star, and *Silphium*) at
Ashland Prairie in Chicago; photo by H. Sampson, circa 1915. Note
horse-drawn mowers in background. (Courtesy Illinois Natural History
Survey, Champaign.)

is the richest of all prairie types, while the wet prairie holds comparatively few species, of which a small number may dominate an entire site.[16] It was in these lush prairies where a rider on horseback in late summer could disappear from view as the curtain of lowland grasses closed behind him.

Although grasses cover more surface area of these prairies than any other plant family, the composites (daisy family) claim the largest number of species present with over 25 percent. Among its members are some of the most magnificent of all prairie species, the ones that inspire protection and restoration of this great biome and that even moved visitors 150 years ago. E. W. Short wrote of the composites he saw during a trip to central Illinois in late summer during the 1840s: "From some elevated position in a large prairie the eyes take in at a glance thousands of acres literally empurpled with the flowering spikes of several species of Liatris. . . . In other situations, where a depressed or flattened surface and clayey soil favor the continuance of moisture, a few species of yellow-flowered coreopsis occur in such profuse abundance as to tinge the entire surface with a golden burnish."[17]

The compass plant (*Silphium laciniatum*) and prairie dock (*S. terebinthinaceum*) are two conspicuous members of this family that are often among the last prairie elements to survive the ravages of mowing and grazing. A small stand of prairie dock still clings to the Northwestern Railroad right-of-way just

9. Wet prairie (with prairie cordgrass and prairie Indian plantain) at
Ashland Prairie, Chicago; photo by H. Sampson, circa 1915. (Courtesy
Illinois Natural History Survey, Champaign.)

south of the Norwood Park station on Chicago's northwest side. This resiliency comes largely from the plant's substantial taproots, which can run to depths of fourteen feet. Aldo Leopold tells of his effort to transplant a compass plant: "It was like digging an oak sapling. After half an hour of hot grimy labor, the root was still enlarging, like a great vertical sweet potato. As far as I know, the Silphium root went clear through to bedrock."[18]

The next best-represented family is the Leguminosae (peas). They are particularly important in contributing to the fertility of prairie soils because their root nodules bear nitrogen-fixing bacteria. Many legumes are very conservative (indicators of nondegraded conditions) and demonstrate a strong fidelity to undisturbed prairie. The false white indigo (*Baptisia leucantha*) and creamy-white indigo (*B. leucophaea*) are two such species, exceedingly showy both in bloom and in seed with their pendulous pods. Another legume restricted to high-quality prairies is the leadplant (*Amorpha canescens*). The species received its name from the early belief that the land on which it grew was heavily infused with lead. This prompted Short to muse that if so, "the whole of the prairies may one day become a mining region."[19] Fortunately, the belief was groundless and the ground leadless.

The milkweed family (Asclepiadaceae), although not a large part of the prairie flora, is of particular interest because it includes some species that thrive in the face of human activities and others that can survive in only the most intact of prairies. Two examples of the former, common milkweed (*Asclepias syriaca*) and whorled milkweed (*A. verticillata*), are numerous and widespread in habitats ranging from undisturbed to ruderal (human dominated). These plants can reproduce vegetatively, forming extensive clones of hundreds of flowering stems that spread widely. They also grow quickly and can tolerate mowing and even applications of herbicide.[20] A final factor aiding the common milkweed is that nonnative insects such as the Eurasian honeybee (*Apis mellifera*) are able to pollinate its flowers.

Toward the conservative end of the milkweed spectrum is the prairie milkweed (*Asclepias sullivantii*), which grows almost exclusively in high-quality prairie and in very small numbers.[21] Referring to this and most of the other nineteen milkweeds they examined, Robert Betz and Herbert Lamp lament that "it is unfortunate that reproductive studies on milkweeds were not undertaken earlier when native plant communities were still intact and available for more definitive studies. Today, having disappeared over most of their original ranges, many of these Asclepias species are difficult to locate."[22]

Mead's milkweed (*A. meadii*) is the rarest of all and one of the most imperiled members of the prairie flora.[23] Once widespread in the Midwest, the species disappeared with its tallgrass habitat. The bulk of its population is now in Missouri and Kansas, where it survives mainly in hayfields and along railroad rights-of-way. Mead's milkweed has been successfully cultivated, but the process is very difficult and time consuming; less than half the seeds germinate and those that do must be cleaned daily with a small toothbrush to remove damaging insects.

For almost eighty years, the only record of Mead's milkweed in the Chicago region was a specimen collected near Crown Point, Indiana, in 1888. Attempts to relocate the species in Indiana had proven unsuccessful. Then, early one Sunday morning in 1966, William Rommel discovered the plant growing on a prairie remnant in Palatine, Illinois. Bob Betz recalls how Rommel, a graduate student of his who had studied Mead's Milkweed in Kansas, phoned him and awash in self-doubt described what he had just seen. A hastily formed expedition was successful in confirming the sighting but unfortunately efforts to protect the site were not. Although a small portion of habitat remains, no one has seen the milkweed there again. Even in the face of a restless and ever-growing human population, rarities manage to hang on in out of the way refugia, some still awaiting the gaze of the discerning naturalist.

The nodding wild onion (*Allium cernuum*) is a member of the lily family (Liliaceae) that inhabits a variety of prairie types. It is famous for having long been considered the origin of Chicago's name.[24] Chicago is based on a word in the Illinois Indian language that is rendered in a variety of ways, "chicagou" and "checagou" being just two. Some early promoters of the city claimed that the term meant "great," but until recently there has been general agreement that it referred to the nodding wild onion. Much of this discussion may in fact now be moot given that the most recent assessment of Chicago's etymological origins concludes that the *Allium* for which the city is named is not *cernuum* but *tricoccum*, wild leek.

A description of the nodding wild onion from the 1890s shows that the species is hardy and can be striking to the eye as well as the nose and palate:

> In late summer, the nodding wild onion decks many fields with showy flowers. . . . They are mostly rose-colored, but pink and white kinds are numerous. This imparts to a field a variegated appearance, bright on the whole, since the reddish hues prevail. They are often in such quantities and grow so thickly that little else is noticeable where they stand. . . . They are common in pastures where the feet of cattle have crushed out the life of less stubborn plants or where the prairie grass has been replaced by cultivated kinds. . . . Their bulbous root serves them admirably in this respect, and bears much rough treatment before its vitality is destroyed.[25]

Two other lilies, the Michigan (*Lilium michiganense*) and prairie (*L. philadelphicum*), also add diversity and color to the low prairies. (Both species are also found in sand prairies, and the Michigan lily can inhabit open woods.) The Michigan lily used to be quite common. Pepoon wrote in 1927 that "the swales east of Dunning [on the southwest side of Chicago] are gorgeous in early July with its blossoms."[26] Although the prairie lily was always much rarer, collectors gathered large quantities of both species to sell in the flower stalls along Chicago's State Street at the turn of the last century.[27]

Although it resembles a desert-loving yucca, the rattlesnake master (*Eryngium yuccifolium*) is a denizen of mesic and wet-mesic sites and a member of the parsley family (Umbelliferae). N. A. Woods, who accompanied the Prince of Wales on a hunting excursion to Dwight, Illinois, in 1861, tells of what is probably this species: "Tall, tufted reedy plants . . . which attract your attention at once. It is the rattlesnake weed, always most plentiful where this deadly reptile abounds, and the root of which, with immense doses of corn whiskey is said . . . to have averted fatal results from the bites of this species."[28] (If this concoction didn't actually save the patient, it no doubt purged him of concern.) While the rattlesnake is now virtually gone from this region (and its last haunts are remote from the rattlesnake master), the even rarer *Papaipema eryngii* is a moth now known to be entirely dependent on the rattlesnake master.

My favorite family of plants is the orchids. Several factors contribute to my fondness for them: their often-elegant beauty, their rarity, and the quality of ground that grants them sanctuary. Many of their members are "errant survivors in a world which no longer offers them the primal niche which spawned them," and to divulge their whereabouts to another is an act of abiding trust—like a secret whispered to a close friend.[29] Indeed, it is a very real threat that the unscrupulous will take them for profit, as likely happened at a nature preserve in Lake County (Ill.) several years ago. (When I refer to a "nature preserve," I mean a high-quality natural area that has been formally dedicated by the state so that it receives maximum protection under state law. All four of the region's states have similar programs; for a more detailed discussion, see chap. 3.)

Of the forty species of orchids recorded in the Chicago region, only the eastern prairie fringed (*Habenaria [Platanthera] leucophaea*) and the white lady's slipper (*Cypripedium candidum*) are endemic to the tallgrass prairie. Although a few large populations of each still exist, both have suffered significant decreases throughout their range as mesic prairie vanishes in the face of agriculture and other purposes. The prairie fringed has become so rare that it is now federally listed as threatened.

Charles Sheviak, in his book on Illinois orchids, notes that although the white lady's slipper once thrived in "extensive colonies," he knows "of but a single station in the state where one can still view hundreds of plants of this species scattered over several acres of low prairie."[30] Unfortunately, most of this site has since been destroyed.

Similar sentiments are expressed by Michael Homoya in his *Orchids of Indiana*: "*Cypripedium candidum* was a common orchid [150 years ago], probably occurring by the millions in mile after mile of the Grand Prairie of northwestern Indiana. . . . Today, only a dozen or so sites in all of Indiana are known to harbor this aristocrat of orchids."[31]

The eastern white fringed orchid is known historically from northwestern Indiana and Berrien County, but today is present only in the region's Wisconsin and Illinois counties. "No other orchid in Indiana has suffered the consequences of habitat destruction as much as *Platanthera leucophaea*," says Homoya. "Its occurrence in prairie remnants in widely separated cemeteries in the Midwest suggests to me that the orchid must have been common throughout . . . much of northwestern Indiana. One can only imagine the great numbers of *P. leucophaea* prior to the coming of the settlers."[32] Although diligent searches for it have been made, the orchid has not been seen in Indiana for more than fifty years.

In the early twentieth century, large numbers of the eastern prairie fringed orchid grew south of Elston Avenue and west of Kedzie in Chicago, and as late as the mid-1980s a small colony persisted in a disturbed prairie remnant near Montrose and Cumberland on Chicago's border with Norridge.[33] Research on the twenty-one prairie white fringed orchid populations extant in Illinois (all but two of which are in the Chicago area) concluded that only one was highly viable and ten moderately viable based on the number of individuals, size of site, diversity of habitat, legal protection, and appropriate land management activities.[34]

Marlin Bowles, a plant ecologist with the Morton Arboretum, has extensively studied both the white lady's slipper and the eastern prairie fringed orchid. He has described how the plants have adapted to their prairie environment and the significance this poses for their conservation. The lady's slipper inhabits wet-mesic to wet sites, where moisture is likely to be sufficient during its spring growing season. It therefore sprouts and flowers every year, although lapsing into senescence soon after blooming. The fringed orchid, in contrast, blooms in midsummer and can occur in drier habitat. This means that the availability of moisture can be a problem during droughts. As a result, some populations go years without flowering and may, in fact, produce no vegetative growth at all, a circumstance that hinders monitoring.

Individuals of both species live a long time. Eastern prairie fringed orchids in a garden bloomed for over thirty years, while seedling white lady's slippers might take twelve years to bloom. This characteristic obviously facilitates long-term survival of populations, assuming, of course, that the habitat remains viable.

The first orchids I ever saw were white lady's slippers that grow in a small forlorn patch of black-soil prairie not far from where I grew up in Mount Prospect, Cook County. I remember one particular overcast May evening when I saw in full display hoary puccoon (*Lithospermum canescens*), cream white indigo, golden Alexanders (*Zizia aurea*), yellow star grass, and the orchids with their purple-lined slippers seemingly crafted for the feet of fairies. A light rain interrupted my musings but also created a remarkable effect: the drizzle rendered the place, already difficult to access, even less inviting to most and thus more remote. The vision at my feet and the drops dampening my hair were both manifestations of ancient and enduring processes that made the scene seem remote in a temporal way as well.

On the Bones of Earth: The Dolomite Prairies

When the outflow draining Lake Chicago finished scouring the valley of the lower Des Plaines River, it left behind a combination of environments unlike any other in the region. Water percolating through the bluffs formed calcium-rich seeps, while the surface water pooling on the flat river plain supported marshes and other wetlands. Stripped of glacial till, the dolomite bedrock was laid bare at numerous points. It is here, from Willow Springs to Joliet, that the dolomite prairies developed.

This stretch of river has maintained its unusual biological features despite a long history of human tampering. During its heyday from 1848 to 1914, the Illinois and Michigan Canal enabled a great traffic in people and cargo to traverse the valley. Then the Chicago Sanitary and Ship Canal was constructed: "Its course was cut deep into the bedrock of the valley, and piles of excavated earth and rock 70 feet high paralleled the new waterway down the center of the valley."[35] Other activities damaging to the ecosystems of the area included the passing of large numbers of livestock on their way to processing plants in Chicago, building of roads to transport quarried limestone, dumping refuse of all kinds, placement of utility lines, and heavy use by off-road vehicles.[36]

Dolomite prairies are composed of plants that can survive on bare or nearly bare dolomitic bedrock. Although these prairies are typed by the same moisture categories as other prairies, researchers have found it particularly difficult to delineate these differences in the field. One reason is that the changes often occur over the course of a very small area, as demonstrated by the community map of Lockport Prairie Nature Preserve painstakingly drawn by plant ecologist Marcy DeMauro of the Will County Forest Preserve District. (See fig. 10.) Another complicating factor, pronounced in a soilless environment, is that areas that are wet in spring become parched in summer. Thus the same piece of ground may support sedges in May but little bluestem in July.[37]

The bluestems, Indian grass, and other grasses predominate here as in other prairies and are distributed according to moisture availability. Over 150 prairie species grow in this area, a number of which exhibit fidelity to the prairies' harsh conditions: slender sandwort (*Arenaria patula*), marbleseed (*Onosmodium hispidissimum*), Ohio horsemint (*Blephilia ciliata*), and tufted hair grass (*Deschampsia caespitosa*). Because so few plants can adapt to pavement-like ground, competition is reduced, and three exceedingly rare plants have found a niche here.

Botanists have recorded the lakeside daisy (*Actinea herbacea*) from two locations in Ontario, a quarry in Ohio, Tazewell County, Illinois (an old station never relocated), the Des Plaines River Valley, and nowhere else on earth.[38] The first specimen of the plant to be described was obtained near Joliet where Pepoon considered it still common in the 1920s.[39]

Floyd Swink and Karl Bartel found the species during the 1950s at Rockdale, south of Joliet. Years later, when Bob Betz attempted to relocate the population using their directions, he discovered that the habitat had been destroyed,

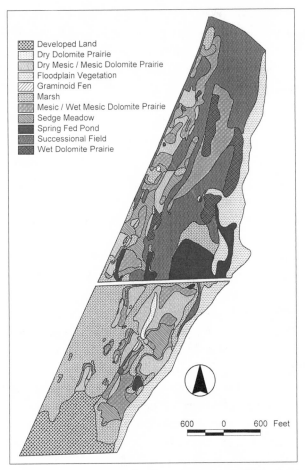

Legend:

- Developed Land
- Dry Dolomite Prairie
- Dry Mesic / Mesic Dolomite Prairie
- Floodplain Vegetation
- Graminoid Fen
- Marsh
- Mesic / Wet Mesic Dolomite Prairie
- Sedge Meadow
- Spring Fed Pond
- Successional Field
- Wet Dolomite Prairie

600   0   600 Feet

10. Plant communities of Lockport Prairie Nature Preserve, Will County; by M. De Mauro. (Courtesy Forest Preserve District of Will County, Joliet, Ill.)

and there was no trace of the plant. Before giving up, however, he crossed Route 6 and came upon a promising parcel within the fences of a Commonwealth Edison Company's coal-fired generating facility:

> I went to the office to ask permission to enter the property. One of the nice things about having a degree is if you say you are doctor so and so or professor so and so they figure you know what you are doing. I was allowed inside and found the population of about two or three dozen plants. I contacted the company and asked if they could set the area aside because it was the only population in the entire state. They said they would take care of it and the next week when I returned I saw that three or four huge cable spools had been placed around the spot to protect it. I'd go back to check on it and things were going along fine. During this time, John Kolar, a plant

propagator, asked how he could get in to see the plants, and I gave the necessary information. Unbeknownst to me, and very fortunately as it turned
out, he made cuttings of the plant and began growing them at his home. A
year or two later, I visited the site and saw the mounds of coal which looked
like giant whales. There was one big mountain of coal over the whole thing,
the whole thing.[40]

So died in 1981 the last population of lakeside daisy in Illinois, the only local
species to have been extirpated through smothering by coal. Betz has never felt
that Edison violated the agreement intentionally: "One hand didn't know what
the other was doing." And out of gratefulness that they weren't slammed, the
company was amenable to certain other conservation initiatives.

The story doesn't end there, however. Marcy DeMauro has studied the
lakeside daisy for many years.[41] She acquired Rockdale plants from Kolar, as
well as specimens from extant populations. Through backcrossing, she obtained plants that are genetically of almost pure local origin. Since a major goal
of her work was the eventual reintroduction of the species into suitable habitat, she also identified a group of candidate sites. Lockport Prairie Nature Preserve was eventually selected due to the large areas of exposed dolomite that it
contained. Lakeside daisies were established there in the fall of 1988 and by
1992 had doubled in population, although DeMauro did not know whether the
increase was through production of seed or vegetative means.

The second great rarity is the leafy prairie clover. It was found near
Geneva, Kane County, in 1862 and at Langham Island in the Kankakee River
in 1872. This second discovery was made by Reverend E. J. Hill, who at the
time was Chicago's foremost field botanist. Although he carefully searched the

11. Lakeside daisy growing on dolomitic limestone at Rockdale, Will
County; photo by F. Swink, circa 1950. (Courtesy Floyd Swink.)

island two years later, he could not relocate the plant. Hill concluded that he had been "unintentionally too good a collector, and probably extinguished the plant, though thinking enough had been left for seed"; he admonished future collectors not to "crop too closely."[42]

Within Illinois, the leafy prairie clover had also been observed in similar habitat in Will and LaSalle Counties. At Ottawa, LaSalle County, a collector found it to be abundant in 1878 and offered to trade specimens of the clover for ferns.[43] A survey of herbaria published in 1973, however, determined that the last collection made in the state was September 12, 1912, at Romeoville in Will County, most likely at the same place where Pepoon stated it persisted at least until 1927.[44] I don't know how long thereafter people continued to see that patch of prairie clover, but by 1973 botanists believed that it was gone from Illinois and represented on the planet by four populations in Tennessee and two in Alabama. These stations were all cedar glades (similar to dolomite prairies in that they, too, grow on bedrock), small areas very vulnerable to habitat destruction. Its precarious status led to the prediction that the leafy prairie clover "will become extremely rare and maybe even extinct in this century."[45]

The leafy prairie clover was not, however, destined for extinction. The plant was actually doing pretty well on the dolomite prairies of the lower Des Plaines River valley, but it wasn't until 1974 that anyone knew. The events culminating in the rediscovery of the leafy prairie clover not only led to the reprieve of a potentially doomed species but represented a personal odyssey for Gerould Wilhelm as well.[46]

In 1972, the United States Army decided that, given Wilhelm's bachelor's degree in biology, he could best serve his country at the Army Corps of Engineers Waterways Experiment Station in Vicksburg, Mississippi. At the time of his arrival, the corps was preparing an environmental impact statement for a project that entailed enlarging the locks at Lockport and deepening the Chicago Sanitary and Ship Canal. Preliminary assessments had identified fifty locations that were potentially suitable as dredge disposal sites. As one of his first tasks, Wilhelm was sent to Chicago to rank each parcel based on its capacity to recover from the proposed dumping. He knew nothing about plants then, so he enlisted Floyd Swink of the Morton Arboretum to accompany him:

> We visited thirteen sites that day. At each, Floyd would rattle off the Latin
> names of 50 or 60 species, all Eurasian or native weeds. I saw sticks and rab-
> bit poop. Floyd couldn't make it the next day so I went with Ray Schulen-
> berg, who would do the same thing: listing off in Latin all these weedy
> plants. (Although I didn't know what they looked like, by now the names
> were becoming familiar.) But when we were finished with each location, he
> would say: 'You can spoil here. You can't hurt it, it will grow back.'

On the afternoon of the third day, we reached spoil site C-2. We stepped across this black mustard berm when Ray stopped dead in his tracks and just looked. In a more hushed voice, he said, "Here is *Sporobolus heterolepis* [prairie dropseed], *Petalostemum purpureum* [purple prairie clover], *Petalostemum candidum* [white prairie clover], *Parthenium integrifolium* [wild quinine], *Potentilla arguta* [prairie cinquefoil], and *Silphium laciniatum* [compass plant]." He put his hand on my shoulder and said, "Jerry, don't spoil here, for this is America and it will not grow back."

I got weak in the knees. Oh lord, I looked at the place and saw America. I knew that this guy was able to identify America by its plants. I collapsed emotionally and decided right then and there that I didn't want to live another day without knowing whether I was in America; whether I could spoil or whether I couldn't.[47]

When he left the army in February 1974, Wilhelm joined the staff of the Morton Arboretum as Ray Schulenberg's assistant. The two of them scoured the region collecting specimens for the 1974 edition of the *Plants of the Chicago Region*. During weekends, Wilhelm would return by himself to the nicer sites that he had encountered during the week. On one of these excursions in August 1974, he entered spoil site C-2 at Lockport and came upon the leafy prairie clover.

Between Wilhelm's discovery and a second station located shortly thereafter, over a thousand individuals were added to the known world population of this species. Under a regime of burning and brush cutting, these plants are thriving, and with the addition of yet another location in Will County, the prospects for the continued survival of the leafy prairie clover are very good.[48]

The third great rarity of these prairies is no longer known in this region. Tennessee milk vetch was collected from Grundy County in the 1800s and on dry dolomite at Joliet by Reverend Hill in 1902. The last known Illinois specimen was found in 1949 along the Illinois River in Tazewell County near Peoria. By 1972, the species' total range was reduced to seven small cedar glades in Tennessee and one in Alabama. Research has shown that as limited as this habitat is, its actual habitat is smaller still, as Tennessee milk vetch only grows in a very narrow zone between open glade and shadowed woods: the former is too dry and the latter too shady.[49]

In 1979, however, Bob Betz was examining herbaria as part of a study on vetches when he discovered a Tennessee milk vetch specimen from Tazewell County that had been misidentified. As the collection was recent, he managed to locate the site from the description on the sheet and, more important, found that the species was still extant. The site has since received state protection and has benefited from careful management.[50]

Is it too much to hope that the species will be rediscovered yet again in old haunts? History demonstrates that the lower Des Plaines River Valley, with its unforgiving bedrock and nourishing waters, doesn't readily give up its secrets.

Dr. Clute's Domain: The Sand Prairies of Braidwood

Sand prairies are concentrated in the Chicago Lake Plain and the Morris-Kankakee Basin. Braidwood Dune and Savanna Nature Preserve, situated in the part of Will County once covered by glacial Lake Morris, comprises 259 acres of sand prairie (from dry to wet), savanna, sedge meadow, and marsh. Typical of so many sites in this region, these different communities coexist next to each other such that it is impossible to characterize a property as being of one type or another: at Braidwood dry prairie is a stride away from wet. The entire area rests on a substrate laced with deep ribbons of coal, like chocolate syrup in an ice cream parfait. In some places the coal is near the surface, while in others it may be sixty feet deep. Mountains of excavated debris marking the entrances of abandoned mine shafts are still evident along Interstate 55 near Coal City, and the nearby Mazon River draws paleontologists from all over the world who seek its fossils.

In the 1920s, the diverse flora of Braidwood attracted the attention of Willard Clute, editor of *American Botanist*, who after several years of fieldwork published the results of his venture in a volume titled *Swamp and Dune: A Study in Plant Distribution*. He concentrated on a six-square-mile block, having concluded that the entire region was "so uniform in character that I soon found the study of a very limited area would serve my purpose."[51] That Clute considered six square miles to be a very limited part of the whole puts in perspective the tiny portion preserved. It was fortuitous that conservationists managed to save anything.

But in Clute's day, the area he chose to investigate was isolated and subjected to little human intrusion. Only six buildings stood, some of which were vacant. Most of the people he encountered were newly arrived immigrants from Europe who would appear in the autumn like the mushrooms they came to collect. The sand ridges and wet swales were not well suited for most agricultural endeavors, but persistent farmers would collect hay every summer, to Clute's obvious displeasure:

> Possibly the cutting depends upon the season that a given swamp is dry
> enough to make haying possible, but it appears as if the haymaker works in
> the fields when he has nothing better to do. . . . The grasses and sedges be-
> gin to brown before the cutting gets to them and one hopes that for once

they may escape, but they never do! . . . Every last spear is cut—even those which shelter a miniature cranberry bog worth much more than grass if the owner only realized it. . . . The hay is of dubious quality owing to the coarse marsh plants which comprise much of it. One might hesitate to offer a bed of it to a self-respecting cow, much less suggest it as food.

From early spring to late fall, Clute recorded the changes that characterized the various plant communities that he observed. After noting the "purplish haze" of the moss *Ceratodon purpureus* in early April, he describes the appearance of the first "real flowers" a few weeks later: "The little sand phlox (*Phlox bifida*) which seems especially created for the purpose, since its range practically coincides with the boundaries of this particular desert, unfolds a myriad of starry blossoms which spreads over the sands in drifts of white and pale lavender like a new kind of Milky Way."

By May, with the flowering of the cynthia or false dandelion (*Krigia biflora*), the lowlands will appear to have ignited. All other vegetation "will be eclipsed by the orange yellow flames of cynthia's dandelion-like blossoms. . . . It spreads great sheets of color in the grassy places and runs up the sands for some distance." The great burst of foliage put forth in June tends to overshadow the inflorescences of the period. An exception is the pasture rose (*Rosa carolina*), which scatters its pinkness across the uplands and even makes tentative forays into moister sand. Swamp (*Asclepias incarnata*) and whorled milkweeds in clusters of varying sizes and the solitary tall green milkweed (*A. hirtella*) appear in the swales of midsummer, while the sand evening primrose (*Oenthera rhombipetala*) sprinkles the bare soil of the driest dunes with circular clumps of yellow.

Colors are at their peak in August—"almost daily new galaxies appear"—but the spectacle is interrupted by the mowing blade. Still, where the ground is too waterlogged or too dry to entice the farmer, the pageantry unfolds. Composites such as the goldenrods, particularly the gray goldenrod (*Solidago nemoralis*), are among the showiest of the late summer blooms, but "the most imposing display . . . comes from the partridge pea (*Cassia fasciculata*). Beginning to bloom in an inconspicuous way in July, by the middle of August it is the most brilliant feature of the landscape. The clear golden yellow of its many blossoms gleam from the roadsides and old fields, and the plant is well represented on the dunes also."

With late August and September, the asters come into bloom: "The New England aster (*Aster novae-angliae*) appears in long drifts of purple in fencerows and along roadsides, mingling with the myriads of small white flower heads of heath aster (*A. ericoides*) and bushy aster (*A. dumosus*). These latter extend sheets of white into all but the driest places, like the premature snow-flurries of which they are the precursors." The same period brings to a peak two species of blazing stars. Marsh blazing star (*Liatris spicata*) tints acres of moist lands with purple, while the rough blazing star (*L. aspera*) graces the drier dunes.

Long after the last flowers are gone, color persists in the vegetative portions of the plants: "Along the roadsides the rich rose-purple panicles of the old witch grass (*Panicum capillare*) make a colorful haze for long stretches and later spread to the vacant fields on the wings of the wind, as tumbleweeds. The longer purple globes of the winged pigweed (*Cycloloma atriplicifolium*) also make movable spots of color in the open places. . . . The clear yellow or wine-color of the flowering spurge (*Euphorbia corollata*) is among the last to disappear and may prolong the color well into November."[52]

Clute could never have dreamed that his most significant findings were the four orchids he included in the book's extensive plant list: grass pink (*Calopogon tuberosus*), bracted orchid (*Habenaria viridis*), wood orchid (*H. clavellata*), and nodding ladies' tresses (*Spiranthes cernua*). Forty years later they would attract the interest of Charles Sheviak, who became so intrigued that he visited Braidwood to see it for himself. Only a small fraction of the landscape described by Clute remained, but Sheviak was impressed enough to alert the Illinois Nature Preserves Commission and the Illinois chapter of the Nature Conservancy. When the property owner, Peabody Coal Company, offered the land for auction, the conservancy purchased 205 acres for $275,000. The land was later "resold" to the Will County Forest Preserve District, which acquired an additional fifty-four acres from the Commonwealth Edison Company.[53] Formal dedication as a nature preserve occurred in 1981.

In the preface to *Swamp and Dune*, Clute had written: "Unless civilization encroaches upon the region more rapidly than present conditions indicate, it will serve as a field in which to hunt the elusive rare species and the vacillating adventive one for many years to come." Civilization certainly did encroach, but over the ensuing four decades it had adopted among its loftier (albeit less acted upon) impulses a conservation ethic. Thus a chunk or two of Braidwood's dazzling ground will continue to showcase the seasonal kaleidoscope described by Clute—thanks, at least in part, to Clute's little book.

In Quality Diminished:
Prairie Settlement and Conservation

O fly to the prairie, sweet maiden with me,

Tis as green, and as wild, and as wide as the sea,

O'er its emerald bosom the summer winds glide

And wave the wild grass like the vanishing tide.

— Dr. J. K. Mitchell (1840)

The vast prairie which lay before them in 1836, now . . . they could scarcely recognize. Indeed, there seemed to be no trace of the original country left, so great had been the changes. —Charles Holden (1882) (Joliet area)

Under the Fleur-de-lis: The French Period

The period of French reign in the Chicago area was of relatively short duration, lasting from 1673 to 1763. No colonies were established and the mission in Chicago was shut down in 1699 when the priests left to proselytize along the Mississippi. The Fox Indians, long-time adversaries of the French, closed the Chicago portage, thus shutting off access to the river thoroughfares. By 1763, the French had relinquished their regional claims to the British.[1]

While they left few marks on the ground, the French produced the first European accounts of the area and gave to us their word for the stunning grasslands they so admired: prairie. What they saw was the land as pristine as it would ever be described, land left by the glacier and modified by those human beings who arrived from Asia so long ago. Illinois, Indiana, and Wisconsin then contained an estimated total of 31,294,000 acres of prairie.

"The Illinois country is undeniably the most beautiful that is known anywhere between the mouth of the St. Lawrence and that of the Mississippi, which are a thousand leagues apart. You begin to see its fertility at Chicago . . .

at the end of Lake Michigan." So wrote De Gannes in the 1690s, echoing the words of Joliet and Marquette quoted in an earlier chapter.[2] Unbridled praise for the beauty and fecundity of the region appears throughout the French writings.

Writing in that vein, René-Robert Cavelier Sieur de La Salle sent the following correspondence to a government minister in Paris: "It is nearly all so beautiful and fertile; so free from forests, so full of meadows, brooks, and rivers; so abounding in fish, game, and venison, that one can find these in plenty, and with little trouble, all that is needful for the support of flourishing colonies."[3]

These unending panegyrics can perhaps be explained in part by the desire of the authors, who were priests (Marquette), entrepreneurs (Joliet), or "soldier-adventurers" (La Salle), to encourage the powers back home to support their work in the wilderness. Failing to find either a shortcut to the Pacific or the mineral riches that sustained Spain in its conquests of Mexico and South America, they emphasized the availability of game and pelts and the potential for agricultural success.

But there is an even larger factor at work here, difficult to visualize after three centuries of Euro-American settlement. Dorothy Anne Dondore, in her comprehensive review of the French chronicles, addresses "the most striking feature of all the exploration literature": "This is for the region of the prairies the use of superlatives. . . . Their praise indicates heartfelt tribute; their glorifying adjectives they seem impelled to use almost without their consciousness or volition. Absolutely every person who enters these regions of delight seems impressed by the fact that they are in quality unexcelled."[4]

The Prairie Resists: Treelessness, Fire, Disease, and Other Barriers to Settlement

The settlers who were to follow the French faced the special challenges posed by prairie habitation. These challenges delayed the influx of immigrants so that prairies were often the last lands to be claimed. Eventually, however, the masses of people pouring into the region shattered the prairie defenses one by one, and in a little more than sixty years these globally unique grasslands ceased to exist as a major landscape feature. And it took another seventy years before systematic and funded efforts were launched to preserve the prairie vestiges that still remained.

◄o► ◄o► ◄o►

When settlers first saw the vast expanses of prairie, the open sea was the image used most often to describe them. Among the similarities they shared were featureless distances broken only by the ephemera of waves. Successful navigation under such conditions required care and skill. On the high seas, there was reliance on instrumentation keyed to celestial order. But a prairie traveler, lacking the knowledge and equipment of his seafaring brethren, could easily find himself disoriented, especially if he were traversing areas of grass taller than himself.

On an afternoon in 1840, for instance, Warren Jackman, Crystal Lake's first schoolteacher, mounted his horse to perform some errands in McHenry, seven miles away. When he failed to appear that evening for choir practice, people became worried. He finally showed up the next morning, admitting that he had lost his way in the thick grass.[5] (A small portion of that prairie, incidentally, still exists as a narrow strip along the Chicago-Northwestern line linking the two towns.)

Like a ship coursing unencumbered by bearings, the wayfarer lost in the grasslands could confront the ultimate calamity, particularly in winter: "John M. Piper, who had come in 1837 to select land, made his choice in the Barkley settlement, and started on the 18th of December on foot for La Porte to make the proper entry. Soon after starting on his journey, a snowstorm set in, and he was never again seen alive. For thirty miles his route lay through the untracked prairie with no guide but a faint Indian trail, and it was thought that . . . becoming bewildered, he had traveled in a circle until, overcome with fatigue and cold, he laid down and died."[6]

Even where roads existed, travel and the transportation of goods were not easy. Since most of the region was far from navigable rivers, overland routes were the only alternatives. But as these crossed low prairie and marsh, commercial intercourse was severely hindered. In 1846, for example, the hundred-mile trip from Chicago to Peru (LaSalle County, just west of Grundy County) took thirty-two hours by stagecoach: "The day was hot, and the horses dragged us through the black mud, which seemed to possess the consistency and tenacity of sticking-plaster."[7]

For many immigrants used to forest, there was a strong prejudice against treeless scapes; lands that were incapable of supporting trees could hardly be suitable for agriculture. James Monroe was the most famous proponent of this view: "A great part of the territory is miserably poor, especially that near Lake Michigan . . . and that upon the Illinois consists of plains which have not had, from appearances, and will not have, a single bush on them for ages." In Jasper County, Indiana, years went by before a house was built beyond the shadows of the woods.[8]

The reluctance to claim land devoid of trees was based on more than attitude. Timber provided the wood that was essential for construction and fuel; remoteness from this critical commodity greatly increased the costs of homesteading. Indeed, to be a successful prairie pioneer one needed the financial resources to obtain lumber for initial improvements.[9] As the choice timbered acres were at a premium, the would-be settler with limited funds found himself in a quandary—woodlands were too expensive to purchase, and prairies were too costly to develop. In a letter written September 1840, Nicholas LePrevost related his experience:

> Up to this time all the lands that I had seen were woody and the farms cleared and for sale were at $10 to $30 per acre, but I was informed that at Racine there were government lands called prairies to sell at $1.25 the acre—I left my family on [August] 13 and proceeded to Racine. Oh! the beautiful grounds, not a tree and full of grass about 15 inches high, and in the lower parts 3 feet high—but as there is wood required for fire and building and it has to be purchased second hand at from $5 to $8 per acre, and from 3 to 5 miles distant—of the prairies I got discouraged.[10]

While the most productive soils in the world lay at their feet, the eastern farmers had never experienced anything like the thick mat of prairie sod. It was almost impenetrable, and breaking through to the bounty below was hell. Operators for hire would travel about with their special rigs and shred the protective husk for an often prohibitive two to four dollars an acre.[11] The introduction of the self-scouring steel plow in the 1830s, however, made it much easier for the average farmer to cultivate his land, which in turn spurred even greater prairie immigration. An old history of Will County provides a vivid description of the deflowering of original grassland:

> On many, many an acre of the virgin prairie of Will County did Lane's plows upturn the sod, drawn by from four to eight yoke of oxen and steers. . . . On, on, over the prairie swells, with steady but ruthless tread, moved the long "breaking team," and on, on came the giant plow, cutting the turf with its sharp colter, and turning over with its moldboard the rich earth in long, black ribbons; before it blooming grass and fragrant herb and beautiful flowers; behind it a dreary waste of black, fat humus, inviting the steps and stimulating the hopes of the sturdy planter.[12]

Fears about contracting disease caused many potential settlers to pause before embarking on new lives in the prairies. Both Illinois as a state and prairies as a type of land had bad reputations for being places where "fever and ague," mostly malaria, were rife: Illinois was widely regarded as a "graveyard." Whether the illness was worse in the state than outside is difficult to judge, but it is a fact that Illinoisans wrote about the topic with greater frequency than

12. Sod being broken by team of oxen and plow in Jefferson County,
Wisconsin (just north of Walworth County), in the 1860s. (Courtesy
Kettle Moraine State Forest Archives, Eagle, Wis.)

anyone else.[13] Charles Latrobe, making his way from Chicago to St. Louis
in 1833, found that "every cottage was full of ghastly faces and emaciated
forms."[14]

Five years later, while on an excursion into the prairies ten miles west of
Chicago, Captain Levinge and his party sought lodging for the night at an establishment where

> we found all the inmates in bed, covered up with blankets, and everything
> which could add to warmth heaped upon them. The driver informed us
> that this was the bad day of their fever, but that the fit would soon be over,
> and that then they would set about our accommodation for the night. We
> did not particularly like stopping in a house where every soul was under the
> influence of remittent fever, but our [guide] comforted us with the assur-
> ance that more or less of it prevailed in every house on the prairies at this
> season of the year.[15]

The history of malaria in the Middle West is fascinating, although any
but the most cursory discussion is beyond the scope of this work. Medical historian Erwin Ackernecht summarizes its occurrence in Illinois: "We see

malaria remain on a very low level from the first settlements up to the 1760's, then rise almost during one decade to epidemico-endemic proportions and hold this position unabated for about 70 years . . . ; we see it decline rather slowly in the 50's, 60's, and 70's, and rapidly in the 80's so that from 1890 on . . . malaria . . . is no longer of any importance." The operative fact here is that malaria flourished during the "pioneering phase of land occupation and development" and diminished as standards of living and physical "improvements" exceeded certain levels. Although malaria is spread by *Anopheles* mosquitoes, no single factor dictates the rise or demise of the disease.[16]

In an example of folk wisdom expressing truths long before they could be confirmed by science, the poet William Cullen Bryant wrote in 1846 that "it is a common remark in this country, that the first cultivation of the earth renders any neighborhood more or less unhealthy. 'Nature', said a western man to me, some years since, 'resents the violence done her, and punishes those who first break the surface of the earth with the plough.'"[17]

Fires played an important role as a protector of the prairie for they "were the most dreaded of all the early contingencies with which settlers had to deal."[18] There was a symbiotic relationship of sorts: the flames nurtured the prairie vegetation and helped discourage settlers, while the rank greenery fed the flames. This was something of a double-edged sword, however, as settlers attempted to break the relationship by attacking the prairie.

One measure designed to protect buildings involved plowing several furrows around the perimeter of the improvements. Settlers burned the strip within the furrows and allowed cattle to graze upon the prairie grasses that sprouted. Over time, with the pressure of intense grazing, the native grasses would give way to such Eurasian adventives as bluegrass and redtop that were not able to carry a fire. When fires did break out, the community armed itself with wet mops and bundles of hazel (precursors to modern rubber flappers), lit backfires, and worked together. The Indiana legislature lent its hand by enacting a statute that specifically banned "setting the prairie on fire," although prosecutions were infrequent, given the difficulty of proving guilt.[19] (Hoosiers were apparently more committed to the legal process than the Kansans, who apprehended a man they thought had accidentally started a fire and hung him.[20])

The Defenses Crumble but Some Prairie Survives

While traversing the prairies themselves might have been difficult, developments such as the opening of the Erie Canal simplified travel to them from the east coast. And although years from completion, the Illinois and Michigan Canal spawned settlement along its anticipated course. As early as 1836, regularly scheduled wagons serviced the districts between Chicago and Kankakee. In a very short time, as the population centers expanded, the "empty spaces" filled with settlers. The process began its final stage in 1848, when the Galena and Chicago Union Railroad provided Chicago's first train service.[21]

In 1830, none of northeastern Illinois was considered settled or had a population density greater than two people per square mile. By 1840, the entire state was settled, save for two small areas in the north and east-central portions, those most distant from transportation corridors. Most of northeastern Illinois was supporting six to eighteen people a square mile, and even the "unsettled" sections were up to two to six people per square mile. During these ten years, more than three hundred thousand people moved to the prairie lands of Illinois and vanquished forever the prairie wilderness. Settlement reached northwestern Indiana and southern Michigan at the same time or even earlier, 1825–31.[22] That the human tide was already reaching the hinterlands of the Chicago region as early as the 1820s is a fact often neglected: an oak tree that is 150 years old is not of presettlement time.

Southeastern Wisconsin was no different. A map depicting "pioneer settlements and associated farmlands in Racine County, 1838–1841" shows that over half of the county's surface was already supporting people and agriculture. In 1843, development in the county was proceeding at a pace of "unparalleled rapidity."[23] In the same year, Reverend A. C. Barry wrote of what he saw on his way to Rochester, on the Fox River twenty-five miles west of Racine: "Our way lay across the prairie the greater part of the distance. All was new, delightful and enchanting. White farm houses and cultivated fields dotted here and there the vast expanse; occasionally large herds of cattle were seen cropping the herbage in the distance; flowers of every hue were blooming all around upon the upturned sod."[24]

Although no one was to act seriously on it until deep into the next century when it was already too late, a few writers in the 1840s and 1850s express regret that the prairie was rapidly disappearing. These writers tended to be visitors in search of new sights and experiences, perhaps the first ecotourists. Some specifically state that seeing prairie was a major goal of their trip. Unfortunately, no entrepreneur saw the proverbial goldmine at her doorstep: picture a Franklin's ground squirrel resting in the shade of a compass plant surrounded by ten horse-drawn wagons brimming with tourists snapping away with their Daguerreotypes, an image reminiscent of today's Serengeti.

Except for his compulsion to collect, Edward Watkin was a good ecotourist, both enjoying the sights of 1851 and contributing to the local economy: "One of my objects was to see a prairie. I hired, one day, a vehicle and good horse, and drove with a friend right out upon the prairie lands, which encircle [Chicago], and, with intervals of cultivation, cover . . . a large portion of the state of Illinois. . . . We found an immense variety of wild flowers, some of them extremely beautiful, growing amongst the grass, and pulled more than thirty separate kinds within a space of half a mile."[25]

Two of the strongest and most explicit statements lamenting the rapidly disappearing prairies come from Fredrika Bremer (1853) and Caroline Kirkland (1858). It is worth noting about these two women that the former was a Swedish national and the latter had also spent considerable time in Europe, as her piece suggests. This background, perhaps, made them more likely to appreciate a landscape not yet filled with people. After having described how wonderful she found the prairie, Bremer wrote: "Chicago is one of the most miserable and ugly cities which I have yet seen in America, and is very little deserving of its name, 'Queen of the Lake.' . . . But in the evening when the sun descends and the wind subsides, I go to some higher part of the city, to see the sun set over the prairie land, for it is very beautiful. And beholding this magnificent spectacle melancholy thoughts arise. I see in this sun-bright western land thousands of shops and thousands of traders, but no temple of the sun and of eternal beauty."[26]

With the passing of every decade, prairie tracts dwindled in number. Those that survived did so only because specific circumstances prevented their annihilation. Sometimes these circumstances were rooted in the land itself: both wet prairie and sand prairie failed to yield satisfactory amounts of produce. In other instances, the land was used but in a way that often maintained some prairie character: pasture, railroad rights-of-way, and cemeteries.

Lowland prairie resisted agricultural invasion until widespread programs of ditching and tiling were inaugurated. In Illinois this commenced in the 1870s, and by 1919 drainage projects within the state exceeded three thousand miles in length.[27] Drainage of the Kankakee River wetlands began in the 1850s and received a boost in 1889 when the Indiana legislature enacted a law appropriating proceeds of land sales in the area to that purpose.[28]

While many people today recognize that wetlands are worthy of protection, the case was very different seventy-five years ago. Landowners who failed to drain every last yard of their property were subjected to derision and scorn. A 1927 master's thesis prepared in the University of Chicago's Geography Department examined land use in Bremen Township in southern Cook County. Although admitting that adjacent drained land "yielded discouragingly small crops," the author lambasted the landowner who left eighty of his acres unditched: "Here is evidence of a human factor, a matter of ignorance, shiftlessness or folly [that] is seen in brambles, weeds, and coppice. . . . These eighty acres of desolate wasteland tell the story of environment winning out over the puny efforts of incompetence, while the present orderly green expanse of the once equally cursed environments along the middle roads speaks eloquently of man's ability, when rightly directed, to cope with nature, even in her sorrier moods, when the odds are not too great."[29]

Ironically, the very railroads whose spreading tentacles opened the prairie to markets also protected strips of right-of-way from farming. Utility companies often strung their lines along the same segments of track, further limiting land use. While railroad maintenance activities tended to be destructive, at least one common practice benefited the prairie remnants: to control the growth of trees, employees regularly burned the rights-of-way.

In Berrien County, virtually the only prairies left are tiny scraps lying along the hundred-foot-wide corridor of the Michigan Central Railroad completed in the late 1840s. When Amtrak took over the line in 1976, planned upgrades in the track bed threatened to destroy these small relics. The Michigan chapter of the Nature Conservancy entered into negotiations with railroad management; working together, the two parties identified and agreed to protect six critical portions spanning four miles of right-of-way. (Three of the tracts are outside Berrien County.) This stretch includes examples of dry, mesic, and wet prairie types, as well as fifteen species of plants listed as rare, threatened, or endangered in Michigan.[30]

West Chicago Prairie, DuPage County, the largest and most diverse black-soil prairie in the region, owes its survival to having been part of the land acquired by the Galena and Union Railroad (now the Chicago and Northwestern) in 1850 and held until the 1960s. Sixty percent of all the native plant species currently known to exist in DuPage County, including six that are state endangered, inhabit the prairie's 248 acres. The Forest Preserve District of DuPage County and the City of West Chicago obtained the property in 1979; although extremely well maintained by the district, the site is probably the finest natural area in northeastern Illinois that has yet to be dedicated as a nature preserve. It would be a tragedy if harm befell this prairie before it received the full protection it deserves.[31]

Parts of the Chicago region supported a large and lucrative dairy industry, particularly Kane and McHenry counties. Prairie subjected to light grazing retains its basic integrity indefinitely, while overgrazing can degrade the original flora in a very brief period.[32] Pasturing was particularly devastating to mesic prairie, both because much of it is highly palatable to livestock—according to John Curtis the *Silphium* were "sought out like hidden candy at a child's birthday party"—and it was fertile ground for weedy adventives such as bluegrass and ragweed (*Ambrosia*).[33]

Dry and wet prairies proved more resilient, largely because they were inhospitable to the exotics. Over time, however, even these prairies would begin to change composition, although some original elements remained. On the dry-hill prairies, for instance, cattle would browse prairie smoke but ignore prairie buttercup because it blistered their mouths. Dairying also encouraged the maintenance of fencerows, which provided valuable enclaves for prairie species. But, when economic shifts favored the production of corn over dairy products and the use of automobiles required the widening of roads, these fallow margins disappeared along with the natives they had sheltered.[34]

Cemeteries have also provided valuable, albeit tiny, reserves for prairie organisms. When the pioneers enclosed small portions of land to bury their dead, they created what would become isolated islands of prairie amid the cultivated miles. Because their soils are intact and have been spared decades of erosion, these cemeteries often lie several inches or more above the adjacent land. Of the 3,923 cemeteries examined, the Illinois Natural Areas Inventory found twenty-four to contain high-quality prairie or savanna communities.[35] One example is the superb prairie at Vermont Cemetery in Will County. For Indiana, however, the situation is even starker: German Methodist Cemetery Nature Preserve near Lowell, Lake County, is one of the very few surviving black-soil prairies in the entire state. Although only an acre in size, it supports over sixty species of prairie plants, which the Indiana Nature Preserves Commission says "may make it the most diverse acre in Indiana."[36]

The only other remaining prairie lands of any extent were the sand prairies. For a long time, their agricultural potential went unrecognized, but beginning around 1910 many landowners turned their property into pine-tree plantations that proved successful in the sandy soil. More recently, truck farmers have found a profit in asparagus, onions, and other produce.[37] Henry Gleason, who was to become one of the foremost botanists of the twentieth century, studied these prairies in 1908, concentrating his time in western Illinois. He spent only two days in the Chicago region, at Saint Anne in Kankakee County. Although the Morris-Kankakee Basin is "undoubtedly the largest sand area represented in the state, . . . at least three-fourths of its total extent lies in Indiana," and much of the upland portion was either wooded or in cultivation.

In the introduction to his study, Gleason makes this bleak pronouncement: "At the present time, [the sand regions] comprise the largest, and virtually only, areas of natural vegetation within the state. With the exception of parts of the sand deposits, of some small swamp areas, of rock outcrops, of ponds and lakes, and of some small tracts of forest, all the original vegetation of Illinois has been destroyed or greatly modified by clearing, planting, or pasturing."[38]

Victor Shelford, an ecologist at the University of Illinois, reiterated the sentiment in 1911 when "he lamented that the prairie was gone, except for a few small patches and remnants along railroad rights of way."[39] In a sense, we have reached the nadir. Two of the most distinguished biologists in the state (indeed, both men enjoyed international reputations) proclaimed the virtual destruction of all prairie land in Illinois. And the situation was no better in southeastern Wisconsin, Indiana, and Michigan.

Several years after these two biologists declared that Illinois's prairie was gone, Arthur Vestal published the first scientific study of a Chicago area prairie.[40] Known as Elmhurst Prairie, the site had been left alone by virtue of its small size and surrounding forest and marsh. Composed of mesic and wet prairie, it provided habitat for such conservative species as Hill's thistle (*Cirsium hilli*), Indian paintbrush (*Castilleja coccinea*), and prairie milkweed. Botanists regarded the tract as the best black-soil prairie extant in Illinois. If, as we shall see, the Great Depression saved the prairies of Markham and Westchester, the affluence of the 1950s decreed the death of Elmhurst Prairie. Slashed and scraped by the blades of the Tollway Authority in 1957, it lies interred under Route 294, a loss now barely remembered.

Beginning around 1915, botanist Homer Sampson undertook surveys to identify prairie still extant in Illinois.[41] He sent letters to each of the 102 county surveyors asking the location of prairies within their jurisdiction. Sampson received seventy-three responses pointing to the existence of several thousand acres of prairie, although some of them proved to be heavily grazed bluegrass fields. Three of the counties were from this area:

> Cook: About 5000 acres on the old lake bed of Lake Chicago and a few small tracts on the Valparaiso Moraine. There are 2000 acres in the vicinity of Ashburn within the city limits of Chicago.
>
> DuPage: Small areas along east branch of the DuPage River between Swift and Lisle.
>
> Grundy: "Hay swamps" north of Coal City; 220 acres five miles west of Morris along the Illinois River. Mostly flood plain; some moraine and mostly pastured.

Sampson studied the Morris site and extensive portions of the Chicago prairie. The Morris location was wet and had been pastured. Because of the intensive grazing, prairie cordgrass and bluejoint grass had been displaced by sedges and redtop grass (*Agrostis alba*), switchgrass by redtop and Kentucky bluegrass (*Poa pratensis*), and big bluestem by Kentucky bluegrass. Sampson concluded that areas less altered by pasturing "would exhibit a mixture of associations of native and cultivated grasses impossible to decipher on an ecological basis."

The Ashburn prairie also manifested the effects of long-term disturbance (see figs. 8 and 9). Due to forty years of July mowing, the lowering of the water table, and grazing, the nonnative bluegrasses and redtop grass had established themselves over large areas as they had done at the Morris site.

Fortunately, the tracts were regularly burned, a circumstance Sampson considered inimical to their well-being but that in reality enabled them to remain prairie.

Neither the citizenry nor its elected officials were moved to protect the properties listed on Homer Sampson's inventory. In fact, it is possible to trace the slow dismemberment of Ashburn Prairie. In his discussion of prairie smoke, Pepoon writes that Ashburn is one of only two places in the region where this hill-prairie plant occurs. It grew "in an area of perhaps ten square rods, . . . a survivor of a more numerous ancient race [which] is doomed in all of the known localities by the encroaching bluegrass."[42]

William Beecher, for many years director of the Chicago Academy of Sciences, has written that he watched the Ashburn Prairie "disappear acre by acre" until the last of it, south of Eighty-seventh Street and Kedzie Avenue, "was subdivided and the querulous notes of the upland plover, the lonely lost-soul cry of the prairie, ceased to be heard."[43] Finally, in 1992, the only remaining shard, tucked away in a corner of the St. Mary's–Evergreen Cemetery complex, was about to be covered by a shopping center. Prairie steward Joe Neumann and others tried to save it, but the parcel was too small and too expensive and the developer was on the verge of moving dirt. Eventually, the Chicago Park District agreed to strip the sod and replant it at Marquette Park, a short distance to the north.

From Sampson's time to the 1960s, interest in whatever remained of local prairie was relatively low. Donald Culross Peattie highlighted prairies in several of the articles he wrote for his series "Hikes around Chicago," which appeared in the *Chicago Daily News* in 1925. Hike number 3 explored the Beverly area of Chicago. Just west of the Rock Island tracks on 103rd Street (east of Western Avenue), "the sidewalks begin to peter out and the pleasant houses are left behind and presently one finds oneself on open prairie—the sort of place where in the spring the meadowlarks whistle and the shooting stars nod in the grass; at this season [summer] the face of the land is gorgeous with purple ironweed and compass plant."[44]

Bill Beecher, after innumerable field excursions, found a sizable tract of mesic and wet prairie huddled against the Glenview Naval Air Station. He came upon it in 1940 and tried to convince the Cook County Forest Preserve District and Illinois Department of Conservation to purchase it. At $1,500 an acre, however, the agencies deemed the parcel too expensive, and the opportunity was lost as the prairie gave way to subdivision.[45]

A city block–sized prairie was still extant in 1942 at the northeast corner of Foster and Neenah Avenues in Chicago. Prairie violet (*Viola pedatifida*), sky-blue aster (*Aster azureus*), yellow stargrass, leadplant, wild quinine, and prairie Indian plantain were among the more conservative species present at the site.

Before its destruction three years earlier, an adjacent tract, slightly drier, had supported such rarities as cream white indigo and Hill's thistle. By the end of the decade, the entire area was covered in the neat rows of homes and lawns that remain today.[46]

Illinois took a giant step toward protecting prairies (and all other natural communities) when it enacted the Natural Areas Preservation Act in 1963. Versions of this landmark legislation, a monument to the brilliance and perseverance of the late George Fell, who both conceived it and worked tirelessly to enhance its effectiveness, were adopted by numerous other states including Indiana (1967), Michigan (1972), and Wisconsin (1985). (Wisconsin has had a "scientific areas" program since 1951.)

Its most important provision establishes a system of dedicated nature preserves, high-quality natural areas—generally those manifesting a minimum of human disturbance—that can only be used for purposes that maintain or increase the well-being of their natural features. Dedication occurs when the landowner, either private or public, grants what in essence is a highly restrictive conservation easement to the Nature Preserves Commission, a body appointed by the governor and composed of biologists and others committed to conservation. Only properties that retain significant natural features are eligible for this protection, which includes immunity from condemnation.

The Turning Point for Prairie Conservation: Goose Lake Prairie

As late as 1966 it was still possible for one conservationist to lament, "You can count on the fingers of one hand those people who are interested in prairies."[47] Common wisdom held that only one prairie should be fought for at a time. There is general agreement that these attitudes changed with the battle to save Goose Lake Prairie, Grundy County. Bob Betz calls it the turning point.[48]

Goose Lake Prairie had been part of a seven thousand–acre spread owned by a family named Collins, who had never drained or intensively farmed these eighteen hundred acres. Bill Beecher surmised that it had been spared the plow because it was surrounded by wetland and littered with glacial erratics, boulders left by the glacier. For whatever the reason, Goose Lake Prairie was the largest remnant still surviving in the entire prairie peninsula, and it contained the full range of landscape types, from dry prairie to marsh and open water. It was not the richest prairie, for it had obviously been grazed and much of it was "beaten up," but its size and diversity offered a unique opportunity to upgrade its quality through a careful regimen of burning and other practices.

Among the many people who contributed to safeguarding Goose Lake Prairie, three in particular stand out for the principal roles they played in the great undertaking. The late Charles Olmsted, then chairman of the University of Chicago's Botany Department, first brought the prairie to the attention of the conservation community and then lent his stature as a scientist to the project. Jeffrey Short, then chairman of the Openlands Project, used the resources of his organization and his moxie as a businessman to help clear the seemingly insurmountable hurdles. And Bill Beecher, in addition to his standing as the biologist best known to the public, made the issue popular through Chicago Academy of Science activities and his writings, particularly an influential piece that ran in the *Chicago Tribune Sunday Magazine* in September 1967. I remember that article well, for it prompted my first visit to Goose Lake Prairie. More important, it inspired an anonymous donor to offer $1.5 million to the prairie's preservation.

Beecher has written in great detail of the events that led to their victory. Allied against the conservationists were the EJ&E Railroad and the Illinois Clay Products Company. (This was just the first of three fights conservationists would have with Illinois Clay Products over properties owned by the company.) One of the firms wanted to industrialize the Illinois River Valley into the "Ruhr Valley of Illinois," while the other desired the clay that lined the bottom of Goose Lake. Numerous meetings were held in Morris and Chicago. A report by the Illinois Natural History Survey convinced William Lodge, director of the Illinois Department of Conservation, that the state should purchase the property.

The final decision came to rest with the Illinois Building Authority, whose approval was necessary before the Department of Conservation could spend any money on the project. The chairman of the Authority announced that before voting he wanted to see the prairie. This spawned another intense round of activity, culminating in helicopters converging at Goose Lake from Chicago and Springfield for one last gathering before the formal vote. At the big showdown a few weeks later in Chicago, the board rendered its decision: to their jubilation, the conservationists had prevailed by a four-to-one vote.

But like most conservation struggles, a single victorious battle does not a victorious war make. Department of Conservation officials started getting cold feet over the cost of the property. In addition, Governor Kerner had resigned to take a federal judgeship, making Sam Shapiro governor. Shapiro, however, was now a lame duck, having been defeated by Richard Ogilvie in the general election. Rather than pressuring Shapiro to act in the waning days of his administration, the brain trust decided to wait until Ogilvie assumed office and named his choice to head the Department of Conservation.

That choice was William Rutherford, who was later to establish Wildlife Prairie Park near Peoria. Rutherford astounded the conservationists by stating his desire to acquire three thousand acres, twelve hundred more than even they had been requesting. Soon after becoming director, he met with the Collinses and arranged the purchase of fourteen hundred acres at $1,400 per acre. Ultimately, the state bought a total of twenty-six hundred acres, which became Goose Lake Prairie State Park. Of that land, 1,628 acres are in the Nature Preserves System and another five hundred acres have become reconstructed prairie. The reconstruction effort, under the skillful direction of department biologists Francis Harty and William Glass, removed more than thirty thousand trees and increased numerous prairie species.

Prairie Tales: A Few Prairies and the Battles to Save Them

As prairies gained in stature, increasing amounts of money and time were spent locating, studying, and protecting them. These searches turned up prairies of varying sizes, types, and quality. A good number had been known before the formal pursuit of them began; a few have been discovered since. Some have been destroyed, either completely or in part. The Illinois Natural Areas Inventory concluded that "the chance of a natural prairie persisting in Illinois is so slight that more than one factor working in combination has often been necessary for the prairie's continued existence."[49] Because the demand for land is now so intense, we are very close to the time when the only surviving prairies will be those owned by conservation interests. And behind every saved prairie there is a story, the successful conclusion of which usually took years and the immeasurable energy, talent, and love of vigilant champions, many of whom are volunteers.

Sometimes, though, energy, talent, love, and even money are insufficient to defeat profound avarice. One of the ugliest stories in these pages is that of Buffalo Grove Prairie (a.k.a. Chevy Chase Prairie and Wheeling Prairie), Lake County (Ill.). Although some question exists as to when and by whom the prairie was first found, conservationists became aware of its importance in the spring and summer of 1976. The fifty-six acres of black-soil prairie contained thousands of white lady's slippers, eastern prairie fringed orchids, the only cream wild indigo in Lake County, and even a large population of massasauga rattlesnakes. As much as a third of the total area manifested no disturbance at all. Alan Haney, a botanist at the University of Illinois, wrote that "it is without doubt . . . the best wet prairie within a 50-mile radius and maybe one of the best left in the state."[50] Bob Betz, Floyd Swink, the state biologists, and others were unanimous in urging the Lake County Forest Preserve District to protect the prairie. The Illinois chapter of the Nature Conservancy offered to buy and hold the land until they could sell it to the district when monies became available. The Illinois Department of Conservation was also willing to help the district obtain the necessary funding. With this information in hand, the district agreed that saving the site was a top priority and quickly began formulating an acquisition plan.

Meanwhile, in the process of extending Lake Cook Road west from Milwaukee Avenue, the Bongi Cartage Company of Cicero began removing soil from the prairie to use as roadbed fill. It turned out the prairie owners had sold the mineral rights to Bongi. Alarmed conservationists attempted to contact the family who owned most of the prairie. Lake County officials found them to be uncooperative, but in an article published on September 3, the Nature Conservancy reported that the family was "in sympathy with preserving it just as we are. The thing is they have to make some money out of it."[51]

The prospects for a successful resolution seemed good. All the conservation forces were working in harmony, the Lake County Forest Preserve District was committed to preserving the property, and the owners had indicated that they would be reasonable. But over the Labor Day weekend of 1976, crews from Bongi worked overtime to plow into obliteration all but one-quarter acre of the owners' prairie holdings. No one doubted that the act was deliberate. Said one district official, "I think we can only conclude that the owners felt this was the best route to avoid delay in the proposed annexation of the land to Buffalo Grove."[52] As far as I know, the destruction of a high-quality natural area specifically to thwart its protection by a willing and able public agency is unique in the annals of local conservation. (The only other incident that comes close is when the same owner attempted to clear the timber from a parcel being purchased by the DuPage County Forest Preserve District.)

The story has a sequel, which to date has been far more pleasing.[53] Ten acres of adjacent prairie owned by Commonwealth Edison and situated under its power lines were spared the Labor Day massacre. (The vandals obviously respected private property rights.) This piece is still very rich, but was threatened by vehicle incursions, dumping, and other incidental activities.

With the help of Meg Bushnell, then chairman of the Illinois Commerce Commission, conservation organizations met with Commonwealth Edison officials to discuss protection of this prairie and other natural areas under company control. At the same time, Beverly Hanson of the Buffalo Grove Prairie Guardians, another of the citizen-conservationists whose contributions are often critical but unheralded, was working with local Edison people to make sure the prairie was preserved. The company ultimately agreed to fence the parcel, erect a sign explaining its significance, and allow land management activities.

13. Only surviving remnant of Buffalo Grove Prairie, preserved under
utility right-of-way; photo by J. Greenberg, 1997.

While Edison has refused to dedicate it as a nature preserve claiming they may some day need to use the property, Buffalo Grove Prairie seems to be secure, at least for now.

⊰o⊱ ⊰o⊱ ⊰o⊱

One of the earliest studies of a local prairie was published by Northwestern University's Ruth Davis Paintin in 1924 at a time when the school still had faculty members who were professionally interested in local natural history.[54] Paintin examined the composition of Peacock Prairie, located in Glenview (Cook County) on Milwaukee Avenue between Central and Greenwood Avenues.

The Peacock and Long families held the property from 1843 to 1953, when they finally sold it to a developer. All evidence indicates that at no time during their reign of ownership did the families ever allow the prairie to be plowed or consistently grazed. It was, however, burned every year. That the prairie was wet and thus less suitable for farming than adjacent land probably explains its preservation.

A family member described to Paintin some of the plants he knew were on the prairie and said that they "were characteristic of all adjoining land before it had been broken but this particular plot had always had more plants and been more colorful than any other." One story, perhaps apocryphal, has it that grandmothers Long and Peacock found the prairie so lovely they would meet there to pass the time, and it was, at least in part, out of deference to these ladies that the prairie was kept.[55]

Starting in 1953, the prairie fell on difficult times and was gradually whittled down in size to 5.3 acres. The new owner derived income from the property through its use as a parking lot for construction equipment, a go-cart raceway, and a miniature golf course. Expansion of the golf course would have destroyed the prairie in 1966 had a group of citizens not intervened. Joining together a year earlier, conservationists led by Bernice Popelka and Evelyn Tyner incorporated as the Peacock Prairie Preservation Society. They contacted the Openlands Project, whose president, Jeffrey Short, convinced the developer to delay further activity. Public agencies from the Glenview Park District to the Department of Conservation all declined to buy the land: it was too expensive and small. Fortunately, the University of Illinois at Chicago stepped in and agreed to obtain the property.

The combined efforts of the university (particularly Professor Albert Rouffa and former chancellor Norman Parker), the Openlands Project, and the Peacock Prairie Preservation Society succeeded in obtaining a grant from the federal Land and Water Conservation (LAWCON) program and the additional funds needed to match it (Chicago Community Trust was a major contributor). The Leslie Family paid for an education center, and the prairie was renamed to honor one of their relatives, James Woodworth.[56]

In the forty years since Paintin performed her study, the prairie had shrunk in size, much of what remained had been abused, and the land around it had been covered with buildings and cement. Bob Betz and Marion Cole wondered how all these changes had affected the vegetation of the prairie. To their surprise, they found that the prairie had actually improved in quality over the years, even without regular management. Ten species of prairie legumes, two lilies, two gentians, and one orchid still inhabited the tract, but, most surprising, a number of the weeds seen by Paintin had disappeared: "It is one of the few prairies in the region that does not contain the ubiquitous [Kentucky bluegrass] and [Canada bluegrass]."[57]

Because it is small, rich, and surrounded by development, Woodworth is a site that epitomizes the term "prairie remnant." Houses abut it on the north side and a McDonald's on the south. A Burger King and an Arby's are across the street: where the prairie meets the fast food restaurant. Fortunately, Rouffa and his volunteers have kept close watch over the prairie, and the terms of the LAWCON Grant discourage the university from ever selling the land. It is still vitally important, though, that the university officials in Urbana follow the recommendations of the Chicago campus and dedicate the prairie as a state nature preserve to ensure that this virgin relict remains safe forever.

◄O► ◄O► ◄O►

Everything about Gensburg-Markham Prairie bespeaks quality: from its richness and diversity—a summer visit leaves you wondering whether the riot of colors is not the creation of a landscaper with a fondness for lysergic acid—to the meticulous care with which it has been protected and studied. [58] Ninety-five acres are dedicated as nature preserve. Additional prairies exist in the vicinity that, along with Gensburg-Markham, are collectively known as the Indian Boundary Prairies. In recognition of all this remarkable prairie in one small area, a proposal, unfortunately never adopted, was made several years ago to erect a sign proclaiming Markham, "the prairie capital of the prairie state."

The area was first surveyed in the summer of 1834. John Clark's field notes indicate that the easternmost portion of the prairie was marsh, while the remainder alternated between wet prairie and marsh, with standing water as deep as eighteen inches. This frequent inundation prompted locals to call the place "Black Slough," and it was a choice spot for spring duck hunting. Although roads were scarce and in poor condition in the early years, cattle and sheep passed through in columns three miles long and bedded down in the prairies between Markham and Blue Island on their way to the stockyards of Chicago, but whether their paths crossed this exact property isn't known.

Sometime prior to 1901, the Thomes family established a farmstead on the western portion of the prairie between Kedzie and Sacramento avenues. As part of the operations, hay was cut once a year, and crops were planted. The assessment of a neighbor was that the farmer "didn't get rich." In fact, due presumably to his labor being so unrewarding, Thomes moved away in 1919 or 1920. The prairie hasn't been commercially mowed since.

By the end of the 1920s, serious plans were underway to convert the prairie into residential housing. Three plats subdividing the prairie were filed in 1926, and over the next couple of years ditches were dug to prepare for the installation of streets. Then, like a governor's last-second phone call of reprieve to the warden, the Great Depression interceded, and designs to develop the prairie evaporated as quickly as the vigor of the world economy. Phil Hanson notes that "of the 700 lots that the prairie was divided into, only two . . . were ever built upon," and they were located on the prairie edge where their effects were minimal.

Although not destroyed, the prairie has been subjected to numerous disturbances arising from surrounding Markham. From the late 1960s to 1972, an acre of vegetation was cut so that it could be used as a field for baseball and model airplanes. Not only did the mowing stunt plant growth in subsequent years, but it decreased soil moisture as well. This was evident by the dominance of little bluestem instead of the big bluestem that flourished on adjacent uncut land.

Of longest lasting effect were the various drainage trenches excavated over the years. While initially reducing standing water, the trenches have since fallen into disrepair and the prairie now keeps most of the water it receives. But these ditches stayed moist longer than the surrounding prairie and thus provided favorable conditions for the invasion of cottonwoods (*Populus deltoides*). As part of the ongoing land management regime, these trees are being removed lest they proliferate and jeopardize shade-intolerant prairie species. Another consequence of these ditches is highly desirable. They have been colonized by a distinctive plant community that thrives where sand has been removed almost to the water table. The highly conservative species whose territory at Markham is confined to these furrows include grass pink orchids, royal ferns (*Osmunda regalis*), and narrow-leaved sundews (*Drosera intermedia*).

The prairie, in addition, has been crossed by snowmobiles, intruded on by utility lines and sewers, marred by illegal dumping, and according to the late naturalist Karl Bartel "harvested" by professional florists, one of whom "came into the prairie each year and cut a station wagon full of [marsh blazing stars]." Careless children, though, might have inadvertently nullified the effects of these harmful activities: it is believed that they set the fires that acted like white corpuscles in fending off floral invaders and keeping the prairie healthy.

By the late 1960s, conservationists had initiated a concerted effort to preserve Markham Prairie. Bob Betz, Ray Schulenberg, and David Blenz of the Cook County Forest Preserve District convinced the Markham authorities to zone the prairie as open space. It had been earlier established that of the three parties owning the prairie, the Gensburg family, residing in California, held the largest portion. Through Betz's labor, Northeastern Illinois University took an active role in the battle, and the Gensburgs agreed to donate half of their share to the school. With assistance from the Illinois chapter of the Nature Conservancy, this gift was used as a match to obtain a $200,000 federal grant that went toward the purchase of the remainder. Ninety-five acres were dedicated as nature preserve in September 1980.

This still left any nearby unprotected parcels of prairie in jeopardy. Most recently, a businessman proposed a restaurant-motel complex on adjacent high-quality prairie. Fortunately, after the U.S. Army Corps of Engineers designated the tract as wetland, the parties were able to reach a compromise that left most of the prairie in place.

Courtesy of Lake Chicago, a ridge of sand supporting mesic prairie occupies the southwest half of Gensburg-Markham Prairie. To the northeast, where the land drops three to four feet, wet prairie flourishes on poorly drained loam (black soil). The preserve entrance opens onto the mesic prairie that harbors the richest assemblage of plants on the entire site. Among these are the most conservative species of Gensburg-Markham's flora: cream white indigo, wood betony (*Pedicularis canadensis*), downy gentian (*Gentiana puberula*), and soapwort gentian (*G. saponaria*).

This portion of Gensburg-Markham Prairie also features one of the most spectacular phenological events that this region offers: the blooming of the blazing stars. By early August the marsh blazing star is in full flower and, as it slides into senescence late in the month, the rough blazing star takes over, prolonging the display another few weeks. When a summer has been cool and wet, there is a good chance of seeing both species in bloom simultaneously. Countless wands of amethyst sway to the irregular rhythm of summer breezes while butterflies such as monarchs (*Danaus plexippus*) and black swallowtails (*Papilio polyxenes*) hang on like rodeo cowboys.

I missed the show one summer, for my July visit was too early; only a few of the marsh blazing stars had reached anthesis. But as compensation, I came across a splendid concentration of Culver's root (*Veronicastrum virginicum*) growing in the company of rattlesnake master, white prairie clover, yellow coneflower (*Ratibida pinnata*), wild quinine, butterfly weed, and other prairie specialties. Culver's root, looking like an oddly shaped candelabra filled with pale pink candles, had not been recorded by Phil Hanson in any of his ten research plots twenty years ago. The increase in this lovely plant is an example of the good things that can happen to a prairie under thoughtful management.

◄O► ◄O► ◄O►

Hoosier Prairie, at four hundred acres, is the largest in Indiana. More than three hundred species of plants have been found in the natural communities that thrive here: black oak savanna, dry sand prairie, mesic sand prairie, wet sand prairie, sedge meadow, and marsh. It harbors such exceedingly rare species as yellow wild indigo (*Baptisia tinctoria*), Wolf's spike rush (*Eleocharis wolfii*), and hair bladderwort (*Utricularia subulata*).[59] Local conservationists had long known the natural value of the prairie but had never given it much emphasis as they had focused their attention on preserving the magnificent Indiana Dunes. But in 1967, Irene Herlocker began a nine-year campaign that didn't end until the prairie was protected more thoroughly than anyone could have predicted.

Herlocker wrote of her first visit to the prairie: "I was stunned. I couldn't believe there was something so beautiful only ten minutes from my home, and

I'd lived within ten miles of this area all of my life."[60] Her initial flurry of activity led to the formation of the Hoosier Prairie Committee in 1969. The group consisted of Bob Betz ("He'll go anywhere to save a prairie," according to Herlocker), William Barnes, director of Indiana's Division of Nature Preserves, and Herman Feldman, chairman of the Division of Arts and Sciences at Indiana University Northwest. The very name they adopted reflected keen political insight. Previous names for the site, Griffith Prairie and Scherville Prairie, were rooted in local geography, but Betz proposed Hoosier Prairie to make its preservation more appealing to those Indianans who saw Lake County as the state's "stepchild."

The family who owned the property agreed to protect the land, but they were not willing simply to give it away in the name of conservation or to preserve it indefinitely: they expected conservationists eventually to secure the funds to buy it. Conservationists saw their opportunity when monies became available to increase the size of the Indiana Dunes National Lakeshore. The committee pushed hard to have Hoosier Prairie included as part of the expansion, and members made numerous lobbying trips to Washington. (Herlocker: "You really need good shoes to walk in those marble halls.") The National Park Service demurred, however, saying that the prairie was ten miles from the closest federal holdings and would therefore be difficult to manage.

About this time, a chance meeting between Herlocker and State Senator Ralf Potesta led to a new possibility: the state of Indiana might purchase all or part of the site. With the aid of Governor Otis Bowen, numerous state legislators, all but one of the Indiana congressional delegation, and both Illinois senators, a federal-state partnership was crafted whereby Indiana would receive $450,000 as a grant from the U.S. Department of Interior and then use $450,000 of its own money to purchase the entire tract. This collaboration has benefited Hoosier Prairie in another way as well: it is both a dedicated Indiana Nature Preserve and a unit of the Indiana Dunes National Lakeshore and is thus afforded both state and federal attention.

◄► ◄► ◄►

Wolf Road Prairie, in Westchester (Cook County), might hold the record in length of time it has taken to be preserved and the number of people who have in one way or another contributed to the cause.[61] Cook County Forest Preserve District staff urged that it be bought as long ago as the 1950s, but the large number of landowners made the process of acquisition so formidable that the district opted for other lands. Alma Greene, fresh from a course in prairies taught at the Morton Arboretum by Ray Schulenberg, "rediscovered" the prairie in 1972 and three years later, along with Jack Shouba and others, founded the Save the Prairie Society.

The society's major strategy had been trying to convince the Westchester Park District to purchase the prairie. Unfortunately, the society lacked local influence, as not one of its members was a resident of Westchester. But that changed when Valerie Spale joined. She agreed to collect signatures from neighbors urging the park district to act. Having presented her petition, she figured the job was done. Only a seer could have known what was to come: Spale ended up playing a key role in the long course of action, detailed below, that led to the dedication of the prairie as a nature preserve, and in the process, she became one of northeastern Illinois's most influential voices for conservation. Along the way, she figures close to five thousand people helped to save the prairie.

At eighty acres, Wolf Road Prairie is one of the two largest and highest-quality black-soil prairies extant in this part of Illinois. The site is further enriched by the presence of a five-acre savanna that has been in place since at least 1821 when it was mapped by the U.S. Government Public Land Survey.

The Chicago fire of 1871 destroyed Cook County's real estate records, and therefore little of the prairie's early history is known. Presumably the prairie was left alone because of its wetness, including periodic flooding by nearby Salt Creek. Development, however, caught up with the tract in the 1920s. Electric train lines radiated out from Chicago to the expanding suburbs, including Westchester. The prairie was plotted, and six hundred lots were sold to more than a hundred owners. Reminiscent of what happened at Gensburg-Markham Prairie, the Great Depression drove the developers into bankruptcy, but not before a grid of sidewalks demarcating eight blocks was installed on the prairie's southeast portion. This, to me, is the most singular feature of Wolf Road Prairie: in between the crisscrossing rows of concrete walkways lies virgin prairie.

Even after the economy righted itself, property owners were unable to develop their holdings. The lots were too small to hold septic tanks, and no single owner was big enough to begin the construction that would open up the eighty acres. Thus, Valerie Spale and Save the Prairie Society had the time they needed to put in place the funding plan that would bring the prairie into public ownership. They enlisted the help of then State Senator Judy Barr Topinka (now Illinois State Treasurer), who helped broker an arrangement by which the Illinois Department of Conservation and the Cook County Forest Preserve District would each purchase forty acres. Federal LAWCON dollars also assisted in the purchases.

For fifty years, the lot owners had done nothing to advance their devel-

14. Wolf Road Prairie in Westchester, Cook County, showing
sidewalks crossing site; photo by J. Greenberg, 1997.

opment schemes; thus, it was surprising that many became intransigent and
forced the state and county to acquire the land through the exercise of eminent
domain. Buying out these small owners lot by lot was a slow and expensive
process, something akin to hand-to-hand combat. Conservation agencies obtained the last parcel of prairie in 1992 and dedicated it as nature preserve a
year later. Fortunately, throughout it all, Spale was there, watching and nudg-
ing, to make sure the project stayed on track.

Protecting the Protected: Prairie Stewardship and Management

The more people studied prairies, the clearer it became that legal protection
alone was not enough. Although remnants had been spared the plow and back-
hoe, they were vulnerable to invasion by the native and nonnative weeds that
thrived on adjacent land. As early as 1856, William Ferguson noted that "indigenous plants and grasses retire before those introduced by man, just as the
Indians retire before the white man."[62]

Alien plants such as Queen Anne's lace (*Daucus carota*), chicory (*Cichorium intybus*), and the sweet clovers (*Meliotus alba* and *M. officinalis*) are quick to exploit trail edges and other wounds invariably present on even the most intact of prairies. Arthur Vestal's study warned that white sweet clover can totally supplant the original vegetation "once the prairie is broken."[63] Kentucky bluegrass appeared so soon after the arrival of the first settlers that many thought it was native to the tallgrass prairie; its ubiquitousness led Homer Sampson to question whether there were any truly virgin prairies left.[64]

The proliferation of woody vegetation poses an even greater threat to local prairies. If left unchecked, such plants would shade into extirpation many of the species so characteristic of open grassland. Some of these trees and shrubs such as the notorious common buckthorn (*Rhamnus cathartica*) are exotics, but gray dogwood (*Cornus racemosa*), hawthorn, cottonwood, and others are native. What these weedy plants have in common is an inability to survive regular burning. Sometimes, however, thick stands of undesirable shrubs or mature trees may persist in the face of frequent fires for long periods. It is, therefore, often necessary to cut and girdle problem plants. One frustrated conservation agency was forced to use flamethrowers to eradicate a large clone of multiflora rose (*Rosa multiflora*).

The reintroduction of fire as a tool to manage protected sites proved to be difficult. Antiburning sentiment was strong until relatively recently. Bob Betz, an early proponent of controlled burns, cites John Weaver's classic *North American Prairie* as an example of how botanists often denigrated the importance of fire. Weaver devotes but three pages to the subject and leads off his discussion with the statement that "fires were damaging and destructive."[65] Betz is pleased to note, however, that some of the staunchest opponents of burning have since become strong advocates.

In presettlement days, fires would hopscotch across the land, scorching some areas and missing others. They would also vary greatly in intensity: weather conditions both before and "during a fire can make the difference between a creeping smoldering fire and a dangerous conflagration."[66] If certain species of plants and animals were reduced in number by the flames, individuals in untouched sections would be quick to recolonize. Given, however, that surviving prairies are usually small and people try to conduct burns under conditions that maximize the potential for combustion, the possibility exists that while some species may flourish with regular burning, others may decline.

Animals such as rodents and snakes are often found dead in the stubble of a freshly burned prairie, but their continued presence in high numbers on managed sites attests to their well-being. Studies assessing the impact of fire on short-tailed shrews (*Blarina brevicauda*), white-footed mice (*Peromyscus leucopus*), thirteen-lined ground squirrels (*Spermophilus tridecemlineatus*), and other small mammals confirm this. Population shifts brought about by burning are largely caused by immigration and emigration, and after two or three years numbers have returned to preburn levels.[67]

Of greater uncertainty is how fires affect the fate of arthropods and other poorly understood organisms. A 1989 review of the question as it regards spiders located only three studies, all of which suggested that regular burning could jeopardize spider populations.[68] Pointing to a different conclusion, research conducted at Woodworth Prairie in Cook County over forty years ago found that short-winged mold beetles (Pselaphids), mites and ticks (Acarina), and other prairie invertebrates were able to survive fire by appropriating the labyrinthine nests of prairie ants (*Formica cinerea*).[69] How they contended with the ants was not addressed.

The most comprehensive study of the issue, in this area at least, is the ongoing work on insects performed by Ron Panzer and his associates at Northeastern Illinois University.[70] Of the thousands of insect species that occur in the Chicago region, Panzer is focusing on one hundred from three orders: Orthoptera (katydids, walking sticks, and grasshoppers), Homoptera (leafhoppers), and Lepidoptera (moths and butterflies). These species were selected because they are largely endemic to prairies (indeed, many have very strict requirements) and have habits that might make them vulnerable to burning.

Although his work is not yet completed, Panzer has some preliminary findings. While over 90 percent of the insects that live aboveground may die in a single fire, their reproductive capacity is so great that recolonization of the site can occur within a year. He believes that less than 5 percent, and it may be as few as 1 percent, of all prairie insects suffer long-term effects from regular burning. Many entomologists are not so sanguine, however, and some are now advocating limiting the use of burning as a management tool. In their view, mowing or introducing bison or even cattle would have a more salubrious effect on prairie inhabitants.[71]

Panzer thinks that the data he has accumulated demonstrate that, except for very few species, prairie biota benefits from carefully conducted burns. A careful burn avoids backfires in better quality areas because they are against the wind and thus burn longer and hotter in one place. Intense burning of degraded portions is encouraged, however, in order to provide additional habitat as quickly as possible. But the most critical element of a successful management program is that no more than 50 percent of the high-quality sections of a given site should be burned at any one time so that fire-sensitive species can find refuge. On large sites, the Illinois Department of Conservation and other agencies divide the property into thirds, only one of which is burned in any one year. Thus, each portion goes two years without being burned.

Unfortunately, this last recommendation sometimes goes unheeded. Many sites are of such small size that establishing firebreaks can be difficult if not dangerous for participants. There is also the understandable hesitation to cancel burns when the requisite number of people has assembled (particularly when the workforce is composed of volunteers), even if circumstances suggest that a partial burn is unlikely.

It is a common trait in human beings to go from one extreme to the other: today we have come to the point where many consider burns to be good whether the safe havens to which and from which immigration and emigration of animals can occur are maintained or not. While there is no question that fire suppression in this region leads to loss of prairie, it is a process that occurs over time.[72] A single event, in contrast, can decimate if not extirpate a fire-intolerant species if flames are allowed to engulf the full extent of its habitat.

Considering what is known, and particularly what is not, prudence dictates that errors should be on the side of caution: on high-quality sites that are under a regular burning regimen, it is preferable to skip a given burn than risk torching the whole thing. And it may even be the case, where a species at risk is known to occur, that a given property not be burned but be subjected to other brush control measures instead. Dennis Figg, an ecologist with the Missouri Department of Conservation, has written that "protecting flora and fauna may not be as simple as 'good' prairie management, but may require specialized management techniques to achieve specific goals that insure invertebrates too are protected."[73] Recognizing that sound management could mean treating different parcels differently merely acknowledges that humans are not omniscient.

The Nearly Vanished Transitions:
Shrublands and Savannas

Immediately after crossing the Fox River [Racine County], a fine broad stream, you enter the
"oak openings." . . . The trees, which are mostly white oaks, are scattered thinly over its
surface, forming natural parks, through which the wild deer roam and where vast quantities
of game are found. . . . In summer the surface is almost entirely covered with red, yellow,
white, and purple flowers spread a gorgeous carpet through the forest as far as the eye could
see. . . . The "oak openings" are fast receiving a hardy and industrious population. . . . And
the period is certainly not far distant when every rod of this rich soil will be upturned by
the busy plow, and when the hum of industry will go up in these wilds, making them glad.
— Reverend A. C. Barry (1843 [in the Eugene W. Leach collection])

Gone So Quickly: The Deep-Soil Shrublands and Savannas

Presented with vistas of unbroken vegetation stretching beyond the horizon,
early visitors could see the patchy continuum of dense woods through open
savanna and shrublands to the varieties of true prairie. Today, however, with
nothing but scraps remaining, it is difficult to distinguish the transitions that
constituted so much of the landscape. Indeed, shrublands and savannas rooted
in deep silt-loam soils are now virtually nonexistent. As with the sand prairies,
sand savannas and sand shrublands were less intensely exploited, and more
have survived. (They also differ floristically from their deep-soil counterparts
and, thus, will be treated separately.)

Early accounts hint at the combinations of woods and prairie present in
the region. Joliet's version of that fateful trip up the Illinois River with Marquette includes this passage: "There are prairies three, six, ten, and twenty
leagues in length, and three in width, surrounded by forests of the same extent;
beyond these, the prairies begin again so that there is as much of one sort of
land as of the other."[1]

Ground that contained both trees and prairies is described by Claude Allouez in 1676. A Jesuit who "sought only to labor and suffer," he voyaged along the Lake Michigan shoreline from Wisconsin to Chicago: "We advanced coasting always along vast prairies that stretched away beyond our sight; from time to time we saw trees, but so ranged that they seemed planted designedly to form alleys more agreeable to the sight than those of orchards. The foot of these trees is often watered by little streams where we saw herds of stags and does drinking and feeding on the young grass. We followed these vast plains for twenty leagues, and often said, 'Benedicite opera Domini Domino.'"[2]

While traveling from Detroit to Chicago in 1834, A. A. Parker attempted to put what he had seen into order: "There are three kinds of land in the Western country—prairie land, entirely destitute of timber and covered with grass; oak openings, land thinly covered with timber like a northern apple orchard; and timbered land having a dense forest of trees."[3]

Finally, Caroline Kirkland, in her *Atlantic Monthly* article chronicling a trip through Illinois, describes a fourth type of landscape: "There are great tracts of what are called bushy prairies, covered with a thick growth of hazel and sassafras . . ."[4]

◄O► ◄O► ◄O►

Understanding savannas and shrublands has proven to be extremely difficult because there are so few intact examples to study. Settlers highly coveted these lands possessed of open timber and fertile earth. The sod was broken, and the trees were cleared. And as fire frequency declined under the dictates of the new occupants, areas of stunted and/or scattered trees grew to become closed forests, further masking their original character.[5]

Lacking a corpus delicti, so to speak, researchers have had to become detectives, relying on the historical record, data from the Public Land Surveys, and degraded remnants. Unfortunately, there was no agreement among early commentators as to what to call the mixtures of woods and prairie, which were variously called barrens, oak openings, savannas, copses, thickets, and bushy prairies. Then, too, the frequency with which a given type appears in the literature could be a function of author preference rather than an accurate depiction of the vegetation. For example, travelers tended to emphasize the orchard-like savannas because they were both prettier and easier to pass through than the shrubland. This historical material is problematic to begin with, but the results are further complicated here where the landscapes themselves are highly variable due to their transitional nature.

Out of this confusion, the orchard-like savannas emerged to become the prototype of the ecotonal woodlands. Since many researchers had this precon- ceived notion of savannas, they ignored or gave a different name to any land deviating from the model. John Curtis, for instance, used the name "brush prairies" to identify tracts "indistinguishable from the true prairies, since the prairie grasses exceeded the oaks in height and protected them from view."[6]

These model savannas consisted mostly of bur oaks scattered across a prairie mix of grasses and forbs. The primary criterion separating savanna from prairie and forest is percentage of canopy cover, although there have been many efforts to determine where the line should be drawn. Curtis defined sa- vanna as land having anywhere from one tree per acre to a 50 percent canopy cover. The Illinois Natural Areas Inventory drew a wider range of the contin- uum: savannas had canopies from 10 percent to 80 percent. Steve Packard and his colleagues distinguished "open savanna" (10–50 percent canopy cover) from "closed savanna" (50–80 percent). A very recent attempt at a consensus definition of savannas appears in the Chicago Wilderness *Biodiversity Recovery Plan* and harkens back to Curtis: 10–50 percent canopy cover with an under- story dominated by grass.[7]

Marlin Bowles and Jenny McBride distinguish three types of transitional landscapes on the silt soils of northeastern Illinois: (1) savanna (open oak can- opy with an understory of grass and forbs and, sometimes, shrubs); (2) shrub barrens (shrublands—no tree canopy and understory composed of American hazelnut [*Corylus americana*], four species of dogwood [*Cornus*], wild plum [*Prunus americana*], New Jersey tea [*Ceanothus americanus*], prickly ash [*Xan- thoxylum americanum*], and other shrubs); and (3) oak grub barrens (no tree canopy and understory of shrubs and oaks, particularly scarlet [*Quercus coc- cinea*], black [*Q. velutina*], and white [*Q. alba*]).[8]

How each of these types formed is not precisely known, although fire is believed to be a key element. Where burns were most common, as on the ground moraines and lake plains, prairies developed. A less intense fire regime killed off all but the most fire-resistant trees and allowed prairies to invade the understory. Then, savannas prevailed. Bur oak was the dominant tree, but white oak was often present as well. A similar frequency of burning reduced less fire-resistant species, such as black oak and scarlet oak, to sprouts and thus produced oak grub barrens. Slightly less fire in a treeless setting promoted the shrub barrens.

An important aspect of these vegetation types is that they were "spatially and temporally dynamic."[9] Shrublands and savannas shifted toward forest dur- ing wet periods and in the absence of fire; fire and drought drove the lines in the other direction toward prairie. On the landscape level, the mix of prairie and forest elements existed in a multitude of combinations.

Beyond wrestling with the general aspect of the transitional lands,

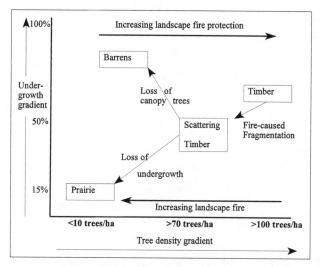

15. Landscape vegetation and fire process model based on Public Land Surveyor notes. "Scattering timber" is synonymous with savanna and "barrens" with shrublands. (From Bowles et al., 1998b, fig. 13. Courtesy Marlin Bowles, Morton Arboretum, Lisle, Ill.)

researchers have tried to determine which grasses and forbs inhabited the silt savannas and shrublands. This task has also been challenging because the surveyor notes and general descriptions focus on woody vegetation. And of course extant examples are rare and have been compromised by grazing, tree cutting, and fire suppression.

Where along the prairie-forest continuum one's definition of savanna lies determines the floral composition of the community. Curtis concluded that savannas share a number of attributes in common with prairies: grasses provide most of the groundcover, forbs dominate as to number of species, and grasses, composites, and legumes are the three most common families.[10] In classifications where savannas include more extensive tree cover, shade-tolerant species become more important.

Curtis's study of savanna flora found forty-six species that were prevalent in savannas and six that were modal. Those six were false sunflower (*Heliopsis helianthoides*), kitten tails (*Wulfenia bullii*), one-flowered broomrape (*Orobanche uniflora*), marsh phlox (*Phlox glaberrima*), early buttercup (*Ranunculus fascicularis*), and white camas (*Zigadenus glaucus*). (Kitten tails and marsh phlox are now thought to be less related to savannas than they are to hilltops and calcareous prairies, respectively.)[11] Studying Illinois silt savannas, and extending the savanna definition to include 80 percent canopy, the Illinois Natural Areas Inventory arrived at a list of fifty-one prevalent understory species. Inventory researchers considered the following species to be characteristic though not necessarily exclusive: American hazel, common carrion flower (*Smilax lasio-neura*), starry campion (*Silene stellata*), false sunflower, veiny pea (*Lathyrus ve-nosus*), and golden Alexander (*Zizia aurea*).[12]

Bowles and McBride compiled a list of shrubland species that occurred in assemblages designated barrens, copse, or thickets. Based largely on four old floras, their compilation contains 243 taxa, including seven tick trefoils, four eupatorium, four bush clovers, seven goldenrods, and five violets. Although no one knows for sure, one difference between the understory of barrens and sa-vannas seems to be that the former had less grass. Dr. Mead's 1846 list of bar-rens plants from Hancock County, Illinois (well to the south of this region) had few grasses, and Bowles and McBride quotes an old manuscript to the effect that "within these shrubby areas the grass was much suppressed."[13]

It appears that although the deep-soil savannas and shrublands have been largely lost as community types, most savanna and shrubland species can read-ily survive in woods, on the edges of woods, or in open prairie, depending on their shade tolerance. Efforts to identify rare, threatened, or endangered species restricted to these communities have failed to find any. Roger Ander-son and Marlin Bowles explain that "this may be the result of the wide distri-bution and transitional nature of savanna, by which no species is restricted to this habitat."[14]

◄o► ◄o► ◄o►

While there may be no known remnant oak grub or deep-soil shrub barrens in this region, some savannas still survive outside the sandy Chicago Lake Plain and Morris-Kankakee Basin. Two of the most intact remnants are Middlefork Savanna in Lake Forest, Lake County (Ill.), and Wolf Road Prairie Savanna in Westchester, Cook County (see chap. 3).

Middlefork Savanna, a five-hundred-acre site on the middle fork of the Chicago River's North Branch in Lake Forest, Lake County (Ill.), protects thirty acres of some of the best remaining savanna anywhere. Four species of oaks dominate the canopy. White oaks are most common in the drier north-western portion of the savanna, while bur oaks, scarlet oaks, and red oaks reach peak abundance in moister areas that merge into wet prairie or sedge meadow slightly downslope. American hazelnut, gray dogwood, and the alien common buckthorn form the shrub layer.[15] Table 2 lists common species of Middlefork Savanna along a light continuum.

Even after ditching in the early 1900s, much of the property's low area proved too wet to farm. The rail line bordering the section was also in-strumental is keeping the site intact. Burning embers from the trains would

Table 2. Distribution of the Most Common Native Nonwoody Plants along a Light Continuum at Middle Fork Savanna

Light	Intermediate	Shade
Panicled aster (*Aster simplex*)	Willow aster (*Aster praealtus*)	Wild onion (*Allium canadense*)
Tall goldenrod (*Solidago altissima*)	Arrow-leafed aster (*Aster saggittifolius*)	Side-flowering Aster (*Aster lateriflorus*)
Common spiderwort (*Tradescantia ohiensis*)	Common oak sedge (*Carex pennsylvanica*)	Avens (sp.) (*Geum* sp.)
Culver's root (*Veronicastrum virginicum*)	Common strawberry (*Frageria virginiana*)	Self-heal (*Prunella vulgaris*)
	Wild geranium (*Geranium maculatum*)	
	Woodland sunflower (*Helianthus divaricatus*)	
	Common cinquefoil (*Potentilla simplex*)	
	Early wild rose (*Rosa blanda*)	
	Early goldenrod (*Solidago juncea*)	
	Upright carrion flower (*Smilax ecirrhata*)	

Source. After Bowles et al. (1997).

periodically ignite the dried grasses, thus ensuring that the curative fires of the early days would continue. Landowners continued to farm or graze the property until the 1970s.

In 1979, the Lake Forest Open Lands Association commissioned Ralph Brown and Wayne Schennum to survey the vegetation of Middlefork Savanna, including the prairie and sedge meadow sections. Additional studies have examined the site for butterflies, beetles, herpetofauna, and other biota. These efforts led to the discovery of several uncommon animal species and three plants listed in Illinois as threatened or endangered: eastern prairie fringed orchid (federally threatened as well), beaked sedge (*Carex rostrata*), and pale vetchling (*Lathyrus ochroleucus*).[16]

At the same time, Lake Forest Open Lands, under Steve Christy's direction, began working with landowners to manage the natural areas. Steve Packard, then with the Illinois chapter of the Nature Conservancy, and Steve Apfelbaum of Applied Ecological Services also pushed hard for preservation of the site. Their combined efforts plus strong interest by the Lake County Forest Preserve District culminated in the district buying much of the land; the district and three private owners now protect five hundred acres of high-quality or restorable property.

In the late 1990s, Marlin Bowles and collaborators examined both Middlefork Savanna and the Wolf Road Prairie Savanna to determine how they were faring.[17] Such efforts are difficult, however, because as the researchers acknowledge, their "interpretations of vegetation change and causal effects of fire management at Middlefork are limited by the absence of detailed information on fire coverage or intensity, the absence of control plots that were not burned, and potential for other vegetation changes."[18] Nonetheless, they did conclude that, true to the dynamic nature of deep-soil savannas, changes were occurring: each site was apparently losing species diversity and its savanna aspect. The lack of fire at Wolf Road Prairie Savanna has allowed the development of a dense thirty-year-old subcanopy of bur oak and scarlet oak, and, even with biannual burning, the same phenomenon (minus bur oak) is occurring at Middlefork Savanna. Now shady understories are being taken over by such exotics as common buckthorn, garlic mustard (*Alliaria petiolata*), and bittersweet nightshade (*Solanum dulcamara*). (At Middlefork, the researchers attributed the absence of some late-successional native prairie species such as leadplant and purple prairie clover to grazing.) The prescription offered to reverse these processes is for land managers to thin the subcanopy, either through more intense burning or the girdling and cutting of trees.

All Sorts of Floral Treasures: The Sand Savannas and Shrublands

Savannas and shrublands have persisted in the sand regions with better success than in the more fertile silt areas. Virtually all of the very few surviving shrublands in Illinois (called "shrub prairie" by the Illinois Natural Areas Inventory) occur in the Morris-Kankakee Basin. Fine sand savannas still populate the dunes fronting Lake Michigan, the Morris-Kankakee Basin, and the Sand Ridge and Thornton-Lansing Nature Preserves in the southern Lake Plain of Cook County. (See chap. 10 for a discussion of the dune savannas.)

The Illinois Natural Areas Inventory identified sixty acres of existing shrubland in the entire state, all but three of which acres are in the Morris-Kankakee Basin. Bristly blackberry (*Rubus setosus* [state endangered]), hardhack

(*Spiraea tomentosa*), haircap moss (*Polytrichum commune*), and the two bluestems dominate the community.[19]

One of the largest surviving tracts of shrubland is the Wilmington Shrub Prairie Nature Preserve in Will County.[20] The entire site is 146 acres, which includes sand prairie, sand savanna, silt loam prairie, sedge meadow, marsh, and eighteen acres of shrub prairie. It is within the swamp and dune province studied by Willard Clute.

Prior to state ownership, the property was divided between the Vesleys and the Simpsons, and before that it was solely owned by James Perry. Cattle grazed on the land, and ditches siphoned water from the wetlands. Coal mining obliterated part of the marsh. Plows intruded upon the silt loam prairie, but ultimately most of the area remained too wet for intensive agriculture. However, the cessation of fire and lowering water tables enabled the proliferation of such woody vegetation as dogwood. The Department of Natural Resources considers controlling these species to be their primary management goal on the land.

Although it would be impossible to tell by looking at the area now, a fine sand savanna cloaked the old Lake Chicago beach ridges at Wilson and Broadway in Chicago. Herman Pepoon used to bring his Lake View High School classes there on field trips in the early years of this century. Nodding trillium, a species now extremely rare in the region and state, grew there in abundance. Pepoon's recollections of the site appeared in the January 15, 1930, issue of the school's newspaper, *The Lake ReView:* "[There were] ponds, thickets, some ridges, and forest growth [that] gave us all sorts of plants—such floral treasures as water lilies, lady slippers, trillium, mayapples, lupines, phlox, Solomon's seal, prickly-pear, asters, puccoons, and a host of others flourished."

Another rich sand savanna survives as part of the unusual mosaic of plant communities that make up the 446 acres of the Thornton-Lansing Road Nature Preserve in Calumet City, Cook County. Other vegetation types present on the site include mesic woods, prairie, and marsh. Because of its diversity and the presence of some very rare species, the area has been drawing naturalists for over a hundred years. Reverend Hill, Henry Cowles, Charles Olmsted, and Floyd Swink are among the distinguished botanists who have studied its flora. At least three papers, including a master's thesis, have focused on the site.[21]

The need to preserve this biologically valuable land was not lost on the Cook County Forest Preserve, but the large number of owners made the district's acquisition plan difficult to carry out. They purchased their first parcel in 1917 and their last in 1964. One year later the area became a state nature preserve.

The fifty acres of sand savanna occupies a beach ridge from the Calumet

Stage of Lake Chicago. Black oaks predominate, with a smaller sprinkling of white oak, scarlet oak, and sassafras (*Sassafras albidum*). Understory plants include early low blueberry (*Vaccinium angustifolium*), late low blueberry (*V. pallidum*), bracken fern (*Pteridium aquilinum*), bird's-foot violet (*Viola pedata*), porcupine grass (*Stipa spartea*), and lupine (*Lupinus perennis*).

Bracken, royal (*Osmunda regalis*), and cinnamon (*Osmunda cinnamomea*) ferns are conspicuous components of the ground layer, and their protection creates a challenge to forest preserve district staffers. Starting in the 1970s, people accustomed to picking young ferns (called fiddleheads because of their shape) in their countries of origin began helping themselves to Thornton-Lansing's bounty. On one Mother's Day, more than seventy-five people arrived at the preserve in search of edibles. They took ferns, wild leeks, honewort (*Cryptotaenia canadensis*), and other plants. A few years later, police arrested a man who had filled his van full of ferns. Naturalist Paul Strand responded by placing an article in the newspaper printed in the offenders' language, pointing out that everything on the property was protected and, further, eating large quantities of fiddleheads increased the risk of cancer. The problem has subsided, a fact that Strand attributes more to increased police surveillance than to his article.[22]

One of the rarest and most beautiful of local plants inhabits a nearby site: orange fringed orchid (*Habenaria ciliaris*). Frederick Case writes that "its rich orange is nothing less than tropical."[23] The orchid is primarily a southeastern species, with disjunct populations in the southern Great Lakes, including a few locations in northwest Indiana and Berrien County. This station is its sole outpost in Illinois. In his *Orchids of Illinois*, Charles Sheviak suggests that its restricted range in this region is because of higher soil temperature caused by the moderating influence of the Great Lakes. Thus it is not found in areas to the west and north that might otherwise have suitable habitat.[24]

The orchid has undergone notable population fluctuations over the years. In the 1970s, before management, the species was most abundant amid bracken fern in the shade of aspens. Then, when the canopy was opened, the orchids increased dramatically. But over time, regular burning enabled grasses to outcompete the orchids, which then declined. Precipitation levels and the lowering of the water table due to nearby quarrying operations may also affect their numbers. In 1993, Paul Strand counted twenty individuals, but this number had declined to five plants by 1996.[25]

Thornton-Lansing has had a long history of disturbance. As early as 1850, cattle grazed the woods, and over the next twenty years settlers cut the last of the old trees. When the Chicago, Danville, and Vincennes Railroad (now the Grand Trunk and Western Railroad) elected to extend its track from Dolton to Chicago in 1873, it purchased wood for fuel and sand for roadbed. Both commodities came at least in part from Thornton-Lansing Woods.

To obtain the sand, pits were dug through and around the savanna areas. The excavations created an extremely unusual situation—a totally human engineered environment colonized by assemblages of conservative plants. Where sand removal reaches the water table, the highly acidic and nutritionally poor depressions repel many species, even many weedy Eurasians. For a while, these barren areas remain without plants but eventually rose pogonia (*Pogonia ophioglossoides*), yellow-eyed grass (*Xyris torta*), sundew, marsh Saint-John's-wort (*Hypericum virginicum*), and hardhack appear. Floyd Swink, who has studied the matter closely, points out that most of these species have at least two things in common: they produce dustlike seeds and they also grow well on moist, sandy flats. Swink believes that the tiny seeds easily adhere to the legs of water birds, who unwittingly provide the transport for these rare plants.[26]

Like Nowhere Else on Earth: The Savanna of Langham Island

Langham Island, also called Altorf Island, is almost twenty-five acres of bedrock projecting out of a shallow and rapid-flowing portion of the Kankakee River, a few miles downstream from the city of Kankakee. Over the years it has been grazed, and at one point early this century the most level part was used as a cornfield. Today, the island is largely open woods, what John Schwegman, formerly of the Illinois Department of Natural Resources, calls gravel savanna.[27]

In 1872, E. J. Hill became the first botanist to visit the island, and over the next twelve years he discovered several extraordinarily rare species: leafy prairie clover, buffalo clover (*Trifolium reflexum* [state endangered and one of only a handful of local records]), and the lobed violet (*Viola palmata* [extirpated from the state]). More recently, controlled burning brought to light Illinois's only population of the northern corn salad (*Valerianella umbilicata*). This collection of unusual plants would by themselves confer on this tiny place a mantle of great distinction. But on June 29, 1872, Reverend Hill found another species, one that made Langham Island globally significant: on that date, he collected the first known specimen of the Kankakee mallow (*Iliamna remota*), not known to occur naturally anywhere else on earth.

Resembling a hollyhock, the Kankakee mallow grows to 5.4 feet in height. Adult plants have strikingly long and thick roots that spread horizontally through the thin soil. Through July and August it is heavily laden with fragrant rose-colored blooms that may be two inches in diameter.

Although limited to the south end of the island, Kankakee mallow is common where it occurs, often forming pure stands. Earl Sherff, a Chicago botanist who studied the plant, visited the island in 1912 and 1916 and noted that the mallow was growing downslope from the cornfield. By the time Sherff returned eight or so years later, the cornfield had been abandoned and the mallow had spread into the now fallow parcel. The plant obviously does well in disturbed areas. Several botanists over the years have planted seeds in their gardens. Dr. Betz reports that it took over his lawn. John Schwegman also had good luck with the plant in his Springfield, Illinois, backyard, until it developed root rot during a wet year. (The easiest place to see the mallow is along the ditch at the west end of Markham Prairie, Cook County, where it was introduced by Betz.)

The island has been part of Kankakee River State Park for more than fifty years and an Illinois Nature Preserve since 1966. Starting in 1983, the Department of Natural Resources has managed the island to help the mallow. Regularly burning the site both maximizes the savanna habitat and facilitates germination of mallow seeds. Those who have artificially raised the species recommend that the seeds be either soaked in water for a day or scarified by abrading them with sandpaper.

In the late 1920s, botanists discovered a plant very similar to Kankakee mallow on Peters Mountain in western Virginia. About nine hundred feet above the New River, small clumps clung to "mere pockets [of soil] in the rock."[28] There are some differences between the Virginia and Kankakee plants, and authors have disagreed on how to treat them. Sherff believed that although they were the same species, the two mallows were distinct as varieties. But Merritt Fernald, in the 1950 edition of *Gray's Manual of Botany*, listed them as distinct species: *I. remota* and *I. corei*.[29]

Whether these widely isolated mallows are one or two species may be of less interest than how they came to inhabit the tiny outcroppings they call home. Both grow on bedrock subsurfaces that have little soil. *Iliamna corei* lives high on the rocky wall of a river-cut gorge. Langham Island receives the brunt of ice chunks as they careen downstream in spring. They smash into the south end of the island, scraping the land like miniature glaciers and providing the disturbance that helped maintain the open woods. (To maximize mallow habitat, state biologists regularly burn the island.) While Peters Mountain and Langham Island have things in common, the bigger mystery is, to paraphrase a much older query, what makes these sites different from all other sites?

Witnesses to History: Forests

By the time the hepaticas are gone to sleep the violets will be up in the woods along the Des Plaines and at Beverly Hills, and a little later in the ravines to the north, and later still the Flossmoor Woods and Stewart Ridge will be blue with them. . . . And take all the children you know with you, lest one should ever send a pang to your heart by saying, as a sweet city child of 14 once said to me very wistfully, "But Miss Emily, I never saw violets growing." —Louella Chapin (1907)

There is no other land in the world with autumns like ours. We pile the treasure of the year into a great burial fire. Tongues of flame go up to the sky, the garnet of black and red oaks, the leaping maples and the flickering aspens and out of the midst of it all one exulting spire of light where a cottonwood shakes primal yellow at the primal blue of the American sky. From the boughs pours down the glory of the vines— woodbine and corded grape and poison ivy. The thickets fill with the cymbal colors of the sumac— orange and scarlet and stain of wine; the leaning dwarf forest of the hawthorns begins to drop its shower of little pomes— ruby color overcast with purple bloom. —Donald Culross Peattie (1938)

Consistent with its ecotonal character, the Chicago region hosts a remarkable diversity of forests. E. Lucy Braun in her classic *Deciduous Forests of Eastern North America* states that this area is within the Prairie Peninsula section of the oak-hickory region, except the districts close to Lake Michigan, which represent western and southern extensions of the beech-maple region. But, as she acknowledges, there also exists here representatives of the maple-basswood region (from southwestern Wisconsin) and hemlock–white pine–northern hardwoods region (from the upper Great Lakes).[1] This last element is concentrated in the dunes and ravines of Berrien County and will be dealt with in chapter 10.

What these forests were like prior to European settlement, what role fire played in their formation and maintenance, and how they should be managed today are questions without definitive answers, however. The lack of consensus has made writing this chapter especially difficult.[2] People continue to wrestle with these questions, and careful science will help provide some of the answers. But, as Marlin Bowles says, we may never arrive at a final resolution.

I have based my treatment of woods on what have been standard classification systems. Under the categories of John Curtis and the Illinois Natural Areas Inventory, there are four principal kinds of forests in the area: lowland or floodplain, mesic or mesic upland, dry or dry-mesic upland, and northern flatwoods.[3] (The last two are composed largely of oaks and are treated in the first section of this chapter, below.) Available moisture, soil, and protection from fire all play a part in determining whether and where these forest types will develop. Often changes between types are abrupt and occur within a very small area, a reflection of varying soils and elevation.

But new typologies have recently been proposed. For example, the Chicago Wilderness *Biodiversity Recovery Plan* and others now recognize a distinct community type they call woodland.[4] It encompasses that portion of the savanna-forest continuum where the canopy cover was originally 50–80 percent. Yet a very different classification system is suggested by the work of Marlin Bowles and Jenny McBride. They studied the public land survey notes and "were able to segregate maple, red oak, and white oak stands as different forest types."[5]

Letting in the Light: Oak Forests

During Pepoon's time (1920s), four-fifths of local timber were oaks, a figure that has no doubt declined, as we shall see later. As lone sentinels on the prairie to clusters in the wooded lowlands, oaks are important in almost all of the region's timbered plant communities. But they are most dominant in at least two kinds of forests: the flatwoods and the dry or dry-mesic forests.

Flatwoods are very limited in acreage and develop in two different contexts. The most frequent is in level areas underlain by clay, as along the Des Plaines River in Lake County. In morainal districts such as Thorn Creek Woods, they occur in clay-lined depressions, the deepest portions of which often become vernal ponds. (These ponds are too wet for trees, and when they dry up they are demarcated with great precision by the oaks that surround them.) The dense, almost impermeable clay soil sets the parameters that define these forests. Plants have to tolerate an abundance of water in spring, which limits the oxygen available to their roots, and parched conditions in late summer when their roots are stymied by the packed hardpan. Fall rains, if they arrive, start the cycle over again. In this environment of moisture extremes, swamp white oaks (*Quercus bicolor*) flourish, along with white oak, scarlet oak, and American elm.

The dry or dry mesic forests are the most widely distributed forests in the region, although their composition changes with moisture, fire exposure, and shade tolerance. For example, the following ranking of oaks is in the order of least to most fire sensitive: bur, black (primarily in sandy soils), white, and red (*Quercus rubra*). This follows from physiological differences of the trees themselves: red oak has bark that is 80 percent as thick as black oak and 50 percent as thick as white oak.[6]

At Thorn Creek Woods, the oaks occur along an elevational continuum that reflects fire frequency and moisture: a few red oaks and white oaks at the slope base (mesic forest), red oak increasing until peaking at midslope, and white oak increasing from midslope to level upland where there are almost pure stands. Bur oaks, in contrast, are widely distributed, enjoying perhaps the widest tolerance of any member of its genus. This resilient species, the classic savanna tree, grows on a variety of soils and moisture regimes, from open plains scorched by prairie fires to sheltered river-bottom forests in the company of cottonwood and silver maple.[7]

The beauty of a summer oak forest is captured by E. J. Hill, in an article he wrote in 1894: "The prevalence of oaks with smooth and glossy leaves gives to many of these woodlands a peculiar distinctness under the glow of the summer sun. A shimmering light plays upon them, as well defined, although not as bright, as that which glances from a water surface, and these bright areas catch the eye from a distance, and in the broad sweep of the green landscape these forest masses rise out of the general level as sources of clear mellow light."[8]

In autumn, the reds and oranges of oak leaves are more muted than the maple, and they don't last as long, quickly fading into a lingering dun. But they are nonetheless striking in their shapes and textures. An open-grown bur or white with its broad, rounded crown represents time frozen in wood. A trunk bereft of boughs started life surrounded by other trees, while layered spreading branches mark a tree that matured unfettered, free to seek the light that engulfed it. Eventually these lower branches die, a victim of the tree's inability to survive its own shade.

Oak bark is also worthy of attention. Lynn Hepler, a superb naturalist with the Lake County Forest Preserve District, points to how remarkably varied it can be. Red oaks have a dark gray bark, but when the sun's rays play on the upper portions, you can see stripes of rough interspersed with smooth. The reflectivity of the latter heightens the effect that appears as a series of vertical rises and dips, like ski runs down a mountain's face. Then there is the bur oak, whose twigs have corky winglike ridges. When silhouetted against a winter sky, the tree appears gnarled and almost arthritic.

Perhaps even more striking is how different the bark manifested by the same tree can be. The swamp white oak provides the best example. At the tips of the twigs and small branches, the gray bark is smooth and tight. But toward the trunk it begins to split and exfoliate like birch. The skin curls and sloughs off in rolls. But as the branch grows, the bark takes on yet another look: loosely connected plates reminiscent of tar shingles on a dilapidated shack. And finally, at the base of larger specimens, the bark becomes ridged and corky.

Even when leafed out, oak woods, with their complementary shagbark hickory (*Carya ovata*), black walnut (*Juglans nigra*), and black maple (*Acer nigrum*), allow far more light to penetrate than do the maple-dominated mesic woods. Thus, the ground flora need not race to complete life's important tasks within a few precious weeks of illumination. In this, the oaks are more forgiving than the maples, for the oaks give rise to a rich understory that can grow all summer long.

An understory layered with subcanopy trees and shrubs is characteristic of modern oak forests, although some believe that the original forests lacked this feature due to frequent fires.[9] Common members of the woody vegetation include hop hornbeam (*Ostrya virginiana*), black haw (*Viburnum ibuprunifolium*), nannyberry (*V. lentago*), maple-leaved viburnum (*V. acerifolium*), blackberry, dotted hawthorn (*Crataegus punctata*), gray dogwood, and hazelnut. Curtis reports that "shrub densities may reach levels of 21,000 per acre or more, of which nearly 19,000 are due to gray dogwood, hazelnut, and blackberry."[10]

The display of spring wildflowers can often be showy, with large clusters of white trout lily (*Erythronium albidum*), Dutchman's breeches (*Dicentra cucullaria*), hepatica (*Hepatica acutiloba*), bloodroot (*Sanguinaria canadensis*), bellwort (*Uvularia grandiflora*), and mayapple (*Podophyllum peltatum*). These typical mesic forest species are also at home under the dense shrub layer of the oaks. Toothwort (*Dentaria laciniata*), smooth Solomon's seal (*Polygonatum canaliculatum*), feathery false Solomon's seal (*Smilacina racemosa*), and wild geranium (*Geranium maculatum*) also lend color to the vernal assemblage.

The aptly named spring beauty (*Claytonia virginica*) is one of the commonest of the spring-blooming forbs, occurring in both oak and maple forests as well as savannas and even prairies. Multiplying by both seed and corm, it forms thick crowds of pink flowers held aloft on dainty stems between the grasslike leaves. But up close you see that the petals are actually white, striped with pink veins that guide pollinators to the pink stamens.

The success of this species is attributable not only to its ability to thrive

16. Spring beauties are often the last woodland wildflowers
to survive the clearing of native vegetation. Photographed
in Evanston, Cook County, by J. Greenberg, May 1997.

in a variety of habitats but to its withstanding the harshest sorts of human intervention. Where woods are converted into residential lots, the spring beauty often lingers with the few remaining trees as the sole survivors: "It forms dense stands competing with the grass, often in circular patches which follow the contours of the oak trees above."[11]

But long after the spring flowers of a mesic woods are spent, the oak woods offer a wide variety of blossoming plants throughout the growing season: hog peanut (*Amphicarpaea bracteata*), white lettuce (*Prenanthes alba*), enchanter's nightshade (*Circaea lutetiana*), purple joe-pye weed (*Eupatorium purpureum*), fire pink (*Silene virginica*), yellow false foxglove (*Aureolaria grandiflora*), sunflowers (*Helianthus*), and asters, among others.

The large yellow lady's slipper (*Cypripedeum calceolus* var. *pubescens*) is a particularly noteworthy member of the upland forest. In some oak woods, where an open canopy exists, this orchid can become one of the more conspicuous members of the flora. It often grows on east- and west-facing slopes, south-facing being too dry and north-facing too shaded.[12]

Although scattered populations occur in a number of counties, this lady's slipper, like other orchids, has declined over the years. This change is reflected in old herbarium sheets. The late Bill Wingate, McHenry County's venerated naturalist, used to receive these volumes when the owner didn't know who else would be interested: "These herbaria are from the 1890s or thereabouts. I think the interesting thing is that people saved these to the point of their death. These pressed plants were the treasures from their school days. And while there are a lot of local plants missing, we have these lady's slippers. Now you can hardly find them at all."[13]

◄◦► ◄◦► ◄◦►

Many Midwestern biologists fear that the oaks may be waning in the face of the more successful maple. Gerould Wilhelm compared original survey notes and older writings with current data to conclude that the oak forests of the Morton Arboretum are in serious jeopardy. Of equal concern, the understory is becoming highly depauperate without manifesting any of the richness characteristic of mesic forests. A more recent study of twenty-eight high-quality forests in northeastern Illinois also found that maples are increasing and overall species diversity is lower in maple-dominated forests.[14]

Focusing on a wider geographic area but based on similar sources, John Ebinger wrote: "It appears, that in many areas, even the best quality oak-hickory communities are undergoing an apparent irreversible change as sugar maple, and other shade-tolerant species, replace many of the original forest components." Mark Fishbein studied the tree composition at Ryerson Woods Conservation Area. Using both demographic data and a statistical model, he predicted that sugar maple will comprise an ever greater portion of the forest canopy, although other species will persist in wet areas and where there are large canopy gaps.[15]

Curtis describes how maples can invade and overwhelm a forest comprising predominantly oaks. In one scenario, which he says "is by no means common," a few red maples get established in a red oak forest but fail to reproduce because there is insufficient shade. Once the oaks fully mature, however, sapling maples are able to survive and when an opening in the canopy occurs, the maples exploit the opportunity to assume a bigger role in the forest. Eventually, the maples overwhelm "the oak community as they grow, much as a cancer destroys its host." In a similar situation, a forest of white oak and black oak encompassed an "island of red oak containing a few sugar maple and basswood." With fire suppression, the mesic trees expanded outward, shading out the plants that thrived under the oaks.[16]

The specter of maples metastasizing and taking over oak forests has had a strong impact on many local ecologists and land managers. The issue raises two questions: (1) Are we losing our oak forests to maples? (2) If so, why is this happening?

The answer to the first question is that in many places maples are indeed becoming more abundant in areas once dominated by oaks. But this is not so everywhere, and it is unclear whether some of the shift is a function of cycles that will switch and favor oaks sometime in the future. Al Westerman, a forester serving on the Lake County (Ill.) Board of Commissioners, believes that most of the oak forests he knows in Lake County (Ill.) are maintaining themselves. Jon Mendelson of Governor's State University holds a similar view of Thorn Creek Woods, Will County: "There are vast acreages of oak woodlands with nary a maple to be seen." [17]

In 1981 Lawrence Leitner of the Southeast Wisconsin Regional Planning Commission examined three woodlots studied thirty-two years earlier to determine how tree composition had changed. [18] The three areas he studied were Zirbe Woods in northeastern Racine County, Thompson Woods in northeastern Kenosha County, and Petrifying Springs Woods in northeastern Kenosha County.

Leitner found that each site represented a different scenario. Thompson Woods was the least mesic, being dominated by white oak, red oak, and basswood. It was free of sugar maple in 1949 as it was in 1981. White oak and basswood, however, had both increased substantially. Petrifying Springs was at the other extreme. Sugar maple was the dominant tree in 1949 and remained so, with red oak and white oak following in importance respectively. During that time, sugar maple had increased slightly along with red oak, indicating that the woods had become marginally more mesic. But it was Zirbe Woods, representing an intermediate stage, that had undergone the greatest change toward mesic. Sugar maple, basswood, and red oak had all increased significantly, while white ash and white oak had all decreased. The 1981 results indicated that the principal species were, in descending order, basswood, white ash, red oak, and sugar maple. Hopefully, someone will do yet another follow-up to see how these woods fared in the 1990s. [19]

A number of factors, some possibly not yet identified, have contributed to the increase of maples. The most commonly advanced explanation for the change is fire suppression. Some say it is the single cause. Thin-barked maple is very sensitive to fire, while the oaks are more tolerant. Even if their thick bark fails to protect them, oak suckers can often resprout. Some oaks, particularly black oaks, retain their leaves late into fall or even through the winter and, thus, provide fuel capable of carrying fires at varying heights.

Marc Abrams documents how the cessation of fires initially benefited oaks by allowing them to spread into areas that were previously grassland. But since oaks are successional species, they are eventually supplanted by maples and other shade tolerant species unless they are regularly burned. "However," Abrams acknowledges, "this phenomenon may vary with regional and edaphic factors and be more pronounced on mesic rather than on xeric sites."[20]

Burning woods would certainly inhibit the growth of maple. But how frequently fire reached local woods in presettlement times is unknown. Mendelson points out that surveyor notes show that many forested areas were composed of all-aged trees, suggesting "continuous recruitment . . . and low levels of disturbance."[21]

Further, the sweeping fires that raced across the landscape and into the accounts of early travelers were among the first things extinguished by settlement. In some places, it has been well over a century since the flames last roared. To the extent that the proliferation of maples and loss of oaks are phenomena of more recent vintage, fire cannot be the only factor at work.

Grazing has had a significant, although often overlooked, impact on these forests. As we saw earlier, dairying was a major industry in much of our area. From the end of the Civil War to World War II, the sight of grazing cattle and horses was common. Mendelson has compiled some statistics on the extent to which local woodlands were subjected to this activity: "In 1925 . . . , 92% of 23,000 acres of woodland in Cook County had been or was being grazed; similar percentages were recorded for DuPage, Lake, and Will Counties. . . . A survey of 430 northern Illinois farmers taken during this same period revealed that over 90% grazed their woods."[22]

Livestock kept the woods open—that is, free of saplings and understory. This both prevented the recruitment of shrubs and trees and enabled the colonization of such nonnatives as bluegrass and Canada thistle. While this stopped the development of both oaks and maples, it helped maintain the status quo by suppressing maples and preserving the oak canopy. With the elimination of cattle, the woods have filled in, contributing to the shaded areas favorable to maple. But even though the cattle may be gone, they left in their wake compacted soil that is poorly suited for oak regeneration. How long the healing process takes depends, of course, on the degree of damage, which varies greatly from tract to tract.

The cyclical nature of oak reproduction may also be part of the answer. Perhaps even more so than maple, oaks vary greatly in the amount of seed they generate every year. In some years, a given species may not fruit at all. On the average, acorn yields peak about every three to five years. For white oaks, this may occur at intervals of four to ten years. For instance, 1992 proved to be an exceptionally good year for white oak, and recruitment was heavy in Thorn Creek Woods. But only in the years of heaviest seed production does reproduction occur, because many species of animals favor acorns as food. Even before they fall, over half the acorns may be damaged by insects and birds: the

17. Cattle grazing along North Branch of the Chicago River, Glenview,
Cook County, May 1913; photo by Chicago Prairie Club. (Courtesy
Westchester Township Historical Museum, Chesterton, Ind.)

acorn weevil (*Curculio*) is particularly notorious for its depredations. On the ground, acorns are vulnerable to squirrels, mice, and white-tailed deer (*Odocoileus virginianus*). One study demonstrated that deer at the density of one per thirty acres consumed the *entire* crop during a modest year. And some woods in northeastern Illinois contain well over five deer per thirty acres.[23]

Because oaks are intolerant of their own shade, a grove expands outward. Acorns, of course, lack the aerodynamic quality of maple samaras, and thus the spread would rarely exceed the reach of the most extended branch. But many do wind up farther, transported by birds or mammals that drop them prior to feeding. Unfortunately, this process is hindered in modern times, by the paucity of open ground to colonize and by competition with buckthorn and multiflora rose.[24]

Perhaps the best overall perspective on the subject is provided by Gerard Donnelly, director of the Morton Arboretum. He knows and respects both forests, the shadiest of the beech-maple and the light-infused oak: "Once you do have a shady forest, it is true that oaks are not likely to regenerate. But is that bad? If fire were not the only factor, maybe the natural progression of things and interbalances would have been such that sugar maple would come to express more dominance in the landscape. I would like to suggest, then, that we rejoice that nature is complex and ascribing broad patterns to a single factor may be naive."[25]

Where Shadows Reign: The Mesic Forests

The Chicago Region supports two principal types of mesic forests: maple-basswood and beech-maple. They are in fact very similar, differing primarily in the presence or absence of the beech. Maple-basswood forests are the most widely distributed of the two and form in a variety of topographic contexts. In morainal systems, mesic forests occur on north-facing slopes, particularly near the bottoms, where humidity and soil moisture are greatest and where fires cannot reach. At Thorn Creek Woods, a well-preserved forest of the Valparaiso Moraine in Will County, the dominant canopy trees of the mesic forest are sugar maple (*Acer saccharum*), basswood (*Tilia americana*), black cherry (*Prunus serotina*), red oak (*Quercus rubra*), and white oak. This composition is typical of maple-basswood communities. This site also has a particularly rich shrub layer that includes maple-leaved arrowwood (*Viburnum acerifolium*), nannyberry (*V. lentago*), and witch hazel (*Hamamelis virginiana*).[26]

Maple-basswood forests also rim the leeward banks of rivers where they are protected from fires and where soil conditions are suitable. The timbered lands along the east side of the Des Plaines River in Lake County (Ill.) provide an excellent example. Maple-basswood forests do best in the section between Deerfield Road and Route 176. Here the soil consists of clay lying atop gravel and sand, products of glacial outwash. This segment of the river, with its better-drained soils, promotes forests with trees that are greater in both diversity and size. Ryerson Woods Conservation Area, Daniel Wright Woods, Lloyd Woods Nature Preserve, and a part of MacArthur Woods Nature Preserve are all on this stretch of the river.[27]

In contrast, the areas riparian to the Des Plaines in the southern portion of the county are underlain by dense and poorly drained clay tills that hinder the growth of mesic forests. (As the glacier retreated, meltwater probably covered this area.) The saturated ground can kill lower roots and even the entire tree during particularly wet years. Further, where the sinker roots have died due to an excess of moisture in the spring, the tree may have difficulty obtaining enough water to sustain itself during the dry summer.[28]

American beech (*Fagus grandifolia*) and sugar maple dominate the mature woodlands of Berrien County, but otherwise beech has a spotty distribution in the region. A peninsula of these forests followed the Valparaiso Moraine south almost as far as Valparaiso, Indiana, before abruptly giving way to oak-hickory.

18. Deep ravine of the Valparaiso Moraine harboring mesic forest at
Palos Park, Cook County, June 1909. Photo by Chicago Prairie Club.
(Courtesy Westchester Township Historical Museum, Chesterton, Ind.)

Wallace Elton, who examined this phenomenon by establishing study plots
from eastern La Porte County to western Lake County (Ind.), discovered that
forest composition was probably a function of soil characteristics.[29] Beech-
maple abundance decreased and oak-hickory increased as the soil texture went
from coarse (sandy) to fine (silt and clay). Consistent with the mesic forests of
the Des Plaines River, the beech-maple prospered where extremes in moisture
were least. In addition to edaphic (soil) factors, Elton also thinks that heavier
snowfalls in the eastern portion of the area he studied may contribute to the
formation of the mesic forests. He discounts fire because the current beech distribution is similar to that suggested by the early surveyor records, made before settlers altered original burn frequencies.

Beech-maple forests developed in pockets in the Indiana Dunes but are
largely absent from the Illinois side of the lake. Until they were cut in 1922, a
small grove of beech persisted along the Chicago River near Edgebrook (now
a part of Chicago), but these may have been planted by Native Americans. The
species also occurs in a few of the ravines of Lake County (Ill.), although some
have suggested that these too were of Indian origin or that they arrived via the
digestive tract of the now extinct passenger pigeon.[30]

Beech-maple forests do not reappear until the northeastern corner of

Racine County. This heavily timbered area forms the southern tip of a peninsula, protected from fire and drought by the southeastern-flowing Root River
and Lake Michigan. One outstanding example of this forest survives: Renak-
Polak Maple Beechwoods. Historically, landowners took some trees for fuel
and allowed some light grazing in one corner of the property, but the woods
have mended. One sign of this is the presence of "wolf trees," irregularly
shaped specimens that are the first casualties in forests managed as lumber. Another sign is the stellar display of spring flowers, including large numbers of the
declined trillium (*Trillium flexipes*), a relatively uncommon species with im-
maculate white petals and stamens of pink to purple.

Writing on the role of the sugar maple in mesic forests, Curtis says that
"the unique features of this forest are dependent almost entirely on the behavior of this species."[31] Pollinated mostly by the wind, the sugar maple flowers
during April and early May. Loosened by autumnal winds, vast quantities of
wing-shaped fruit known as samaras twirl to the ground and coat the woodland
floor. Trees begin producing seed at the age of forty years, but crops are light
until an additional thirty years pass. The size of the crop, like most things in
nature, is cyclical, peaking every two to five years in correspondence with optimal weather conditions. During one of these good years, maples can produce
more than 5 million seeds per acre, although half may be infertile.

Few of these seeds ever become trees, however. Canopy maples have numerous branches and broad leaves, thus enabling little light to reach the forest
floor. These young maples can survive light deprivation for up to twenty years,
but unless a canopy tree comes down, creating an oasis of light, the saplings will
never reach their full potential.

Competition for light is the driving force behind the success or failure of
mesic forest plants. Tulip tree (*Liriodendron tulipifera*) and black cherry maintain themselves as minority members of mesic forests by inhabiting areas of
topographic and hydrologic variation. By rooting on ridges or adjacent to vernal ponds that are sparsely canopied, they make do with the light that pene-
trates obliquely. Basswoods survive by producing root sprouts that encircle the
adult tree. When the elder finally dies, these sprouts can then mature and the
process begins over again.

A number of ecologists have studied the competition for light at Berrien
County's Warren Woods, a superb site that I will discuss more broadly later.
In 1935, Stanley Cain of Indiana University inventoried the woody vegetation.
He found that maple was the overwhelmingly dominant species among trees
less than a foot tall, beech and maple numbers were roughly equal in trees over
a foot tall and under an inch in diameter, and beech was by far the most abundant in the largest size category, outnumbering maple by as much as eight to
one. These demographics led Cain and others to conclude that "the balance

will be in favor of sugar maple as time goes on and that the tract will approach closer to a codominance of maple with beech."[32]

Fifty years later, however, tiny maples still covered the Warren Woods floor and beech still dominated the canopy. Gerard Donnelly focused his doctoral research on why the status quo was being maintained. When a canopy tree falls, the opening creates a microhabitat fundamentally different from the climax forest that surrounds it. Suddenly, critical resources such as space, light, and warmth become available, and there is a rush by competing organisms to exploit the temporary abundance. Maples spurt upward to join the beech, and with their superior numbers, their accession to the canopy seems assured. But the small gaps generally close during the course of a fifteen- to thirty-year period, too quickly for a sapling maple to take its place in the sun. Thus, there is a large population of "trees in waiting," condemned to endure a lifetime in the shade. During this time, maple growth virtually stops; counting rings of trees that were so trapped becomes an exercise in microscopy. Eventually most of these also-rans will die.

Although not as swift growing as the maple in full light, the beech continues to rise even after a canopy rent is mended. The beech is better suited to the waiting game because of an evolutionary trade-off. The speed with which it increases in height is sacrificed for lateral growth. In the summer forest, muted flecks of light drizzle through little slits in the canopy. Beech send forth long horizontal branches that seek out these glints and, thus, over the centuries, can pierce the maple curtain. (One beech took more than three hundred years to reach the canopy.)[33]

Gerard Donnelly's conclusion that beech will maintain its position in Warren Woods is predicated on the assumption that the rate of disturbance, natural or human, will remain low. If large openings in the canopy develop, closure will not be rapid enough to exclude maples.

Since 1975, a series of severe storms has dramatically increased the rate of windfall in the woods. This most recent chapter in the life of Warren Woods has been documented by Tom Poulson formerly of the University of Illinois at Chicago. For the first three-quarters of this century, the rate of windfall at Warren Woods was about one-tenth of a tree per year per hectare. It is now one to one-and-a-half trees per year per hectare. Poulson reports that the forest looks very different now: "There are seas of maple of all sizes." The ratio of beech to maple in the canopy has dropped to four to one, and in about a hundred years it is likely to be only two to one, or even one to one. But he doubts that Warren Woods will lose its magnificent beech, for enough will win the race to the canopy to ensure survival.[34]

These mesic forests feature some of the most beautiful scenes to grace the region. The beech in any season is an exquisite mixture of form, color, and texture that has few equals among its arboreal relations. Open-grown trees are wider then they are tall; limbs of ancient trees bend to touch the earth, the strain of carrying the burden of their age. But lending grace to the massiveness of beech trunks and major branches, delicate twigs reach out with thin and sharply pointed buds.

The slate gray bark of the American beech, smooth and taut, seems muscular but not sinewy as in the blue beech (*Carpinus caroliniana*). In the fall, it contrasts with the pale golden leaves in an elegant combination of muted hues. Unfortunately, beech bark creates another effect: whether it is Daniel Boone marking the place where he "cilled a bar" in 1760 or a fevered young man proclaiming his first conquest, some citizens get an irresistible urge to carve memorials on the fair surface of the tree. Few local beeches have escaped defacement.[35]

The sugar maple can draw human attention as few other local trees can. A sugar maple in fall is arguably the major jewel in an arboreal crown studded with gems. Again I quote from Peattie who singles this tree out among the many others who contribute to this "most magnificent display of color in all the kingdom of plants": "Clearest yellow, richest crimson, tumultuous scarlet, or brilliant orange—the yellow pigments shining through the over-painting of the red—the foliage of sugar maple at once outdoes and unifies the rest. It is like the mighty, marching melody that rides upon the crest of some symphonic weltering sea and, with its crying song, gives meaning to all the calculated dissonance of the orchestra."[36]

But the sugar maple doesn't just dazzle the eye, it also provides a culinary treat that humans have appreciated since the sweet stickiness first touched their tongues.[37] Native Americans harvested maple syrup and turned it into sugar that they used as a flavoring for dried meat and other foods. The first mention of its use by Europeans in this region is by La Salle's "trusted subordinate" Henri Joutel, who spent the early spring of 1684 in Chicago: "There being but very little game in that place, we had nothing but our meal of Indian wheat to feed on; yet we discovered a kind of manna, which was a great help to us. It was a sort of tree, resembling our maple, in which we made incisions, whence flowed a sweet liquor, and in it we boiled our Indian wheat, which made it delicious, sweet and of a very agreeable relish."[38]

Maple syrup became very important to the settlers for whom it was their only source of sugar. Sugar bushes, as maple groves were called, were of such value that the Illinois legislature early on imposed a fine of eight dollars per tree to anyone caught tapping maples on government land. Eight dollars exceeded by almost three times what the government paid as daily wages.[39]

Near Three Oaks, Berrien County, the production of maple sugar became an industry from 1835 to 1850.[40] Sap began running in February and continued for up to six weeks, depending on the weather. Flows remained heavy in periods of cool temperatures, but diminished during warm spells. On a daily basis, workers extracted three to six gallons of sap per tree to be stored in troughs made of tulip tree. They then boiled, stirred, and skimmed the sap for hours until it became a concentrated syrup that eventually hardened into sugar as it cooled. When conditions were optimal, "five or six gallons of sap made a pound of sugar, each large tree supplying about four pounds of sugar in a season." What settlers didn't use for home consumption, they traded for other products or sold for up to ten cents a pound.

◄◦► ◄◦► ◄◦►

There is one period during the growing season when these otherwise dark mesic forests are open to the nurturing rays of the sun. During that time, from mid-April through May, the herbaceous understory races into color like fireworks across the sky of a July night. Some of these plants, collectively called spring ephemerals, must flower and absorb sufficient energy during that narrow span before the thick foliage of the canopy casts them into shadow. After that, little or no sign of them remains and they disappear until the following spring. This group includes trout lilies, Dutchman's britches, and toothwort. Other species, not truly ephemeral, retain their leaves and stems throughout the summer, fruiting in the fall or carrying on the photosynthetic process as best they can with the minimal light. They possess bulbs or corms that enable them to store up the nutrients ingested during those busy days of spring. Curtis writes that this "adjustment by a group of herbs to a whole set of growth patterns and to a particular timing cycle produced by another member of the community is to be taken as an indication of a very long period of coexistence."[41]

For me the quintessential spring woodland flower is the great white trillium (*Trillium grandiflorum*). Its large snowy flowers bleach extensive sections of the understory in many high-quality forests throughout the area. As the days pass, however, the snowy corollas become pink, adding yet more color to the living bouquet that includes spring beauties, bellwort (*Uvularia grandiflora*), woodland phlox (*Phlox divaricata*), swamp buttercup (*Ranunculus septentrionalis*), and several violets, of which yellow violet (*Viola pubescens*) and common blue violet (*V. sororia*) are the most abundant.

Another flower of the vernal forest, although not an ephemeral, is the mayapple (*Podophyllum peltatum*). When they first emerge from the rich humus of the forest floor, their folded leaves look like the knuckles of a tiny clenched fist. Later, when the stem comes up, the leaves unfurl in the distinctive parasol of the adult plant. As if neurotically modest, the waxy white flowers bloom half-hidden at the junction of the leaf pedicels. Mayapples spread vegetatively in large circular clones that average forty years of age. The abundant and showy white trout lily forms the same kinds of clones, but enjoys a longer lifespan: an average of 125 years, with an extreme of 313 years.[42]

A very beautiful but rare member of the spring flora is the showy orchis (*Orchis spectabilis*). I have seen it but once in the area, at a place above the Fox River where it was likely planted many years before. Reverend Hill describes it well: "It is a plant of the rich damp woods, rooting in the mold of decayed leaves and wood, and often growing in little patches. It makes a pretty picture amid the dry leaves and fresh verdure with its two shining, rich green leaves near the surface of the ground and its pink or purplish flowers with white oval lips on the short stem between them. It is one of the handsomest of the Orchids, its showy flowers well entitling it to precede the others of the family."[43]

The most imperiled of local forest flowers is also an orchid, the small whorled pogonia (*Isotria medeoloides*). Recently reclassified by the U.S. Fish and Wildlife Service from endangered to threatened because of newly discovered stations in the eastern part of the country, this species is known in the Chicago region from one small population in Berrien County. William Schwab first found it in 1968 and over the next three years the number of plants varied from a high of twelve to a low of seven. The site is a low red maple (*Acer rubrum*) forest with bare sandy soil save for a modest growth of royal ferns, marsh ferns (*Dryopteris thelypteris*), and Canada mayflowers (*Maianthemum canadense*). A private conservation group now owns the property, so the orchid is safe from development. Unfortunately, when orchid authority Frederick Case (who had seen the plants with Schwab) revisited the site a few years ago, he found that the vegetation had grown very dense and he was unable to relocate the pogonias. But more than most orchids, the small whorled pogonia has a way of vanishing only to reappear again; there is still hope that this diminutive rarity may survive within this area.[44]

While the sight of prairie blooms moved both early settlers and modern scientists to rapturous poetry, the incredible local displays of spring woodland flowers have for some reason failed to elicit the same response. Several naturalists point out that the woods were old hat to the settlers and thus they were less likely to comment on it. Perhaps too, the best of the local woods have long been under protection, and thus there was no need to rally the troops with inspiring prose, as was the case with prairies. Gerard Donnelly offers another perspective: "Spring wildflowers are delicate, and I think there is a more intimate sense about forest wildflowers that you might not quite feel when you look at . . . a display across the broad landscape of a prairie. But the spring flowers couldn't be any more abundant, for the whole forest floor is carpeted with them."[45]

Probably every local naturalist has a favorite forest where the pageant of spring wildflowers is particularly beautiful. It might be the East Woods of the Morton Arboretum, O'Hara Woods in Will County, Glenview Woods in Cook County, Renak-Polak Beech Maple Woods in Racine County, somewhere in the Indiana Dunes, or one of any number of other places. One such spot, well known throughout the region and breathtakingly beautiful, is Messenger Woods, a dedicated nature preserve owned and managed by the Will County Forest Preserve District. It lies in the swells of the Valparaiso Moraine, on the banks of Spring Creek, where a narrow band of floodplain forest segues upslope into seventy acres of high-quality mesic forest. The heart of the woods, about fifty acres, has miraculously escaped both lumbering and grazing.[46]

In late April and early May the gently undulating ridges appear as a giant battleground, pitting armies of annual blue-eyed Marys (*Collinsia verna*) against those of Virginia bluebells (*Mertensia virginica*). The blue and white of the former holds the field in one sector, particularly in the floodplain, only to give way elsewhere to solid stands of the latter's cobalt blue. From afar, the bluebells look robust and full of fight, but a closer inspection reveals droopy stems, like old celery stalks. The diminished stature of the plant is mitigated by the greater appreciation of its succulent leaves, which hold the droplets of a recent shower like diamonds on green-velvet backing. This nearer view also shows the minute white flowers of the false mermaid (*Floerkea proserpinacoides*), another of the few annuals in the mesic forest, infiltrating the ranks of the taller principals. And great white trillium, red trillium (*Trillium recurvatum*), Dutchman's breeches, and others appear upslope in various configurations of their own, perhaps as guerillas waiting for a chance to advance.

Three other plants of these forests are noteworthy, not because of their looks or ecological significance but because of their medicinal properties, alleged or real. Golden seal (*Hydrastis canadensis*) has been used for a host of medical purposes, including the treatment of cancer and stomach ailments. One author asserts that "there is no disease for which golden seal would not be useful."[47] There is genuine medical evidence that it increases "rhythmic contractions of the uterus" and "contains an antibiotic that is effective against broad-spectrum bacteria and protozoa."[48]

In 1918, the federal government "estimated that between 200,000 and 300,000 pounds of the drug produced from the root were used annually."[49] This kind of demand for golden seal almost brought it to extinction. Herman Pepoon was not optimistic about its local survival, citing the plant's popularity and disappearing habitat, "the richest and deepest leaf mold in dense shade." He related the following incident: "In a . . . bit of woodland on the Chicago River, ten years ago, a small patch of Hydrastis, numbering possibly a hundred plants, was found in bloom. Today there are none, due to botanists, picnickers, herb gatherers, the cutting off of the trees, and possibly other causes. . . . The chance location of a wood path, leading within ten feet of the above-mentioned patch, was the initial, unpremeditated death call of this little group. As effective, however, as willful destruction, for the traveler could not but see the curious and coveted plant."[50] Golden seal, however, seems to have increased since Pepoon's day, persisting in a number of counties throughout the region.

Human obsession with the second of these plants, ginseng (*Panax quinquefolius*), originated long ago in China where it was seen as "the crystallization of the essence of the earth in the form of man. . . . It is further believed that a small portion of ginseng can cure the sick, strengthen the weak, rejuvenate the aged, and revitalize the dying."[51] This is a lot of baggage to place on the roots of one small plant. But ginseng does contain numerous complex chemicals that suggest it possesses medicinal properties, and researchers are sorting out the bogus claims from the genuine.

Courtesy of a French Jesuit, China first learned in the early 1700s that North America had an acceptable variety of ginseng. This launched a ginseng trade that "produced . . . as much passion and greed as much later did the announcement of the gold mines of California." Thousands of people found work as ginseng hunters. An illustration of their success is the ship that left Boston in 1773 bound for China with fifty-five tons of dried ginseng root.[52]

Ginseng has steadily climbed in price, and exports from the United States to Hong Kong have also increased. This rising popularity has led to widespread cultivation of the plant. At least one such operation is in McHenry County. But Asian consumers strongly prefer roots of wild plants, which now bring $300 a pound. The pressure on wild stocks prompted officials to list ginseng in the Convention on International Trade in Endangered Species of Wild Fauna and Flora. As a result, the U.S. Fish and Wildlife Service mandates that every state must regulate ginseng harvesting.[53]

In 1983 the Illinois General Assembly enacted the Ginseng Conservation Act, which includes the following provisions: digging can only be conducted during a set season; ginseng collected in any one season cannot be kept beyond March 1 of the following year; landowners must give their permission to allow digging; and both diggers and dealers must be licensed. Licenses for diggers cost $7.50, and for dealers $50.00 or $100.00, depending on whether they are resident or nonresident. There are currently twenty-nine licensed dealers in the state, two of whom are in this region.[54]

Ginseng is rare but widely distributed in high-quality forests throughout most of the region. But the plants are vulnerable to unscrupulous diggers operating outside the bounds of the regulatory scheme. Bill Wingate told me about an elderly veterinarian in McHenry County who had ginseng on his property. He protected the plants, except on occasion when he allowed a grandchild to dig one up for Christmas money. One day the doctor received a call from an individual claiming to be from a national conservation magazine that was doing a story on ginseng and wanted to photograph the local plants. Two men arrived, and the doctor showed them the patch. Feeling fatigued, he went back to the house, leaving the visitors in the field. When he returned to the site some days later, the ginseng was gone and the conservation organization denied ever sending anyone.

The story of white snakeroot (*Eupatorium rugosum*), a common and weedy species found in a number of wooded habitats, is very different from that of ginseng or golden seal. Its effects on the body are devastating and were known long before anyone associated them with the plant.

During the summer, pioneers commonly let their cattle wander through the woods eating whatever was edible. In some places this led to tragic consequences for both livestock and the people who consumed their milk. Milk sickness, also referred to by such colorful names as trembles, puking fever, bilious sick stomach, and mukosma, claimed the lives of many early settlers in the Midwest. The most famous victim was Nancy Hanks Lincoln, mother of Abraham, whose death in Indiana prompted the remaining family members to relocate to Illinois. The legislatures of Michigan, Illinois, Indiana, Ohio, and Kentucky all offered rewards for discovery of the pathogen and its cure.[55] Doctor W. E. Walsh of Morris, Grundy County, a student of the malady who wrote several articles on it, summed up its impact: "No wonder pioneer families by whom malaria and typhoid were accepted as a matter of course, fled back east in terror from this mysterious disease from which they died so suddenly. Their cattle and horses, apparently well, died after exercise, and no one knew what it was."[56]

Not only was the illness mysterious, but it also produced horrible effects. Breath became so malodorous many people had to leave the room of the patient. Constipation was common, in one instance lasting fifteen days before death finally ended the child's misery. And as one of its names suggests, vomiting was a characteristic symptom: "The patient brings up whatever is taken into [the stomach], mixed with dirty looking mucus, which hangs from the patient's mouth in long strings like frog's spawn."[57]

Although some physicians figured out the cause of milk sickness relatively early, and even published their findings, many decades elapsed before there was conclusive evidence that the origin of the illness was white snakeroot. Its leaves and stems contain the poisonous alcohol tremetol, which is soluble in milk fat. Thus, butter and cream were more toxic than milk. It ceased being a major problem in Illinois by the late 1800s, thereby becoming the first of the great pioneer diseases to disappear, although Walsh reported twentieth century cases from the Joliet and Morris areas.[58]

Raised in Flood and Drought: The Lowland Forests

Lowland or floodplain forests tend to occur along rivers or, less frequently, lakes and are marked by seasonal inundation, often followed by water scarcity. Floodwaters strip the soil as they speed downstream and deposit new soils as they recede. The material left behind can be heavy in sand or gravel and thus quick to drain. This kind of disturbance regime inflicts havoc on understory plants, and among the few that persist are vines such as poison ivy and river-bank grape. (In the wake of development, this pattern of disturbance has increased tremendously, to the detriment of many riparian woods.) The dominant trees include the highly tolerant black willow (*Salix nigra*), American elm (*Ulmus americana*), slippery elm (*Ulmus rubra*), sycamore (*Platanus occidentalis*), silver maple (*Acer saccharinum*), cottonwood, box elder (*Acer negundo*), and green ash (*Fraxinus pennsylvanica*). In this region, the Kankakee River was the only river that had extensive floodplain forest.

It is not a coincidence that several of these floodplain trees show up as ornamentals lining the thoroughfares of urban America, where only species whose genetic heritage was forged in flood (low oxygen), drought, and scoured earth can survive. These rapidly growing trees are also handsome. The silver maple flashes green and then silver as the wind tugs at its leaves, while the American elm stands tall and straight before branching at the top to cast a cooling shadow. James Schmid reported in his splendid *Urban Vegetation* that these two trees occurred on the residential lots and parkways of this region far more frequently than any others, although ash was also well represented. Box elder is even tougher, showing up unwanted in pavement cracks, along fences, and wherever else little patches remain unattended by human hands.

American elms hold a special place not only in our neighborhoods but in our history as well. One prominent local elm grew on an estate in Racine, Wisconsin, where it eventually reached a height of ninety-five feet and a basal diameter of eight feet. The city was formally chartered by the state legislature in February 1841 and held its first election in April of the same year: "Another seed—an elm—was taking root that spring. Both apparently were on fertile soil. Through several wars and many storms, as well as periods of prosperity and sunshine, the village and the elm grew." The dying tree was eventually cut down in 1953 as a precautionary measure.[59] Of all the historical trees in this country, more are American elms than any other. That the tree becomes the mnemonic for events or persons otherwise forgotten prompted Donald Peattie to remark that "if you want to be recalled for something that you do, you will be well advised to do it under an elm."[60]

Although American elm remains a lovely component in many local forests and neighborhoods, its survival was thrown into doubt by the arrival of the fungus *Ophiostoma* (*Ceratocystis*) *ulmi*, or Dutch elm disease. Believed to have crossed the Atlantic on logs from Europe, the fungus appeared in Indiana in 1930, Michigan in 1950, Illinois in 1954, and Wisconsin in 1956. The effects were devastating: "It is not possible to suggest another species whose removal from the Midwestern urban landscape could begin to be so disruptive as that of the American elm."[61]

Feeding on both healthy and infected trees, the nonnative European bark beetle (*Scolytus multistriatus*) is the principal agent responsible for the spread of the fungus. Another pathway for the disease arises where elm roots of one tree graft with those of another, a common occurrence where trees are closely spaced. Once established, the fungus lodges in the vascular system of the tree, cutting off the flow of water and other nutrients.

The primary means of control is removal of all sick and dead trees. Nationwide, such efforts cost over $100 million a year, but where practiced diligently, they greatly reduce overall elm mortality.[62] A few examples make the point clear. The following Illinois municipalities had no control programs and lost almost all of their elms between 1955 and 1966: Elgin, 94.0 percent; Zion, 93.8 percent; Joliet, 92.1 percent; and Aurora, 91.1 percent. The towns that follow did use comprehensive control measures, and from 1957 to 1971 suffered far fewer losses: Kenilworth, 10.0 percent; Lincolnwood, 27.5 percent; Homewood, 31.3 percent; Highland Park, 42.0 percent; and Lombard, 46.8 percent.[63]

Much less information is available concerning elm mortality in natural environments. The Cook County Forest Preserve District removes diseased elms found on its holdings. Elm loss peaked in the period from 1965 to 1970, with the single highest year being 1967, when district personnel took down and disposed of 19,393 trees. But elms continue to suffer as district removal figures demonstrate: 1992—8,109; 1993—3,157; 1994—4,098; and 1995—1,723.

Al Westerman says that when the infestation was at its worst some lowland forests lost as much as 50 percent of their canopy almost overnight. Dead and rotting elm trunks were everywhere, particularly at Gurnee Woods, which has the largest floodplain forest in Lake County [Ill.]. Silver maples and green ash replaced the elms, but there are still places where the gaps have yet to fill in, like open sores that fail to heal.

The cottonwood is a pioneering species of damp ground, daring to take root where no tree has gone before. It produces huge quantities of cottony seeds, whitening the ground as in the aftermath of a spring snowstorm. In many places, these blizzards coincide with the recession of spring floods, thus maximizing the surfaces hospitable to seed germination.

No tree in this region grows taller than the cottonwood, and several giants have attained notoriety. A huge specimen, Illinois's largest tree, grew in Morris, Grundy County, until 1990. People routinely crowded into its hollow trunk, some actually living there on a temporary basis. In Racine, there was the "Sentinel of Wind Point." It grew on the shore of Lake Michigan in a dense woodland owned by David Felix, who died in 1855. Felix cleared the entire woods, except for this one cottonwood that "he did not have the heart to level." It towered more than a hundred feet and became a landmark for lake-going vessels. Shipmasters watched for it, knowing that Racine Harbor was but a few miles to the south.[64]

An even more remarkable cottonwood sprouted near what is now the intersection of Glenview Road and the Edens Expressway in Glenview (Cook).[65] Some called it the "Potawatomi Tree," while to others it was simply "The Big Tree." Said to have been the largest tree in the country that was not a sequoia, the cottonwood was 130 feet tall and had a girth of forty-one feet. At its base was a cavity supposedly large enough to hold thirty people. The first branches appeared seventy feet up the trunk. Contemporary accounts quote various experts as saying the tree must have been between five and six hundred years old. Modern scientists say the species can grow to 190 feet, but this is more a testament to its fast-growing nature than its longevity, for the cottonwood rarely lives beyond its 125th season.

Whatever its true age and size, the tree became the subject of lore nearly as rich as the soil that anchored its mighty roots. Originally in the middle of "a great grove of cottonwoods and poplars surrounded by hazel bushes," the Big Tree survived an 1832 fire that swept through the copse, killing most every other tree. The locals saw its survival as a miracle, and from then on "viewed the 'Big Tree' . . . with something akin to veneration."

A few years after the fire, a black bear and her two cubs took up residence in the tree's hollow. They stayed until their depredations on livestock led to their discovery, and a fight between a knife-wielding hunter and the sow. According to the story, both parties succumbed to their injuries, the bear outright and the "terribly mutilated" human several weeks later.

In the 1860s, a ring of local thieves stashed their horde of silverware and other valuables in the bears' former home. Not many years after the gang leader died, a boy found the trove of silver. Among the pieces was a sugar bowl filled with hickory nuts "stowed away by some provident member of the squirrel family."

The tree grew on the farm of Charles Kotz, who had known the cottonwood since childhood. Kotz attributed the tree's success to permanent springs that kept the thick soil perpetually watered. He was interviewed in 1898, five years before the "Big Tree" was taken down for safety reasons:

As long as I live and can raise potatoes, and there is firewood on the place, no ax shall harm the tree. I don't believe anyone, after I'm dead, will be mean enough to cut it down. When the city grows out this way, as it certainly will within fifty years or maybe less, this place may be a park, and with that tree would be one of the sights of Chicago, wouldn't it? . . . We would have one of the most wonderful natural attractions in the country. No, I have no objection to people coming here to look at it. It don't cost anything to be decent, and I am glad to have people appreciate our wonder.

Mostly on or under the Trees: Lichens and Mushrooms

Although not exclusively of the woods, lichens and mushrooms reach their greatest diversity in that environment. William Wirt Calkins, whose *The Lichen Flora of Chicago and Vicinity* was published in 1896, and Gerould Wilhelm, whose work is ongoing, are responsible for much of what is known about local lichens. Both authors imbue their writings with a strong sense of history that document changes in lichen status. Calkins wrote: "Localities in and around Chicago formerly rich in lichenose vegetation are now destitute of it. The species were and are mostly corticolous [growing on trees], with a few on rocks, where exposed, and even on the boulders of our prairies. But the tidal waves of civilization have changed the conditions under which lichens grow, and to find them abundantly we must seek the country where the air on which they feed is pure and the substrates suitable." [66]

Taking into account modern nomenclature and taxonomy, Calkins recorded 109 species of lichens, of which fifty have not been found since. As of 1993, Wilhelm and his colleagues were aware of eighty-six local species not encountered by Calkins. Of the nineteen species considered common by Calkins, only *Endocarpon pusillum* and *Physcia stellaris* remain so, the former growing abundantly on "weathered concrete and flagstone" and the latter on numerous trees. At the same time, *Caloplaca feracissima*, *Lecanora dispersa*, and *Phaeophyscia rubropulchra* went unreported by Calkins but are common today. [67]

Wilhelm and Wayne Lampa, both now with the Conservation Design Forum, offer two explanations to explain the eighty-six species missed by Calkins. First, lichens are very sensitive to air pollution, and their increase may be in response to improved air quality. More important, though, there are undoubtedly more trees present in the area now than there were in the latter part of the nineteenth century. This provides corridors for "less modal lichen species . . . to extend their ranges." [68]

While lichens may interest only a few botanists, mushrooms are sought by legions. More than three hundred species inhabit the region, but only a

19. The giant cottonwood known as the "Big Tree" or "Potawatomi Tree," Glenview, Cook County, 1898. (Courtesy Wilmette Historical Museum, Wilmette, Ill.)

relatively small number are either delicious or dangerous. Most are simply too tough, small, or bad tasting to eat.

Morels (*Morchella*) are one of the choicest of all. They need well-drained soils, and indeed the only places I have ever found them were on low dunes near Lake Michigan. Mycologist Anthony Jandacek told me one of his favorite mushrooms is hen-of-the-woods (*Grifola frondosus*), a species that sprouts under oaks. He found one specimen in Cook County that weighed fifty-six pounds. Puffballs (Lycoperdales) are also very popular because as a family they are almost all edible and relatively easy to identify. Certain species can grow to the size of basketballs.[69] If you are squeamish about taking your butter straight, fried puffballs are perfect, as they have little flavor of their own and possess a tremendous capacity to absorb shortening.

The most notorious group of mushrooms is the amanitas. Even their names are chilling. Called the "beautiful yet dangerous monarch of mushrooms," the destroying angel or death cup (*Amanita virosa*) has killed more local mushroom eaters than all other species combined.[70] To put things in perspective, however, only seventy fatal mushroom poisonings are known to have occurred in the entire United States from 1900 to 1972. Most of these happened in the first decade or two of the century, when large influxes of European immigrants brought mushroom collecting to this country. Their example increased collecting by native-born U.S. citizens who knew nothing about mycology, and the new arrivals themselves were unfamiliar with the mushrooms they were encountering here for the first time.[71] (The most recent surge in immigration has also produced an increase in mushroom poisonings.)

Dr. Denis Benjamin refers to *Amanita* poisoning as "a triphasic illness," which can destroy the liver and other organs.[72] The first phase is marked by sudden and severe gastrointestinal distress, including stomach pains, vomiting, and diarrhea. After twenty-four hours or so, the symptoms often, though not always, subside and the patient feels well enough to believe he has recovered. A false hope, however, for the amatoxin has been working steadily and soon the stomach problems return, along with all the other manifestations of a failing liver, most notable of which are progressive coma and death. In some instances, the patient survives the liver damage, only to suffer kidney or heart failure. And if he does survive, it may be with permanently impaired organs.

Traditionally, most mushroom hunters were of southern or eastern European origin. Mushroom collecting was both a form of outdoor recreation and a way to augment the family larder. In the early part of the twentieth century, large groups of immigrants would leave Chicago and head for the country in search of their quarry. One writer from Deerfield, Lake County (Ill.), complained that the suburb was invaded by over four hundred mushroomers, many intoxicated, who arrived on trains from the city and left havoc in their wake.

The xenophobic commentator would probably be more comfortable with today's mushroom devotees, who represent a range of ethnic backgrounds and are less likely to have accents. They tend to be more knowledgeable about identification, but some mycologists are concerned that they may lack some of the conservation ethic allegedly possessed by the old-timers. But even among informed mushroomers, there is the notion that all public lands are open to their picking. This is clearly not so, and collectors should make sure that they are conducting their searches where it is permissible.

Mushroom collecting was particularly popular during the Great Depression, and even those who knew nothing about it began participating. In Racine County, 1929 may have been rough on the working classes, but it was a good year for mushrooms. People gathered various kinds in large numbers, but were shaky on their identifications. Edwin Sanders, a Racine schoolteacher and amateur mycologist, spent two whole weeks going through the piles people brought him. One destitute fellow walked two miles to consult with Sanders; as he told the teacher, he was out of work and felt this was one way to help his family. With regret, Sanders had to inform the man that there wasn't an edible mushroom in the bunch.[73]

Recently scientists have begun to examine the relationship between mushroom populations and the health of the forest ecosystems of which they are a part. The cap and stem of the mushroom are really just the fruiting body of the fungus "plant," known as the mycelium. The mycelia surround or invade the rootlets of trees and other plants to the mutual benefit of both—the fungus receives carbohydrates while providing nitrogen, phosphorus, and other nutrients that would otherwise not be available to the plant. What happens when that relationship is broken is the subject of worldwide research. Locally, mycologists at the Field Museum are examining the effects of air pollutants on this process.[74]

From Lumber to Ecosystems: Utilization and Conservation

Two fundamental differences exist between settlement of the prairies and of the woods. First, once prairie disappeared on a large scale, it never grew back. There is also no such thing as selective plowing in the same sense as there is selective logging. Once the prairie sod was torn to bits, there were insufficient reservoirs of extant native plants to overcome competition by the ubiquitous hordes of alien species. Taking only some trees ensured a continuation of some forest. And even where a forest is clear-cut, indigenous trees will probably grow back, even if takes a long time and a different set of pioneering species appears. Of course, a stand of cottonwoods and box elder on an abandoned city lot can hardly be called a forest, but at least some forest elements exist.

Further, and this is the second of the differences, the commercial value of prairie lies largely in the richness of the soil rather than the native flora that springs from it. To be sure, livestock need pastures, but intensive grazing diminished native grassland. In addition, market fluctuations would shift land use back and forth between animal crops and vegetable crops. A farmer with healthy and well-fed stock had no particular interest in prairie plants. Forest plants, however, had value in their own right. From maple syrup to ginseng to mushrooms to the timber itself, people harvested forest products for home use or sale. Although profligacy was rife, there was at least some incentive to husband the resource.

Virtually all of the original timber disappeared under the first waves of settlement. Studies in Lake County, Illinois, and at Thorn Creek Woods reveal that most canopy trees date to a fifty-year period from 1830 to 1880. There are

20. Timber hauled on sleds, Kettle Moraine, Walworth County, circa 1900. (Courtesy Kettle Moraine State Forest Archives, Eagle, Wis.)

older trees, generally in the 230-year range, but they exist as individuals rather than forests. Still, Marlin Bowles believes that these ancient trees are present with enough frequency to link many of the region's highest quality forests to presettlement times.[75]

Then there is a gap of about forty to fifty years when few trees germinated. This might be due to cyclicity of reproduction, massive die-off, or most likely, grazing pressure. With the 1920s came a second boom in tree reproduction, which continues to the present.

How people settled and used the region's woods varied from place to place, depending on the nature of the forest. To illustrate the process, I have selected the Des Plaines River Valley in Lake County (Ill.), the Big Woods of Evanston in Cook County, and the vicinity of Three Oaks in Berrien County. Conservationists have carefully documented the history of forest utilization in each, in large measure because surviving remnants provide a direct link to those early times.

◂◦▸ ◂◦▸ ◂◦▸

Lake County offered a wide variety of landscapes.[76] Settlers chose savanna first, as it provided both timber and rich soil. When these lands became occupied or too dear, open prairie was the next choice. But to ensure access to timber, these homesteaders would often buy small tracts of forest to use as woodlots. They cropped these trees judiciously, beginning with the dead and the largest. Most of the lumber was used as fence posts and fuel.

Later settlers had fewer options and wound up in the forested areas. Unlike those who had preceded them, they saw the timber not as a valuable resource to be husbanded but as an impediment to farming. They spent all of their spare time removing the trees. If the tree was smaller than eighteen inches in diameter, these new homesteaders would cut it down and then grub or, later, dynamite the stump. If greater than eighteen inches, they would girdle the tree and then pile brush around it so that it could be burned. This rapid clearing produced so much timber, most of it was simply discarded as it had little market value.

By the mid-1800s, many farmers found that it was cheaper to buy milled pine than to cut and hew their own wood. Later, companies from Chicago would travel into the county to buy timber. They would cut it into firewood, haul it on wagons to the Chicago and Northwestern train, and then send it by rail to Chicago. The demand for this lumber, and the importance of the woodlots, subsided greatly when coal became the fuel of choice at the end of the century.

Some accounts mention that wildflowers were noticeably thicker in the first spring following the cutting of the woods, but the introduction of wheat, which has allelopathic properties, made the phenomenon short-lived.[77] Wheat production was the number one crop in Lake County until the Civil War. Settlers with wooded property were particularly fond of wheat because it required minimal care and could be sown around the stumps.

But the grain depleted soil fertility, and when prices collapsed, a large dairy industry developed in its stead. This peaked in the 1870s and 1880s and stayed strong until World War II. Allowed to roam through the woodlots, the cattle destroyed the shrubby understory, making the oak woods look like parks. When the Ryersons first bought their riverside property in the 1920s, the woods were open. It took decades to mend, to where spring flowers were once again thick.

Starting in the 1920s, many of the woodlots in the southern part of the county were subdivided into small lots for summer homes. Some developers sought out wooded parcels from which they could obtain elms and hawthorns for landscaping. The depressions that resulted were still evident on portions of the Ryerson Conservation Area sixty years later.

With the end of World War II and increased affluence, people sought out these timbered parcels for one- or two-acre estates. The ongoing trend is to tear down smaller homes to build larger ones. An example of this situation

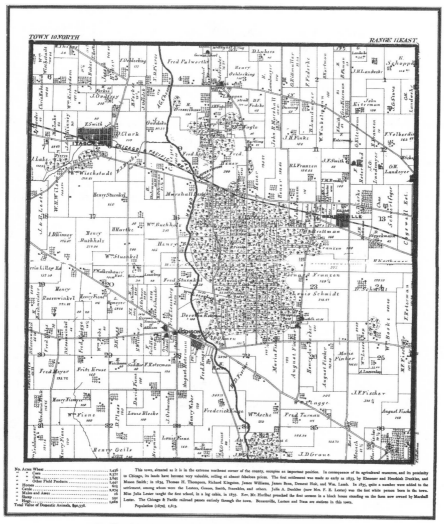

21. Plat of northeastern Addison Township, DuPage County, showing
that the forests along the east side of Salt Creek were subdivided into
small woodlots. This map appears in the 1874 atlas of DuPage County,
reprinted in 1974. (Reproduced with permission of DuPage County
Historical Society, Wheaton, Ill.)

gone amok exists on Portwine Road in Riverwoods, where a choice wooded
setting has been obliterated by a castle.

There are a few places in Lake County, like Lake Forest, Lake Bluff, and
Riverwoods, where the residential landscaping has incorporated old-growth
trees. (Wilmette, Evanston, Beverly Park, Morgan Park, and other communities in the region can also boast old-growth trees as part of their urban setting.)
Economics, however, militate against preserving any original vegetation. Developers find it easier and cheaper to clear a site of everything, regrade it as

necessary, and then plant whatever is available in local nurseries. Even where preservation of standing trees is desired, compaction of soil, changing drainage patterns, and damage during construction usually proves fatal to most upland species. And it is the rare homeowner who tries to maintain native understory.[78]

Fortunately, the Lake County Forest Preserve District has acquired much of the Des Plaines River woodland in the county. Three large tracts are dedicated nature preserves: Ryerson Woods Conservation Area, Lloyd Woods (privately owned but managed by the district), and MacArthur Woods. All of these sites contain high-quality examples of the forest types we have just examined. But as with all land in this region, there are threats that do not recognize legal boundaries. The burgeoning deer population is a problem of large proportions that has proven to be a political nightmare (see chap. 12). When a new technique in veneering drove the price for black walnut sky high, tree rustlers, armed with silent saws, cut hundreds of trees up and down the Des Plaines River. When they were done, few large black walnuts remained. The worst single incident occurred in the winter of 1970–71 when seventy-six walnuts were cut at MacArthur Woods. Soon thereafter, authorities arrested several people for taking walnuts on Cook County Forest Preserve land. Whether because of the arrests or lessening market pressure, similar incidents of that magnitude have not been repeated.[79]

Nonnative species also pose major threats to the woods of Lake County and the rest of the region. They become entrenched in abused areas and make healing difficult because they outcompete the natives. Common buckthorn established itself in southeastern Lake County in the 1930s, having originally been planted on the grounds of the lakefront mansions. Dense stands allow little else to share the understory. The spread was slow, appearing in scattered locations in the south end of the county by 1971. Ten years later it was widely distributed in the north, and now is ubiquitous.[80]

Another pestiferous alien that plagues local forests is garlic mustard (*Alliaria petiolata*), now the dominant spring flower of many woods. Europeans used the plant as a seasoning, and may have brought it with them for that purpose. In any event, garlic mustard was first noted in the United States in 1868 and has thrived ever since. The first record of the species for the region and state occurred at Ravinia, Lake County in 1918. Since then, in Illinois at least, "the rate at which new populations were detected approximately doubled every ten years."[81]

Garlic mustard thrives in most wooded communities, establishing itself in areas of disturbance such as flood plains, trails, and roadsides. The plant disperses easily and widely because its tiny seeds can be transported by water, pets, people, or machinery. Controlled burns can also benefit the species by uncovering seedbeds. Given all of the vectors that facilitate its spread, garlic mustard will undoubtedly increase further.

◄◦► ◄◦► ◄◦►

From Evanston to Winnetka, a diverse forest arose from the ridges and swales that demarcate the changing levels of glacial Lake Chicago. Protected from most fires by the broad wet spaces that separated them, these timbers became known as the Big Woods and covered much of the ground from Lake Michigan to the east banks of the Chicago River's North Branch. With one remarkable exception, little if any of its living glory has endured. Most of what follows focuses on Evanston, where the historical record of the forest has been meticulously and lovingly documented by naturalist Libby Hill.

One of the earliest floras of this region appeared in 1891 and focused on Cook County and a portion of Lake County, Indiana. Authors William Higley and Charles Raddin highlight the Big Woods as one of the "localities of special interest":

> Here many of our representative trees are found as well as less frequent forms, while around their trunks twine the wild grape, woodbine, bittersweet, and poison ivy. In the spring parts of this area are submerged and marshy, and abound with species of Trillium, Arabis, and Cardamine. Species of the [orchids] Habenaria, Cypripedium, and Orchis are here met with, as well as the *Sanguinaria candadensis* and *Oxalis violacea*. During the summer and autumn the undergrowth is marked by species of Solidago, Aster, Helianthus, Eupatorium, [Laportea (wood nettle)], . . . and many others, while the fallen logs present a great variety of mosses and fungi.[82]

Writing in 1910, Charles Atwell, professor of biology at Northwestern University and later Evanston's chief forester, stated that the principal trees in the drier portions were oaks—black, red, white, and bur—and shagbark hickories, "with white birch, [white] pine, juniper and occasional black cherry trees along the [easternmost] ridge." Within the clay-lined swales, there were places slightly elevated and drained sufficiently to support forest, also, but of a different type. These lowlands were the domain of swamp white oaks, American elms, basswood, ash, silver maple, sugar maple, bitternut hickory (*Carya cordiformis*), and butternut (*Juglans cinerea*).[83]

Ten years later, Lillian Simmons of Northwestern University published a systematic study that she had conducted of the woods.[84] Although urbanization had altered much of the area, she found that extensive forest still survived.

Using the terminology current at the time, she noted the presence of meso-phytic upland forest, xerophytic sand ridge forest, and morainic swamp forest.

The mesophytic upland forest and xerophytic sand ridge forests were re-stricted to a few small areas. They still contained the same trees recorded by Atwell, but much less of the understory remained. Some of those species per-sisting in the upland forest included chokecherry, mayapple, wild geranium, and red trillium, and in the sand ridge forest, red trillium, feathery false Solomon's seal, and strawberry (probably wild strawberry, *Frageria virginiana*).

Of the three kinds of forests, the morainic swamp was the "most exten-sive and least disturbed." In addition to the trees mentioned by Atwell, Sim-mons recorded red oak, various haws, and pignut hickory. The understory was rich and "very luxuriant" with young trees, chokecherry (*Prunus virginiana*), elderberry (*Sambucus canadensis*), prickly ash, poison ivy, bristly green brier (*Smilax hispida*), large white trillium, red trillium, bulbous cress (*Cardamine bulbosa*), smooth sweet cicely (*Osmorhiza longistylis*), and other species. She does not mention the orchids that so impressed Higley and Raddin; perhaps in the intervening years these conservative forbs had disappeared.

Of course, few of the people who knew the woods in the early days ap-preciated its floristic diversity. The first settlers, able to purchase land for a dol-lar an acre, arrived in the late 1820s with one mission: to carve a homestead out of the woods. Evanston historian J. S. Currey described the result:

> The new arrival in a region covered with virgin forest was to clear a space
> for his dwelling, and continually enlarge such a space so that in a season or
> two he could form the outlines of his fields of which his future farm was to
> consist. He attacked the forest growth with such furious zeal that daylight
> began to penetrate the gloom of the original forest in many places, and so
> great was his eagerness to extirpate every vestige of the obstruction to open
> farm land that he did not even allow a single tree or bush to remain near
> his dwelling. . . . Many of the early pictures of pioneer dwellings show a
> bare log cabin surrounded by stumps but not a tree within a long distance
> to the edge of the retiring forest lines.[85]

Much of the downed timber was transported to Chicago, where a cord of oak wood sold for 75 cents. Haulers lashed the logs into rafts and then moved them across the dunes and swales to the lake. But this was only possible during winter when the marshy expanses had frozen solid enough to support the weight. A team of oxen powered the rafts that were towed south along the shore toward their destination. Even the stumps had value. Settlers would pile them ten or fifteen feet high, and ignite them. After burning for two or three weeks, the charcoal brought five cents a bushel.[86]

Ditching began in the 1850s, shortly after the Illinois Legislature authorized drainage districts. These projects dewatered much of the lowland and established the roads that still crisscross Evanston. The direct loss of habitat and alteration of hydrology took its toll on the Big Forest. A local resident writing in 1903 attributed a decrease in oaks to "the change in soil resulting from better drainage."[87]

Architect Dwight Perkins moved to Evanston in 1904, an important event in the history of the Big Woods. Called the father of the Cook County Forest Preserve District, he was instrumental in creating the district and guiding it in its early years. Among the properties he sought to protect was a 7.8-acre tract in north Evanston, bounded by the streets Grant and Colfax and the avenues Bennett and Ewing. In May 1918 the district purchased the land for $35,000; seven years after Perkins's death in 1941, the district formally named the parcel Perkins Woods.[88]

Simmons, in her paper, singled out Perkins Woods as "the most characteristic patch" of the swamp forest.[89] Now, seventy years later, it is the only surviving patch, and may in fact be the only forest of its kind in Illinois. Too small and disturbed to be included in the Natural Areas Inventory, it differs from the categories recognized by the inventory. To my eye, it comes closest to Curtis's lake plain lowland forest, which is also called hardwood swamp.[90]

Perkins Woods has suffered the damage associated with being an urban park. For a site so small, it is laced with trails, including a few official ones that are paved (in excess of five feet including mowed edges) and numerous footpaths. In 1966 concern for public safety led to massive cutting of the understory.[91] Dutch elm disease cleared the woods of some its oldest and largest members, although fine specimens remain. Despite these and other impacts, Perkins Woods has retained almost all of its arboreal diversity.

For many years, bird-watchers have walked the trails of Perkins Woods in search of migrants, and local residents have enjoyed the spring wildflowers. But there has been less appreciation for the woods as the last living vestige of something that was once huge, dark, mysterious, daunting, and so very full of life. These were the woods that harbored fishers and martens 150 years ago. Libby Hill, who works with the forest preserve district in her role as steward of the woods, has been successful in connecting the Perkins Woods of today with the Big Woods of yesterday. Most important, in the tradition of the wood's namesake, she is working to help ensure that the woods are treated kindly in the future.

It was 1835 when Richard Love became the first settler of Three Oaks Township, Berrien County. He and the many who followed built their cabins and opened modest patches in the heavy forest. Yellow poplar was the wood of choice for house building, but basswood, black cherry, beech, or oak were acceptable substitutes. A few lumber mills sprang up over the next ten years, but they catered to local markets, as transportation to farther reaches was impossible.[92]

Wendell Paddock, chairman of Ohio State University's Horticulture Department, wrote a long lovely letter to the Three Oaks newspaper, *The Acorn*, in 1917. He was too young to recall the days when the vicinity "was covered with virgin forest," but he did not miss that period by much: "My earliest remembrance of the home farm is that there was not more than fifteen acres of cultivated land, most of it very stumpy, a few acres of chopping, and the rest unbroken forest. The woods shut us in in all directions, and they extended for miles with only occasionally a small clearing where some settler was slowly chopping out a farm. Timber was the one thing that was plentiful, and every boy had to learn to take care of himself in the woods."[93]

By the 1840s and 1850s, entrepreneurs began investing in infrastructure that would allow them access to new markets. They built piers to service Lake Michigan steamships and horse-drawn rail lines to connect the piers with outlying areas. When rail service to Chicago became available in 1853, however, the importance of ship transport was diminished.

Local forests fell quickly in the race to exploit the new business opportunities. Henry Chamberlain, one of the area's wealthiest, wrote of Three Oaks Township and adjacent Chickaming Township: "Except for the small clearings made by the few earliest settlers, nearly all the trees in that part of Chickaming Township which lies north and west of the Galien River, and [on several sections] which lie south of the river, were manufactured into square timber, lumber, spokes, staves, ties, broom and fork handles, and cord wood, and shipped from the piers, or by the Chicago and West Michigan Railroad."[94]

The trees in parts of Three Oaks Township fared no better. Those deemed unsuitable for lumber wound up as fuel for the railroads, which used up to twenty thousand cords annually to run trains between Galien and New Buffalo. Following the completion of the track to Chicago, Chamberlain contracted with the railroad company to supply "2,000 cords of beech, maple, white ash, and hickory wood" at $1.50 a cord. But the railroad was particular: each piece "was to be full four feet from point to kerf, and all split wood; there were to be no limbs which were not straight and large enough to split." Although these specifications cut into Chamberlain's profit, he notes that at the time "we did not put much value on the timber, as land along the line of the railroad could yet be purchased for five dollars an acre."

The railroad's actual demand reached five-to-ten thousand cords a year. Chamberlain assumed that the company would take whatever he supplied, and so "in the winter of 1857 a very large quantity was cut and much of it was drawn and piled near the track." But the financial panic of that year crippled firms everywhere, and the resulting decrease in business meant that the railroad could make do with the wood it already had. Consequently, Chamberlain's product "rotted where it was piled." This was a serious blow to the local economy, forcing, among other things, men to wear pants made of meal bags.

Many people escaped total impoverishment by shifting their energies to other wood-based industries. Elm, oak, basswood, poplar, and sycamore became "blocks for staves and headings." Black ash (*Fraxinus nigra*) barrel hoops were also popular at the time, and those who could make them earned a steady income. They flocked to the few lowlands where the tree grew commonly, taking what they wanted without regard to the landowner.

Wood rose in value during the 1860s, and the region prospered. As coal became the principal fuel, the demand for wood dropped once again. Still, the railroad companies continued to buy wood in reduced quantities until 1892. By then, however, most of the timber was gone.

Paddock, too, recalled those uncertain times: "Finally there came a day when it was evident that the timber supply would soon be exhausted. The question of how to meet the changing conditions was often discussed and the change came so rapidly that our family at least was scarcely ready. We came to be very careful of the final woodlot and we saw with regret the rapid passing of the most familiar object, the stately forest. I am glad now that I left the farm before the advent of the coal stove."[95]

Because of Edward Warren, however, one magnificent tract of virtually untouched beech–sugar maple forest still shades the banks of the Galien River near Three Oaks. Warren Woods, as it is now called, may be the finest example of its kind in the world.[96]

Edward Warren, who was born in 1847 and died in 1919, invented the "featherbone corset," which substituted turkey wings for whalebone. The popularity of this item secured his fortune, later enlarged by successful real estate and banking ventures. While I have not made an extensive study of the man, he seems to have been fair-minded and ahead of his time in conservation matters, for he also purchased 250 acres of Berrien County dunesland. To ensure that the woods and dunes would be safeguarded in perpetuity (as well as the Chamberlain Memorial Museum, which he founded and named for his father-in-law, whose fortunes were discussed earlier in this section), he established the E. K. Warren Foundation two years before his death. Eventually the museum disbanded, but the natural areas became Warren Dunes State Park, which is managed by the State of Michigan, although it is still owned by the foundation.[97]

Warren bought the 150-acre forest in 1879 (part of a three hundred–acre tract that has also been preserved), and for some years after logged a small portion of it for charcoal. According to Greenberry King, an elderly resident interviewed in 1933, about 10 percent of the timber was removed between 1882 and 1891. The targeted trees were basswood, yellow poplar, white oak, black cherry, and a few sugar maples but no beech. These operations were never very profitable, and over time Warren realized that his woods were far more valuable than the sum of its lumber. He curtailed all logging, and even the tapping of maples for syrup lest the trees be damaged. The one thing he continued to allow was the collection of dead trees for firewood, a practice that ended when the state assumed control of the land in 1949.[98]

The least disturbed portion of the site is a thirty-nine-acre parcel north of the Galien River. After a long absence, Wendell Paddock visited his boyhood home in Three Oaks in 1917. Although looking forward to seeing Warren Woods, he was concerned that his recollections of the old forests had become enhanced with the passage of years, such that any reality would be wanting by comparison. But to his great pleasure, it was as he remembered:

> Everything about the woods is just right and no detail is lacking. The underbrush is all there, spicebush, buck beech, ironwood, and alder and no doubt in the spring of the year there is a wealth of flowers. A woods to be just right should be provided with ravines and running water. The Galien River furnishes these details and on the bottom land I saw, just as I expected, butternut and walnut trees. . . . Here and there a tree has fallen in years gone by and now lies in a state of decay covered with mosses, lichens, and ferns. . . . I know of no other locality in the State or surrounding states that can boast of such a sight as this. Surely there are no other forests of this extent anywhere in this region that have not been mutilated by the hand of man.[99]

The uniqueness of the forest has been attracting scientists for decades; I know of at least fifteen different scientific publications that have addressed various aspects of Warren Woods. Over that time, the woods have changed. Butternut is gone, and walnut is rare; and as we have seen, maples will likely assume a greater role in the canopy at the expense of beech. But stasis is foreign to nature's way, and Warren Woods grants the opportunity to catch the subtle undertones of a living system as it evolves with a minimum of human interference. We have Mr. Warren to thank.

22. View of Galien River at Warren Woods, Three Oaks, Berrien
County, July 1914. Photo by Chicago Prairie Club. (Courtesy
Westchester Township Historical Museum, Chesterton, Ind.)

Knotty Questions: How Best to Treat Local Forests

At the turn of the century, conservationists saw their mission as protecting woods, and thus there are "forest preserves." The legislation that created
forest preserves in 1913 contains this language: "Any forest preserve district
organized under this act, shall have the power . . . to acquire . . . and hold lands
containing one or more natural forests or parts thereof" (emphasis added). Later,
the words "or land or lands connecting such forests or parts thereof" were
added. In the 1927 case Washburn *v.* Forest Preserve District, 327 Ill. 479, the
Illinois Supreme Court blocked the Cook County Forest Preserve District's
attempt to acquire part of the Skokie Swamp because the lands in question nei-

23. "A big beech and two peaches" was the original caption describing
this photo of Chicago Prairie Club's outing to Warren Woods in
July 1914. (Courtesy Westchester Township Historical Museum,
Chesterton, Ind.)

ther contained nor connected forests. The General Assembly has since
changed the section again to give the districts wider latitude in the lands they
can purchase.[100]

True to their mission, forest preserve districts concentrated on purchasing wooded lands. A high percentage of these were in morainal areas (such as the Palos) or along rivers, precisely the places where timber most likely always did exist. Because so much forest was in public ownership, they did not receive as much attention as wetlands and prairies that required special efforts to protect.

In more recent years, interest has again shifted to local woods. This time it has been marked by serious disagreement. A strong difference of opinion over the management of forests ignited one of the most acrimonious fights in the annals of local conservation. Aggressive attempts by volunteers working on Cook County forest preserve land to thin woods into savanna provoked a powerful backlash by those who opposed such efforts. The controversy, which quickly became highly personal and allowed little room for middle ground, jeopardized most, if not all, land management carried out by the district. Ultimately, the Cook County Board did impose restrictions on what volunteers can do on its property, particularly the requirement that district staff had to oversee certain management activities.

◄o► ◄o► ◄o►

A commonly held view is that many of the region's forested communities are heavily stressed: the various kinds "of forests all degrade quickly in the absence of grazing ungulates, with major hydrologic changes (especially dewatering), and without recurrent burning. In all woodlands the trends in the degradation process are similar. This can be characterized by the development of an over-stocked canopy of native trees and dense shrub layer, often comprised of non-native species. Under this woody vegetation growth, a dense shade prevents the establishment and growth of soil stabilizing ground cover grasses, sedges and forbs."[101]

This model leads to the conclusion that intense human intervention is necessary to maintain the region's woods. Some have advocated bringing them back to presettlement times. A more viable goal is to "focus on creating stable, naturally diverse assemblages of native plant and animal systems." In order to accomplish this, it is necessary to fix or remove the factors that may be stressing one or more wooded communities, including watershed restriction, hydrologic and hydraulic changes, fire suppression, native shrubs and trees of early succession, dense subcanopies of native trees including oaks, nonnative plants, erosion of topsoil, and overabundance of deer.

An alternative analysis of this region's forests is the far more optimistic one put forward by Jon Mendelson. He believes that local woods are recovering from a long history of cutting and grazing. The profusion of such understory shrubs as hawthorn, and even the nonnative buckthorn and honeysuckle, which tend to colonize the most heavily disturbed sections, is but an early manifestation of a forest mending itself:

> The early stages in the recovery of grazing are, first, the spread of existing thorny or unpalatable species, of which hawthorn is usually most prominent, which is followed by the arrival of light-seeded and bird-disseminated tree species: ash, slippery elm, sugar maple, basswood, and black cherry. . . . Oaks generally appear later in the process. This sequence seems to describe very well the pattern of species in appearance in northeastern Illinois woodlands, where white ash, slippery elm and black cherry are frequently found beneath a much older, oak-dominated canopy, and where once vigorous stands of hawthorn are already in decline.[102]

Mendelson fears that the removal of virtually all non-oaks seriously jeopardizes the future of the region's forests. His is a decidedly minority view, however. Many more believe that doing nothing will lead to an inevitable loss of floral variety, and most agencies are actively involved in woodland management, targeting the various stressors mentioned above. Possibly, time will tell whether the local woods are healing on their own or are gravely ill and requiring massive human aid. And if the latter, what aid is most efficacious in restoring the full diversity of both plants and animals that is possible within these arboreal assemblages? Opportunities exist for gaining important insights into these profound questions, but only if action, or inaction, is accompanied by rigorous scientific scrutiny. May the interest and resources be there.

6

Of Two Worlds: Wetlands

There is a certain grandeur about a big marsh with its reedy vegetation billowing out to a flat horizon. Even in a tamed countryside, it still holds itself aloof as a symbol of wilderness. Land-going creatures are unwilling to flounder in its mud and grassy water. —William J. Beecher (1981)

Even to the casual observer the marsh offers many living and shining things of great interest and beauty which are attracted to it by its springs of water and its friendly cover. But it is forever jealous of its real secrets which it guards with care, revealing them only to those who with love in their hearts seek and find them. —Samuel Harper (1928)

The Pilgrim's Progress to Section 404: Destruction and Conservation of Wetlands

No landscape has undergone a greater change in the public's mind than wetlands. They have been traditionally viewed as unwholesome places best avoided or, better still, eliminated. John Bunyan's seventeenth century classic *Pilgrim's Progress* describes "one of the most famous wetlands in western literature": "This miry slough is such a place as cannot be mended; it is the descent whither the scum and filth that attends conviction for sin doth continually run, and therefore it is called the Slough of Despond."[1]

As we have seen, the initial aversion to the tallgrass prairies rested in part on the lowlands that harbored malarial mosquitoes, made transportation an ordeal, and provided little in the way of potable water. Those who did choose to live in these places were themselves stigmatized as being criminal or unhinged. And perhaps for many, such characterizations were accurate, for where better to avoid scrutiny than the impenetrable mires. Whether a reflection of prejudice or fact, it is revealing that the marshes of the Chain O' Lakes contained a "Bogus Island" and those of the Kankakee, being more extensive, had

115

both a "Little Bogus Island" and a "Big Bogus Island," all three so named because they allegedly provided safe haven for horse thieves and counterfeiters.

Legislators, responsive to the desires of their constituents, enacted laws
designed to facilitate drainage. The Swamp Land Act of 1849 was a landmark
piece of legislation that reflected federal policy for well over a century. (The
original act pertained to Louisiana but was expanded in subsequent years; by
1860, its provisions covered the four states of the Chicago region.) Congress
ceded control of wetlands to the states, to encourage flood control and land
"reclamation" measures. The states responded by building levees, straightening streams, and ditching lowlands.[2]

Drainage ditches became commonplace in many low areas. In Cicero
Township, Cook County, for example, open trenches "12 feet wide at the top,
two feet wide at the bottom and four feet deep" ran every half mile. Every road
was bordered by at least one water-filled ditch, a potential trap for the unwary.
To protect their offspring, "some mothers tied their children together with a
clothesline for the trek to school so that if one child fell into the ditch, the others could pull him out."[3]

Unwanted water, otherwise prone to linger, now flowed elsewhere in a
rapid, if not orderly, manner. And with the water went the troublesome marshlands. Illinois, for instance, has lost around 95 percent of its original wetlands.

It is an old story that humans often fail to perceive value in something
until it is almost gone. Of course, naturalists, hunters, and anglers had long recognized the value of wetlands, but it took others a longer time to appreciate
these special places.

For those millions of people who live on the flat plain of old Lake Chicago, flooding is a very tangible manifestation of eliminating wetlands. It matters not to water whether the lowest point on the landscape is a marsh or a basement. As we saw earlier, much of this now excess water winds up in local rivers,
which overflow their banks with increasing frequency. (It is also important to
remember that upland ecosystems likewise made important contributions to
water retention.) An article published in the April 25, 1993, issue of the *Southtown Economist* estimated that eighteen thousand residences are damaged in the
area by river flooding and "tens of thousands of additional homes have experienced sewer backups or land drainage problems." The same piece reported that
over $1.45 billion of public monies have been expended on combating flood-
ing in the Illinois portions of the Des Plaines and Little Calumet watersheds.

In August of 1987 the heaviest rains on record produced flooding that
damaged more than sixteen thousand homes. Colonel Jesse Franco, then commander of the Chicago office of the Army Corps of Engineers, met with flood
victims to discuss the various issues raised by the unwanted water. People

stepped to the podium and lashed out at officials who allowed the destruction of wetlands and permitted the building of homes in flood plains. Instant conservationists—just add water.

Wetlands generate benefits beyond flood control. Their edges often provide some replenishment to shallow aquifers. And water improves in quality when it wends its way through the biological filtering system of a wetland. Sediments settle out and are buried in debris, while certain chemicals are broken down and/or removed from the water through various organic processes.[4] However, the very effectiveness of wetlands in removing impurities from water may put at risk the organisms that make these ecosystems so wonderful in the first place. Before humans employ these havens of biodiversity as water treatment facilities, we must be confident that the stuff left behind in these marshes poses no threats to their long-term health.[5]

As attitudes about the environment in general and wetlands in particular became kinder and gentler, the government changed its position and cloaked wetlands in a mantle of federal protection that uplands sorely lack. This stems from article 1, section 8, of the U.S. Constitution, which gives Congress the power to regulate interstate commerce. Under this constitutional authority, federal jurisdiction includes migratory birds, navigable waterways, and wetlands adjacent to waterways.

There are several federal laws and policies that embody the new desire to protect wetlands. President Carter, in two executive orders announced in 1977, declared that the protection of wetlands and riparian areas would now be a federal goal. The primary mechanism for implementing the goal is section 404 of the Federal Water Pollution Control Act (Clean Water Act), which requires that before some threshold area of wetlands or waters of the United States can be filled, dredged, or drained, the U.S. Army Corps of Engineers must issue a permit. The U.S. Environmental Protection Agency and U.S. Fish and Wildlife Service also have input in whether a permit should be issued and, if so, what conditions should be attached. A party who is granted the desired permit will probably have to mitigate the loss by creating or preserving a greater area of wetland elsewhere.[6]

Under the national scheme, three elements define a wetland: saturation or periodic inundation, presence of hydric soils, and presence of wetland vegetation. The first of these elements has been the subject of intense battles. Pro-developers have sought to exclude lands that are wet only part of the year. Fortunately, these efforts to delist large acreages have generally been unsuccessful.

This is not to say that wetland losses have stopped. Wetlands isolated from navigable waterways are vulnerable, and illegal filling continues, as it is impossible to monitor every site that merits protection. And many of the replacement wetlands have proven to be failures. But in a short period wetlands have gone from being "sloughs of despond" to being the only type of natural land that can often be protected by agency fiat.

On a Cusp: Sedge Meadows and Marshes

Wetlands of several principal types lie scattered unevenly across the Chicago region: marshes, sedge meadows, bogs, fens, pannes, and swamps. They occupy yet another kind of contested ground, an ecotone between open water and dry land. Although this hybrid zone differs from the terrestrial and the aquatic, it is heavily reliant on both.[7] (Pannes, which are the wet flats that form where interdunal swales reach the water table of Lake Michigan, are treated in chap. 10, and swamps, here characterized as a forest type, are treated in chap. 5.)[8]

Concentrated on the beds of ancient lakes, along rivers, and in morainal depressions, marshes are the most extensive of the wetland types. Their key feature is vegetation emerging from standing water. Forming on soils that are saturated but not submerged, sedge meadows represent an intermediate zone on the hydric continuum between marsh (wetter) and wet prairie (drier). Few high-quality examples of sedge meadow remain. In Illinois, for example, only 670 acres were found in the entire state, almost all of which were in this region.[9]

Bogs and fens formed a much smaller part of the local landscape. The Chicago region is near the southern limit of where bogs occur, and fens tend to be small and rare everywhere. Their distinctiveness rests on the chemical composition of the waters that sustain them: bogs need acidic water that is poor in nutrients, while fens require flowing water laden with calcium and other minerals.

‑◄o►‑ ‑◄o►‑ ‑◄o►‑

The overriding issue confronting sedge meadow inhabitants is their struggle to endure the stress of living on soil that is sometimes under water and sometimes above. This is, of course, the challenge that all wetland species must face, but it is particularly acute for the sedge meadows that thrive on the cusp of a cusp. Looking at Racine and four other southeastern Wisconsin counties, David Costello found sedge meadows could tolerate moisture variations from pools two feet deep to water tables eleven inches beneath the ground.[10]

The dominant plant of this community is one that lingers in the memory of anybody who has walked into a sedge meadow. Although in late summer dense greenery may mask what lies underfoot, the first few steps reveal a treacherous field of knolls, spaced one to four feet apart. It is an exhausting and

24. Tussock sedge meadows, Illinois Beach State Park, Lake County
(Ill.), April 1997. Photo by J. Greenberg.

slow process to avoid twisting an ankle or losing balance as you make your way across the obstacle course: you are enduring the tussock sedge (*Carex stricta*).

Upon closer inspection, the tussocks show their stool or pedestal shape: "They appear as clumps of closely packed culms [stems] at the bases of which masses of underground branches and dead culms build up a rounded hummock of from six inches to three feet in diameter and often a foot or more in height."[11] In their early years, the clumps enlarge relatively quickly, trapping debris when the first stems appear. An individual tussock can survive more than fifty years, but its growth rate slacks off after the first few years. Where flooding is more frequent, as near deeper ponds, the pedestals reach their maximum size. This reduces the chances that the plants will ever be completely submerged.

The tussock sedge possesses other features, not obvious to the pedestrian, that also protect it from flood or drought. It produces two kinds of roots: one, which is straight and cylindrical, descends eight inches or more, while the other, branched and thin, forms a dense mat just below or at the surface. Thus it has access to moisture at various levels. Both roots and rhizomes contain a layer of unusually thick and hard cells that also protect the plant from desiccation. And along the midrib of its relatively narrow leaves, the sedge has other cells that collapse when deprived of sufficient moisture. The leaf thus folds down the middle in yet another measure to help the plant conserve water. Also in the leaves, as well as in the roots and stems, are air spaces called aerenchyma. This is a common feature of wetland plants, for it promotes the easy flow of oxygen when saturated soil threatens root anoxia (insufficient oxygen).

In many sedge meadows, the tussock sedge can comprise up to 90 percent of the vegetation. But on other sites its share is smaller, and bluejoint grass comes in a strong second. A. B. Stout conducted his study near Madison, Wisconsin, and counted 52,377 individual plants to determine species composition. Of these, 21,127 (40 percent) were tussock sedge, and 9,765 (19 percent) were bluejoint grass.[12]

Besides tussock sedge, numerous other sedges also occur in these damp environs. Wayne Schennum, who inventoried the sedge meadows of Lyons Prairie and Marsh Nature Preserve (Lake County, Ill.), and Costello each tallied about twenty species, of which six were found in both studies.[13] These six were tussock sedge, flat-stemmed spike rush (*Eleocharis compressa*), dark green rush (*Scirpus atrovirens*), common lake sedge (*Carex lacustris*), running marsh sedge (*Carex sartwellii*), and brown fox sedge (*Carex vulpinoidea*). Three other sedges should also probably belong to this group, as Costello encountered them in the wet end of the sedge meadows but Schennum called their habitat marsh—common yellow lake sedge (*Carex utriculata*), great spike rush (*Eleocharis palustris*), and river bulrush (*Scirpus fluviatilis*).

Sedge meadows, of course, also support plants that are not sedges. Costello's work yielded 135 species, and Schennum tabulated 141.[14] In southern Wisconsin, seventeen herbaceous plants reach their highest abundance in sedge meadows, and, of these, five were frequent: meadow anemone (*Anemone canadensis*), great angelica (*Angelica atropurpurea*), wild madder (*Galium obtusum*), marsh vetchling (*Lathyrus palustris*), and woundwort (*Stachys palustris*).[15]

A number of plants thrive in the shady flats between the tussock sedges. These include horsetail (*Equisetum arvense*), orange jewelweed (*Impatiens capensis*), and the bryophyte *Marchantia polymorpha*. Another group, those reproducing by seed, often manages to germinate on the tussocks themselves. Costello singles out the common beggar's ticks (*Bidens frondosa*): "As the season progresses the tap roots grow down the sides of the pedestals, apparently keeping pace with the lowering water table."[16]

Reed canary grass (*Phalaris arundinacea*) also flourishes in sedge meadows (as well as wet prairies and marshes). In fact, it can replace the other species that are present. Although apparently native to North America, the plants that are in this region arrived as introductions from Europe. Grazing, siltation, and other disturbances enable the species to establish itself, after which it can form dense monocultures. A striking example of how dominant this plant can be is provided by research done at a wetland near Woodstock, McHenry County. Wetland soils often contain dormant seeds of many plants: one marsh in Iowa proved to have a seed bank of forty species. But after forty years of bearing reed canary grass, the soil underlying the Woodstock site yielded nothing but reed canary grass.[17] (At least one bird has adapted to reed canary grass: sedge wrens often breed in the midst of solid stands.)

Sedge meadows provided a valuable commodity for those who settled near the large marshes. The grasses and sedges proved to be excellent hay. The early farmers put such a premium on these meadowlands that in some places none were available for later settlers. The *Whitewater Register* of April 30, 1896, described the process as it occurred at the Honey Creek marsh near East Troy, Walworth County:[18] "There has been no government land in the [marsh] for more than a generation. . . . Most of the town north of the big marsh consisted of oak openings, and in the time of the pioneers the marshes afforded the only natural hay lands of the section. This fact caused them to purchase small tracts of marsh so that they might be able to have hay for their farm stock until they could cultivate the tame grasses and also for a reserve in case of a failure of the upland crop in a dry season."

During midsummer haying, marshes would often be swarming with men and boys. In dry years, a farmer could accomplish the task by hand with a scythe or small mower and then remove the hay himself. (Later, draught animals would pull large mowers wherever the substrate would allow.) But when the crop was heavy with precipitation, he needed help hauling it to firm ground. Often he used a sled, drawn by two horses that could negotiate the soggy footing with the aid of special "sandal-like shoes." Other times the hay would be "carried out on a pair of poles by two individuals walking tandem fashion."[19] When the distance out was too great or the terrain too difficult, the hay would be piled into stacks and retrieved in winter when the frozen ground made travel easier.

Prices and uses of hay varied considerably with its composition and texture. Stout said that, in southern Wisconsin, hay could go anywhere from four dollars to ten dollars a ton, depending on "the varying ratio of grasses to sedges and the degree of coarseness of the latter. The grasses are regarded as having higher feeding value although little distinction is made between them and such grass-like sedges as *Carex sartwellii* and *Carex stricta*."[20]

25. Stacks of marsh hay at Skokie Swamp, Cook County 1909. Photo
by Chicago Prairie Club, 1909. (Courtesy Westchester Township
Historical Museum, Chesterton, Ind.)

Besides its use as feed, hay became popular as a packing and insulating
material to help keep ice frozen. This was particularly true in southern Wisconsin, where the firms that made Milwaukee famous brewed vast amounts of
product that needed to be cold throughout the year. In the Kankakee region,
the ranker grades of hay often wound up as bed stuffing.

As the terrestrial sedge meadow segues into the aquatic marsh, plant variety
declines. Schennum's work on the marshes at Lyons yielded only thirty-five
species.[21] And Curtis's surveys of Wisconsin marshes, which he acknowledges
as limited, found only eleven species to be prevalent: blue flag iris (*Iris virginica*)
(the only one not also modal), needle spike rush (*Eleocharis acicularis*), common
reed (*Phragmites australis*), pickerelweed (*Pontederia cordata*), common arrowhead (*Sagittaria latifolia*), hard-stemmed bulrush (*Scirpus acutus*), chairmaker's
rush (*Scirpus pungens*), great bulrush (*Scirpus validus*), common bur reed (*Spar-
ganium eurycarpum*), broad-leaved cattail (*Typha latifolia*), and wild rice (*Ziza-
nia aquatica*).[22]

The blue flag iris is as exquisite a plant as there is in the Chicago region. It spans the wetland continuum from wet prairies to these cattail marshes. When Earl Sherff studied the Skokie Marsh (Cook and Lake Counties [Ill.]) in the early years of the twentieth century, he found "many large but somewhat scattered patches of [blue flag] and *Acorus calamus* [sweet flag], occurring in the outer parts of the reed swamp and often extending into the swamp meadow formation. These constitute an association of a very definite stamp."[23]

Wild rice was once very abundant in the Chicago region. All of the large wetlands held substantial quantities of this beautiful plant, highly coveted as a food source. Gurdon Hubbard's description of Mud Lake, near Maywood, Cook County, in the 1830s is typical: "The mud was very deep, and along the edge of the lake grew tallgrass and wild rice, often reaching above a man's head, and so strong and dense it was almost impossible to walk through."[24]

Unfortunately wild rice does not do well in the face of disturbance. Swink and Wilhelm assigned the species a ten in their conservative rating index, denoting it as being among the most conservative of plants, and remark that it is currently much less widespread than the old records indicate.[25] Alfred Meyer searched for the plant in what was left of the Kankakee Marshes during the 1930s. His comments provide a fitting eulogy, as much for the wetlands as for the species: "Wild rice, once the harvest haven of wild fowl, was found by the author in only one locality—in a drainage ditch."[26]

The common reed, in contrast, thrives under disturbed conditions, particularly in areas that have been ditched or filled. It reproduces through stolons, horizontal stalks that send forth roots and thus create new plants. Through this mechanism, the species forms solid and virtually impenetrable stands often devoid of other plants.[27]

Inhabiting a broad range of hydrologic conditions, cattails are the signature plants of many local marshes. Because of the dominant role they play in many wetlands, cattails have been the subject of more scientific research than any other wetland plant; in 1993 it was estimated that more than four hundred articles have addressed the genus *Typha*.[28] Two species of cattails occur in this region: the broad-leaved cattail predominates in shallower areas, while the narrow-leaved cattail (*Typha angustifolia*) prefers those that are deeper. Despite this habitat difference, however, both species achieve their maximum growth when they are in about twenty inches of water. These two plants also interbreed. The hybrid that results, *Typha* × *glauca*, thrives in water up to three feet deep, a depth exceeding what either parent can tolerate.

Milton Weller describes the ecological position held by cattails: "The edge between a cattail bed and open water becomes a tension zone: The plant edge–water interface shifts back and forth from season to season with changes in water depth, wind action, and animal density. At the shoreward edge of the wetland, it is probably the availability and constancy of moisture, competition with better-adapted shallow-marsh plants, and perhaps nutrient dynamics that influence the success of cattail and hence their extent in the upland edge."[29]

The image that Weller presents is of an uneven edge, where cattails are interspersed with water at the deep end and sedges and other plants on the shallower end. Under this kind of scenario, cattails provide essential habitat for a host of wildlife, of which muskrats and birds are most conspicuous. Where the ratio of water to cattail is between 50 and 75 percent, the bird diversity reaches its maximum. But where closed stands of cattail monocultures form, only one or two avian species may be present.[30]

Unfortunately, these monocultures are becoming increasingly common, and many local marshes have lost the diversity they once had. Ecologists have attributed this trend to such disparate factors as fire suppression, road salting, extreme fluctuations in water levels, increased sedimentation due to runoff, and the ability of the cattail to recolonize lands once used for agriculture.[31] The narrow-leaved cattail may not even be an indigenous species. Two botanists from Ohio State University have presented strong evidence that it may have arrived with European settlers. They trace its spread westward via the canals of New York and Ohio and conclude that it reached the southern end of Lake Michigan during the 1880s.[32] Swink and Wilhelm, however, list the species as a native.[33]

As cattails spread and threaten the quality of many wetlands, researchers have begun investigating techniques for controlling the plant. Land managers have experimented with such diverse approaches as cutting, crushing, shading, spraying with herbicide, manipulating water levels, and burning. The key to success is suppressing the plant so that no part of it protrudes above water for one to three years. To accomplish this, the most effective strategy seems to be one incorporating either burning or mowing, water drawdown, and inundation.[34]

But long before people cared about the decrease of biodiversity in wetlands, they were interested in cattails. The genus *Typha* occurs throughout the world, and human beings have long utilized the plants for a variety of purposes. Ancient Egyptians planted and then harvested cattails as a way of removing salt from the soil. Native Americans wove the leaves into mats and rope and consumed roots and young shoots for food. And many have spoken of its medicinal properties. The pollen has been used as a diuretic and the leftover stamens as a laxative, while the rootstock can be both an aphrodisiac and, conveniently, a cure for gonorrhea.[35]

Throughout the twentieth century, a substantial amount of effort has gone into discovering commercial uses for cattails. During World War II, one Chicago company purchased a large quantity of cattails and processed several million pounds of fluff from the seed heads or spikes. Testing showed that the

26. Marsh with cattails, arrowleaf, and spatterdock, Worth, Cook County, circa 1900. Photo by Frank Woodruff. (Courtesy Chicago Academy of Sciences.)

material could be used to stuff life jackets as an adequate substitute for kapok, supplies of which had been disrupted by the war. In addition, "the seed hair was suitable for sound and heating insulating purposes, spinning and weaving, and had good felting characteristics."[36]

Growing in water deeper still, a small group of plants survives almost totally submerged. The white water lily (*Nymphaea tuberosa*), yellow pond lily (*Nuphar advena*), bullhead lily (*Nuphar variegatum*), coontail (*Ceratophyllum demersum*), and lotus (*Nelumbo lutea*) are rooted to the bottom but possess leaves or flowers that float on the surface. Most of the region's bladderworts (*Utricularia*) are true floaters, unattached to the bottom and buoyed by tiny bladders that also act as traps to catch small invertebrates.

The huge yellow flowers of the lotus have caught the eye of more people than perhaps any other local plant. Chicago's great architect Louis Sullivan became so taken by the sight of this species that he incorporated their shape into some of his buildings, including the Auditorium Theatre at 50 East Congress Parkway in downtown Chicago. Sullivan's inspiration dated to the 1870s when he saw the plant growing in great profusion on the Calumet River. Over the next few decades, unfortunately, the lotus disappeared from there, another casualty of the radical changes that overtook the Calumet area.

But it was in the Chain O' Lakes of northwestern Lake County (Ill.) where the lotus became a botanical landmark unlike any other in the area. Here, the green and gold plant spread over the water in great beds. This sight became an attraction that probably constituted the first successful attempt at ecotourism in the region. As early as 1873, the Wisconsin Central Railroad guidebook "gushed," as one correspondent described it, over the view that awaited visitors:

> Here in the northwestern part of Grass Lake, and covering an area of more than a hundred acres are the . . . beautiful water lily that so closely resembles the water lily of Egypt. . . . There are few places in the world where the soil permits the rooting of this wondrous flower that loaded the air of the ancient world with such fragrance that the people called it the breathing of a divinity, and bowed the knee in worship. But we have chanced to find one, and when the sunset lingers o'er the scene, and soft the winds come floating on the deep, there is a sweetness in the air and dreaminess that makes the soul forget the woes of earth.[37]

Later, promoters would allege that China, Egypt, and the Chain O' Lakes were the only places on earth that offered this spectacle. During the summer

27. Postcard of lotus beds at Grass Lake, Lake County (Ill.), circa 1900.
(Courtesy Art Doty Collection, Antioch, Ill.)

Table 3. Acreage of Lotus Beds on Grass Lake, Fox Lake, and Pistakee
Lake, 1939–59

	1939	1946	1954	1959
Grass Lake	700	736	341	0
Fox Lake	253	249	65	0
Pistakee Lake	104	129	0	0

of 1887, the tourist-laden steamboat *Mary Griswold* left McHenry regularly for visits to the lotus beds. Thousands more provided their own power, and rowed into the floating forest, where the saffron flowers hung above their heads on robust stalks. By the beginning of World War I, the *Gladene* was charging twenty-five cents a head for the tour, and along with postcards, local businesses sold small souvenir bottles of lotus perfume.[38]

In 1912 the expanse of lotus was said to be "continually extending its bounds."[39] But by the early 1920s the lotus beds were in trouble. While appreciative crowds flocked to the flowerbeds in summer, Chicago entrepreneurs took truckloads of the equally striking seedpods during the fall, which they gilded and sold as decorations.[40] Flooding in 1924 was even more devastating, however. Herman Pepoon reported that "the high water . . . appears to have at least temporarily destroyed the Fox Lake plants, as none were seen in 1925 or 1926."[41] Lotus numbers did not significantly increase until 1930, when once again thousands of blossoms and thousands of visitors met on the placid surface of Grass Lake.[42]

Keith Ryder of the U.S. Army Corps of Engineers has documented the decline of the lotus in the Chain by examining aerial photographs from 1939, 1946, 1954, and 1959 (see table 3).[43] Beginning in the late 1970s, lotus has made a modest resurgence that continues, so perhaps its quiet elegance will again ennoble the Chain. Meanwhile, the colonies at Willow Slough Fish and Game Area, Newton County, are probably the largest existing in the region today.

A discussion of wetlands must include the purple loosestrife, one of the most aggressive exotic plants in the region.[44] A native of Europe, the species has been moving steadily westward from the east coast since the early 1800s, when it was introduced deliberately as a medicinal plant (for treating diarrhea, sores, ulcers, and other ailments) and accidentally via ballast water.

Early on, the construction of canals boosted its expansion. Then, purple loosestrife's striking appearance led to its widespread planting for ornamental purposes, although its commercial sale is now illegal in Illinois and other states.[45] More important, the plant can put forth an extraordinary number of seeds: "A single stalk can produce 300,000 seeds, and densities as high as

80,000 stalks/acre have been recorded, with the potential of producing as many as 24 billion seeds an acre."[46] These seeds are very easily transported by humans, other animals, and floods, and can remain fertile even after being in water for almost two years. As a consequence of these various factors, by 1980, purple loosestrife had become a serious problem in the Chicago region.

An aerial photograph of the once diverse Weingart Road Sedge Meadow Nature Preserve, in northeastern McHenry County, reveals almost fifty acres of solid purple. This site and others have been overwhelmed with dense stands of purple loosestrife in a short period. Because this alien outcompetes other plants and offers little shelter or food to animals, land managers have worked diligently to protect wetlands from this scourge. Hand picking and spraying with appropriate herbicides can be effective if the infestation is caught early enough. But once that early threshold is exceeded, combating loosestrife is very difficult.

Concern that the rampant expansion of loosestrife was endangering the quality of many sites led local conservationists to obtain federal help in devising new methods of control. (The work of the late Congressman Sidney Yates was instrumental in securing this assistance.) Researchers focused on Europe, and sought to discover natural enemies that could control loosestrife here without posing any threat to native species. They identified three insects that seemed to meet these requirements and thus were promising as candidates for export to the United States. The beetles *Galerucella calmariensis* and *Galerucella pusilla* feed on the leaves and stems and can strip a plant of foliage. *Hylobius transversovittatus* is a weevil that also eats loosestrife leaves but, in addition, has a larva that causes most of the damage by feeding on roots.

In 1994, about a thousand *G. calmeriensis* were released at six wetland areas in Cook, Lake, Kane, and McHenry counties. The following year, all but one of the sites plus three new ones received *G. pusilla* and *Hylobius*, as well as additional *G. calmeriensis*. By the end of 1996, thousands of these insects had been liberated into selected sites throughout the region. At this early stage in the project, the most encouraging news is that the three species are hardy enough to survive Midwestern winters, for biologists have found evidence of successful overwintering. Any significant reductions in purple loosestrife, however, are a long way off for research suggests it takes five to six years for the insects just to become established. But according to one group of experts, if all goes well, the introductions may reduce "purple loosestrife abundance to 10% of its current level over approximately 90% of its range."[47]

In late summer, disturbed marshes throughout the area are stained by the colorful spikes of purple loosestrife. Often a great egret forages against the deep magenta backdrop. This is a tableau, both beautiful to the eye and discouraging to the heart and mind, that might well serve as a metaphor for one aspect of the modern landscape. A fine native species is enjoying a strong recovery, while a foreign pathogen unleashed by humans is contaminating what little habitat survives. Perhaps if we are fortunate, the loosestrife will decline until it becomes a minor part of local wetlands. Meanwhile, the mixed vision remains.

Wiggly Fields: Bogs and Fens

The bogs of this region developed in two ways. On the Chicago Lake Plain, bogs in the Indiana Dunes and the Grand Mere area of Berrien County formed in what were once lagoons of the ancient lake. Most local bogs, however, were born in declivities filled by the meltwater of abandoned ice. Over thousands of years, these depressions lose the character of lakes as they fill up with vegetation in a two-pronged process. Sedges, sphagnum moss, and other plants creep outward from the shore to form floating mats, while at the same time they begin to fill the basin with their decaying remains. Eventually, the peat builds to the point where there is no longer any open water and the mat is grounded.

Sphagnum moss is a key element in bog formation because it creates and maintains the acidity characteristic of the community. This acidity persists most often where the basin retains its hydrological isolation, for calcareous or neutral inflows lower acidity through dilution, and outflows could wash away the peat and inhibit the expansion of the mat. Where acidic conditions do not develop, the Illinois Natural Areas Inventory calls the floating vegetation a calcareous floating mat, which is a type of fen.[48]

It happens, however, that groundwater does enter most bog systems, creating a deeper layer of calcareous water. The result is a "minerotrophic or alkaline bog" that supports both acidophilic plants (whose short roots remain in the acidic mat) and fen species (whose longer roots can reach the more calcareous depth.). Heavy precipitation favors bog plants, for it drenches them with rain (relatively acidic), while drought conditions create the opposite effect when capillary action draws the neutral water to the surface.[49]

The greatest concentration of bogs in the Chicago area is in the northwestern counties. (See chap. 10 for a discussion of the Chicago Lake Plain bogs.) The sites vary considerably from one to the other, and fortunately conservationists have managed to protect high-quality examples of this diversity. Volo Bog Nature Preserve, Lake County (Ill.), is undoubtedly the most celebrated and best studied, for it is one of the few local bogs that manifests all the various stages of bog succession. (Beulah Bog in Walworth County and Silver Lake Bog in Kenosha County are the other two.) And visitors can easily

28. Aerial view of Volo Bog by Illinois Department of Natural Resources.

traverse these seral rings on a boardwalk, a stroll backwards through time
and changing panoramas that is as evocative as any in the region. Volo Bog,
then, provides an excellent model for discussing the structure of local bog
communities.[50]

Five primary plant communities form concentric circles around the
small opening of water, often called the eye of the bog, which remains in the
center. The outermost ring, encircling the bog like a moat, is a cattail marsh.
Reed canary grass (*Phalaris arundinacea*), broad-leaved cattail, marsh shield
fern (*Dryopteris thelypteris*), and marsh bluegrass (*Poa palustris*) are common
species.

The next ring of vegetation is the tall-shrub bog, a dense amalgam of red-
osier dogwood (*Cornus stolonifera*), winterberry (*Ilex verticillata*), and glossy
buckthorn (*Rhamnus frangula* [a nonnative]). Growing in the perpetual shadows of the understory are marsh cinquefoil (*Potentilla palustris*), sensitive fern
(*Onoclea sensibilis*), cinnamon fern (*Osmunda cinnamomea*), and marsh marigold
(*Caltha palustris*).

Poison sumac (*Rhus vernix*) is a conspicuous member of this community as
well, particularly in fall when its white waxy berries droop in loose clusters and
its foliage turns bright red. It is extremely abundant at Volo, and so dominates
parts of the tall-shrub community that some ecologists believe it constitutes
a separate vegetation type. Contact with the plant can produce multicolored
blistering that is extremely painful. This perhaps explains why Herman Pepoon,

an otherwise passionate defender of native flora, "cut off some 5000 shoots from three acres of swamp land, using a mattock, in the hope that they might be killed out."[51]

The tall-shrub bog then gives way to the tamaracks, a tree that contributes so much character to local bogs. While the tamarack has a wide distribution and can survive in many environments, here, at the southern edge of its range, the species tends to inhabit bogs. It possesses the unusual combination of being both coniferous and deciduous. In summer, as Donald Culross Peattie describes it, the tamarack is "the most tenderly beautiful of all native trees, with its pale green needles like a rime of life and light." But in winter, the lingering cones on bare branches convey the false impression of a blight or killing fire.[52]

And in fact tamaracks have decreased in this region. Various bogs have been logged, including the northern portion of Volo some time before 1920. Lower water tables and infestations of bark beetles (*Dendroctonus simplex*), particularly one in 1942, have combined to kill many tamaracks. The water issue remains a problem, although it can be double-edged: the removal of a beaver dam to increase water levels at one site wound up drowning adult trees, although the action seemed to promote the establishment of seedlings. Finally, the tall shrubs, particularly the invasive buckthorn, have spread so aggressively and are so dense they prevent the survival of young tamaracks. Charles Sheviak and Alan Haney, after a careful study of the bog, believe that some of these changes would occur naturally, but anthropogenic forces have accelerated the loss of tamaracks.[53]

Three of the same shrubs that make up the tall-shrub bog grow commonly under the tamaracks—winterberry, poison sumac, and glossy buckthorn. Herbaceous plants include starflower (*Trientalis borealis*), three-seeded bog sedge (*Carex trisperma* [state endangered]), common fox sedge (*Carex stipata*), and smooth white violet (*Viola pallens*). Once or twice I have seen Indian pipe (*Monotropa uniflora*), a ghost-white saprophyte that lends a touch of otherworldliness to this lovely forest.

Beyond the tamaracks the low shrubs form their own distinctive layer, although it "is narrow, irregular, and in places poorly defined or absent."[54] The woody species that define this community include the now familiar poison sumac, along with dwarf birch (*Betula pumila*) and leatherleaf (*Chamaedaphne calyculata*). Not as common, three willows are also part of this community: pussy (*Salix discolor*), beaked (*S. bebbiana*), and bog (*S. pedicellaris*). The herbaceous plants of this zone also occur on the floating mat, but buckbean (*Menyanthes trifoliata*) and marsh cinquefoil are most abundant here.

At this point, the boardwalk broadens into a viewing platform overlooking the floating mat and the shallow pond (about nine inches deep). In 1973,

Haney and Sheviak estimated the pond to be about 132 feet long and 82.5 feet wide, and the encircling mat to range from a few to almost two hundred feet wide. This signifies an expansion of the mat, and a concomitant decrease in the open water of several feet since Northwestern University's W. G. Waterman first studied the bog in the early 1920s. And Waterman was told by elderly neighbors that, fifty years earlier, there was no mat at all, and the pond covered the entire clearing.[55]

The mat is primarily moss (*Sphagnum recurvum*) woven together with red-rooted spike rush (*Eleocharis erythropoda*). Other important components of the mat include porcupine sedge (*Carex hystericina*), marsh shield fern, cinnamon fern, buckbean, and broad-leaved cattail. Three exquisite orchids occur here and between the low shrubs, of which the rose pogonia (*Pogonia ophioglossoides*) is found locally in few other places. (It is known from only four other sites in Illinois.)

This is also the realm of two carnivorous plants: round-leaved sundew (*Drosera rotundifolia*) and pitcher plant (*Sarracenia purpurea*).[56] These species live in environments where the chemical nature of the substrate reduces the nitrogen and other nutrients available to plants. (Besides bogs, the sundew is found locally in sand areas of high acidity and the pitcher plant in a few fens.) Thus, to augment their "diet," the sundew and pitcher plant consume small insects.

Sundews are so tiny that they can only be located after searching on hands and knees. Their broad leaves are covered with gooey hairs that attract and hold prey. It takes a day for the entire leaf to fold over the unfortunate insect, whose vital juices will be absorbed over the course of about five days. The leaf then opens, ready for new customers.

Pitcher plants, with their vase-like leaves and large purple flowers on tall stems, are the strangest looking of all local plants. Because of their novel appearance, collectors have depleted many local populations, including those at Volo Bog. For the benefit of observant visitors, however, preserve staff have transplanted one within view of the boardwalk. (My lips are sealed.)

Scientists first became aware of the pitcher plant when a drawing of it reached Europe sometime before 1600, but it would take literally centuries of research before the mysteries of the plant were unlocked. The inside of the pitcher consists of four zones: the first marked with reddish venation which lures insects, the second with ridges that guide victims into the interior, the third slick with no footholds, and the fourth with hairs that make it impossible for most insects to escape. At the base of the leaf is a small pool of fluid rich in enzymes and bacteria that digest prey.

While many insects fall victim to the pitcher plant, others reside within the leaves to form a unique ecosystem known as a phytotelm (from the Greek

29. Narrow-leaved sundew with prey, Pinhook Bog,
Indiana Dunes National Lakeshore, Porter County.
Photo by and courtesy of Greg Neice.

words for "plant" and "pool"). Researchers have found at least fourteen species of insects associated with these tiny reservoirs. Members of the moth genus *Exyra* lay their eggs inside the leaf and secure them to the surface with webbing. Newly hatched larvae produce more floss that enables them to feed on the leaf tissue without falling into the abyss. In some instances, they may even enclose part of the pitcher's mouth in webbing. Certain flies (*Blaesoxipha*) deposit their larvae into the fluid so that they may feed on the floating corpses of distant relatives. When it matures, the fly has large footpads, long claws, and the strength to scale the treacherous walls. And finally, in early spring, the mosquito *Wyeomyia smithii* lays its eggs in newly opened leaves. As the pitcher fills with liquid, the eggs hatch, and the larvae mature on a diet of bacteria. Encased in ice, the insects overwinter and emerge as adults in the spring.

The full story of Volo Bog must also contain the struggles to preserve it.[57] In 1958, under the leadership of botanist Margery Carlson and businessman Cyrus Mark, the Illinois chapter of the Nature Conservancy spearheaded the drive to purchase forty-seven acres of Volo Bog and sixty-seven acres of Wauconda Bog. This was the first time in the chapter's history that it appealed to the public for help in raising funds, which in this instance amounted to $40,000. Upon succeeding in its campaign, the conservancy conveyed Volo

Bog to the University of Illinois, which then assumed responsibility for its protection.

Twelve years after this great success, a private developer unveiled plans to construct a $94 million project incorporating a shopping center and housing for ten thousand people spread across 655 acres. And, as William Beecher has written, "right in the middle, bordered by a proposed golf course, was Volo Bog." Conservationists mobilized and launched their counterattack. At one stage in the fight, a hostile local official referred to them as "boggists." Fortunately, Attorney General William Scott and Governor Richard Ogilvie were sympathetic to the boggists, and with their support, the Illinois Department of Conservation purchased enough land to ensure protection of Volo Bog and nearby Pistakee Bog. Both sites have since been dedicated as state nature preserves.

But Volo and its neighboring bogs are still not safe. The irony is that it is an agency of the state that now wants to destroy them. The Illinois Department of Transportation holds an easement that would allow it to construct a major highway through the bog complex. If the Department of Transportation were to succeed, it would not only prove catastrophic to the bogs but would be a serious blow to the state's conservation programs as well. Surely the agency could formulate a new alignment and bypass the bogs, assuming, of course, that the construction of the road is not stopped altogether.

◄◦► ◄◦► ◄◦►

In the 1920s, W. G. Waterman published the first systematic accounts of the bogs of Lake and McHenry counties. His three articles described, contrasted, and analyzed several of these sites. His comments on Volo Bog and Pistakee Bog illustrate the great differences that can exist in bogs situated less than a half mile of each other: "These formations are alike in most of their characteristics, even to the presence of a floating mat, but they differ absolutely in floristic content and in acidity of substratum. Of the commonly accepted bog plants, with the exception of the doubtful *Larix*, not one is found in the [Pistakee] formation, either on the mat or in the forest, while they are prominent in all portions of the [Volo] bog."[58]

Bogs differ from one another not only in their pH levels but also as to where they are successionally. Cedar Lake Bog Nature Preserve, Lake County (Ill.), thirty acres in size, encompasses a bog in the earliest stages of development. It consists of a narrow strip of floating mat sandwiched between a marsh and the open water of 285-acre Cedar Lake. The dominant plants forming the mat are *Sphagnum*, dwarf birch, sedges, rusty cotton grass (*Eriophorum virginicum*), and large cranberry (*Vaccinium macrocarpon*), while other distinctive bog species such as pitcher plant, buckbean, and sundew are also present. At one end of the mat is a small grove of tamaracks, dating from the beginning of this century.

Cedar Lake Bog is also noteworthy because people exploited it commercially, albeit with trepidation: "The bog is of local importance economically because of its annual crop of cranberries. These plants grow luxuriously and produce many berries, but on account of the unstable character of the mat, many people are afraid of venturing on it. Within the last five years at least one horse and one cow have wandered out on the surface of the bog and have gone down in a soft spot and been drowned."[59]

The bog at Gavin Bog and Prairie Nature Preserve, near Lake Villa, Lake County (Ill.), is at the other seral extreme. Peat-filled since before 1934, the bog lacks any open water or floating mat. The heart of the bog is a tamarack forest surrounded by a tall-shrub layer and a small area of short shrubs. All three of these community types are marked by "hummocks" covered with various mosses: *Sphagnum centrale, Aulacomnium palustre,* and *Calliergon* sp.

The prairie and bog complex was carefully described by John Taft and Mary Kay Solecki in their 1990 article. Comparing their results with plant lists from Volo Bog, they found that only 41 percent of the species occurred in both sites. Present at Gavin but not Volo, box huckleberry (*Gaylussacia baccata*), Canada blueberry (*Vaccinium myrtilloides*), and northern gooseberry (*Ribes hirtellum*) grow under the tamaracks; chokeberry (*Aronia melanocarpa*) is a locally common component of the tall-shrub zone; and box huckleberry, rusty cotton grass, and small cranberry (*Vaccinium oxycoccos*) inhabit the short-shrub zone. The discovery of the small cranberry, by the way, is the first confirmed record for the state.

◄O► ◄O► ◄O►

Fens most often occur in morainal areas where water can percolate through calcareous soils, particularly sand and gravel, before coming to the surface.[60] At Wagner Fen Nature Preserve, Lake Barrington, Lake County (Ill.), for example, the fens are concentrated where water seeps from the bases of ridges that surround two sides of a peat-filled lake bed. Beyond that limited area, surface runoff and overflow from a small stream dilute the calcareous waters, and the fens give way to the sedge meadow and marsh that constitute the bulk of the site. Another scenario governs Bluff Spring Fen Nature Preserve in Elgin, Cook County. Here, the fens are nurtured by waters emanating from a series of surface springs.

Tending to be small, the graminoid or nonforested fens share many species in common with the sedge meadow (similarity index of 54 percent) and wet prairie (similarity index of 59 percent). A study of Bluff Spring Fen found

30. Bluff Spring Fen, Elgin, Cook County, with oak-covered kame in
background, April 1997. (Photo by and courtesy of Bob Thall.)

the following plants to be dominant: tussock sedge, Ohio goldenrod (*Solidago ohioensis*), starry false Solomon's seal (*Smilacina stellata*), common valerian (*Valeriana ciliata*), and shrubby cinquefoil (*Potentilla fruticosa*). The four dominant species at Wagner Fen are fen star sedge (*Carex sterilis*), big bluestem, little bluestem, and Indian grass.

The globally endangered butterfly Mitchell's satyr (*Euptychia mitchellii*) only occurs in fens, including a few in Berrien and La Porte counties (see chap. 11). Although found in a wider range of habitats elsewhere, queen of the prairie (*Filipendula rubra*) and bog valerian (*Valeriana uliginosa*) are two plants locally restricted to a small handful of fens. Another group of species is also closely associated with fens: marsh marigold (*C. palustris*), skunk cabbage (*Symplocarpus foetidus*), small fringed gentian (*Gentiana procera*), grass of Parnassus (*Parnassia glauca*), swamp thistle (*Cirsium muticum*), marsh wild timothy (*Muhlenbergia glomerata*), and bog lobelia (*Lobelia kalmii*). And where minerals precipitate out of the water to form marl flats, wicket spike rush (*Eleocharis rostellata*), low calamint (*Satureja arkansana*), slender bog arrow grass (*Triglochin palustris*), and twig rush (*Cladium mariscoides*) are often among the few species present.

One of the region's most unusual fens, and unlike any other in Illinois, perches on the bluffs above the Fox River at Trout Park Nature Preserve in Elgin, Kane County.[61] Sheltering ravines and many cold seeps and springs create a microclimate that is hospitable to an array of boreal plants and aquatic invertebrates, many surviving as glacial relicts south of their usual haunts. (See chap. 8 for a discussion of Trout Park's aquatic ecosystem.) The old-timers called the tangle of wet vegetation a cedar swamp, but in the parlance of the Illinois Natural Areas Inventory it is a forested fen.

The defining feature of Trout Park is the isolated population of white cedars, here approaching the southern limit of their range. Although cedars can live more than four hundred years, their shallow roots make them vulnerable to windthrow, and many of Trout Park's oldest specimens succumbed to a tornado in 1920. Young trees now sprout from many of the fallen trunks.[62]

Other common members of the woody flora are black ash, basswood, butternut (*Juglans cinerea*), and wild black currant (*Ribes americanum*). Spotted touch-me-not (*Impatiens capensis*) is a common woodland associate, but many of the herbaceous plants are typical fen species: skunk cabbage, angelica, tussock sedge, slender sedge (*Carex leptalea*), marsh marigold, and fragile fern (*Cystopteris fragilis*).

For more than a hundred years, local botanists have been attracted by the many rarities found here, particularly those plants that share their northern affinity with the white cedar: northern bog orchid (*Habenaria hyperborea*), low water parsnip (*Berula erecta*), spikenard (*Aralia racemosa*), and alternate-leaved dogwood (*Cornus alternifolia*). Although down to one individual, hemlock parsley (*Conioselinum chinense*) is still present (or at least it was until recently), the last of its kind in Illinois.[63] A majority of the others seem to have disappeared, having gone unrecorded for decades: purple avens (*Geum rivale*), alder buckthorn (*Rhamnus alnifolia*), hairy white violet (*Viola incognita*), white camas (*Zigadenus glaucus*), and round-leaved orchid (*Habenaria orbiculata*). The only confirmed state and regional record of the white adder's mouth orchid (*Malaxis brachypoda*) was collected here over a century ago, the label identifying the place simply as "Elgin Swamp. Ill."[64]

The history of Trout Park is decidedly bittersweet. One of the first owners stocked the streams with trout, providing the site with its current name and no doubt causing havoc with the aquatic fauna that scientists would later celebrate. By the end of the last century, a large amusement park operated below the bluffs, offering roller coaster rides and riverfront tours from a miniature train. Its popularity grew, and on Sunday mornings large coteries of Chicagoans left the Wells Street terminal bound for the park aboard special round-trip excursion trains.[65]

The natural attractions of Trout Park also figured in the promotions. A brochure from 1905 touted the park as "one of the garden spots of

31. A spring running through the white cedar fen at Trout Park, Elgin,
Kane County, April 1997. (Photo by and courtesy of Bob Thall.)

Illinois, with boating, baseball, and music." Venders sold water freshly bottled
from Trout Park's own springs. A 1969 article from the *Elgin Free Press* has this
to say about the water: "That water became very popular with the Chicago
people for a time, but the fact that it was very hard and would need much care
in making it safe to drink put an end to plans to sell it on a big scale in large
cities."[66] (One can only wonder what the Chicago people did do with it.)

Fearing that Trout Park might soon be "threatened with extermination,"
local conservationists began a "Save Trout Park" campaign. In 1922, the City
of Elgin responded to their entreaties by acquiring eighteen acres of the property as a public park. Two years later, Elgin bought thirty-five more acres,
thereby owning most of the cedar fen. At the time of these purchases, city representatives didn't know whether "the park will be left in its natural condition
or whether attempts will be made to remove some of the underbrush and trees."
Perhaps feeling insecure about their purchase of the property, they also pointed
out that "if it ever becomes necessary, [the water] can be used for city purposes."
Eventually, the city named the Elgin Audubon Society and the Elgin chapter
of the Wild Flower Preservation Society of America as park custodians.[67]

The city selected Trout Park as the location for its new Elgin Botanical

Gardens established in 1933. As part of this effort, concerned citizens placed numerous plants in the park, ostensibly to replace species that had become extirpated. Existing records indicate that much of the material came from a firm in Marshall, North Carolina. What impact, if any, these plants have had on extant species is unknown, but it makes sound ecological management of the site difficult. For example, at least thirty-six yellow lady's slippers and twenty-four showy orchises were obtained from North Carolina and introduced into Trout Park. A few individuals of both species still grow here, but no one is sure of their origin or whether the species were ever native to the park.

But whatever harm questionable introductions caused Trout Park was completely overshadowed by the Illinois Tollway Authority in the late 1950s, which bisected the site by running Route 90 through its heart so that Illinois now has two small forested fens rather than a single substantial one.[68] Almost thirteen acres of the richest ravine were destroyed and a number of species once known here have not been found since. This damage can never be repaired, but Trout Park still has cold clear brooks that bathe the roots of white cedar—it is still a southern outpost for boreal species otherwise long gone from this region.

The Last Wilderness: Lake Michigan

There is a fascination in the infinite variety of changes that come upon the ocean, but here are changes as great and much more sudden, for every surface phenomenon that the ocean presents, Lake Michigan presents as well. It has its tides, waterspouts, fogs, moments of peace and moments of passion. —John Rathom (1910 [in Harpel, ser. A, vol. 2])

As everywhere, civilized man disturbs the balance of nature, and becomes the great enemy to all forms of life that do not conform to his artificial methods for their protection. Not only by the hundreds of artifices for the capture of the white-fish, but in the foul drainage from the cities, smelting works, and manufactories, and in the quantities of sawdust from the mills, they are driven from their favorite haunts and spawning grounds, and their food destroyed by waters tainted with fatal chemical combinations. —John W. Milner (1874)

Unpredictable, rebellious, sublime, and essential to the people who live here, Lake Michigan's vast expanse is the closest thing to a Chicago wilderness that still survives. A litany of its dimensions demonstrates how awesome the lake is: 307 miles long, 118 miles at its widest, and a total area of 22,400 square miles. It has a mean depth of 276 feet and holds 1,180 cubic miles of water. Of the five Great Lakes, Michigan ranks third in surface area and second in volume. It is the sixth largest lake in the world and the largest to lie entirely within U.S. borders.[1]

The southern half of Lake Michigan is shallower than the northern, with a maximum depth of 558 feet versus 923 feet. It is also much more uniform, lacking the islands and bays that mark the upper stretches of the lake. The bottom tends to be smooth and gently sloping, although rock formations of differing size do provide some relief. A survey of the lake from Great Lakes Naval Base on the north to Indiana Harbor on the south located over a hundred of these rocky reefs and shoals. Most lie at depths between fifty and one hundred

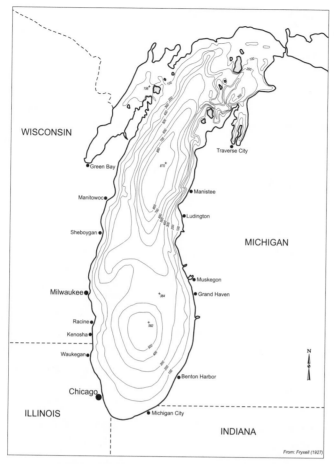

WISCONSIN

Green Bay

Manitowoc

Sheboygan

Milwaukee

Racine

Kenosha

Waukegan

Chicago

ILLINOIS

Traverse City

Manistee

Ludington

MICHIGAN

Muskegon

Grand Haven

Benton Harbor

Michigan City

INDIANA

N

From: Fryxell (1927)

32. Lake Michigan. (From Fryxell 1927. Courtesy University of Chicago Press.)

feet. The largest is Julian's Reef, situated fourteen miles east of Lake Forest and rising to within ninety-nine feet of the surface. Historically, fishermen knew it as a lake trout spawning ground.[2]

Lake Michigan is characterized as oligotrophic, or poor in biological production. (A eutrophic lake is one rich in nutrients.) This is typical of deep and cold lakes, where most of the water lies far beyond the reach of light, and photosynthesis can only occur within a narrow stratum known as the euphotic zone. As Randy Eshenroder and his colleagues at the Great Lakes Fishery Commission have written, "Lake Michigan has been a major producer of fish more because of its great size than its fertility."[3]

Lake Michigan has been affected by Euro-American settlement in three principal ways: pollution, fishing, and the introduction of nonnative species. The first two of these had already been occurring long before the commencement of research. Most of the interest was on fish, and what was known about their status was learned through commercial fishing. The nonnative species came later, and proved to be even more destructive than the fishing. Indeed, Ellen Marsden, formerly of the Illinois Natural History Survey, says that "the history of the Great Lakes ecosystem is a history of introductions."[4]

This parade of harms, some predating recorded information, makes it very difficult, then, to set a presettlement stage in the same way that early descriptions can convey the character of terrestrial environments. I therefore intend to tell the story of Lake Michigan by focusing on four subjects: the impacts of pollution, changes in the plankton and benthos, factors that have had an impact on native fish (fishing and alien species), and the native fish that have felt those impacts.

The Sullying of Lake Michigan: Pollution

John Milner's 1874 report on the fisheries of Lake Michigan was probably the first publication to draw attention to the effects pollution was having on Lake Michigan's fish. He warned that careless fishermen who dumped fish wastes on the catching ground were responsible for driving whitefish away. Of greater consequence, probably, was the timber industry: prolific discharges of sawdust into the lake from milling operations would wash offshore, burying the spawning and feeding areas.[5]

The clear-cutting of the Great Lakes forests brought numerous changes to the watershed, including the elimination of shade, higher water temperatures, greater influx of siltation, and accelerated erosion. The conversion of lake plain rivers into open sewers both deprived Lake Michigan of the beneficial inputs these waterways contributed when they were healthy and, more directly, blighted substantial portions of the lake. Milner observed that there had been no net fishing off Chicago for a long time but "now [that] the filthy current of the [Chicago] river no longer flows into the lake, there may be some success with nets." By 1875, three pound nets stood at the mouth of the Chicago River, each yielding profitable returns.[6]

Fortunately, it was possible to curtail many of the worst abuses before impacts could spread beyond bays, harbors, and inshore areas. And the curative powers of the lake have mended many of these blemishes. An early attempt to divert Chicago's effluents away from Lake Michigan was the Chicago Sanitary and Ship Canal, which will be discussed in greater detail later. By 1966, industrial dischargers had contaminated the Indiana Harbor ship canal so severely that some thought its flow alone could permanently damage the lake.[7] In the years following, however, control programs have led to significant improvements.

Despite the progress, problems certainly remain. The lake has been sullied by a mishmash of various chemicals, a thousand of which are deemed toxic. Some of these poisons remain locked in lake sediments, while others, like mercury originating from power plants, descend from the sky. To make matters worse, some contaminants (particularly certain organic compounds such as DDT and PCBs) increase in concentration as they ascend the food chain, ultimately manifesting their effects at the higher tiers. This phenomenon is known as bioaccumulation. Thus, fish-eating double-crested cormorants (*Phalacrocorax auritus*) nesting on islands in northern Lake Michigan produce abnormally high numbers of offspring so deformed they cannot survive. Concerns about human health have led various agencies to warn against consuming too much lake-caught fish, an unwelcome message for the angler who just hooked a three-foot-long lake trout (*Salvelinus namaycush*).[8]

Ironically, perhaps, the misfortunes of downstream Lakes Ontario and Erie (including its widely publicized if not exaggerated death in the 1960s) have benefited Lake Michigan. Their examples led to ongoing efforts to spare Lake Michigan the same fate. Although these efforts must be continued and indeed intensified, they have been largely successful, a conclusion reflected in the words of a November 1995 report of the Great Lakes Fishery Commission: "Lake Michigan proper has not been severely impacted physiochemically by human settlement around the basin."[9]

Floaters, Bottom Dwellers, and a Filter Feeder Run Amok: The Plankton and Benthos

The Great Lakes Fishery Commission report mentioned above provides a succinct description of the two major biological communities of Lake Michigan:

> Lake Michigan's food web can be viewed as consisting of two separate but overlapping parts: the pelagic food web associated with offshore open water, and the benthic food web associated with the bottom. Both parts of the food web are based on planktonic algae (including bacteria that photosynthesize) produced in surface waters where light penetration is adequate for photosynthesis. . . . The pelagic food web is based on consumption of algae by small invertebrates. . . . The benthic food web is based on the direct conversion of detritus (decomposing algae and other organisms) that rains down to the bottom from the photic zone.[10]

Thus tiny free-floating algae are the agents primarily responsible for converting the lake's chemical nutrients into living tissue. (These algae are also known as phytoplankton, as distinguished from zooplankton, which are planktonic animals.) Three major groups of algae totaling hundreds of species provide this base for Lake Michigan's biota: diatoms (Chrysophyta, also known as yellow-green algae), green algae (Chlorophyta), and blue-green algae (Cyanophyta). Diatoms and green algae are the most abundant and, thus, contribute more oxygen to the lake than any other source. For their part, blue-green algae act as aquatic legumes, capable of making nitrogen from the atmosphere available to other members of the food web.[11]

Although supporting relatively modest concentrations of algae, Lake Michigan boasts a high diversity of species. Competition between these species sorts itself out into a loose temporal pattern. Diatoms extract silica from the water to produce their protective and intricately marked cell walls. Their need for silica, as well as their ability to reproduce at lower temperatures and light levels, means that their populations peak in early spring and late fall when the substance is most plentiful due to seasonal turnover. As spring turns into summer, green algae become the dominant group as the silica becomes depleted, water temperature rises, and the days become longer. But green algae require nitrogen and phosphorus, and when those nutrients begin to dwindle the blue-green algae come to the fore. Not only do certain blue-green algae have the unique capacity to absorb nitrogen from the air, but they can also sequester phosphorus for later use. And the cycle repeats itself.

Pelagic zooplankton include a highly varied microscopic group of animals. Based on data collected from 1983 to 1992, eleven species of rotifers (phylum Rotaforia) and thirteen species of crustaceans (four cladocerans and

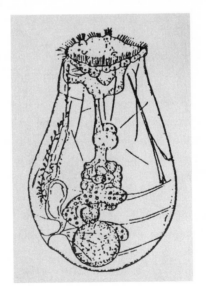

33. *Asplanchna,* genus of rotifer found in
Lake Michigan. (From Thorp and Covich 2001.
Courtesy Academic Press, Walter Koste,
and Museum Am Schölerberg.)

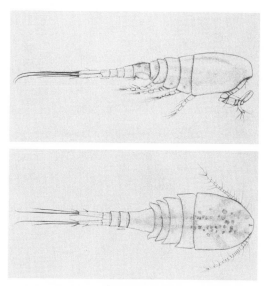

34. *Diacyclops thomasi,* one of the most common and widely distrib-
uted copepods in North America. (Length up to 1.4 millimeters.)
(From Balcer et al. 1983. Courtesy University of
Wisconsin Press, Madison.)

nine copepods) constitute more than 95 percent of the total zooplankton in
Lake Michigan. Many rotifers move through the water by means of tiny cilia
arranged in a circle on the animal's front end; the constant beating of the cilia
makes it appear as if they are revolving rotor-like. *Asplanchna, Conochilus, Poly-
arthra, Notholca,* and *Keratella* are genera commonly found in Lake Michigan.
A majority feed on algae and bacteria, but *Asplanchna* prey on smaller rotifers.
Many copepods also eat algae, but some have jaws that enable them to feed on
other zooplankton. Cladocerans ingest algae through perpetually moving legs
that create a current leading to the mouth. One particularly interesting predatory cladoceran is *Leptodora kindti,* said to be "almost perfectly transparent and
consequently invisible—a true microscopic ghost."[12]

The few benthic organisms that live in water below one hundred feet depend on the downward drift of surface plankton.[13] Two distinctive inhabitants
of this zone are both crustaceans: the amphipod *Diporeia affinis,* which is often
the most abundant species, and the opossum shrimp *Mysis relicta.* They both
depend on well-oxygenated sediments, and both are important food items for
several fish. The shrimp is also noteworthy because it is one species that routinely crosses the boundary between benthic and pelagic. As it seeks water
between 45° and 55°F, the animal resides on or hovers over the bottom (as deep
as nine hundred feet in Lake Superior) at midday and ascends to the surface at
dusk, where for short periods it can survive temperatures of 70°F.[14]

The benthic community produces its own sustenance where the lake

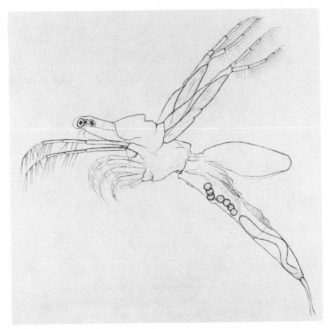

35. *Leptodora kindti*, a transparent cladoceran commonly occurring in lakes and
ponds, but usually in relatively small numbers. (Length up to eighteen millimeters.)
(From Balcer et al. 1983. Courtesy University of Wisconsin Press, Madison.)

bottom is accessible to light. Until the recent introduction of zebra mussels
(*Dreissena polymorpha*), however, the only places in southern Lake Michigan
where this condition existed were the shallower parts of such manmade harbors
as Jackson Park and Montrose.[15] In such places thrive different bacteria, algae,
and invertebrates that attach themselves to rocks, sand, and other surfaces, an
assemblage called the periphyton.

   Bacteria are the first to colonize a clean surface, followed approximately
twelve hours later by diatoms.[16] These algae possess sticky pads that enable
them to adhere to substrates; but they can also relinquish a grip to search for a
more favorable home if the substrate is becoming buried and no longer inhabitable. *Cocconeis* and *Achnanthidium* are among the first genera to arrive and are
excellent food for snails, crayfish, and other grazing benthic invertebrates.

   Once the periphyton community has been established, other species
begin piling on top until a thick felt-like layer of diatoms coats the substrate.
The pioneer species find themselves being outcompeted by the newcomers,
whose different shapes enable them to stick out from the surface like pins in a
cushion to exploit a larger area. Then, later, the green algae *Cladophora* and
Chara appear, eventually forming long waving strands. The forest of littoral algae supports a distinctive community of macroinvertebrates, including several
fingernail clams (*Pisidium*). The snails *Lymnaea* and *Elimia* graze on the algae,

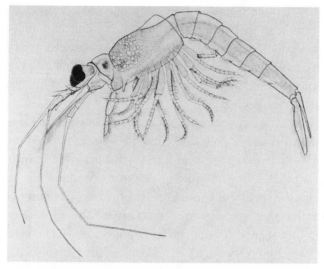

36. *Mysis relicta,* the only opossum shrimp in the Great Lakes. (Length up to twenty-five millimeters.) (From Balcer et al. 1983. Courtesy University of Wisconsin Press, Madison.)

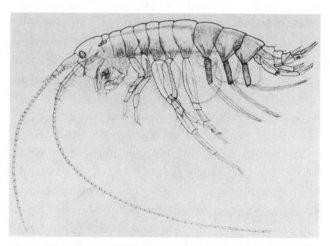

37. *Diporeia affinis,* characteristic amphipod of Lake Michigan. (Length up to nine millimeters.) From Balcer et al 1983. (Courtesy University of Wisconsin.)

while scuds (isopods) and sow bugs (amphipods) scavenge. Crayfish (*Orconectes propinquus* and *O. virilis*) split their diet between algae and detritus.

An early study of Lake Michigan's plankton, published in 1927, drew this conclusion: "The stability of the lake as a biotic factor is strikingly demonstrated by our comparisons of data covering a period of forty years, for little or no change has occurred in the composition of the plankton over this long period."[17] Documenting fluctuations in planktonic organisms, however, has been difficult because methodologies have differed from study to study. But changes have clearly taken place. Some of these are probably responses to the increasing eutrophication of inshore areas as a result of human activity. The diatoms *Stephanodiscus*, *Thalassiosira*, and *Coscinodiscus*, all characteristic of degraded waters, have increased in this section of Lake Michigan, particularly at the mouths of major harbors. At the same time, diatoms of oligotrophic conditions, *Cyclotella*, are decreasing.[18]

Three introduced species have generated more concern about the lake's planktonic health than has pollution. The first species is the spiny water flea (*Bythotrephes cederstroemi*), a native of Europe that probably arrived in the ballast water of a ship. Feeding on other species of zooplankton, the water flea escapes predation by small fish because of its prickliness: diminutive predators may ingest it, but then quickly spit it out. Larger fish do forage on the water flea and may keep its numbers in check. Biologists have found that since the water flea's arrival in 1986 a cladoceran community of ten species has been reduced to three, with one species, *Daphnia galeate mendotae*, now making up 95 percent of the total.[19]

The better-known alewife is a fish that I will discuss in much greater detail later. Suffice it to say here that in the period between 1954 and 1966 when alewives were most abundant, seven of the largest and most common planktonic crustaceans (three cladocerans and four copepods) virtually disappeared, although smaller species did increase. But two years later, as the fish numbers dropped, the seven larger crustaceans rebounded while the smaller ones decreased. By 1983, after a prolonged period of decreased alewife numbers, these larger species reached or exceeded the abundance they enjoyed in 1954. (Unfortunately, the spiny water flea also benefited by the alewife fall.)[20]

But it is the one-to-two-inch-long zebra mussel that seems to be most profoundly disrupting Lake Michigan's plankton.[21] Whereas plankton were historically the foundation for most life in Lake Michigan, there has now been a shift in primary production toward the benthic layer. The diminution of plankton could cause havoc for the many species that depend on it.

Native to the Black and Caspian Seas, zebra mussels have been expanding their range westward through Europe for the past two hundred years. In 1988, their successful crossing of the Atlantic was confirmed when scientists identified specimens from Lake St. Clair near Detroit. The mussels presumably made the transoceanic voyage safely ensconced in the ballast water of a freighter.

Their exponential increase in population has been nothing less than astounding. The first Lake Michigan record of the mussel was established at Chicago in 1989; two years later the species had spread throughout the southern basin of the lake. Ellen Marsden and her colleagues began monitoring

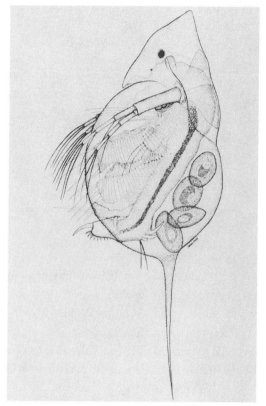

38. *Daphnia galeate mendotae,* the most abundant cladoceran in
Lake Michigan. (Length up to three millimeters.) (From Balcer et al.
1983. Courtesy University of Wisconsin.)

populations in the early months of 1991 and encountered mussels everywhere
along the Illinois shoreline, but at low densities of "less than a few hundred
per square meter." Those findings, however, just hinted at what was to follow:
"By late October, more than 600,000 mussels were counted per square meter
in the warmest southern portion of the lake [and] in one extreme case, over
4 million tiny mussels per square meter were noted on experimental settling
plates."

The key to this animal's remarkable penchant for expansion is its extraordinary fecundity. One female can spawn as many as 1 million eggs, and
these can hatch within hours, producing larvae called veligers. The veligers are
microscopic and can be readily transported any time water is moved, whether
by gravity, machines, or human exertion. In some instances, the larvae can
breed a few weeks later.

Zebra mussels can withstand depths of two hundred feet and can stick
to surfaces as smooth as Teflon. Even other animals find themselves coated

39. Zebra mussels covering pink heelsplitter mussel.
(Photo by and courtesy of Kevin Cummings, Illinois Natural
History Survey, Champaign.)

with mussels. Dr. Marsden described a half-inch-long snail on which seventy-five mussels had taken residence: "The thing was gallantly plodding along the substrate dragging this huge tumor-like mass. The mussels must have some effect." The direct effects on other organisms are clear: "Crayfish can be rendered immobile and unable to shed their exoskeleton if large numbers of mussels settle on their carapace. Dense settlement . . . on native clams and mussels, many of which are already threatened with extinction, can result in growth deformities, suffocation, or starvation due to competition for food."

Like other mussels, zebra mussels are filter feeders. A single individual processes twelve liters of water a day, and in so doing eliminates from the water all organisms smaller than 450 microns. Everything that fits becomes food for the mussels. And what goes in must come out—digested material as feces and undigested in little mucous balls called pseudofeces.

The mussels are having an impact on the lake in two principal ways. First, the water is becoming much clearer. When I did several open water dives off Chicago in 1989, water visibility was between a foot and three feet; there was a very fine line between losing sight of the diver in front and being kicked in the face by his flipper. Nancy Tuchman of Loyola University tells me that the visibility is now thirty or more feet. Her data from a reef a mile off Chicago's north side show that illumination levels at six meters (twenty feet) increased almost fourfold from 1990 to 1994. A pretty but ominous manifestation of greater water clarity is that the lake is noticeably bluer now than it used to be, back when chlorophyll-laden plankton absorbed the sunlight.

Enhanced light penetration has enabled the benthic community to flourish. This process has been aided by the second of the two impacts. Not only are there fewer planktonic organisms in the water column, but there is also more organic material on the bottom. The zebra mussel excretions have created a rich humus-like carpet on the lake floor. Tuchman's research reveals a tremendous growth in benthic algal biomass from 1991 to 1994: a half gram per square meter to fourteen and a half grams.

"The net result of all this," says Marsden, "is that food suspended for planktonic feeders is now sediment for bottom feeders." Whereas in pre-mussel times the inshore benthic fauna was depauperate, and midges were the dominant species, the variety and number of macroinvertebrates have now increased dramatically to exploit the newly available resources. Marsden illustrates the point: "When you pick up a group of zebra mussels, it will literally drip chironomids, leeches, planarians, amphipods, and isopods."

The possibility of ecological devastation is not usually by itself enough to provoke large-scale human action. But as the zebra mussel conquered new territory, evidence mounted that municipal and corporate users of Great Lakes water were at risk. Thick crusts of mussels clogged pipes and impeded water flow. Monroe, Michigan, drawing from Lake Erie, presented a horror story when it suffered a 60 percent reduction in the water it could provide for citizens. The public and private sectors were forced to respond to the threat. They devised ways to foil their tiny foe, and at great expense have managed to hold it at bay.

Several techniques are now employed to thwart mussels, two of which seem particularly effective, although expensive. One of these employs chlorine, which is highly toxic to mussels. Water departments prevent veligers from entering the system by introducing the chemical at the point of water intake rather than deeper into the pipes, although no chlorine is put into the lake itself. At a cost of $5.87 million, Chicago's Water Department began installing a new network of lines designed to carry chlorine to the offshore cribs. Evanston, Wilmette, and Glencoe have each adopted similar strategies for their much smaller treatment facilities. Implementation will cost these three municipalities almost $1.4 million. Abbot Laboratories of North Chicago, dependent on free-flowing water to manufacture its pharmaceutical products, followed suit and spent $150,000.[22]

The second approach works at electric generating stations that produce hot water as a by-product of keeping equipment cool. Recirculating that heated water through infested areas cleanses them of mussels, but care must be taken not to violate legal prohibitions on releasing hot water into the lake. Where the capacity for this "thermal backwashing" already exists, as it does at Edison's State Line plant in Hammond, Indiana, the procedure may cost about $10,000 per treatment. But for other facilities, retrofitting can run as high as $500,000.

While there are new waters for the zebra mussel to colonize, its population growth cannot continue indefinitely. Marsden cautions, however, that the species' expansion through North America has already exceeded every limit that scientists originally hypothesized. Its spread through western Europe has typically been in three stages: incredible growth during its first three to five years on the scene, then a leveling off at the high population for about the same period, followed by a one-third drop in numbers. Two conspicuous and still unexplained exceptions exist, however. In England, zebra mussels never underwent the fantastic increases, and in Sweden they never reached the third step of decline. Everyone is hoping that the Swedish model is not repeated here.

Agents of Change: Commercial Fishing and Alien Species

Commercial fishing first reached Lake Michigan in the late 1830s. [23] During those early years, the industry consisted largely of shore-based seining operations. The lakefront from Michigan City, La Porte County, to New Buffalo, Berrien County, was particularly well known as a "seining ground": "About 1860 it was not unusual to take 1,000 or 1,500 pounds of fish at a single haul, but within ten years nothing has been done in this branch, the fish having kept farther from shore than formerly." That the fish no longer frequented inshore areas was attributed to "the foulness of the rivers." [24]

Seining gave way to the more profitable pound net and the gill net that Lake Michigan fishermen still use today. The pound net was an elaborate contraption anchored by stakes or weights that took two full days to set up. It consisted of a mesh lead extending up to eighteen hundred feet lakeward from the shore to a depth of maybe fifty feet. Fish would encounter the lead, and attempt to circumvent the obstruction by following it down slope. Indeed, the fish would come to a break but instead of finding freedom it faced two wings or enclosures (one on each side). These in turn led to another enclosure, the crib or pot, from which escape was exceedingly unlikely. [25]

Pound nets were extremely efficient, catching most everything that happened by a given section of shoreline. But more important, the fish stayed alive in the crib until the boats arrived to scoop them out. This resulted in less waste (only quantities that could be processed were removed) and a fresher product. One particularly harmful aspect of the pound nets was that they caught large quantities of young fish, particularly whitefish, that concentrated inshore. Milner believed that the loss of these individuals was a major factor in decreasing fish stocks. [26]

The gill net allows much greater flexibility, as it can be set up at any depth or distance from shore. Cables with a float on one end and an anchor on the other are set vertically in the water. Nets three hundred to four hundred feet long, also with floats on the top and weights on the bottom, are strung up between the cables, creating in essence an aquatic fence. Sometimes fishermen would string nets together, doubling or tripling the length. To extricate prey, many of which are dead, the operators have to raise the net, which in Milner's time was an arduous task. Today they use power winches. By changing the depth and mesh size, however, fishermen can target the fish they want.[27]

Because gill nets were placed in deeper water, they tended to trap larger fish. But precisely because they were farther offshore, fishermen often visited them less frequently, particularly during periods of inclement weather. Thus, many fish would spoil while still in the nets. And even when full nets were adequately tended, many fish would turn bad before the fisherman could process his load. Finally, gill nets ripped from their moorings by storms became free-floating pestilences: "They have been grappled up, two years afterwards . . . full of decayed fish."[28]

Although gillnetting remains the technique of choice in this region, advances in technology have increased efficiency. Better craft enable fishermen to work waters farther offshore. Before the 1997 ban on commercial perch fishing in Illinois, Bert Atkinson, one of the state's last commercial fishermen to fish Lake Michigan, sought the yellow perch (*Perca flavescens*) up to seven miles out. Sonar facilitates location of the schools. And the nets themselves have changed. Originally they were made of coarse cotton webbing, then of a finer linen, and still later a flexible cotton cord. Starting in the late 1940s, nylon replaced cotton, which more recently has given way to nylon monofilament.[29]

Even with pollution and commercial fishing, "until the 1940s the fishery of the Great Lakes as a whole was stable and productive despite loss of the sturgeon and the collapse of a few stocks in certain lakes."[30] Then a series of invasions began which forever altered the fish life of Lake Michigan.

The first nonnative species of consequence was the rainbow smelt (*Osmerus mordax*), indigenous to the northern Pacific and Atlantic oceans. Although there are questions as to how the smelt entered Lake Ontario, experts agree that its presence in the upper Great Lakes is the result of deliberate introductions into Crystal Lake, Michigan, in 1912. Other attempts by the state to stock smelt into the St. Mary's River at various times between 1906 and 1921 failed. The motivation behind all these smelt releases was to provide forage for what some dreamed would become a world-class Atlantic salmon (*Salmo salar*) fishery. In the end, however, the salmon never took, and the dreamers had to settle for smelt.[31]

Given that Crystal Lake drains into Lake Michigan, it was only a matter

of time before smelt began showing up in the larger body. The first was a specimen caught off Frankfort, Michigan in 1923. Eight years later commercial
fishermen took eighty-six thousand pounds of smelt from the Wisconsin portion of Lake Michigan. The species grew in numbers rapidly thereafter, peaking in 1941 when 4,775,000 pounds were caught.[32]

But over the next three years something happened to the Lake Michigan smelt population, for in 1944 the commercial harvest plummeted to five
thousand pounds. Called the "smelt disaster," the collapse has never been fully
understood, but the most likely cause was a disease. The species has since
rebounded, and although there have been fluctuations, commercial production is more closely correlated to market price than abundance. Still, scientists have blamed the alewife explosion for another major smelt decrease
that saw production go from over 9 million tons in 1958 to 927,000 tons
in 1965.[33]

Smelt feed on plankton and thus compete with other planktivores. Lake
herring fortunes seem particularly related to those of smelt, decreasing when
smelt are most abundant and rebounding when smelt have ebbed. While not
tied as closely to smelt, whitefish also seemed to benefit from collapsing smelt
populations. On the other hand, smelt have become important prey for lake
trout (especially), burbot (*Lota lota*), walleye (*Stizostedion vitreum*), yellow
perch, and other fish.[34]

Commercial fishermen are not the only ones interested in smelt. The
smelt-run in early spring attracts droves of people to the lakefront. I remember
well my family going to Gillson Park in Wilmette in early April to try our hand
at smelting. My father would throw the anchor offshore as far as possible and

40. Lamprey on Lake Trout. (Courtesy of Great Lakes Sea Grant Network Exotic
Species Graphics Library, Ann Arbor, Mich.)

secure the line to a plank wedged into the rocks of the pier. He then attached the net to the line with a pulley, and we waited. On good nights we plucked fish from the meshes until our hands became too cold to continue.

◄O► ◄O► ◄O►

Every local environment is plagued by one or more exotic species. But few if any exotic species have proved to be as catastrophic as the sea lamprey (*Petromyzon marinus*), which by itself, some scientists say, drove several fish to virtual or total extirpation.

Lampreys, of which there are thirty-one species in the world, belong to their own class (Cyclostomata) of animals, which taxonomically makes them as different from the typical bony fish (Osteichthyes) as they are from reptiles or birds.[35] They are eel-like in shape, and lack jaws and paired fins. Instead of jaws, lamprey possess circular sucking mouths lined with tiny teeth. As adults, sea lampreys attach themselves to other fish, preferably those with soft scales, and rasp a hole into the host that can be an inch or more in diameter.

Lampreys produce a glandular secretion that both dissolves muscles and prevents blood from coagulating. Thus, so long as it hangs on and the unfortunate host remains healthy, the lamprey is assured of comestibles. In the oceanic waters where this species evolved, the three-pound lamprey pursued fish like halibut that might weigh four hundred pounds. In that circumstance, the behemoth could support a passel of lampreys with no ill effects. Not so, of course, if the host is a twenty-pound lake trout.[36]

After fifteen months of adulthood, the lamprey leaves deep water and may travel 120 miles upstream to spawn. They require clear water between 50° and 79°F, substrates of sand or gravel, and a strong current that does not vary in direction (this has prevented them from breeding in otherwise suitable offshore areas). Spawning streams in the Chicago region are confined to Indiana and Berrien County. During this period, the final chapter in the individual's life, the adults stop feeding, and begin metabolizing their own tissues, including the eyes.[37]

Once the eggs hatch, the tiny young, known as ammocoetes, burrow into the bottom where they feed on diatoms and other algae for up to twenty days. They then drift downstream until they reach areas of deeper water and detritus-lined beds. Again they wriggle into the bottom where they exist as filter feeders for anywhere from three to seventeen years. At that point they are ready to tackle more substantial prey and become the parasites so loathed by humans.

The above facts are certain, but mystery attaches to the expansion of lampreys through the Great Lakes. Indeed, in the wake of its early conquests, the lamprey left behind not only lakes devoid of large fish, but perplexing questions that scientists have not yet fully answered. It has generally been assumed that lampreys are native to Lake Ontario, the one Great Lake with unimpeded access to the Atlantic. Apparently, however, no one saw any lamprey in the lake until the 1830s, and sixty more years had to elapse before lampreys became a problem. Some now believe that the invader made its way into Lake Ontario through the Erie Barge Canal, completion of which in 1819 linked Oswego, New York, to New York City. Still others have suggested that lamprey were inadvertently introduced to the Great Lakes via bait buckets, ship ballast, or American eel introductions.[38]

If the lampreys were native to Lake Ontario, or even if they arrived through the Erie Canal, there remains the question of why it took them so long to decimate Lake Ontario's lake trout. At least two answers, by no means mutually exclusive, have been offered. The first posits that an equilibrium existed until human activities began to have an impact on lake trout populations. A combination of pollution and intensive fishing began to stress stocks in general and removed the larger lake trout that could best withstand lamprey parasitism in particular. Lampreys were forced to go after smaller fish and thus accelerated the trout decline. The second possibility addresses the availability of spawning streams. This theory claims that the clearing of riparian timber and other vegetation raised the water temperature of Lake Ontario tributaries above what was suitable for lampreys. In addition, many streams in the watershed were inaccessible to lampreys because they had been dammed during early settlement. But by the beginning of the twentieth century, lamprey habitat was on the increase because vegetation had grown back and the dams had become fewer due to disintegration and deliberate removal.[39]

Niagara Falls ensured that the connection between Lake Erie and Lake Ontario was exclusively downstream. The completion of the Welland Ship Canal in 1824, however, enabled small boats to bypass the obstacle. But lampreys failed to negotiate the canal until it was enlarged and reconfigured over the course of the next century, when Lake Erie's first lamprey appeared in 1921.

Upon reaching Lake Erie, the lampreys created nary a stir. Their populations remained low, and it took them nearly ten years to reach the western outlet that led to Lake Huron. There are reasons why Lake Erie was less hospitable to the lamprey than the other lakes would prove to be. Human activities had silted many potential spawning streams, thus rendering them unsuitable to lampreys that prefer beds of gravel and sand. The relative shallowness and warmth of Lake Erie also provided poor lamprey habitat.[40]

But havoc ensued once the invaders entered Lake Huron in 1933 and Lake Michigan in 1936, when the first individual was taken on March 23 fifteen miles east of Milwaukee. It was sixteen inches long and, fittingly, had attached itself to a lake trout. Although lampreys went after every species large enough to get a grip on, its first victims were the large deepwater predators, burbot and lake trout. Because of its commercial value, the lake trout became the most celebrated casualty of the lamprey onslaught. During its relatively short life as an adult, one lamprey can destroy forty pounds of lake trout. That lake trout numbers collapsed under this pressure is documented by grim statistics. In 1943, 6,860,000 pounds were taken. Nine years later the yield plummeted to four thousand pounds. In 1954, Lake Michigan's commercial fishermen reported a total lake trout catch of thirty-four pounds—representing, perhaps, a single fish. By the end of 1956, the species was probably gone from the lake.[41]

As lake trout ceased being viable prey, lampreys concentrated on other species. When lamprey populations peaked in the mid-1950s, they were destroying an estimated 5 million pounds of fish a year, largely deepwater ciscoes.[42] Commercial fishermen also turned their attention to ciscoes and other species that were still commercially exploitable. In essence, the combination of fishing and lampreys eliminated the top predators, and then the large planktonic feeders (deepwater ciscoes). With their competitors gone, other species increased in population and became the new targets of commercial fishing interests. What had been a stable fishery for a hundred years was suddenly in turmoil.

The first coordinated reaction to the crisis was the creation of the Great Lakes Sea Lamprey Committee in 1946. Representatives from each of the Great Lakes States, Ontario, and the U.S. Fish and Wildlife Service served on the committee, which initiated a comprehensive study of the lamprey. That work provided the foundation on which the eventual control strategy was based. In 1955 a treaty between Canada and the United States established the Great Lakes Fishery Commission, which then assumed the leading role in fighting lampreys.

Control measures focused on the spawning streams, where the animals swarmed in vulnerable concentrations. Biologists installed mechanical traps across thirty-one streams, including two in Indiana. Although potentially highly effective, these weirs were expensive and difficult to maintain. During floods, for example, large numbers of lampreys could pass upstream unmolested. Another technology proved more successful: "A simple, alternating-current electrical field could be substituted for the usual screens or gates of the lamprey weirs, which would control all lamprey and fish movement while permitting free downstream passage of flood water, ice, and debris." By 1958, 132 of these devices were in operation, and from 1953 to 1969 they claimed the lives of over 750,000 adult lampreys.[43]

Despite the results of the electric barriers, many believed that the only truly effective control would be a lamprey larvicide. A group of federal scientists ran almost sixty thousand tests on six thousand different chemicals before they found the right formula: 3-trifluormethyl-4-nitrophenol (TFM). Later studies proved that a mixture of TFM and the compound 5,2'-dichloro-4'-nitrosalicylanilide was even more toxic to ammocoetes without increasing its effects on other species. What these researchers had accomplished was unprecedented: "These compounds for controlling the sea lamprey represent the first known selective toxicants discovered and used to destroy a particular vertebrate without harming other vertebrate or invertebrate animals occupying the same habitat."[44]

By 1966, every stream in the Lake Michigan basin known to support spawning lampreys had received at least one chemical treatment. As one measure that the program is succeeding, three traps yielded a total of 12,886 adults in 1961 and only 1,168 in 1966. Although many fewer fish exhibit lamprey scarring than before, there are signs that the current strategy needs to be reevaluated.

Continuing research indicates that TFM is not as benign toward other organisms as biologists originally thought. Walleyes are almost as sensitive to the larvicide as are lampreys, and invertebrate numbers dropped by 88 percent after exposure to TFM, although they rebounded within several months. These findings bolster the growing political opposition to placing poisons into streams, even for a good cause. Recently, the U.S. Environmental Protection Agency ruled that the German manufacturer of TFM had to reregister the chemical. But the procedure would have cost the company $5 million and, thus, became prohibitive. The agency ultimately changed its original decision, and TFM remains available. The antilamprey program is also very expensive. Lamprey control and research costs $11,400,000 a year, and Congress has threatened to cut funds.[45]

Two more factors may be in the lamprey's favor. First, as water quality improves and riparian areas revegetate, more streams are becoming suitable for lamprey spawning. Any expansion of TFM applications would, due to the issues discussed above, be extremely difficult. And second, the 10–20 percent of lamprey larvae that do survive exposure to TFM may be passing on an immunity to it.[46] They certainly won't be wanting for food, given the abundance of introduced salmon that now occupy the lakes.

For all these reasons, the Great Lakes Fishery Commission is seeking alternative ways of controlling lamprey. Some of these include better barriers, the release of sterile males, and development of lamprey diseases. The specter of burgeoning lamprey populations is incentive enough to succeed.

◄◦► ◄◦► ◄◦►

The alewife, too, claims the Atlantic Ocean as its place of origin. It also shares with the lamprey similar questions as to its spread through the Great Lakes. A number of theories have been advanced to explain its presence in Lake Ontario: (1) it was native (as it is in several landlocked lakes in Ontario) but went undetected until 1873 because of low populations; (2) its presence in the Erie Barge Canal in the 1860s is evidence that it used the artificial waterway to expand its territory; and (3) it was introduced accidentally as part of efforts to establish American shad in the 1870s.[47]

It is presumed that the alewife skirted Niagara Falls through the Welland Ship Canal. But, like the lamprey, the alewife evidently found the earliest versions of the canal difficult or impossible to traverse and did not appear in Lake Erie until 1931. W. J. Christie has suggested that the alewife expansion into Lake Erie was hindered by the presence of other fish that either preyed on it or competed with it for food. It was not until other species declined that alewives began to increase. Be that as it may, the alewife eventually made its way to Lake Huron in 1933 and Lake Michigan in 1949.[48]

Alewife populations in Lake Michigan grew from north to south. Two were captured in the Chicago region in 1953; three years later they had already become a nuisance as commercial fishermen found their gill nets filled with alewives instead of the intended ciscoes.[49] Bert Atkinson told me the lake was so thick with alewives it made him want to quit fishing.

Lampreys had eliminated the predatory lake trout and burbot, and commercial fishermen had reduced the ciscoes, which competed with alewives for plankton. Without any checks, alewives took over Lake Michigan like no fish had ever done before or since. Samples taken in southern Lake Michigan showed that immature alewives had increased "56 times between 1962 and 1964, and the number of adults increased 5 times between 1962 and 1966." According to estimates made in 1965, 85 percent of everything alive in Lake Michigan was alewives.[50]

No aquatic habitat, from the shallowest to the deepest, escaped the alewife for at least some portion of the year. In winter they shared the depths with various ciscoes, which responded to the alewife hordes by declining. From 1954 to 1964, the cisco known as kiyi (*Coregonus kiyi*) went from being abundant to virtually extinct.[51] In spring and summer, alewives utilize both streams and offshore areas for spawning. As huge schools swarmed toward shore, they preyed on the eggs and fry of other shallow water species, most particularly

41. Dead alewives at Monroe Harbor, Chicago, 1966.
(Courtesy of Shedd Aquarium, Chicago.)

yellow perch, emerald shiners (*Notropis atherinoides*), and lake herring (*Coregonus artedii*). Being outcompeted for food and space by the superior numbers of alewives, these other fish underwent displacement and dramatic losses of population.

At its height in 1977, the Lake Michigan alewife fishery produced 48,405,000 pounds. Indiana fishermen caught 694,000 pounds in 1967 and 113,000 pounds in 1971. Other than those two years, the harvesting of alewives has been limited in this region. Most of the Wisconsin catch is out of Milwaukee and points north. Although alewives never commanded a high price, their sheer quantity suggested that they must have some economic value. Efforts to entice the public with pickled alewives, dry salted alewives, alewife hors d'oeuvres, and alewife fish sticks never met with much success. More lucrative was the plant in Oconto, Wisconsin, which converted alewives into fertilizer and cat food.[52]

George Becker dryly remarks that "one aspect of [the alewife's] behavior which distresses man is its dying, a biological end point over which the alewife has little control." But modern man is not used to seeing die-offs in the magnitude that struck the alewife in 1966 and 1967. Bert Atkinson recalls seeing miles of dead alewives floating in windrows three feet deep and three hundred yards wide. To the revulsion of landowners and beach users, but the delight of blowflies and beetles, vast numbers of dead and dying fish washed up on the sandy shorelines of southern Lake Michigan. Biologists with the U.S. Fish and Wildlife Service estimated that 1967 alewife mortality within Lake Michigan amounted to several billion fish, a reduction in population of 70 percent.[53]

Edward Brown, a biologist with the U.S. Bureau of Commercial Fisheries, examined die-off victims but could discover no particular physiological cause for the mortality. Indeed, the fish he collected seemed "robust." One explanation of the events relates to weather. Alewives survive best in waters between 46.4° and 71.6°F. Thus in winter the fish descend to the lower depths, where the water is least affected by the air temperature. But in particularly cold years, alewives have difficulty finding thermal conditions suitable for survival. Many of these winterkills go unnoticed, since the evidence settles to the bottom and decays. But it is during spawning when alewives are most at risk, for they are sensitive to rapid changes in temperature. Already weakened by the demands of reproduction and diminished feeding, they gather in shallow water, where they are easily trapped by surges of cold or warm water, either of which can be fatal.[54]

Alewives, like other members of the herring family, experience extreme fluctuations in their populations. Within a decade of the huge die-offs, the species had rebounded, prompting writer Tom Kuchenberg to comment that "recovery from a nearly three-quarter drop is an indication of how powerful alewife dominance has become."[55] It crashed again, but it never reached the extremes of that first cycle. For by this time, the alewife no longer had free reign of the lakes.

◄○► ◄○► ◄○►

In April 1898, Lake Ontario's last known specimen of the Atlantic salmon was netted off Scarborough, Ontario.[56] At that moment, Lake Ontario both relinquished the distinction of being the only Great Lake with an indigenous salmon population and gained the distinction of being the first to lose an entire fishery. But as early as 1873, efforts had been underway to stock salmon in the other lakes. With one strange exception in the mid-1950s, these attempts were unsuccessful until 1966.

In that year, the Michigan Department of Natural Resources liberated 850,000 coho salmon (*Oncorhynchus kisutch*) into Lakes Michigan and Superior. The following year, the agency added eight hundred thousand of the much larger chinook salmon (*Oncorhynchus tshawytscha*) and another 1.7 million coho salmon. By this time, lamprey dominance had waned, but alewife numbers

42. Stocking rainbow trout at North Avenue Pier, Chicago, 1987.
(Courtesy Illinois Department of Natural Resources, Champaign.)

were exploding. Agencies saw the salmon as a way to reestablish predators so that the lakes could regain some semblance of a balanced ecosystem. Not incidentally, they also hoped to create a sport fishery.

In the ensuing years, all the state agencies together stocked hundreds of millions of trout and salmon into Lake Michigan, 274,000,000 from 1976 to 1994 alone. Besides the coho and chinook, these consisted of lake trout, brook trout, brown trout, and rainbow/steelhead trout.[57] (Steelhead is the anadromous form of the rainbow.) All of these stocked species have been caught in local waters, but the two kinds of salmon and the lake trout are the most important. Although biologists always assumed that continuous stocking would be necessary to maintain populations of the nonnative trout and salmon, they hoped that the lake trout would become self-sustaining and recolonize its former haunts. Lake trout goals have proven difficult to attain (more on this later), but the other salmonids have behaved more or less according to plan.

Another species, the pink salmon (*Oncorhynchus gorbuscha*), proved to be a big surprise. It was accidentally established in 1956 when leftovers from a stocking program designed for Hudson's Bay were dumped into a sewer that ultimately led to Lake Superior. No one thought any more about it until strange fish caught in 1959 were identified as this species. Considered the most saltwater dependent of all salmon, the pink managed to spread throughout the lakes. Although not common on the south end of Lake Michigan, they occasionally appear and may be increasing, but they tend to be small and of little interest to anglers.[58]

From an economic perspective, these introductions have been an incredible success. For the first time, Lake Michigan anglers could focus their energies on large and feisty prey that were also delicious to eat. Lake Michigan became "the most popular salmon-fishing center in the world." In twenty years, a sport fishery has developed on Lake Michigan that generates annual revenues of over $450 million. (Yellow perch is still the most important quarry of local inshore anglers.) Charter boats operate out of harbors all along the lake, including 140 based in Illinois. There is, of course, no such thing as a free lunch, even if it is fillet of fish. A single salmon might cost as high as $15 to raise, release, and catch. Between 1966 and 1988, the states spent over $75 million to maintain their salmon fisheries. There has also been a spurt in lakefront development, with marina madness leading the way as one of the principal excesses.[59]

The salmonids have done their part to reduce alewives. Coho, chinook, and steelhead rely on alewives for 90 percent or more of their diets. Brown trout and lake trout also depend on alewives but to a lesser extent.[60]

While lake trout could shift to other fish when alewives crashed, the chinook and coho could not and suffered their own declines. In part, this is because the salmon prefer different water temperatures than ciscoes, perch, or other possible prey. They are left with alewives, whose cyclical ways impose limits on the salmon.[61] Yet despite these limits, from the 1960s to the mid-1980s agencies continued to stock salmon without regard to alewife levels. The result has been salmon that are a half or third the size of what they had been earlier.

An even more ominous development began in 1988, when chinooks became infected with bacterial kidney disease and died in large numbers. Some scientists attributed the outbreak to individuals infected in hatcheries, a conclusion that prompted Michigan to destroy all the chinook it was currently raising so it could rid its facilities of the pathogen. Another theory, however, held that the commonly occurring illness turned virulent because stocks had become weakened through insufficient forage.[62]

For many years, sport-fishing interests have dictated the stocking regimens followed by state agencies. The more salmon placed in the lake, the better. When alewife numbers dropped, the response was to ban commercial harvesting of alewives. But of late, there is finally agreement that stocking levels must be in line with prey levels. As a result, in recent years the Lake Michigan states have all reduced their salmon introductions by as much as 25 percent.[63]

Victims of Change: Native Fish

Seventy-nine native species of fish are known from Lake Michigan.[64] The warmer and nutrient-rich inshore areas supported a greater variety of species than the deeper and cooler water offshore. Some of these inshore fish dwelt locally exclusively within Lake Michigan, while others were equally at home in rivers. The most important commercial species in this group include whitefish (*Coregonus clupeaformis*), lake herring, yellow perch, and, in the early years, lake sturgeon.

The deep waters offshore gave rise to a smaller but very distinctive guild of fish. Six species of ciscoes, three sculpin, lake trout, and burbot were the dominant species. Lake trout and burbot would also utilize shallower areas during spawning season.

Several small fish are common in the shallowest portions of the lake. One of the most abundant is the spottail shiner (*Notropis hudsonius*). Every one of ninety fish caught in a sample of several sites off the Indiana Dunes was of this species.[65] This distinctive species is also easy to see in September at the mouth of the Dead River at Illinois Beach State Park, where throngs writhe at the edge of the wet sand.

The longnose dace (*Rhinichthys cataractae*) is restricted to the surge zone, where the waves break on the shore in endless repetition. Although a tough environment, the setting provides the same cold and highly oxygenated water as the fast-moving streams that are the dace's preferred habitat in northwestern Illinois. Living at depths as shallow as six inches, the lake chub (*Couesius plumbeus*) seems to need even less water, and it tends to congregate at the mouths of small creeks. Larry Page, former director of the Center for Biodiversity at the Illinois Natural History Survey, discovered just how little water this species requires: he found it in north shore ravines spawning in the tiniest of trickles.[66]

Lake Michigan harbors four kinds of sculpin. The spoonhead sculpin (*Cottus ricei*), described from a specimen washed ashore at Northwestern University, was once common from shore to 450 feet. But for unknown reasons, the fish has since largely disappeared from southern Lake Michigan. Today, only the mottled sculpin (*C. bairdi*) is common in the shallows, although the slimy sculpin (*C. cognatus*) also occurs near shore. The mottled sculpin can tolerate a wide range of ecological conditions, from streams to depths of two hundred feet. It is one of the more conspicuous members of the lake's benthic fish community and is a favorite among scuba divers who enjoy its antics: "They are friendly little fish, which rear up on their fins and gaze at you."[67]

Unfortunately, the mottled sculpin is yet another victim of an alien species. Known in this region only since 1993, the round goby (*Neogobius melanostomus*) originated in the Black and Caspian Seas and turned up in the St. Clair River of Michigan in 1990. No one knows whether the fish spread from the St. Clair or whether it arrived in southern Lake Michigan directly via tanker ballast. It feeds on fish eggs, which scares those biologists who have worked so long to reestablish lake trout in Lake Michigan.[68]

The emerald shiner was, until about forty years ago, one of the most common fish in the shallower portions of Lake Michigan. It dwells near the surface and was important prey for fish, birds, and people, who took large numbers for bait. And as recently as November 1956, there were enough of them to choke utility cooling intakes and boat engines. But then in the early 1960s the shiner virtually disappeared, experiencing what McLain and Wells called "the most extraordinary change in abundance of any species in Lake Michigan." There is not much to say about this, however, for the authorities agree that a single cause was responsible: the unrestrained multiplication of alewives, which feed on shiner eggs.[69]

◄◦► ◄◦► ◄◦►

Reporting on conditions in 1875, Edward Nelson wrote that commercial operators took nearly thirty species of fish at Chicago, South Chicago (at the mouth of the Calumet River), and in the Calumet River, miles upstream at Riverdale.[70] His annotated list is a fascinating glimpse of how the status of certain species has changed over time. Of course, back then both the Chicago and Calumet Rivers fed Lake Michigan, contributing water and organisms. And because pound nets were in vogue, more inshore fish wound up as commodities.

Nelson found walleye (*Stizostedion vitreum*) to be common; fish production records for Illinois and Indiana show that the species has gone virtually unrecorded since, except for four years in the 1930s when Indiana produced a total of thirteen thousand pounds. The freshwater drum (*Aplodinotus grunniens*) is an even better example of a fish whose population has plummeted, although it seems to have increased in recent years. Prior to the early 1980s, the species was thought to be gone from southern Lake Michigan and northeastern Illinois.[71] But Nelson could write: "Much more abundant [off South Chicago] than Chicago. They commence running about the first of June, and are taken in large numbers the remainder of the season. In July 1873, a large run occurred, and in one day over 10,000 pounds were taken."

Modern authors have seemingly overlooked Nelson's comments concerning at least three species he found to be of regular occurrence in Lake Michigan. Bowfins (*Amia calva*) were "often taken by the seines near shore. They swarm in the water about the fish houses near the mouth of the [Calumet River] where the offal is thrown." Although the scientific literature records a single instance of a muskellunge (*Esox masquinongy*) in this portion of Lake Michigan (off Lake County, Ind.), Nelson stated that this magnificent game fish "occurs in the pounds in sparing numbers throughout the season." And finally, despite a 1990 article documenting what the authors believed was the first channel catfish (*Ictalurus punctatus*) for the Illinois waters of Lake Michigan, Nelson found the species to be abundant off South Chicago.[72]

The species of commercial significance have, of course, garnered most of the scientific attention. In the early years, herring and whitefish constituted the bulk of the inshore fishery, but both have declined due to exploitation, pollution of shallow areas, and competition with exotics. Writing for the U.S. Fishery Commission, Walter Koelz summarized the wantonness of the early fishermen: "The whitefish . . . was sought for the markets with the aid of every device that human ingenuity could invent. At no season was the pursuit relented, and no fish were too small to be taken. The smallest, together with the herring and sturgeon, often were carried out onto the beach because they were so numerous that they interfered with the capture of the larger whitefish."[73]

The herring has suffered the most. A combination of heavy fishing and depredation by alewives and smelt has shrunk its numbers below the point where it still constitutes a fishery. Whitefish have fared better, increasing in recent years as lampreys declined.

The sucker fishery, composed primarily of white suckers (*Catostomus commersoni*), has maintained itself over the years, no doubt because consumers valued it much less than they did other species. However, they were not able to escape the ravages of lampreys, which seriously decreased their population during the 1950s. Numbers have since rebounded concomitant with lamprey control. Since 1953, most of the sucker catch in Lake Michigan originated in Green Bay, although for reasons I cannot determine, Indiana produced a whopping 209,000 pounds in 1971.[74]

◄◦► ◄◦► ◄◦►

Sturgeon and yellow perch are unique in their own ways. Of all the Lake Michigan fisheries, that of the sturgeon was the first to collapse, and that of the yellow perch persisted as one of the last two local species to be pursued commercially. The sturgeon is large and rare, while the charm of the perch lies in its familiarity—a fish easily caught by children from Chicago's piers.

The lake sturgeon has inspired the human imagination like no other fish native to this region. Henry Wadsworth Longfellow wrote of it in his epic "Hiawatha":

> On the white sand of the bottom
> Lay the monster, Mishe-Nahma,
> Lay the sturgeon, king of fishes.

And these words by ichthyologist Howard Walden: "One thinks of the sturgeon as a kind of philosopher among fishes, as if its ancient lineage had bred, over the thousands of centuries, a curious old wisdom and a quiet acceptance of change. The sturgeon has seen more years when it first spawns than many fish see in a life time." [75]

Not only philosopher-king, a sturgeon was probably the central figure behind the region's only sightings of a "lake serpent," as the *Chicago Tribune* dubbed it in a series of articles running on August 5 and August 7, 1867. The crews of the *George Wood* and the *Skylark* first reported a strange creature off Evanston on August 4, 1867. From there, the animal headed south around the lake, appearing off Chicago's south side (Hyde Park) on August 5 and Michigan City on August 6. As summarized by the newspaper, the descriptions from the first and third days are virtually identical, down to the admission that the observations were very brief and from a substantial distance. The Michigan City sighting was made from shore by Charles Sanger, justice of the peace, who estimated the object to be one and a half miles away: "He was on the surface of the water only for a minute or two; appeared to be, as far as we could judge, about forty feet in length, of a dark color, and resembled a snake, both in appearance and motion. He was at such a distance from shore and in sight for so short a time, that we could form little idea of his real character."

There were two reports on August 5. One very short communication was from a boat captain who said that he and his first mate saw the largest fish they had ever seen swimming about four miles away. The captain watched the animal for a minute or two through a glass but could determine nothing more.

The second observation that day was made by a lone fisherman, Joseph Muhlke, who was working his lines one and a half miles from shore, "just below Hyde Park," when the strange apparition approached him. Muhlke's detailed statement, as published by the *Tribune*, constitutes an excellent description of a sturgeon except for two purported features: a length of forty feet and, just in front of its anal fins, "two well-developed legs that . . . ended in a webbed foot."

The *Tribune* offered its opinion that the creature was a giant member of the "newt family, indigenous to the lake." After talking with Muhlke, two different experts from the Chicago Academy of Sciences also proffered identifications. Colonel Daniels believed it was a whale that managed to squeeze through the Welland Ship canal as a youngster, but then grew too large to return. (First whales, and then lampreys and alewives.) Dr. Johnson, in contrast, felt "confident that the animal is only an immense sturgeon, and the legs exist only in the imagination of Mr. M." It is difficult to disagree with Dr. Johnson.

Several attributes contribute to the sturgeon mystique. They are of a primitive family, direct descendents of fish that thrived 100 million years ago during the upper Cretaceous Period.[76] Sturgeon are covered in bony plates and share with the sharks cartilaginous spinal cords and heterocercal tails (upper lobe longer than the lower and containing the end of the spinal column).

But their most striking physical quality is their great size. Becker cites an 1881 Fond du Lac, Wisconsin, newspaper article that reports the taking of a nine-foot-long sturgeon weighing 297 pounds. W. J. K. Harkness and J. R. Dymond list all sturgeon records that they could find of fish over a hundred pounds. They missed the nine footer, but include two specimens of 310 pounds, the longest of which was seven feet eleven inches, caught off Benton Harbor, Berrien County, in 1943.[77] Another giant sturgeon, overlooked by the commentators, was caught in 1906 off Chicago's north side and christened Bismarck by its captors. By weight, it would place sixth on Harkness and Dymond's list and by length, third: "Instead of roaming, a conqueror up and down the long stretches of the feeding ground, the monarch of fishdom gasped today for life in a narrow cell of a boat on the beach in Rogers Park, his lease on life depending upon a barefooted boy, who has the task of pumping water for his majesty. Bismarck is seven feet six and a half inches long and weighs 245 pounds. He was captured yesterday and for twenty minutes made a terrible fight to free himself from the meshes of a seine where five men fought to subdue him."[78]

The lake sturgeon was the first of Lake Michigan's fish to suffer catastrophic declines due to exploitation. Ironically, although few people valued the species as food until the 1870s, sturgeon were killed with great abandon nonetheless. Because of their large size and plated bodies, sturgeon ripped many of the nets in which they became entangled. Fishermen also believed, mistakenly as it turns out, that the species fed heavily on other fish deemed more desirable. This led to a wasteful carnage that is reminiscent of what humans did to the passenger pigeon, but fortunately in this instance the killing ended before the species did: "Many picturesque accounts are given of early efforts to dispose of sturgeon. In places, they were piled on the beach like cordwood and, after they had been lying in the sun long enough for the fat to run, they were set afire and burned. . . . In the days of wood-burning steam-boats on the Great Lakes, sturgeon were piled on the wood-dock at Amherst-burg, taken aboard the boats and burned under the boilers. Another use was to dig them into the ground as fertilizer."[79]

Most of the efforts to make something valuable out of sturgeon seem to have originated in Sandusky, Ohio. It was here where Great Lakes caviar was first produced in 1855. And though once fed to pigs, caviar was the product that first generated commercial interest in sturgeon. While there had been devotees of sturgeon soup and pickled sturgeon, it was the Schact brothers of Sandusky and their smoked sturgeon that created a big demand for the fish, at least in the larger cities. One Chicago company reported in 1871 that they had many more orders for the product than they could fill. A third item derived from sturgeon is known as isinglass, a gelatinous substance obtained from the air bladder. It was formerly used in the processing of wines and jellies but has since been replaced by various substitutes.[80]

During his 1871 study, John Milner found that sturgeon were common at the southern end of Lake Michigan. A few years later, Edward Nelson reported that sturgeon were still "very abundant" off south Chicago, near the Calumet River: "The largest haul of this species ever taken amounted to 8,000 pounds of dressed fish." They were also quite common in Lake Calumet.[81]

Sturgeon would spawn in June, at the mouths of various rivers. On July 1, 1871, "at the mouth of the Calumet River, South Chicago, . . . a large lift of sturgeon were brought ashore, looking flaccid and emaciated, and but one specimen out of over twenty individuals contained spawn." Two counties north of the Chicago region, at Saugatuck, Michigan, sturgeon would gather in the Kalamazoo River at dusk, "leaping from the surface [and] throwing their bulky forms entirely out of the water."[82]

But it only took about twenty years to destroy the sturgeon as a har-vestable species. Beginning in 1929, the Lake Michigan states had banned all commercial fishing.[83] Why this species was unable to withstand intensive fishing can be explained by their reproductive biology. Female lake sturgeon don't breed until they are about twenty-five years old and, thereafter, breed only once every four to six years. Males mature more rapidly, being able to re-produce at age fifteen, and generally breed every other year.

Given the time that must elapse before a female sturgeon can breed, it would be an evolutionary necessity that they have long life spans. Sturgeon can live to be a hundred years or more, and thus without human pressure a female would have ample opportunity to contribute progeny. But where large fish are removed, the reproductive capacity of the population dwindles. And even

43. The late Waukegan restaurateur Mathon Kyritsis with the day's catch of yellow perch and one
bloater, 1967. (Courtesy of John Kyritsis.)

when conservation measures are implemented, only the passage of many decades will bring the numbers back to safe levels, although probably never to
original abundance.

◄o► ◄o► ◄o►

Apparently almost nothing has been written about the history of Lake Michigan's sport fishery. But the few early accounts that exist make it clear that
yellow perch has always been a sought-after species. In 1885, large numbers
of people fished for perch from Chicago's piers. They used the simplest of gear,
dip nets or hand-held lines with minnows as bait.[84] Another author described
the Grand Calumet Heights Club, "situated directly upon the shore of Lake
Michigan": "The lake fishing off the Calumet beach is good. Two ladies have
taken as many as 100 perch in a morning's fishing, and although perch fishing
does not afford very exciting sport, it serves to pass away an idle day for gentlemen as well as the ladies."[85]

Over a century later perch remain the primary reason people cast their
lines from the Lake Michigan shoreline. Illinois anglers spent almost half a
million hours in 1994 catching 309,839 perch. Those who fish from Indiana's
piers also ranked perch as their favorite, and even those with access to boats
picked perch second only to coho salmon.[86]

Perch spend most of their time in waters of intermediate and shallow depths. During the summer they come in shore to lay a remarkable cluster of eggs, accordion in shape and up to seven feet four inches long.[87] Their preference for shallow water makes them accessible to all who fish. Added to their availability, perch are a culinary treat that few species can match, particularly panfried in butter.

Data on the commercial perch fishery are much more complete. Edward Nelson reported that pound nets off Chicago frequently yielded yellow perch throughout the season. At the mouth of the Calumet River in autumn, "large numbers are taken with the seine and gill net." They became even more common in the 1880s when whitefish and sturgeon decreased. Based on Lake Michigan–wide figures, commercial operations have netted an annual average of 2.4 million pounds from 1889 through 1970. Two bulges have occurred over that time, when 6.3 million pounds were taken from 1894 to 1896 and 4.3 million pounds from 1961 to 1964. While the higher numbers in those periods reflect both larger populations and more intense fishing efforts, the latter is probably the more important of the two factors.[88]

During the last half of the 1960s, the average catch dropped to 890,000 pounds but then rose again in the early 1970s. This fluctuation correlated closely with the rising and falling of alewives, but the record high harvest of 5.8 million pounds in 1964 probably contributed to the initial drop that occurred the following year.

Biologists now believe that every four or five years a particularly large number of perch offspring survive. The next year's production of young is usually (although not always) poor, with each succeeding year improving until another peak is reached. This cycle can be altered by such factors as fishing pressure and the abundance of other fishes. During the period when they were most common, alewives depressed perch numbers through competition for food and predation on young. But two years after the 1967 alewife crash, perch rebounded with a very large class of offspring.[89]

In recent years perch have hit hard times of unprecedented proportion: "Catch-per-effort of adult yellow perch declined by 90%–95% in Wisconsin and Indiana between 1990 and 1995, and by 86 percent in Illinois from 1992 to 1995. Trawling and seining for young-of-the-year yellow perch have yielded minimal or zero catches since 1989."

What this means is that no significant numbers of young perch have been produced since 1988 (a very large class) and 1989. With virtually no recruitment, the population decreases at the rate of mortality. Twelve million yellow perch were caught in Lake Michigan in 1993, and 6 million in 1994. Scientists now fear that "the adult population may already be too reduced to maintain adequate recruitment."

Not only are the low numbers distressing, but also those adults that still survive are getting old. Perch can live up to sixteen years, with the average maximum age being ten or twelve. Sexually maturing at three years, a female may only have six productive years. Thus, there is the real possibility that the reproductively efficient adult population may reach senescence before it is replaced by a younger age class.

The absence of young perch means that something is affecting the fish at the very early stages of its life cycle. Fishing, therefore, for example, is not the cause of the problem, although under the current situation it will destroy the fishery in a short time. Ellen Marsden believes that in reducing Lake Michigan's plankton layer, zebra mussels have been major contributors to the perch's decimation. Perch fry forage entirely on zooplankton and thus are exceedingly vulnerable to starvation. Also, the clearer water column makes the young perch easier for predators to find. Other scientists blame alewife predation. Although alewives have decreased, their numbers still exceed the threshold levels below which young perch are able to thrive. But because alewife densities vary across the lake, this hypothesis is difficult to evaluate. Harsh spring weather has also been suggested as a factor contributing to the problem.[90]

Meanwhile, despite all the evidence pointing to impending disaster, no jurisdiction wanted to curb its share of the perch take unilaterally. Recognizing the need for a coordinated approach, the Great Lakes Fishery Commission in 1994 created the Yellow Perch Task Group, which consisted of experts from tribal governments and the four states. Eventually the states did agree to impose a moratorium on all commercial perch fishing in 1997. Current daily limits on the number of perch that anglers can take are: thirty-five in Michigan; fifteen in Indiana; fifteen of between eight to ten inches in length in Illinois (with no fishing during the June spawning period); and five in Wisconsin (also with no fishing in June).

In the fall of 1998, biologists caught enough young perch to suggest that a relatively strong class of fish might have been produced that year, particularly in the waters of Indiana and southern Michigan. If these indications prove true, there may yet be hope for a commercial perch fishery in Lake Michigan.[91] But some biologists point to the rapidly shrinking number of adult perch, many approaching the end of their reproductive lives, as evidence that the time for effective action may have already passed.

◄o► ◄o► ◄o►

Because Lake Michigan is only about ten thousand years old and thus relatively young, the deep-water fish community consists of few species. Prior to the lamprey, lake trout and burbot were the top predators. They fed primarily on seven species of chubs or ciscoes (Coregonids) and the deepwater sculpin (*Myoxocephalus thompsoni*). These prey species, in turn, relied for food on the larger members of the zooplankton, particularly *Mysis relicta* and *Diporeia hoyi*.

Neither the burbot nor the sculpin has been subjected to the concerted fishing pressure experienced by the trout or ciscoes. Sculpin are too small to be of commercial value, although some were caught in the early 1960s for use as animal food. Burbot, members of the cod family, have never been popular despite their large size and apparently good taste, although their livers were considered "a rare dish by experienced persons."[92] Fishermen catch them while seeking other fish and have destroyed many because there was no market. Burbots have suffered far more, however, because of lampreys, and sculpin fluctuate in line with alewives.

As whitefish stocks declined in the late 1800s, fishermen turned their attention to lake trout. By 1890, the trout became the most valuable fishery in Lake Michigan, a position it was to hold for fifty years. Although ever-increasing fishing pressure caused a slow decline in both numbers and size, this long-term stability was, perhaps, the most striking attribute of the lake trout fishery. (Research from Great Slave Lake in western Canada suggests that lake trout abundance is not nearly as cyclical as many other species.)[93]

Biologists generally agree that the lamprey onslaught caused the virtual if not complete extirpation of the lake trout in Lake Michigan. (Very recently, some scientists are suggesting that PCB pollution might have been a factor in lake trout declines as well.) There is, however, some debate as to whether overfishing contributed to the collapse. Stanford Smith points to Illinois, where trout production leapt from 259,000 pounds to 972,000 pounds between the years 1927–39 and 1940–44, an increase of 275 percent. He suggests that the overexploitation "may have been sufficient to initiate the decline of the lake trout stock, which then became weakened further by sea lamprey predation." Other writers have thought that Illinois constitutes too little of Lake Michigan to cause lakewide extermination but did believe that long-term overfishing was a factor. And still others argue that no "convincing evidence [exists] of overfishing in Lakes Huron and Michigan," and thus lampreys are the sole culprits.[94]

Whatever the causes behind it, lake trout had disappeared from Lake Michigan by 1956. But once lamprey control had proved to be effective, the Great Lakes Fishery Commission began coordinating efforts to reestablish lake trout. From 1965 to 1973, agencies placed an average of 2 million yearlings a year into Lake Michigan. The average increased during the 1976–94 period, when 2.46 million entered the lake annually.[95]

It was easy enough to establish a lake trout sports fishery: continue dumping huge numbers of fish into the lake for anglers to catch. This was the goal behind salmon stocking. But since lake trout were native species, biologists hoped to create self-sustaining populations that would facilitate replication of the prelamprey ecosystem.[96]

To increase the chances for success, lake trout were obtained from at least three different sources: Seneca Lake (New York), Lake Superior, and Green Lake (Wisconsin), where trout originating in Lake Michigan had been stocked decades earlier. These strains were all believed to lay eggs in deep water, thus making them easier to protect. Unfortunately, the inaccessibility of the deeper areas prevented biologists from finding eggs, even if the fish were spawning. Julian's Reef, for example, yielded females heavy with roe, but no one could confirm whether spawning had occurred.

Soon after arriving on the scene, Ellen Marsden decided that, at 125 feet, Julian's Reef was too deep to study adequately. She shifted her efforts to shallower areas. For two years she searched the shoreline for suitable substrate—cobble piles where lake trout deposit their eggs in the sheltered spaces between stones. When she found such sites, she placed egg-collecting equipment and discovered eggs at each one. Thus, Marsden had demonstrated that the ostensibly deep-spawning trout strains could lay eggs at depths of less than forty-five feet. More recently, she has found eggs at Julian Reef at 110 feet. But despite the presence of eggs, there is as yet no evidence that young fish are entering the population.

The fisheries biologists who began the work on reestablishing lake trout in the Great Lakes retired without seeing the fruition of their labors. Many had lost hope that those labors would, in fact, ever prove successful. But the tide may have begun to turn, and this splendid predator might once again be a reproducing member of Lake Michigan's fauna. It will have ample alewives for food, but most of the ciscoes on which it preyed for ten thousand years are now gone forever.

◄◦► ◄◦► ◄◦►

Of all the organisms within Lake Michigan, the deepwater ciscoes have suffered most profoundly. In 1974, the U.S. Fish and Wildlife Service stated that "the ciscoes of the Great Lakes probably represent the most significantly endangered fishery, the most significantly endangered fish populations, and the most significantly endangered combination of fish species in the freshwaters of the United States." At one time the dominant commercial fish of the Great Lakes, four are now biologically extinct, two are endangered, and only the smallest still survives in Lake Michigan in sufficient numbers to harvest.[97]

The deepwater ciscoes resemble one another so closely that "even present-day experts are confused."[98] It is understandable, therefore, why fishery data do not distinguish between them. Indeed, it wasn't until 1929, when

Walter Koelz published his great monograph on the group, that all the current species were even scientifically described. Ichthyologists have not unanimously agreed with his taxonomy, but most of the literature recognizes seven species of deepwater ciscoes.[99] (The lake whitefish and herring are also in this genus but tend to inhabit shallower water.) They fall into three size categories: blackfin (*Coregonus nigripinnis*) and *C. johannae* are the largest; shortjaw (*C. zenithicus*), longjaw (*C. alpenae*), shortnose (*C. reigardi*), and kiyi (*C. kiyi*) are intermediate; and bloater (*C. hoyi*) is the smallest.[100]

The cisco fishery began around 1869 in Grand Traverse Bay, Michigan, and had spread to Racine and other locations by the early 1880s.[101] Sold fresh or salted, cisco was popular primarily because it was inexpensive. That all changed, however, when C. H. Fischer of Milwaukee decided to smoke the nuisance ciscoes that filled his lake trout nets. Over the next decade, the demand for this new product burgeoned, a fact Koelz attributed to the "predilection for smoked fish of the Teutonic peoples." From Sheboygan, Wisconsin, to St. Joseph, Michigan, the southern part of Lake Michigan became a major fishing ground for ciscoes, with annual catches in excess of 10 million pounds. Most of these were undoubtedly blackfin and *johannae*.

Twenty years after it began, the fishery started to collapse. In response, the fishermen began using nets of smaller mesh size. Three-inch and $2^7/_8$-inch nets were replaced by those of $2^3/_4$ and $2^1/_2$ inches. By the end of the 1950s, some fishermen were using $2^3/_8$-inch nets, while others employed deepwater trawls with no restriction on mesh size.[102] With these adjustments, the industry again flourished, for now they could exploit the smaller species.

The impact of this intensive harvesting on specific cisco species was documented by the U.S. Bureau of Fisheries and the Fish and Wildlife Service. From 1930 to 1932, the bureau engaged in extensive sampling in various parts of Lake Michigan, including stations off Racine and Grand Haven, Michigan. While species abundance varied to some extent according to location, the blackfin and *johannae* were virtually gone. The bloater, kiyi, and shortnose were the most common.[103]

The Fish and Wildlife Service repeated the study in the years 1954 and 1955. Not only had fishing continued unabated, but lampreys had increased as well. The combination was devastating: the researchers failed to catch one single *johannae* or blackfin, and with one exception, the remaining species had declined by 63 percent. That one exception was the bloater.

Once part of a balanced ecosystem, the bloater found itself in a lake with few predators or competitors. And because the bloater grows at a slower rate than the other species, it can breed several times before it attains the ten inches in length that makes it vulnerable to lampreys and fishermen. Other ciscoes can breed only once or twice before reaching that size. Bloaters soared in abundance, and whereas fishermen used to discard them for being too small, they were now the mainstay of the fishery.

By 1964, 99 percent of all deepwater ciscoes taken by researchers were bloaters. The other species were being pummeled by growing numbers of alewives that both outcompeted them for food and preyed on their young. In addition, biologists began to notice that the few shortnose and kiyi still encountered "were not as distinct morphologically as formerly," their appearance suggesting hybridization with the bloater.[104] As if they didn't have enough difficulties, the surviving remnants of the larger species were being genetically swamped by the abundant bloater.

Some extinctions are well documented and accompanied by appropriate lamentations. Others occur with little comment and are remembered only by a few specialists. That human activity was solely or partially to blame for the global destruction of four species of ciscoes is a fact that should be recorded plainly. The last *johannae* was caught in Lake Huron off of Wolfsell, Ontario on August 4, 1952. The last blackfin cisco was caught in Lake Michigan off of Marinette, Wisconsin, on May 26, 1969.[105] The last longjaw cisco was caught in Georgian Bay, Ontario, on June 12, 1975. And finally, to conclude this litany of obituaries, the last shortnose cisco was caught in Lake Huron in 1985.[106] In addition to these four, the kiyi and the shortjaw are now gone from Lake Michigan, although still present elsewhere.

As for the bloaters, they have experienced fluctuations that seem to be inversely related to the fortunes of alewives. Currently, they are holding their own, but there is an ominous trend. Although individuals can live thirty years and spawn every year, little recruitment seems to be taking place, for people are finding few young. Most biologists believe that fry are not surviving, probably due to predation by alewives. No one knows for sure what is happening, but it is possible that the last of the deepwater ciscoes may be on the verge of a population crash.

Approaching the Way: Rivers and Small Lakes

He thought his happiness was complete when . . . suddenly he stood by the edge of a full-fed river. . . . The mole was bewitched, entranced, fascinated. By the side of the river he trotted as one trots, when very small, by the side of a man who holds one spellbound by exciting stories; and when tired at last, he sat on the bank, while the river still chattered on to him, a babbling procession of the best stories in the world, sent from the heart of the earth to be told at last to the insatiable sea. —Kenneth Grahame, *The Wind in the Willows* (1908)

Because water excels in benefiting the myriad creatures without contending with them and settles where none would like to be, it comes close to the way. —Lao Tzu, *Tao Te Ching* (late fourth or early third century B.C.)

Just as two great biomes come together here, so do two of the continent's principal watersheds. The rivers of the Chicago Lake Plain discharged into Lake Michigan. These include the Root, Pike, Chicago, Calumet, St. Joseph, Paw Paw, and Galien Rivers. The rest of the region is in the Mississippi River drainage.

Three tributaries of the Mississippi receive water from the area. The Rock River draws from McHenry and Kane counties via the Kishwaukee and Piscataw Rivers and from Walworth County via Turtle Creek and the Bark River. The Ohio River drains the four small parts of Jasper and Starke counties that lie within the Tippecanoe River watershed. But most of the region contributes water to the Illinois River.

The Illinois River begins here, at the confluence of the Des Plaines and Kankakee Rivers near Morris, Grundy County. The Des Plaines takes form near Union Grove in southern Racine County and is fed by Mill Creek, Salt Creek, Hickory Creek, and, its largest tributary, the DuPage River. The

Kankakee River starts near South Bend, Indiana, and flows west, picking up the waters of the Yellow River, Rock Creek, Prairie Creek, and the Iroquois River.

Starting north of the region in Waukesha County, Wisconsin, the Fox River is the third largest tributary of the Illinois. It accepts the White River, Nippersink Creek, Flint Creek, Big Rock Creek, and Aux Sable Creek before entering the Illinois in LaSalle County. Also contributing to its flows are the numerous lakes in its upper stretches, including Lake Geneva, Lake Delavan, the Chain O' Lakes, Cedar Lake, Deep Lake, and Elizabeth Lake.

Rivers in Flux

Influenced by beer commercials or trips to the Rocky Mountains, some people imagine the rivers of the Chicago region to have been torrents of clear water cascading year round over rocky bottoms. And some of the smaller rivers might have approached such scenes. Hickory Creek, for example, a tributary of the Des Plaines flowing through Cook and Will Counties, looked like this in the late 1830s: "Hickory Creek was a well behaved stream which never failed to furnish abundant water for cattle farmers and the mills, some of which operated year round. It was a well defined body of water lasting the whole year. It was well stocked with fish of the pickerel and pike species, with bullhead and catfish."[1]

In reality, many of the larger rivers were often little more than marshy swales that dried up in summer. As the early commentators make clear, negotiating many of these waterways was difficult or impossible for most of the year. La Salle, writing in the 1680s, says that "the Chicago River is not even navigable for canoes, except after [the spring] flood." Even at its mouth, the Chicago was a stream "ten to fifteen yards wide, and only a few inches deep."[2]

Describing the mouth of the Des Plaines in 1721, Father Charlevoix comes close to capturing in a single image the essence of the Chicago Region prior to settlement: a bison fording a river so shallow that the water barely reached its knees. During one drought year, Gurdon Hubbard found that there were segments of the Des Plaines that he could cross without dampening the soles of his feet. During the summer even the Illinois River was unnavigable upstream of Starved Rock in LaSalle County, a distance of thirty miles from its origin.[3]

William Darby visited the region in 1818 and had this to say about the rivers: "The Chicago and the [Des Plaines] . . . have not the character of streams, but of canals; the water hardly moves in their deep and narrow channels. The Illinois itself is more a canal than a river, having hardly current enough to bend the lofty grass which grows in its bed."[4]

The early conditions of the Chicago and Des Plaines Rivers are better

documented than perhaps any other, thanks to a lawsuit filed by the U.S. Department of the Army against the Economy Power and Light Company in
1904. At issue was whether the Des Plaines River was navigable and thus
under federal jurisdiction. Both litigants poured tremendous resources into
the proceedings, and produced what has been called the most comprehensive
study ever made of a river.[5]

In addition to travelers' descriptions, the case made use of readings derived from a depth gauge installed at Riverside, Cook County, in 1886 and still
in operation. From 1886 to 1904, the river on average discharged water at levels that were less than measurable for ninety-two days of the year. For "an additional 117 days per year the river had 60 cubic feet per second or less discharge which was equal to a depth of less than 3 inches."[6] Thus for 209 days of
the year, the Des Plaines had little or no water.

Ecologist Steve Apfelbaum took the above data and compared it with the
period from 1943 to 1988. He found that median discharges increased from
four cubic feet per second to seven to eight hundred cubic feet per second.
Flows also changed dramatically: high flows increased in frequency from an
average of 1.5 per year to the current three to five; median flow levels increased
by four hundred times; and low flows are now 250 times higher.

These greater flows reflect changes in the watershed. Six hundred and
thirty-three square miles feed the Des Plaines at Riverside, Cook County.
Apfelbaum estimates that by the late 1800s "about 40% of the watershed had
been tilled and/or developed [while] at present approximately 70–80% of the
watershed is developed or under annually tilled agricultural land-uses." So long
as the land was spongy marshland, prairie, and woods, little precipitation left
the region via the river. Sixty to 70 percent "was lost through evaporation or
evapotranspiration" and much of the remainder gradually seeped into streams
and wetlands. But the river has been gaining water steadily as once absorbent
surfaces become veneered with pavement and other impermeable coverings.

◄○► ◄○► ◄○►

There were at least two low places where floodwaters breached the divide between the Mississippi and the Great Lakes. The marsh that gives birth to the
Des Plaines also shares its water with the Root River. Farther south, near Maywood, Cook County, the Des Plaines enters a small portion of the Chicago
Lake Plain. Here there was a slough called Mud Lake, which routinely served
as a conduit allowing heavy flows of the Des Plaines to escape into the south
fork of the Chicago River.

As early as 1673, Louis Joliet suggested that the digging of a canal
through Mud Lake would create an unbroken waterway between the Illinois

River and Lake Michigan.[7] The need for such an undertaking was manifest to every trader who had to cross Mud Lake during periods of low water. Gurdon Hubbard described what it was like in 1818:

> We remained [in Chicago] about a week to rest our men and prepare for the fatigue and hardships of crossing our boats and goods to the Des Plaines River. Our goods were transported across the prairie on the backs of our boatmen. The boats thus lightened were passed through the eastern outlet of and into Mud Lake, known now as Ogden's Ditch. This lake was well named; it was but a scum of liquid mud, a foot or more deep, over which our boats were slid, not floated over, men wading each side without firm footing, but often sinking deep in this filthy mire, filled with bloodsuckers, which attached themselves in quantities to their legs. Three days were consumed in passing through this sinkhole of only one or two miles in length.[8]

On March 30, 1822, Congress gave the state of Illinois permission to begin a canal through lands still in federal ownership and appropriated $10,000 for the surveys necessary to begin the project. But political wrangling, changes in route, and substantial increases in cost all contributed to delays that plagued the effort. It wasn't until July 4, 1836, that construction of the Illinois and Michigan Canal was finally authorized. Far more ambitious than Joliet's vision of a 1.5-mile-long channel, the canal as built extended ninety-six miles from the town of LaSalle, Illinois, to Bridgeport in Chicago. The city and state spent nearly $10 million on the project, two-thirds of which was raised by selling public land. And although its construction proved far more arduous than its supporters could have guessed, the canal's completion in 1848 did spur tremendous growth of the local economy.[9] (At the same time, a series of other canals was being constructed throughout the eastern Great Lakes that also facilitated the east-west flow of materials.)

Commerce would not be the only use to which the canal was put. All living things must ingest varying amounts of water. All living things also produce and dispose of waste. Chicago's conundrum was that Lake Michigan served both as its tap and its toilet (either directly or via the Chicago River). As the city's population grew, this flaw in the system became deadly obvious. One early (1871) attempt at a solution was to send the effluent through the Illinois and Michigan Canal into the Des Plaines and then the Illinois River. Its effect on the Illinois River and its tributaries was spectacular:

> When the current of the Chicago River was first turned through the canal and the rivers, it caused the fish in them to bloat to a large size, and rising

to the surface they floated down the stream in large numbers. It was estimated at the time that several tons of dead fish passed through one of the canal-locks just after the foul water commenced running through the canal.

When these bloated fish chanced to float into the clear water at the mouth of some tributary of the river they would revive and swim up the clear stream. Such large numbers of the fish revived in this manner that all the small streams flowing into the Des Plaines and Kankakee rivers were filled with fish in such numbers that many were taken with hook and line, one man taking over 300 in a day. . . .

When the spring freshets occur, the current is so rapid and the amount of pure water in the river is so great, that the foul water does not have much effect upon the fishes, and large numbers of the species mentioned ascend the rivers and are caught with hook and line. Later in the season as the water subsides, and the water from Chicago River predominates, the fish which came up in the spring die and are floated down the river. In July and August when the water is the worst even the mud turtles leave the river in disgust and seek less odorous homes. . . . [Bowfin] are the last to die. Next to this species the [brown] bullhead are the longest lived, but finally they succumb and are floated down like their predecessors.[10]

Although routing sewage through the Illinois and Michigan Canal provided some relief to Chicago's problem, canal hydraulics were a barrier to the long-term remedy that the city sought. Waterborne diseases remained at epidemic levels. At its worst in 1891, the death rate due to typhoid fever reached 172 per hundred thousand population.[11] So long as the waste disposal problem remained, Chicago's future was in jeopardy.

In response to the ongoing crisis, the state legislature created, in 1889, the Sanitary District of Chicago to, quite literally, save Chicago.[12] (That a separate entity was formed reflected Springfield's distrust of Chicago's politicians.) The district immediately began work on the Sanitary and Ship Canal (or Main Channel), which it completed in 1900. Stretching twenty-eight miles between the South Branch of the Chicago River at Damen Avenue in Chicago and the Des Plaines River at Lockport, this channel in essence reversed the flow of the Chicago River so that it became a tributary of the Des Plaines and Illinois rather than Lake Michigan. To increase the canal's effectiveness, district engineers straightened thirteen miles of the Des Plaines.

Lake Michigan and the people of Chicago benefited tremendously from this engineering triumph. For decades after this, however, the upper stretches of the Illinois River remained virtually bereft of life. Stephen Forbes and Robert Richardson of the Illinois Natural History Survey studied the river extensively in 1911 and 1912.[13] They took bottom sediment near Morris,

Grundy County, and found only sludge worms (Tubificidae), an organism that can thrive where oxygen levels are so low that literally every other animal is dead. The sediment was chemically tested and compared with sludge obtained from the septic tanks of two municipal sewage systems. There was less oxygen and more carbon dioxide in the river sludge.

During the winter and summer of 1912, the two scientists engaged in intensive fish sampling at Morris, an activity that included the detonation of twenty half-pound sticks of dynamite. Their efforts produced a few emerald shiners (*Notropis atherinoides*), five black bullheads (*Ictalurus melas*—some of which "were 'fungused'"), one rock bass (*Ambloplites rupestris*), and one bluegill (*Lepomis macrochirus*), all of which were taken near the mouth of Mazon Creek. Seventeen years later, Natural History Survey biologist David Thompson could still report that "there are no fishes of any kind above Utica [in eastern LaSalle County]." It wasn't until the sanitary district commenced effluent treatment in the 1920s that the Illinois River began to heal.

From 1900 to 1920, the district constructed two more channels. The North Shore Channel runs from Wilmette Harbor to the North Branch of the Chicago River at Lawrence Avenue in Chicago, and the Calumet-Sag Channel goes from the Little Calumet River just east of Blue Island to the Sanitary and Ship Canal. Thus, like the Chicago River, the Calumet River was also shunted into the Illinois drainage. Because of these changes, very little of Illinois is any longer in the Lake Michigan watershed.[14]

At the Lake Michigan end of all three waterways, the district installed locks to control flow. These allow the diversion of Lake Michigan water to flush the channels in the desired direction, as well as to dilute the sewage to reduce downstream effects. They also enable the district to discharge sewage overflows into the lake during storms.

The channel system was the main element in the dilution approach to waste water ("dilution is the solution to pollution"). But the ever-greater demands placed on the district by growing population and industry required that it find new techniques. In addition, the federal government, Canada, and other states began challenging the district's diversion of Lake Michigan water.

In the face of these pressures, the district began treating waste water to remove impurities prior to release.[15] It became a world leader in developing treatment methodologies and was subjecting all waste water to secondary treatment by 1940, decades before it became mandatory under federal and state law. When the oxygen content is too low, the Illinois Pollution Control Board now requires the district to run flows through artificial instream aeration systems to increase directly the dissolved oxygen levels in the waterways.

The district's remaining challenge was to overcome the inability to handle major rain events, which create combined sewer overflows that discharge the equivalent of raw waste from 1 million people per day into the waterways. In the 1970s, the district therefore launched the highly ambitious $3.8 billion Tunnel and Reservoir Plan, better known as the Deep Tunnel project. The purpose of this project is to collect overflows in a series of huge tunnels and reservoirs until the water can be processed in district facilities.

These efforts have dramatically improved the quality of the district's waterways. In the North Shore Channel, for example, until the early 1980s the benthic fauna consisted almost entirely of sludge worms and midge larvae. But when the district began aerating the water and stopped adding chlorine, snails, fingernail clams, leeches, and other invertebrates appeared as evidence of a recovering ecosystem. Even more striking is the increase that has occurred in fish species. From the period 1974–77 to 1988–91, the fish recorded in the Chicago Sanitary and Ship Canal went from three species to twenty-two, and other district waterways experienced similar gains.[16]

Focusing on point-source emissions, federal and state water pollution laws have successfully reduced many of the most insidious discharges. But regulations have lagged behind in the control of non-point-source runoff. Sediments and chemical residues wash into waterways to the detriment of aquatic biota and pose one of the major threats to the continued existence of many local species (e.g., native mussels). This is of particular concern in agricultural areas. Research has shown that strips of riparian vegetation as narrow as twenty-five or thirty feet can block 80 percent of incoming phosphates and nitrates, but changing human behavior can be a slow process.[17] Perhaps ironically, the waters that were most degraded in the early years of urban pollution have experienced the greatest improvements, while waters only more recently disturbed by agriculture and construction continue to decrease in quality as runoff proceeds without controls.

The water column is only part of the aquatic habitat, however. Much more difficult to clean up is the bottom sediment, with decades worth of accumulated pollutants. Benthic organisms that make their living on the bottom, particularly the less mobile invertebrates, are often absent or represented by few species.

Channelization has harmed many waterways by increasing siltation and destroying habitat diversity. In May 1972, the then Illinois Department of Conservation tabulated all the miles of channelized streams in the state and arrived at a total of 8,129. The extent of channelization in northeastern Illinois can be seen from the following sample of counties: Cook County— 184.3 miles; Kane County—152 miles; Kankakee County—340.7 miles (third most in the state); and McHenry County—257.6 miles (sixth most in the state). These figures do not reflect the actual damage that ditching entails, for the removal of meanders may reduce the length of a stream by as much as one-half.[18]

The Indiana portion of the Kankakee River is entirely channelized and appears on some maps as a series of ditches (see chap. 9). This holds special significance for the Kankakee, because it had the most extensive floodplain of any local river. Ecologist Thomas Kwak explains: "Twenty-five fish species have been associated with the floodplain of the Kankakee River near the Momence Wetlands. A high proportion of juveniles (55%) and the tendency of juveniles of some species to remain in isolated backwaters demonstrated the value of the Kankakee River floodplain as spawning and nursery habitats."[19]

Dams inflict a host of challenges on river organisms. At their least subtle, dams turn rivers into lakes. In fact many larger rivers are now less rivers than "a series of impoundments."[20] They also block the movement of organisms, create extremes in flow that exceed what many organisms can tolerate, and alter water temperature. The Illinois, Des Plaines, Kankakee, Fox, and others have dams of various sizes and configurations.

Even the scientific management of lakes and rivers has traditionally benefited a few popular fish to the great detriment of the rest. Fisheries biologists have treated these waterways as farms rather than ecosystems. They have introduced huge numbers of predatory game fish (trout, bass, pike, etc.) into waterways without much regard for the consequences. Nongame species become "rough fish," considered only as food for game fish or, worse, pests to be eliminated.

The most extreme measure employed by fishery managers is "rehabilitation," a euphemism for poisoning lakes and rivers with rotenone and other toxicants that are indiscriminant in what they kill. The idea of sterilizing a terrestrial site because of a problem species is unthinkable: no one would suggest plowing up Markham Prairie because white sweet clover is present on the edges. During the early 1970s, over two thousand miles of streams and a hundred thousand acres of marsh within the Rock River watershed in Wisconsin received doses of the poison antimycin A. (Antimycin A is no longer approved for such uses.) Follow-up studies found that the program effectively reduced not only the targeted carp, but (oops!) also the game fish. Black bullhead remained the only species still being caught in reasonable numbers. To fix the unintended consequences of such programs, game fish are restocked, but very little time or money is spent reintroducing the other piscine casualties. Fortunately (one hopes) such poisoning campaigns are now being conducted with greater circumspection and are increasingly limited to small artificial lakes that were stocked to begin with. This reflects a combination of new attitudes, endangered species laws, and the high cost of biocides. (Rotenone sells for $35 a gallon.) But as the rotenone poisonings of Lake Delavan, Walworth County, in 1989 and Eagle Lake, Racine County, in 1991 demonstrate, old practices are tough to rehabilitate.[21]

Despite all the abuses to which they are subjected, rivers remain very difficult to kill. Their long tendrils reach areas that have not yet been rendered unfit for aquatic organisms. And so long as these stretches of headwater streams act as refugia for conservative species, recolonization of former haunts is possible.[22]

Current Affairs: River Ecology

Flowing waters are characterized in a number of ways.[23] From a nonbiotic perspective, streams are often classified by order, first through fifth. One head-water stream is a first order; when it joins another of equal or higher order the resulting stream becomes a second order, and so forth.

With respect to biota, the ordination of aquatic communities in general is not nearly as well established as it is for terrestrial ecosystems. This is par-ticularly true of streams, due in part to the numerous and shifting variables that influence the composition and distribution of its inhabitants.

Being cold-blooded, the animals of these aquatic environments can be very sensitive to water temperature, which is affected by air temperature, shade, water origin (springs vs. marsh), depth, movement, wind, currents, and thermal pollution due to direct discharges. Aquatic insects such as deerflies, mayflies, and winter stoneflies suffer decreased larval development as well as the possibility of delayed adult emergences when subjected to cold weather. Metabolic rates for fish can double with every increase in water temperature of 18°F. This can be particularly stressful because, with warming, the water loses its capacity to retain oxygen just when the fish require more.[24]

Gradient is another critical factor that has an impact on aquatic organ-isms. The speed with which water moves is an important variable unto itself, but in addition it affects oxygen content and substrate type. As the slope of a stream decreases, so does the particle size lining its bed. Thus, the stony riffles characteristic of upstream segments disappear as the water gains in volume and loses velocity downstream. Organisms have to adjust accordingly: some attach themselves under rocks, some bury into mud and silt, and still others survive on the surface of sheltered pools. Something is adapted to every possible niche.

Still another variable is riparian vegetation. Arching trees limit light, and the patterns of shadow help determine where aquatic plants and animals situ-ate themselves. This applies both to depth and distance from shore. Per-haps even more important is the organic contribution made by terrestrial organisms. From newly fallen leaves to rotting wood to indistinguishable detritus, vegetable debris feeds many varieties of aquatic invertebrates. Among the groups that avail themselves to this sustenance are caddis fly larvae, midges, stoneflies, and crayfish. Providence from the shore also includes numerous animals that become prey for both surface and benthic feeding fish.

Considering these and other physical factors, P. S. Maitland underlines the difficulties in classifying aquatic ecosystems: "Some species are limited by temperature, others by substrate, amount of suspended matter, calcium, etc. Not only are those factors usually transitional in themselves from the extremes normally found at source and mouth, but if by chance there is a sharp change in one of them . . . there would rarely be a change in any of the others at the same point. Thus the general theme of the change in biotic associations from source to mouth in a river will tend to be one not of zonation but transition."[25]

Creatures adapted to life under water do not spring forth upon the rain's first contact with the earth. Some moisture must linger before distinctively aquatic organisms have an opportunity to colonize. When the water's force is sufficient to scour a channel deep enough to hold such moisture, blackflies (*Simulium*) and mayflies may appear. These are insects that spend their youth in water and their maturity in the air. Often, however, these temporary wet places dry up before the inhabitants can escape. (In the following discussion, a species is mentioned where it first appears in the continuum; many are found in a range of waters, from the first permanent pools and first-order streams to large rivers and lakes.)

The first permanent water in a budding stream is naturally a pool, a depression capable of holding water until the next downpour replenishes it. These pools are subject to great variations in water volume and temperature and attendant oxygen levels. The species that establish themselves here are all hardy and well adapted to the changing conditions.

Insects such as dragonflies (*Aeshna constricta* and *Cordulegaster obliquus*), predaceous diving beetles (Dytiscidae), and crane flies appear, all of which possess wings as adults. The beetles (both as adults and larvae) are particularly noteworthy for their predatory behavior, routinely attacking prey much larger than themselves such as minnows and tadpoles. The brook amphipod (*Gammarus fasciatus*) and the sow bug (*Asellus communis*), which are also present, can bury into wet vegetation during times of drought. All of these species are able to move against the current, a necessity in times of heavy flow.

These pools also attract several species of fish, including johnny darter (*Etheostoma nigrum*), blacknose dace (*Rhinichthys atratulus*), southern redbelly

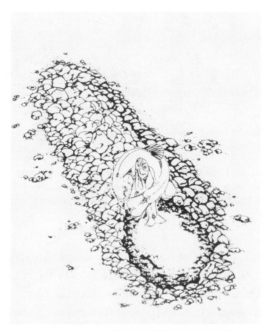

44. Typical pit ridge nest of creek chub with breeding fish;
drawing by M. Sabaj. (Courtesy M. Sabaj and Academy of
Natural Sciences, Philadelphia.)

dace (*Phoxinus erythrogaster*), and creek chub (*Semotilus atromaculatus*). Of
these, the creek chub is often the first pioneer. Twenty-eight percent of the
Wisconsin streams that contained creek chubs were less than six feet wide.
That this species can thrive in marginal habitats has enabled it to increase in
population and range as anthropogenic changes have reduced predators, less-
ened flows, and raised turbidity levels of many streams.[26]

One reason that the creek chub may be doing so well is that it constructs
an elaborate nest to shelter its eggs: "Prolonged activity forms a ridge of gravel
one to several feet long and about a foot wide covering a previously excavated
trench and a shallow pit (newest section of the trench) just downstream to the
ridge. . . . Spawning occurs when a female enters the nest and approaches the
male, which clasps her between pectoral fin and body. . . . Since spawnings are
interspersed with nest-building the eggs become imbedded in a shallow gravel
pile that probably deters predators . . . and protects the eggs from sediments."[27]

Two other pioneering animals that share the first permanent water are
the northern clearwater crayfish (*Orconectes propinquus*) and the virile crayfish
(*Orconectes virilis*).[28] Both can live in an extraordinarily wide range of waters,
from the pristine to polluted, and from small pools to the depths of Lake
Michigan. Indeed, the virile crayfish is the most common crayfish in Illinois.
Unfortunately, both are now giving way to the newly introduced rusty crayfish

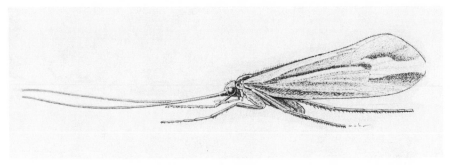

45. Adult caddis fly *Hesperophylax designatus*, a locally rare species
restricted to spring-brooks with high-quality water, such as those found
at Trout Park, Elgin, Kane County. (From Ross 1944. Courtesy Illinois
Natural History Survey, Champaign.)

(*Orconectes rusticus*). A native of Kentucky and Ohio, this species grows more rapidly, is larger, and behaves more aggressively than the native crayfish.

The intermittent stream becomes permanent as its drainage area grows and other streams merge with it. As part of this process, a phenomenon known as stream capture (or stream piracy) often occurs. Through erosion, one stream will breach the divide separating it from another, thus enabling one flow to capture the other. This also allows fish to traverse drainage divides and move from one stream to another.[29]

Another scenario of stream development avoids the intermittent stage altogether. These flows originate, instead, from permanent water sources, such as marshes, lakes, or springs. Springs, because they are cold and heavily laden with minerals, support their own characteristic assemblage of organisms. The pearl dace (*Margariscus margarita*) is a fish that is locally known only from springs in Walworth County.[30]

With its numerous brooks, springs, and seeps, Trout Park Nature Preserve, Kane County, provides an excellent example of the spring brook community. It harbors at least forty-eight taxa of macroinvertebrates, including three caddis flies not found elsewhere in Illinois: *Glossosoma intermedium*, *Hesperophylax designatus*, and *Wormaldia moesta*. Dilution by surface water, however, soon begins to erase the distinctiveness of the spring brook community.[31]

With year-round water, sufficient grade, and a substrate composed of varying sized particles, the classic riffle-and-pool configuration often develops. This alternation of shallow and deep water maximizes types of habitat.[32] In smaller streams, it is easy for species to cross from one patch of preferred habitat to another, thus blurring the distinction between the two communities. But in larger streams, the extent of each habitat is greater and thus more discrete.

The riffles are layered. Finer gravels on the bottom trap increasingly larger stones so that even boulders may appear on the surface layer. Because these bars tend to angle toward one bank or another, the stream curves as well, creating even greater variations in habitat. Pools, in contrast, are lined with gravel and sand that provide fewer spaces for bottom fish and invertebrates to inhabit. The more uniform substrate results in a reduction in both the abundance and diversity of species. This tendency is stronger in disturbed watersheds, where heavy silt loads settle to the pool bottoms, further reducing habitat. Providing a counterweight of sorts, the greater depth supports a larger variety of mussels and a fish fauna more characteristic of sluggish waters downstream.

As the flow increases, various anchored plants begin to appear. *Cladophora*, *Nuphar*, and *Chara* cling to submerged rocks, and the nonnative watercress (*Nasturtium officinale*) lines the channel along narrow springs. Where there is enough calm and clear water, pondweeds (*Potamogeton*) can sprout.

Swift-moving water provides habitat for invertebrates that require highly oxygenated water. Survival in the fast lane, however, means that animals have to prevent themselves from being at the total mercy of their medium and washing away. Some, like midges (*Chironomidae*), prefer sheltered stream edges where they can feed more easily. In many streams, midges are the most abundant insects, providing so much food for other species that it drives the ecosystem.[33]

Other species have evolved highly specialized adaptations. The river snail (*Elimia livescens*) has a large shell to act as ballast and a powerful foot that adheres tightly to the flat surface of rocks, enabling it to travel upstream in the face of forty-inch-per-second flows. Certain blackfly (*Simulium*) larvae have

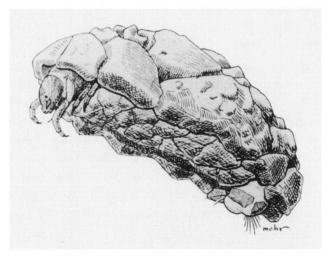

46. Larval caddis fly *Glossosoma intermedium*, a locally rare species that encases itself in stones. (From Ross 1944. Courtesy Illinois Natural History Survey, Champaign.)

the ability to secrete a sticky web that secures the animal to its rocky base. In times of flood, as its anchorage becomes precarious, it can double over and encase itself into a tight cocoon-like ball that provides even further protection. Perhaps most remarkable, however, the blackfly has a backup in the form of a safety line, another thread that connects to the rock. If, despite all of its precautions, the larva finds itself adrift, it can work its way back to home via its line.

Caddis flies (Trichoptera), a common group in fast streams, cling to the irregular surfaces of rocks with their claws. They further resist the current, and gain protection from predators as well, by encasing themselves in a sheath of pebbles, sand, and/or plant material. Some species utilize fairly heavy stones, arranging the largest ones toward its front. Thus, if they are pried loose, "they merely slide off the stone and fall into sheltered dead water."[34] One family (Hydropsychidae) also spins webs, which can be thick enough to clog water passages. The principal purpose of these webs, however, is as seines, trapping food items hurling through the water.

A larger group of animals resides under or among the stones. The larvae of various mayflies (*Heptageninae*), damselflies (Zygoptera), and stoneflies (Plecoptera) all wriggle their way under rocks. The round and flat water penny beetle (*Psephenus herricki*) sticks to its rock like a suction cup, head and legs concealed. Numerous small spikes rim its body to strengthen the seal further. The inconspicuous sponges (Porifera) also prefer the undersides of rocks, which provide shelter from drought, strong currents, and scouring. Should they be wiped clean from the surface of logs or rocks, their immobility makes it difficult for them to recolonize lost territory.

Fish must also adapt themselves to fast water. Inhabiting the bottom (benthos), whether in the riffles or the pools, the darters are the group most characteristic of this habitat. Streamlined in shape, they have well-developed pectoral and anal fins that give them footing, if you will, on the coarse bottom. Even more profound, perhaps, darters have air bladders much smaller than most fish. This is the organ that enables fish to control their buoyancy. But the option of rising or falling in the water column is unnecessary to most darters.

Darters have long fascinated ichthyologists, including pioneering ecologist Stephen Forbes, the first director of the Illinois Natural History Survey. In his and Robert Richardson's classic *Fishes of Illinois*, he alludes to their small size and brilliant coloration by saying, "they are to the fishes of North America what hummingbirds are to the birds of South America." At another place, he writes this about the darters:

> These are the mountaineers of fish. Forced from the populous and fertile
> valleys of the riverbeds and lake bottoms, they have taken refuge from their

47. Johnny darter, a widespread species able to live in a diverse range
of habitats, from streams to Lake Michigan. (Courtesy Lawrence Page,
Illinois Natural History Survey, Champaign.)

enemies in the rocky highlands, where the free waters play in ceaseless torrents, and where they have wrested from stubborn nature a meager living.
Although diminished in size by their constant struggle with the elements,
they have developed an activity and hardihood, a vigor of life and a glow of
high color, almost unknown among the easier livers of the lower lands.
Notwithstanding their trivial size, they do not seem to be dwarfed so much
as concentrated fish.[35]

Shallow streams afford an unusual opportunity to actually see fish. An interesting array of species is often visible around nests of the hornyhead chub
(*Nocomis biguttatus*). This fish collects small pebbles and deposits them in shallow depressions, either preexisting or of the chub's own making. Spawning and
nest building proceed alternately so that eggs become sheltered soon after they
are laid. Because these piles of marble-sized gravel are often the only clean
patches in the stream, other species also lay their eggs there. In April and May,
red shiners (*Cyprinella lutrensis*) and redfin shiners (*Lythrurus umbratilis*) swarm
over chub nests, punctuating the gray mounds with glints of rose. Blacknose
dace (*Rhinichthys atratulus*), central stoneroller (*Campostoma anomalum*), rosy-
face shiner (*Notropis rubellus*), and common shiner (*Luxilus cornutus*) also deposit eggs in the gravel heaps.

Of the species that take advantage of the chub's labor, the common shiner
is unique in assisting the chub in protection of the nest. It doesn't gather gravel,
but when the chub is so engaged it stays at the nest and drives away small in-
truders such as other species of shiners. The chub takes on more formidable
adversaries, even those four times its size: "A hog sucker . . . crept slowly up on
a chub nest; its protective markings seemed to conceal it from the guarding fish
for a time, but suddenly it was noticed by the male hornyhead, which was carrying stones. The hornyhead immediately gave the sucker a blow on the side
of the head with his tubercle-roughened snout of sufficient force to send the

sucker several centimeters over to one side. A few more blows started the sucker on an upstream retreat, with the hornyhead following for four or more meters."[36]

Of the various aquatic habitats that once graced this region, the rarest may be streams that have the combination of clear water, vegetation, and soft substrates of sand and mud. The brassy minnow (*Hybognathus hankinsoni*) is a characteristic species of this environment and has declined precipitously as these waterways became choked with vast amounts of silt.

Ichthyologist Greg Seegert has made a special effort to locate brassy minnows in Illinois.[37] It remains secure in other parts of Wisconsin but hasn't been recorded from any of the three counties of this region since specimens were taken from four streams in Walworth County during the 1970s. In 1976, one specimen was collected in Jelkes Creek, a small tributary of the Fox River in Kane County, and in earlier years the species had been found in Poplar Creek in northwest Cook County. All told, the brassy minnow was known historically from about twenty sites in Illinois, but Seegert found it only twice. One location that had formerly held the species, a tributary of the Kishwaukee River in McHenry County, looked extremely promising, complete with vegetation and a sandy bottom. Seegert put on his waders, stepped into the water, and sank to his chest in unconsolidated silt! The entire stream was like that.

Pools, with depths of ten feet, support a different composition of species. Among insects, inhabitants include midge larvae (*Chironomus*), lancet clubtail (*Gomphus exilis*), and burrowing mayfly (*Hexagenia*). Mollusks are well represented there, with several genera of snails and nine or ten species of mussels.

The fish fauna of the larger pools and sluggish rivers is similar, and even share much in common with lakes. One of the richest segments of this habitat is a two-mile stretch of the Kankakee River near Custer Park, Will County. (This is downstream of the historic marsh discussed in chap. 9.) Michael Sule and Thomas Skelly studied the site for five years and found seventy species, only nineteen less than all the fish that have ever been recorded in the entire watershed. The list spans the gamut from the most common to the rarest.[38]

About a third of the Kankakee's fishes are considered to be ecologically sensitive.[39] The northern brook lamprey (*Ichthyomyzon fossor*), pallid shiner (*Notropis amnis*), weed shiner (*Notropis texanus*), and western sand darter (*Ammocrypta clara*) are state endangered and the ironcolor shiner (*Notropis chalybaeus*), blacknose shiner (*Notropis heterolepis*), and river redhorse (*Moxostoma carinatum*) are state threatened. The lamprey and the blacknose shiner, however, haven't been found in the river in over twenty years and so may be extirpated.

Two of the rarest and most elusive of this group are the western sand darter and the pallid shiner. Despite many efforts over the years to sample the Kankakee's fish population, Greg Seegert is the only person ever to find the western sand darter in the river.[40] (The closest population is in the main stem of the Mississippi River.) Even though he has searched for it intensively, he has only caught it three times. The first was completely accidental, a larval specimen sucked up by the Braidwood Nuclear Power Plant. Two adults were later caught together off a sandbar downstream of Wilmington. Seegert surmises that the population must be very small and in deep water where seining is not practical.

The pallid shiner is a poorly known species that has largely disappeared from the northern portion of its range. By the 1990s, the species' territory in Wisconsin had contracted to a small area near LaCrosse, in the far western part of the state. It disappeared from Missouri in a period of under twenty years. With the use of rotenone, fourteen individuals were collected from one location on the Yellow River near Knox, Starke County, in June of 1971. The only records of its presence in this part of Illinois were of three specimens taken at Berwyn, Cook County, in 1900 and eight in the Kankakee River near Ritchie, Will County, in 1963. For fifteen years, no one found it in Illinois, and many thought it extirpated. But in 1978 Michael Sule caught one at his study site near Custer Park. Additional work has determined that a small population survives on a short segment of river. They appear to prefer warm and shallow water that moves slowly over a bottom of sand and silt.[41]

Because they receive contaminants from throughout the watershed, large rivers like the Kankakee are populated by the fish most tolerant of adverse water conditions. These include some of the best-known species: black bullhead, rock bass, largemouth bass (*Micropterus salmoides*), bluegill (*Lepomis macrochirus*), several sunfish species, and the introduced common carp (*Cyprinus carpio*).

Many fish are limited in their abundance by the scarcity of adequate spawning sites. What makes the bluegill, sunfish, and bass successful is that they build their own nests. By fanning away silt with their tails, they create a clean microhabitat. They also aggressively defend the nest, further increasing chances for successful reproduction.

The black bullhead is widespread because it thrives in streams of virtually all widths and substrates, be it sand, gravel, mud, or silt. Its ability to survive in seemingly marginal habitats is illustrated by one of the first discussions of the species' behavior to appear in the scientific literature: "During the early summer of 1899 I was able to make some further observations on the habits of the larvae. In one of the drainage ditches on Cottage Grove Ave., Chicago, they were so numerous that in walking a distance of a hundred yards one would see from seventy to eighty schools. The larvae are usually huddled so closely together that they form a dark mass, which at a distance appears as a shadow moving to and from. They rarely move in straight paths, but are ever circling, apparently in quest of food."[42]

In many of the region's waters, the carp is likely to be the most conspicuous (and, to some, infamous) fish. It thrives in all sizes of rivers and lakes (including Lake Michigan), making it highly accessible to many anglers. In spring, during spawning, they are a common sight as they thrash the surface of shallow waters throughout the area. As I waded along a flooded road next to the Fox River one June morning, I felt them bumping into my legs. Ironically, though now considered a nuisance by many, this Eurasian native was enthusiastically introduced for food and recreation.

The U.S. Fish Commission started the process by importing 345 carp from Germany in 1877. Progeny of these fish arrived in Michigan, Illinois, and Indiana two years later. A single female carp, depending on her age and size, can produce up to 2,208,000 eggs a season. Hatcheries were thus able to raise enough fish in six years to introduce 30,900 into the Fox, Des Plaines, and Illinois Rivers. Wisconsin received its first batch in 1880 and began releasing fish in 1881. The introductions peaked in 1890 when thirty-five thousand carp were liberated into the waters of the state.[43]

In those early years, there seems to have been little or no carping in reaction to the establishment of the species. A number of testimonials from the time are so out of sync with contemporary ideas as to be both comical and sad. One Colorado Fish Commissioner suggested damming small streams where carp could be raised "after extermination of the inferior native trout." Increase Lapham of the University of Wisconsin stated his support of the carp thus: "The day will come when the people of the state [Wisconsin] will thank the men who have introduced and planted this extra fine species of fish."[44]

If that day ever did arrive, it passed quickly. By the 1890s, stocking programs were truncated severely, as criticism mounted. Forbes and Richardson listed the four major objections to carp: "Carp roil the water and spoil the breeding and feeding grounds of other fish; that they eat the spawn of other fish and prevent the nesting of such species as bass and sunfishes; that they spoil the feeding grounds of water birds by eating and rooting up the wild rice and other aquatic plants; and, that they are of no value as either a food or game fish."[45]

Forbes and Richardson evaluated these issues at some length before eventually coming down in favor of the carp for economic reasons: "As a cheap flesh food it compares favorably in price with any of the products of either fresh or salt water." The wholesale price of carp would drop from a winter high of two and one-half cents per pound to a spring low of a third of a cent per pound. What wasn't sold for food became fertilizer. Despite the inexpensiveness of carp, an official of the Illinois Fisherman's Association could say: "From all points along the Illinois River, the carp have brought more money than the catch of all the other fish combined. Long live the carp!"

From an ecological perspective, a major question is whether carp are symptomatic of degraded waters or the cause. They proliferate in damaged waters, where turbidity, low oxygen levels, and high temperatures would kill most other fish. But they also spread into less stressed systems and impede the restoration of waterways by their habit of stirring up the bottom and hindering the growth of plants.[46] Millions of dollars have gone into carp control measures, among which have been poison, diseases, seining, manipulation of water levels, and electrocution.

Given modern-day realities, the consensus is that carp will remain common: "Unless we are willing to spend millions of dollars to pull out dams and restore the watersheds of our streams, . . . we will have carp in abundance."[47] And, as Dr. Becker concludes, so long as carp are here, people should be encouraged to catch them and eat them.

River Atrophy: The Disappearing Mussels

The native freshwater bivalves of this region belong to three families. The fingernail clams (Sphaeriidae) are small and very difficult to distinguish from one another. Irwin Polls of the Metropolitan Water Reclamation District has identified fifteen locally occurring species of three genera, but hardly anyone else pays them much mind except to note they have vanished from many places where they were once common. Biologists are, however, beginning to focus more attention on the larger Margaritiferidae (of which the spectaclecase is the only local representative) and Unionidae, the subjects of this section.

Scientists have become concerned because these mussels are disappearing. Of the 297 species and subspecies indigenous to this continent, 72 percent are considered extinct or in danger.[48] Mussels evolved with their rivers, forging relationships resilient enough to survive the upheavals wrought over millennia, but which crumbled in the torrent of anthropogenic change. Their strong and beautifully patterned shells, their habitat, their method of feeding, and their intricate reproductive strategies, all the elements that made mussels so successful for so long, have become liabilities in the world of modern human beings.

◄○► ◄○► ◄○►

The unionid mussels inhabit all stretches of a river, and a few species commonly occur in lakes. (See table 4.) Their abundance and diversity, however,

Table 4. Abundance of Selected Mussels along River Gradient

	Small Brooks to Small Creeks to Large Creeks	Small Rivers to Medium Rivers	Fairly Large to Large Rivers
Creek heelsplitter (*Lasmigona compressa*)	C, A, C	C, R	...
Squawfoot (*Strophitus undulatus*)	C, C	C, C	R, R
Cylindrical papershell (*Anodontoides ferussacianus*)	R, A, C	C	...
Slippershell (*Alasmidonta viridis*)	A, A	R, R	...
Spike (*Elliptio dilitata*)	C	A, A	A, R
Rainbow (*Villosa iris*)	R, C	A, A	R, R
Elktoe (*Alasmidonta marginata*)	R	C, C	R, R
Snuffbox (*Epioblasma triquetra*)	...	R, C	R
Fluted-shell (*Lasmigona costata*)	...	C	R, R
Purple wartyback (*Cyclonaias tuberculata*)	...	C	C, R
Paper pondshell (*Anodonta imbecillis*)	C	C, C	C, C
Wabash pigtoe (*Fusconaia flava*)	R	C, C	C, R
White heelsplitter (*Lasmigona complanata*)	C	C, C	C, R

Source. After Van der Schalie in Hynes (1973, 388); Cummings and Mayer (1992), and Kevin Cummings (written review of this table, 1995).

Note. R = rare; C = common; A = abundant; ellipses dots indicate species not present.

increases in a downstream direction, peaking in a transitional zone between small and large rivers.[49] Unfortunately for mussels, however, the harmful effects of watershed disturbances accumulate as one goes downstream. And significant alteration of the physical or biological properties of a river can prove catastrophic to these animals.

Mussels bury themselves either partially or completely into river bottoms, where they spend their entire adult lives, rarely venturing beyond a range of several hundred yards. To support a diverse mussel fauna, then, a riverbed can be neither too hard nor too soft. Bedrock is impossible to penetrate, and unconsolidated silt, sand, or mud provides inadequate anchorages. Prime mussel habitat consists of clean gravel shoals, with deposits of stable sand and mud.[50]

Since their sedentary ways preclude the pursuit of prey, mussels rely on the current to bring them diatoms, protozoans, and other tiny organisms. Protruding from the mussel and exposed to the upstream flow are two siphons, one to receive food and one to excrete the same after digestion. Thus, mussels are sensitive not only to changes in the substrate but also to water quality and flow.

When exposure to pollutants is of short duration, mussels can survive by shutting their valves. However, mussels cannot withstand long-term contact with heavy metals, chlorine, ammonia, or other effluents. Equally detrimental to mussel well being, and virtually uncontrolled, is the silt and other sediments generated by agriculture, mining, and construction activities. These slugs of small particles "degrade . . . substratum, clog gills, reduce feeding efficiency and growth, and eventually smother mussels if sufficient accumulation occurs."[51]

Dams are yet another blight on the mussel world. The giant floater (*Pyganodon grandis*), paper pondshell (*Anodonta imbecillis*), fragile papershell (*Leptodea fragilis*), and pink papershell (*Potamilus ohiensis*) are among the local species that thrive in impoundments, but numerous others cannot. Dams can reduce mussel diversity by a third to two-thirds.[52] This destruction stems from reduced flows, changes in temperature, and bottoms now coated with thick layers of mud and silt. The most serious harm, however, may be the effect dams have on the fish that form such an essential part of mussel reproduction.

The relationship between fish and mussels is quite remarkable and forms an integral stage in the survival of young mussels. Female mussels can produce huge numbers of eggs, estimates of which range from seventy-five thousand to 3.5 million, depending on her size and species. The fertilized eggs develop within her gills where they receive sufficient oxygen. They then hatch into tiny versions of the adults called glochidia. Like living castanets, they snap about in search of the right fish to grab. Some, like floaters and heelsplitters (Anodontinae), are triangular and equipped with a hook that enables them to attach to fins. Others, round and hookless, are ingested by the host fish and mature within its gills. The Lampsilids (muckets, pocketbooks, and black sandshells, etc.) are among this group.

Parasitizing fish in this way enables mussels to colonize upstream areas, for they would otherwise be at the mercy of currents. But this reproductive

48. Plain pocketbook mussel showing its worm-like mantle used to lure
fish that are hosts for mussel glochidia. (Photo by and courtesy of
K. Cummings, Illinois Natural History Survey, Champaign.)

strategy also makes the mussel vulnerable to changes in the status of its host. Many mussels are thought to be dependent on specific fish or, in the case of the salamander mussel (*Simpsonaias ambigua*), a single amphibian—the mud puppy (*Necturus maculosus*). Growing evidence suggests that particular fish groups support particular mussel groups. As examples, darters, bass, and sunfish host lampsilids, while catfish and minnows provide homes for pigtoes (*Pleurobema*). Much more research is needed in this area of mussel ecology, but to date, "host fishes have been identified, with various degrees of certainty, for 33 genera and about 65 species of mussels."[53]

This is a seemingly inefficient way to reproduce, for if the glochidia can't connect with a suitable host quickly, they are likely to be eaten or starve. To minimize these risks, a number of mussels have evolved strategies to lure the right host. Some species possess mantles, a layer of tissue extending beyond the shell, that resemble ever so closely the favored prey of bass or sunfish: a minnow (complete with eye spot), darter, or hellgrammite (larval form of dobsonfly). As the predator moves in to procure a supposed meal, the mussel releases its glochidia. Other mussels cast a baited line, emitting a nearly invisible mucous strand two or three meters long attached to a bundle of glochidia. The bundle looks for all the world like a wounded minnow, and when the fish bites, it winds up with a mouthful of baby mussels.

Mussels also benefit their hosts. Mud puppies, for example, feed on the adults of the same mussels whose glochidia they carry around for seven months. Thus, in this instance the mussel itself is the bait. There is also evidence that mussel beds are the favored substrates of white crappies (*Pomoxis annularis*), saugers (*Stizostedion canadense*), bluegills, river shiner, and other fish. Several reasons might explain this. Mussel beds provide shelter for smaller fish and spawning grounds for walleyes and other lithophilic (among rocks) breeders. Some fish, although none currently known from this region, utilize mussels as brood chambers for their eggs.[54] And, most important, fish gather in mussel beds to forage on the dense populations of invertebrates that seek protection among the shells, feed on mussel feces and pseudofeces, and find mussel shells ideal for attaching eggs, pupae, and feeding nets. Mussels are particularly valuable in this regard because, unlike rocks, which are easily buried under sediments, "the living mussel actively maintains its position at the sediment surface [and] the supply of solid substrate continually accumulates through the death of individual mussels."

The Chicago region once held a diverse mussel population. In Illinois, the Des Plaines River and the Lake Michigan tributaries are known to have supported thirty-four species, while the Fox had thirty-one. The Kankakee and its basin had between thirty-five and forty species. But these figures reflect times past. Most of the streams within the Des Plaines watershed are almost devoid of mussels, while even the best of the local mussel streams support assemblages that are poorer than they used to be: Nippersink Creek (fourteen species), the Illinois portion of the Kankakee (roughly twenty), and the Tippecanoe (about thirty-five), which barely touches this region.[55]

It is in these streams, particularly the last two, where the rarest species are making their final stands. The salamander mussel once enjoyed a large population in Hickory Creek, where Arthur Howard obtained the specimens that enabled him to prove that the mud puppy was the host, but it has since disappeared from there and everywhere else in Illinois except possibly the Kankakee and a few other streams.[56] Although still present, the snuffbox (*Epioblasma triquetra*) and sheepnose (*Plethobasus cyphus*) may be losing their struggle, for most of the few recent finds consist of dead specimens from widely scattered locations. Doing slightly better, perhaps, are the purple wartyback (*Cyclonaias tuberculata*), ellipse (*Venustaconcha ellipsiformis*), rabbitsfoot (*Quadrula cylindrica*), and Wabash pigtoe (*Fusconaia flava*).

Some mussel species, however, have manifested a remarkable tenacity that allows them to thrive in degraded streams. Among this relatively small group are white heelsplitters, giant floaters, fatmuckets, and plain pocketbooks. Kevin Cummings, of the Illinois Natural History Survey, suggests that most of these can probably use a wide range of fish as hosts for their glochidia. Others are probably adapted to natural disturbances and, thus, do reasonably well when confronted with such stresses as heavy silt loads. Cummings emphasizes, however, that much more work needs to be done on these issues.

In their survey of the Kankakee basin, Charles Wilson and H. Walton Clark describe the ability of mussels to survive under hostile conditions on a section of the Yellow River in Starke County:

> Instead of a good current running over a sandy or gravelly bottom and keeping everything clear and clean, we now find lagoons and bayous in which the water is practically motionless. . . . Consequently, they are rich in algae and other water plants, and the firm bottom has been covered with soft mud and in many places with fine ooze, 2 feet or more in depth. [Except for the pimpleback (*Quadrula pustulosa*), the other mussels] have succeeded in climbing up on top of the mud and ooze as fast as it was deposited. Even the large and heavy [black sandshell], [pocketbook], and [three-ridge] are found on the very top. How such an unwieldy bulk as a full-grown [three-ridge] can move about and actually lift itself up through mud so soft that it will not hold up an empty shell is difficult to understand. . . . A noticeable peculiarity [is] of algae around the siphonal (upper) end of the shell. These would . . . aid in oxygenating the stagnant water in which the mussels live, and might also be of assistance in keeping them on top of the mud.[57]

The decline of mussels in the Illinois River has been carefully documented.[58] From 1870 to 1900, the river and its connecting lakes yielded forty-nine species of mussels. By the time William Starrett conducted his study from 1966 to 1969, this number dropped to twenty-four species. More striking was the fate of mussels in the upper portion of the river, defined as the forty-two miles that extend from its origin east of Morris downstream to Utica, LaSalle County. Whereas the earliest researchers found thirty-eight species in this stretch, Starrett failed to detect a single one. (Conditions in the upper Illinois were already so bad by 1900 that few if any mussels remained even then.) They simply could not withstand the raw sewage of Chicago, the construction of high dams at Dresden Island (twenty-four feet high), Marseilles (twenty-four feet), and Starved Rock (nineteen feet), constant dredging to maintain the nine-foot deep navigation channel, and heavy boat traffic that resuspends silt and other sediment.[59] Fortunately, since Starrett's work, a few of the more tolerant mussels have reappeared in small numbers.

Most of the Kankakee River also lost its mussel fauna. Recently published surveys have concentrated on the Illinois portion, possibly because the ditch that runs through Indiana is so depauperate.[60] In 1909, Charles Wilson and H. Walton Clark sampled throughout the watershed, finding abundant mussels wherever conditions allowed. But in many places conditions did not allow: "Dredging entirely annihilates the mussel fauna of such a basin throughout the portions operated upon, no matter how prolific and varied that fauna may have been previously. And it establishes artificial conditions, every one of which is antagonistic to any reestablishing of the fauna. The most fatal condition is the constant movement of the fine sand and silt along the bottom of the dredged channels. Until that has ceased there can be no chance for mussels to live."[61]

◄o► ◄o► ◄o►

There is another reason mussels have fallen by the wayside of modern civilization. They were, and still are, the targets of an industry that flourished on the Illinois River, and to a lesser extent the Fox and Kankakee. In three succeeding waves, men came to rip out the riches that lie half buried in the soft beds of these gentle rivers.

The first to come were the pearlers. Called the "pioneers of the mussel industry," they combed the Illinois River from 1892 to 1907 and the Fox River from 1906 to 1909.[62] The pearlers were single minded in their pursuit, leaving behind tons of shells as their legacy. Beardstown, on the middle Illinois River, attracted pearl buyers from as far away as New York and even Paris. Over a twenty-day period, one claimed to have purchased $20,000 worth of pearls and slugs. (Besides rounded pearls, mussels also produce nacre-covered objects of various sizes and shapes that are known as slugs or baroques, but these are of much less value than pearls.)

The Fox River was particularly well known for its pearls. John Eldridge, in his study of the river's mussel fishery, said that the lower Fox, from Millington to Sheridan in LaSalle County, was "one of the most fertile pearl producers in the country." The river had yielded many pearls in the $1,000–$1,850 range. Results, however, were less rewarding upstream. On average, a pearler working between Geneva, Kane County, and Yorkville, Kendall County, would find about $100 worth of pearls in a season. One pearl worth twice that amount was found at McHenry Dam in July 1911.[63]

Pearling was not restricted to these rivers alone. Although the upper Yellow River still supported a varied mussel fauna in 1909, "many of the finest shells in this part of the river have been killed by pearlers." Wilson and Clark found a pile of shells weighing three thousand pounds, said to be the consequence of "a severe attack of the 'pearl fever.'"[64] Donald Culross Peattie encountered two fellows on the Little Calumet near Miller, Lake County (Ind.), who proved that pearlers didn't have to be successful to be destructive: "One of them quietly stepped out [of the boat] and commenced to pull up what seemed like the entire bottom of the stream. . . . Great numbers of clams were opened and in none of them was the pearl of great price, nor any price, nor any pearl at all."[65]

When it came to pearl production, not all mussels were created equal. On the Illinois, most pearls originated from the washboard (*Megalonaias nervosa*), while slugs were common in the three-ridge (*Amblema plicata*), and to a lesser extent the wartyback (*Quadrula nodulata*).[66] On the Fox, muckets (*Actinonaias ligamentina*) were the most important, and on the Kankakee purple wartybacks, three-ridges, and spikes (*Elliptio dilatata*) yielded most of the pearls.

Mussel harvesters employed several techniques. In deeper waters, the crowfoot dredge, a ten-to-eighteen-foot-long piece of metal from which were hung up to two hundred hooks, trailed behind flat john boats and raked the river bottom. Usually partially opened, the mussel valves would close on the hooks as they entered the animal's soft innards. Where the river is shallow, as along much of the Fox, the only equipment needed was a bag or pail to hold the mussels and a knife to open them.[67]

Once the mussels were collected, they were boiled in large vats to facilitate removal of the meat.[68] The insides were then carefully examined to see if they held any slugs or pearls. Slugs were dropped into water for cleaning while pearls were "tempered by being placed in the mouth for a while, then wrapped loosely in cotton, and put in a small tin box . . . for safe-keeping."[69]

The second wave of entrepreneurs sought the shells themselves and gobbled up far more mussels than the pearlers, in their grotesque wastefulness, ever did. Shellers obtained mussels in the same way but went after a greater variety of species. The most desired species were those possessing thick shells, the outer surface smooth and the inner "with nacre of clear, lustrous white without stains or color." Of the five hundred mussel species then recognized within the United States, Robert Coker wrote that forty-one were used in the shell trade, but only seventeen were of any real commercial significance. For the Illinois River, twenty species had value but only six or seven were common enough "to be of practical worth." The following are among the most economically important of this region's mussels: ebony shell (*Fusconaia ebena*— "the most valuable button shell of the United States"), wartyback, washboard (*Megalonaias nervosa*—"the best button shell of the Illinois"), pigtoe, and white heelsplitter (*Lasmigona complanata*).[70]

It seems that John Boepple single handedly inspired this demand for shells. A button maker from Ottensen, Germany, Boepple came to the United States in 1887 and settled in Muscatine, Iowa. His great genius was being the first to recognize that freshwater mussels would make a marvelous substitute for the bone, antlers, and marine shells that then provided the raw material out of which buttons were fashioned. Mussels were abundant, and their nacre-lined shells were both beautiful and tough. And far from least, they were easy to work with: "Take a clean shell and cut round blanks out of it with a cylindrical saw blade driven by a lathe. Grind the blanks to uniform thickness on a revolving emery wheel, then drill two to four holes. A little polishing, and you had a pearly white button that might even give off a little iridescent glimmer."[71]

In 1891, Boepple opened his button factory and a new industry blossomed. By 1912, 196 such factories were operating in twenty states, twenty-one of them along the Illinois River. The Fox River supplied mussels to a blank factory (where the buttons were cut from shells) at Yorkville with sixteen machines, and another at Somonauk with ten. Most of the shells collected on the Indiana side of the Kankakee wound up being processed by the Benoit Company in Saint Joseph, Berrien County.[72] The late Gordon Graves told me that he used to clam on the river at Aroma Park, Kankakee County, when he was a youngster in the 1930s. A man would come around in a small truck to buy the shells, which he then sold to a local button factory located on Wall Street in West Kankakee.

Between 1912 and 1927, the demand for buttons consumed between forty and sixty thousand tons of shells annually. And of all the rivers that contributed to this total, the Illinois was "the most productive stream per mile of any in the country, and it has been reliably stated that only two or three years ago more than 2,600 boats were engaged in the mussel fishery between Peru and Grafton." In 1913 alone, the river gave up 5,890 tons of shells.[73]

The Fox River yielded its share as well. John Eldridge provides the following estimates for a three-year span when production was at its height: 1909—ten to twelve railroad carloads; 1910—twenty-five to thirty carloads; and 1911—twenty-two carloads. In March 1915, thirty tons of shells were shipped from Spring Grove, McHenry County, to Muscatine and yielded $11 a ton. Sixty tons of three-ridge mussels sprawled on the shore near Cary because no buyer could be found. As a section of river became depleted, attention would turn to other stretches, until there was nowhere else to go:

> The shelling of recent years . . . has in some places nearly exhausted the mussels, and there is a great difference in those remaining. On the river north of Carpentersville, where little shelling has been done previous to this year, 15 to 20 tons of shells were the usual catch per man in 1911; below Elgin on the Five Islands bed, which has been worked for two years, the catch averaged 10 to 12 tons per man; farther down below Yorkville, 7 tons per man were considered a good yield; on the Millington-Sheridan bed, which is the oldest and hardest worked in the river, but four tons could be caught. It was the general opinion that shelling for 1911 was 50 per cent less than that of the previous year. The only cause for this is the ravages of man.[74]

49. Fox River at Yorkville, Kendall County, where mussel beds were
commercially exploited during the early 1900s. Photo taken
August 1910 by Prairie Club. (Courtesy Westchester Township
Historical Museum, Chesterton, Ind.)

The second wave of mussel exploitation foundered on plastic, for buttons made of this new substance were both cheaper and more durable than those of shells. The industry shrunk, and by the mid-1960s the last shell button factory at Muscatine closed. But by then a third wave had commenced: the Japanese had discovered that the best cultured pearls develop in oysters seeded with pieces of mussel shells. Such pearls are hard and consist purely of nacre. This new market had an impact on the middle and lower Illinois, the Mississippi, the Wabash, and other rivers still being harvested, but the rivers of the Chicago region had long before ceased being commercial sources of mussels.

Like Crystals on the Landscape: The Small Glacial Lakes

The small lakes of this region fall into two categories. On the Chicago Lake Plain, lakes Calumet, Hyde, Wolf, Berry, and George were legacies of the big glacial lake as it receded into what is now Lake Michigan. (See chap. 9 for a

50. In 1896, Charles Johnson published a book entitled *Angling in the Lakes of Northern Illinois*. It contained figures of the various lakes depicting features pertaining to fishing, including areas of emergent vegetation. This is Johnson's rendition of Sand Lake, Lake County (Ill.). (Redrawn by C. Kerchmar.)

discussion of the Lake Plain lakes.) Most of the local lakes, however, are morainal, water either held within receptacles of glacial deposition or left by the melting remnants of buried glacial ice. There are scattered representatives in northwest Indiana and Berrien County: Cedar (in Lake County, Ind., and not to be confused with Cedar Lake in Lake County, Ill.), Hudson, Stone, Flint, Pine, Paw Paw, and Pipestone among them. But the greatest concentration lies within the watersheds of the Fox (mostly) and Des Plaines Rivers, in the counties of Lake (Ill.), McHenry, Kenosha, and Walworth.

The morainal lakes vary tremendously by size, depth, and extent of fringing vegetation. At one extreme is Lake Geneva. Contained within the steep slopes of a valley, the lake covers 5,262 acres and reaches a maximum depth of 135 feet. More than three quarters of its expanse is greater than twenty feet deep, and there is little or no emergent vegetation on its borders. Grass Lake represents another scenario. One-fourth the size of Lake Geneva, it was a shallow slough whose open water increased with the construction of McHenry Dam in 1939. Almost surrounded by cattail marsh, Grass Lake reaches a maximum depth of six feet, although 60 percent of it is no deeper than four feet.

As for the smallest lakes, many have lost their original character through

51. This aerial photo shows Sand Lake in 1998. (North is in the direction of the three small lakes to the upper right.) The shallows and the sandbar noted by Johnson are discernable in the photo, but the only remaining emergent vegetation are two small patches of spatterdock on the south side. Filling of the lake edge, increased water levels created by a dam on the outlet stream, and inaccuracies in Johnson's drawing explain why the shape of the lake differs from one picture to another. It is also worth noting that the lake had recently been treated with herbicides (to remove, in particular, European water milfoil) and that its once gradually sloping shoreline has been replaced by abrupt changes in depth due to the installation of a retaining wall. (Courtesy Mark Pfister, Lake County Health Department, Waukegan, Ill.)

damming, dredging, filling, and the use of biocides. Sun Lake, with a surface area of only thirty-one acres, is a lovely exception, being among the very few lakes in Lake County inaccessible to automobiles. And it should remain safe, now that it is under the protection of the Lake County Forest Preserve District.[75]

Set like crystals amid the verdant rolls of the Valparaiso Moraine, these beautiful lakes have long attracted visitors. Colbee Benton reached Lake Geneva in 1835 and recorded his impressions:

> We came to the most splendid lake and the largest that I have seen since I left Chicago. It has a smooth, stony bottom, clear, pure water, and it was surrounded by high banks covered with the heavy prairie grass and the great variety of flowers which are everywhere to be found in this country . . . I became so deeply in love with it and so much interested with its romantic and delightful appearance, that I felt quite unwilling to leave; and I did not, until I had selected a location for my wigwam, which was a gentle elevation in the beautiful grove and overlooked the calm and pure

52. Day's catch of northern pike and bass at Grass Lake, Lake County
(Ill.), 1915. (Courtesy Art Doty Collection, Antioch, Ill.)

waters of the lake. It seemed the sweetest, the most calm, the most peace-
ful and retired spot that I ever saw.[76]

The March 4, 1845, issue of the *Little Fort Porcupine and Democratic Ban-
ner* wrote glowingly of the Chain O' Lakes: "These lakes have long been noted
for their romantic scenery, as well as for being the favorite resort of the Indians of the west, for ages past; and there is probably no spot which they left more
reluctantly than these favored lakes. . . . The lakes abound in almost every kind
of freshwater fish, and in the spring and fall of the year, the surface of the water is covered with almost every description of waterfowl known in the western country."

Lodges catering to the hunter and angler were among the first developments to affect these lakes. An 1885 atlas of Lake County listed twelve different resorts on the Chain O' Lakes alone, and most of the other larger lakes had
at least one. By 1910, Fox Lake had thirty hotels and seven saloons, while Pistakee Bay on the south end of the Chain could already boast over eighty hotels
and cottages. Then, later, shoreline property became clogged with summer
homes. Those lakes closer to Chicago tended to offer more modest dwellings,
while Lake Geneva provided a dramatic backdrop for the summer palaces of
many of the region's gentry.[77]

Now many lakes are enveloped by urban sprawl and plagued by summer blooms of speeding boats. The consequences of this development are a loss of wetlands, littoral areas, rooted aquatic plants, and water clarity, elements integral to the lakes' biological diversity.

◄○► ◄○► ◄○►

Organisms in these smaller lakes arrange themselves in zones as they do in Lake Michigan: pelagic, littoral, and benthic. But because these lakes are shallower and have gentler slopes, more of the benthic community lies within the littoral zone, thus contributing even more to the lakes' overall productivity. These lakes also tend to lack the deepwater fauna characteristic of the Great Lakes.

Most of the attention paid to the planktonic populations of these lakes involves the "water blooms" that sometimes erupt in still shallows. Blue-green algae of the genera *Microcystis* and *Anabaena* spread across the water surface on warm sunny days, only to break up and sink with periods of prolonged cloudiness. In life, these algae offend the aesthetic sensibilities of visitors and block light from penetrating the water; in death, their decomposition consumes oxygen to the detriment of other organisms. During the late 1960s and early 1970s, this was a serious problem in the Chain O' Lakes, particularly affecting Fox Lake and Pistakee Lake. These eruptions are nurtured, if not caused, by fertilizers and other nutrient-heavy runoff.[78]

Lake Geneva is one of the few lakes whose plankton has been carefully examined. A study in 1976 found that the phytoplankton was relatively sparse and varied in composition throughout the season. In the spring, because of water turnover, the algae are at their most diverse: 48 percent blue-green, 49 percent green, and 3 percent diatoms. But the blue-green increased through the summer until it constituted 99 percent of all the algae just before the October turnover. One species alone, *Anacystis thermalis*, made up over 90 percent of the total.[79]

The same study identified twenty-two species of zooplankton, of which two cladocerans (*Daphnia longiremis* and *Eubosmina coregoni*) and two copepods (*Tropocyclops prasinus* and *Cyclops thomasi*) were the most abundant. (See fig. 34) Similar surveys had been conducted in 1901 and 1974, and a comparison of the results reveals that Lake Geneva went from being a clean oligotrophic lake to one experiencing accelerated eutrophication. The most striking example of a change involves the copepod *Limnoclaenis marcrurus*. Found during the 1901 research, this sensitive species, requiring cold water and high oxygen levels, is now quite rare in most inland water bodies except the Great Lakes.

Life in the benthic zone is heavily regulated by such factors as temperature, dissolved oxygen, type of substrate, food availability, cover, and competition. Few organisms survive on the bottom of the deepest lakes, for this abyssal region is covered with a layer of fine organic debris and is often deficient in oxygen. In Lake Geneva, for example, life below fifty feet was dominated by snails (*Viviparus* and *Lymna*), fingernail clams (*Sphaerium*), segmented worms (*Tubifex*), and midges (*Chironomus*).

But even in shallow areas, the bottoms of many lakes are depauperate. After studying a number of the morainal lakes, Stephen Forbes wrote:

> When one sees acres of the shallower water black with waterfowl, and so clogged with weeds that the boat can scarcely be pushed through the mass; when, lifting a handful of the latter, he finds them covered with shells and alive with small crustaceans; and then, dragging a towing net for a few minutes, finds it lined with myriads of diatoms and other microscopic algae . . . , he is likely to infer that these waters are everywhere swarming with life, from top to bottom and from shore to shore. If, however, he will haul a dredge for an hour or so in the deepest water he can find, he will invariably discover an area singularly barren of both plant and animal life, yielding scarcely anything but a small bivalve mollusk, a few worms, and red larvae of gnats.[80]

Forbes attributed this situation to the substrate, "black, deep, and almost impalpable mud or ooze, too soft and unstable to afford foothold to plants even if the lake is shallow enough to admit a sufficient quantity of light to its bottom to support vegetation." Unfortunately, the impoverishment of the littoral zone in many areas seems to be accelerating. After studying several sites in the Chain O' Lakes, researchers were surprised that every one of their samples "showed a low, relatively undiversified population" of benthic organisms. They ascribed the damage to excessive siltation, much of it generated by a surfeit of powerboats that churn the shallow lake bottoms into uninhabitable barrens.[81]

Gravity and water movement tend to shift the finely textured muck offshore, leaving behind coarser particles that are favorable to rooting aquatic plants. These substrates underlie the sun-enriched littoral zones that ring the morainal lakes at widths varying with slope and water clarity. The littoral zones range in depth from thirty feet at Lake Geneva to about ten feet at most of the Illinois lakes.

Aquatic vegetation is highly varied. Riding the surface, the duckweeds are tiny vascular plants that can carpet the top of still waters. Seven species occur in this region, with small duckweed (*Lemna minor*) being the most abundant. Another group of plants contains members that are rooted but submerged.

Among the algae, these include stonewort (*Chara*) and green algae (*Clado-phora*). Coontail (*Ceratophyllum demersum*), milfoil (*Myriophyllum*), common waterweed (*Elodea canadensis*), and eelgrass (*Vallisneria americana*) are vascular submergents that are also frequent in these waters.

Depending on the species, pondweeds are either submerged or have leaves that float on the surface. Botanists have identified twenty species growing in this region. Some, like the leafy (*Potamogeton foliosus*) and long-leaved (*P. nodosus*), are common and widespread, while white-stemmed (*P. praelongus*), stiff (*P. strictifolius*), and other species are confined to lakes with very high water quality.[82]

Invertebrates in large numbers are drawn to the vegetated areas for a myriad of reasons. Predacious diving beetles (*Dysticidae*) and water scorpions (*Ranatra*) lay their eggs inside plant tissue, while mayflies, caddis flies, and numerous snails attach theirs to leaves or stems. Many aquatic animals rely on vegetation as ladders to the surface, which they climb for oxygen. This group includes water scavenger beetles (Hydrophilidae), giant water bugs (Belostomatidae), long-horned leaf beetles (Donaciinae), water boatmen (Corixidae), and snails (*Physella* and *Planorbis*). Predatory dragonfly nymphs use the foliage as cover to ambush prey.[83]

◄◦► ◄◦► ◄◦►

Between sixty and seventy species of fish have been recorded in these lakes. The most common are ecological generalists such as bluegill, largemouth bass, sunfish, white sucker (*Catostomus commersoni*), bullheads, and bluntnose minnow (*Pimephales notatus*). Other species are limited to specific lakes or have undergone population fluctuations in response to changing conditions. And one, except for recent stockings, is now completely gone from the region.

The muskellunge was one of those large predators that disappeared early and with little trace. Apart from a small population in Lake Michigan, its presence in the region seems to have been limited to the Chain O' Lakes and nearby Fox River. In 1889, E. Hough reported in *Forest and Stream* that several muskies had been caught in Fox Lake, ranging in size from eighteen pounds to 42½ pounds. One thirty-two pounder was hooked by "a 14-year old boy with a common cane pole." By 1914, the Illinois Rivers and Lakes Commission could write its obituary: "Formerly the muskellunge was rated as one of the finest game fish, but it has practically disappeared from the waters of the lake district."[84]

The lake herring (*Coregonus artedii*) has perhaps the most limited local range of any lake fish. Except for Lake Michigan, Lake Geneva and Lake Beulah (Walworth County) are the only local lakes deep enough to maintain the cold and oxygenated water it requires. For most of the year, lake herring inhabit depths in excess of sixty feet, but in late fall they move inshore to spawn. During the last century at Lake Geneva, herring were caught for market, and a single fisherman could capture over two hundred in a day.

Starting in the 1940s and continuing until 1973, Lake Geneva's herring periodically experienced massive die-offs, presumably from sudden fluctuations in water temperature and from oxygen depletion at lower depths.[85] Human depredations, however, are now relatively modest, thanks to the tapeworm *Triaenophorus crassus*, which now infects the herring in Lake Geneva. The parasite is not harmful to people and is readily killed through cooking, but few are willing to eat the fish.

Although found more widely than the lake herring, six small species form an assemblage that is virtually restricted, at least regionally, to the morainal lakes. These relict fish are the pugnose shiner (*Notropis anogenus*), blacknose shiner (*Notropis heterolepis*), blackchin shiner (*Notropis heterodon*), banded killifish (*Fundulus diaphanus*), Iowa darter (*Etheostoma exile*), and lake chubsucker (*Erimyzon sucetta*).[86] They all enjoy relatively wide ranges but have generally declined in many of their Midwest locations. Camp (Kenosha), Silver (Kenosha), and Beulah (Walworth) are the only local lakes that have all six of these rare fish. Four lakes—Elizabeth (Kenosha/McHenry), Mary (Kenosha), Benedict (Kenosha), and Cross (Kenosha/Lake)—lack only the Iowa darter. Eleven other Wisconsin lakes have at least three species. (These totals are based on data accumulated between 1970 and 1996.)[87]

The most imperiled of the bunch is the pugnose shiner, which once occurred in small and scattered populations from eastern South Dakota to Lake Ontario. Today, the species is apparently most "secure" in Minnesota and Wisconsin, where it is rare in the former and threatened in the latter.[88] The species is known to inhabit at least ten of this region's Wisconsin lakes, including two that straddle the state line. But Don Fago, senior fisheries biologist at the Wisconsin Department of Natural Resources, believes that few, if any, of these populations are secure and that the species is probably declining.

No one knows for sure why this species is in so much more trouble than its associates, particularly the two closely related shiners. One possibility is that the pugnose has a very limited diet, for its small and upturned mouth suggests it can only feed on tiny prey at the surface.

Greg Seegert surveyed a number of the Illinois lakes to find how many held pugnose shiners and located only two. Although only eighty-seven acres in size and thirty-four feet deep, Cross Lake yielded thirteen pugnose shiners and supported healthy populations of other glacial lake specialties as well: two-hundred-plus blacknose, two-hundred-plus blackchin, and more than a hundred killifish. East Loon Lake, 164 acres and twenty-six feet deep, produced

53. Pugnose shiner, a rare species restricted locally to morainal lakes in the northwest part of the region. Specimen from Lake County, Illinois. (Photo by and courtesy of Lawrence Page, Illinois Natural History Survey, Champaign.)

much smaller numbers of pugnose (two), blacknose (three), blackchin (three), and killifish (three).[89] Given that Lawrence Page collected several pugnose shiners in Deep Lake in 1985, the species may persist there as well, but otherwise that appears to be the extent of the fish's Illinois population.

What distinguishes these lakes from all the ones that have lost the special six? Seegert told me that not too long into his study he could eyeball a lake and determine with reasonable confidence whether it was suitable for the species he was seeking. He looked for water clarity and diversity of submerged vegetation, two very closely related features. Seegert explains:

> Most small glacial lakes at this latitude should have between six to ten species of rooted aquatic plants. But what you find in degraded systems are virtual monocultures of exotic Eurasian water milfoil [*Myriophyllum spicatum*], and maybe one or two other species such as coontail. I don't think it is the species as much as variety. But that is only part of it. Theoretically a pugnose shiner could live in a system dominated by *Myriophyllum*. But you have to ask yourself what happened that created this monoculture. The answer is eutrophication and the associated turbidity. These factors, more than the plants themselves, are most detrimental to the fish.[90]

Systemic abuses to the lakes such as pollution and speed boating take their toll of the littoral bounty that these sensitive fish require for food and shelter. Other assaults are more direct. Many lakeside residents seem to detest the submerged plants that so enrich the water bodies they claim to like. Through chemicals or aquatic combines that mow swaths eight feet wide and five feet deep, the vegetation is poisoned or minced. The perpetrators lessen the occasions when their fishing lines become entangled, while destroying something that was once wonderful.

As mentioned earlier, fishery agencies have traditionally seen lakes and rivers as farms for the production of game fish. They stock bass, northern pike, and other predators with little or no regard to the fate of prey species. Then, there is the process of rehabilitation, whereby the fish fauna is destroyed for the benefit of game fish that will be introduced later. A 1972 report on the surface waters of Lake County included these remarks on Cross Lake: "The lake is dominated by small bluegill, pumpkinseed, warmouth bass and yellow bullhead. Largemouth bass are moderately abundant. . . . Carp are also present. Total rehabilitation has been recommended by Wisconsin fisheries personnel. . . . There is no pollution problem on the lake."[91] That one of the richest lakes in the region might have been deliberately sterilized is a chilling thought. Thank the inertia or opposition that averted this potential disaster.

◄o► ◄o► ◄o►

Another group of fish share with the common species discussed above an ability to tolerate degraded water and to be equally comfortable in streams, rivers, or lakes. But the channel catfish (*Ictalurus punctatus*), bowfin (*Amia calva*), and longnose gar (*Lepisosteus osseus*) have all undergone changes in population that reflect changes in the conditions of the morainal lakes.

The channel catfish generally prefers warm water, although while young it will seek the shallow riffles of low-order streams. With its direct connection to the Fox River and large expanses of warm water, the Chain O' Lakes holds far more channel catfish than any of the other morainal lakes. (Channel catfish, having been extensively stocked, now live in places they would never have reached on their own.) Over the years, however, the Chain's population of this species has undergone some striking shifts. From 1954 to 1984, channel catfish grew in abundance to become the second most common fish, an increase attributed to the growing turbidity of the Chain. But over the course of the next eight years, it steadily declined from 21.2 percent of the total catch to 5.8 percent. An optimist would say that this reflects decreasing turbidity, but no evidence supports such a view, and the fluctuations have not been explained.[92]

The longnose gar and the bowfin (also known as dogfish) share several characteristics. They both favor warmer waters and feed almost exclusively on fish. This latter trait has earned them the undying enmity of fishermen and biologists alike. Some of the most scathing denunciations of animals that I have ever read appear in the gar and bowfin accounts by Forbes and Richardson, two renowned scientists who might have been expected to have a more ecological view of the situation. They say that the gar "is a wholly worthless and destructive nuisance in its relations to mankind [having] all the vices and none of the virtues of a predacious fish." Later, they lump the bowfin and gar together: "The time will doubtless come when thoroughgoing measures will be taken to keep down to the lowest practicable limit the dogfish and the gars as useless and destructive in our productive waters as wolves and foxes formerly were in our pastures and poultry-yards."[93]

The only bowfins I have ever seen were in a garbage can at Fourth Lake, Lake County (Ill.). This is the common reaction of many anglers, but they acknowledge that a fighting bowfin is at least fun to catch. While landing a gar can also be exciting, the toughness of its narrow snout makes it difficult to hook in the first place, so gar provide little in the way of recreation. (The way to catch them apparently is to rig up little wire loops at the end of a baited line so the fish can lasso itself.) Many anglers toss gar back into the water but not before ramming a stout stick down the unfortunate fish's throat. Thousands more have been killed over the years in efforts to eradicate nuisance fish. In Pewaukee Lake, Waukesha County, just north of this region, a Wisconsin Department of Natural Resources rough-fish removal crew caught more than ten thousand pounds of gar on one occasion in 1937. The fish were eventually used as fertilizer.[94]

A singular anatomical feature of gars and bowfins, unchanged over eons of evolution, is that their swim bladders are connected to their throats. When oxygen levels in the water are insufficient to sustain the fish through ordinary gill respiration, the bladders then act as auxiliary lungs, enabling the fish to draw air directly from the atmosphere. The retention of the dual breathing system has given the gar and bowfin a great advantage over other fish: "The ability of gars and bowfins to breathe air enables them to live in polluted waters unfit for any other fish. . . . We have seen cases of total oxygen depletion where all the other species were killed, but the gars and bowfins still swam about unconcernedly."[95]

The bowfin has a behavioral characteristic that has also contributed to its survival. Bowfin parents, particularly the male, zealously guard offspring. The babies mass into tight balls, and any threat to this defenseless bundle of fry elicits a swift response by the father. One vigilant parent actually left the water several times as it charged eight inches up a bank to drive off a human intruder standing on the shore.

Both species are very prolific, as a large gar can lay thirty-six thousand eggs and a bowfin sixty-four thousand. But they spawn in thickly vegetated waters, and the loss of marsh and littoral plants has brought a decline in both species. The bowfin has fared better, particularly at Turner Lake, this species' Lake County stronghold. (Turner Lake is both part of Chain O' Lakes State Park and largely surrounded by high-quality marsh.) But gar have become quite rare in the lake region. Between 1972 and 1995, the Wisconsin Department of Natural Resources located small numbers of gar in at least ten of the region's lakes, although some of those populations may no longer be extant. As for Illinois, from 1954 to 1984, gar were found in the Chain during every Illinois Department of Natural Resources study, but not one has appeared in a sample catch since. A fish is still caught every five to ten years in Bangs Lake and Cedar Lake, reminders of the tenacity that marks this ancient predator.

9

Casualties of a Modern World: The Marshes of the Kankakee and Calumet

The Kankakee of old has gone. . . . The despoiler tore relentlessly through ferny aisles in the green embowered woods and across the swamps and flowing fens, the glittering lakes, the meandering loops and bends disappeared and the fecund marshlands yielded their life currents. The thousand night voices on their moor-flooded stretches were stilled. . . . The currents that once widened in silvery magnificence to their natural barriers, and wandered peacefully among the mysteries of the woods, now flow madly on through a man wrought channel. In sorrow the gloomy waters flee with writhing swirls from the land where once they crept out over the low areas and rested on their way to the sea. —Earl Reed (1920)

Efforts to stem water pollution have made progress towards cleaning up the streams, but they have had negative impacts on the [Calumet] wetlands. The effects of expanding land disposal activity are irreversible. While riverine environments can rebound from degraded conditions when discharges are curtailed, marshland buried by landfilling activity is unlikely to return to its natural state for centuries, if at all. —Craig E. Colten (1985)

The stories of the Kankakee and Calumet wetlands deserve to be told in memory of their original splendor. The Kankakee marshes were systematically drained, largely for agriculture, and ceased to exist by 1917. (Interestingly, just a few years after the last of the Indiana portion of the river became a ditch, books appeared that very passionately lamented what had just been lost.) Tragically, they were destroyed before anyone had studied them. Accounts of the more conspicuous bird life, larger mammals, and general vegetation have been preserved, but apparently there were no naturalists the likes of Willis Blatchley, Robert Kennicott, or Philo Hoy among its intimates.

The Calumet wetlands were filled in piecemeal. Their proximity to the scientific institutions of Chicago made them a convenient place for fieldtrips, and so their biota is much better known. In a way, though, the history of the Calumet area seems to me sadder. The difference, perhaps, is between a quick death that is mourned, and slow torture allowed to continue through indifference or worse. As we begin the twenty-first century, there is now a serious effort to allow the Kankakee River to regain portions of its former domain, but the fate of the Calumet region remains unresolved.

Two Thousand Bends of a Silver Thread: The Kankakee's Great Marsh

The Kankakee River lies in a shallow and broad valley between the Valparaiso Moraine and the Outer Uplands. For the first two-thirds of its length, the 110 miles from South Bend, Indiana, to Momence, Kankakee County, the river originally twisted into two thousand bends as it dropped in elevation just a little more than a hundred feet. (With the 250 miles of meanders, this decline averaged about five inches per mile.) The sluggish water rolls over a thick bed of gravel and sand, until it reaches a four-mile-long limestone outcropping or ledge at Momence. This divides the river basin in two and acts as a natural dam to impound the drainage of the upper valley, a watershed exceeding two thousand square miles.[1]

The natural reservoir cradled the "Great Marsh," one of the largest freshwater wetlands in the United States. Just how large seems to be a matter of some disagreement, for estimates of acreage range from 400,000 to 1 million.[2] For most of the year, sheets of water three to five miles wide and one to four feet deep flanked each side of the river channel.[3] Charles Bartlett described the river as it curled its way through the valley: "The river has been a mere thread of silver meandering through the sloughs, lily beds, and the rice; now trending over to the ancient bank on the right, and now wandering far off to the left; here creeping around and between the members of a group of islands, and then quite losing itself in ten thousand acres of rushes and reeds."[4]

The vastness of the Kankakee labyrinth was matched by the heterogeneity of its character, for virtually every natural community in the region was represented here. There were even a few small "tamarack swamps." More extensive was the floodplain forest that bordered the riverbanks from English Lake to Momence. It was rarely more than a mile wide, except to the south and east of Hebron where it flared to three miles. The trees included silver maple, black ash, white ash, American elm, black birch, yellow birch, bur oak, swamp white oak, and sycamore. In 1911, a few years before the river was to be straightened, Indiana's Commissioner of Fish and Game could still enthuse that the Kankakee "courses through a forest of great elms, and trees such as grow on wet ground, and the branches of these hang near, or touch the water. . . . All in all the scenery is altogether unlike that of any other river in Indiana."[5]

In woods like these near Schneider, Lake County, the botanist Charles Deam observed a spectacle that no one else has likely seen in this region: Indian pipe in such profusion "that it reminded one of a woods in winter when the snow was on the ground. Acres of these woods were carpeted with it. I revisited this woods several years later at the same time of the year but I was able to find only a plant here and there."[6]

A greater variety of trees cloaked the islands. Besides the lowland species already mentioned, there were beech, white oak, black oak, butternut, black walnut, sassafras, red maple, wild cherry, and pawpaw. Many of the islands provided outstanding displays of spring flowers—spring beauties, Dutchman's breeches, and violets.[7] Charles Bartlett depicts one particular island he calls Eagle Point, possibly Little Eagle Island in Lake County:

> This island . . . was covered in most parts with an oak-grove, with here and there a giant shell-bark hickory. The soft turf spread beneath this grove screened from view on all sides by the tops of dense thickets of dogwood, and marsh maples and soft willows that rose from the low ground surrounding the island. . . . Here and there, over the interior, was a clump of sassafras or a billowy area of wild roses. There was a place where a few white birches lifted their graceful, though ghostly, forms. . . . Where a boggy indentation at the base of the island completed the latter's heart-shaped outline, there stood a dark, compact mass of tamaracks. The delicate foliage of their tender green rose in exquisite contrast against the dull gray wall of massive oak-trunks.[8]

Most of the Kankakee country was marsh, the background through which the river and forests wound. Geographer Alfred Meyer, who devoted more scholarly attention to the Kankakee than probably anyone else, described it thus:

> Here as far as the eye can see, is an expanse of marsh interrupted only by an occasional upland oak grove on a sandy knoll or ridge, or possibly by a cluster of closely set pin oaks rising out of the water. . . . Miniature mounds with clumps of grass just emerging from the water betray the somewhat undulating character of the otherwise markedly far-flung flatness of the submerged terrain. Rank sedges and grasses and flags mark the shallower stretches. With these alternate the wild-rice swales; the cattail, spadder-dock, and smartweed sloughs; and the reed and lily ponds, water sites throughout the year.[9]

In the 1830s, the wandering bands of Potawatomi who seasonally inhabited the marshlands began leaving the area as required by the federal treaties of 1832 and 1836, and the first white settlers started taking up residence. Trappers and hunters, what Meyer calls the pioneer squatter, preferred the remote wooded island close to the marshes or river, while farmers opted for sites on the marsh periphery. Starting about 1880, a tourism industry was born, whereby lodges and guides would cater to urban hunters and anglers. So long as the life-giving waters continued to gather, the marsh enabled those who resided or visited to reap a mighty harvest.

The limited stands of timber were exploited heavily. "Swampers," as the Kankakee lumbermen were called, targeted white oak on the higher ground and elm, ash, maple, pin oak, and bur oak among the lowland species. But other trees, such as poplar and beech, were also taken.

Although much of the timber grew on the river's edge, the circuitous channel was a serious obstacle to floating the logs out. The swampers compensated by working in winter, when the logs were tied to the runners of horse-drawn sleds and pulled to the marsh edge for collection later. On cold winter nights, the road to Hebron, Porter County, would be clogged with "as many as one hundred sled loads of cut and trimmed trees, slowly moving toward town as one great procession." [10]

Around 1870, the Indian Island Sawmill Company launched the Kankakee River's first steamboat. The vessel's engine both powered a portable sawmill and pulled scows of cut lumber downstream to Momence. But the most notorious lumbering effort was undertaken by a Chicago furniture company in 1907. They bought acres of standing trees and imported both men and special ox-powered rigs from Kentucky to clear as much timber as possible in the shortest time. Fay Nichols says, "People came from miles around to witness the slaughter, to clasp their hands and to weep at the absolute destruction of that which they had enjoyed and admired for years." Ironically, because the foreign talent was unfamiliar with the convolutions of the river, most of the lumber was lost: "Millions of feet of the finest of hardwood lie strewn along the river for a distance of over twenty miles."

On a smaller scale, marsh inhabitants also collected other plant materials for home consumption or market. Huckleberries added to many a family's larder and, at times, could bring two cents a quart in trade with local merchants. One particularly enterprising store owner made annual pilgrimages to New York to replenish both his wares and to sell goods he brought from home. For months prior to his trip, he saved "for the eastern market any choice commodities which the environment of a wilderness village might supply cheaply and abundantly." Cranberries, maple sugar, dried huckleberries, and hickory nuts all appealed to sophisticated eastern tastes. Most valuable, though, were medicinal herbs like snakeroot and ginseng. The former could fetch a dollar a pound, while the latter's value depended on the size of the roots.[11]

The flooded immensity of the Kankakee Valley was a giant nursery, producing wildlife in unbelievable numbers and attracting hordes of others during migration. Throughout the literature of the marsh are glimpses of this lost world, most describing fishing or waterfowl hunting.

Fish provided a ready source of food and recreation. Walleyes (up to fifteen pounds), bullheads, buffalo, pickerel, catfish, bluegills, and crappies were among the popular species.[12] The recollections of F. E. Ling, a dentist from Hebron who spent days on the river as a child, are among the most detailed I have found:

> One season the river was alive with small pickerel weighing about a pound and a half. A boy friend and I caught eighty-seven in about an hour. He caught thirteen fish in thirteen straight casts of about thirty feet. . . . He threw his steel casting rod down in the boat and said, 'This is not fishing; it's slaughter.'
>
> In the spring of the year, after the ice had gone out and we had our first thunderstorm, the old fishermen would go dogfish [bowfin] spearing. They would anchor their boats on the shallow side of the river bend on a sand bar. . . . The fish would come drifting along from singles to droves of six or eight, and the fisherman would spear boatloads and salt them down.[13]

Ling regrets that the bowfin runs stopped after the river was dredged and that there are few left in the ditch. But even before the river was straightened, people feared the consequences of overfishing. At English Lake, Starke County, in 1874 the problem became particularly acute, for the superintendent of the Mak-saw-ba shooting club reported that "the fish were being exterminated by constant netting, seining, and spearing." Netting had already eliminated the pickerel, and "lawbreakers" had started employing dynamite.[14]

If there was one natural feature on which the Kankakee's fame rested, it was the incredible concentrations of waterbirds. One of the choicest locations for waterfowl was the thirty-six thousand acres of water and marsh known as Beaver Lake in Newton County. Hunters measured the birds by the acre rather than by individuals, and at times most of the lake was covered. Burt Burroughs describes the lake in early spring: "At this time small, red-head [green-winged] teal occupied these waters literally by the hundreds of thousands. Out on the broad expanse of the lake proper and the open reaches of that famous hunting ground known as the 'Gaff Ranch,' there dwelt mallards, geese, and swans literally by the acre. Judge Hunter recalls that often as he lay in his blind he has watched a flight of these red-heads go over, scarcely six feet above his head, a veritable cloud of them acres in extent, a living blanket four or five feet in thickness."[15]

Swans congregated here in large numbers as well: "There was an element of the spectacular and the beautiful in this moving picture of the wildlife of the lake, especially at such times when the swans rose in numbers from the surface of the water, a roaring, turbulent, billowy mass, their white breasts and wings glowing with an iridescence like mother-of-pearl where the sunlight was reflected from them." One hunter remembers shooting a whole wagonful and then drying the skins for feathers, only to have moths ruin the entire load.

There is evidence that swans nested in the environs of Beaver Lake until 1872 or 1873. Such swans would have been trumpeters, known to have bred in few other Midwestern locations and none nearly as recent (excluding reintroductions). Farmers would occasionally raid nests and place the eggs under poultry for hatching. Lanier Barker told an interviewer how he and his brother took two swan eggs in 1869 or 1870. It was not an easy task, for the nest was in a section known as the "Black Marsh," "a quagmire of . . . ooze and slime . . . eight or ten feet in depth."[16]

In the more wooded parts of the valley, wood ducks were especially abundant. Possessed of singular beauty and a haunting call, the wood duck personifies the flooded river bottom: "For about two hours before dark in certain areas of bayous, ponds, or sloughs that had lots of old logs, floating flag roots and puckerbrush, the air was full of wood ducks, from singles to flocks of fifty coming to roost. It was not uncommon to see 500 wood ducks in the air at one time, in these areas."[17]

Only three roads crossed the Kankakee Valley in the 1830s. The western route went around the marsh at Momence, where the limestone ledge made fording the river easier. Clinging to ridges, the eastern and central routes minimized the distance needed to traverse the lowlands. By 1836, a ferry at the central crossing was transporting passengers across a mile and a half of marsh and river.[18] But in the eyes of many the situation remained intolerable. The almost impenetrable swath virtually segregated northern Indiana from the rest of the state, and to many it represented hundreds of thousands of idle acres.

Early attempts at draining the marshes were poorly organized and performed by laborers wielding spades. But by the middle 1800s, fortunes began favoring marsh destruction. Indiana enacted the 1852 Drainage Act, a law providing that the proceeds from the sale of state-owned marshland would be held in a fund and distributed to promote drainage of these properties. Counties became responsible for administering the program.[19]

Unfortunately for Indiana, but fortunately for the marsh, widespread fraud and corruption squandered much of the money earmarked for drainage purposes. In counties such as Newton and Lake, the swampland fund dried up

54. Marshy bayou on Kankakee River near Hebron, Porter County, circa
1910. Photo by F. E. Ling. (Courtesy John Spinks, Sr.)

55. Logging on the Kankakee River near Kouts, Porter County, 1900.
Photo by Frank Woodruff. (Courtesy Chicago Academy of Sciences.)

56. Trappers camp with muskrats on Kankakee River, near Hebron,
Porter County, circa 1910. Photo by F. E. Ling. (Courtesy
John Spinks, Sr.)

before the swampland did. A major investigation later documented the improprieties, but not one party was indicted or forced to return tainted gains. Unbridled greed provided the marsh with but a temporary reprieve, however.
With new legislation and the introduction of the steam dredge in 1884, the
technology, money, and political power were in place to annihilate the Great
Marsh.[20]

A state-commissioned report in the 1880s concluded that removal of the
limestone ledge at Momence would go a long ways toward drying the basin.
Indiana appropriated $65,000 for the project, which was completed in 1893.
For the money, 66,447 cubic yards of rock were removed, leaving "a channel
not quite 1½ miles long, 300 feet wide, and 2½ feet deep."[21] Also left was the
marsh, and it became clear that more of the ledge had to be removed (Illinois
refused) or the river had to be channelized.

Channelization began on the upper stretches of the river in 1896. W. H.
Frazier and S. R. Sapirie, engineers with the Indiana Department of Conservation, explained: "The improvement of the channel of the river began at the
upper end by straightening the bends and cleaning the natural channel. This
being a comparatively small project, it was executed by individual effort and resulted in the making of a channel seven miles long, which greatly benefited
eight thousand acres. The effect of this and succeeding changes of the river,
which speedily followed, was to increase the flood conditions upon the lower
lands so that it became imperative to continue their drainage systems."[22]

Two thousand loops of river were converted into seven ditches dredged
end to end from South Bend to the Illinois line. There were Miller Ditch, Kankakee River Improvement Ditch, Danielson Arm of the Place Ditch, Kankakee
Reclamation Ditch, Marble Ditch, Davis Ditch, and William's Ditch. When

57. Steam-powered dredge that made the channelization of the
Kankakee River possible. Near Hebron, circa 1915. Photo by
F. E. Ling. (Courtesy John Spinks, Sr.)

58. Kankakee River near Hebron soon after river was channelized,
circa 1915. Photo by F. E. Ling. (Courtesy John Spinks, Sr.)

the William's Ditch reached the Illinois border in 1917, less than thirty thousand acres of the wetlands, and none of the original Kankakee River, was left
in Indiana. All that remained of the curving river were the eight miles in Illinois below Momence, and the crews from Indiana would have mutilated that
stretch as well if the old swamp folk hadn't driven them off with rifles.[23]

The draining of Beaver Lake began in the 1880s and ended in 1917. The
final act brought about a carnage that was probably repeated throughout the
Great Marsh, but at Beaver Lake people saw it and remembered:

> In the nesting places of the shallow swamps the geese had but recently
> brought off their broods. . . . There were tens of thousands of these big,

59. Aerial photo of Kankakee River taken in 1973. The river's channel is
a series of ditches in Indiana but retains its winding character upon
reaching Illinois, marked by arrow. (Photo by U.S. Department of
Agriculture and other participating agencies.)

soft, fuzzy goslings suddenly bereft of their native element—water. . . .
The sight was pitiable, says A. L. Barker, who, as a boy witnessed it all.
They walked and rolled and dragged themselves painfully to the few depressions in the marsh bottom where water still remained and crowded
these places to suffocation. For days the sandy spaces roundabout the
sloughs were alive with the roly-poly forms of these goslings, some dead,
others dying, while the remainder toiled persistently though painfully
landward, under a burning sun, in search of water.

The geese were not the only ones to suffer. With the passing of the
waters of the lake the hosts of buffalo, catfish, and pickerel contained
therein were left marooned in shallow pools or stranded helplessly in the
black muck of the lake's bottom. There were buffalo and pickerel of enormous size, patriarchs of these primeval waters, whose carcasses littered the
bottom of the lake so thickly that one could step from one to another in any
direction, like upon so many stepping-stones. For weeks, after the release
of the waters, this spot was like a charnel house, from which emanated odors
of fish and game, rotting under the rays of a hot sun, that smelled to Heaven
and hung over this citadel of the wilderness like a pestilential blanket.[24]

Levees were then constructed to protect the now extensive croplands from flood damage. But it soon became apparent that portions of the former marsh would always hold water. Several years after it was established in 1919, the Indiana Department of Conservation began acquiring chunks of this "sub-marginal" land to create refuges. Ten square miles of restored marsh are now protected within the following state fish and game areas: LaSalle, Willow Slough, Kankakee, Jasper-Pulaski, and Kingsbury. Other state and county holdings in or near what was the former marsh include Grand Kankakee Marsh County Park, Lake County (960 acres); Beaver Lake Nature Preserve, Newton County (640 acres); Round Lake Conservation Area and Nature Preserve, Starke County (140 acres); and Koontz Lake Conservation Area and Nature Preserve, Starke County (148 acres). Adding to the protected acreage, the Indiana chapter of the Nature Conservancy acquired 7,209 acres of grassland and savanna in Newton County. In Illinois, much of the Momence wetlands is preserved under state ownership.

The recent history of the upper Kankakee valley is also driven by concerns over unwanted water. Indiana has tended to opt for moving the water downstream as quickly as possible. Illinois, with little of the marsh, has seen the river as a place for enjoyment rather than as a threat to economic growth. Consequently the two states have often been at odds, with Illinois resisting Indiana's drainage schemes.

This schism flared in 1979 when a series of floods prompted Indiana to approve clearing the main channel of snags and other obstructions. Gordon Graves and fellow conservationists alerted Illinois officials, who went into federal court to have the river put under the jurisdiction of the Corps of Engineers. Illinois prevailed, and the corps ruled that the environmental damage caused by the clearing outweighed the benefits. Indiana retaliated by using its political muscle to divide federal control over the river between three different Corps of Engineers' offices: Rock Island, Chicago, and Detroit.[25]

Two years earlier, the Indiana legislature had created the Kankakee River Basin Commission to oversee water issues. When the corps shot down the channel cleaning proposal, the commission looked to other approaches to managing flood water. Not only had the regulatory climate changed, but there was also almost no undrained land left and agriculture was giving way to subdivisions. It was physically impossible to contain all the runoff into the main channel, regardless of how high the levees rose.

Jody Melton, director of the commission, says that the new strategy relies heavily on a wide levee system. Constructing levees away from the river would shield seventy thousand acres of land from inundation by holding water from a hundred-year flood on 30,714 acres that would develop into wetlands. The rebuilding of the Williams Levee, Lake County, in late 1987 proved to be a highly successful pilot project, "protecting cropland to the north and allowing land between the levee and the river to become permanently intertwined with the river system."[26] The total cost of the program has been estimated at $100 million, so for now it is a goal to be implemented on a piecemeal basis as funds become available.

The latest chapter in the story of the Kankakee River bodes well for the future. People such as the late Gordon Graves, J. R. Black, and Jody Melton understood that Illinois and Indiana have to collaborate on river-related issues. They enlisted the support of their local U.S. Representatives, and on September 14, 1995, Congress authorized the U.S. Army Corps of Engineers to conduct a multiyear study with the two states to identify and evaluate measures that integrate flood control, ecological protection and restoration, and recreational enhancement within the bistate Kankakee River Basin. The project marks the first time since Illinois allowed Indiana to remove part of the Momence ledge in 1893 that the two states have agreed to cooperate with respect to the river.

One element of the study is a U.S. Fish and Wildlife Service proposal for a thirty thousand acre national wildlife refuge in the Kankakee's upper basin. Another idea under consideration is to reconnect the river with the meanders that were so critical to its original character. If these and other conservation proposals reach fruition, and combined with existing preserves, nearly a hundred thousand acres of the old marsh would be protected and subject to restoration. While no one is contemplating re-creating the marsh to its former size, the lollygagging river that looped its way through marshland and forest may once again become a reality and not merely the stuff of dreams.

The Marsh That Will Not Die: The Calumet

Five shallow lakes stretched across the Chicago Lake Plain on either side of the Illinois and Indiana border. From west to east they were Lake Calumet, Hyde Lake, Wolf Lake (bisected by the state line), Lake George, and Bear Lake (or Berry Lake). Just to the south of these bodies and extending east, "a curious and interesting stream," sometimes called the Calumet River, literally doubled back on itself so that it flowed in opposite directions through two nearly parallel channels before entering Lake Michigan at Miller Beach in Gary.[27] Extensive areas of marsh and wet prairie fringed the open water or formed in shallow depressions between sand and gravel ridges supporting various types of woodland. One local historian recollected that one-third of the land was upland woods and the remainder "prairie and swamp."[28]

This was the Calumet region of the pioneer era.[29] James Landing, for

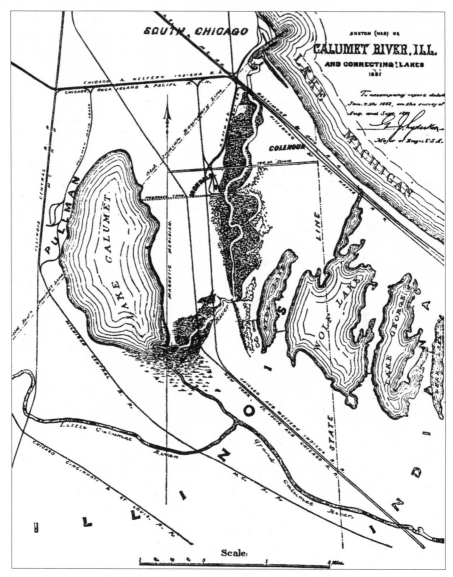

60. The Lake Calumet area in 1881, with the dark areas indicating
marsh. (Map published by U.S. Senate, Exec. Doc. 1881, 1st sess.,
No. 77. p. 5, and reprinted in Colten [1985, 17]).

many years on the geography faculty at the University of Illinois at Chicago,
estimates that the Illinois portion north of 138th Street once held twenty-two
thousand acres of wetland, fifteen thousand of which were in Chicago. The
Cady Marsh, south of the Calumet River near Dyer, Indiana, consisted of
thousands of additional acres, as did the Indiana Dunes area to the east.[30]

Inhospitable terrain kept most settlers at bay, and the majority of travelers avoided the region by following the Lake Michigan shoreline. An ardent

hunter and angler, S. C. Clarke was one who did make many visits to Lake Calumet during the 1840s. The ride from Chicago crossed heavy sand and took three or four hours, "chilling northers whistling about our ears."[31] He described what awaited: the lake "was then a solitary sheet of water, two or three miles long, in a dense swamp, with a deep border of reeds and rushes around it, accessible only through a winding creek from the Calumet River; so blind an entrance that it was necessary to put a flag or other signal to mark it, or one might wander over these miles of lake and water plants for hours or days without getting back to the river."

Farther east, along the Little Calumet River near Tolleston (south of what would be Gary), the Tolleston Club kept two thousand acres for its membership that still looked wild into the 1880s: "The whole of the area . . . is covered with innumerable sloughs, bayous, morasses, ponds, and mudholes of endless variety of shape, in size all the way from a small pool up to a forty-acre pond or lake, divided and interspersed with fields of wild rice and cane, bogs, lily pads, rushes and muskrat houses, and yet so formed by nature that a hunting boat can pass through openings . . . almost over the entire ground and even to the river proper. Still even to this day there are many sloughs totally inaccessible to boats."[32]

Wolf Lake drew the attention of botanists who were impressed by the variety of its wetland vegetation. Dr. Pepoon found fourteen species of willows along one four-mile strip on the western side of the lake from Lake Michigan to Hegewisch. Black (*Salix nigra*) and peach-leaved willows (*S. amygdaloides*) inhabited wet woods next to the lake, and bog willow (*S. pedicellaris*) and hoary willow (*S. candida*) were restricted to the "boggy grounds" at the southern end of the stretch. In wet sand, Bebb's willow (*S. bebbiana*) grew in scattered clumps, while drier sand harbored prairie willow (*S. humilis*).[33]

Most of the local pondweeds were also in Wolf Lake, prompting Pepoon to comment on "the richness of this comparatively small body of water in this genus of pondweeds." Of the fourteen species he encountered in the lake, Richardson's pondweed (*Potamogeton richardsonii*), Fries's pondweed (*P. friesii*), stiff pondweed (*P. strictifolius*), grass-leaved pondweed (*P. gramineus*), and fern pondweed (*P. robbinsii*) are particularly intolerant of pollution and have disappeared from most places in the Chicago region. Some, however, still persist at Wolf Lake.

Donald Culross Peattie considered a walk around Wolf Lake's "curving reedy shore" to be one of the most beautiful in the Chicago vicinity. In September, he cherished the ripening "spikes of Indian rice, . . . looking like aquatic corn." And a little farther to the south, the hike traversed a "fairy meadow of scarlet and blue lobelia."[34]

The wetlands of the Calumet area were also home to *Thismia americana*,

61. *Thismia americana,* in situ near Lake Calumet, where it was found by N. Pfeiffer
between 1912 and 1916. The oldest flower appears on the right.
(From Pfeiffer 1914.)

one of the most perplexing mysteries of North American natural history.[35] The half-inch tall saprophytic plant first became known to science when Norma Pfeiffer, then a graduate student in botany at the University of Chicago, discovered the species in a damp prairie near 119th and Torrence Avenue, just north of where the Ford Motor Company is now located. Thismia grew amid marsh club moss (*Selaginella apoda*) and the moss *Aneura pinguis*, although most commonly where they were sparse. Many decades later, she revealed that she also found a few of the plants at a nearby cattail marsh.

Her initial find was on August 1, 1912, and she saw specimens at the site over the next four years. With the exception of one flimsy claim from Arkansas in 1948, no one has reported the species again anywhere since Pfeiffer's last observation on September 1, 1916. Based on a letter Pfeiffer wrote to Robert Mohlenbrock in 1984, it appears that the only other people who ever saw *Thismia* in situ were three graduate students to whom she showed the plant.

Adding to the plant's mystique is that the genus *Thismia*, of which there are about twenty-five species, is entirely tropical except for *T. americana* and the very similar *T. rodwayi. Thismia rodwayi*, however, lives in the forests of New Zealand and Tasmania on the other side of the globe. The biogeographical aspects of the two plants are remarkable: somehow, during the few thousand years since Lake Chicago's recession, *T. rodwayi* or a common ancestor arrived on a prairie near Lake Calumet and evolved into a new species. (Of course it might not have arrived directly here, but that is pure conjecture since it has never been found anywhere else.) The ranges of these two very closely related plants may represent "the most anomalous disjunction of all."[36]

Away from the wetlands, woods grew on the higher ground that was coveted by settlers. Frequent and unpredictable changes in the local water table made such dry sites attractive to Miami, Potawatomi, French, English, and Americans alike. These woods were cleared early, and few old descriptions remain. Near Lansing, where Torrence Avenue intersects the Bloom Township boundary, an old dune line contained "a heavy growth of black oak forest, an average of about forty large trees of two feet in diameter per acre and a dense growth of smaller trees of both white and black oak variety ranging in size of from three to ten inches in thickness and about forty feet tall." Another notable parcel of heavy timber lasting until the 1850s was called Roches Woods, located between Maple Avenue, Stony Creek, Union, and York Streets in Blue Island. It was protected by a fence, which helped maintain its original condition. Lady's slippers of unknown species survived here "after they had disappeared everywhere else in the neighborhood." There are still a few old growth oaks in such forest preserves as Beaubien Woods and Dan Ryan Woods.[37]

The combination of the Calumet River, extensive wetlands, lakes, and connection with Lake Michigan endowed the Calumet area with an exceedingly rich fish fauna. Edward Nelson's report to the federal fish commission in 1878 includes a fascinating account of how Lake Michigan, Lake Calumet, and the river interacted, sharing their water and fish:

> When a strong north wind prevails for several days the lake water gradually forces the river water back, and sometimes the lake water extends up the river 12 miles from its mouth. . . . The lake water has a greenish tint and is much colder, while the river water has a dark-brownish color and is quite warm. As the lake water gradually ascends the channel the river fish retreat, and in a day or two lake fish take their places. When the wind stops blowing the lake water gradually flows back, the lake fish going with it, and the river fish return.[38]

During these northerlies, some Lake Michigan fish would leave the main channel of the river and enter the small artery that leads to Lake Calumet. Many were unable to find their way back and were trapped. The old fishermen favored this theory as a way to explain the large fish population within the smaller lake.

In his conversations with Lake Calumet fishermen, Nelson compiled a list of frequently caught species: burbot, black bass, rock bass, perch, white bass, pickerel, mullet sucker, buffalo, bullhead, lake catfish, bowfin, gar, sturgeon, and lampreys (probably brook lampreys). Of these, bullheads were exceedingly abundant in the lake; three thousand pounds were taken in a single net on January 13, 1876. Ten years earlier pickerel and black bass had also been commonly taken in the river, but over the preceding five years their numbers had plummeted so that "a person might troll for several days without getting a fish."

One major cause of fish decline was pollution, which Nelson attributed to a large distillery at Riverdale. In summer and fall, no fish were caught down-river of the discharge, while immediately above, several species were prevalent. To further corroborate his conclusion he related "the remarkable run of fish" he observed at Riverdale in January 1875. On his arrival, he encountered a large group of men and boys:

> They were armed with shovels, pitchforks, muskrat-spears, dip-nets, and indeed any implements that could be used in throwing or pulling the fish out of the water. Joining one of these groups I was astonished to find the water filled with a struggling mass of fishes, all striving to get their noses to the surface of the water. . . . On the ice, to one side of the hole, was a pile of buffalo fish, large perch, bullheads, a few pickerel and black bass, which had been caught by one man with a dip-net. When he removed them, there were two one-horse wagonloads, amounting to over 2,500 pounds. Scattered about on the ice were hundreds of fishes not edible. Garpike were especially numerous. I counted over two hundred and seemed no nearer the end than when I had commenced.

The fish "were very stupid," even those just taken out of the water barely moved. Later in the season, when the ice had melted and water levels dropped, Nelson could see the full effects of the distillery. For five miles downstream, the river's banks were strewn with thousands of dead fish. In some places they formed a layer several inches thick.[39]

◄○► ◄○► ◄○►

What the marshland of the western Calumet area first offered the Potawatomi, it also offered to the Euro-Americans until well into the 1870s. And it remains the primary reason the extant marshes so richly deserve to be protected: the great concentrations of birds that collect here. In fact, and I have considered this carefully, I believe that with the exception of the refuges in southern Illinois and certain areas along the Illinois and Mississippi rivers, no place in the state attracts more birds than the western Calumet. Thus, although this history of the western Calumet avifauna focuses on waterfowl and waders, it should be borne in mind that most other locally occurring birds also use the area for migration, breeding, and/or wintering.

Early evidence of the Calumet's abundant bird life is provided by James Watson Webb, who as a young officer stationed at Fort Dearborn in 1822 would join his comrades on hunting excursions into the Calamink swamps, as they were then called. On fall mornings they would awaken early, so that dawn would find them properly positioned amid the rushes of Lake Calumet:

> The wildfowl was so incalculably numerous that it is scarcely possible to give you any adequate idea of their numbers. . . . The bay was literally filled with game, old and young, and they simultaneously rose, and at times absolutely obscured the sun from the beach over which they passed and around which they circled. As this cloud of game passed each officer fired and then took another of his guns to repeat his shot until all his guns had been discharged. . . .
>
> Then followed the picking up and collection of game. I dare not name the number we would then collect of a morning lest you might doubt the accuracy of my memory. . . . There were swan, pelican, geese, brandt [sic], canvasbacks, redheads, mallards, teal of every variety, and ducks of every kind which breed upon this continent.[40]

Henry Eenigenburg, born in the region in 1859, wrote of Lake Calumet that "when one would look upon the water from a distance, it would look like plowed ground, for the water was so covered with the feathered army in the spring and fall of the year." The fruit that arose from that liquid field became known nationally. Senator Stephen Douglas (most famous for his debates with Abraham Lincoln) told Chicago friends in 1859 how he and such colleagues as Henry Clay and Daniel Webster would formulate federal policy over meals of Chesapeake Bay canvasbacks. But when it was his turn to host, Douglas ordered a healthy quantity of Lake Calumet canvasbacks "whose toothsomeness fairly carried the day with his senatorial table guests." (In those days, canvasbacks could be obtained in the Chicago markets for thirty to fifty cents a pair.)[41]

A local hunter, calling himself "Bluewing," waxed nostalgic in the *American Field* of April 5, 1884: "Calumet! What a host of recollections this well-known name will recall to the memory of Chicago sportsmen, old as well as young! How many have stood on the river bank and heard the whiz and flutter of the blue-wing teals as they wheeled in countless thousands on some beautiful clear crisp frosty morning in the latter part of September, just arriving from their northern summer homes. How the blood fairly races through one's veins as just at daybreak the first flocks are seen skimming along the river!"[42]

Waterfowl in the early times brought the hunters, and sandpipers in the modern era brought the bird watchers. Thirty-eight species have been recorded in this century. Sandpipers gather wherever water collects, which in the Calumet lowlands is in many places. Favored locations were the cinder flats at 103rd Street and Doty Avenue at the north end of Lake Calumet and the Sanitary District Sewage Plant at the lake's south end. One species, the Wilson's phalarope, nested on the flats in larger numbers than anywhere else in the region or state. Birders found eleven nests in 1962, and six in 1963, but no breeding was detected after 1968, save for two nests in 1981.[43]

A glimpse of how many sandpipers and other waders move through the Lake Calumet area was given in 1968. Half of the lake was drained, and by early September thousands of birds swarmed to the exposed mud, including such rarities as marbled godwits, avocets, and one black-necked stilt. Charley Clark, in four decades of Chicago birding, had never seen anything like it. The spectacle was short lived, however, as the population had dropped to six hundred individuals by the following week.[44]

◄o► ◄o► ◄o►

The western Calumet area has experienced every abuse that a wealthy society can subject to a small surface of the earth except significant radiation exposure and warfare. (Two efforts to place an airport here failed.) Because these activities have been concentrated in such a confined and biologically important area as the Calumet, the consequences are apparent. A detailed account of what happened here would fill volumes, and even then it would be incomplete, for much went unrecorded. By necessity, therefore, what follows is portrayed with broad strokes.[45]

The earliest commerce and transportation through the Calumet were conducted along ridgelines that became trails and stagecoach routes and later railroads. The first to enter the area was the Lake Shore Railroad, which arrived from the east in 1851. It wasn't long, though, before railroads crisscrossed the district, necessitating the construction of large switching facilities. Artificial embankments augmented the natural ridges, thereby filling marsh and disrupting drainage patterns.[46]

Agricultural development to the south had been slowed by frequent flooding and the presence of the Cady Marsh, which in places was eight feet deep. To relieve the problem, farmers from Thornton to Hobart began diverting water from the marsh into the Little Calumet in 1862, and within six years they had successfully drained the area. The newly exposed land was said to be the most fertile of all, producing three hundred bushels of potatoes per acre.[47]

At the time of European settlement, the primary outlet of the Calumet River was near Miller, Indiana. Sandbars frequently blocked the entrance, however, and another even less well-defined passage shunted water north between Lake Calumet and Wolf Lake into Lake Michigan. After evaluating this western outlet, the U.S. Army Corps of Engineers in 1869 issued a report saying that "the Calumet River is susceptible to being made a capacious and good harbor," though they concluded that the economic benefits were insufficient. Despite this opinion, Congress responded to citizen prodding and initiated the project.[48]

The corps spent $296,000 during the years 1869–82 building the harbor, including two piers that kept it from clogging. Next on the agenda was creation of a channel through the low area to accommodate commercial boats. This process included further blocking the Miller outlet, thereby reversing the Grand Calumet so that it flowed west. Where the Grand Calumet met the Little Calumet, the two rivers proceeded north through the newly widened channel, now designated the Calumet River. Various companies began locating on the river in anticipation of the changes, among them "three steel mills, a shipyard, several grain elevators, an ice company, and a linseed oil maker." Some of these firms engaged in their own dredging operations and used the material to fill marshes so they could expand the usable land available to them.

The corps, however, was reluctant to complete the project until it had acquired the right-of-way from Lake Calumet to the mouth. Although most riparian owners gladly cooperated, there was still enough resistance to stall commencement of the final stages until 1888. Three years later, the upper stretches of the widened river began taking traffic, and by 1896 a smaller channel extended to Lake Calumet.

Meanwhile, in 1880 George Pullman started to build his immense railcar factory and the city designed to house his workforce. The one-half- by two-mile parcel was on the western shore of Lake Calumet, and by 1893 accommodated 12,600 residents. By dredging the lake, laborers obtained enough fill to raise the site from two to four feet above the surrounding marshland. The lake bottom also supplied the clay from which Pullman's bricks were made, an operation that averaged 18.5 million bricks a year.[49]

Besides its marshes and abandoned factories, the western Calumet is best known for the dumping that has gone on there for well over a century. Nelson's discussion of fish mortality at the hands of the distillery may be the first complaint to appear in print. Another early statement condemning pollution was made in 1893 by the commander of the Army Engineers, who found that keeping the Grand Calumet River channel clear was a fruitless exercise because it "filled up rapidly by slaughterhouse refuse and filth from manufacturing establishments and solid matter from the sewage poured into the dead stream."[50]

Table 5. Estimates of Iron and Steel Waste Production, 1885–1920 (in Pounds per Year)

Year	Phenols	Cyanide	Lube Oil	H$_2$SO$_4$	FeSO$_4$
1885	13,283	5,583	1,108,800	1,090,800	4,068,000
1890	38,730	10,904	2,165,699	2,130,541	7,945,584
1895	68,509	28,794	5,718,636	5,625,801	20,980,710
1900	86,098	36,186	7,186,813	7,070,144	26,367,205
1905	18,651	49,868	9,904,128	9,743,347	36,336,574
1910	222,377	93,463	18,562,347	18,261,010	68,102,117
1915	155,525	65,366	12,982,089	12,771,341	47,629,093
1920	267,792	112,550	22,353,279	21,990,401	82,010,405

Source. After Colten (1985, 27).

Note. H$_2$SO$_4$ = sulphuric acid; FeSO$_4$ = iron sulphate.

In a perverse way, this may have helped prolong the life of some wetlands, for the corps spent so much of its budget redredging that it couldn't afford to complete its original plans.

Navigational problems arising from dumping solid effluent directly into waterways underlined the advantages of using marshes and lakes instead. The North Chicago Rolling Mill, located at the mouth of the Calumet River just north of the federal piers, deposited so much slag and dredge that the area around it grew at four acres a year. With the aid of lake currents, the area of fill eventually reached three hundred acres. Another case was that of the Wisconsin Steel Company, which bought a large parcel of marsh in 1908 as a place to heap slag. And similar activities occurred throughout the Calumet.

The first attempt to capture industrial and residential waste was made at Pullman. The city's model sewage system pumped wastes away from Lake Calumet, where the factory obtained its water, and onto fields where they could percolate through the soil. (Celery from the Pullman farms was particularly prized for its high quality.) But by 1907, the system was no longer operating, and the raw sewage, both industrial and domestic, went directly into Lake Calumet and the Little Calumet River. Until the early 1920s, waste generators of every stripe discharged most, if not all, of their varied effluents directly into the shallow and slow-moving local waters. Table 5 shows some of what one single industry contributed to the pollution stream from 1885 to 1920. This period also coincides with the elimination of commercial and recreational fishing from the Calumet River and offshore waters of Lake Michigan.

In 1922 the Metropolitan Sanitary District completed two major projects that would have profound effects on waste disposal in the Calumet. First, the Calumet Sag Channel was opened. The Cal-Sag did to the Calumet River what the Sanitary and Ship Canal did to the Chicago River: it reversed the flow away from Lake Michigan and into the Des Plaines, where it eventually reached the Mississippi. From that point on, the Calumet region was no longer in the Lake Michigan watershed. Second, the district finished its Calumet Sewage Treatment works, which began processing domestic and some industrial wastes. Many companies resisted cooperating with the district, and significant changes did not begin until 1927 when the Illinois legislature granted the district explicit authority "to control and regulate the discharge of industrial wastes." (Interestingly, although Indiana also passed laws restricting water pollution, the Gary, Whiting, and Hammond areas were specifically exempted from having to comply.)

Unfortunately, local and state laws still proved incapable of curtailing irresponsible companies. Geographer Craig Colten observes that "when contrasted with national developments in waste disposal technology, industries in the Calumet area generally lagged in accepting new technology and dallied in adhering to regulations." Federal legislation, too, was enacted and ignored.

In 1954 the Corps of Engineers sued three large steel companies for continuing to dump in the waterways the corps was responsible for maintaining. Court records revealed hideous violations by the defendants, behavior suggesting that few advances had been made since the nineteenth century. Thousands of tons of solid waste flowed from their sewers directly into the Calumet River every year: Republic Steel added ten thousand tons, Interlake Iron twenty thousand tons, and Wisconsin Steel (International Harvester) twenty-seven thousand tons, which was just one part of the company's total daily discharge of 4.9 million gallons of untreated waste.

Although the court ruled in favor of the corps, a 1965 federal report found that at least two of the defendants were among eight polluters contributing 376 million gallons of liquid waste per day into the Calumet area. (Almost two-thirds of this was cooling water from Commonwealth Edison.) The study further concluded that the Grand Calumet River was incapable of even maintaining populations of sludge worms (Tubifex), animals whose toleration of low oxygen enables them to survive when literally every other living thing is gone. Eventually, tougher laws, heightened awareness of environmental issues, and decades of legal skirmishing "finally forced industries to halt untreated discharges in the late 1970s." Yet, at least as recently as 1996, there were places along the Grand Calumet River so saturated with chemicals that a person's weight could cause an oily substance to ooze from the bank to form a sheen on the water surface.

Ironically, even efforts at environmental protection led to the continuing desecration of the Calumet marshes. Emerging as an alternative to helter-skelter dumping into waterways was the designation of specific tracts of land as disposal sites. These landfills would consume hundreds of acres of marshland and become one of the Calumet's primary industries.

The first official landfill began operating in 1940. It was owned by the city of Chicago and was established as a disposal site for the city's municipal waste. Located at Lake Calumet's northern end, the site consisted of three hundred acres of marsh and water deemed by the city to be suitable for a landfill because of its remoteness, availability, and underlying clay soils. This facility remained active until about 1970, by which time it had filled over a fourth of Lake Calumet.

The Army Corps itself also contributed significantly to the loss of marshland. Starting in 1924, the corps had deposited dredge material into Lake Michigan at specifically chosen locations. But once again, it dawned on the authorities that dumping contaminated waste into Chicago's drinking water was an unwise thing to do. Consequently, in 1967 the corps changed its policy and began disposing dredge spoil at eleven "inland" locations within the Calumet region. From 1967 to 1976, these sites received over 2 million cubic yards of material.

At least fifty-one locations within the Calumet area are known to have been used for waste disposal. A 1990 study characterized these by type: thirteen hazardous waste sites, fifteen solid and industrial waste landfills, and twenty-three unauthorized and random dumps.[51]

Various other activities over the years also consumed habitat. Highways and collateral development necessitated major filling and disruption of surface hydrology. Railroad embankments in the 1870s separated Wolf Lake from its western sibling, Hyde Lake. Less than twenty years later, additional filling reduced Hyde Lake from 520 acres to 120 acres, and the distance between the two water bodies grew to almost three-quarters of a mile. Today, only twenty acres of beat-up marsh remain uncovered by the activities of Republic Steel. The construction of a Nike military facility obliterated yet more of the Wolf Lake wetlands. Because existing marshes are so small and isolated, it is difficult to appreciate their original pattern and extent. Jim Landing points out that the marshes at Eggers Woods Forest Preserve and Powderhorn Lake Forest Preserve were all once connected to Wolf Lake but are now miles apart.[52]

On June 7, 1925, the City of Chicago authorized a huge project to turn Lake Calumet into "a great industrial harbor." Alderman Guy Guernsey, sponsor of the bill, referred to the lake as "nothing more than a breeding place for mosquitoes and mud turtles." Under the plan, the city would give the Nickel Plate Railroad land to perform massive dredging and filling operations in the lake. This property would enable the company to build a rail line around the lake and to construct the facilities necessary to service its activities. One effect of this was to segregate the lake from adjacent marshes. Twelve hundred more acres would be filled directly by the city.[53]

62. Great blue heron, black-crowned night heron, and great egret
amid industrial landscape at Big Marsh, near Lake Calumet.
(Photo by and courtesy of Greg Neice.)

Within the past fifteen or so years, developers illegally destroyed wetlands west of Eggers Woods, and the Illinois International Port Authority
legally filled marshland on Lake Calumet's northern shore for a golf course.
The single greatest threat to the entire Calumet area in recent years, however,
was the proposed airport, which would have needed 9,400 acres of mostly wetland and existing neighborhoods.[54] It was telling that at the 1990 press conference where the plan was first announced, not one newsperson asked one question about the loss of marshland or endangered species. And when the proposal
was mercifully defeated by the state senate in the summer of 1992, it was due
more to a struggle between two powerful politicians than concerns over conservation or residential displacement.

According to Landing's estimates, of the twenty-two thousand acres of
wetland that once occurred in the Illinois part of the Calumet only five hundred remain. Of these, only Burnham Prairie and a section of prairie in Powderhorn Lake Forest Preserve have high-quality plant communities. Other
sites are of statewide significance, however, because they harbor threatened or

endangered species. Powderhorn Lake has one of Illinois' largest populations of banded killifish. Wolf Lake still has banded killifish and Iowa darter, as well as at least two state-listed pondweeds: grass-leaved and fern (still found there in 1987 but not 1991). Van Vlissingen Prairie provides habitat for the state-endangered false golden sedge (*Carex garberi*).

The best-known remnants, however, are the open water marshes that are so attractive to birds. The Big Marsh, Indian Ridge Marshes, Dead Stick Pond, the shores and open water of Lake Calumet, and Hegewisch Marsh are among the premier sites. Most, if not all, of these marshes have formed over fill, so they have little plant diversity, being dominated by *Phragmites* and cattails. This fact has been used by some to minimize their importance, but it is indisputable that they have provided vital nesting and foraging habitat for many state-threatened and -endangered birds, including pied-billed grebe, double-crested cormorant, great egret, black-crowned night heron, least bittern, common moorhen, black tern, and yellow-headed blackbird. Migrants also flock to these places in large numbers.

Conservation victories in the Calumet have been slow in arriving. At the turn of the century, Dwight Perkins authored an official report that advocated turning Lake Calumet and three thousand surrounding acres into a park, citing its interesting geological and botanical history.[55] Many of the sites identified in the report as being worthy of protection did become forest preserves but, alas, not this one. In 1952, there was apparently a modest, and unsuccessful, effort by Field Museum botanists and others to prevent the destruction of the *Thismia* site.

It wasn't until the late 1970s that there began a systematic effort to build coalitions and enlist public officials to improve the environmental conditions of the Calumet region. After decades of neglect, the area is currently enjoying a flurry of attention: a compilation made in 1997 listed thirty-eight government and private organizations actively involved in furthering environmental protection. One stellar example involves the City of Chicago. Seven years after the demise of its airport proposal, the city is now moving forward on a different plan: to build a major environmental education center near the Indian Ridge Marsh, which it is purchasing as a preserve.

This recent interest in the Calumet area is the product of hard work by many people on both sides of the state line. I am compelled to single out the contribution of Marian Byrnes, even though she would probably demur. Over the many long years, her Zen-like patience and persistence, along with considerable perspicacity, have been critical in helping mold a new vision for the Calumet area.

An important event in the struggle to protect the Calumet wetlands occurred in 1985 when Jim Landing prepared the "Conceptual Plan for the

Lake Calumet Ecological Park: Chicago, Illinois." This document identifies the sites within Illinois that should be protected, restored, and made part of a comprehensive park. Implementation of the plan received a boost in 1996 when, with the urging of Congressman Jerry Weller, the National Park Service undertook a detailed study to determine the feasibility of including the Calumet region in the national park system. What emerged from the effort was a proposal to wed the natural, cultural, and historical features of the region into a bistate Calumet National Heritage Area. A federally funded entity made up of local people would be formed to provide oversight of the park. To ensure that there is maximum support for the proposal in both Indiana and Illinois, work is underway to resolve boundary details and other issues before legislation creating the heritage area is formally introduced.

It is not clear to me why official recognition and protection of these wetlands have been so long in coming. Perhaps it was because certain influential people eyed them as additional landfill space. (As active dumps exhaust their capacity, the revenue accruing to those who can still legally accept material is astronomical: landfills are goldmines.) And Craig Colten points to psychological factors: "The rusting industrial skyline and the view of an open wasteland east of Pullman give the public the impression that the Calumet area is nothing more than an outdated manufacturing district. Landscapes of dereliction do little for an area's public image, and imagery is critical in future development. Demolition crews and waste heaps define the area as incapacitated and suggest that garbage disposal is the most fitting use for this property. As long as the Calumet area is associated with such an image, politicians and policy makers will be predisposed to think of it in those terms."[56]

But above the "landscapes of dereliction," particularly at the ebb of a summer's day, the sky is transformed into a busy thoroughfare used by the flocks that depend on the Calumet waters. Ring-billed and herring gulls are ubiquitous as they circle between their great nesting colony in Lake Calumet and the dumps that provide them succor. Loose wedges of double-crested cormorants, sated from a day's feeding on the open water of the lakes, return to their roost amid the cottonwoods that fringe the quarry at Riverdale. Great egrets and great blue herons slowly work their way across the horizon as well, but singly or in small groups. Then, just before darkness, the black-crowned night herons appear, headed for foraging grounds sheltered by the cover of night.

I know of no other place in the region where the skies are so constantly filled with birds across such a wide front. In this respect, the Calumet is almost maritime. Far from an ocean, of course, it is but the tatters of a once great marsh—a marsh that refuses to die.

10

Lake Michigan's Rim:
Beaches, Dunes, and Bluffs

Here, on the shores of a great freshwater sea, whose moisture is constantly being carried southward by the prevailing northwest winds, and tempered both in summer and winter by its position on the lake, is a region so wonderful that it should be kept for all time as a great natural park for study and the recreation of millions of people of the middle west. —Orpheus Moyer Schantz (1919)

Setting the Scene

In its variety of landforms, plants, and animals, the land ringing Lake Michigan is a virtual microcosm of the entire region. This circumscribed province harbors superb prairies, savannas, forests, and wetlands. Beach communities and pannes (a type of wetland) are found only here.

Much of this diversity is attributable to the most recent glacial incursion. We have already discussed Lake Chicago, the imprint it left as it receded, and the lake plain that emerged. But to understand the lakefront, we have to look more closely at the changes wrought during the thousands of years it took for the glacier to disappear.

Geologists now recognize twelve major phases in the 14,500-year history of Lake Chicago and Lake Michigan, each of which represents expansions or contractions of the lake. (See fig. 63.) Lake level changes were caused by four principal factors: advances and recessions of glacial ice within the larger Great Lakes Basin; isostatic rebound, whereby land slowly rises once relieved of glacial weight; enlargement of outlets through erosion; and the varying amounts of water entering the lake.[1]

Some dune formations that mark the various lakeshore boundaries are distinct, while others have become obscured. The Indiana Dunes National Lakeshore is a good place to see both scenarios. At the lakeshore's western end,

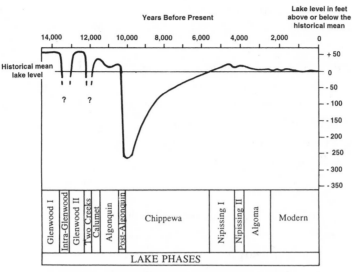

Years Before Present

Lake level in feet
above or below the
historical mean

63. Phases of the glacial lakes in the southern part of the Lake
Michigan basin. (Figure by and courtesy of Mike Chrzastowski, Illinois
Geological Survey, Champaign, Ill.)

the near-shore Nipissing dunes are separated from the inland Tolleston dunes by the Long Lake marsh complex. (The Tolleston dunes formed during the Algonquin phase of Lake Chicago.) Where the wetland ends at Midwest Steel, the two dune systems merge so that the high dunes extending through the state park to Beverly Shores are Nipissing on the lakeward side and Tolleston on the landward side. At the south and east parts of the lakeshore, Tolleston and Calumet dunes are separated by the Great Marsh. Calumet and Glenwood dunes are also separated by a low area on the west but eventually abut each other farther east (near Ly-co-ki-we Trail, close to the visitor center).

At Illinois Beach State Park and Spring Bluff Forest Preserve in Lake County, the sand deposits are all Nipissing dunes or younger. The dunes lie on a northeast to southwest axis and become progressively more recent as they go south. In the northwest portion of the area, sand deposits are approximately 3,500 years old, while in the southeast corner they may be less than eighty years old.[2]

The most dramatic sandscapes are products of modern and Lake Nipissing deposits. With the help of southerly currents and westerly winds, these sand deposits have mounded into huge dunes from Porter County to Berrien County. Their height blocks the western winds, creating moist and fire-free pockets where rich mesic forests have developed.

On the beaches of Illinois and Wisconsin, however, the same prevailing westerly winds push sand into the lake. The modest dunes that form result from less frequent easterly winds, particularly the fierce autumn storms that rush out of the northeast.[3] With no dunes substantial enough to provide shelter from the wind, the areas free of water support fire-climax prairie and oak savanna.

Wave-transported sediment has created beach ridges of varying ages, sizes, and vegetational stages, which in turn enable a wide range of natural communities to thrive in remarkably close quarters. At Illinois Beach State Park, for example, it is often possible to start with feet submerged in the open water of Dead River and, in ten strides to the east, traverse marsh, sedge meadow, and three kinds of sand prairie before reaching a dry oak savanna ridge.

In the northeasternmost corner of Racine County and from Winnetka to Waukegan, the lakeshore consists not of the sandy bottom of vanished lakes but rather of the moraines of the Lake Border Upland. Here, steep ravines and eroding clay bluffs provide unique assemblages of plants rich in northern relicts. A few of the species found here are unknown elsewhere in the region.

In addition to topographical variation, Lake Michigan contributes to the biological diversity of the lakefront by creating climatic conditions different from inland areas. These include increased moisture, warmer winters, and cooler summers that enable disparate floral elements to thrive in close proximity to each other. Perhaps the classic example is the boreal bearberry or kinnikinnick (*Arctostaphylos uva-ursi*), sharing a dune with the eastern prickly pear cactus (*Opuntia humifusa*), of a genus with southwestern connections.

Much of the lakefront has been altered by urbanization and industry. For example, nothing of the original Chicago lakefront remains. Although much of it is park, most rests on "manmade fill." Debris from the great fire of 1871, earth from construction projects, and even offal from the stockyards literally support the realized dreams of entrepreneurs and officials alike. Its principal significance to local natural history is as habitat to migrating birds and for the populations of such rare plants as sea rocket (*Cakile edentula*) and seaside spurge (*Euphorbia polygonifolia*) that persist on a few beaches, including Montrose and Rainbow.[4]

Both Pepoon and Watts write of substantial dunes that once studded the city's lakeshore, from Edgewater to Graceland.[5] John Caton's lakefront account from the early 1830s provides an even earlier glimpse:

> There were along where Michigan Avenue now is walled with palatial mansions innumerable sand hills rising to a considerable height, overrun by the wild juniper loaded with its fragrant berries at the feet of which stretched away to the southeast the soft smooth beach. . . . A pleasant ramble was also found along the beach north of the river where also the drifting sand had

been piled by the shifting winds into a thousand hills stretching farther back from the waters than on the south, but here the juniper bush was replaced by a stunted growth of scraggly pines often hilled high up by the drifting sand.

At Chicago alone does the Grand Prairie actually abut upon Lake Michigan for the distance of four miles between Oak Woods, now Hyde Park, and the mouth of the Chicago River. Here alone do the waters of the lake actually lave the head of this great prairie. Everywhere else are these two great bodies of land and water separated by bodies of timber of greater or less width along the shores of the lake.[6]

W. H. Caulkins wrote in 1906 of "the many live or dead swamps or swales—that not long ago existed back of the sands—as in Washington and Jackson Parks."[7] Although these kinds of swales are now known to be rich and rare, and far more valuable than mowed bluegrass and manicured trees, park planners and enthusiasts held (and still hold) them in contempt. In her 1972 history of Chicago parks, Lois Wille writes with enthusiastic approval of the conversion of "nearly 2,000 acres of meadow and wasteland and marsh into gardens and playgrounds." She then addresses Fredrick Law Olmsted's work on the two south-side parks: "He studied the series of marshes and ponds and sand ridges along the shore from 56th Street to 67th Street, relieved only by a few stunted oak trees covered with mold, and called it a 'forbidding place.' The soil was so sandy that water quickly drained away, and large plants died for lack of moisture. He proposed that the marshes be deepened into lagoons, with the fill used to elevate the surrounding land."[8]

While meadow and marsh were still forbidding to most people in the 1890s, the beauty of the lakefront changed enough attitudes over time to protect many extraordinary places. The most prolonged battle was waged over the magnificent Indiana Dunes, a struggle that eventually led to the establishment of the first national park in an urban area. Less well-known campaigns have saved important parts of Chiwaukee Prairie, Illinois Beach State Park, the Lake Border Upland, and the Berrien County shore. The fate of other valuable sites remains an open question.

So Many Fine Examples of Rare and Beautiful Species:
Natural Communities of the Indiana Dunes

Large swatches of the Indiana Dunes have been obliterated, but the surviving habitat supports a variety of life virtually without equal in this country.[9] This is not hyperbole. Based on National Park Service data, the Nature

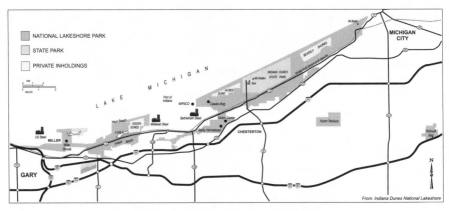

64. Map of Indiana Dunes National Lakeshore showing place names.

Conservancy's Great Lakes Program has reported that the Indiana Dunes National Lakeshore "ranks third of all U.S. National Parks in plant diversity, even though its acreage totals less than 3% [of] either of the top two (Great Smoky Mountains and Grand Canyon)."[10]

Scientists have long recognized the importance of the Indiana Dunes, and consequently the area has been studied far more thoroughly than any other portion of the Chicago region. Most celebrated of the work was initiated over a hundred years ago by Henry Chandler Cowles and his associates at the University of Chicago. Cowles became a seminal figure in the development of plant ecology, the study of the relations between plants and their environment.[11] Because of the changeability inherent in dunes, Cowles could relate ecological succession to dynamic geological processes, and he found the Indiana Dunes to be an ideal research site. His efforts conferred on the dunes an aura of scientific significance that has been amplified by successive generations of biologists, many of whom either worked for or received support from the Indiana Dunes National Lakeshore.

◄○► ◄○► ◄○►

Among the harshest of all natural environments in the region is the lower beach or wash zone. No plant permanently inhabits this narrow strip where the waves of Lake Michigan continuously break on the shore. If an odd seed were to germinate, the pounding water would soon dislodge it from its precarious anchorage.[12]

While depauperate in living vegetation, this wet desert is not without organic material, for it becomes a graveyard where Lake Michigan deposits its casualties on the darkened sand. Victor Shelford described a June walk along the Indiana shoreline:

The waves were rolling moderately high, and the beach was covered with a host of insects, chiefly alive, though many were dead. . . . Often the live ones were still clinging to small sticks upon which they had floated ashore by the fifties. These insects represented all orders, belonging to various habitats near the lake. . . . With them were occasional fish, some with large round scars showing the work of the lampreys; others that had evidently died from other causes. On other occasions dead muskrats, dogs, cats, [and] birds of all kinds have been found in these lines of drift.[13]

This organic debris attracts, at least on a temporary basis, skunks, sandpipers, gulls, toads, tiger beetles, blowflies, spiders, and other animals that seek the accumulating protein.

The middle beach, usually unscathed by the storms of summer but swept by those of winter, supports a unique but sparse flora. These plants have specific adaptations that enable them to survive the inhospitable conditions, and all are annuals, for the lashing by winter storms would prove fatal to species requiring stability. They must also survive the scourges of wind-driven sand and the scorching summer heat.[14] Sea rocket, the dominant member of this community, has thick fleshy leaves resistant to desiccation. Another frequent species, the seaside spurge derives protection by growing along the sand in low mats, possessing small glossy leaves, and having a thick latex sap. A third species of the open beach is bugseed (*Corispermum hyssopifolium*). In fall, the dried plant snaps at the base and, propelled by the wind, tumbles across the sand as it leaves an invisible wake of tiny seeds.

Although the beach may be rough on most species, it attracts summering human beings in throngs (if not thongs). Many beaches have lost their characteristic plants due to raking, vehicular travel, and trampling, activities conducted for and by these summer visitors. At some sites, sea rocket and seaside spurge remain only where they are protected by boat racks and other structures or by the abundance of sandbur (*Cenchrus longispinus*), which discourages human strolling.[15]

When conditions are just right—high lake levels, absence of severe storms, and cool wet summers—marram grass (*Ammophila breviligulata*) and cottonwoods become established on the middle beach.[16] These plants are particularly effective in catching and holding sand and, thus, provide the essential first step in the formation of foredunes. The process is rare, however; Tom Poulson found that marram grass colonized open sand at his study area near Miller, Lake County (Ind.), on just two occasions during the past twenty-five years. Cottonwoods have been successful even less often—twice in seventy-five years.

The classic view of succession holds that marram grass and cottonwoods stabilize dunes and promote humus development, thereby enabling the next set of plants to take hold. But Poulson's work demonstrates that a dense mass of dried and living marram grass stymies succession. For other species to become established, something must open up the marram grass, and that something appears to be fire. Cottonwoods may even act as lightning rods, increasing the likelihood that the marram grass litter is burned. Once a fire moves through, numerous species take root in no particular order. These include sand reed grass (*Calamovilfa longifolia*), little bluestem (*Andropogon scoparius*), switchgrass (*Panicum virgatum*), dune goldenrod (*Solidago racemosa*), sand cherry (*Prunus pumila*), hairy puccoon (*Lithospermum croceum*), sand cress (*Arabis lyrata*), and wormwood (*Artemisia caudata*).

◄◦► ◄◦► ◄◦►

Jack pine (*Pinus banksiana*) and black oak (*Quercus velutina*) savanna distinguish the next successional phase. Because acorns just drop and jack pines produce small seeds that travel not much farther than eight feet, these trees would be incapable of spreading far on their own. Another group of organisms, however, provides the transportation: birds of various species use the cottonwoods as perches, and undigested seeds germinate underneath. It has been suggested that these plants then become nesting sites for blue jays, which carry acorns and pine seeds up to thirty-five miles away. Jays drop some seeds and cache others, thus introducing the oaks and pines.[17]

The youngest dune benefits from the protection afforded it by its older siblings. Thus over time, the older dune appears to be moving inland. And in open areas amid the black oaks and jack pines there is an increasing array of other species. Hop tree (*Ptelea trifoliata*) and common juniper (*Juniperus communis*) grow among the sand cherry and little bluestem. Black willow (*Salix nigra*), dwarf fragrant sumac (*Rhus aromatica* var. *arenaria*), red-osier dogwood (*Cornus stolonifera*), red cedar (*Juniperus virginiana*), prickly pear, and early wild rose (*Rosa blanda*) can also be in the mix. E. J. Hill, writing in 1893, describes such a dune: "The play of sunlight on the masses of foliage formed by the various bushes, with their differing shades of green, is very beautiful. There is a charming variety of color, subdued and restful to the eye, which is dazzled by the glitter from the white sand or the reflection from the water. The groups also have a wavy outline, due to the little mounds of sand heaped about them along the common dune. One or two kinds may occupy the top of a hillock and others clothe its sides or skirt its base, the colors blending or contrasting."[18]

Once the groundcover becomes sufficient to carry a fire, regular burning selects for a fire climax or, in Poulson's words, a "guild of arsonists." At Poulson's research site, fires generally occur every three to six years. Few of the oaks have gained the height and thick bark necessary to survive these burns; most of the large trees probably matured during unusually long periods between fires. The first fire after such a hiatus is often intense, as the fuel load is abundant. Such a conflagration kills many trees and forbs, leaving in its wake extensive areas of bare sand favorable for oak recruitment and species not adapted to fire.

◄○► ◄○► ◄○►

On the interior dunes, fire climax communities take the form of either black oak savanna or prairie. Miller Woods manifests the dune and swale aspect characteristic of the younger beach deposits. The oak savanna there is one of the finest in the Chicago region. Its quality arises from two primary factors. First, before it became part of the lakeshore, it was owned by U.S. Steel, who protected it from trespass. And second, its proximity to railroad tracks ensured that the savanna would burn periodically. Thus, the site fell into the rare circumstance of being free from anthropogenic degradation but not fire. Ecologist Carl Krekeler, in his comprehensive survey of dunes ecosystems, points to the magnificent spring displays of American columbine (*Aquilegia canadensis*) and Indian paintbrush (*Castilleja coccinea*) that thrive here.[19]

These savannas have an exceedingly rich understory populated with many species locally rare or even unknown outside the dunes. Among them are fame flower (*Talinum rugospermum*), three species of wintergreen, two species of pyrola, rattlesnake plantain (*Goodyera pubescens*), one-flowered broomrape (*Orobanche uniflora*), and trailing arbutus (*Epigaea repens*). H. S. Pepoon advised that "unless the explorer traverses practically every foot of the ground many of these will escape him, as the localities are often very circumscribed."[20]

The rarest of these is the fame flower, a species thought extirpated from the dunes until naturalist Barbara Plampin rediscovered it in 1985. Noel Pavlovic, an ecologist at the Indiana Dunes National Lakeshore, characterizes the plant as "an interstitial species that occupies bare soil patches created by fire, drought, sand deposition, and biotic disturbances."[21] Fame flower seeds need light to germinate, and thus without fire or other disturbances they would be shaded out by accumulating litter.

Not as rare, the trailing arbutus seems to be a special favorite for many people. Pepoon used a photograph of the species as the frontispiece for his great book. Barbara and Geoffrey Plampin selected their homesite in Dune Acres, a private subdivision within the national lakeshore, largely because it harbored a population of the plant. Some eighty years earlier, Louella Chapin, perhaps clairvoyant, had written that the arbutus is secure "because it takes long and patient search to find them, and he who will take that trouble, loves them too well to harm them."[22]

Howes Prairie near Dune Acres is an outstanding example of a dunes-style prairie-savanna mix. The prairie proper is 49.2 acres, but the entire site is roughly 185.3 acres. Because of fire suppression, oaks became dense, and the contrast with the open prairie was well marked. Since 1985, as park biologists have reintroduced burning, the borders between oak and prairie have begun to blur, no doubt resembling earlier times.

After extensive study, the prairie's ecological history is better known than most. It lies in a bowl-shaped basin that was originally a panne during the Lake Nipissing period four to five thousand years ago. A few persisting panne species such as Kalm's Saint-John's-wort (*Hypericum kalmianum*) and blue-hearts (*Buchnera americana*) provide a link with that earlier period. But for the past 3,200 years, Lake Michigan elevations have not been high enough to have an impact on the hydrology.[23]

White pines (*Pinus strobus*) and jack pines dominated the scene for a thousand years, beginning in about 3200 B.P., and were then largely replaced by oak savanna and prairie as climate shifted. Fossil pollen suggests, however, that within the past 150 years tree density and canopy cover have increased at a rate far more rapid than before. These changes have been attributed to a number of anthropogenic events: extirpation of large herbivores, virtual elimination of white pines through logging (much of it done to help rebuild Chicago after the 1871 fire), declines in fire frequency from the 1930s to 1985, and deposition of nitrates and sulfates originating from nearby industrial complexes.

Despite the above changes, Howes Prairie has to a large extent maintained its open canopy and collection of conservative species. Ecologists believe that this has occurred due to the hydrologic stability; because it lies north of the main groundwater drainage divide between Lake Michigan and Dune Creek, the prairie has escaped the threats posed by efforts to ditch nearby wetlands. Possibly more so than fire, naturally induced flood events have benefited the mesic element of Howes Prairie.[24]

Howes Prairie is one of the most scenic places in the national lakeshore. Owing to Lake Michigan's chilly breath, there is no early spring in the dunes, so June is a good time to make the first pilgrimage. At the southeast end of the prairie, a trail leads to an overlook from which it is possible to look down into the bowl and then across to the open savanna on the far slope. Directly below, false white indigos (*Baptisia leucantha*) appear as exclamation marks emphasizing the blue carpet of lupine (*Lupinus perennis*). A mild winter with abundant spring rains produced an uncommonly fine lupine display in 1995, for on many plants all the blooms were in flower simultaneously.

A little later in the season, goat's rue (*Tephrosia virginiana*) embroiders the open sand beneath the oaks with its thick clusters of pale gold and pink, while in other places there are Indian paintbrush and two rare species of blue-eyed grass. Then in August, and particularly in a year that has seen fire, extensive splashes of blazing star, mostly marsh (*Liatris spicata*) but also some rough (*L. aspera*) and cylindrical (*L. cylindracea*), tint the prairie like dye on the heaving waters of a small pond.

◄O► ◄O► ◄O►

The dunes of Indiana are products of a dynamic interplay between vegetation, lake levels, and wind. In Porter and La Porte Counties, this interplay results in Mount Tom (192 feet), Mount Holden (184 feet), and the other high dunes that are signature features of the entire area. The largest dune of all no longer exists, however: Hoosier Slide, near Michigan City, stood at two hundred feet but, by the beginning of the twentieth century, had been hauled away to become jars and plate glass.[25]

Perhaps the most spectacular example of dune destabilization is the blowout, where gusts of wind enlarge rents in the vegetative armor of the dune. Weak spots can be created by off-road vehicles and excessive pedestrian traffic or by circumstances as natural as wave damage, drought, and dune interstices. Once exposed, the sand is at the mercy of the wind, as May Watts describes: "The vegetation was losing ground, actually losing ground. Common juniper was holding mounds of sand with its roots; but we could see where the wind was prying its fingers in under a jack pine. It would topple soon. The others are doomed too—the few white pines, the carpets of kinnikinnick and the scattered black oaks. As they go down, one by one, this will become another great dune blowout."[26]

As the sand streams from the punctured dune, like grain from a torn sack, it buries adjacent areas. Dunes have traveled sixty feet a year, on occasion engulfing an entire forest. Black oaks perish without much of a struggle, but cottonwood and basswood can persist even though all but their uppermost branches are submerged; they defy the sand by sending out roots from now-covered trunks and branches. But what is being covered today can be revealed tomorrow. So it is that tree graveyards sometimes emerge from a disintegrating dune. Dr. Pepoon refers to one such discovery, "an ancient forest" of white pine and white cedar having trunks two to three feet in diameter.[27]

Although areas of moving sand are mostly without vegetation, there are sections along the rim made inhabitable by the stabilizing effects of sand reed grass. Frugiverous birds deposit the seeds that enable poison ivy (*Rhus radicans*), climbing bittersweet (*Celastrus scandens*), and river grape (*Vitis riparia*) to gain footholds on the fixed sand. Other species include the plants typical of early succession, such as marram grass, dune goldenrod, and sand cherry.[28]

But the rarest of dune plants is, locally at least, now virtually restricted to

65. Pitcher's thistle at Indiana Dunes National Lakeshore.
(Photo by and courtesy of Noel Pavlovic.)

the partially stabilized blowouts of the Indiana Dunes National Lakeshore. The federally threatened Pitcher's thistle (*Cirsium pitcheri*) is endemic to the Nipissing dunes and upper beaches of Lakes Michigan, Huron, and Superior.[29] Botanists believe that Pitcher's thistle is of recent origin, most likely having evolved from the similar Platte thistle (*Cirsium canescens*) of the Great Plains.

Pitcher's thistle matures in five to eight years. It then blooms for the first and only time, sends forth seed, and dies. The plant has large heavy seeds that increase the chances of germination in the dry sand. But this comes at a cost, for dispersal rarely exceeds six and a half feet. In addition, many seed heads and seeds are eaten by rabbits, the caterpillars of artichoke plume moths (*Platyptilia carduidactyla*), and American goldfinches.

The ever-shifting sands destroy and create habitat for the Pitcher's thistle, which therefore continually colonize the mosaic of open habitats within the dunes. That the species inhabits only small portions of a given dunal area and only for a limited time means that its long-term survival rests on the maintenance of large tracts free from development. Even though a lakefront parcel may currently be without thistles, the construction of a condominium denies habitat that might later provide a critical refuge. But these are the very properties that are in greatest demand for residences, marinas, and recreation.

Fortunately, most local thistle populations are on protected land, but they are still at risk from thousands of moving feet.

◄◊► ◄◊► ◄◊►

At many locations throughout the dunes, oak savannas have been without fire for so long they have become oak forests. To combat this trend, lakeshore ecologists have begun burning an increasing amount of acreage. But a variety of forests grew in places that were never subjected to fire on a frequent basis.

Between the high dunes, there is often a depression known as a mesophytic pocket or cove, so deep that it escaped the flames. Fire would ride the west winds, creep up the dune slope, and sputter as it hit the damp crater. Other areas, along flood plains or in interdunal wetlands, were also too wet to burn. Farther inland, fires raged less often due to topography, water barriers, and finer soils that held moisture longer than sand. (It is also possible that these richer soils promoted forest growth.)

One of the largest pockets, about four or five acres, lies within Indiana Dunes State Park. Species characteristic of these small forests include sugar maple, red oak, basswood, tulip tree (*Liriodendron tulipifera*), witch hazel (*Hamamelis virginiana*), blue-stemmed goldenrod (*Solidago caesia*), and maple-leaved arrowwood (*Viburnum acerifolium*). Some of these enclaves also have a very rich spring flora.

Two wet forests, what Gerould Wilhelm calls "hydro-mesophytic," are among the outstanding forests in the dunes.[30] For the initial half-mile of its length, Trail 2 in the state park parallels Dune Creek and winds through a lovely tract of lowland woods of sugar maple and beech. In spring, the creek side is ablaze with yellow: a carpet of marsh marigolds (*Caltha palustris*) is complimented by an overhead layer of spicebush (*Lindera benzoin*).

The second such woods is a forty-acre tract east of Kemil Road near the visitor center. Wilhelm considers this site to be one of the most remarkable areas in the Chicago region. A part of the Great Marsh, the forest was spared the ax because even after the installation of drainage ditches it remained wet. It consists of little hammocks interspersed with damp areas, all of which are shaded by old-growth beech, maple, black ash, red oak, and swamp white oak. Marsh marigolds and skunk cabbage (*Symplocarpus foetidus*) are conspicuous in spring, and numerous rare species find refuge here, including one of the region's biggest populations of paper birch (*Betula papyrifera*).

Black oak dominates in the upland forests of the Calumet and Glenwood ridges, with a greater number of species in the latter due to its greater age and increasing mesic character. The shrub layer of these two forests also differs. Early low blueberry (*Vaccinium angustifolium*), box huckleberry (*Gaylussacia baccata*), and late low blueberry (*V. pallidum*) are the most common elements in Calumet-aged sites, while Virginia creeper (*Parthenocissus quinquefolia*) and spicebush predominate in the Glenwood forests. Very few if any of these shrubs inhabit both Calumet and Glenwood.[31]

As the sandy soils of the Chicago Lake Plain give way to the clays of the Lake Border Upland, black oak disappears. In its stead grows red oak, white oak, and shagbark hickory, together with spring beauties.

More mesic yet are the beech-maple forests that are local in the dunes. The largest and best example is the Heron Rookery (where forty pairs of great blue herons nest), bisected by the Little Calumet River. The southern half is in much better condition, having been logged less recently and apparently not grazed. In the spring, the forest sparkles with three species of trillium, one of the national lakeshore's premier floral displays.[32]

◄○► ◄○► ◄○►

Pannes form behind the foredunes, shallow troughs of sand kept wet by the water table and/or springs within nearby dunes. Classic examples are those at Miller and West Beach in the Indiana Dunes National Lakeshore. (Pannes also exist at Illinois Beach State Park and in Berrien County.) The calcium-rich (alkaline) water that supports this community gives rise to a fenlike flora that includes lakeshore rush (*Juncus balticus*), hair beak rush (*Rhynchospora capillacea*), false golden sedge (*Carex garberi*), green yellow sedge (*C. viridula*), rose gentian (*Sabatia angularis*), Kalm's Saint-John's-wort (*Hypericum kalmianum*), common bog arrow grass (*Triglochin maritima*), and horned bladderwort (*Utricularia cornuta*).

Pannes are extraordinary for several reasons. In North America, they are restricted to the Great Lakes Basin, where development pressure has led the Nature Conservancy to rank them as globally imperiled (G2). There is also tremendous variation among them. A study of Indiana Dune pannes tabulated a total of seventy-four plant taxa, but of these only thirteen were found in all five pannes.[33] These results are explained by changes in alkalinity due to the age of the panne and its distance from the lake.

Pannes are also home to a large number of plants whose range is principally on the Atlantic coastal plain. Known as Atlantic coast disjuncts, seventy species occur in this region.[34] Among those that inhabit pannes are winged oval sedge (*Carex alata*), twig rush (*Cladium mariscoides*), round-leaved sundew (*Drosera rotundifolia*), knee spike rush (*Eleocharis geniculata*), black-fruited spike rush (*E. melanocarpa*), and marsh Saint-John's-wort (*Hypericum virginicum*). One of the most beautiful coastal disjuncts is purple bladderwort (*Utricularia purpurea*). In 1976, extensive drifts of this species empurpled the surface of Little Lake. It was reminiscent of a canvas by Monet, if he had abandoned Giverny for the Dunes.

The Dunes region has more Atlantic coast plants than any other inland area, and a few of the species are not otherwise known within several hundred miles. Botanist Donald Culross Peattie observed that substantially more of these plants occur near Lake Michigan than Lake Erie, even though Lake Michigan is four hundred miles farther west. He concluded that many of these plants once enjoyed a larger presence throughout the eastern Great Lakes, but changes in water level associated with the various stages of the lakes wiped out the damp sandy flats the species required. But where those conditions persist, as they do in no more glorious fashion than at the southern end of Lake Michigan, so do the plants.[35]

The most superlative manifestation of this glory was Goose Lake (also known as Mud Lake and Walker Lake), in the central dunes of Porter County. The great Indiana botanist Charles Deam considered it his favorite site. He once wrote Floyd Swink about the shore's edge, outlined in the red of sundews. Soldier rush (*Juncus militaris*) grew here, and at no other place closer than northern Michigan. The concentration of coastal disjuncts was unlike anywhere else, and Swink believed that its destruction in April 1963 to make way for a large industrial complex was one of the greatest losses ever suffered by American botanists. Although the richness of Goose Lake will never be replicated, nearby Little Lake and a Northern Indiana Public Service Company (NIPSCO) settling pond have yielded good mixes of rare coastal disjuncts, including umbrella sedge (*Fuirena pumila*), which was thought to have disappeared along with Goose Lake.[36]

◄◙► ◄◙► ◄◙►

The changing levels of Lake Michigan and its predecessors over six thousand years marked northwestern Lake County in a unique way. A series of 150 old beach ridges and intervening swales spread across the otherwise level plain. Although most of this wetland complex has been destroyed, conservationists have managed to protect several outstanding tracts such as Clarke and Pine Nature Preserve (three hundred acres), Tolleston Ridges Nature Preserve (thirty-nine acres), Ivanhoe (143 acres), and Gibson Woods Nature Preserve (120 acres). Efforts are underway to preserve several other remaining parcels.

Because the early botanists knew this area so well, and discovered within its watery province "so many fine examples of rare and beautiful plants," excellent descriptions of it exist: "Many islets, peninsulas, coves, and flats with long stretches of deep water, steep and sloping banks, water-logged trunks of huge pines, shallow water marshes of cat-tail, bur-reed, sedge, and similar plants afforded abundant shelter for delicate forms. The water was always clear, and, before the days of sewage, palatable as the writer many times proved."[37]

Of the many plants that occurred here, the profusion of orchids was a major attraction. Floyd Swink has written that thirty-two species of orchids have been confirmed from the Indiana Dunes, and most of them grew in these sandy swells and swales.[38]

Unquestionably a candidate for most beautiful local flower, the showy lady's slipper (*Cyprepedium reginae*) was once abundant in the damp places, thriving by the tens of thousands. Not only was its habitat wrecked by development, the lady's slipper was cursed by being so singularly gorgeous. Plants were harvested for the florist trade wherever they could be found; thousands were cut for placement on Chicago restaurant tables. But some botanists also succumbed to the impulse to overcollect.[39] In her delightful book of 1907, Louella Chapin confesses to a past indiscretion: "Years ago they grew thickest where East Chicago now is, and once I stood on a low sand ridge and counted more than 200 bordering a swampy spot. They tossed, proud and free in the full sunshine, at the top of their tall, straight stalks, yet I picked them down to the ground, all I could carry, and they made my neighbors and child garden glad. Now I would not harm one on any account. I am more civilized than I was, but that does not bring back the vanished orchids."[40]

A particularly celebrated site within this dune and swale complex was the Tolleston Bog and Swamp, located at Seventeenth and Whitcomb Streets in Gary.[41] Floyd Swink called it "a Mecca for hundreds of wildflowers." It was the first place he ever found large cranberry (*Vaccinium macrocarpon*). In one small area, fifty rose pogonias (*Pogonia ophioglossoides*) and fifty grass pink orchids (*Calopogon pulchellus*) sprouted from the low sandy ground. And later in the season, these would be replaced by the subtle blooms of nodding ladies' tresses (*Spiranthes cernua*) and "tens of thousands of fringed gentians, many of them with 60 or more blossoms per plant in the surrounding neighborhood." Fame flower, club moss, and bluehearts were three rare nonorchids that also found refuge here.

In the late 1950s when Swink decided that the area ought to be documented photographically, he commissioned Al Reuss, an accomplished naturalist in his own right, to visit the site. Swink was in his office when he received Reuss's phone call. Reuss was perplexed: although Swink's directions seemed fine, he could not find the wetland. Swink jumped in his car and to his dismay learned that since he had last visited, Seventeenth and Whitcomb had become a subdivision with five hundred houses.

It is a testament to the richness of this complex that the remaining pieces,

66. White pines and jack pines along Grand Calumet River, near Miller,
Lake County (Ind.), April 9, 1909. Photo by Chicago Prairie Club.
(Courtesy of Westchester Township Historical Museum, Chesterton, Ind.)

representing but a fraction of what once was, are among the premier natural areas of the Chicago region. Ken Klick thinks there are few places in the Chicago area as beautiful as Clarke and Pine Nature Preserve, located near the Gary airport. During June, one sixty-five-foot-wide ridge might be studded with Indian paintbrush, bluehearts, prairie lily, and Robin's plantain (*Erigeron pulchellus*). In due time, false foxglove, grass of Parnassus, and fringed gentian begin their tenure, until they too fade from the sandy stage. And because of the nutrient-poor soil, the grass never grows tall enough to hide the colorful procession. Separated by the intervening wet depression gilded with yellow pond lily and purple bladderwort is yet another ridge, similar to the first except it may have a twisted jack pine or black oak.[42]

◄◦► ◄◦► ◄◦►

In addition to the pannes and swales of the recent dunes, the Indiana Dunes has examples of virtually every kind of wetland and aquatic community that occurs in the Chicago region. Sixty-six-acre Long Lake, sandwiched between Tolleston and Nipissing dunes at West Beach, is the largest inland water body in the National Lakeshore.[43] Extensive marshes include those that surround Long Lake, Inland Marsh (to the south), and the Great Marsh. There is fen at Cowles Bog, bog at Pinhook Bog, swamp in the Indiana Dunes State Park, sedge meadow at various locations such as Inland Marsh and Dune Acres, and a seep at Crescent Beach in the state park. (A seep is where the water comes directly out of the ground.)

The Great Marsh is an elongated wetland situated along the north side of the Calumet ridge. From Lake Street in Gary, it extends across Porter County almost to Michigan City. Subjected to grazing and ditching, the marsh has mostly weedy species whose presence signifies traumatized wetlands. Willows and quaking aspen are the dominant woody plants growing on the periphery. The wetter portions are almost exclusively solid stands of cattails, with reed canary grass, common reed, purple loosestrife, and tall goldenrod.[44]

Within the territory of the Great Marsh is a smaller 260-acre section that includes swamp, marsh, sedge meadow, wet prairie, and Cowles Bog, perhaps the most famous of all natural areas in the Indiana Dunes. Recognized early on for its ecological import, it was the first property purchased by Save the Dunes Council. Even its name is noteworthy. The Cowles part of it is easily explained: a memorial to the great ecologist who spent so much of his life studying and working toward the preservation of the Indiana Dunes. But "bog" is a misnomer dating from the 1920s before biologists distinguished wetlands as they do today. For in reality, Cowles Bog is not a bog but rather a forested fen centered over an artesian spring. The ten-acre fen is dominated by white cedar, with a mix of tamaracks. Either because of mineral deposition or the force of the discharging water, the mat is elevated about five feet above the adjacent marsh and swamp. Unlike a bog, the mat is almost devoid of sphagnum moss, which is present only in small clumps at the base of trees. Northeast of the forested fen lies a graminoid fen, now dominated by cattails.[45]

A remarkable array of rare plants has been found at Cowles Bog over the years. In 1990, Jerry Wilhelm compiled a list of forty-one conservative plants ("special vegetation"), mostly of northern affinity, that currently or formerly occurred here. His compilation includes six kinds of orchids, twinflower, pitcher plant, muck sedge (*Carex limosa*), dwarf birch, bunchberry, and goldthread.[46]

Despite the attention that it has garnered, Cowles Bog has been harmed by hydrological alterations and fire suppression. Its spring-fed center apparently remains "in decent shape," but the larger marsh portion has lost much of its diversity, and is now mostly cattails. The biggest single problem is an increased variability in water levels. Much of this originates from NIPSCO, Bethlehem Steel, and the other industrial neighbors to the south and west. Northern Indiana Public Service Co. has installed a dike restricting water flowage, dug pits that filled with contaminated water and then leaked into the marsh, and made excavations for an aborted nuclear power plant. Air-borne pollutants have altered water chemistry, and construction of mills blocked fires that used to roll north from the railroad tracks. (In the 1940s and 1950s, it was common for residents of Dune Acres to interrupt their routines to fight fires.)[47]

Some of these abuses have stopped. The National Park Service took NIPSCO to court to prevent the runoff of polluted water into the Cowles Bog. If water flows can be stabilized and fires reintroduced, it may be possible to restore the floral diversity that once distinguished the wetlands surrounding Cowles Bog.

Pinhook Bog, in contrast to Cowles Bog, is a bona fide bog, having formed in an impermeable clay-lined depression on the Valparaiso Moraine. Five hundred eighty total acres are protected, of which ninety are bog. It is in an advanced stage of succession, with tamaracks distributed throughout. As one of the finest bogs in Indiana, Pinhook Bog holds several distinctions, discussed in Jerry Wilhelm's fascinating *Special Vegetation of the Indiana Dunes National Lakeshore*.[48] Over half of the twenty-eight species of *Sphagnum* moss known from Indiana occur at the site, including three not known elsewhere in the state, and one, *Sphagnum bartlettianum*, not otherwise known from outside the southeastern coastal plain.

Another outstanding find was the discovery of the first bog bladderwort (*Utricularia geminiscapa*) in Indiana and the Chicago region. Closely resembling the widespread great bladderwort (*U. vulgaris*), which also occurs at Pinhook Bog, it remained undetected by local botanists until the University of Michigan's Anton Reznicek, on a brief visit to the bog, brought it to their notice. The bog bladderwort has subsequently been found at a few other spots in northwestern Indiana.

Pinhook Bog also harbors the most accessible, and probably the largest, population of pink lady's slippers (moccasin flowers) in the region. The flower can be viewed effortlessly from the safety of a boardwalk, but visitation is limited to days when staff is present. Overall, the fate of this orchid has been similar to that of the showy lady's slipper. Dr. Pepoon lamented, "*Cypripedium acaule*, your regal beauty is your doom."[49]

In at least two different locations within the dunes, distinctive plant assemblages have arisen in the presence of seeps. At one narrow topographic level, a seep zone exists where the Calumet Dunes slope into the Great Marsh. The calcareous water that dribbles out of the ridge supports a forested fen for several miles. Butternut (*Juglans cinerea*—increasingly infected by canker fungus [*Sirococcus claygigenti*]), golden saxifrage (*Chrysosplenium americanum*), and swamp saxifrage (*Saxifraga pensylvanica*) are three conservative species characteristic of this habitat. Another smaller seep occurs at Crescent Beach in the state park, where a bed of clay provides the conduit for water that originates inland and surfaces at the base of Mount Baldy. The wet area that results, three hundred feet long and twenty feet wide, provides an oasis for marsh species like common arrowhead, hard-stem bulrush, and cattails that are not otherwise found on the open beach.[50]

By Their Deeds Ye Shall Know Them:
Utilization and Conservation of the Indiana Dunes

The beauty of the dunes has moved people for over a hundred years. Novelists, poets, and painters have devoted careers to memorializing its splendor. A large cadre of scientists has studied its wonders and, in so doing, illuminated some of nature's fundamental processes. These people and others, including teachers, business people, architects, lawyers, and a remarkable U.S. senator, gave of themselves without respite to prevent desecration of the land they loved.

Passion for the dunes has produced a literature dwarfing that of any other part of the region except the City of Chicago. Dunes scholar Ronald Engel summarizes the "hundreds of items" that focus on the dunes: "novels, histories, children's stories, plays, poems, pageants, masques, travelogues, nature-essays, natural history, speeches, newspaper reports, etchings, watercolors, paintings, sculpture, films, songs, and a seemingly endless number of scientific monographs."[51] Since 1983, at least three excellent book-length accounts have documented the conservation struggle alone: Ronald Engel's *Sacred Sands*, Kay Franklin and Norma Schaeffer's *Duel for the Dunes*, and Ron Cockrell's *A Signature of Time and Eternity*. And Herb Read, a heroic veteran of the recent wars, says the full story has yet to be told.

Given the voluminous literature on the history of the area, a comprehensive retelling here would be both impractical and repetitive. What follows is an abbreviated sketch that I hope will spur the reader to explore the lengthier works.

◄o► ◄o► ◄o►

Early descriptions of the dunes region were largely unflattering. In May 1821, Indiana Boundary Commissioner John Tipton observed the dunes and marshes and concluded that they "never can admit settlement nor ever will be of much service to our state."[52] Twelve years later, Charles Latrobe reached the shoreline where massive dunes rose two hundred feet: "The aspect of the broad expanse of the lake swelling to the horizon, and for hundreds of miles beyond, was sublime, but it was hardly beautiful. A narrow band of sand, with a few trees, stretching away from us to the east and west, and a shore strewed with huge trunks of trees and the wrecks of boats and vessels bleached with wind and wave, formed the sandscape. All vegetation appeared choked by the fine white sand, swept up from the deep, and gradually driving back the waters by its rise and accumulation."[53]

The first permanent settlement came in 1822 when Joseph Bailly set up his home and fur-trading business on the Little Calumet River, south of the marshy moats and barren dunes that seemed so inhospitable. He had chosen his location carefully, for the river was crossed by the north branch of the Sauk Trail. This maximized the number of trappers with whom he could do business and enabled him to send the products to markets on Lake Michigan.[54]

Within ten years three towns had been platted, which for various reasons failed. Michigan City grew to be the area's commercial center, and settlement gained momentum with the construction of railroad tracks in 1850–52. The steady income the railroad provided attracted yet others who were interested in agriculture and fishing.

Already changes in the landscape were becoming evident. The first victim of the European presence was the beaver, trapped out even before Bailly's arrival. But perhaps the most obvious organism to suffer was the white pine. When William Keating visited the region in 1823, he found the tree to be abundant, and one early resident remembered when the lakefront dunes "was well covered with beautiful white pine."[55]

As one forest scientist has written, "the lumber industry in the United States was founded on the Eastern white pine." In part, its value rests on the fact that it has been put to a greater variety of uses than any other tree. The wood is light, soft, and yet very resilient. These qualities, in addition to proximity to burgeoning Chicago and the treeless prairie, led to the rapid decimation of the white pine in this region. The largest existing population of white pines in the dunes inhabits the Keiser portion of the state park, but the species is scattered throughout much of the lakeshore.[56]

Sawmills were already beginning to spring up by the 1830s, and during the following decades lumbering became a big business. The first formally established road in Porter County supposedly linked two of the mills. By the time Dr. Pepoon arrived in Chicago in 1875, the "largest area most fully occupied by the white pine, in places almost a pure stand, was the swampy land now embraced by Indiana Harbor, East Chicago, and the neighboring grounds." In the vicinity was also a busy sawmill, which remained in operation until it was consumed by the fires of 1871. As late as 1885, lumbering was still considered the largest industry in Pine Township, La Porte County, even though only one sawmill remained. (Of course, oak and other trees were also utilized.)[57]

Berry gathering was another important economic activity in the dunes. Professor E. T. Cox, Indiana's state geologist, commented that huckleberries were "highly esteemed and much sought after" in 1873 in the Michigan City area: "The shipments in the height of the season reach near three hundred bushels per day, being, to the berry gatherers, a dispensation of ten thousand dollars per annum."[58]

Cranberries were also popular. Cox reported that "about two miles northwest of Michigan City is a marsh of sixty acres . . . which, it is asserted, yields annually from one to two hundred bushels of berries per acre." First noted in 1830, another much smaller cranberry marsh flourished near Dune Acres until 1924, when the site was turned into a golf course.[59]

The Great Marsh and other wetlands also figure prominently in the settlement of the area. They were difficult to traverse and, thus, protected the high dunes for many years. During that time, the marshes were used for hunting, gathering, hay, and pasturage. Once the beaver disappeared, the bulk of the later fur trade was in muskrat, with some otter and mink. Many plants were collected in the lowlands and dunes by Indians and settlers alike. These included sassafras, arrowroot, calamus, and mint for medicine and food; poison sumac, poison ivy, and deadly nightshade for their toxic properties; and bloodroot and golden thread for dyes. In trying to develop a cattle industry, several landowners began using the marsh for grazing and haying.[60]

Ultimately, however, these wetland areas paid dearly for the difficulties they presented. When the early efforts at commercial exploitation of the lowlands were deemed insufficient, speculation began that if these properties could be drained, and their fundamental character altered, they would be ripe for agriculture and habitation. John Peyton, an easterner who visited the dunes in 1848, wrote of his time with local landowner Judge Douglas: "Here we were upon a frozen lake or swamp, with alternate ridges of sand. . . . It was not supposed possible to drain this swamp, and consequently the land was considered valueless. We spent the residue of the day making our reconnaissance, and ascertained that . . . it was . . . susceptible at an inconsiderable cost comparatively, of being drained. . . . Next morning Judge Douglas informed me of his purpose to purchase a large portion of this apparent waste. By draining it, he believed it would yield a fortune to himself and children."[61]

By 1897, at least three ditches drained the upper stretches of the Little Calumet River. They were followed by many more, some public and some private. In addition, numerous farmers constructed smaller channels that carried water off of their property and into the main ditch.[62]

Burns Ditch was the most ambitious drainage to hit the dunes region. Opponents, including the Michigan Southern Railroad that would have needed to build a bridge over the channel, contested the proposal all the way to the U.S. Supreme Court. The ditch was ultimately completed in 1926, and it drained more than twenty thousand acres of Lake and Porter Counties. More recent ditching in the dunes has primarily benefited residential, commercial, and industrial development rather than agriculture.

◄◦► ◄◦► ◄◦►

By the late 1800s, new economic interests began to overshadow hunting, gathering, and agriculture. Among the first were mining companies that provided sand from the dunes to Chicago landfills and building industries.[63] These firms profited not from the continuing productivity of the land but from the land itself.

The next major player was the U.S. Steel Company. It saw land in yet another way: "When one purchases the land for business or industrial purposes, he does not purchase the land but [instead] the location."[64] In 1904, it began buying property in Lake County to build the world's largest steel complex. Nine thousand acres lying along seven miles of lakeshore became steel mills and the city of Gary, which like Pullman would be a model city, providing housing for the workforce. Plant Superintendent William Gleason detailed the prodigious construction effort. Over a thousand men labored to raise the mill site fifteen feet, "move as much dirt as the Panama Canal," straighten two miles of the Grand Calumet River, use over 160,000 tons of steel, and "lay a giant water tunnel 80 feet deep and a mile out into the lake that had a capacity of five million gallons a day." Not only did this undertaking represent a magnificent display of America's industrial might, it "destroyed the Lake County dune forever."

The building of the Gary works and the ensuing loss of the Lake County lakeshore did, however, focus attention on the still wild, still beautiful Porter County dunes. There, a small group of visionaries coalesced into a force that would lead to the creation of the Indiana Dunes State Park in 1925. A respite of three decades followed before new threats launched the mother of all local conservation battles, "perhaps the most savage conservation-industry confrontation in history."[65]

Perhaps the first organized attempt to protect the Dunes began in 1914. The Prairie Club, formed three years earlier to promote the love of nature and the preservation of sites for outdoor recreation, convened a meeting of other interested groups, which became the Conservation Council of Chicago. Led by Jens Jensen (a leading landscape architect who became known as the "Apostle of the Dunes") and Dr. Cowles, the organization unsuccessfully sought private money to purchase dunes property. The University of Chicago rejected a faculty recommendation to buy three thousand acres as a field station. Julius Rosenwald refused to establish a school of horticulture in the dunes, and Henry Ford declined the opportunity to fund a 5,000–6,000-acre arboretum. After about a year of setbacks, the council turned to the public sector for help.[66]

The year 1916 proved to be one of great significance, for three events occurred that would directly contribute to dunes preservation. In July, three thousand dune supporters met at Waverly Beach to establish the National Dunes Park Association, which formally joined the Chicago and Indiana advocates. Among the first board members were Cowles, Jensen, and William Allinson from Chicago and A. F. Knotts, John O. Bowers, and Bess Sheehan (who would receive the sobriquet "Lady of the Dunes") from northwest Indiana.[67]

67. Removal of sand during construction of facilities at Gary, Lake
County, April 9, 1909. Photo by Chicago Prairie Club. (Courtesy of
Westchester Township Historical Museum, Chesterton, Ind.)

On August 25, the National Park Service came into being, and Chicagoan Stephen Mather became its director.[68] Long a supporter of dunes protection, he used his new position to advance the creation of a Sand Dunes National Park. If he succeeded, it would be the first time in U.S. history that the federal government spent funds to purchase land for a national park. (Previous national parks had already been federal property at the time of their establishment.)

The high point of Mather's effort was a hearing held in Chicago on October 30. More than four hundred people attended, of whom forty spoke in favor of the park. Although opponents were present, not one dissent appeared in the record. Mather and his assistant Horace Albright wrote the report in which they strongly urged that Congress authorize $1.8–$2.6 million to acquire the necessary nine to thirteen thousand acres. The recommendations were given to the secretary of interior and then distributed to members of Congress. And there it stalled. Indiana Senator Tom Taggart, a strong proponent of the park, lost his campaign for reelection and resigned before his term expired. Mather suffered a debilitating breakdown in early 1917. Most important, though, the nation went to war, and among the casualties was the Sand Dunes National Park. The idea of a national park would languish for four decades.

Not even a world war, however, could extinguish the resolve of the dune preservationists, and they soon adopted a new approach. Indiana had become a state in 1816, and as part of its centennial celebration created a State Park

Memorial Committee. By unvarnished good fortune, Richard Lieber became chairman. Few, if any, conservation causes have attracted as many distinguished advocates as the efforts to preserve the dunes. And Lieber was one of the most extraordinary among them. An immigrant from Prussia, he was a respected journalist, an accomplished musician, a successful entrepreneur, and a master of six languages. University of Chicago President William Rainey Harper was so impressed by Lieber's knowledge and intellect that he offered him a year to get a doctorate in either Greek, Latin, or history, after which Lieber could join the faculty. (Family commitments forced him to decline.) And, far from least, the man also had a fine sense of humor.[69]

Before the year was over, Lieber had raised the private funds needed to purchase Indiana's first two state parks: Turkey Run and McCormick Creek. As chair of the memorial committee, he worked successfully for the creation of a state Department of Conservation, which he headed for fourteen years. Through his efforts, Indiana became the first state to have a state park system.[70] But getting the state to acquire its third park proved very difficult.

The National Dunes Park Association elected to drop the large national park in favor of a more modest state park. Lieber sought legislative approval for the park and received tremendous assistance from Bess Sheehan, an unwavering supporter of a dunes park and respected officer of the Indiana Federation of Women's Clubs. Through the offices of that highly regarded organization, she contacted every legislator in the state. On the evening of January 26, 1923, she spoke for two hours before a special joint session of the Indiana legislature to which the lawmakers' spouses had been invited. Sheehan enlisted the aid of former Senator Taggart, and along with Lieber won Governor Warren Mac-Crae's assistance. By a vote of fifty-two to fifty-one, the state house approved the measure on March 1, the last day of the session. The senate concurred by a much larger majority.[71]

After prolonged wrangling, the private money finally started flowing. Lieber convinced Judge Elbert Gary of U.S. Steel to contribute $250,000 and Julius Rosenwald $50,000. Samuel Insull donated some land and lent the state $200,000. By 1927, Indiana had purchased two thousand acres of land: the state park had become a reality. And on the seventh day, the dune advocates rested. For twenty-two years.

In the face of the Great Depression and World War II, the dunes seemed safe. But in the late 1940s, there began rumblings about a deep-water port at Burns Ditch in the central dunes. The port was an old idea, but this time around, the Army Corps of Engineers found merit in it.

The Indiana Dunes Preservation Council tried to shake off the lethargy of a twenty-two-year quiescence, but most of the old leadership was gone, either claimed by death or headed in other directions. Dr. Reuben Myron Strong was one who did remain. At age seventy-seven, he despaired that unless a new energetic leader emerged, a great tragedy would be inevitable. Although he was unable to pick up the mantle himself, Strong found the right person in Dorothy Buell.

Dorothy Buell was sixty-five years old and had no experience as an activist. But she possessed an absolute certainty in the righteousness of her cause and a "calm and inspiring dignity respected by friend and critic alike."[72] The writings I have in front of me all attest to this latter quality. There is unanimous agreement that this woman had a remarkable presence—a combination of charisma, integrity, and strength—that stoked the dunes preservation movement despite the awesome power of their adversaries. In the words of Schaeffer and Franklin, "she personified saving the Dunes for a quarter of a century."[73]

On June 20, 1952, twenty-two women met at Buell's home to hear Bess Sheehan talk of the earlier battles. This gathering became the first meeting of Buell's newly formed Save the Dunes Council. Buell stated the members' credo: "We are prepared to spend the rest of our lives, if necessary, to save the Dunes!"[74]

The new campaign to save the dunes had two agendas. The first was to stave off destruction of the central dunes, an almost five-mile stretch of lakefront located between Ogden Dunes and Dune Acres. This area, "considered by conservationists as the most desirable parcel in the entire Dunes region for preservation," encompassed the highest dunes still extant, the widest expanse of dunes, and some of the best wetland and savanna.[75] The second aim was to actualize the long-held dream to create a park that protected the full diversity of the dunes in perpetuity.

Proposals for the deep-water port, two state-of-the-art steel plants, an electric generating station, rail lines, and assorted collateral development all threatened the central dunes. Proponents of these sundry facilities included the Army Corps of Engineers, National Steel (its local operations were part of its Midwest Steel Division), Bethlehem Steel, Inland Steel, New York Central Railroad, Northern Indiana Public Service Company, nearly every elected official in Indiana, and most of the Indiana press. More than any other prominent person, Republican minority leader of the U.S. House of Representatives Charles Halleck became the most unyielding opponent. He represented Porter County and, unlike those politicians who became park supporters once the central dunes were destroyed, he retained bitter animosity toward the conservationists to the end of his long life.

Dorothy Buell believed that the path to preservation was education. Toward that end she enlisted conservationists of national stature, and her organization generated a half million signatures in support of the park. But the forces arrayed against the council were hardly open to conversion through exhortation. Clearly, the Save the Dunes Council had to expand its approach. Leonard Rutstein and Edward Osann pursued legal strategies, Thomas Dustin worked on public relations, and Herbert Read, an architect whose father was an avid dunes advocate during the first battles, became the group's principal engineering and economics expert.

Despite the successes they had wrested, Buell and the others knew they could not win on their own, and in Senator Paul Douglas they found a powerful ally, as enchanted with the dunes as they themselves were. Herb Read says that "Senator Douglas could not have prevailed without the 'grassrooters,' nor could they have succeeded without Douglas. It was a hand-in-hand relationship."[76] Once more the story touches on a truly extraordinary person. Paul Douglas was raised by his stepmother in a remote lumber town in Maine, where he developed his love of nature and disdain for injustice.[77] After earning his doctorate in economics from Columbia University, he taught at various schools before accepting a faculty position at the University of Chicago. He married Emily Taft, daughter of sculptor Lorado Taft, who had campaigned vigorously with Jens Jensen on behalf of the dunes decades earlier. Emily introduced Paul to the dunes, and the two built a small house at Dune Acres where they spent weekends and holidays.

Douglas was elected to the Chicago City Council in 1939 and established himself as an independent voice for the city's poor. His honesty, erudition, and dedication earned him the respect of the Democratic leadership that would later slate him for the U.S. Senate. Then, in 1942, when he was fifty years old, Douglas joined the U.S. Marines as a private. Franklin and Schaeffer comment that "seemingly he did not accept the notion that his mind, his training, and even his political abilities might have had greater value for his country than his aging body and a desire to prove his worth to some unnamed authority." Four years later, Douglas left the service, having climbed in rank to a lieutenant colonel. His military activities left him with two purple hearts and a crippled left arm.

Douglas entered the Senate in 1948 and was returned there two more times before being defeated by Charles Percy in an acrimonious campaign. In a wonderful passage expressed late in his career, Douglas described his goals as a senator:

> I'm now in my 16th or 17th year in the Senate and when I first came it was a big jump from alderman to the Senate, and I knew I was going to save the world. I was into my second term and knew I'd be doing very well to save the Western Hemisphere. Now at the end of my second term, they'd got me down to North America. Into my third term I realized I couldn't do a

damn thing about Canada and Mexico, so I was going to save the United
States, which was not a bad thing to do. Christ, it wasn't very long before
I gave up everything west of the Mississippi and south of the Mason Dixon.
They pushed me and squeezed me and took away everything I wanted to
save, but Goddamn, I'm not going to give up the Indiana Dunes. That's the
only thing I can save because my days are slipping away.

Senator Douglas introduced the first of his many dune bills on May 26, 1958.
Senate Bill 3898 called for the creation of a 3,800-acre Indiana Dunes National
Monument that included the contested central dunes. It would take eight long
years and more than a hundred bills before a federal park in the dunes finally
became a reality.

Much of the battle centered on the federal funding of the port, on which
the private interests were hinging their own resource commitments. In October of 1962, Douglas learned that President Kennedy was prepared to include
the harbor in the newly prepared public works bill. He had his staff inform the
president's office that although he had no appointment he needed to see the
president immediately. He also instructed them to call Herb Read to find out
if Read had any ammunition he could share with Kennedy. Read suggested that
Douglas tell Kennedy that the latest Corps of Engineers' report contained
"new and glaring errors." When asked what they were, Read replied: "I don't
know. But by tomorrow we'll find something." That night he and dunes colleague George Anderson were on a train to Washington for a seven-hour
meeting with high officials of the corps and various agencies. Before they
reached their destination, they had uncovered the new and glaring errors. The
president backed off, and the conservationists gained a reprieve.[78]

A stalemate developed. Senator Douglas and his forces could prevent the
harbor, and Congressman Halleck could stop the park. While factions within
government fought, the steel companies took matters into their own hands: in
early 1963 they leveled the central dunes, thereby denying the conservationists
their most desired treasure.

Although the destruction was horrendous, it enabled a compromise to
emerge. Some of the Indiana officials who had been committed to the harbor
could now support a park encompassing other properties. Kennedy liked this
approach as well. But victory remained elusive until November 5, 1966, when
President Johnson authorized the federal government to spend $28 million for
the purchase of 8,100 acres.[79]

Anticonservation forces need only to win once, while conservationists
must fight forever. Ten years later, a battle ensued over park expansion. Many
of the old players were gone, among them Halleck, Douglas, and Buell. This

68–73. These remarkable photos were taken by Herbert Read, who graciously allowed their use. Each before and after shot was taken from the exact same spot and illustrates in a powerful way what was at stake in the struggle to save the central dunes. Figure 68 (above). *Before:* Looking southeast from future Burns Waterway Harbor in central Dunes, Porter County, June 1962.

69. *After:* Looking southeast toward Bethlehem Steel, July 1971.

70. *Before:* Looking south from future Burns Waterway Harbor toward
large dune known as Howling Hill in the central dunes of Porter County,
June 1961. The bare trunks protruding from the sand are a "graveyard"
of white pines that had been buried and then exposed.

71. *After:* Dune removed and steel shipped to the port placed
in foreground.

72. *Before:* Looking north from future Bethlehem Steel site, May 1963.

73. *After:* Bethlehem Steel Site, February 1965. The same white pine appears in the left side of both pictures.

time Indiana Senators Birch Bayh and Vance Hartke and local Congressmen Edward Roush and Floyd Fithian pushed hard for a larger park, although an unsympathetic Ford administration whittled the area down from 7,023 acres to 3,663. On September 24, 1976, in the midst of Senate consideration of the final compromise bill, Senator Percy announced to his colleagues the death of Paul Douglas earlier that day. Each of the seventy-four Senators present voted in favor, and President Ford signed the measure into law the following month.[80]

Including the state park, the Indiana Dunes National Lakeshore now comprises a little more than fifteen thousand acres. The Save the Dunes Council, the Shirley Heinze Environmental Fund, and the Indiana chapter of the Nature Conservancy are working to preserve additional tracts. These include corridors along the Little Calumet River and Salt Creek, and pannes in Lake and Porter Counties. Because of the Endangered Species Act and the presence of Karner blue butterflies, Midwest Steel has restored some of its property to black oak savanna. Conservationists hope that the company may some day convey that land to the national lakeshore.

Steeper and More Mesic: The Dunes of Berrien County

The dunes of Berrien County share the loftiness of Indiana's but differ principally in being steeper and supporting a more mesic type of vegetation. Along with black oak on the foredunes, there is red oak. And in protected pockets next to Lake Michigan, hemlock, black walnut, and sugar maple can thrive. There are a number of reasons why this is so.

As you travel from the Indiana Dunes into Michigan, you cross both climate and fire gradients. Berrien County experiences greater precipitation and more moderate temperatures that produce a longer growing season. The fire issue is more complex. First, there are a number of rivers that act as firebreaks. Among these are Trail Creek in Michigan City and the Galien River at New Buffalo. Second, the Indiana Dunes are aligned east to west and the Berrien County Dunes north to south. This makes the Indiana Dunes more accessible to the prevailing westerly winds and the fires they carry, while the Berrien County dunes act as barriers that flames have to skitter up and over. That the Michigan dunes are often steeper further reduces their frequency of burning.[81]

Industry has long coveted these dunes for their sand, and mining has posed an ongoing threat. It seems that dune sand is especially valuable for the manufacture of metal molds used in producing machinery. Because of its chemical composition, this sand can tolerate the extreme heat necessary to melt metals. As a result, conversion of dune sand into foundry sand yields a 10 percent loss, while the same process using inland sand creates a 50 percent loss.[82]

Concern over the destruction of these scenic and biologically important lands prompted Michigan to enact the Sand Dunes Protection Act in 1978. Under the regulatory scheme, the state has designated certain dunes as critical, where sand mining is forbidden. Little if any such mining still occurs in Berrien County, but its legacy lives on. A valuable area near Bridgman was stripped, while a far more satisfactory conclusion was reached at Grand Mere, where a mining controversy led to permanent protection.

◄o► ◄o► ◄o►

The first of the Berrien dunelands to be protected was Warren Dunes State Park, which also includes Warren Woods. E. K. Warren bought the lakefront parcel specifically because "it would be of great value to thousands of people as a place of education."[83] Local residents enjoyed access to it, and many evidently came to believe they had a proprietary interest in the land, for they were unhappy when the state assumed control of it. Warren Dunes now has parking spaces for twenty-five hundred cars and is very popular among summer beachgoers. For some reason, however, little seems to have been written on the park's natural features.

Much more can be said about Grand Mere. Located farther north, it comprises a mixture of natural communities unique to the region. James Wells and Paul Thompson studied this diverse area in the late 1970s and published their valuable results in 1983. Much of what follows is based on their article.

Formed as an embayment flooded during the Glenwood stage of Lake Chicago, the sixteen-mile-long and one-mile-wide lowland that is Grand Mere features three interconnected lakes in different states of succession. The water flows north, beginning with South Lake, which is the shallowest and most heavily vegetated. Intermediate in location, size, and vegetational cover is Middle Lake. Finally there is North Lake, the largest and possessing the most open water. On the west side of North Lake, a channel carries the flow into Lake Michigan.

A large assemblage of wetland plants inhabits the lakes and their adjacent lowlands. Floating vegetation includes fragrant water lily, yellow water lily, pickerelweed (*Pontederia cordata*), and various pondweeds (*Potamogeton*). Because of its shallowness, South Lake holds the most emergent species, such as wild rice, pitcher plant, and humped bladderwort (*Utricularia gibba*).

The most significant plant of South Lake, at least from a cultural perspective, is large cranberry. A wooden dam enabled workers to control the water levels of South Lake to maximize the crop. From the 1890s to 1912, Stevensville exported hundreds of pounds to Chicago and other Midwestern cities: "During the height of the cranberry harvest . . . , nearly 500 people could be found picking cranberries, moving slowly across the bog in a kneeling position, in long unbroken lines. . . . Pickers were not allowed to take leads or pull away from their neighbors, thereby retaining a line that was truly a sight not easily forgotten. . . . For working on the marsh, horses were shod with a special set of removable wooden muck-shoes to prevent bogging down."[84]

In a portion of the low area south of the lakes is one of the Chicago region's few hemlock (*Tsuga canadensis*) swamps. This swamp represents an example of the hemlock–white pine–Northern hardwood forest type that extends south just into Berrien County. Hemlock stands form a very dense canopy, which creates a microclimate that is moister and cooler than adjacent sites.[85] These conditions enable many forbs of northern affinity to survive here: starflowers (*Trientalis borealis*), bunchberry (*Cornus canadensis*), goldthread (*Coptis trifolia*), purple avens (*Geum rivale*), and twinflower (*Linnaea borealis*).

A thin band of post-Algoma sand lies interposed between the two northern lakes and Lake Michigan. Starting at the southern end of Middle Lake and heading south, this border widens into an extensive system of large dunes derived from Algonquin, Algoma, and Nipissing Lake stages. (The highest of these dunes is known as Johnson Dune, which stands 180 feet above Lake Michigan.) Grand Mere manifests evidence of all the various lake stages except for Tolleston.[86]

One of the most unusual communities discovered by Wells and Thompson was what they called a "heath bald," which consisted of a shrub-covered dune dominated by huckleberry and low blueberry. Although a small area, "the very dense assemblage of the shrub heath and the paucity of canopy layer and ground cover rendered a unique aspect for sand dunes vegetation."[87] Unfortunately, the spot was later mined for its sand.

Close to Lake Michigan, the botanists discovered an unusual valley between two dunes. A grove of black walnuts, perhaps fifty years old, grew within the mesophytic pocket. Lichens coated the trunks, evidence of the moisture created by offshore winds. The dominant shrub was hop tree, and common species of understory included poison ivy, wild bergamot (*Monarda fistulosa*), and starry false Solomon's seal (*Smilacina stellata*).

Serious efforts to protect Grand Mere began in 1965, when three landowners, Philip Shapiro, Manley Brothers, and Victor Peters pooled their holdings and offered twelve hundred acres for sale to interested companies. The property encompassed two of the three lakes, which development would damage if not destroy.[88] Announcement of the plan ignited a battle between conservationists and developers that would last twenty years.

The Grand Mere Association quickly formed to promote conservation interests. They convinced the state legislature to appropriate money to purchase critical parcels and successfully challenged the township planning commission's support of rezoning by initiating and winning two referenda. At the association's behest, out-of-town experts such as Charles Olmsted of the University of Chicago and Herbert Read visited to speak on behalf of preservation.

A key event occurred in 1967 when Shapiro died. He had been less hostile than his two partners, and thus conservationists were hopeful that the state could acquire the 383 acres in his estate. After six years of negotiations and the strong support of State Senator Charles Zollar, the Michigan Department of Natural Resources bought the land for $613,700.[89]

Meanwhile, Manley Brothers had been actively seeking state permission to mine sand. Every time they made an application, the conservationists rose to meet the challenge. The Michigan Department of Natural Resources was prepared to buy the Manley holdings, but the asking price was excessive. Then, "right in the middle of one hearing," British Industrial Sand acquired Manley, and the controversy took a turn for the better.

The new company realized that pursuing Manley's tack would lead to endless litigation, so they sought a compromise. British Industrial Sand was allowed to mine forty acres at the southern end of the site in return for their selling 490.5 acres to the state. There was so little trust between the parties, however, that Tom Woiwode of Michigan's chapter of the Nature Conservancy entered the fray as an intermediary to hammer out a resolution. In 1985, after three years of negotiations, a fifty-four-page agreement spelling out every possible contingent was finally signed, and a year later the state took possession of what had been the battleground. A total of 950 acres are now protected within Grand Mere State Park.

Not All Treasure Is at the Rainbow's End: The Western Dunelands

Almost ninety years ago, Frank Caleb Gates began his study of the beach area in northeastern Illinois and southeastern Wisconsin. This narrow crescent of dunes and swales, called by early authors the Waukegan Moorlands or Waukegan Flats, then stretched without interruption from southern Waukegan to Kenosha. Gates described what the region looked like from a seat on the Chicago Northwestern Railroad, whose tracks follow the Glenwood ridgeline at the area's western edge.

The southern portion, extending north to roughly what is now Greenwood Avenue, "is characterized by marshy swales separated from one another by very low sandy ridges. . . . The vegetation is essentially prairie-like. It is very monotonous in appearance, except during July, when the lilies are in bloom, and during September, when it is covered with blazing stars."[90]

A passenger would not recognize the southern sector today. Instead of grasslands, there is Waukegan Harbor, the city's public beach, the Outboard Marine Company, a large water treatment facility, Commonwealth Edison's coal-fired generating plant and slip, and the Johns Manville plant and dump. But a thin strip of land between industry and the lake lying just north of the public beach is still a wonderful place for the naturalist. Several years ago, following the direction of local authority Jim Neal, I found three species of orchids: green twayblade (*Liparis loeselii*), Northern bog orchid (*Habenaria hyperborea*), and helleborine (*Epipactis helleborine*), the only nonnative member of the family to have become established in the region.

But this beach's singular feature is its attractiveness to birds. Common terns (*Sterna hirundo*) have nested (or at least tried to nest) in the immediate vicinity since at least 1935, and until 2001 nowhere else in the region.[91] Edison, to its credit, has allowed state biologists to manage a part of their land for the benefit of the terns. (The terns left this nesting site in 2000 and moved to the Great Lakes Naval Training Station to the south.)

The beach is best known, however, for migrating sandpipers. Numerous species find a haven on the deserted sand, including red knots (*Calidris canutus*), whimbrels (*Numenius phaeopus*), and federally endangered piping plovers (*Charadrius melodus*). In fact, the last nesting pairs of piping plover in the state and region raised young on Edison property in the summers of 1973 and 1979. To see the birds, it was necessary to circumvent a thick growth of willows by wading into the lake. I remember showing the plovers to longtime birder Amy Baldwin. Frail and in her eighties, she held my arm for support as she trekked through knee-deep water to enjoy a once-familiar sight for the final time.

Proceeding north to the mouth of Dead River, the lay of the land remains roughly the same but leaves an entirely different impression because of the groves of pines that occupy the ridges. These pines were the survivors among the two hundred thousand trees of twenty-five-plus species (including many deciduous types) that nurseryman Robert Douglas planted. He began his reforestation project with the purchase of six hundred acres in 1873 and then proceeded to place surplus seedling stock in plowed furrows over the next fifteen years or so. Among the pines in Douglas's forest were white, Austrian (*Pinus nigra*), Scotch (*P. sylvestris*), Table Mountain (*P. pungens*—now gone), and pitch (*P. rigida*).[92] (Some articles erroneously point to the white pines as relics of an original forest.)

Douglas's handiwork created a habitat that was both beautiful and locally unique. Over the years, the pines have yielded numerous bird vagrants, the most astonishing being the nonmigratory red-cockaded woodpecker (*Picoides borealis*) that spent five months here in 2001. In some winters, pine grosbeaks (*Pinicola enucleator*), white-winged crossbills (*Loxia leucoptera*), and red crossbills (*L. curvirostra*) visit to feed on the abundant cones. A few times, red crossbills even nested. But the trees are introductions, and the Department of Natural Resources appropriately manages for native species. Thus, under a regimen of periodic burning the pines are dying out, and, in not too distant a time, it will be as if Douglas had never pursued his fancy.

The northern third of the journey, from Dead River to Kenosha, is by far the longest and the most varied:

> It is wooded, but in this case the trees are oak instead of pine. There are many blowouts, those toward the north being larger and slightly more numerous that those in the southern part. The interridgial depressions, which are not so low as those toward the south, are, for the most part, wider, and are occupied by prairie rather than by marsh plants. At the Illinois-Wisconsin state line the innermost oak ridge has been cut away, leaving an area of level sandy ground, one kilometer in width, from the lake to the bluff. . . . Nearer Kenosha occurs the last oak ridge, which is quite wide and

has several large blowouts in its sandy soil. . . . The part between the oak ridge and the railway track is a sodded sandy plain.[93]

Along with the oaks and ridges, today's traveler would see a hotel complex at Illinois Beach State Park, Commonwealth Edison's Zion Nuclear Power Plant, a huge marina operated by the Illinois Department of Natural Resources, and a smaller marina and residential developments in Pleasant Prairie, Kenosha County. Interspersed with the wide range of development is some of the highest quality natural land in the region, much of which is protected. This mixture of land use may, in fact, be the most striking feature of today's Wisconsin-Illinois dunelands.

Although nothing of the southern third is formally preserved, landowners afford at least some protection to a significant portion of the rest. (Opportunities for further conservation efforts still exist, and should be exercised.) Moving northward from Johns Manville, there is the southern unit of Illinois Beach State Park, prairie protected by Commonwealth Edison (although presumably still vulnerable), Hosah Prairie of the Zion Park District, more state park, Spring Bluff Forest Preserve of the Lake County Forest Preserve District, and Chiwaukee Prairie, a joint project of the Wisconsin Department of Natural Resources, University of Wisconsin—Parkside, and the Wisconsin chapter of the Nature Conservancy.

◄◦► ◄◦► ◄◦►

Well over 650 species of plants have been recorded at the south unit of Illinois Beach State Park; more high-quality natural communities occur here than anywhere else in the state. A good way to sample the place is to start at the nature center and walk south along the Dead River to its mouth. This stretch of the route traverses fine sections of mesic and wet prairie, sedge meadow, marsh, and open water. Return via the gravel road through the oak savanna.

On the low dunes at the mouth of the Dead River a regionally unique plant community has arisen that some believe is one of the prettiest natural landscapes in the state. It may be the defining image of the Illinois dunelands: "The high and dry ridges are covered with the lustrous leaves of the bearberry and with the prostrate sprays of Waukegan Juniper, one of the most beautiful of evergreens—silvery green with whitish berries that turn into purple in the winter."[94]

Waukegan juniper (*Juniperus horizontalis*) spreads outward from its center, its branches sprouting roots along the way. An individual plant may cover sixty feet. Eventually, as the plant moves, the point where it began may die.

Sometimes the ensuing bare patch of sand becomes enlarged and forms a blowout. At other times, however, the space becomes occupied by the common juniper (*J. communis*), the third most significant member of the heath, as Gates calls this community. Although horizontal juniper once occurred as far south as Lawrence Avenue and Lake Michigan on Chicago's north side, it has never been recorded from the Indiana Dunes.[95]

While its runners are less conspicuous, bearberry is similar in its growth to the spreading juniper. Both species trap debris and thus promote the accumulation of humus, but with its thicker tangle of branches, the bearberry does so more effectively. Bearberry is also an important food source for wildlife. Numerous birds eat its scarlet berries, and three insects feed on nothing but this plant: hoary elfin butterfly (*Callophrys polios*), bearberry leafhopper (*Texananus cumulatus*), and bearberry aphid (*Tamalia coweni*).[96]

Spring comes late to the park, but by mid-May, conspicuous bursts of color have begun to variegate the tawniness of the sand. Fragile-looking sand cress (*Arabis lyrata*) emerges early. At the same time that their small white blossoms appear, so does the small white Olympia butterfly (*Euchloe olympia*), whose larvae feed on the plant. Joining the sand cress on the open ground of the savanna are lupine, common blue-eyed grass (*Sisyrinchium albidum*), hoary puccoon (*Lithospermum canescens*), starry Solomon's seal, and several violets. In wetter areas, yellow star grass (*Hypoxis hirsuta*) and the exotic-looking wood betony or lousewort (*Pedicularis canadensis*) thrive.

The plants that bloom in summer are far too numerous to enumerate, and the aspect changes throughout the season. Jesse Lowe Smith, a prominent north-shore educator and naturalist in the early part of the twentieth century, provides his impression of the dunes, or as he calls them, the Waukegan Flats: "It is in early summer that the flats begin to show at their best when the coreopsis, the black-eyed Susans, orange-red [prairie] lilies, and the spiked lobelia appear together with two beautiful native orchids, the calopogon and the rose pogonia. . . . These two orchids are as yet abundant in the low grassy shallows of the Flats. . . . Later on come into bloom the shrubby potentilla with yellow blossoms, the prairie clover, evening primrose, Pitcher's thistle, several species of milkweed, of which, the butterfly weed, is very conspicuous with its orange-red flower masses."[97]

Smith's description of Illinois Beach includes at least three species that are apparently no longer present in the western dunelands. (Gates also recorded the now missing three.) These are the tamarack, Pitcher's thistle, and showy lady's slipper.[98] Smith noted that the lady's slipper was sliding toward oblivion because collectors sought its roots for medicinal purposes and its flowers for decorations.

The purple fringed orchid (*Habenaria psycodes*) was another species that Smith believed was flirting with extinction. Fortunately, this plant has survived. It is most frequent at the north end of the park, but in 1994 it appeared where, as far as I know, it had not been seen in recent years. I was leading a bird walk when, looking down, I spied an orchid in a copse of shrubbery. After stopping suddenly, I began exclaiming incoherently and by so doing convinced the rest of the group that I had been stricken by a debilitating illness. The fact is that numerous people with strong interests in botany have walked that trail for years, and few if any ever witnessed what we were seeing. The orchids were almost certainly not new arrivals to the mucky sand, but some special set of circumstances coincided that year to trigger the rising of the plant and its scepter of amethyst flowers. One might devote hours patrolling that path every August and yet never see the purple fringed orchid again.

Late summer and early fall are lovely times as well. Blazing stars of three species sort themselves in appropriate niches from dry foredunes to mesic prairie. Six asters, six goldenrods, and two coneflowers lend another range of hues to the landscape. Inconspicuous and dainty, two ladies' tresses—the nodding (*Spiranthes cernua*) and the much rarer slender (*S. lacera*)—are scattered through the swales.

The most regal of all autumnal flowers is the fringed gentian (*Gentiana crinita*), which is endowed with an intense blue that can best be likened to a cloudless sky. Although the species is now reduced to little clumps here and there along the damp swales, it wasn't always that way. There was a time, now beyond the memories of living souls, when fringed gentian "pastures" spread for acres across the Waukegan flats. As Minnie Horton wrote, not all treasure is at the rainbow's end.[99]

◄○► ◄○► ◄○►

As early as the late 1880s, people began thinking about preserving the western dunesland.[100] In a 1944 letter preserved in the Dunesland Preservation Society files, the great Jens Jensen reported that in 1888 Robert Douglas raised the subject "of conserving the rich flora in the Waukegan Flats for all times." And in 1914, Dean Howard Ganster, a member of the Waukegan Park Board, tried in vain to get Waukegan to buy the area as a park.[101]

The years that followed saw large blocks of the area converted to industrial purposes. Commonwealth Edison built its coal-fired generating station in 1920, and Johns Manville completed its plant in 1922. These projects no doubt led to a growing sense of urgency on the part of conservationists, and it is probably not a coincidence that the first legislation authorizing a dunes park was

74. Beach pool at southern end of "Waukegan Moorlands" (Waukegan, Lake County, Ill.), with feeding sanderlings, August 17, 1909. Photo by F. C. Gates. (Courtesy of Illinois Natural History Survey, Champaign.)

75. South end of Illinois Beach State Park, depicting the nonnative pine forest planted by Robert Douglas in the 1870s. Photo by Jesse Lowe Smith, taken between 1910 and 1921. (Courtesy Park District of Highland Park, Highland Park, Ill.)

76. Aerial photo of Dead River, Illinois Beach State Park, which receives
its name from the sand dam that often forms at its mouth; it is believed
to be very similar to the presettlement form of the Chicago River.
(Courtesy of R. Grosso and S. Wright, Illinois Beach State Park, Zion.)

77. Bearberry and juniper on the dunes near the mouth of the Dead
River at Illinois Beach State Park, May 1914. Photo by J. L. Smith.
(Courtesy Park District of Highland Park, Highland Park, Ill.)

introduced into the Illinois General Assembly in 1923. It may also be the case that once Manville and Edison sated their appetite for land, politicians became more comfortable backing conservation initiatives.

That first legislative effort went nowhere, for the $2 million price tag for the land was deemed excessive. Similar bills followed, and support gradually grew. A staunch proponent of the park was State Senator Ray Paddock of Wauconda, and in 1928 he convinced five of his colleagues on the appropriations committee to tour the area. The senators were "impressed beyond expectation [with the] rare beauty of the site" and declared they would recommend that the land be bought. They were also motivated by another consideration, as stated by downstate Senator Stewart Cuthbertson of Bunker Hill (near St. Louis): "The state will have to do something for the Chicago district, and I believe it can be done with providing this park."

Despite the senators' endorsement, the assembly failed to pass Paddock's bill. In 1930, in fulfillment of his promise to Paddock, Governor Louis Emmerson visited the property. He was accompanied by his advisory committee on state parks and Secretary of State William Stratton. Again, there was unanimity that the park was a worthwhile project deserving state action. This time the price tag was $5 million. A flurry of reports indicated that private and public sources had committed to the land acquisition, but for whatever reason both the philanthropy and the state resources evaporated, and the land remained in private ownership.

A new initiative began under the auspices of the State Board of Park Advisors. As part of this effort, a group calling itself the Illinois Dunes Park Association was created. It proceeded to lease fifteen hundred acres for five years. The purposes of their activities were to "keep the natural beauties of the dunes intact, to protect the piece from ultimate destruction, and to save the hundreds of pine trees which in the past few years have been badly mutilated and dug up." The association charged visitors a dime, the money going for upkeep of the site.

In 1938, at the request of Governor Henry Horner, the state prepared a document titled *Illinois Park, Parkway and Recreational Area Plan*. On page 110, the report made the following statement: "Public acquisition is urgently recommended of about 3,500 acres, fronting on Lake Michigan, north of Waukegan. . . . This is the only remaining beach frontage on Lake Michigan of adequate length and available for public ownership. If publicly owned, its recreational value to the state and particularly, to the huge population of northeastern Illinois would be incalculable. It is the most important recreational area in Illinois which could be added to the state park system."

As I read the articles that appeared in the Chicago and Waukegan papers at the time, I was struck by the lack of opposition to the park plan. Local officials (both county and municipal), citizens, the press, governors, and legislators (from northeastern Illinois as well as downstate) all endorsed the park. If commercial interests did fight, they did so quietly and without newspaper coverage. Yet, it wasn't until May 10, 1943, under the administration of Governor Dwight Green, that the state at last bought its first parcel of 450 acres.

The reality of the park spawned the creation of a new organization called the Illinois Dunesland Preservation Society. (The Illinois Dunes Park Association seems to have faded into nothingness, perhaps considering its mission completed with the establishment of the park.) This new group evolved out of the Illinois Dunesland Garden Club, and among its most active members were Dean Howard Ganster, Jeanette Aiken Black, and George Pavlik. The society worked closely with the state, particularly Walter Rosenfield (Illinois's director of public works), to ensure that plans were compatible with nature preservation.

One issue that the society struggled with was burning. They strongly supported fire lanes and urged local fire departments to respond more quickly to brushfires. George Pavlik hooked his tractor up to a wagon, the vehicle being called "a dunes taxi," and gave educational tours designed in part to show the damaging effects of fire. The well being of the pines was of major concern to society members. Over time, however, the group sought input from others, and their views changed. In the society's archives, for example, is a 1954 letter from John Curtis answering University of Chicago botanist Charles Olmsted's query on the effects of fire on prairie: "It would indeed be tragic if the [Lake Michigan] prairies were allowed to proceed to biological destruction through the misguided application of total fire protection."

The price of conservation is constant vigilance. When Governor William Stratton announced in May 1957 the building of a large hotel complex on park grounds, the society and other conservationists, including the State Park Advisory Board, actively opposed its location. It was to be plunked in the middle of a panne system, destroying Illinois's largest colony of horned bladderwort, along with grass of Parnassus, purple false foxglove, bog lobelia, and fringed gentian. But in the end, Governor Stratton ignored the pleadings of his own board, and the hotel opened in June 1960. For most of the past forty years, the lodge has been a financial bust, although it is currently in a rare period of operation.

Mayor Robert Sabonjian of Waukegan initiated what could have been a devastating assault on the park. In the fall of 1961, he asked the state to lease Waukegan 160 acres at the far south end of the park so the city could construct a marina, swimming pool, and golf course. Sabonjian, claiming to respect "lovers of nature," said that he personally inspected the south prairie and found few if any native plants. He further emphasized that his plan "would not take one tree out of the park." Regarding the latter point, the *Chicago Tribune* (November 11, 1961) quipped, "The southern third of Illinois Beach State Park is significant not for the trees that it does not have, but for being the largest piece of natural sand prairie surviving in this region." By January 1962, state authorities had firmly rejected Sabonjian's attempted land grab. Today, the state of Illinois has about 4,210 acres of the flats. Lake County's Spring Bluff Forest Preserve contains another 233 acres and Hosah Prairie (Zion Park District) twenty-three acres. Substantial portions of both Illinois Beach and Spring Bluff are dedicated nature preserves.

On September 1, 1948, five years after the state finally purchased its first dunelands, Jeanette Black wrote the following words of thanks to Walter Rosenfield. It is a sentiment easily understood by any park visitor:

> I feel as though I had reached the top of the mountain and could look over after waiting, working, and hoping for all this for thirty-four years. If I were a spiritualist, I would say as I walk through the trails my father's spirit walks with me, for he skated as a boy all the way up the swamps 8 miles to court my mother. . . . But always in my father's mind (he too was a dreamer) there would be a park of that land from the lake to the railroad, so you can see I was born with this dream, and the fulfillment is something so deep how can I express my appreciation.

◄○► ◄○► ◄○►

Chiwaukee Prairie is one of the outstanding natural areas in the region and state. The site comprises approximately 330 acres of low dunes and swales. Most of it is treeless, a function of fire and possibly, to a lesser degree, flooding in wet years.

Wet, mesic, and dry prairie flourish within feet of each other. This rich mosaic is sustained by the subtle variations in topography that assures adequate moisture regardless of precipitation levels in a given year. Thus during droughts, the swales provide habitat for wet and mesic species, and in times of high water the ridge tops can support mesic and dry plants.[102]

Botanists have recorded over 475 species of plants at Chiwaukee Prairie, including such rarities as pink milkwort (*Polygala incarnata*—currently known to exist in the region at only two or three sites), prairie Indian plantain (*Cacalia plantaginea*), and one of the largest eastern prairie fringed orchid (*Habenaria* [*Platanthera*] *leucophaea*) populations in the Midwest. In the lowest places, roundstem bulrush, swamp milkweed (*Asclepias incarnata*), blue flag, and spotted joe-pye weed (*Eupatorium maculatum*) find sanctuary. Further up the slight slope, mesic species predominate: big bluestem, lead plant, colic root (*Aletris*

78. Spring flora at Chiwaukee Prairie, Kenosha County, including
shooting star, hoary pucoon, and wood betony. (Photo by
and courtesy of Greg Neice.)

farinosa), Indian paintbrush, tall green milkweed (*Asclepias hirtella*), false toad-flax (*Comandra umbellata*), all three prairie silphia, rattlesnake master, and six milkworts. At the driest level, the guild of plants includes prairie dropseed, little bluestem, purple prairie clover (*Petalostemum purpureum*), stiff goldenrod (*Solidago rigida*), and hairy puccoon.

Shooting stars (*Dodecatheon meadia*), above all other species, characterize Chiwaukee Prairie. The plant is not particularly uncommon, but in late May it blankets the prairie in such profusion that it attains a level of splendor not exceeded elsewhere in the region. The flowers cluster along the narrow dune tops, delineating these elevations in lines of azure, pink, and white. One anonymous writer describing the area early in the past century called the shooting stars the particular glory of the low ridges. She said they were plucked in great armfuls.[103]

Often, when the shooting stars are in bloom, the weather fashions another equally stunning image of the prairie. Although the earth has already begun to warm, Lake Michigan remains chilly. Drifting back and forth from water to land, the moist air condenses into a translucent cloak of fog that settles over the bejeweled plain. Not quickly forgotten is this muted expanse of shooting star vignetting into the distance.

◄O► ◄O► ◄O►

In 1924, a woman of substantial means bought eighteen hundred acres of Kenosha County lakefront. Mrs. Edith Rockefeller McCormick intended to erect "a model city with retail shops, a golf course, a school, playgrounds, and marina."[104] Named Edithton Beach, the project moved forward as Barnes Creek was straightened, roads were built, and bridges constructed. To the south, another group of developers began their vision of luxury living that included as special attractions an eighteen-hole golf course and clubhouse (both of which were completed), as well as a hotel.

But it seemed that nature conspired to thwart the various developers: the golf course failed, houses could not be completed or were washed into the lake, and access roads collapsed. Then in 1929 the economy also collapsed. With Mrs. McCormick's own permanent collapse three years later, her holdings were sold to a group who shared her aspirations and, fortunately for the prairie, her success.

From the late 1930s to the mid-1940s, a serious effort was made to incorporate the area as part of a state park. But Wisconsin was short of money, and many believed that the establishment of a park would mostly benefit Illinoisans. The passing of this opportunity led to the gradual conversion of prairie into subdivision.

Conservationists were keenly aware of Chiwaukee Prairie's importance. Floyd Swink recalled visiting Albert Fuller, Botany Curator of the Milwaukee Public Museum, some time after World War II. Fuller was nearing retirement: "He just put his head in his hands and said, 'I don't know how we're going to do it, but we have to save the Ridges [in Door County, Wisconsin], and we have to save Chiwaukee Prairie.' And he was almost crying."[105]

By the spring of 1964, time was running out. But then Alfred Krampert and Phil Sander rose to the challenge, after convincing themselves that they could save Chiwaukee Prairie. Their timing was auspicious, for less than a year later, developers announced plans for a giant marina called Pompeii on the Lake, which would take a huge chunk out of the prairie.

The developers first had to convince the County Board to rezone the land from residential and agricultural to commercial. The night of the board meeting was bitterly cold, with fierce winds and heavy snow. Undeterred, the conservationists made the meeting, some driving all the way from Madison. Krampert recalled Professor Hugh Iltis's presentation: "I'll never forget Hugh Iltis standing there looking like a skinny Santa Claus with a black beard covered with half-melted snow pleading with the County Board not to rezone in these words, 'You are rezoning land in Pleasant Prairie Township. Your children will ask, "What is a pleasant prairie," and you will have no answer—for you will have destroyed it.'"

The County Board voted in favor of the marina. But in response the conservationists formed the Kenosha-Racine Project Committee of the Wisconsin chapter of the Nature Conservancy and began the process of raising funds, identifying landowners (one of whom was traced all the way to Portugal), and acquiring property. In 1965, the grassroots efforts evolved into a new organization, the Chiwaukee Prairie Preservation Fund, which actively assists the Nature Conservancy and the Department of Natural Resources.

Twenty years later the Southeast Wisconsin Regional Planning Commission developed a comprehensive land use plan for the 1,825 acres that comprise the Chiwaukee Prairie–Carol Beach portion of Pleasant Prairie. They determined that within the study area there were 818 acres of wetland, 368 acres of high-value prairie, and 343 acres of medium-value prairie. Of this and other vacant land, the County Board eventually agreed to protect through zoning 52 percent while allowing 39 percent to become developed.

By the end of 1994, the University of Wisconsin—Parkside and the Nature Conservancy co-owned 226 acres of Chiwaukee Prairie. They are acquiring the remainder, platted into 168 lots, bit by bit.

Cool Shadowy Slopes: The Bluffs and Ravines

Along two very circumscribed segments of lakefront, the Lake Border Upland abuts Lake Michigan: in northeastern Racine County (Cliffside Park in Crestview) and from Winnetka to Waukegan. Bluffs rise as high as 140 feet above the lake and are often dissected by deep ravines running up to a mile long. This dramatic variability in topography, combined with soil diversity and the effects of Lake Michigan, produces an array of plant communities, including the unique eroding bluff. Botanists have discovered over 367 species of plants in the Lake County portion alone.[106]

Little of this area is open to the public, and even less has escaped serious human abuse. A few sites do exist, however, that are both high quality and accessible. Cliffside Park, owned and managed by the Racine County Public Works Division, is 232 acres, which include wooded ravines, slopes, and eroding bluffs.[107] Rosewood Park in Highland Park (which may soon be dedicated as an Illinois Nature Preserve) consists of eleven acres. Probably the most intact and definitely the most extensive bluff and ravine system in northeastern Illinois spans McCormick Ravine (Lake Forest Park District) and Fort Sheridan. Rival interests have debated the fate of Fort Sheridan for years, but it now appears as if the Lake County Forest Preserve District will obtain the natural areas. Dedication of this unique complex as a nature preserve should be a high priority for both the municipality and the county.

◄o► ◄o► ◄o►

Dr. Cowles asserts that "there can be almost no other habitat in our climate which imposes such severe conditions upon vegetation as an eroding clay bluff." Extremes in temperature, exposure to sun and wind, and the consistency of clay which changes from mush to concrete as it dries provide few advantages to pioneering plants. In fact, during periods of erosion, "all vegetation is impossible."[108]

Eventually, enough material sloughs off the bluff face to reduce its steepness and susceptibility to erode. Sufficient soil stability allows the formation of a highly distinctive plant community, referred to by Dr. Cowles as "the shrub stage of the captured cliff." These slopes are surprisingly rich, for they are enhanced by seeps and small trickles.

Although botanizing on these unsteady slumps was very treacherous, it was often equally rewarding. Trees that tend to be more abundant to the north such as paper birch, common juniper, red cedar, and white pine thrived here. The balsam poplar (*Populus balsamifera*) used to be common as well but is now extirpated, save for a population at Cliffside Park. The Chicago region's only record (and one of only two from Illinois) of red pine (*Pinus resinosa*) was collected "at the base of a clay bluff at Lake Forest in 1955." The beautiful shrub buffalo berry (*Shepherdia canadensis*) is now largely restricted to the bluffs, particularly at Cliffside Park, where the largest population resides. Taking advantage of the open aspect, smooth blue aster (*Aster laevis*), wood betony (*Pedicularis canadensis*), fringed gentian, and other prairie species have also established themselves.[109]

Organisms that do best on eroding bluffs lead inherently precarious lives, especially in this region, where potential habitat has always been limited. For example, because of erosion caused by Lake Michigan, the bluffs at Lake Bluff, Lake County, "have receded an average of . . . 267 feet since 1872," thereby eliminating habitat.[110] Landowners fearful that their stately homes will become rubble on the beach below respond with measures to stop the erosion. Thus bluff plants are caught in a catch-22: either they literally lose ground through the erosion that creates the conditions they require or they are replaced by the new guild of plants that colonize the now-stabilized bluff.

Bluffs that have been long stabilized are dominated by oak forests; white oak and red oak were the most common species, followed by scarlet oak and swamp white oak. Witch hazel is by far the most abundant shrub, and Pennsylvania sedge the most abundant herb. When one early botanist did her survey of the forests of Glencoe in the fall of 1919, she found numerous sugar maple saplings in these upland woods and predicted they might soon match the oaks in frequency and numbers. But fifty-five years later, Robbin Moran could still report that the primacy of the oaks had not diminished. What had diminished in the intervening years were the forests themselves: "Picturesque bluffs, trenched by ravines, and the high rolling upland with its wealth of trees make this section almost ideal for home sites." [111]

The lakefront ravines have also attracted the attention of local ecologists for many years. Devoting much of his discussion to the north shore, Henry Cowles describes ravine formation in the context of the evolving physiography of rivers: "Wherever there is an elevated stretch of land adjoining a body of water, such as a lake bluff, one is apt to find excellent illustrations of the beginning of a ravine." In its first stage, the ravine "is essentially a desert," erosion preventing the establishment of vegetation. But as the descending water declines in its velocity, the effect is less to deepen than to widen the ravine. Under these new conditions, "the vegetation leaps as it were by bounds through the herbaceous and shrubby stages into a mesophytic forest." [112]

79. Eroding morainal bluff at Lake Bluff, Lake County, (Ill.). Photo
by Chicago Prairie Club, June 1913. (Courtesy Westchester
Township Historical Museum, Chesterton, Ind.)

80. Showy orchis, a rare species restricted to mesic forests, on Ravine
Drive in Highland Park, Lake County (Ill.), 1912. Photo by J. L. Smith.
(Courtesy Park District of Highland Park, Highland Park, Ill.)

It is this mesic forest, consisting of sugar maple, basswood, red oak, white ash (*Fraxinus americana*), and hop hornbeam, that garners so much interest. At Crestview and Highland Park, there are healthy colonies of beech trees. The outstanding herbaceous growth within the ravines has yielded such extremely rare species as dwarf scouring rush (*Equisetum scirpoides*—two of the region's only three records of this plant), Hooker's orchid (*Habenaria hookeri*), heart-leaved plantain (*Plantago cordata*), and male fern (*Dryopteris filix-mas*), known locally only since 1979 from a single ravine in Glencoe, Cook County.[113]

As is characteristic of mesic forests, the spring flora is striking. The most vivid images come from the pen of Louella Chapin:

> The most beautiful of the flowers in the ravines is the great white trillium, tall and spotless in a circle of its own green leaves; but of these you must never take but a handful, and a very small handful at that, for they are sadly diminishing year by year, as the city reaches farther and farther out. Best of all, take just one apiece to those at home . . . ; and for yourself, enjoy them where they stand fluttering beside the waxy May apples, in the misty green of the maidenhair and meadow rue on the cool shadowy slopes.[114]

Many More Than We Know: Insects

Of all the many forms of life which exist upon the surface of this old earth of ours, and which are our daily companions for good or ill during our few years stay hereon, none are more numerous or less known than the insects. Not only are they abundant as individuals, but the number of species is also many fold greater than that of all other animals put together. Both on land and in water, they occur by millions, yet the life history of even the housefly is known to few. —Willis S. Blatchley (1910)

Civilization from a fly's eyeview is the increasing proliferation of organic waste and garbage. — Bernard Greenberg (1991)

Some recent estimates place the world total of insect species at over 40 million. State biologists estimate that seventeen thousand occur in Illinois alone. Among these are 1,485 hoppers, cicadas, and aphids (Homoptera), 5,000 beetles (Coleoptera), 2,000 ants, wasps, and bees (Hymenoptera), 4,100 flies (Diptera), and 2,000 butterflies and moths (Lepidoptera). It is often said that if people aren't careful with their treatment of the earth, insects will take over. Tom Eisner of Cornell University has quipped that insects already own the earth, so humans may as well make peace with the landlords.[1]

Millions of years of insect evolution have produced a fantastic array of forms, yet all are marked as insects by possessing three pairs of legs, a three-segmented body (head, thorax, and abdomen), and a pair of antennae. Many also have wings and are the only invertebrates that do. Unfortunately, however, unless there is an economic or medical impact associated with them, few insects receive much study.

Most of what has been written on insects consists of highly technical taxonomic treatises that offer elaborate identification keys difficult for the nonspecialist to use. For example, shape of adult male genitalia (many larvae and females cannot be identified) is often a diagnostic character. This requires dissection and a microscope, but even then when the entire animal is only a millimeter or two in length subtle differences are not easy to discern.

Some specimens can only be identified through close comparison with others. This requires access to a large collection and someone familiar with it. But there may only be one or two people in the entire country who specialize in a given insect group. (Because of research priorities, these taxonomists are themselves becoming rare.) And it's sometimes worse than that. Andrew Williams of the University of Wisconsin—Madison, who works with prairie insects, is still searching for someone willing and able to identify the many species of leaf miner flies (Agromyzidae) that he has found.[2]

Under these circumstances, it is not surprising that little if any information exists on the changing status of insects, which forces me to treat insects differently than other subjects. I will focus on three topics, each of which illustrates a different aspect of insects in this region: two sections on rare species (whose very presence says something about the landscape), one section on forensic entomology (a unique interaction between humans and animals), and two sections on swarms (manifestations of the region's biological wealth).

Beleaguered Beetles, Mystery Moths, and a Rediscovered Dragonfly:
A Smattering of Endangered Insects

Very little conservation work has focused on insects.[3] An early attempt to address the subject was a paper that zoologist Walter Hahn published in 1910 titled "An Analytic Study of Faunal Changes in Indiana."[4] He concluded that among insects, the increase has been more marked than the decrease. This is largely because available data caused him to focus on agricultural pests such as the cabbage butterfly (*Pieris rapae*) and horn fly (*Hematobia serrata*), species that had only recently been introduced into the United States. Among native species, the black swallowtail also increased dramatically. In 1891, it was deemed the second rarest swallowtail in the state; nineteen years later it was the most common.

Hahn did identify species and groups that had declined: "But we know these so little that it is not possible to point out many instances." Most of these were woodland species, hurt by the clearing of timber. Many of the Hymenoptera also suffered either because farming destroyed burrowing species or people killed them out of fear. Two species, the walking stick (*Diapheromera femorata*) and the praying mantis (*Stagmomantis carolina*), became rare because they were conspicuous and thus easily killed. To make matters worse for the walking stick, it "is known as the devil's darning needle and doubtless the word 'devil' in association with it has created something of a superstitious fear of it."

In 1962, a somewhat peculiar effort in insect conservation was made when Northwestern University's Walter Suter and Orlando Park produced a "microcoleopterological ordination of natural communities."[5] Without explaining why, these two experts on short-winged mold beetles (Pselaphids) began with the premise that the presence of the beetles "can be regarded as indices of some measure of natural stability, albeit only at the level of microhabitat occasionally. Therefore, localities in which these beetles have been found are regarded as natural areas." Their list of sites range from such well-known gems as Volo Bog, Lake County (Ill.), and Trout Park, Kane County, to mounds of horse manure near Harms Woods, Cook County, and piles of sawdust at the Interstate 294 toll plaza near Waukegan, Lake County.

In 1995, after twelve years of surveying local natural areas for insects (concentrating on sixty families in nine orders), Ron Panzer and his associates published their study identifying species that required high-quality prairie and savanna habitat or, in their words, were "remnant dependent." They concluded that approximately 25 percent of the insects they looked at were remnant dependent. The authors acknowledge the challenges inherent in their work: "Efforts to identify and monitor imperiled insects have lagged far behind those for other taxa, primarily because of the enormity of the task. Where does one start on a site supporting more than 2,000 unknown, tiny, elusive, and often unidentifiable species?"[6]

Andrew Williams and Daniel Young of the University of Wisconsin reiterate how difficult such an assessment is. They believe it is imperative to look closely at the widest possible range of insects, which means using a variety of capture techniques and seeking expertise that may not even exist. Further, insects have very different life stages; while a winged adult may frequent ruderal habitats, the less mobile larvae may cleave to a single conservative plant. Because so few people are working on insect conservation, many species will undoubtedly perish before biologists can get a handle on these important creatures. (This underscores the critical point that land managers should employ a wide range of techniques in the most careful manner possible.)[7]

Some local insects are known to science through only a few specimens, and there are undoubtedly species yet to be discovered. The thrip (Thysanoptera) *Illinothrips rossi* belongs to a monotypic genus that was first collected at a site now known as Shoe Factory Road Prairie Nature Preserve, Cook County, in 1944. Entomologists have since found it there again and at two sites in Mason County, Illinois, but nowhere else. The species appears to be restricted to little bluestem.[8]

Entomologists have even less experience with two other insects. James

81. Winter stone fly (*Allocapnia granulata*), a species mysteriously declining throughout the region. (Courtesy Illinois Natural History Survey, Champaign.)

Lloyd of the University of Florida found an undescribed firefly of the genus *Photuris* in cattails and low moist fields in Berrien and Washtenaw Counties of Michigan. And all anyone knows about the leafhopper (Cicadellidae) *Paraphlepsius lupalus* is that a handful of individuals have been caught in prairie and sedge meadow at Illinois Beach State Park in late summer.[9]

Several insects have suffered major population crashes for reasons not understood. Until 1975, the stonefly (Plecoptera) *Allocapnia granulata* was found on streams throughout Illinois. It is considered a generalist, not needing particularly high-quality water. But now the species has disappeared from most of northeastern Illinois.[10]

Two beetles once known from this region are in a more precarious situation, having virtually disappeared everywhere. The rove beetle (Staphylinidae) *Platydracus vulpinus* was formerly common throughout the eastern United States. In scouring collections across the country, Alfred Newton of the Field Museum discovered a dramatic drop in the number of specimens that have been obtained in the past thirty or forty years. Three have been taken in the Chicago area since 1945, the last of which was collected in Chicago in 1960. The only information on this species' life history is that many of the specimens were caught under rocks or ground litter and, often, on the sandy shores of lakes.[11]

More celebrated is the American burying beetle (*Nicrophorus americanus*), a large beetle (over an inch in length) that eats carrion. The carrion is buried and then tended by the adults who produce fluids that prolong the freshness of the meat. Both parents provide food and protection to the larvae.[12]

During a fifty-year period beginning in the 1930s, the range of the American burying beetle shrunk from the entire eastern half of the United States to isolated pockets in Oklahoma, Nebraska, Arkansas, and an island (Block) ten miles off the Rhode Island coast. (The Field Museum has four specimens from Cook County; the most recent local record in the museum's holdings is of one collected at Beverly Shores, Porter County, in 1934.) This population collapse may be the most dramatic of any insect on record, and no one knows for sure why it happened. Since the U.S. Fish and Wildlife Service listed the beetle as an endangered species in 1989, several entomologists have begun studying the species for clues as to its decrease. Several factors have been suggested: habitat loss through human activity; loss of carrion through increases in dogs, raccoons, skunks, and other scavengers; and presence of a pathogen that destroyed all but the few peripheral populations.[13]

◄○► ◄○► ◄○►

The *Papaipema* moths have caterpillars that bore into roots to feed and pupate. There are about thirty species in this area, twenty-five of which inhabit high-quality prairie. Most of these moths are uncommon, but two are more than that. In all the world, biologists have located only three extant native populations of *Papaipema eryngii;* one of these is in Will County and the other is in Grundy County. (The third was discovered in Oklahoma by Ron Panzer.) The second moth hasn't even been named yet—a few specimens have been collected on the same two local prairies as *P. eryngii.*[14]

82. *Papaipema eryngii,* an extremely rare moth whose global range
is virtually restricted to a few prairies in the Chicago region.
(Photo by and courtesy of Ron Panzer.)

Most of the *eryngii* known to science were collected in the 1920s and 1930s in the southern suburbs of Chicago. During the decades that followed, entomologists in several states searched for it unsuccessfully, and most people assumed that it was extinct. Among the seekers were Ron Panzer and his colleague George Derkovitz, who performed many insect surveys on natural areas throughout the region. One of their techniques is to use blacklights to attract nocturnal species such as the *Papaipemas*. For ten years they conducted their research and became leading authorities on this group of moths.

Derkovitz would often collect by himself and then bring the live animals back to Panzer for identification of challenging specimens. After one evening's work at Goose Lake Prairie State Park (Grundy), Derkovitz had a large batch of mostly *P. baptisia*, one of the more widespread members of the genus. He dropped them off for Panzer to examine and then headed back to Goose Lake. When Panzer finished looking, he was to join Derkovitz and they would release the moths. It was getting toward dark as Panzer completed his task: "Then in amongst all the *baptisia* there it was. I thought, it cannot be. The problem was another species, *P. birdi*, is ridiculously close to *eryngii* in appearance. *Birdi* feeds only on wild hemlock, *Cicuta maculata*, but we had never previously caught it either. So whichever moth this turned out to be would make it a great find. I thought, 'Oh man, we found *birdi*.' I couldn't say to myself that we found *eryngii*, although deep down I was holding out hope."

By the time the two met later that night, Derkovitz had concluded that the moth didn't look right for *baptisia*. Panzer said, "I know George. They are *birdi*. It could even be *eryngii*, but at least its *birdi*." They caught about twenty of the moths that evening and kept two as specimens. The next day Panzer dissected one of them to examine the genitalia, on which the identification keys are based. Although the species are almost the same in physiognomy, their genitals differ in shape: *birdi* has a little knob at the end, while *eryngii* is shaped like a French horn. It was definitely *eryngii*. They sent it off to Eric Quinter at the American Museum of Natural History in New York for confirmation. Despite their confidence, they had restless nights until they received Quinter's excited call: "Do you know what you have?" And Panzer answered, "Yes, I think we do."

The most intriguing question this species poses is why it inhabits so few sites. Panzer believes that the two Illinois prairies harbor scores and scores of them; four to five thousand caterpillars inhabit Goose Lake Prairie every year. It feeds solely on the rattlesnake master, from which it received its specific name. But other papaipemas also rely on a single host plant. *Papaipema sciata*, for example, is dependent on Culver's root and yet is found on a couple of dozen prairies in Illinois alone.

One element that bestows uniqueness on Goose Lake Prairie is its size.

Few tallgrass prairies are fifteen hundred acres, and none east of the Mississippi. While the Will County prairie where Panzer and Derkovitz have also found *eryngii* is small, Goose Lake is nearby and prairie remnants exist between the two sites.

More than some species, *eryngii* is sensitive to fire, and Panzer considers this the principal reason behind its rarity. He has compared burned prairie with unburned and found fifteen times more *eryngii* in the latter than the former. On prairies that have been burned in their entirety once or twice, the species may have been incinerated out of existence. Because Goose Lake and the Will County prairie are under careful burn regimes that torch no more than a third of either site in any given year, the moth can repopulate an area in one season. It is this ability to recover that Panzer offers as proof that burning does no harm to the species, and since fire is good for the rattlesnake master, the moth ultimately benefits as well.

Believing that a secure species needs to be represented on the planet by more than three limited sites, Panzer and Derkovitz have successfully introduced *Papaipema eryngii* to Markham Prairie. They started their project by raising a hundred caterpillars to adulthood. While rattlesnake master root stays fresh longer, the magnitude of their effort dictated the substitution of carrots. A small hole would be made in each carrot, inside of which would be placed a larva. After five days, the vegetable would begin to rot and so the caterpillar would be removed, cleaned, and placed in a new carrot. ("The poor caterpillar would be covered in orange swill—washing it off just seems the right thing to do.") This process went on for three months until they stopped eating, built their cocoons (pupated), and the beautiful adults appeared. Seventy-five moths survived and were liberated to seek out the one or two thousand rattlesnake masters that thrive on Markham. An additional patch of earth now harbors *Papaipema eryngii*.

Precisely two things are known about the unnamed *Papaipema*: (1) it lives on Goose Lake Prairie and the Will County prairie, and (2) Ron Panzer and George Derkovitz are the only two human beings who have ever found it. Six is the greatest number they have caught in a year. For decades, entomologists have searched prairies for moths and not one has ever recorded this species.

The moth is very distinctive, grayish with dandruff-like scales, and is undoubtedly an undescribed species. It should receive federal protection but that can only occur after scientists have formally described and named it. Quinter is reluctant to do this, however, until the food plant is discovered. He feels that the additional information will enable him to better assess its relationship to other species. Unfortunately, the few specimens that Panzer and Derkovitz have obtained were adults attracted to black lights. Thus, every plant that is common to the two prairies is theoretically a candidate, and since the two sites differ little in their composition the possibilities are staggering. The two men keep searching and, although they find known *Papaipemas* on new host plants, the solution to their mystery continues to elude them.

◄○► ◄○► ◄○►

During the early 1980s, Ron Panzer surveyed insect and spider fauna for the Will County Forest Preserve District along the lower Des Plaines River Valley.[15] He found a total of 190 species of nine orders and sixty-four families. In comparison to other sites in the region, he thought the results were low. Several species were, however, locally uncommon: broad-winged dragonfly (*Calopteryx aequabile*), Texas katydid (*Scudderia texensis*), striped sedge meadow grasshopper (*Stethophyma lineatum*), and cordgrass leafhopper (*Hecalus lineatus*). And one proved to be extraordinary, resurrected from the obituaries of organisms thought to be extinct.

On July 14, 1983, Panzer collected a strange dragonfly: "It was so rare it wasn't even included in the standard treatise on dragonflies. I worked through the book and couldn't confidently identify it, so I set it aside. Four years later, I was in a McDonald's with Tim Vogt, who works almost exclusively with dragonflies. I told him that I have a dragonfly that is a real enigma, and that he would probably want to look at it because it doesn't fit in the key. I left the restaurant, drove home, and returned with the specimen. He almost had a heart attack because he knew what it was."

The insect on the table was a Hine's emerald dragonfly (*Somatochlora hineana*), a species that hadn't been found since 1956. Collections held a total of twenty-eight specimens taken from three counties in Ohio and one from Gary, Indiana. No description of the habitat accompanies the Indiana record, but the Ohio sites included "a bog meadow," "a shallow pond," and a small stream thickly vegetated with lizard's tail (*Saururus cernuus*), willows, and "heavy swamp woods." But recent searches of these locations led biologists to conclude that the dragonfly was no longer present: none of the insects were discovered and habitat had "been severely altered."[16]

In June 1988, Vogt and Everett Cashatt, a dragonfly expert with the Illinois State Museum, launched a hunt for Hine's emerald, which turned up several individuals. When word of their success circulated, representatives of the Will County Forest Preserve District (Marcy DeMauro) and the Illinois Nature Preserves Commission (me) met Cashatt on site.

The summer of 1988 was one of the hottest and driest on record—it convinced many people of global warming. Due to heat and drought, some trees were already displaying autumn coloration in their foliage. We were concerned that the weather might reduce seeps and other water sources that the dragonfly presumably required. But just before dusk, Cashatt identified a Hine's emerald as it foraged the ecotonal strip between woods and wet prairie. And before dark terminated our effort, we saw yet another. (A lovely way to make a living.)

Since 1990, a number of researchers have intensively studied the species and its requirements. Eight breeding colonies are now known in this area. Entomologists have also found populations in Door County, Wisconsin, Mackinac County, Michigan, and Missouri.[17]

Like other dragonflies, the Hine's emerald leads a double life. The female lays her eggs in muck or shallow water. When they hatch, the larvae that emerge are exclusively aquatic, a stage that can last two years. At the end of that period, the nymph climbs out of the water never to return. The final metamorphosis occurs with the emergence of the adult, now a creature of the sky.

The bimodal life cycle of the Hine's emerald poses a strong challenge to the conservationist. Most larvae inhabit slow-moving but high-quality water flowing through cattails and/or sedges. Although all but one of the local sites are on public land, the dragonflies are threatened by the polluting capabilities of a refinery, asphalt plant, golf course, several quarries, and residential development. Beaver activity can also be detrimental by changing surface hydrology: reductions in water flow can be harmful to eggs and larvae in the summer, and flooding can result in the contamination of springs by degraded surface water.

The adults have a different set of requirements. Their foraging habits suggest a need for diverse plant communities: over sedge meadows, along marsh edges, and through wooded borders. In addition, they frequently use shrubs for shelter, mating, and resting between feeding forays.

Maintaining the variety of elements that the dragonfly seems to require necessitates land management on most local sites. But these must be conducted with the utmost care and flexibility. Burning and brush removal will preserve the open sedge and cattail areas the larvae need. These same techniques, however, can also severely harm the insect if they remove perches on which the adults depend, reduce the plant litter required by larvae, and lead to the drying out of larval habitat, particularly during droughts.[18]

Tim Cashatt believes that the dragonfly can survive if certain steps are taken on its behalf, the first of which was implemented when the federal government formally listed the dragonfly as an endangered species in January 1995. The remaining actions generally relate to maintaining water quality. Foremost of these, Cashatt urges the appropriate agencies to acquire enough additional land to assure watershed integrity and habitat viability.[19]

83. Hine's emerald dragonfly, a federally endangered species
restricted locally to the lower Des Plaines River valley. (Photo by
and courtesy of T. Cashatt, Illinois State Museum, Springfield.)

Flitting on the Edge: The Mitchell's Satyr and the Karner Blue

Of all the organisms known to exist in the Chicago region, the one that may be
in greatest danger of global extinction is the small brown butterfly named
Mitchell's satyr (*Neonympha mitchellii mitchellii*). The butterfly was known historically from thirty locations in four states, but an intensive 1993 survey revealed that its extant range is now limited to twelve sites in Michigan and Indiana. And only two of those were in public ownership. During the survey,
investigators counted a total of 264 butterflies in populations ranging from one
to fifty-six. John Shuey, an authority on the species with the Indiana chapter of
the Nature Conservancy, considers only five of these populations to be solid.[20]

The Chicago region holds three of the four largest populations: one in
La Porte County (fifty-six) and two in Berrien County (fifty-two and thirty-
five). In conferring endangered status on the species in 1992, the U.S. Fish and
Wildlife Service (USFWS) said that it was unlikely that new stations would be
located, and if they were, such sites would undoubtedly be of lower-quality
habitat, capable of supporting few butterflies. The USFWS concluded that
"the findings of a few such sites will do little to alter the probability of extinction for *N. mitchelli*."[21]

Investigators engaged in a special search for the species discovered the
La Porte County site in 1991. It is part of a wetland complex several miles long,
but Mitchell's satyrs only use fifteen acres. Although privately owned, the
owner is a strong conservationist who is actively acquiring adjacent land to
protect. The butterfly numbers are stable, but biologists worry that invading
shrubs might soon pose a threat.[22]

Mitchell's satyr has never been common as far as anyone knows. Although
it can inhabit sedge meadows and swamps, it most often occurs in fens, which

are rare themselves. But very few fens support the species, and even where it does persist, it tends to use only a portion of the habitat that is available. Another limiting factor, therefore, is also at play. The larvae apparently feed on sedges, particularly the common and widespread tussock sedge, suggesting that food is not the key element. However, the possibility remains that some rare sedge is an essential component of its diet. John Shuey believes that the key may lie in the vegetational structure of satyr habitat. Mitchell's satyr seems to prefer fens with a narrow woody border, be it tamarack, cedar, or small shrubs.[23] Unfortunately, this is the kind of ecotonal environment that many wetland managers aim to eliminate in their desire to increase the open fen.

Other aspects of the butterfly's biology also contribute to its precarious state. Unlike many other species, the Mitchell's satyr produces but a single brood per year. The adults emerge in summer for a two- or three-week span, thus making it difficult for researchers to study the species. Finally, the adults are weak flyers, which reduces the possibility of recolonization or genetic mixing between nearby populations. It also means that the butterfly is easy prey for collectors.[24]

But like all species, Mitchell's satyr is well adapted to its environment and could flourish in suitable pockets indefinitely. Only in the face of current events do its requirements become an obstacle to survival. Fens are highly vulnerable and are difficult to protect, because they are fed by calcareous waters that may originate far offsite: both water chemistry and quantity must be maintained. Because fens are usually small, people can easily destroy them, sometimes even inadvertently. Known Mitchell's satyr locations have been wrecked by urban development, agriculture, pig farming, and off-road vehicle use.[25]

84. Mitchell's satyr, a federally endangered butterfly restricted locally
to a few fens in the northeastern portion of the region. (Photo by
and courtesy of John A. Shuey.)

Another threat to satyr habitat is succession. The invasion of woody plants would destroy the character of the fen, but in presettlement times this process was deterred both by fire and the alkaline water that is a poor medium for species not adapted to its chemical properties. Fire suppression and tampering with hydrologic regimes (i.e., lowering the water table) have removed these barriers, to the detriment of the butterfly. Thus land management activities are an essential part of Mitchell satyr conservation, but biologists know so little about the species that anything done on its behalf must be conducted in the most gentle manner possible.

Most insects have such a tremendous reproductive capacity that collecting poses little threat to the well being of the species. But as Ron Panzer points out, the serious collector focuses his attention on those species that are the most vulnerable, "like a plant collector who only wanted to take orchids."[26] There seems little doubt that collectors have had a devastating impact on some Mitchell's satyr populations. They apparently denuded two New Jersey sites, and according to USFWS, "all known [Mitchell's satyr] sites are believed vulnerable to local extinction by overcollection."[27]

There is agreement that this species is flirting with extinction. During the comment period required under the federal Endangered Species Act, USFWS received forty-two statements, all but one in favor of listing the butterfly. Conservation departments from the states that currently have or once had Mitchell's satyrs supported federal protection. Yet, it is highly likely that a road extension jeopardizing 20 percent of the world's Mitchell's satyrs will be built.

The completion of U.S. 31 in Berrien County has been in the works for twenty-five years. From the beginning, the Michigan Department of Transportation routed the final 1.5 miles through the guts of a forty-acre fen now known to harbor the second largest population of the butterfly on the planet. An alternative that would avoid the fen was, and is, available but the transportation department has refused to yield.

When Mitchell's satyr was added to the federal endangered species list, USFWS had to determined that the proposed road would likely cause harm to the butterfly, and, thus, became involved in the project. Whether it would have asserted jurisdiction on its own is an open question, but fortunately a dedicated group of local conservationists led by Charles and Judy Sirk and Al Puplis sought out the scientific expertise that helped convince the service. (Their tireless efforts to save the fen go well beyond this one skirmish. If twenty years from now, Mitchell's satyr remains secure at the fen, it is because of these three more than anyone else.)

The original project called for running four lanes of concrete through the site, thereby obliterating Mitchell's satyr and the rest of the fen community. With the input of Fish and Wildlife, a new plan has emerged. The road will now span the critical area on two bridges fifty feet high. In addition, the transportation department must obey other requirements including the following: implement a bridge design that prevents discharge or drainage of runoff into the fen, use sterile fill material as a guard against introduction of invasive plants, apply calcium magnesium acetate instead of salt as a road deicer, conduct a four-year study of Mitchell's satyr life history and perform annual censuses until the species is no longer federally listed, station on site during construction a "biological observer" who has the authority to stop activities deemed harmful to the butterfly, and protect through acquisition or conservation easement thirteen to fifteen hundred acres of butterfly habitat.[28]

Unquestionably, these revisions represent a vast improvement, replacing certain destruction with possible destruction. The USFWS acknowledges that shading by the bridge will kill three acres of habitat. The area of shadow may prove to be an uncrossable barrier that divides the population. Additionally, shade-induced temperature differentials may affect maturation of the butterfly, which in turn could cause disynchrony between larvae and food plants or reduce the number of adults that can breed at any one time. And then there are the procedural issues, which are as problematic as the bridge itself. For example, how long will there be vigilant scrutiny of what kind of deicing agent is used? (A very small quantity of salt can create changes in the composition of the vegetation.) Who will check to make sure no contaminated water is entering the site? Once a project starts rolling, expenses and politics make it very difficult to stop. And in this case, any damage is likely to be irreparable.

Federal monies for the road seem to have dried up, but funding for the research and land acquisition has been forthcoming, and these important mitigation measures have gone forward. Perhaps, in the end, the road proposal will have lengthened the Mitchell's satyr's tenure on the planet.

◄◦► ◄◦► ◄◦►

As the Mitchell's satyr demonstrates, an endangered insect needs more than a bleak future to receive the attention it deserves. Though only a subspecies, the Karner blue has these extra attributes: (1) it is pretty; (2) it was described to science by the most famous of all lepidopterists, the novelist Vladimir Nabokov (every popular account of the butterfly that I have ever read mentions this fact); and (3) it suffered spectacular declines: the largest population known went from eighty thousand individuals in 1979 to less than two hundred in 1990 as its habitat was replaced by the State University of New York at Albany

85. Adult Karner blue, a federally endangered butterfly whose larvae feed exclusively on wild lupine. (Photo by and courtesy of John A. Shuey.)

and various office buildings. (This conspicuous loss, accompanied by others throughout its range eventually led to its listing as a federally endangered species in 1992.)[29]

The largest number of Karner blues in the region reside in the Indiana Dunes National Lakeshore where somewhere between five and ten thousand of the butterflies thrive. But federal listing presented a challenge to park staffers. They had just put in place a burn plan and had assembled crews when the question arose as to how fire affected Karner blues. Because so little was known about the species, park scientists Ralph Grundel and Noel Pavlovic initiated an ambitious research program.

The Karner blue is distinct from all similar species in that its larvae feed on only one plant, wild lupine (*Lupinus perennis*). Lupines grow in open oak woods with sandy soils. This savanna community requires fire, yet the insect itself is vulnerable to burning. Biologists resolved the conundrum by burning no more than 25 percent of a site at any one time. If the site is small, biologists identify what portion is most thickly inhabited by the butterfly and burn around it.

Beyond resolving the burning issue, the biologists learned a great deal about other aspects of Karner blue life history. While males spend almost all of their time in large open areas, females occupied all portions of the shadow-light continuum. Almost all egg laying occurred in locations with moderate to heavy shading, even though lupine grows most abundantly in sunny places. Gathering nectar and mating both tended to happen in the less shaded openings.

In late summer, Karner blues lay eggs that overwinter and hatch in April. The larvae go through four stages before they pupate in late May. Four or five days later they emerge as adults that can survive for nearly three weeks. These butterflies then lay their eggs to begin the cycle that culminates in the second batch of adults in mid-July. Changes in the vegetation over the course of the summer dictate that each phase of each brood must make a living off of different plants or plants at different developmental stages.

Apart from the humans who are working on its behalf, the Karner blue seems to have other friends. Ants of seven species have formed a relationship with Karner blue larvae that biologists do not yet fully understand. In the Indiana Dunes, this occurs most commonly with the ant *Lasius neoniger*. The caterpillars produce a fluid rich in amino acids that the ants strongly crave. Ants consume the secretion as they run up and down the caterpillars. No one knows for sure whether this arrangement constitutes appeasement by the caterpillar to prevent it from becoming ant food or whether the ants provide protection against other predators. Most research suggests the latter. A study in New York, for example, indicated that 67 percent of ant-attended caterpillars survived versus 38 percent of unattended. But it is also true that some of the same ant species that tend larvae may also prey on them. The possibility exists that the individual caterpillars so targeted have failed for one reason or another to provide their quota of juice.[30]

Barriers to dispersal pose the greatest threat to the Karner blue, yet are the least understood element of the species' biology. This is particularly significant in the Indiana Dunes. The building of the Inland Steel Plant in the 1960s interposed what amounted to a mile of barren wasteland between the remaining Karner blue populations. This expanse of metal and concrete was enough to prevent mingling of the two groups, for those on the east side gradually decreased to the point where they are now gone. Although this obstacle proved insurmountable, female Karner blues have shown themselves to be very adept at locating lupine in the middle of a forest a mile away. Thus, although colonization of suitable habitat and genetic mixing between isolated populations is theoretically possible over the long term, some unknown factor militates against it. And this has biologists worried.

The seeming inability of Karner blue to disperse over long distances makes its recent Illinois occurrence a genuine mystery. All anyone knows for sure is that Illinois Beach State Park held a population of five individuals for three days in August 1992. On August 16, Irwin Leeuw, a longtime student of local insects, was checking favorite spots in the park when to his amazement he discovered the Karner blues. The only previous state record was a pair collected a century ago and labeled simply "Northern Illinois." Leeuw contacted a downstate collector, who arrived on August 18 to confirm the sighting.[31]

All five of the Karner blues were collected; this touched off a controversy that eventually appeared in a front-page story of the *Chicago Tribune* a year later.[32] The collector possessed the proper permits, but that every butterfly was taken raised ethical concerns. All agreed, however, that the loss of five individuals should not wipe out an entire population. But, alas, such appears to be the case. Although many people have searched the location in the summers that followed, no one has seen another Karner blue, and the brief appearance of this weak-flying butterfly at such a well-scrutinized place is difficult if not impossible to explain.

Another local Karner blue population also faced annihilation but was rescued at the last minute.[33] National Steel Company's Midwest Division in Portage, Lake County (Ind.), needed to establish another landfill on their property and contacted the U.S. Environmental Protection Agency to begin the permitting process. On an inspection of the proposed site, personnel from the agency and the USFWS discovered a male Karner blue. Although notified, the company apparently did nothing until their waste problem became critical. By then it was fall and impossible to evaluate the butterfly population. They were, however, able to count lupine stems.

Because time was at a premium, Midwest Steel agreed to transplant every one of the 1,613 lupine stems to another site they owned. Lupine possess deep roots and to move them the company needed to dig ten to fifteen feet down. Although some biologists were skeptical about the attempt, many Karner blues emerged the following summer. Two years later, both the lupine and the insect are thriving. Following federal directions, the company has spent $2 million on behalf of the butterfly. Most notably, it purchased and then gave to the Indiana Dunes National Lakeshore a fifty-one-acre tract of habitat.

Mere Patches in Time and Space:
The Corpse as Ecosystem and Forensic Entomology

In the mid-1970s, a lawyer in the Cook County State's Attorney's office called the entomology department of the Field Museum with a query.[34] He was prosecuting a double murder case in which the time of death had become a major issue. As part of the evidence, he had photographs of fly larvae and puparia found on the corpse and wondered if anyone could evaluate that material to help resolve the timing question. The museum staffer said, "Oh, maggots. You want Greenberg." And so Bernard Greenberg of the University of Illinois at Chicago, an internationally recognized authority on flies and public health (and no relation to the author, unfortunately), entered the world of forensic entomology.

Forensic entomology is based on the concept of the corpse as an ecosystem: "Although cadavers, compared with other ecosystems, are a mere patch in time and space, they have a distinctive faunal succession."[35] There are four stages in the life of the corpse: (1) fresh, (2) bloat, (3) active decay, and (4) dry decay.[36] How quickly the process runs its course varies tremendously. A researcher in Australia killed what appeared to be two identical sheep and let them rot side by side. The rate of decay between the animals varied by 25 percent. It is also true that some parts of the body decompose more quickly than others—a hand will desiccate more quickly than the trunk and can therefore support a different guild of insects. In assessing the temporal aspects of decomposition, scientists must consider such factors as ambient temperature, weight of the deceased, location of cadaver, and nature of clothing (how substantial, whether it's soaked in paint, gasoline, or other insect repellent, etc.). Even other insects may stall decomposition by preying heavily on scavenging flies: ants such as *Prenolepis imparis* and *Camponotus pennsylvanicus* can dramatically reduce the number of eggs, and rove beetles (Staphylinidae) target larvae.

Blowflies (Calliphoridae) are usually the first on the scene. They rely on their sense of smell and can detect carrion from a mile away. Within minutes of the appearance of meat, flies in the neighborhood arrive to feed, mate, and lay eggs. These flies have soft mouthparts designed for sucking rather than puncturing. Thus, they concentrate their initial attention on the oases of wounds, eyes, and orifices. Being so desirable, these moist openings are often covered by thousands of eggs deposited by different females of the same or other species.[37]

There are a thousand species of blowflies in the world and seventy-five in the United States. Of the twelve blowflies most important for forensic considerations, three are abundant in this region. *Calliphora vicina* has a life cycle of twenty-one days from egg to first instar larvae to second instar larvae to third instar larvae to post–feeding stage to pupa to adult.[38] *Phaenicia sericata* and *Phormia regina* each complete the same number of steps in fourteen days. Another species, *Cochliomyia macellaria*, breeds in the south and disperses northward into this region during the summer.

A crucial variable in using insects to determine postmortem interval is temperature: warmth spurs development and cold retards development. But the animals themselves moderate the effects of changes in ambient temperature. Maggots, for example, produce heat; in one experiment, Greenberg found that this "peaked at 18°C above ambient."[39] Larvae are also mobile enough to burrow deeper into the carcass, thereby taking advantage of the insulative properties of meat.

The investigation of Verneta Wheat illustrates Greenberg's methodology. The nine-year-old lay dead in the bathroom of an abandoned building in downtown Waukegan. She was the first known victim of Alton Coleman and Deborah Brown, whose murder spree would eventually claim at least four lives in three states. Sharing the tiled floor with Wheat were swarms of *Phaenicia sericata* and *Phormia regina*, both with life cycles of two weeks. Authorities asked Greenberg to determine when the girl had died. His challenge was ascertaining whether the adult flies were from the first eggs laid or subsequent generations, in which case his estimate would be significantly less precise.

Fortunately, *C. vicina* had not yet emerged, so Greenberg knew that Wheat had been dead between two and three weeks.

Pathologists rely on body temperature and the degree of rigor mortis to calculate postmortem periods. But these indices are variable and lose their value after one and a half days. By knowing the life histories of these flies, Dr. Greenberg can estimate the time of death more accurately. To maximize the effectiveness of his work, he asks that the police collect as many specimens as possible. Identification of larvae can be difficult, so Greenberg requests living examples that can be raised to adulthood. Dead maggots should be boiled and then placed in preservatives that don't cause shrinking: a shrunken larvae could create the impression of a much younger specimen and throw off the time assessment by twenty-four to thirty hours.

The first stage of decomposition is the most important for forensic purposes because a majority of bodies are discovered within a few weeks after death. But as the corpse dries up, blowflies give way to dermestid beetles (Dermestidae) and cheese skipper flies (Piophilidae) that leave behind only bone and hair. If a desiccated carcass becomes wet, the remnants of jerky can again become palatable to the blowflies, further complicating the work of the forensic entomologist.

Even though there may be little if any tissue remaining at this stage, dead or living flies are often present and useful to investigators. Because maggots concentrate chemicals ingested with their food, they can provide insights on the pharmacological habits of the victim. Thus the adult flies might be more suitable for toxicological evaluation than whatever is left of their ecosystem.

Conspicuous on a Large Scale: Insect Swarms

Although insects thrive on, around, and over human beings in uncountable numbers, they usually go unnoticed. When their presence is noted, it is generally because the insect has just mounted a direct attack on the larger species or its property. Thus we are aware of the mosquito as she bites (but who has seen the male that spends his short adult life sipping plant juices?), the persistent yellow jacket exploiting the bonanza of a Labor Day's picnic, and the termite and its legacy of pulp. From time to time, however, insects form huge swarms that are conspicuous on a large scale. Depending on the species, these concentrations may arise from adult emergences, migration, feeding frenzies, and nuptial displays. And they can be incredible.

◄O► ◄O► ◄O►

Undertaking flights to wintering grounds in central Mexico, monarch butterflies (*Danaus plexippus*) are the most famous and beloved insect migrants of
all. Orlando Park studied monarch migration as it occurred in his backyard in
Evanston in 1948. Although he concluded the total migration lasted two to
three weeks, he maintained a careful estimate from September 7–13. During
that week, 1,940 monarchs drifted over in "loosely integrated assemblage[s]" at
an average speed of 31.5 yards in ten seconds. All migration ceased in the face
of rain and sunset.[40]

Park's observations represent typical numbers, but there have also been
reports of truly extraordinary monarch concentrations during September. In
1868 at Racine, "swarms appeared and settled on trees soon after midday," and
in 1912 a similar phenomenon occurred on the Chicago lakefront.[41] But the
largest single massing that I know of occurred on September 9, 1989, at the
Hammond (Ind.) Lakefront Park and Sanctuary, which is also called the "Migrant Trap." One of the two observers wrote what she saw: "As we walked past
the weighted shrubs, the Monarchs took to the air, and we found ourselves
enveloped in a cloud of hundreds of these marvelous winged creatures.
Their presence was observed throughout the entire length and breadth of the
Trap. . . . There were places where entire trees were adorned with them, each
leaf being covered and even the adjacent weed stalks held their share. It would
be difficult to estimate accurately the number of monarchs present but one
hundred thousand is probably a conservative figure."[42]

During his observations, Park never saw a bird attack a monarch, and that
is because monarchs taste terrible. Birds even avoid a number of butterflies that
are palatable but have evolved a physical resemblance to the monarch. The
viceroy (*Limenitis archippus*) is probably the best-known example.

Given this defense mechanism, the behavior of a merlin (*Falco columbarius*) at Illinois Beach State Park is worth noting. On September 20, 1987, a female and/or immature merlin repeatedly sallied over Lake Michigan to capture
monarchs. This happened four times, and in each instance the merlin released
the butterfly, which then proceeded on its way as if nothing happened. During
one of its flights, the falcon caught and freed the same monarch twice.[43]

Green darner dragonflies (*Anax junius*) also gather in huge numbers on
the Lake Michigan shore. Depending on the time of year and their behavior,
they might either be drawn together for food or migration. Alan Stokie found
himself surrounded by thousands of these dragonflies as he birded the south
end of Illinois Beach State Park on September 18, 1993. Fifteen American
kestrels were also on the scene, enacting in miniature the same drama as gray
wolves following herds of caribou. Stokie watched individual birds launch forays into the dense ranks of the massing dragonflies. Often, the hawk would
emerge clutching an insect in its talons. It would then fly to a perch where the

prey was consumed. By the following week, the dragonflies had moved on, and only one kestrel, probably a resident, remained.[44]

Springtails (Collembola) of the families Poduridae and Entomobryidae are minuscule insects that live within the darkness of soil, leaf litter, and rotting logs.[45] They are among the most common animals of the forest floor and contribute greatly to soil creation. But on rare occasions, they erupt into gargantuan swarms. One such incident occurring in Europe "held up a Swiss train, the minute insects covering the rails so heavily that the driving-wheels of the locomotive revolved ineffectually." Nothing that dramatic has happened here, but two local massing incidents are on record.

On the morning of December 7, 1946, a "lot of pinkish bugs" began streaming out of three abandoned thirteen-lined ground squirrel (*Spermophilus tridecemlineatus*) dens in the grass of Northwestern University's Dyche Stadium (now known as Ryan Field). Later identified as *Achorutes bengtssoni*, 450,000 springtails were collected along with a small soil sample of fifty-nine grams. Professor Park estimated that the three openings combined, located within an area of six square feet, held at minimum 4,050,000 individuals but more likely 9 million per square meter next to the exit holes. He attributed the concentration to the organic material left in the burrows by the former inhabitants. Another springtail infestation enveloped two blocks of South Holland, Cook County, for two weeks in July 1976. It was particularly unusual because the species involved, *Entomobrya unostrigata*, had only twice before been recorded east of the Mississippi, and never in Illinois.[46]

◄O► ◄O► ◄O►

Fireflies (Lampyridae) are beetles that share with some forty other animal orders the power to produce light. This capacity usually emanates from the ventral side of their abdomen, where two chemicals, luciferin and luciferase, come in contact to generate the light. The process radiates very little heat, converting 98 percent of the energy directly into light. One estimate holds that it would take more than eighty thousand luminous beetles of one of the largest species to equal the heat of one small candle flame.[47]

These beetles flash for the same reasons most organisms do anything—breeding and feeding. Typically, the male firefly flashes a particular color at a particular time and in a particular pattern to attract a female of his species. Of these cues, the last seems to be the most important and differs greatly between species. One of the most distinctive fireflies is the locally common *Photinus pyralis*, whose flight path creates a J-shaped swath of yellow luminescence. *Pyractomena angulata* is another conspicuous species found in this area. Not as bright as *Photinus pyralis*, its golden-orange lights appear as "a flicker of 8–10 pulses emitted at a rate of about 9 pulses per second." An interested female then responds with her own unique signals of light so that the male may join her.

But if a male receives the right flash back and charges after the origin, he may well find himself as the evening's meal. Females of certain predatory species in the genus *Photuris* can imitate females of the other genera. (There are six Photurids in this region.) Other *Photuris* fireflies use a more direct approach to procure victuals: lacking lights, they simply pluck shining males right out of the air.

The foremost firefly expert in the country, James E. Lloyd of the University of Florida, has recorded twenty-eight species of seven genera in the nineteen counties of the Chicago region, including one species that he has yet to describe formally. Fireflies inhabit a variety of habitats, including the barren alley outside my former apartment in the Jefferson Park portion of Chicago's northwest side. But there are times and places when the abundance of individuals and species create a show of living pyrotechnics that remains etched in the memory forever. Twenty-five years ago I watched such a display in a field next to the Ryerson Conservation Area in Lake County (Ill.). The range of colors and patterns was mesmerizing.

Edwin Way Teale devotes an entire chapter of his *Journey into Summer* to "River of the Fireflies," a beautiful account of his enchanting experiences along the Kankakee River on several nights in July 1959. As he and his wife followed the course of the river through what had once been the Great Marsh, they witnessed magnificence: "The beauty of the day was gone. But the beauty of the night had replaced it. For, from end to end, the field was spangled with winking, dancing lights. They rose and fell. They flashed on and off. They waxed and waned in brilliance. At this same moment, over hundreds of square miles around us, this eerie beauty of the fairy-dance of *Wah-Wah-Taysee*, Hiawatha's little firefly, was part of the summer night. . . . Around us always, wherever we went, streamed the sparks of living fire."

People have been moved by the sight of fireflies for centuries. The earliest known effort at insect conservation occurred in 1835 when the Queen of Spain asked a scientific adviser how they could best protect fireflies. It appears that twentieth-century Americans also need a plan to conserve this group of beetles.

Mounting evidence suggests that night skies throughout the east and Midwest are losing their "sparks of life." Habitat loss, pesticides, and streetlights that interfere with mating displays all contribute to declining numbers. In addition to these ubiquitous assaults, fireflies have to contend with something else altogether: "In the U.S., one predator goes by the dubious name of the Firefly Scientists Club, operated by a St. Louis chemical company that pays a penny a bug to members who collect millions of fireflies a year." One woman in Vinton, Iowa, employs 329 people to catch fireflies. In a single year alone, her army of vandals killed over a million of the insects. This carnage is particularly distasteful because the chemical sought can now be artificially produced, but the company stays in the firefly business for the sake of "tradition."

◄o► ◄o► ◄o►

The burrowing mayfly (Ephemeridae) spends two years as an aquatic larva, buried in the muddy bottoms of lakes and rivers as it undergoes the molts that eventually lead to its emergence as a subadult. A winged creature floating on the water surface or clutching a strand of emergent vegetation, the subadult discards its skin one more time before it commences the aerial dance that consumes the remaining day or two of its life. (This last molt is unique among insects.) During this frenzied period, the adults mate and lay eggs.[48] Millions upon millions drift with the wind to form billowing clouds that darken streetlights and are cast on lakeshores in lines a yard deep.

Apparently no one has documented the local mayfly decline; scientists have devoted more attention to Lake Erie. Nonetheless, Lake Michigan supported huge hatches of the mayfly *Hexagenia limbata* until the early 1960s, when lake sediment became too contaminated with industrial pollutants. As recently as the late 1950s, workers shoveled mayflies from Chicago gas stations, and piles of mayflies drifted like snow at the base of the Covenant Club, on Randolph Street.[49]

A wonderful account of what a mayfly hatching in Chicago used to be like appears in the July 25, 1888, *Chicago Tribune* article entitled "The Sand Flies Have Taken Possession":

> The sand flies are becoming a terrible nuisance. Last night they were out in such numbers that walking along a well-lighted sidewalk was exceedingly disagreeable. Madison, Dearborn between Washington and Monroe,

86. Adult mayfly *Hexagenia limbata,* a species that used to appear locally in huge numbers during its emergence into the winged adult stage. (Courtesy Illinois Natural History Survey, Champaign.)

Clark, and State around the Palmer House were taken by storm by these pestiferous little creatures. . . .

For hours a crowd of people stood at the northeast corner of Madison and Dearborn watching those who had business in the office making a dash through the buzzing cloud, struggling to retain a foothold in the moving, greasy carpet of flies on the sidewalk, grabbing the door handle to demand admittance, and finally, half-choked with flapping buzzing insects, wading blinded through the mass to the side entrance on Madison Street.

The electric lights at the Illinois Central suburban depot at the foot of Randolph Street attracted untold thousands. The planking under the light on the building—perhaps fifty feet square—was covered at least three inches deep on the level, and in places there were heaps containing bushels. . . . Occasionally some whooping urchin would come along and with a run take a slide through the mass, to his great delight and the disgust of the spectators. When the women went through, there was an elevation of skirts and a chorus of feminine shrieks that made things interesting.

The Musical Brood: Periodic Cicadas

Every seventeen years, two marvelous insect species issue from innumerable subterranean crypts in such numbers as literally to coat trees and ground. These are the periodic cicadas (Homoptera: Cicadidae) *Magicicada septendecim* and the smaller *M. cassini*.[50] They engender varying combinations of fear, curiosity, and wonder among the citizenry, and a fascination among some scientists that has spawned decades of research.

Encountering one of the first groups of cicadas to emerge in 1888, commuters at a Chicago train station in May were baffled by the "multitude of large bugs unlike anything anybody had seen before." Some trainmen "pinned several of them upon a big placard and threw knives at them." By early June, the cicadas were particularly thick in the Wheaton area of DuPage County: "They literally cover all kinds of bushes, hedges, trees, and even perch on the fences. . . . Great apprehension is felt over their general devastation and it is feared the shade and fruit trees will be ruined." The following day's *Chicago Tribune* had a statement from Illinois's State Entomologist Stephen Forbes assuring people that apart from the cuts it makes on twigs for egg laying, the adult cicada is harmless. It has a mouth designed for sucking, not chewing. (The cuts are made by the ovipositor, the organ for egg laying.)[51]

Thirty-four years later, the *Tribune* reported: "With kettledrum-like instruments on their bodies, a million musicians of the cicada's symphony issued loud, piercing notes from the tree tops around schoolhouses up and down the Fox River valley yesterday, causing great excitement among teachers and children. In Aurora and Joliet hundreds of persons armed with long sticks turned out to fight the pests. The hoppers were knocked out of trees where they had settled to lay eggs. Humming of the bugs was so pronounced that a shout could not be heard across the street."[52]

The oddest thing people do with cicadas these days is eat them. Whether or not anyone bought any I don't know, but during the 1990 emergence stores were allegedly selling cicadas at the same price per pound as sirloin. Their flavor has been likened to a raw potato with a dash of avocado or clam juice. But after sautéing the insects in butter, naturalist Lynn Hepler found that they tasted largely of butter, which of course is not a bad thing.[53]

The scientific literature devoted to periodic cicadas is extensive and goes back a long way. At the turn of the century, C. L. Marlatt, a biologist with the U.S. Department of Agriculture, mapped out eruptions of periodic cicadas throughout their range and devised a naming system based on when these occurred. He identified seventeen discrete broods of seventeen-year cicadas (broods I–XVII) and twelve broods of the more southerly thirteen-year cicadas (broods XVIII–XXX). Habitat loss and shifts between broods have reduced the number of seventeen-year broods to thirteen and thirteen-year broods to three. The seventeen-year cicadas in northern Illinois and southern Wisconsin are part of brood XIII (appearing in 1803, 1820, . . . 1990, 2007, etc.) and those in northern Indiana and southwest Michigan belong to brood X (appearing in 1800, 1817, . . . 1987, 2004, etc.)[54]

Periodic cicadas have the longest known life cycles of any insects in the world. The adults, which have life spans of about three weeks, make tiny slits in branches and twigs and then deposit their eggs in the incisions. Almost two months later, after the hoopla of the adult emergence has faded, the eggs hatch, and the larvae burrow into the soil. They attach themselves to roots, out of which they suck nutrition until the plant dies or it is time to seek the bright lights. If the former happens, the larvae are mobile enough to find another lifeline. Toward the latter part of their sixteenth year, they begin burrowing upward, creating tunnels that open into capped "turrets" rising an inch or more above the ground. When the soil temperature reaches 64°F sometime in late spring, the cicadas enact their spectacle.[55]

Researchers believe that this unique scheme evolved over the millennia as a way to overwhelm predators. If at one time there were predators whose biological clocks were in sync with the cicadas, they were unable to keep pace with the increasingly long periods of cicada dormancy. Eventually the hypothetical predator either became extinct or adapted to a more frequent food source. It is true that skunks dig up the larvae waiting to emerge, numerous birds pick adults out of the air, and chipmunks, squirrels, daddy longlegs (Phalangida), cats, dogs, and a host of other critters feast on the dying adults. But these predators can barely dent the cicada hordes.[56]

Periodic cicadas are the loudest of all insects. The adult males gather in trees to form "chorusing centers," each composed of a single species. From these platforms, they "fill the daytime spring air with the unearthly din of rasping, burring, coughing, crescendoing jackhammer choruses." The noise can make it impossible for one person to hear another even though they are face to face.[57]

All this serenading is for the benefit of females, who find the dulcet tones irresistible. Upon alighting in the midst of the boisterous males, she sits quietly. A suitor may reach out with a foreleg to test her receptivity. If she moves, he has been rejected. If she does nothing, she may be interested. Or she may be "resting, feeding, frightened, sick, wounded, dead, . . . or doing nothing because it is unnecessary to do anything."[58] As difficult as this may be for the males, who have been observed courting various inanimate objects, it is almost impossible for the researcher trying to unlock the keys of cicada behavior.

The Chicago region has been blessed with having two of the world's foremost cicada scholars: Monte Lloyd, who was for many years at the University of Chicago, and the late Henry Dybas of the Field Museum. They conducted much of their research at Raccoon Grove Forest Preserve in Will County. Dedicated as a nature preserve in 1989, the 210-acre site has well-defined upland and floodplain forests. In 1956, after meticulous censusing, Dybas and a colleague found that the upland woods supported 133,000 cicadas per acre (mostly *M. septendecim*) and the lowlands (mostly *M. cassini*) 1.5 million per acre. This latter figure translates into a biomass of 1,707 to 3,288 pounds per acre, "the highest mean biomass per unit of habitat recorded for a terrestrial animal under natural conditions."[59]

Yet by the 1990 emergence, Lloyd found very few cicadas at Raccoon Grove. He was not surprised; indeed he predicted the decrease. The culprit is a fungus *Massopora cicadina* that renders the cicada infertile but doesn't affect its ability to fly. Thus, the pathogen is spread to both other adults and washed into the ground where it affects future generations. It builds up over seven or eight emergences so that after two big years there is a collapse in cicadas, as occurred at Raccoon Grove. At Ryerson Woods, Lake County (Ill.), 5–10 percent of the cicadas manifested resting spores in 1990. In ruderal environments such as orchards and suburban lots, however, the fungus does not do well and cicadas can persist in huge numbers.[60]

When cicada densities reach a certain level, they will often vacate a given location, possibly as a defensive response to the fungus.[61] This would be particularly effective in an ecotonal area such as ours, where woods and grass-lands shift. After seventeen years, trees might have sprouted where they hadn't been during the previous emergence. In modern times, landscaping and empty lots provide new habitat that facilitates cicada dispersal. Lloyd has noted their spread toward Chicago, as trees are planted on land that was once lake plain prairie.

Survivors in Trouble:
Reptiles and Amphibians

The ungainly toad
That crawls from his secure abode . . .
Oh, mark the beauty of his eye,
What wonders in that circle lie!
—William Wordsworth (Dickerson 1969, who erroneously
attributes the lines to W. Shakespeare)

Eels are not known, but snakes are, to an extent to supply all deficiencies. . . . It is an
excellent precaution, when going to bed in the dark, to take the bedclothes off and shake
the snakes out of them, before getting in yourself. —M. F. Lawson (1841, Warren Township,
Lake County, Ill. [Lawson 1974])

Approximately sixty species of reptiles and amphibians inhabit the Chicago region. Reptiles are represented in the area by turtles (Order Testudines), snakes (Order Squamata, Suborder Serpentes), and lizards (Order Squamata, Suborder Lacertilia). Amphibians comprise frogs (Order Anura) and salamanders (Order Caudata.)

Reptiles and amphibians differ from one another in a number of ways. The former have scales, clawed toes (not applicable to snakes or glass lizards, which lack feet altogether), shelled eggs, and young that are not fundamentally different in appearance from adults. The latter have bare skin, unclawed feet, shell-less eggs, and generally undergo radical transformations from the larval to the adult stage. All local frogs and toads hatch from their eggs as aquatic tadpoles; most salamanders also have an immature aquatic phase except that the red-backed salamander (*Plethodon cinereus*) is wholly terrestrial and the mud puppy (*Necturus maculosus*) and lesser siren (*Siren intermedia*) are wholly aquatic.

With the possible exception of the five-lined skink (*Eumeces fasciatus*), which was last collected over ninety years ago, no species confirmed to have been in this area has become extirpated. Most, however, have been seriously reduced in numbers, some to the point where long-term survival would be surprising.

Reptiles and amphibians are shy creatures that generally manage to elude people by clinging to the security of darkness or the safety of water. And woe to them that are discovered. Snakes are often killed on sight; if not, they along with turtles, frogs, and salamanders often wind up as pets, frequently destined to starve, desiccate, or drown according to the ignorance of their captors.

As with many plants and animals of this region, habitat loss and degradation pose major threats to their survival. For the amphibians that lead bimodal lives, changes in water quality and land use create synergistic effects that often are devastating. Ecologists are documenting their declines throughout the world. But some reptiles and amphibians are also being jeopardized by a lucrative and illegal pet trade. Common species such as bullfrogs (*Rana catesbiana*) and midland painted turtles (*Chrysemys picta*) may bring only a couple of dollars apiece, but individual spotted turtles (*Clemmys guttata*) and Blanding's turtles (*Emydoidea blandingii*) go for as high as $100.

In the Soup and Pets of Plunder: Turtles

On August 8, 1881, noted book dealer Mr. Chapin traveled the thirty miles from Chicago to Oswego, Kendall County, for a day of fishing on the Fox River. To maximize the chances of success, he armed himself with three hundred feet of line, to which were connected a hundred hooks. Unable to find any frogs or minnows for bait, he purchased a pound of "grizzled beefsteak." Finally, all of his preparations completed, he had his rig set by 2:00 P.M. and waited for his rewards. After an hour, he and a local fisherman eagerly checked the line. The weight convinced them they had caught at least fifty large fish:

> They pulled it a little higher, and then, great Caesar! what a sight. There, in line one after the other, they counted eight big soft shell turtles, that were turning in every conceivable shape; some turning somersaults and standing in the water, kicking, jerking and wriggling to get off. The first they piled in the boat and took the hook out of his mouth; the second they pulled in the boat, and cut his head off, as the first one was crawling around in the bottom of the boat (the local was barefoot and was afraid the turtle would bite a toe off); the third they pulled to the edge of the boat and cut his head off;

the fourth they pulled up to the top of the boat, he hissing like a snake. To make a long story short, they cut the line off of them and let them go.

Although the anglers failed to hook a single fish in six hours, they wound up catching a total of twenty-three softshell turtles, all weighing between fifteen and twenty pounds.[1]

With their emphasis on fish, these two seemed unaware that spiny softshell turtles (*Apalone spinifera*) were highly coveted for their flesh. At the time Alvin Cahn wrote his great monograph on Illinois turtles in 1937, hunters were taking tons of softshell turtles annually from the state's major rivers, to be sold at handsome prices in local markets. In fact, local demand was so high there were none left to ship to markets elsewhere.[2]

Of turtles occurring in the Chicago region, it was the snapping turtle (*Chelydra serpentina*) that most contributed to the turtle-meat trade. In a 1920 federal report, the snapper is described this way: "One could not exactly call him handsome; a better statement would be that he looks good enough to eat." These imposing animals can weigh up to thirty-five pounds in the wild and eighty pounds in captivity, and half of this is edible. Snappers caught in the Midwest were transported alive to Chicago and other large cities for use by the restaurant industry. One wholesaler in Chicago maintained a pen in the basement of his warehouse that could hold up to two and a half tons of live turtles.[3]

Demand for snapping turtle fell in the 1920s, only to rise again in the 1930s when it far exceeded supply.[4] Perhaps the turtle's biggest attraction as food was its low cost. Trappers received a nickel to eight cents a pound per living animal while consumers paid a quarter for a pound of dressed turtle. During the depression years, it was the cheapest meat available.[5] And since turtle was most often served as an ingredient of soup, a little went a long way.

Snapping turtles are most vulnerable to human depredation when they come together for the winter in large hibernacula. One example from this region involved Earl Bixby, a turtle hunter from Berrien Springs, Michigan, who "took five hundred pounds of snappers in the early spring of 1937 from a small channel between two of the Grand Marais Lakes just west of Stevensville, Berrien County. These turtles were buried under from one to two feet of the soft bottom material in this channel and were located and hauled out by means of an iron rod with a hook at one end."[6]

Commercial hunting of turtles is no longer an issue in this region, as most turtle meat now originates in the southern states. It is outlawed in Illinois, where a maximum of eight turtles can be taken per day under a fishing license. According to the 1999 Illinois Sport Fishing Survey, of the 37.75 million days spent fishing in the state, anglers devote only 30,148 days to catching turtles, most of which are snapping turtles.

Even though they were victims of market hunting, the snapping and spiny softshell, along with the painted, remain the most abundant turtles in the region. A number of factors contribute to their success. First, they can live in a variety of waters. Painted turtles prefer the shallow water of streams, rivers, ponds, marshes, and retention ponds. Softshells are more restricted to large streams, rivers, and lakes, although they are even found in quarries and marshes. You can see them in Lake Michigan where they bask on the sand in the Northwestern University lagoon (Evanston, Cook County) or on the breakwaters at Waukegan. Snapping turtles are the most widespread of all, occurring in nearly every type of aquatic habitat, including Lake Michigan.[7]

Second, turtles flourish in highly polluted waters. Snapping turtles, in particular, can persist under wretched conditions. Herpetologist Tom Anton has found them in drainage ditches glazed with the sheen of gasoline. The species also has a remarkably high tolerance to some forms of mercury and PCBs. (It is important to realize, however, that many animals appearing to be healthy have in fact suffered losses of reproductive capacity and/or other harms through the bioaccumulation of various pollutants.)

And third, these turtle species produce numerous offspring. Painted turtles begin to breed from the age of five to seven years and snapping turtles from eight to ten. All three breed every year and produce many eggs. And since they all enjoy relatively long life spans, the opportunities for adults to more than replace themselves is high.

Despite their abundance, however, these turtles face a major threat: an extremely high rate of nesting mortality. Although turtles spend most of their time in their aquatic habitats, they seek well-drained uplands for nesting. In presettlement times, satisfactory sites were scattered across the landscape. But today, development has circumscribed the lowlands so that turtles must either make long hazardous treks to preferred nesting territory or make do with manmade substitutes fraught with danger. These three species have adapted and now utilize railroad beds, road embankments, and even golf course sand traps. While these sunny places with their porous substrates seem ideal for turtles, they also serve as smorgasbords for predators; some studies indicate that raccoons, skunks, opossums, and coyotes can cause nesting losses in excess of 90 percent.[8]

The Blanding's turtle and spotted turtle have been the focus of growing attention precisely because they are rare. The Blanding's turtle is a prairie species, the first scientific description of which was based on a specimen collected locally near the Fox River. The eighteenth-century naturalists considered it common or abundant. With the destruction of the prairie lowlands,

87. Snapping turtle killed on railroad track while seeking a dry area to lay eggs, which are visible in picture. Cuba Road Marsh Forest Preserve, Lake County, Illinois, June 1996. (Photo by J. Greenberg.)

however, it declined to the point of being listed as threatened in Wisconsin, Indiana, and Illinois.

The Blanding's turtle would be even rarer if it hadn't adjusted to new circumstances: "This would account in a measure, then, for the diverse habitat selections we find today, some individuals of an original swamp species attempting to adapt themselves to the dry land conditions they find, others to a more aquatic existence where large rivers and an abundance of water afford such an environment." The variety of its habitat led one early biologist to state the oxymoron that although it is more frequently found in water than on land, "it is essentially a terrestrial species."[9]

Cahn commented that there is no Illinois turtle more poorly known than Blanding's. Fortunately, this species has been the subject of ongoing studies. Focusing on DuPage County, Dan Ludwig of the DuPage County Forest Preserve District and herpetologist Michael Redmer conducted an ambitious local examination of the turtle.[10] They identified eighteen sites distributed across the county that support Blanding's turtles. The two largest populations contained twenty-eight and fourteen individuals, respectively.

During the summer of 1995, Ludwig and Redmer radio-tagged twenty-four turtles so that the species' movements and habitat requirements could be better understood. To manage sites for the well-being of the turtles, it is necessary to learn about the factors that most affect them, including vegetation density and diversity and the presence of other animals. This is especially important, given that Blanding's turtles spend 90 percent of their time in wetland areas. More problematic is the 10 percent of the time that the turtles are moving from one wetland to another and to and from nesting sites. Blanding's turtles travel substantial distances in search of suitable nesting places, which puts them at tremendous risk of becoming at one with the pavement. One of the marked turtles showed up in a marsh over a mile away from where it was originally released, crossing two busy roads in the process.

Females will brave the same hazards year after year to lay eggs at favored spots. As an experiment, researchers erected barriers and created artificial sand mounds to entice the turtles to nest closer to their foraging areas and thus obviate the need to wander as much. The turtles, undaunted, trekked around the barriers, over the mounds, and on to their original destinations. Redmer's hope is that by optimizing Blanding's turtle's foraging habitat, the animals may be less likely to roam. Another option is to install underpasses that enable turtles to cross roadways in safety.[11]

The spotted turtle represents a very different situation. It is an eastern species that reaches the western limit of its range in the Chicago area. A number of populations exist in Berrien County, northwestern Indiana, and the lower Des Plaines River Valley. Illinois's first record was established in June 1927 when Cahn collected two specimens near Wolf Lake, but drainage and development have since wiped out whatever animals might have been present.[12]

Until 1985, spotted turtles were reported only three more times in the state.[13] But in that year, a live turtle was photographed and another was found as a roadkill. To determine the status of the species, David Mauger, now of the Will County Forest Preserve District, led a group of us in May 1987 to survey the area where the animals had been located. It was a thrilling moment when Mauger yelled that he saw one. A little while later, I spied a bright adult turtle basking on a sedge tussock. We found a total of six that day.

Mauger has been studying and protecting these turtles ever since.[14] He believes that their presence in the lower Des Plaines Valley can be attributed to the combination of wet prairie, sedge meadow, and shallow marsh. When the marshes are deeper than three feet, snapping and Blanding's turtles begin to dominate. Another important factor is the cold clean water bubbling up from the dolomite bedrock. Spotted turtles prefer cooler temperatures than many other turtles and are primarily active in the spring and early summer. Because they are so susceptible to overheating, they spend most of the summer huddled deep in the shade of rank vegetation.

Using radiotelemetry and infinite patience, Mauger and his colleagues have made several important discoveries regarding this species, particularly with respect to nesting. The female begins digging her nest in late afternoon and then sits all night without laying any eggs. Come morning, she deposits her eggs and then covers the hole quickly before departing. Mauger surmises that this behavior thwarts nocturnal predators. If a raccoon appears, the turtle can leave the site without having lost any eggs, and by first light the risk of predation has decreased.

There is little evidence that spotted turtles are being poached in large numbers in this region, but herpetologists worry nevertheless. Dave Mauger would like to publish his spotted turtle findings some day but fears that the information may jeopardize the animals. Alan Resetar of the Field Museum heard secondhand that a poacher took fifty to a hundred of the turtles from a site in Lake County, Indiana; and Jim Harding of Michigan State University told me that the only three spotted turtles he found in a Berrien County bog were too ugly—damaged carapaces and no spots—to be of value. Harding tells a first-hand horror story concerning a population he was studying near Lansing, Michigan. Of twenty-five spotted turtles he had marked, poachers took every last one and later boasted of how many other colonies they had ravaged.

Without doubt the pet trade is a major threat to local spotted turtles. This is an animal too beautiful and pleasant for its own good. Chapman Grant, an Indiana herpetologist, wrote of the species: "The spotted turtle is the most likable of Indiana pond turtles. It is slow and methodical, cannot be induced to bite, feeds readily on raw beef in captivity, allows its legs to be extended, and will project its head and neck in a trusting manner when newly captured."[15]

The pet trade has long had an impact on turtles. As youngsters, many of us had the tiny green turtles (red-eared turtle [*Trachemys scripta*]), and their transparent bowls complete with plastic palm trees. During the height of the craze in the 1960s, 10 million of these turtles were distributed throughout the United States and 3 million more in Canada.[16] These were largely the progeny of wild caught animals from Louisiana, and many either died at the hands of our mistreatment (the turtle food pushed by pet stores was mostly ant eggs, woefully inadequate to maintain turtles) or were liberated into local waters. When researchers linked outbreaks of salmonella poisoning in children to the turtles, authorities imposed regulations that limited the domestic industry.

While red-eared turtles are indigenous to the Kankakee River drainage, releases of nonnative stock have allowed the species to become established north of their original range and to mix with native gene pools. This opens up the possibility of spreading disease and damaging local biota. Researchers in South Africa and France have attributed declines in certain native species to the spread of the red-eared turtle, now referred to as the Norway rat of turtles because of its capacity to establish itself worldwide.

Much more recently, the popularity of the "Teenage Mutant Ninja

Turtles" created a new demand for turtles. Apparently, baby boomers objected to the ersatz violence of their children's play, preferring instead the option of actual violence on a live turtle. (Oh, what has my generation become?) There were even reports that animals were mutilated to resemble more closely Michelangelo, Leonardo, and the rest. But children tire quickly of their toys: Steve Swanson, director of the Glenview Park District's The Grove, received more turtles during that period than before or since.

Far more insidious is the international trade in these animals. As the economies of western Europe and the Pacific Rim expanded in the 1960s and 1970s, so did the desire for turtles. In 1993, the United States exported 1.38 million red-eared turtles to South Korea and 665,624 to Japan. More exotic species such as spotted turtles also have become popular. (North Carolina is the only state in the country that has not banned commercial trade in spotted turtles, and so long as that exception remains, it enables thieves to claim that their turtles are legal.)

For years, Mediterranean tortoises of the genus *Testudo* were popular as pets throughout Europe. From 1967 to 1971, over a million spur-thighed tortoises (*T. graeca*) were sent to England. But in 1984, all of that stopped when the European Community outlawed trade in these animals. Undeterred, dealers turned to the United States and discovered box turtles: "From 1991 to 1994, over 100,000 box turtles were exported to Europe."[17]

For some reason, box turtles were excluded in the official tallies until the early 1990s. Two species occur in this region. The ornate box turtle (*Terrapene ornata*) exists as an isolated and fast disappearing population in the sand country of the Morris-Kankakee Basin.[18] The eastern box turtle (*T. carolina*) still inhabits the woods of the Indiana Dunes and Berrien County, but in greatly reduced numbers.

Table 6 shows the number of turtles belonging to local species that were exported out of the United States from 1989 to 1997. (These figures represent individuals taken from the totality of the species' U.S. range; while some individuals might have been caught in this region, the vast majority, of course, were not.) It is from an illuminating study by the Humane Society of the United States, using data from the U. S. Fish and Wildlife Service. Although the most accurate information available, these government figures likely undercount the full extent of the trade by anywhere from one-third to two-thirds because the data reflect only the number of animals listed on dealer invoices (which are notorious for underreporting) and do not consider turtles that died before arriving at market. It is also important to keep in mind that every North American turtle made grist for this industry either is taken from a wild population or is offspring of such an individual; in virtually no case is the animal a

Table 6. Individuals of Locally Occurring Turtle Species Exported from the United States, 1989–97

Species	1989–93	1994–98	Total
Eastern spiny softshell	...	5,061	5,061
Softshell (species)	...	17,398	17,398
Common snapping	...	67,961	67,961
Midland painted	...	54,730	54,730
Blanding's	150	179	329
Map (species)	71,552	220,035	291,587
Stinkpot	...	6,238	6,238
Musk/stinkpot (species)	20,076	28,773	48,849
Eastern box	50,439	28,683	79,122
Ornate box	14,296	12,302	26,598
Red-eared	...	540,962	540,962

Source. Data courtesy of the Humane Society of the United States (1999).

product of captive-bred parents. As demand increases and wild populations decrease, captive breeding programs will grow, but current economics still strongly favor pillaging.

It is these developments, spawned by events far from the marshes, lakes, and rivers of the Chicago region, that generate concern on the part of local herpetologists. The Illinois Department of Natural Resources' Law Enforcement Division has launched successful sting operations against poachers. In 1993, they targeted a swap meet in Streamwood, Cook County, where poachers gathered to dispose of their victims. Twenty-three arrests resulted in twenty-two guilty pleas, over $7,000 in fines, and the confiscation of hundreds of animals. Although this aggressive stance by the state should be lauded, both the chances of getting caught and the penalties remain too low.[19] As the financial rewards grow and large turtle populations become depleted, these criminals will be forced to plunder new locations, most of which in this area are on protected land. Citizens can assist the conservation agencies by reporting any suspicious activity.

Given the reproductive strategies of many turtles, the loss of even a few adults, particularly females, can severely damage a local population. That possibility becomes even more likely if the population is already small and stressed by habitat loss or other factors. Blanding's turtles, for example, do not start breeding until they are thirteen years old. And like other turtles, few if any of their young live to adulthood. Spotted turtles may lay eggs only every other year, and when they do, clutch size is around four. These species rely on long life spans and the odds that over the decades a handful of offspring will survive.[20]

Long and Suffering: Snakes (and Three Lizards)

Spanning both centuries and cultures, snakes have evoked within human beings a multitude of powerful emotions. Throughout southern Asia, for example, king cobras and other snakes are venerated symbols of rebirth, fertility, water, and even life itself. Certain rituals require unspeakable intimacies between person and reptile.[21] How different in our society, where the feelings roused by the sight of a snake tend to be fear and loathing. (Glenview Park District's Steve Swanson says he wishes that Adam and Eve had received the apple from a squirrel.)

The first snake I ever saw was at Waldheim Cemetery in Chicago while my family was walking to the grave of my maternal grandmother. Carried away by the moment, I pointed out the garter snake, even knowing that my mother is deathly afraid of snakes. She ran back to the car, vowing to restrict any future visits to winter. She acknowledges that her phobia is irrational and has never tried to push it on to my sister or me.

Henry Eenigenburg, writing of the 1860s and 1870s in the Calumet area, had a different experience: "My mother would teach her babies that snakes were dangerous by taking a big stick and pounding them to death."[22] Perhaps many parents of the Lower Calumet region adopted this practice, a possibility suggested by Eenigenburg's description of his contemporaries: "A few farm boys would get together and spend a few hours around the sloughs with their clubs and kill four or five hundred snakes of all kinds in one drive, and they were big fat fellows too."[23]

The deliberate slaughter of snakes is a common theme in this discussion and continues to be a serious conservation issue. This gratuitous mortality combined with the usual culprits of habitat loss, lower water quality, and reduction of prey have caused severe population declines in every locally occurring snake species. Despite this ominous trend, however, the massasauga rattlesnake (*Sistrurus catenatus*) may be the only species in danger of total extirpation from the region.

Snakes require places to hide, hunt, thermo-regulate (being cold blooded, they are sensitive to ambient temperatures), and hibernate. Where these sites occur, snakes will often mass in large gatherings. A buried cistern served as a hibernaculum in Kane County. Tom Anton watched forty midland brown snakes (*Storeria dekayi*) pour out over the course of an hour; as he returned to the location several times during the day, there were always brown snakes and garter snakes present. Another large group of hibernating snakes was uncovered in Indiana Dunes State Park during the 1940s. Bulldozers ripping through a dune exposed a huge ball of blue racers (*Coluber constrictor*).[24]

In the early 1930s near Dune Acres, Porter County, Karl Schmidt discovered what was probably the most remarkable hibernaculum in the region. Hundreds of blue racers used vacated woodchuck burrows on the south face of a dune. In the fall, they would congregate in the vicinity, draping themselves over bushes. Upon emerging in spring, the snakes would withstand the still cool air by basking in the unobstructed sun. Schmidt and his colleagues at the Field Museum marked up to a hundred snakes every fall during the early years of the study. The site was periodically monitored for about twenty-five years, but unfortunately, Schmidt's notes and results have disappeared. As for the hibernaculum, the dune is still there, but as the locale became increasingly shaded through succession, the snakes moved on.[25]

As open land fills with human traffic, the discovery of these concentrations becomes inevitable and often spells disaster. Gary Casper, of the Milwaukee Public Museum, says that he not infrequently receives phone calls from alarmed citizens who want to rid themselves of the plains garter snake (*Thamnophis radix*) den they just uncovered. There is little doubt that they eventually succeed.

Casper believes that the northern water snake (*Nerodia sipedon*) is one species whose habit of gathering in hibernacula places it at particular risk. The water snake uses the rubble around bridges for winter denning. But these sites are also popular for fishing, and when anglers have the opportunity to kill one of these big snakes they do, even though the species poses no threat to game fish. While still found in all three of the area's Wisconsin counties, they are much less common. For example, five years ago at a site in Walworth County, Casper could see one to six live snakes on every visit. On recent trips, he could not find even one. Once or twice he came across dead water snakes lying on the bank, undoubtedly victims of human ignorance. Overall, this snake is found in suitable locations throughout this region and is quite observable at such places as the Little Calumet River near Bailly's Homestead, Porter County, and McDowell Grove Forest Preserve, DuPage County.

Fifty years ago common wisdom held that water snakes were major predators of trout. A fishing magazine in 1938 titled an article "Control the Watersnake." Research has since demonstrated, however, that in natural waters the snake feeds almost entirely on nongame fish, frogs, and salamanders. And as Casper points out, since trout need to be stocked regularly anyway, who cares if native predators take some. From an ecological standpoint, the loss of these trout is also meaningless since they aren't even natural species but rather, in

Casper's terms, "hybrid monsters." The one setting where water snakes can be a nuisance is at fish hatcheries where there are artificial concentrations of fingerling trout, easy pickings for the snakes.[26]

Extraordinary summer concentrations of snakes are also found from time to time. The 298 plains garter snakes discovered by Henri Seibert and Charles Hagen on 3.2 acres near Lake Calumet in 1945 represents one of the highest densities ever recorded for a North American snake.[27] Three summers earlier, Ed Lace, who later in life was for many years a naturalist with the Cook County Forest Preserve District, found a smaller site that had even more plains garter snakes. He and a group of fellow high school students used to ride the streetcars to the end of the line and then hitchhike in search of snakes. The report of a Kirtland's snake (*Clonophis kirtlandii*) at the corner of School Street and Odell Avenue, near the Chicago/Elmwood Park border, intrigued them and they decided to investigate. On their way they stopped at the Brookfield Zoo to talk with their mentor Emil Rokosky, curator of herpetology. During the conversation, Rokosky said he was looking for live snakes as dietary supplements to the snakes in the collection, and he offered the boys a dime for every garter snake they brought to the zoo. They knew a few spots where they could collect twenty or thirty garter snakes in an afternoon, and they heartily agreed.

The group headed off toward its destination and discovered that the intersection of School and Odell consisted of four abandoned lots surrounded by buildings. World War II had put a hiatus on any construction so the boys could roam around at their leisure. Very quickly, Lace and his friends realized the site was unbelievably rich in snakes. In an hour and a half, they caught 452 snakes: four hundred plains garter snakes, with the remainder being eastern garter snakes (*Thamnophis sirtalis*), smooth green snakes (*Opheodrys vernalis*), and one Kirtland's snake curled up in a hambone. Keeping their haul of plains garter snakes, they returned to the zoo and asked Rokosky if his offer still stood. He assured them of his sincerity but quickly retreated when he saw the 400 snakes: $40 was a week's pay. The disappointed entrepreneurs rejected Rokosky's compromise offer to buy forty snakes and marched to the middle of the zoo and released the entire kit and caboodle.[28]

Although most snakes prey on a wide range of food items, a few have narrow requirements that limit their range and abundance. The smooth green snake is a prairie species that has adapted to nonnative meadows. Seventy-eight individuals were discovered in the same 3.2-acre old field that held all of those plains garter snakes in 1945. White sweet clover dominated the site, although there was a smattering of other nonnative species also characteristic of ruderal plant communities. Unfortunately, this kind of habitat is far more common and widespread than the snake. Since green snakes live on insects and other soft-bodied invertebrates, a number of herpetologists believe that the widespread use of pesticides has limited the distribution of the species. Supporting this explanation, Sherman Minton of Indiana University found two green snakes in a field that had just been doused: one snake was dying and the other succumbed shortly thereafter. Apparently though, no biologist has performed the toxicological studies to confirm the vulnerability of this snake to specific insecticides.[29]

Two species of snakes feed heavily on crayfish. Graham's crayfish snake (*Regina grahamii*) reaches the eastern edge of its range in the Illinois portion of the Chicago region, and herpetologists have yet to find it in Indiana or Wisconsin. Inhabiting wetland edges, the species spends most of its time in crayfish burrows and is rarely found. A DuPage County Forest Preserve District employee discovered a specimen in the spring of 1995; it was the county's first record in thirty years.[30]

Queen snakes (*Regina septemvittata*) require cool clean water over a cobble bottom that supports the macroinvertebrates preyed upon by the crayfish. The species is most common in the lower Des Plaines Valley, where the exposed bedrock provides shelter and the springs improve water quality. But its future is bleak in Wisconsin, where only two extant populations are known. One of these is in Walworth County along a two-mile stretch of river, but unfortunately runoff and silt from nearby farms are choking the stream to death.[31]

As cold-blooded creatures, terrestrial snakes must take measures to mitigate extremes in ambient air temperature. Hence, they hibernate in winter. But more challenging are the other three seasons when snakes need to conduct their more taxing affairs and yet withstand the vagaries of Midwestern weather. To accomplish this, snakes seek out sites that offer a variety of temperature gradients. And in an urbanized region like Chicago, this creates the seemingly anomalous situation of trash-strewn wastelands with numerous snakes.

Picture the scene: A tortured tract of land slopes down into a cattail ditch or is pocked with pits of stagnant water. Strewn about are sheets of metal, rocks, rubber tires, or pieces of cardboard, a corner of which lies in the wet ditch. Closer scrutiny reveals a healthy food supply in the form of small rodents, leeches, earthworms, and maybe crayfish that dig narrow burrows. The snakes will find sanctuary under the heat-absorbing metal or tires in early spring and late fall, the rocks and brush in May and June, and the damp cardboard in the torrid days of July and August. If crayfish are present, their moist burrows are ideal late summer hideouts. Thus in one small area the serpents can avoid cold, heat, drought, and hunger.

Many species of snakes thrive in such environments. Milk snakes (*Lampropeltis triangulum*—a decreasing species still found across the region) are strongly attracted to piles of sheet metal. They move from one level of the stack to the next in search of the ideal temperature. But the one species above all others that seems to occur most often, although not exclusively, in the degraded areas just described is Kirtland's snake.[32]

For his master's thesis, Mark Bavetz investigated the status of the Kirtland's snake in Illinois: "All of the sites I visited were to some degree, disturbed. Pristine sites in Illinois containing the original habitat for *C. kirtlandii* are unknown." During the 1980s, the most reliable local spot for the snake was thirty-five acres of highly degraded prairie surrounded by an industrial park in Palos Hills, Cook County. The parcel was being used as a garbage dump and off-road vehicle track. Over a three-year period, the site's discoverer removed over twenty-five of the snakes, claiming that the property was for sale and could be developed at any time. Unfortunately, this species is notorious for dying in captivity.[33]

The prospects for the Kirtland's snake are not especially bright. As early as 1892, an Illinois herpetologist commented that "tiling, ditching, and cultivation of the soil have destroyed its haunts and nearly exterminated it."[34] There are no certain records of it for Wisconsin, and both Indiana and Illinois list it as threatened; the snake also is being considered for designation as federally threatened. Unfortunately, and understandably, there has been no zeal to purchase and protect the often-damaged land that harbors this and other snake species. There is not, to my knowledge, widespread popular support for buying and maintaining trash heaps at the public expense. Private conservation groups have also refrained from launching fundraising campaigns to secure these biologically important but ugly properties. Ornithologist James Herkert has sagaciously noted that many grassland birds that shifted to old farmland when prairies disappeared have been neglected by conservationists and thus are victims of their own adaptability. Surely, no species better exemplifies this irony than the Kirtland's snake.

Two species of snakes and all three locally occurring lizards live almost exclusively in the sand areas. Old records indicate that some of these once had wider ranges, but they now rarely if ever occur outside the Chicago Lake Plain and Morris-Kankakee Basin.

The eastern hognose snake (*Heterodon platyrhinos*) is limited not only in range but in diet as well. It feeds almost entirely on toads, as manifested by its "hognose" that facilitates digging out prey. Hognose snakes also engage in the most distinctive defense behavior of any local snake. A hognose will hiss and flatten its hood like a cobra, although unlike a cobra it is entirely harmless. If this display fails to drive off its adversary, the snake resorts to tactic number two: playing dead by turning on its back with tongue protruding limply from its mouth and blood oozing from its gums. If placed on its belly while in this state, it flips back over, undermining the otherwise convincing nature of its ruse.[35]

Attaining a length of six feet (with a record of over eight feet), the bull snake (*Pituophis melanoleucus*) is the region's largest snake. Previously known from only south of the Kankakee River, the species has moved as far north as Crown Point and Hoosier Prairie in Lake County, Indiana. Alan Resetar believes that the draining of the Kankakee Marshes eliminated a natural barrier to this species. He also suspects that railroad corridors have helped the bull snake on its northward journey by providing an amenable corridor across the Kankakee lowlands.

The five-lined skink is the one reptile that may be gone from the region, although Alan Resetar has cautioned me that too little work has been done in the Kankakee River area to proclaim the species extirpated. This lizard has been recorded sporadically from a handful of counties, but the last specimen was taken at Miller, Lake County (Ind.), at the end of the nineteenth century. Another sighting, unconfirmed, occurred decades later near a sawmill east of Chesterton, Porter County. Six-lined racerunners (*Cnemidophorus sexlineatus*) are common in the Indiana Dunes and the Morris-Kankakee Basin. Ken Mierzwa has seen up to fifty in one morning at Will County's Braidwood Dunes and Savanna Nature Preserve.[36] Although recorded from Michigan City, La Porte County, it has never been found in Michigan, less than a dozen miles away. While presettlement forests might have kept it out of the state, subsequent human activities have created strips of open habitat that the lizard could easily colonize.

To the uninitiated, the slender glass lizard (*Ophisaurus attenuatus*) strongly resembles a snake. Although legless, it does have the movable eyelids and external ear openings characteristic of lizards. The most remarkable thing about this species is its long tail. If caught by this appendage, the lizard by a single wrench can effect its escape by leaving its writhing tail behind. Although the tail never grows back, the wound discharges no blood and a pointed stump soon forms.[37] Records from Evanston and the Palos region show that the glass lizard once enjoyed a range more extensive than its current one, but it remains in the Indiana Dunes and the Kankakee area.[38]

Winding through History: Massasauga Rattlesnakes

As the only venomous snake in this region, the massasauga rattlesnake has attracted more comment than any other local reptile. From the 1830s on, the historical record of its presence is more complete than for all but a few birds and mammals. Early settlers and modern herpetologists have written at length on local populations of this species. Many biologists share Tom Anton's enthusiasm for the massasauga:

> The massasauga rattlesnake is a very unusual species. In some areas it is a desert grassland animal, a chaparral-scrub animal, a peat bog animal, and a tall-grass prairie animal. The underlying reason for this adaptability is that massasaugas are pit vipers, the Lamborghinis of snakes. Pit vipers are the most recently evolved of snakes, and they are extremely successful ambush predators, although a few are active foragers. If the conditions are right, if there is limited management, or the habitat is left alone and protected, massasaugas can maintain stable populations so long as people don't go in and wantonly kill or collect them.[39]

Most people probably would be surprised that rattlesnakes still hold on in isolated pockets throughout the Chicago metropolitan area. I hope they would find such knowledge gratifying. But how much longer the snake will continue to survive is an open question.

In my view, the massasauga rattlesnake ranks with the prairie chicken as being among the two most potent faunal symbols of the land that was once the Chicago region. It has been over a quarter of a century since the last local prairie chicken crossed the line from reality to memory. And as those of us deep in middle age begin to falter, those last few birds in Indiana will cease being even memories. That the massasauga rattlesnake has displayed greater resilience by continuing to reproduce within the confines of this area is both a gift and a challenge. We will have learned nothing if we allow its dry rattle to be stilled.

◄○► ◄○► ◄○►

Most of the early authors express the same two notions concerning massasauga rattlesnakes. First, the animal is common.[40] And second, they are personally committed to making the first less true.

Frances Barker saw her first rattlesnake in the late 1820s about fifteen miles west of Chicago. As she ran barefoot through the fudge-like soil of newly plowed prairie, she felt a "sharp prick and saw a large snake retreating." After being ill for several weeks, she recovered, and then it was the rattlesnake's turn to suffer: "From that time on we waged war on snakes. It seems wonderful now that we killed them in the way we did, by putting a piece of timber, or even a foot upon their heads, and holding them down until someone could come and sever or bruise their bodies."[41]

As they made their way from Chicago to St. Louis, R. Tinkham and his party killed dozens of rattlesnakes in August 1831. Captain Levinge wrote that the species was "very numerous" in the low grassland near Fox Lake in 1838. He goes on to say that if it were not for the prairie fires that kill so many of them, the snakes "would increase to a fearful extent."[42] On the prairie twenty-five miles west of Chicago in DuPage County, William Pearse found rattlesnakes to be "very plentiful" in 1847: "The snakes are awfully thick. At first they annoyed me considerably, but now I care little for them. A stroke with a switch or whip breaks their joints and disables them and then it is the custom of the country to put the foot on their heads, catch hold of their tails and pull their heads off. I killed four the other day."[43]

Southeastern Wisconsin had its share of massasaugas as well. Writing in 1883 from Racine, Philo Hoy said they "were once abundant" on the "marshy grassy prairies where meadow mice live."[44] The April 30, 1896, *Whitewater Register* reported on the fate of local rattlesnakes after farmers began using horse-drawn mowing machines for their haying operations in the large marshes near East Troy, Walworth County:

> One season the snakes were very numerous, the next season there were few to be seen and the next not any; since that time a [rattlesnake] on the marsh has been a rarity. . . . The users of machines had noticed from the first numerous bodies of snakes without heads on the marsh and amid the hay. Then they . . . found that the click of the machine roused the sleeping snake in the grass in front of the mower; he raised his head from the coil to see what was coming, and the sickle took the head slick and clean from the body. Of course it was only a question of time when the snakes would be exterminated, for the machine swept every foot of the surface for acres.

In the early years, rattlesnakes were common in the Calumet region, but the last one was seen "about 1860 on Vermont Street west of Maple Avenue near Stony Creek." At the time Joseph Bailey established Baileytown in 1822, the Indiana Dunes harbored such large populations of the snake that Indians from across the region visited to secure venom for their poisons. A century later the species was still common in the dunes. Workers who cut marsh grass wrapped burlap around their lower legs to shield themselves from snakebite. And over the course of constructing the Bethlehem Steel plant that destroyed the highest dunes and best marshes of the Indiana Dunes area, one bulldozer operator reported seeing from forty to fifty rattlers.[45]

Along with destruction of the prairies (particularly draining of the lowlands) and direct slaughter by people, the introduction of livestock proved to be a serious blow to the massasauga. Pigs, in particular, seemed to have both an aversion to the snakes and the ability to withstand the bites, presumably because their layer of fat is thicker than the length of the snake's fangs. Writing of southern Lake County (Ill.), Charles Bushey tells of the impact feral pigs had on rattlesnake numbers: "A large population of 'wild boars' came to occupy the forested areas and edge in a very short time. . . . A decline in the local rattlesnake population was noticed by residents as the pig population increased. Later 'wild boar' hunts became a sport for many of the residents. They not only 'enjoyed the hunt', but eliminated the potential pig hazard at the same time. The last 'wild pig' killed was claimed . . . around 1890. Within a few years residents noticed a rapid increase in the number of rattlesnakes."[46]

Just how dangerous are massasauga rattlesnakes to people? Being no more than two to three feet in length, the animal carries too little venom to kill most healthy people, including children. The effects are even less if the animal is unable to deliver a full complement of poison. This could arise either because the snake was unable to inject all the venom it had or because its venom supply had not yet been replenished since striking a previous victim.

Arlie Schorger found seventy references to rattlesnakes biting people in Wisconsin before 1880. Of these, twelve related to fatalities, but nearly all the deaths occurred in areas occupied by the larger timber rattlesnake. In his study of the massasauga in Illinois, Bertrand Wright concluded that "the bite of the massasauga according to authentic records has never been fatal."[47] There is, however, at least one well-documented instance of a fatality in the Chicago region.

In August 1935, a four-year-old boy was bitten on the back of the middle finger by a massasauga and was brought to the hospital in La Porte, Indiana. The attending physician had successfully treated four other snakebite patients during the preceding ten years, the last two of whom recovered without the use of antivenin. (Although presumably, they were adults.) Motivated further by the absence of antivenin in town and his belief that its cost would be a serious burden to the family, the doctor waited forty-eight hours before he finally administered a dose to the child. The first injection seemed helpful, but subsequent shots were not. The young patient languished for a total of seven days before succumbing to anemia produced by hemolysis (destruction of red blood cells and the freeing of hemoglobin).[48]

While a massasauga bite is unlikely to kill, it can be a painful experience requiring intensive medical attention. A seventy-two-year-old farmer, bitten on the left little finger in Saint Joseph County, Indiana, arrived at a doctor's office in South Bend an hour later. He received antivenin about eleven hours after that. After six days in a hospital, much of which time he was in severe pain as his arm swelled and his finger appeared gangrenous, he recovered and left without further difficulty. Another patient had a much easier time. A snake collector, accidentally bitten by a small locally caught massasauga, was out of the hospital in less than nineteen hours. He had immediately made incisions near the wound, began using suction to remove venom, and was in the care of a doctor within ten minutes. (Current thought advises against incision and suction in most cases.)[49]

Today's snakebite victim has the benefit of modern medicine, but years ago some of the antidotes were possibly more deleterious than the bite itself: "A man at Fennimore, bitten by a massasauga while binding grain, underwent heroic treatment. When questioned by Bishop Kemper, he replied that after reaching the house he drank half a pint of alcohol and camphor, then a quart of whiskey, followed by a quart of pure alcohol, and all of this with no symptoms of intoxication. The following morning he drank a pint of alcohol and swallowed a quarter pound of finely cut tobacco boiled in milk. In a way, it is disappointing that he did not die."[50]

Whatever risk massasauga rattlesnakes posed to the people of this region when the snake was common is now a subject of historical interest only. The chances that a resident in the twenty-first century would even be near a massasauga are extraordinarily remote. And most of the few remaining populations may have already dipped below the point of viability. Despite the loss of habitat, pigs, boys under the influence of testosterone poisoning, guys being guys, and lunatic moms, massasaugas presently occur in the following counties: Cook, Lake (Ill.), Will, Walworth, Lake (Ind. [although possibly extirpated]), Porter, La Porte, and Berrien.

The Will County massasaugas first came to the attention of the forest preserve district in 1990, when it received a specimen that the caretaker of a local golf course had deliberately run over with a lawnmower.[51] Dave Mauger, who has since studied the population using radio telemetry, estimates that a twenty-acre site adjacent to the golf course supports forty to fifty animals. Farmed until 1950, the area does contain some wetland and two acres of degraded prairie. Mauger believes that these tiny tracts were enough to enable the snakes to persist, and that is where they are most concentrated, though cessation of farming has increased the fallow land tenfold.

Although small rodents and other prey already use the site, Mauger hopes to improve snake cover by increasing the prairie character of the vegetation. He is reluctant to disk the area for fear of harming the snakes, so he is employing the slower method of hand seeding. Mauger is also burning the site with less frequency than he otherwise would. His concern is not that the snakes would be burned—they are still in hibernation at the time—but rather the bare ground that would await them on their emergence would make them more vulnerable to hawks and other predators.

Of all the surviving massasaugas, those in northern Cook and southern Lake Counties (Ill.) have been the most thoroughly studied, with articles on them dating back to at least 1935. The building of roads, subdivisions, and golf courses has diced the once contiguous population along the Des Plaines River into three small pockets. For instance, the construction of Deerfield Road and its bridge over the river destroyed many massasaugas: the bridge reportedly wiped out an important hibernaculum and work crews killed another forty. Paralleling the Des Plaines, Portwine Road buried prime rattlesnake habitat and left at least one hundred snakes dead at the hands of workers.[52]

Other calamities befell the species. A large hibernaculum on Cook County Forest Preserve District land was inadvertently destroyed when the site was turned into a wood-storing and -burning facility. The most infamous attacks on the species, however, were the twice-annual snake hunts conducted from the 1930s to the 1960s. Organized by Ed Belmore, a barber from Wheeling (Cook), teams would go up and down Portwine Road in search of prey. Hundreds of snakes of all species perished, many of which were massasaugas, then still common in spots. Belmore decorated his shop with jars of dead massasaugas, creating a unique ambience for those seeking tonsorial splendor.

Eventually, this exercise in wanton carnage ended as the participants brought back less quarry every year. Ray Schwarz, who became the naturalist at River Trail Nature Center in the early 1960s, also mitigated some of the harm by convincing hunters that they should bring him live massasaugas because he had a friend who needed them for research. Schwarz, along with Steve Swanson who is a relative of Barber Belmore, would then release the snakes back into local areas. (Swanson believes that his lifelong interest in natural history and conservation is in part a response to his relative's actions.)

Tom Anton has photographed virtually every surviving adult and recorded their markings so that he can monitor the populations with great precision.[53] One of the biggest threats to the species is that their grassy and ecotonal habitat is becoming increasingly wooded, but burning and other management techniques must be conducted with great care. For example, Anton points out that buckthorn, a nonnative species that is the bane of many land managers, provides important shelter to the massasauga. Complete removal of the buckthorn all at once would make the snake more accessible to predators.

Anton's work has led him to another conclusion, but one that is difficult to prove. Massasaugas exist in enclaves devoid of milk snakes and fox snakes (*Elaphe vulpina*). Competition among them would not be surprising given that all three species live in ecotonal areas and feed heavily on rodents. Between milk snakes and massasaugas, there is probably even cross-predation: adult milk snakes may eat juvenile rattlers and juvenile rattlers (which unlike their parents prey on cold-blooded animals) may take juvenile milk snakes. Dave Mauger's work lends support to Anton's suggestion: in four years of studying massasaugas on the twenty-acre Will County location, he has yet to find a single fox snake.

Aside from my parents, my first natural history mentor was Richard Horwitz, now an ecologist at the Philadelphia Academy of Natural Sciences, who took me on my inaugural bird-watching excursion in November 1966. It was he who informed me that massasauga rattlesnakes inhabited old fields and open woods not far from where I lived. Although I looked for them whenever I was in the field, it wasn't until many years later that I learned their exact locations.

During the summer of 1983, I went three times a week to the best spot and turned over the boards placed there by the herpetologists studying the species. Oh, there were snakes—garters and browns—but never *the* snake. To improve my chances, I even accompanied Ken Mierzwa and Tom Anton but to no avail. My failure to find it became one of life's great frustrations; the snake became my great jinx organism.

Then, on Labor Day Weekend 1987, Lynn Hepler and I were walking through the prime field when I detected a noise different from any I had heard before. It sounded more like an insect's buzz than a rattle, but moving slowly through the thick vegetation was the consummation of my twenty-year quest: a lovely foot-long massasauga. We followed it for a brief time and then watched it disappear into the shadows of heavy grass.

Under Cover or on the March: Salamanders

Of the thirteen species of salamanders in the region, three are particularly widespread. Tiger salamanders (*Ambystoma tigrinum*) inhabit prairies and savannas, blue-spotted salamanders (*A. laterale*) inhabit areas ranging from savannas to forests, and spotted salamanders (*A. maculatum*) inhabit forests. Fidelity to specific habitats is stronger among members of this group than most other vertebrates. A fourth species, the red-backed salamander, is restricted largely to the Indiana Dunes and Berrien County but is prevalent in the woods where it is found. Some ecologists say this salamander is the most abundant vertebrate in its preferred habitat.

Because salamanders are among the most retiring of creatures, species with limited ranges and small populations may go undetected and appear rarer than they are. Making this even more likely, there are far too few herpetologists to survey all the promising sites adequately. There is always the possibility, then, that something totally unexpected may lie under or inside the next rotting mass of carbon. So it was for Tom Anton in the spring of 1995 when he made one of the most unexpected herpetological discoveries in recent years.[54]

His major objective in inventorying this woods near Crete, Will County, was to confirm the presence of wood frogs (*Rana sylvatica*), spotted salamanders, and blue-spotted salamanders. After one and a half months of working the site, Tom had successfully accomplished his mission and was preparing to leave. He decided to do some last minute poking around: "I remember turning over the log and finding it. I stared at it awhile. I was kind of frozen and thought, 'My god, what is this?' When I got close enough, I knew that it was a four-toed salamander."

A female with eggs, it was the first definite report of the four-toed salamander (*Hemidactylium scutatum*) in northeastern Illinois in over sixty-five years. The last previous records were from the now destroyed Skokie Marsh on the border of Lake and Cook Counties. It belongs to a group of terrestrial yet lungless salamanders that absorbs oxygen through the skin and mouth directly from the moisture of wet humus and moss. Thus, it requires cool and wet environments, with thick growths of spongy *Sphagnum* and or other mosses. (The lone four-toed salamander specimen from Walworth County has puzzled herpetologists for years, given that it seems remote from any suitable habitat.[55])

Two species of salamanders are exclusively aquatic, and therefore infrequently detected. The more common of these is the mud puppy, which spends its days under rocks on the bottom of rivers and lakes. Even though the species is sighted throughout the region, herpetologists lack solid information on its status because it is so difficult to survey.

In the old days, mud puppies were quite common, especially in Lake Michigan. During the late 1860s, an Evanston fisherman "had nine hundred hooks set in the lake, and in one day took from these five hundred [mud puppies], removing them all himself, as his men, sharing the popular notion on the lakes, believed them to be poisonous, and preferred to cut away hook and all to taking hold of the slimy amphibian."[56]

The most reliable source of specimens is still the lakefront, where anglers perched on piers and jetties will occasionally hook one. Unfortunately, the typical human tends to respond to this completely harmless animal in the same way his forebears did 140 years ago: killing the captured mud puppy because it looks so strange and/or is perceived as a threat to good fishing.

Much rarer is the lesser water siren. Local records are concentrated from the sand prairies of Indiana, where a reliable location is Jasper-Pulaski Fish and Wildlife Area. Most of Michigan's records were casualties of official programs that dispensed rotenone into waters of the state to eliminate undesirable fish.

Therefore, as Jim Harding told me, in many places the siren was being discovered at the same time it was probably being extirpated.

Ed Lace is one of the few herpetologists who have reported the water siren locally. And if the microhabitat in which he found it reflects a strong preference by the siren, it is understandable why people encounter it so infrequently. About fifty years ago, Lace and some companions were on a field trip at Ogden Dunes (now part of Indiana Dunes National Lakeshore), Porter County. They were considering the best way to cross a water-filled ditch, when one fellow spotted what he took to be a rock. Lace knew that boulders were unlikely in the dunes area, but before he could issue a warning, his companion leapt onto the object. And sank waist deep into dead horse. This not only released a terrible stench, but several lesser water sirens as well.[57]

As they head toward breeding ponds in the spring and fall, salamanders often congregate in impressive numbers. Peter Dring, formerly a naturalist with the Cook County Forest Preserve District, recalls when he first moved to the Palos area in the early 1960s. Driving down Willow Springs Road one spring evening after a rain, he came upon a quarter-mile stretch covered with hundreds and hundreds of salamanders. Dring estimated that there was a tiger or spotted salamander for every foot of highway.

Along the Des Plaines River in southern Lake County (Ill.), herpetologist Ken Mierzwa recorded more than six hundred blue-spotted salamanders at two small ponds. Perhaps the best salamander habitat in the region lies within the morainal forests of Thorn Creek Woods Nature Preserve in Will County. Researchers have identified more than thirty breeding ponds, one of which attracted three hundred salamanders. Of these, roughly 80 percent were spotted salamanders, 20 percent blue-spotted salamanders, and the small remainder tiger salamanders.[58]

The wet summer of 1993 produced a bumper crop of tiger salamanders, many of which wandered into newly built subdivisions during September. Rainbow Hills, outside Saint Charles, Kane County, earned the sobriquet "Salamander City." One swimming pool attracted as many as thirty salamanders at a time, while the window wells of another residence contained fifty.[59] In McHenry County, officials closed a road because it was getting slick with the goo of crushed salamanders. But the strangest salamander-related incident that fall was the mass of three hundred tigers that someone apparently dumped in the parking lot of Shoe Factory Road Woods in Cook County.

Current thought holds that the tiger salamander represents a species complex; what scientists now call subspecies may really be nine separate species. This becomes problematic because tiger salamanders are raised commercially for medical research and bait. Anglers can even buy them in bait-vending machines, two for $1.50. (Ron Brandon, of Southern Illinois University, calls them "vend-a-manders.") Most of these salamanders currently are of North Dakota stock. Thus, anglers are releasing large quantities of nonnative tiger salamanders into local waterways. Such introductions not only bring nonnative salamander DNA but also a host of tiny parasitic and commensal organisms that can potentially decimate local salamanders by causing disease outbreaks.[60]

The Plight of the Choristers: Frogs and Toads

Frog music is undoubtedly the most conspicuous attribute of any locally occurring amphibians. In its September 10, 1836, issue, the *Chicago Democrat* describes a series of prairie sloughs, complete with waterfowl and muskrat houses, located in the center of Chicago's downtown. One of these, extending to the corner of Lake and LaSalle Streets, "was inhabited by innumerable frogs, annoying the editor exceedingly by their vocalizations at night."

On the south side of Foundry Road, between Wolf and River Roads, there was a small marshy area that my father and I used to pass on our daily runs to and from the Mount Prospect (Cook County) train station. Beginning in March, I would roll down the window and ask him to slow down so I could listen for western chorus frogs (*Pseudacris triseriata*). Time after time, the exercise yielded nothing but silence. But eventually, one warm night would be graced with the staccato notes of their song, widely described as sounding like a fingernail moving along the short tines of a plastic comb. At that moment, spring had arrived.

If that editor were around today, he could sleep soundly without batrachian disturbances. (El trains are another matter.) And with the passage of a decade, that lowland near where I grew up holds neither water nor frogs. Perhaps more than any other small animals in this region, frogs have experienced precipitous declines. Just how precipitous depends on the area and species.

Bullfrogs seem to be increasing in most areas, and it is still possible to encounter large concentrations of other species. In the frenzy to mate, common toads (*Bufo americanus*) swarm by the hundreds at places like Beck Lake and Big Bend Lake in Cook County. And on a few rainy days in July, tremendous numbers of newly formed adult wood frogs, looking like tan popcorn dancing on a hot pan, continue to hop across certain roads in the Indiana Dunes. Chorus frogs are still deafening if you visit the right places in spring, although even they have declined.

Reflecting on the changes that he has seen in the Des Plaines River region of northern Cook County, Steve Swanson sadly concludes that "over the years you forget what it was like. We may have 20 chorus frogs in a pond now. I just came back from Texas where we could hear frogs even though we were driving down a gravel road with the windows rolled up and the air conditioner on. Thirty years ago, it used to be like that here."

The first direct assault on frogs was mounted by an industry that utilized the animals for food and research. Because of their appearance and association with things occult, frogs were shunned for many years as a food item in most of Europe. The one exception was France, whose citizens early recognized the palatability of the animals. Gradually, the popularity of frogs spread to other countries, including the United States. By the end of the nineteenth century, this country consumed more frogs than any other.[61]

A report on edible frogs written in 1900 says that the commercial trade in frogs was "of economic importance in fifteen states," and the total annual take was just under 1 million animals. Froggers used a plethora of techniques to capture their prey: baited lines, small-bore rifles, gigs, and even crossbows. Consumers spent about $150,000, while hunters received one-third of that amount. Indiana was one of the eight states that produced most of the frogs that were marketed. And the Hoosier frog capital was the Kankakee River Valley. Here, hunters received from five to seventy-five cents a dozen, the amount depending on the size of the frogs.

It was also here, on seventeen acres in North Judson, Starke County, where Alfred A. Sphung established his reputation as "Sphung, the frog man."[62] For thirty years, he dealt more frogs than any one else in the country. Sphung also trafficked in turtles, clams, and crayfish. Most of his clients were in the food business, but he also made regular shipments to research and teaching institutions across the nation; the University of Chicago, Northwestern, Stanford, Harvard, Yale, and the federal government were all regular customers.

The volume of his business was tremendous: "He handles these water products by the thousands and by the tons, and in his place at North Judson he frequently has as high as thirty-five tons of frogs at one time." He had a second site in Wisconsin, where additional frogs were held prior to shipment to Indiana. Both facilities were often called "farms," but "no frogs are raised at either place; they are shipped out as fast as they are caught. From early spring until late in autumn and through the winter his ponds and sheds are full of the little animals."

Because it is the largest of local frogs, the bullfrog was the most exploited of all the species. (Next in size and therefore desirability was the green [*Rana clamitans*], followed by the leopard.) The same 1900 report already cited issues this warning: "The unrestricted hunting of frogs threatens their practical extinction in all places where their abundance and shipping facilities or proximity to market render the business profitable."[63] The solution offered was "frog culture." This did not mean artificial propagation but, rather, stocking suitable areas with the preferred species and then protecting the tadpoles and adults until harvesting. One consequence of this effort was that entrepreneurs introduced bullfrogs into places where they were not native. Local populations were also augmented by bullfrogs obtained as pets and released when the owners tired of their playthings.

How this history of slaughter and introduction affected bullfrogs in the Chicago region is difficult to assess. In his 1855 list of animals inhabiting Cook County, Robert Kennicott omits any mention of the species.[64] Whether this was an error or not, the bullfrog has since become one of the region's most widespread and common frogs because it has actually benefited from the changes wrought by development.

Bullfrog tadpoles take two years to mature into the adult form, and during that period they require permanent bodies of water. But since few of the wetlands and rivers of this poorly drained region remained sufficiently wet throughout two consecutive summers, bullfrog range was limited. However, as the land was excavated, drained, and covered with the hard surfaces of urbanization, the waters raced into farm ponds, retention basins, reservoirs, and the rivers whose flows increased concomitantly. And as their preferred habitat has increased, so have bullfrogs.

Alan Resetar had studied the reptiles and amphibians of the Indiana Dunes for ten years before he encountered his first bullfrog. One day in 1988, he was driving down Route 12 near Long Lake when he spotted a large dead frog on the road side that he felt sure was a bullfrog. Traffic prevented him from jamming on his brakes but he eventually found a place where he could turn around. As he approached the carcass, he slowed, opened the door, and grabbed the specimen as his car rolled by. He tossed it on the floor of the passenger side and was immediately hit by the odor of rotting frog, rotting bullfrog to be precise. The species remains rare in the Dunes, but Resetar is finding it with increased frequency.

Has the spread of the bullfrog harmed other frogs? Bullfrogs are highly tolerant of heat and can eat a tremendous range of food. Tom Anton calls them amphibian garbage cans. At degraded sites, without vegetation for shade or shelter, bullfrogs dominate and prey heavily on other species that are unable to find protective cover. In the spring of 1995, Mike Redmer found a bullfrog that had just eaten two leopard frogs. Where there is a thick growth of aquatic and emergent plants, however, green frogs and leopard frogs can coexist with the bullfrogs in large numbers. And because the two smaller species mature more rapidly than the bullfrog, they can thrive where water is temporary.

Northern leopard frogs (*Rana pipiens*) underwent a sudden and unexplained population decline during the 1970s. Ditches at Hoosier Prairie that used to boil with tadpoles yielded only three or four in a season.[65] Researchers in various areas began finding dead adults, lacking any of the apparent damage predators would cause. Then, after about ten years, leopard frogs began to rebound. The frogs are now common in many places but have yet to reach their former abundance. Whether these population fluctuations reflect regular but uncharted cycles, unusual weather, or something else altogether, no one knows. This is just one more illustration of how little is known about amphibian population change, habitat, and health.

Apart from the common toad and to a much lesser extent the chorus frog, every species of small frog has suffered greatly in the face of recent human activity. And each has its own story.

The spring peeper (*Pseudacris crucifer*) has fared better than some. Like many other amphibians (frogs and salamanders both), this species lays its eggs in small vernal pools shaded by woods where, upon hatching, the tadpoles make their living until they morph into adults. Because these wet depressions are so easily altered by precipitation and the deposition of material, they may become unsuitable as spawning areas in a short time. It is therefore imperative that spring peepers can exploit newly created sites. Dave Mauger found a small colony at Thorn Creek Woods, Will County, that was breeding in a foot and a half of algae-covered water at the bottom of an abandoned swimming pool. These frogs have even made do with trail ruts, gouged out by off-road vehicles.

Fifty years ago, spring peepers, whose distant chorusing has been likened to the sound of sleighbells, used to "gather in great numbers wherever they find a combination of quiet, shallow water and low vegetation."[66] Today, despite their capacity to adjust to changes in their microhabitat, that combination more often than not is sans spring peepers. Though still easily found in parts of southern Cook County, they are almost gone from northern Cook County. Spring peepers remain common in the Kettle Moraine of Walworth County but are absent from Racine and Kenosha counties. Other viable populations are scattered through the region but are decreasing for reasons no one knows.

Wood frogs are also holding their own in some places, but not in others. As its name suggests, it prefers forested areas, and it is doing best in the Indiana Dunes, Berrien County, and the Kettle Morain portion of Walworth County. Mike Redmer's ongoing search for the species in northeastern Illinois, however, has confirmed only three extant populations: one in Will County and two in Cook County. Efforts to locate a small population that was once present at Ryerson Woods in Lake County have failed.

Redmer offers some explanations for the decline in wood frogs. In general, this species does not do well in heavily urbanized areas. He believes that the fragmentation of suitable habitat makes it difficult for populations to maintain healthy genetic diversity. Further, since this species is the only ground-living woodland frog (the others cling to trees or other vegetation), it is harmed by decreases in ground moisture and humidity. And the forest floor is becoming drier as urbanization lowers water tables and groundcover disappears in the face of deer and buckthorn.

The frog whose presence in the region is the most precarious of all is the pickerel frog (*Rana palustris*). Requiring cool and high-quality streams in association with dense vegetation, the frog apparently was never common here. A recent study of the species in northern Illinois found that several old records including museum specimens were actually the similar-looking leopard frog.[67] Pickerel frogs are now limited to two fens in Walworth County and possibly another in Berrien County.

The circumstances of the Fowler's toad (*Bufo fowleri*) are different yet again. In the Chicago region, it is restricted to the sand regions. It used to inhabit the moorlands near Waukegan; development of the area shrunk the toad's range so that it was limited to Illinois Beach State Park. Isolated and small, this population persisted until at least the 1930s.[68] But decades have now passed without further sign of it. Fowler's toad has never been reported in Wisconsin, although Illinois Beach and Chiwaukee Prairie were virtually contiguous. It now seems likely that this gap in Wisconsin's batrachian fauna will remain indefinitely.

The local strongholds of Fowler's toad are the Lake Michigan dunes of Indiana and Berrien County, where they occur in sizable but isolated populations. (They are also found in the sand country south of the Kankakee River.) At night, during the summer and early fall, hundreds of these animals leave their daytime haunts and, traveling distances up to a mile, make pilgrimages to the beach. For many years, biologists thought that the toads worked the strand line for food. But research at the Indiana Dunes proved that the toads were really seeking damp sand to hydrate themselves, which they accomplish by absorbing moisture directly through their skin. Toads avoided the lake itself, and if a wave reached them, they usually retreated for the night.[69]

No frog has undergone a more dramatic or mysterious decline than the cricket frog (*Acris crepitans*). From 1961 to 1981, three monographs were published on the amphibians and reptiles of Illinois, Indiana, and Wisconsin, respectively. In the first of these, Philip Smith wrote that the "cricket frog is the most common amphibian in Illinois." Eleven years later, Sherman Minton could still call the species "the most frequently seen of Indiana's smaller amphibians." But by the time the third book came out, the decline was in full force, for Richard Vogt wrote: "During the last three years, populations of cricket frogs have diminished rapidly. This once very common frog is becoming extremely rare in Wisconsin." It is now gone from Wisconsin and hangs on in isolated populations of varying sizes in this portion of Indiana, Illinois, and Michigan.[70]

The cause of the decline seems to go beyond habitat loss. In southern Wisconsin, for example, the cow wallows and other degraded areas where it used to thrive have not disappeared. Other factors such as climate, natural fluctuations in the population, and an increase in ultraviolet rays have all been offered as possible explanations.

A common theme running throughout this book is that there is too little research being carried out on regional natural history subjects. But the riddle of the cricket frog is a refreshing exception to this scientific inactivity. Val Beasley and his colleagues at the University of Illinois College of Veterinary Medicine have undertaken a major project designed to elucidate the reasons behind the decline of this small animal in particular and amphibians in general.[71] Although they have yet to reach any final conclusions, detailed toxicological, pathologic, and parasitological testing have produced some notable findings.

Cricket frogs are about an inch and a half in length, take a year to mature, and have a life span of one and a half years. They require small pools, preferably devoid of predatory fish, with thick vegetation in the water and gradually sloping banks that have some cover. This set of elements provides the frog with both easy egress and shelter when it leaves the water to feed on insects, as well as enhanced protection while in the water. An abundance of green algae also provides food for the tadpole. Any alteration of these conditions represents degradation of habitat and imposes an additional level of stress on the frogs.

Beasley and his team have identified several current trends that are militating toward such changes. First, there is the ever-increasing habitat fragmentation. Breeding sites become bisected by roads or surrounded by agricultural or other unsuitable land. Genetic homogeneity increases, as does mortality induced by predators and vehicles. Further, ponds are becoming oxygen deficient due to nutrient loading and algal blooms. During periods of prolonged drought, cricket frogs inhabiting such environments must either defer breeding until suitable water is available or find another site. Because they live for such a short period, the first option might be disastrous, while isolation may prevent them from successfully executing the second. As one authority suggests, the cricket frog may be the Yossarian of anurans, caught in its own catch-22.[72]

Second, landowners often deepen ponds and stock them with game fish. They replace gentle slopes with steep sides to create a more orderly appearance. Further grooming leads to the removal of aquatic and emergent vegetation.

Third, herbicides enter the water from nearby fields or lawns or when landowners decide to remove aquatic plants. These chemicals effectively reduce protective cover (terrestrial, emergent, and aquatic) and the oxygen content of the water. They may also directly harm the frogs. Beasley has suggested that heavier concentrations of herbicides may be creating another more subtle change: the hardier and more poisonous blue-green algae are replacing the less tolerant and more benign green algae. Whether this in turn is having an impact on the algal-feeding tadpoles remains to be explored.

One of the largest populations of cricket frogs still extant in this region is at Midewin National Tallgrass Prairie, Will County. But even here the frog is not secure, for in the mid-1990s Beasley and his group discovered that the herbicide Atrazine was entering the ponds via runoff from an adjacent corn-field. Again, it isn't clear whether this pollution is having any effects on the frogs, but close monitoring is warranted.

Although the final conclusions have yet to be drawn, the cricket frog does seem to be up against intractable foes. But perhaps it is not too late for home-owners, farmers, and developers to see the need for more linked, structurally diverse, and intact aquatic habitats. And whether or not these attitudinal changes occur in time to save local populations of cricket frogs, a host of other organisms, including our own, will certainly benefit.[73]

Of Extinction and Resurrection: Passenger Pigeon, Prairie Chicken, Sandhill Crane, and Colonial Nesters

There comes a point in the existence of every living species, if its population drops extremely low, when it straddles a precarious line. If things go well and the forces of man and nature refrain from dealing it further deleterious blows, it may survive and increase and over the years return to a semblance of its former abundance. But one little push over that line in the opposite direction seals the fate of the species. —Allen W. Eckert (1965)

The subjects of this chapter have historical records that make it possible to trace in detail their changing status in the region. They can also be seen as metaphors, representing four different scenarios that have emerged in the past 320 years. Passenger pigeons (*Ectopistes migratorius*) were here in astounding numbers, but through market hunting and gratuitous slaughter the species is now globally extinct. Greater prairie chickens (*Tympanuchus cupido*) were also abundant, although to a much lesser extent, and because of hunting and habitat loss they are now locally extinct. With destruction of the lowlands and some hunting, sandhill cranes (*Grus canadensis*) seemed destined to follow the prairie chicken, but unlike that species has managed to rebound and is once again a common sight. And finally, there are the double-crested cormorants (*Phalacrocorax auritus*), gulls, and certain herons (all colonial nesters), some of which now breed here in greater numbers than they ever have before, or least since interested people left written records. Within this chapter, then, stories range from the bleakest to the most encouraging.

Remembering Martha and Her Kin: Passenger Pigeon

Arlie Schorger was a chemist in Madison, Wisconsin, who combed the collections of the State Historical Society of Wisconsin in search of all references to wildlife (apparently excluding waterfowl). This included reading every newspaper held by the society. He produced numerous papers based on this research, a wonderful body of work that has been a major inspiration to me. His crowning achievement, though, was *The Passenger Pigeon: Its History and Extinction*, one of the finest biographies ever written about a bird. (In researching it, Schorger went well beyond the confines of his hometown and wound up consulting over ten thousand references.) It is impossible to disagree with Schorger's primary assertion: "Viewed from all angles, the passenger pigeon was the most impressive species of bird that man has known."[1]

The story of the passenger pigeon and its extinction has been told often, and it should be. I believe that its demise may represent the greatest act of vandalism ever perpetrated by our species against another. Schorger estimates that at the time of settlement, the species enjoyed a population that was between 3 and 5 billion birds. Given that in the early nineteenth century one flight in Kentucky was conservatively calculated as being of 2,230,272,000 individuals and another in Ontario exceeded 3,717,000,000, the high end of Schorger's range seems plausible. It was the most abundant bird the world has ever known and may have comprised 25–40 percent of this country's avian population.

For the last century of its life, the passenger pigeon was subjected to human depredations of a magnitude and ferocity as difficult to imagine as the bird's abundance. The huge concentrations were attacked in every conceivable way: gunners by the hundreds emerged with the arrival of the flocks; birds were netted; chicks were knocked out of their nests with poles and blunt arrows; cannons were filled with scrap and discharged into the trees, clearing large swaths of nests; trees heavy with nests would be carefully felled so as to knock over others; roosting and nesting sites were deliberately set ablaze; sulphur was burned in attempts to asphyxiate squabs and brooding adults; and there were instances when men lured pigeons using grain laced with strychnine. Pigs were turned loose to feed on the maimed and dead surplus. And for every adult killed, the chances plummeted that its fledgling would survive. With the advent of the railroads and telegraph, information on gatherings was quickly disseminated, and the birds were pursued year round. Hundreds of people would descend on the sites, resulting in trainloads of pigeons sent to such markets as St. Louis and Chicago.

It was still possible to find huge concentrations of passenger pigeons in the 1870s, a fact that disguised the true plight of the species and thwarted conservation attempts. These survivors represented but a fraction of the previous numbers. In addition, the almost total collapse of successful reproduction meant that the population consisted largely of older birds past their prime breeding age. Wild birds were for all intents and purposes gone by 1900, and the last member of the species, twenty-nine-year-old Martha, died in her cage in the Cincinnati Zoo sometime before 1:00 P.M. on September 1, 1914.

The biggest and best-documented nestings occurred north of the Chicago region, mostly in central Wisconsin and Michigan. A few instances of large local nestings have been recorded however. According to George Brennan, author of *The Wonders of the Dunes*, "myriads" of pigeons nested among the pines of the Indiana Dunes. One old resident spoke of going "many times at night with his father to the nesting and roosting places of the big pines and knock[ing] over the birds with a club. . . . They were so common the settlers got tired of them." One commentator refers to a nesting in the vicinity of Racine that was acres in size: "Every tree is literally covered with their nests, so much so that branches a foot in diameter are frequently broken down by their weight, and squabs are taken and carried off by bushels and wagon loads."[2]

Another example is the 1864 nesting in Berrien and Van Buren Counties, characterized by Schorger as being "aberrant" because it involved the breeding of birds still in immature plumage: "Thirty-two years ago there was a big nesting between South Haven and Saint Joseph on Lake Michigan. About one week after the main body commenced nesting, a new body of great size, covering hundreds of acres, came and joined them. . . . I found they were all young birds less than a year old, which could be easily explained from their mottled coloring."[3]

A newspaper in Whitewater, Walworth County, described the young pigeons in a nesting of unrecorded size: "The squabs lie blinking in their nests for hours. On finding themselves deserted, they toddle to the rims of their baskets [nests] and balance themselves. After a preliminary flutter of the wings they strike out for a limb, reach it, lose their equilibrium and tumble to the ground. They then wander about like drunken men for three or four days ere they know enough to seek food or water. Fully a week elapses before they are in good flying condition."

During this weak period, the chicks were both vulnerable and desirable, for they fed on beech and other nuts that made them exceedingly plump and delicious. Harvesters would shake them off branches, and the resulting thud resembled falling apples. Live chicks were then "grasped between the first and second fingers and with a snap the crop and head were removed in one operation." Many others wound up on roadways where they were crushed by traffic, particularly during inclement weather.

A nesting in Van Buren County, Michigan (just north of Berrien County), in 1872 illustrates one of the purposes for which the pigeons were used. A dealer bought 8,400 live birds for shooting contests: back then pigeons were not clay. Mortality during transport was high, depending on the weather and care received by the birds. Forty thousand out of a total of sixty thousand captured in Missouri died before they reached market for want of water.

Chicago was a center for handling live birds. Two local firms seemed to have dominated the business here. Bond and Ellsworth had the space for keeping twelve thousand birds, while Thomas Stagg could make available twenty-three thousand pigeons. One of Stagg's facilities was a former barn that could hold five thousand birds. Henry Coale relates what he saw on a visit: "When the pigeons were put into this huge cage they were so thirsty, that many drank themselves to death, or were killed in the scramble for water."[4]

The shooting tournaments that consumed so many birds were quite popular. Forty to forty-five thousand pigeons were used in a single shoot held in New York in 1874 and fourteen thousand at a similar exercise in Peoria. Among the participants, one Captain Adam Bogardus was the preeminent shooter of his day, the Michael Jordan of bird blasters. During one competition conducted in Dexter Park, Chicago, he won $1,000 by killing five hundred birds in 528 minutes.

Passenger pigeons were most successful when they nested in huge masses. But much smaller groups ranging down to individual pairs often nested as well. Relatively few of these have been recorded for this region. In Warren Township, Lake County (Ill.), Edward Lawson reported that twenty-five pairs nested on his grandfather's property in 1883 and one in 1885. Charles Douglas of Waukegan wrote of the species in his area: "You know the nests in this locality were few and only one pair of birds to each nest. . . . All the nests I found were in the same place each year, and in groups of three or four, not many rods apart, in the big pines near the Lake at Beach (a mile north of Waukegan), and in a small hard-wood grove about a mile west."[5] *The Birds of Indiana* mentions breeding in La Porte, Newton, Porter, and Starke Counties but gives no further details except that "the birds were said to have nested . . . 'in great numbers' along the Kankakee River."[6]

If local writers rarely noted actual nestings, they chronicled in detail the huge flocks that passed over and roosted during migration. In the fall at Racine, passenger pigeons would appear from the north, hugging the lakeshore until they reached the mouth of the Root River and headed inland. Their numbers would blot out the sun for a half hour at a time as they swept by at elevations no greater than twenty-five or thirty feet above the ground. That the birds flew so low made them easy victims of human ingenuity. A number of young men rigged up a "pigeon killer," a long pole stuck in the ground on a high point along the river and to which they attached cords "in opposite directions." When the pigeons arrived, the fellows "would vibrate the pole rapidly by pulling the cords alternately, the top of the pole knocking hundreds of them to earth." At another location, just south of the city, two brothers fished for birds by tying a hundred-foot long seine as high up in two trees as possible. As the birds smashed into the net, "some would fall to the ground and others would become entangled in its meshes." Other residents took a much more literal approach to harvesting pigeons and resorted to garden rakes and pitchforks.[7]

Ferdinand Schapper writes of the species in southern Cook County: "Wild pigeons were here in such immense flocks that it seems incredible today. . . . I have seen the trees so full that you could hear the branches breaking off all around you. There were millions of them, and when they arose for a flight, it sounded like a tornado, and the sun would be obscured by the flocks."[8]

He augments his own recollections with old Chicago newspaper clippings. On September 17, 1836, the press reported: "A few days ago our town was swarming with pigeons; the horizon in almost every direction was black with them." Similar sights were observed by Lucien Yoe, a student at Lake Forest Academy (Lake County, Ill.) from 1860 to 1863: "In the spring, the passenger pigeons flew north in flocks that almost obscured the sun. In the autumn during their migrations south, when they lit in the oak trees to feed on acorns, one could bag three and four in a single shot."[9]

A correspondent to the *American Field* reported on the events that transpired in Morgan Park, Chicago, on September 28, 1883: "Wild pigeons were about in large numbers in the woods, and even in the yards, and perched on the houses all day. The birds were very young, as I discovered by shooting ten of them before breakfast, and which I enjoyed in pot pie at supper."[10]

By the 1890s, the species' fate was reasonably clear. Efforts to document the last sightings were made by ornithologists across the country. E. B. Clark wrote a vivid article for the *Chicago Tribune* of his last passenger pigeon, seen in Lincoln Park in April 1893:

> He was perched on the limb of a soft maple and was facing the rising sun. I had never seen in any cabinet a more perfect specimen. The tree on which he was resting was at the southeast corner of the park. There were no trees between him and the lake to break from his breast the fullness of the glory of the rising sun. The pigeon allowed me to approach within twenty yards of his resting place, and I watched him through a powerful glass that permitted as minute an examination as if he were in my hand. I was more than astonished to find here close to the pavements of a great city the representative of a race which always loved the wild woods and which I thought had passed away from Illinois forever.[11]

The species was not quite gone, however. A specimen was taken from a small group encountered at Liverpool, Lake County (Ind.), in March 1894. One was shot in Lake Forest on August 7, 1895, and another near Delavan

Lake on September 8, 1896. The last local specimen about which there is apparently no dispute was collected in Rogers Park, Chicago "about" 1897.[12]

Several specimen records vie for the "honor" of being the last passenger pigeon killed in the wild. George Clingman collected a young male at Bryn Mawr, Chicago, on either September 30, 1891, or September 30, 1901.[13] Schorger lists the record under the latter date but, ultimately, rejects it because the mounted bird was destroyed in a fire, thereby making it impossible to examine. He concludes that the last wild passenger pigeon was a young male shot in Pike County, Ohio, in 1900 and now housed at Ohio State University.[14]

In an effort to determine whether the species was still extant, members of the American Ornithologists Union began offering in 1909 various rewards totaling $2,200 to locate remaining birds. At the end of three years, no credible claims for the money had been received.

A Chronicle of the Boom Times: Prairie Chicken

Bennett's Comet blazed in the predawn sky, taking our minds off the penetrating cold of single digit temperatures and a northeast wind of fifteen miles per hour. The date was March 29, 1970, and four of us were standing on a roadside near North Newton High School (Morocco, Newton County) listening for prairie chickens. At the same place a year earlier, we watched and heard two males displaying, their orange neck sacs conspicuously inflated as they danced furiously for the hens that would never come. Eventually, on this morning, the haunting boom of a lovelorn cock reached us through the creeping light. We never saw the bird, although we might have heard a second.

According to state records, Indiana Department of Natural Resources biologist Robert D. Feldt would be the last person ever to see a prairie chicken in the state and the Chicago region. He saw one male at the above location on April 3, 1972. (None were observed in 1971.) While unsubstantiated reports were made as late as 1974, it is safe to conclude that, within a year or two of Feldt's sighting, the prairie chicken was no longer a part of the local fauna.[15]

That the prairie chicken hung on in this region as long as it did is a thing to marvel. Having lost the tallgrass quarters out of which it evolved, the bird had to fend for itself in a world dominated by a species too stingy to share. But on crystalline mornings in early spring, prairie chicken music would conjure up the bygone images. In the loveliest passage in his fine book *Where the Sky Begins*, John Madson describes the magic: "It is a lonely wild sound made by a lonely wild bird. It has the quality of an ancient wind blowing across the smokeflap of a wickiup—companion noise to an Indian courting flute, and the dream of unshod pony hooves on bluestem sod. In all of modern America, there is no more lost plaintive old-time sound than the booming of a native prairie chicken."[16]

With Feldt's final observation of that lone bird, the history of the prairie chicken in this region came to an end, one more connection with the glorious and wild past severed forever. But what a past it was.

◄o► ◄o► ◄o►

Prairie chickens were commonly noted by the earliest of European explorers. Father Marquette has the distinction of being the first European to encounter the prairie chicken in the region and perhaps the first anywhere to describe it. The priest records in his entry of December 12, 1674, that "Jacques brought a partridge which he had killed, quite similar to that of France, except that it had, as it were, two little wings of three or four feathers a finger long near the head with which they cover the neck where there are no feathers."[17] It is, in fact, these little appendages of feathers, thought by Linnaeus to resemble the wings of a Roman god, that give the bird its Latin name of *cupido*.

In 1828, as John Fonda followed the Des Plaines south from Wisconsin, prairie chickens "were to be seen budding on the trees, and we killed [an] abundance of them as we passed along." Five years later at nearby Fort Dearborn, Daniel Tasker recalled huge numbers of this species: "Dear me, what a pest they were for several years, for they destroyed the cornfields rapidly. I have seen thousands on a tree close to Kinzie Bridge and have killed them by the hundreds. Once, at Naperville, [DuPage,] I shot into such a flock as I spoke of and I verily believe I killed more than can be put in this house." Also writing about DuPage, although in the 1840s, William Pearse remembers things a little differently: "The prairie swarms with wild hens . . . , but the natives don't care to waste their powder and shot on them."[18]

From the 1840s through the 1870s prairie chickens were killed in incredible quantities and in a variety of ways, some of which were even unintentional. Old news articles report that many birds lost their lives because they flew into the telegraph wires that were being strung in and around Chicago; as many as five birds from a single flock were known to have died this way.[19]

Fire often proved highly destructive to prairie chickens. Fall burns would eliminate winter cover and food. But more harmful were burns in late spring. Robert Kennicott, northeastern Illinois's first naturalist, singled out fire as being particularly injurious because of the damage it caused to eggs. One writer stated his view that "if their nesting grounds had not been desolated by fire, and they had been allowed to increase to their natural limit, the cornfields of Illinois could not have fed them all."[20]

In some areas, residents set these fires to facilitate the gathering of eggs for their own consumption. Garrett Landwehr, of Barrington, told his son that in March 1855 he collected seventy eggs to see if he could raise them. After setting the eggs under domestic hens, the prairie chickens hatched but quickly thereafter ran away.[21]

While populations had already begun to decline by 1850, market hunters and "sportsmen" continued to exploit the birds with great gusto. Although much has been written on the taking of prairie chickens by shooting, Schorger says that many thousands were also obtained by trapping. Settlers near Racine used a large box with an open bottom and a top constructed of wooden slats. On either end, wicker doors swung easily inward but not the reverse. Thus once the birds entered the contraption in search of the grain bait, they couldn't get out.[22]

Robert Saunders had been a merchant in Chicago's famous South Water Street Market since the 1840s. In 1889, he told of the prairie chicken trade in those earlier years: "I paid the young men who procured the game for me seven shillings per dozen for [ruffed] grouse and prairie chickens, and sold them at wholesale for eight shillings. Such grouse and chickens as they were, big and fat! Two men would go out a few miles from the city with shotguns and a covered wagon to bring the game back in. The fowl would fill themselves with grain and then sit moping, hundreds of them, on the fences and in the fields. The hunters would fire into them, and bring down ten at a shot."[23]

Saunders and his fellow merchants regretted their inability to sell their game to eastern markets where prices were higher. Trains were not yet an option, and transport via the lakes was limited because ice was unavailable for refrigeration in the warm months and too plentiful to allow the passage of ships in winter. As an experiment, "a four-horse prairie schooner" loaded up with 1,650 ruffed grouse and 3,500 prairie chickens left for New York in November 1850. A year later, six thousand prairie chickens were shipped from Michigan City, La Porte County, and over a six-week period around the same time twenty thousand birds were sent from Lake County (Ind.) to Detroit. Even as late as 1873, an incredible 600,000 prairie chickens were sold to Chicago markets.[24]

By 1850, Colonel Arthur Cunynghame embarked on a hunting excursion south of Chicago. In Thornton, Cook County, he met a "rough-looking hunter," perhaps one of Saunders employees, who said he had taken more than two thousand prairie chickens that season. Another fellow said he once shot 160 in one day. As for his own efforts, Cunynghame found that it was easy to bag fifty to eighty birds a day, but such results were no longer possible within fifty miles of Chicago.[25]

Three records from 1873 reveal that the species was still widespread and even plentiful in places. A flock over Racine was thought to be migrating, something the species did regularly in the northern part of its range in the days when it was abundant. In tandem with his dog Joe, a hunter obtained ten to fifteen plump prairie chickens over the course of a two-hour session in the vicinity of Palatine, Cook County. Finally, that fall a party of six men and four dogs spent ten days hunting near what was then Remington, Jasper County. In their first several hours of morning shooting, they brought down forty prairie chickens. But not wanting to kill more than they could use, the group limited itself to a total take of two hundred birds.[26]

Schorger devotes the last twenty-two pages of his brilliant article on the history of the prairie chicken in Wisconsin to a year-by-year "prairie chicken annals" spanning the period from 1855 to 1900. The last twenty-five years reflect a not surprising downward trend mixed with upward blips. The year 1875 was a good one, with "several hundred" being shot on the first day of the season at Lake Geneva. The birds were down the following year—the highest daily total was the dozen taken by two men at Delavan. In 1880, numbers were generally depressed, but by the next year prairie chickens rebounded modestly, especially at Kenosha where one hunter had a single-day tally of forty-seven. A few short years later, however, a newspaper article in 1887 proclaimed that the prairie chicken was gone from Elkhorn. That twenty-one were killed on September 1, 1888, near Racine is the last mention of the Chicago region to appear in the annals.[27]

Schorger ends his piece saying that from 1898 to 1900, "the population remained at a low level, and it is unnecessary to go into details." Apparently, prairie chickens lasted in the Kettle Moraine area until the 1940s. Sam Robbins gives 1939 and 1949 as the last years for this species in Racine County and Kenosha County, respectively. (Prairie chickens still exist farther north in Wisconsin.)[28]

Robert Ridgway, probably the greatest ornithologist Illinois ever produced, published his book *The Ornithology of Illinois* in 1895. He devotes two short paragraphs to the prairie chicken, the first of which states: "To describe in a work intended especially for Illinois readers the habits of the prairie chicken, seems almost as superfluous a proceeding as 'carrying coals to Newcastle.'"[29] When those words were written, the species had already begun its plummet toward virtual extinction within the state, but small populations persisted in a variety of places, including the Chicago region. (Two flocks, under careful management, still survive near Effingham, in south-central Illinois.)

Benjamin Gault wrote of his experiences with the species in the late 1800s: "My first experience with [the prairie chicken]. . . was in Chicago. I accidentally stumbled on a nest in that portion of Garfield Park, then Central Park, south of Madison Street, a section left wild and unchanged. The nest contained 15 eggs, and I remember it as well as though it happened yesterday. . . . Chickens were then fairly common on the virgin prairie lands all the way to the Des Plaines River and beyond toward Lombard and Prospect Park (now Glen Ellyn)."[30]

88. Hunter with prairie chicken, Melendy Prairie, Kettle Moraine,
Walworth County, circa 1920. (Courtesy Kettle Moraine
State Forest Archives, Eagle, Wis.)

Born in 1904, William Klingenberg grew up on a farm on Harbor Road between Route 22 and Cuba Road in Lake County (Ill.). In the springtime, on his way to school, he would "hear the prairie chicken booming its call and drumming its wings." And retired naturalist Chuck Westcott tells of his father visiting the Edward Hines racetrack in Maywood (Cook County) in 1915 to watch the legendary Barney Oldfield compete in his "Golden Bug" automobile. On spring evenings, the elder Westcott would hear the courting prairie chickens whose lek (booming ground) was located across First Avenue where the Hines Hospital and Loyola Medical Center now stand. Westcott still possesses two mounted birds shot by his father and grandfather in the 1920s along the East Branch of the DuPage River close to the present site of the Morton Arboretum.[31]

Howard Christian remembers a flock of about forty individuals that gathered on a particular hill near his home in Newark, Kendall County. They "would have any foliage stamped down, so a large spot would be just dust." The birds disappeared soon after 1935, but the county game warden reported in a 1944 state survey that two flocks still inhabited the county. Paul Spittel informs me that there was a lek in Saratoga Township, Grundy County, until 1943.

This was perhaps one of the four flocks reported from the county in 1944 as part of the state survey, which also recorded the last Will County occurrence, identified as "one small group of seven or eight."[32]

Prairie chickens were sighted from the McGinnis Slough area (Orland Park, Cook County) as late as 1946, but the last published record for northeastern Illinois is that of a single bird reported by a Cook County Forest Preserve naturalist near Elmhurst on July 26, 1948. It flew in front of his car and across Route 83 into a large marsh now occupied by a Wal-Mart. The most remarkable claim, however, is that the species survived near Starke Station, Kane County until the mid-1960s. Robert Morris, a former Kane County commissioner, says that he first became familiar with the bird in November 1953, when as a ten-year-old he shot one with his first .410. At that time there were two flocks in the vicinity, totaling forty to fifty individuals. They lived on a large tract of land bounded by Highway 20, Plank Road, Route 47, and Marshall Road. Portions of it were not plowed until the 1950s and the center held a thirty-acre marsh. Morris's family home was adjacent to this area, and over the next ten years he watched the gradual diminution of the population until only one or two birds remained.[33]

On more than one occasion, the Cook County Forest Preserve District has released prairie chickens onto its holdings. The most recent and ambitious attempt began at Crabtree Lake Nature Center (Barrington) in the summer of 1964 when site manager Charles Westcott received forty-two prairie chickens from a captive flock maintained at the University of Illinois. He and his wife Lorraine spent many an eighteen-hour day caring for their valuable wards. They planned on liberating half the birds in early September. However, when two succumbed to histomoniasis, an illness of domestic poultry also known as blackhead disease, they decided to keep the flock until spring.[34]

But in January an ice storm damaged the pens that held the birds. Four prairie chickens escaped, and two fell prey to a raccoon. A month later, just prior to the new release date, a long-tailed weasel managed to enter the enclosure and kill fifteen prairie chickens in one night. Several survivors managed to produce and raise young that spring. That number was augmented by sixty-six eggs obtained from the university flock; of those, thirty-four chicks survived through the eighth week. Later in the summer, ten more young birds arrived from Champaign.

In the summer of 1965, Westcott began to release birds at both Crabtree and Spring Creek Forest Preserves, two and a half miles away. He saw broods at Crabtree until September and at Spring Creek until August. But after that they vanished, and on August 28, 1967, the last of the captive prairie chickens were returned to the University of Illinois. In hindsight, Westcott believes that failure was inevitable. The amount of land the district was committed to keeping as grassland, free from heavy recreational use, was simply not enough to allow the survival of a viable prairie chicken population.

This discussion ends, as it began, in northwestern Indiana. Although by 1940 prairie chickens were still present in a number of Indiana counties, the only sizable populations left totaled about a thousand birds in two Newton County townships. State biologist William B. Barnes probably spent more time on preserving these last birds than anyone else. He tells of the fate of the largest gathering: "In Newton County by far the largest concentration was on the old Bogus Island Ranch owned by E. S. Earling of Chicago. He had large switchgrass and bluestem pastures. The one on Section Nine held the most chickens. The next owner destroyed everything . . . in his greed for money for corn and soybeans."[35]

When the opportunity arose in 1943, Barnes optioned a large parcel of prairie chicken range. With federal money and the help of the Izaak Walton League, Indiana Audubon Society, and other conservation groups, the 640 acres were bought and eventually became the Beaver Lake Prairie Chicken Refuge. The purchase was significant, but Barnes and others considered "it too little, too late"; there simply was not enough interest by the public or official-dom to preserve the species. While it still provides sanctuary to a host of prairie organisms, Indiana's prairie chicken refuge after 1953 had no more prairie chickens than downtown Indianapolis.

Surveys of displaying males over the next twenty years document the in-exorable decline in the few sites where they still remained: biologists counted 212 birds in 1955 and only one in 1972. Besides the ongoing loss of habitat, the occasional bird would be "shot [by] some old time hunter who wanted to shoot one more chicken before he died."[36] Far more vicious, a new landowner delib-erately set fire to a lek in the spring of 1962 or 1963 and reportedly incinerated many of the birds that used it.

Jim Swartz, a longtime outdoorsman from Morocco, related his final memories of the species: "I don't know for sure when I saw my last chicken. It just happened that they disappeared real gradual-like . . . and one day I woke up and they was gone. At times like this, when I get to remembering them . . . by God, I miss them. I miss hearing them cocks booming and seeing them dance in spring. Yeah. They was really something."[37]

The Triumph of the Trumpeters: Sandhill Crane

In March 1967, several months after I started bird-watching, my mother took my sister and me to Grand Island, Nebraska, to see one of the continent's pre-mier ornithological spectacles. For sixty or so miles along the Platte River, a hundred thousand sandhill cranes gather to feed and display before dispersing northward to their nesting grounds. As we approached our destination late in the day, we could see clouds of birds in the distance, the individuals too indistinct to identify. With the certainty of a twelve-year-old, I rejected my mother's suggestion that they were cranes; geese I could believe, but surely there could not be that many cranes. She was right, of course, and after two days of watching and listening to these magnificent birds, we fell under their spell.

Years later, I read Aldo Leopold's "Marshland Elegy," which appears in the standard edition of *A Sand County Almanac*, and learned that our reaction was not unusual. In this essay, almost as gorgeous as its subject, Leopold wrote: "Our ability to perceive quality in nature begins, as in art, with the pretty. It expands through successive stages of the beautiful to values as yet uncaptured by language. The quality of cranes lies, I think, in this higher gamut, as yet beyond the reach of words."[38]

◄o► ◄o► ◄o►

In the old days, sandhill cranes nested abundantly in the wet prairies and marshes that were so common in the region. Writing in 1854, Kennicott says that "a few years since this species was very abundant here, and flocks of over a hundred birds might be seen in their uncouth dances." Dr. Philo Hoy, referring to the 1840s, provides a similar story from Racine: "Sandhill cranes were so common that one could not go any considerable distance on the prairies without seeing numbers of these stately birds."[39]

But perhaps the largest concentration of sandhill cranes occurred in the Beaver Lake section of the Kankakee Marsh: "At such times numbers of these birds gathered on a high spot of the prairie adjacent to the water. They formed in a circle, each one equidistant from his neighbor, and thus disposed they went through a series of movements strangely akin to the figures of a quadrille. Always there was a dignity of movement and a seriousness of mien and deportment altogether amusing, interesting and quite out of the ordinary."[40]

Sandhill cranes declined rapidly. When and where the last sandhill crane nested in the Illinois portion of the Chicago region seems to have escaped notice, but the last breeding anywhere in the state was in Champaign County in 1872. Jasper County, near Parr, was the scene of Indiana's last nesting in 1929. Nesting cranes were still present in Walworth County in 1903, but a quarter century later, these too were gone, and a statewide survey could find only five pairs in all of Wisconsin. (If the bird ever bred in Berrien County, Walkinshaw fails to mention it, despite his detailed county-by-county discussion of Michigan.)[41]

As with the passenger pigeon and the prairie chicken, sandhill cranes suffered from habitat loss and hunting. Attempts to drain Horicon Marsh in central Wisconsin (not very successful), the Kankakee Marsh (very successful), and other wetlands reduced crane range by millions of acres. Fire suppression enabled willows and other woody plants to take hold of many wetlands, rendering them unsuitable for cranes. Areas otherwise too wet for agriculture were subjected to grazing and haying. This was particularly true in southern Wisconsin where hay was used to insulate ice and pack the golden output of Milwaukee's breweries.[42]

Lawrence Walkinshaw, in his classic *The Sandhill Cranes*, gives voice to his belief that shooting was most responsible for the species' decimation. In Indiana, market hunters took birds, but in Wisconsin evidence suggests that subsistence hunting had a more deleterious effect on the cranes than either market or sport hunting because the difficulty in obtaining birds exceeded what was either fun or profitable. An 1884 account from Lacon, Illinois (in Marshall County, two counties southwest of the Chicago region), describes how cranes could be shot:

> Where corn adjoined a wheat or oat stubble, they would alight in that and then approach the corn in the most wary skirmisher style. . . . Shy birds? I should say they were. Here they were always very careful in looking out for the safety of companions . . . with this one exception: the cranes . . . are very greedy and nearly always hungry, hence sometimes when a bunch would visit a field . . . and the grub was good and plentiful, they all fall to eating at once, leaving no sentries. At such times one with good care could get quite close to them. . . . Many a one have I laid low with my little old single shotgun.[43]

Another incident throws light on one of the culinary uses of sandhill cranes. "Uncle Joe" wrote of an acquaintance with a sweet tooth who lived near Chicago during the 1830s: "Thanksgiving time was drawing near, and Mrs. Peters wanted to make some mince pies. Meat was pretty scarce at the time and fruits and sugar were costly articles. But her mind was set on pie, and pie she must have. The chopped breasts of sandhill cranes and mashed crab apples, sweetened with a spoonful of molasses and well-spiced, made that mince meat. A wedge of that pie was enough to break the courage of the stoutest settler and never failed in a single instance."[44]

Although an inconsequential factor in the decline of the species, sandhill cranes were coveted as pets. Robert Kennicott kept one at his family home ("The Grove") in Glenview during the 1850s: "It had the run of the place, followed the children around, and was always present when plowing and digging were going on because it relished the insect larvae, mice, shrews, and moles that were turned up." In the spring of 1855, Garrett Landwehr caught two crane chicks near his home in Barrington. As the birds matured, they would take food from his hand. Unfortunately, "one day the wind blew so hard, they got hurt and died." The strangest story of a captive crane refers to the one killed in California in 1881. The bird allegedly had a silver quarter hanging from its neck by wire and on the coin were inscribed these words: "Captured at Fort Duquesne, May 25, 1783. Released at Fort Dearborn [Chicago], November 17, 1846."[45]

In contrast to the passenger pigeon and prairie chicken, however, neither changing land use nor hunting was intense enough to doom the resilient sandhill crane. In fact, one form of agriculture proved to be highly beneficial. The cranberry industry in central Wisconsin protected marshes and maintained adequate water levels for the birds. Sandhill cranes also demonstrated they could make do with small marshes (some less than twenty acres in size have supported cranes) and survive in relative proximity to people. Even when populations were low during the 1940s, cranes bred within fifty miles of Detroit.[46]

In assessing the decrease of cranes in the Midwest, Walkinshaw wrote: "The prairie and plains areas, which the cranes deserted when the human populations there were still small, lacked one of the characteristics of other crane marshes: the isolation produced by mountain ridges, woodland, and water. On the plains, isolation was merely of distance; the grasses and sedges of the marshes, which human vision was readily able to penetrate, were the only cover." Requiring neither actual remoteness nor vast wetlands, sandhill cranes needed most of all to be left alone. With legal protection and the restoration of some marshland, the birds have increased dramatically. This manifests itself in the growing numbers of both migrants and breeding pairs.[47]

There is one place in the region where sandhill cranes gather in proportions of continental significance. During spring and fall, most of the sandhill cranes in the eastern United States stop at Jasper-Pulaski State Fish and Wildlife Area near Medaryville, Indiana (Jasper County). Their use of this site mirrors the rising fortune of the species itself.

Jasper-Pulaski came into being when the Indiana Department of Fish and Game purchased 520 acres of woods and marsh in 1929 as a "game reservation." This tract was located in a corner of where Beaver Lake used to be and was drained ("reclaimed") land that remained "unsuitable for agriculture." Over the next two years, state holdings had increased to 4,908 acres at a cost of $86,482. (Jasper-Pulaski has expanded in size over the decades to its current eight thousand acres.) The first land management done on the property consisted of planting trees and blocking ditches to create marshland. Predator control was also initiated. A partial list of the "vermin count" for 1931 includes "sparrow hawks 9, marsh hawks 23, monkey-faced owl 10, barred owl 10," and assorted other birds, mammals, and reptiles.[48]

Sandhill cranes first appeared at Jasper-Pulaski in 1935, when nine were reported. By the fall of 1942, 135 birds used the site at one time. Over the next forty-five years, the increase was slow, with twenty-five hundred counted in 1967. But then peak numbers rose dramatically: from five thousand in 1972 to an incredible thirty-two thousand in 1991. Since 1988, the high tallies have hovered around fifteen thousand.[49] (Counts are made in the fall when the crane population is at its highest. The results are based on single day censuses, derived by placing observers at strategic points throughout the refuge and then combining their numbers.) The majestic displays enacted before the eyes of the early settlers, as choreographed by the forces of history and described by Burroughs, now unfold on the same stage to the pleasure of moderns.

As the cranes make their way to and from Jasper-Pulaski, their trumpeting drifts gently out of the sky like rain on parched fields. Until the recent population explosion, their migration route through the region was along a fairly narrow front. Steve Mlodinow in his *Chicago Area Birds* describes it as "a line from Jasper-Pulaski to Willow Slough [Newton County] to Flossmoor to Longjohn Slough to Crabtree Lake to Chain O' Lakes and then into Wisconsin."[50] They tended to stay inland from the lake, but when weather conditions dictated, exceptions occurred. Over several hours on a bitterly cold day in November 1971, a group of us watched flocks of cranes totaling over four hundred individuals stream south along the Chicago lakefront. The birds were too high to hear, as they passed in front of skyscrapers fighting the thirty-five-mile-an-hour west wind. Charley Clark, who had been birding in Chicago for more than forty years, had never seen them along the lake before.

Tichigan State Wildlife Refuge in northwestern Racine County was the only site in the Chicago region to have nesting sandhill cranes in 1968. Five years later, the three Wisconsin counties had five breeding locations, and the number has been steadily increasing ever since.

On May 24, 1979, I found an adult with two downy young at Deer Lake, near Antioch, Lake County. It was the first nesting in Illinois in over a century, but many more have followed. Breeding, or at least summering pairs, has been seen in most of the region's Illinois counties. Indiana's first recent breeding record occurred in 1982 in Steuben County in the northeastern part of the state, but another nested at Willow Slough in 1993.[51]

In the same essay I quoted earlier, Leopold laments the loss of cranes: "Amid the endless mediocrity of the commonplace, a crane marsh holds a paleontological patent of nobility, and revocable only by shotgun. The sadness discernible in some marshes arises, perhaps, from their once having harbored cranes."[52] Although Leopold did not live to see it, that sadness has now lifted, like the shrouds of fog he alludes to in his essay. The cranes have retaken their own.

Changing Status of the Colonial Nesters: Herons, Cormorants, and Gulls

Certain water birds tend to nest in colonies, often consisting of several species. In this region, these include two species of gulls, three species of herons, and double-crested cormorants. As rookeries expand in size, the sight, sound, and even smell become impossible for people to ignore. This has proven to be both detrimental and advantageous. The birds were easy to exploit for commercial purposes but also easy to monitor to determine changes in their status. And perhaps most important, they confer a distinction on otherwise drab places that is easily appreciated by a wide range of citizens.

These species were among the many that suffered terribly at the hands of the millinery trade during the nineteenth and early twentieth centuries. Fashion favored women's headwear adorned with the body parts of birds. One ornithologist surveyed hats while strolling through Manhattan and found that 542 out of seven hundred contained at least some portion of twenty different species. The millinery industry consumed more than 5 million birds a year in this country alone.[53] Herons were affected most dramatically, as their long plumes were especially coveted. The immaculately white great egret (*Ardea alba*) and snowy egret (*Egretta thula*) almost disappeared from the United States as a result. Fortunately, this bloodbath produced another consequence as well: it spawned the country's conservation movement, with the National Audubon Society leading the successful fight for legislative protection.

As the egrets declined, gulls and terns were killed in increasing numbers. And unlike the herons, gulls and some terns nest on the ground where they are vulnerable to egg collecting. Reductions in these species led to the virtual extinction of the least tern (*Sterna antillarum*—which is still federally endangered) and the survival of but one herring gull (*Larus argentatus*) colony along the entire Atlantic Coast. The Great Lakes gull colonies fared poorly as well. Samuel Robbins describes the assaults suffered by herring gulls on islands off Door County, Wisconsin: "Early in the nineteenth century Indians and early settlers made many trips to them to obtain eggs for food and for sale. Later in the nineteenth century plume hunters valued the sleek white feathers for millinery use. Early in the twentieth century fruit growers trying to raise grapes on Strawberry Island attempted to drive off the gulls. Oologists came to collect eggs. Fishermen paid visits to cut down the population of birds that they perceived as a threat to their industry."[54]

The status of these birds in the Chicago region must be evaluated in this larger context. By the time the first naturalists, Philo Hoy of Racine and Robert Kennicott of Northfield (Cook County), began their work in the 1840s, populations were already ebbing. Thus there are no historical breeding records of double-crested cormorants, herring gulls, and ring-billed gulls (*Larus delawarensis*) from this area, and great egrets were concentrated on the Kankakee River. (Although they did nest to the north of this region in Wisconsin.) The expanded breeding ranges that these birds now enjoy in the area is a recent phenomenon that represents partial recovery from the days of wholesale slaughter.[55]

Without question, ring-billed and herring gulls have done the best. Over the years, I have been asked several times why there are so many more gulls, particularly away from Lake Michigan. The answer is food. Huge landfills have provided a year-round supply capable of sustaining vast numbers of birds. Indeed, some commentators have said that the increase in gulls is a manifestation of the ultimate in landscape abuse. Since landfill space is being depleted at a rapid pace and it is politically almost impossible to establish new ones, this bounty will shrink in the future; time will tell whether gull numbers decrease as well.

The densest concentration of dumps in the area is at Lake Calumet, and so it is not surprising that gulls nested here first and in the largest numbers. In July 1975, eight hundred ring-billed gulls, including seventy-one chicks, were found on an island in the southeast corner of the lake. By the summer of 1993, the colony had grown to ten thousand nests. Herring gulls joined the colony in 1978, at which time three of their nests were discovered. Fifteen years later, observers estimated the number of herring nests as being between one and two thousand. Indiana established its first ring-billed gull nesting record in 1990 at East Chicago, a little more than ten miles from Lake Calumet. On a steel company landfill jutting into Lake Michigan, a thousand adults produced around seventy-two young, most not yet ready to fledge.[56]

Other habitats also attract nesting gulls. Two ring-billed colonies formed on dikes within the restricted and fish-stocked confines of Commonwealth Edison cooling ponds. The larger one, at Heidecke Lake in Grundy County, contained 249 nests at the peak of the 1993 breeding season, while the Dresden Power Plant in Will County had only twenty. Although a few young fledged from Dresden, not a single surviving chick could be found at Heidecke, presumably because of intense predation.[57]

The double-crested cormorant is the most recent of the colonial waterbirds to begin nesting in the region in large numbers. Birds began summering in numbers in the 1970s; by the 1980s they were nesting at numerous sites and are now common throughout the summer.[58]

In the face of pesticides and habitat destruction, herons have not fared nearly as well as the gulls and cormorants. A 1950s survey of Wisconsin great blue herons (*Ardea herodias*) was compared to a similar one conducted twenty years later. Results showed that heronries increased significantly in the northwestern part of the state and decreased significantly in the northeast and south. Further, the number of nests per colony declined from an average of fifty to forty. The Grabers, whose brilliant bird monographs for the Illinois Natural History Survey should be much better known than they are, and their collaborator Ethelyn Kirk found that great blues, great egrets, and black-crowned night herons (*Nycticorax nycticorax*) all declined in the 1970s after several decades of increase. They pull no punches: "Human activity could hardly be more destructive to heron populations if that were the goal." But recognizing the complexities at issue, they conclude with these words: "The problem of determining population trends of the herons is the problem of conducting studies that are both intensive and extensive in terms of area (hundreds of square miles) and time (20 years or more). The natural oscillations of any population are generally unknown, and the abandonment of a colony site cannot be assumed to be either a change of nesting locale or a population loss."[59]

Old accounts of heronries tend to lack detail as to species composition and numbers. It is not surprising that the largest concentrations in this region were along the Kankakee River. "Crane Heaven," located in Lake County, comprised thirty or forty acres of nesting herons. Most of the thousands of birds were great blue herons and black-crowned night herons, but great egrets were also present in large numbers.[60] Dr. F. E. Ling described another heronry, this one located near his home in Hebron, Porter County: " At different places in the swamp the cranes had what we called 'crane towns.' Hundreds of them would meet in one locality in the cottonwood trees. Many times I have seen as many as four or five nests in one tree. The largest town, the one we called 'lower crane town,' was estimated to have 1,000 cranes and, believe me, there was some music when the young were in the nests!"[61]

The Lake Calumet area supports the largest nesting groups of black-crowned night herons in this region and in Illinois as a whole. Seemingly more often than the larger herons, this species shifts location, abandoning one site to occupy another as water levels, disturbance, space, and other factors change. In the early 1990s, the night herons concentrated in the Big Marsh, but more recently they have moved to Indian Ridge Marsh and an adjacent site. This suggests that to keep black-crowned night herons, multiple nesting areas need to be available to accommodate their nomadic ways.[62]

Two of the premier heron rookeries in the Chicago region are Baker's Lake in Barrington, Cook County, and Lake Renwick in Plainfield, Will County. Human activities created the lakes that surround them, pose the greatest threats to their continuation, and provide the protection that offers the best promise for their survival. Perhaps no better examples exist locally of nature's resiliency: degraded land surrounded by development has been colonized by large, beautiful, and rare birds. Excluding only the cranes of Jasper-Pulaski, these two places feature the most striking and dependable display of avian life in the region. At your next summer visit, close your eyes for a moment; upon opening them, you will swear you've been transported to a swamp deep within the Okefenokee or Everglades.

What was to become Baker's Lake started out as a peat bog that flooded often.[63] Starting in the 1920s, tiles were laid and the property was drained—so successfully, in fact, that it caught fire in 1932. By 1935, the local citizenry had grown so tired of the smoke from the smoldering peat that they installed another set of pipes that was intended to reflood the area. That project also worked and led to the birth of 112-acre Baker's Lake.

Grebes, geese, ducks, coots, and other waterbirds soon began using the shallow lake as a migration stopover. Impressed by the birds, the Cook County Forest Preserve District bought Baker's Lake and much of the land around it. The Village of Barrington and the Barrington Park District also own key parcels on or near the lake.

In the middle of Baker's Lake is a small wooded island on which black-crowned night herons (an Illinois endangered species) began breeding in 1978. Observers counted thirty-three nests the first year, and the numbers grew steadily to a peak of 227 in 1984. That there were, for example, only five other black-crowned night heron colonies in the state (two of those are in this region) in 1983 underlined the significance of this discovery. Beginning in 1982, great blue herons and great egrets also joined the rookery: one nest of the former and two of the latter were found. Four years later, there were forty-seven great blue and eighteen great egret nests.

The three public owners have worked closely together to protect the biological resources of their holdings. They entered into a cooperative agreement that established a "nesting/rookery zone" to ensure minimal disturbance of the site. In 1984, the property was dedicated as a state nature preserve, one of the few focusing exclusively on animals. When a major shopping center/residential complex was proposed for a tract catty-corner from the lake, the two districts joined thousands of Barrington residents and others in convincing the Village Board to deny the petitioners request for a zoning change, thereby ending the threat.

Despite responsible owners and highly supportive citizens, the heronry at Baker's Lake was far from secure. Studies of the lake revealed that the island was losing its best nesting trees due to high water levels. This was particularly ominous for the night herons, which were being outcompeted for nesting sites by the earlier arriving great blues and egrets. The solution required installing a water control structure by which lake levels could be regulated. This was eventually done, but in the short term it was necessary to augment available nesting space. The various agencies decided to erect high-rise structures, a sort of CHA, Ciconiforme (the order of birds containing herons) Housing Authority. These "consisted of a star-shaped horizontal support, with 30 nesting platforms, raised approximately six feet above the ground. An additional 40 individual nesting platforms were mounted at varying heights on six poles which supported the horizontal support, and three additional poles located near the horizontal support."

On arriving in the spring, the herons were clearly skeptical of these new "trees." Disappointment among the biologists mounted as time passed and the birds continued to avoid the structures. But on the fourteenth day, black-crowns started using the artificial nests; they were followed by great blues on the nineteenth and great egrets on the thirty-seventh. The CHA was a success.

The rookery has continued to grow. A 1986 population of five summering double-crested cormorants mushroomed into thirty-five nesting pairs during both the 1992 and 1993 breeding seasons. Over the past ten years, a small colony of herring gulls has established itself as well. Five nests produced five fledglings in 1993. Great blue herons were up to ninety-four nests in 1992 and 117 in 1993. During the same two years, great egret nests increased to forty-five and seventy, respectively.

89. Biologists working on heron nesting structures at Baker's Lake, Barrington, Cook County. (Photo by and courtesy of Bob Montgomery.)

Sadly, the expanding numbers of the bigger herons produced a casualty. The black-crowned night heron, the pioneering heron of Baker's Lake, was absent throughout much of the 1990s, although a few have since returned. They tend to be outcompeted by their larger relatives and forced to utilize increasingly marginal nesting locations.

An excellent article by Joe Milosevich documents the history of three hundred–acre Lake Renwick and its rookery.[64] The earliest recollection of the property was from one elderly resident who said a Ku Klux Klan rally was held there in the late 1800s. (Where else have white herons replaced white supremacists?) Some years later, the county began removing gravel from the site for road grading, and by 1904 commercial operations were extracting over two hundred rail cars of crushed rock per day. A year or two after the Chicago Gravel Company bought the land in 1913, their digging reached springs, whose cool waters began to fill the pit. Although quarrying equipment had to be relocated to other portions of the property, the new lake was soon contributing to the firm's prosperity.

"Ice harvesting" became an important winter moneymaker. An early reference says sixteen people were employed in the mining, but 140 were needed to cut, haul, and store Lake Renwick's ice. Recognizing a potential summer market, an entrepreneur constructed a sand beach, pier, diving board, and bathhouse, where patrons could rent swimsuits. All of this was offered for three dollars a season. In the 1920s, a dancing establishment opened across Renwick Road from the lake; not to be missed, it boasted "big city dance music by Formento's Singing Syncopators." More important, in the same period Chicago Gravel stocked the lake with two carloads of unspecified fish.

The last business to reap the benefits of Lake Renwick's amenities was a popular restaurant called Powell's Mill, which served customers in the 1930s. It not only provided dining, dancing, and fishing but, apparently, pollution severe enough to force the closing of the beach. By the 1950s, Lake Renwick was encircled by a fence and largely devoid of human traffic.

Milosevich has carefully traced the probable antecedents of the Lake Renwick rookery. A large black-crowned night heron colony had been known for many years five miles north of the lake. At its peak in 1942, the heronry held eight hundred individuals. By 1960, apart from a few lingering birds, all that remained was a three-foot-thick layer of droppings. Another smaller group nested in a catalpa grove about the same distance from the lake. It disappeared in the mid- to late 1950s. The closest known great blue heron and great egret colony was one of modest size that inhabited a small quarry in Plainfield until the late 1940s.

The presence of breeding herons at Lake Renwick was first substantiated

Table 7. Number of Nests per Species at Lake Renwick Rookery

	1983	1986	1990	1993
Double-crested cormorant	0	6	109	211
Great blue heron	38	101	321	412
Cattle egret	12	8	12	14
Great egret	63	63	233	253
Black-crowned night heron	273	196	106	74

in 1961, when Dr. Bruce Wallin photographed nesting great egrets and black-crowned night herons. Two years later, great blue herons appeared. Cattle egret (*Bubulcus ibis*) nests were first found in 1971, and the lake remains their only breeding location in the region. Their population fluctuates between eight and twenty-two nests. The first and largest double-crested cormorant colony in the region began in 1986, with the discovery of six nests. (Table 7 illustrates the composition of the rookery in selected years.)

As was the case at Baker's Lake, the other birds at Lake Renwick are taking over nesting space once occupied by the black-crowned night herons. Fortunately, besides the four islands on which most of the nesting now occurs, Lake Renwick and its immediate environs contain a number of smaller islands ripe for colonizing. The night herons selected one of these in 1984 but wound up abandoning two hundred nests. As the birds relocate to more heavily vegetated sites, accurate censusing becomes difficult, if not impossible.

After owning Lake Renwick and adjacent holdings for almost seventy years, the Chicago Gravel Company made public its intent to sell the property. Similar to the birds their plans would displace, developers began flocking. One proposal envisioned "Renwick Shores," purportedly a series of townhouses gently nestled on the lake's edge in such a way as to be attractive to herons and people alike.

Having been raised in the vicinity of the lake, Gayle Peterson reacted to its threatened destruction by initiating the effort to preserve it. She enlisted the support of the Will County chapter of the Illinois Audubon Society, which adopted Lake Renwick as their "ongoing project." Years of hard work by society members produced important results. The Will County Forest Preserve District and the Illinois Department of Conservation joined forces and initiated condemnation proceedings against Chicago Gravel because no mutually agreeable price could be reached. Finally, on January 18, 1990, the two agencies purchased the land for $776,000. (A host of other entities also contributed financially.) When you are fighting to save something that is undeniably unique and spectacular, your chances of success increase immeasurably. But even with that in your corner, the struggle seems to take forever—nine years in the case of Lake Renwick.

As the agency with primary responsibility over Lake Renwick, the Will County Forest Preserve District had a problem on its hands: how to allow the public to enjoy the birds of Lake Renwick without disturbing them.[65] The first step was to install an observation deck 750 feet from the nearest nesting island, a water buffer considerably more conservative than published recommendations. Second, the site remained closed to visitors until late May when all species had established nests. Third, to monitor possible disturbances, volunteers were recruited to document "bird response to visitor use." Birds roosting on the shore of the public area flushed with the approach of people, and individuals in flight avoided passing directly over the observation structure. (This could be an advantage to the people standing there.) But, happily, observers discerned no reaction by birds on the nesting islands. Of potentially greater impact, low-flying planes, a nearby railroad, and a loud auction held offsite all produced noticeable agitation of the birds.

The thoughtful approach of the forest preserve district accomplished a number of excellent results. It identified the need to educate potentially disruptive neighbors so that the birds can be afforded maximum protection. By using volunteers in this important study, support for the site and the district was strengthened. And most gratifying of all, the agency has proven that with sensitivity it is possible to balance the well being of the birds with that of the people who helped protect the site.

For Everything There Is a Season: Birds through the Year

The flow and ebb of the mighty feathered wave has been sung by poets and reasoned of by philosophers, has given rise to proverbs and entered into popular superstitions, and yet we may say of it still that our ignorance is immense. — Alfred Newton, *A Dictionary of Birds* (1896)

Nesting Season: Birds of Woodlands

Most of the region's birds have shown themselves to be surprisingly resilient. Few, if any, manifest fidelity to pristine plant communities: such a species would certainly have become extinct long ago. In fact, the total number of species that breed locally has probably not decreased much over the centuries, although increases and decreases in populations are continous.[1] Some species have become extirpated, but others have expanded their ranges into this region. In modern times, at least, woodland species have generally fared better than those dependent on the ever-decreasing grasslands and marshes.

But nothing in nature is simple. The fate of birds hinges on more than quantity of breeding sites. Healthy populations depend just as heavily on quality of breeding habitat (the fragmentation issue) and suitability of wintering and migration range. A single bird may, over the course of a year, travel thousands of miles; along the way it must find sustenance in places as different as tropical rain forests, suburban backyards, and spruce bogs. As John Terborgh of Duke University has written, "migration is a chain whose strength is its weakest link."[2]

Some early changes in woodland birds can be documented. Wild turkeys (*Meleagris gallopavo*) were once widespread and not uncommon. Father Marquette, while at Chicago on December 12, 1674, noted that two members of his party "contented themselves with killing three or four turkeys out of many which came around our cabin, because they were dying with hunger." Into the

1850s, the species was common in the timbered portions of the Calumet area. Twenty years later, hunters were still taking birds in Lake County, Illinois, and the last of them persisted in the Indiana counties of Lake, Newton, and Porter until 1880, 1884, and 1886 respectively.[3]

The ruffed grouse (*Bonasa umbellus*) was present in larger numbers than the turkey and, on occasion, even foraged with domestic chickens in barnyards. It disappeared first from the Illinois counties. Notes appearing in the Illinois Audubon Society *Bulletin* state that one was "almost stepped on" in the spring of 1916 at La Grange, and another, the last published record, was flushed on May 7, 1932, near the Des Plaines River close to where Devon Avenue crosses it in Park Ridge. From time to time there have been sightings at various places in northeastern Illinois, but these are certainly based on game farm escapees, intentional releases, or misidentifications.[4]

In Wisconsin, the last ruffed grouse was seen in Kenosha in 1949 and Racine in 1955, although the bird still lives in counties just to the north. Samuel Robbins quotes a brief passage from a Walworth County newspaper dated October 26, 1887: "A Ruffed Grouse in its mad course the other day struck the subscriber's house kerthump! dropped onto the ground, got up, spread its tail, shook its feathers and resumed its flight. Later one went through Mrs John Meig's pantry window, the misguided bird cutting itself so badly with the broken glass that it was a mercy to kill the poor thing."[5]

The Indiana Dunes provided one of the last refuges for the species. An ornithologist at the Field Museum reported in 1920 that "grouse are much more numerous in the Dunes this year than usual; as many as eight being seen in one day's tramp, two individuals being noted within a half mile of the Gary Steel Mills." On April 4, 1931, Charley Clark flushed one that "sped like a bullet between the trees over the dune ridge and out of our sight. The squarish tail with black bar at its end made us believe what we had not expected to find." For thirty years, it seemed that a 1955 observation would be the last time anyone would see the bird in the Indiana Dunes. But, in the decade from 1987 to 1997, three sightings were made, presumably of wanderers from Berrien County. A reintroduction program has also been launched at Jasper-Pulaski State Game Area.[6]

Although gone from eighteen of the region's counties, the ruffed grouse never left Berrien County. In boglands from Berrien Springs to Eau Claire, the drumming of this local relict still reverberates through a handful of woods. The Michigan Breeding Bird Atlas, conducted from 1983 through 1988, found that ruffed grouse probably or definitely bred in nine blocks within the county. Like many northern birds, this species increases and decreases in regular cycles of about ten years.[7]

Bald eagles (*Haliaeetus leucocephalus*) nested at a few places up until the

1890s. One nest was situated on the bluffs near Lake Forest, but the last haunts of this huge fish eater were the Kankakee Marshes and the Indiana Dunes. Over a twenty-year period ending in 1880, a pair nested in a large elm tree on "Little Eagle Island," a small rise in the Lake County portion of the marsh.[8]

In his *Birds of the Chicago Area*, Frank Woodruff documented the bald eagle's final nestings in the Chicago area. Of the bird at Kouts, Porter County, he wrote: "On the Kankakee marshes . . . there were two nests of this species, both of which were occupied during the spring of 1896. One of the nests was in a dead oak tree and not over fifty feet above the ground and within twenty feet of a haystack. The female would allow us to approach within seventy-five yards of the nest before she would leave it." The following year the region's last nesting took place in the dunes near Miller, Lake County: "Mr. Edward Carr obtained the young birds," and later in the season Woodruff collected one eagle out of a group of five.[9]

◄o► ◄o► ◄o►

Certain species that nest in hollow trees or cavities have undergone changes in behavior and/or status. At one extreme, the Carolina parakeet (*Conuropsis carolinensis*) became extinct. But the chimney swift (*Chaetura pelagica*), purple martin (*Progne subis*), and Eastern bluebird (*Sialia sialis*) are unique in the degree to which they have successfully adapted to the human presence. The first two are splendid flyers that catch insects on the wing, above whatever covers the earth below. Therefore, the nature of the vegetation mix is not as important to them as it is to the bluebird, which prefers orchards, open woods, or woodland edges.

Chimney swifts were quick to exploit chimneys, which they found to be a more abundant and preferable version of the hollow trees they had been using since the species came to be. For many years, Paul Downing of Highwood, Lake County (Ill.), banded roosting swifts along the north shore. One old chimney near Plaza Del Lago on the Kenilworth/Wilmette border (Cook County) accommodated up to three thousand birds. Some swifts still use trees, while others have diversified into wells, buildings, and even outhouses. A pair nested for three years on the interior side of an outhouse door servicing a depot near Lafayette, Indiana. Each patron was asked to open and close the door gently so as to minimize disturbance of the birds. Fortunately, the birds were not sensitive to olfactory insults.[10]

While nights in a chimney tend to be predator free, the hollow brick columns provide their own risks. During a rainstorm on May 13, 1908, a large number of swifts sought refuge in an operating chimney in Waukegan (Lake County):

At first the chimney . . . was so obstructed by the birds as to choke the draft, and for more than an hour the boys were busy in taking out the swifts which had accumulated and were still flying in. . . . There were . . . one hundred and five dead and probably five times that number that revived sufficiently to enable them to fly off when liberated. After the numbers had largely decreased in flying down the chimney . . . , I went to the flue and extricated sixty-six more, of which eight were so injured by the heat that I had to kill them.[11]

Purple martins have now virtually abandoned the use of natural nesting sites in many areas. Mumford and Keller, for example, find but a single instance of a martin nesting in a tree in Indiana, and that was in 1899. A description of Fort Dearborn in 1830 includes the observation that, "adjoining the east front of the blockhouse, was a tenement for the martins." Martin houses, in fact, predate European arrival, for a number of Native American groups fastened gourds to poles to attract the birds.[12]

Eastern bluebirds have undergone two major adaptive changes over the past century and a half. Preferred nesting locations shifted from dead trees (before 1900) to fence posts to nest boxes (after 1950). The establishment of bluebird trails has now become a widespread activity. People carefully place the wooden boxes in opportune locations and conscientiously monitor the results. In five northeastern Illinois counties alone, an informal group of about a hundred people work with more than seven hundred bluebird houses. An increasing number of golf courses and corporations are also installing boxes on their property.[13]

Both the bluebird and purple martin are vulnerable to inclement weather and competition from other birds. Severe cold spells in early spring, particularly accompanied by ice storms, can doom many individuals to starvation. Bluebird numbers dropped deeply following the winters of 1894–95, 1959–60, and the three bitter ones in the late 1970s, while martin populations plummeted throughout the Midwest during below freezing conditions in the springs of 1966 and 1982. Breeding bird surveys from Berrien County suggest that the two species have fared very differently from 1975 to 1991: martins have decreased over 90 percent, and bluebirds have increased 400 percent.[14]

Two nonnative birds, the now ubiquitous house sparrow (*Passer domesticus*) and Eurasian starling (*Sturnus vulgaris*), have successfully usurped both natural holes and many artificial nesting structures intended for use by martins and bluebirds. Because they are permanent residents, they can take over sites before the indigenous species return from their winter quarters. It is therefore important that nest boxes be properly maintained so that martins and bluebirds find vacancies upon their arrival.

The final cavity-nesting bird I wish to discuss neither engendered affection nor could adapt in the face of human activity. The Carolina parakeet, the only parrot endemic to the United States, became extinct some time in the early twentieth century, but no one is certain why. It was hunted as a pest but not in any systematic way. If it had specific habitat requirements, the bird vanished before they were discerned. An interesting theory offering at least one reason for its disappearance has been advanced by Daniel McKinley, the bird's principal biographer. He suggests that the rapid spread of the Eurasian honeybee, brought to this continent by the first European settlers, forced the parakeet to lose many potential nesting sites. During the same time that hollow trees all across eastern North America were becoming beehives, swifts and martins responded by switching to cavities of human origin. Thus confronted with a new competitor, two species adjusted, and one declined.[15]

The Carolina parakeet was never common in this region, being of more southern origins. As McKinley painstakingly documents, claims to the contrary were based on unsubstantiated reports that were repeated until they became accepted. But the species did at one time occur here, at least during the period of French occupation. Marquette referred to parakeets, as did the author of the DeGannes Memoir (written in 1702), who encountered them in what is now Grundy County: "Three leagues from the fork (of the Illinois River) is the river Mazon . . . where flocks of parakeets of fifty to sixty are found. They make a very strange noise. They are a little bigger than turtle doves."[16]

In addition to those early observations, two nineteenth-century specimens of Carolina parakeet exist that may be from northeastern Illinois. But both are surrounded by so much uncertainty, however, that after spending pages discussing them, McKinley can reach no conclusion as to their origin. Eliot Downing of the University of Chicago reported one on June 11, 1912, "in the sand dune region on the shore of Lake Michigan, not far from Chicago." (Given Downing's interests and the distribution of sand dunes around Chicago, this record clearly pertains to the Indiana Dunes, and not somewhere in Illinois.) He claims to have seen it well, but doubt attaches to the record because it is generally believed that by 1912 the few surviving birds were largely confined to the most inhospitable swamps of the southeastern states.[17]

⊰o⊱ ⊰o⊱ ⊰o⊱

Without looking back in time, it would be impossible to know that such widespread permanent residents as the Northern cardinal (*Cardinalis cardinalis*), tufted titmouse (*Baeolophus bicolor*), Carolina wren (*Thryothorus ludovicianus* [populations rise and fall in step with the severity of winters]), and red-bellied woodpecker (*Melanerpes carolinus*) are all relatively recent arrivals from the south. Although more localized than these, other southern woodland birds have also been extending their ranges northward. These include mockingbirds (*Mimus polyglottos*), white-eyed vireo (*Vireo griseus*), hooded warbler (*Wilsonia pusilla*), and Kentucky warbler (*Oporornis formosus*). A warm spell lasting from 1920 through the 1950s may have enabled some of these species to expand their ranges, but no single reason can explain all of the changes.[18]

The cardinal is now very common throughout the region, thriving in habitats ranging from undisturbed to heavily urbanized. The state bird of both Indiana and Illinois, the cardinal is perhaps the best known of any native bird. But prior to 1900, it was rare or absent from this area: Racine had its first record in 1902, Walworth in 1927, and Kenosha in 1931. Samuel Robbins characterizes its spread through Wisconsin as one of "a series of limited invasions . . . following the major waterways, and then gradually fanning out into the neighboring areas."[19] This scenario pertains to other parts of the region as well. Urbanization has also no doubt aided the cardinal in its move northward: bird feeders and large-scale plantings of sheltering ornamentals have buffered the effects of winter.

The increase of the red-bellied woodpecker can be traced in the loose-leaf binders of Charley Clark, one of the most meticulous observers ever to bird Chicago. From 1929 to 1942, Clark was in the field on 557 days. During that period he saw three of the woodpeckers. From 1943 to 1961, he logged 552 days and seventy red bellies. From 1962 to 1977, he went on 910 field outings and saw 249 of the woodpeckers. Perhaps even more telling than Clark's data, two major works on the birds of the Indiana Dunes, one written in 1918 and the other in 1923, fail to mention the red-bellied woodpecker as occurring at all, even in this heavily wooded area. By 1986, Ken Brock in his *Birds of the Indiana Dunes* could give it an abundance ranking of three, meaning that a single observer should see one for every half day of birding.[20]

At least three major factors have been advanced to account for the species' increase. First, as with the cardinal, people have augmented natural food supplies. In southern Wisconsin, this bird glides through winter by frequenting open corncribs, which bird-watchers regard as "gigantic winter feeders." Second, the many trees weakened and killed by Dutch elm disease provided a bounty of insect prey and nesting habitat. And third, although the reasons aren't well understood, the red-bellied woodpecker seems to prefer woods that have a heavy woody understory. Such conditions have increased with fire suppression and the maturing of fallow land now under protection.[21]

The changing status of the Northern mockingbird also presents a complex history. Prior to 1856, Dr. Hoy found six nests in the vicinity of Racine. From Newton County, a contributor to the *Indiana Audubon Quarterly* reported that in 1884 enterprising locals augmented their incomes by catching and raising mockingbirds to sell as songsters.[22] During the first two decades of the twentieth century, however, mockingbirds retreated southward, ceasing to be a nester in the region. Then, about 1920, they made a modest comeback, which accelerated in the 1940s. Cold winters, such as those of the late 1970s, reduced the mockingbird presence, which then took several years to build back up. Some authors attribute the twentieth-century recolonization of this area to the planting of multiflora rose hedges. A 1984 assessment still holds true: it is rare in the northern tier of counties and uncommon in the southern.[23]

◄○► ◄○► ◄○►

A majority of the woodland birds that breed in this region winter in the Caribbean or Latin America. Known as Neotropical migrants, this group includes such local breeders as cuckoos, flycatchers, vireos, veery (*Catharus minimus*), wood thrush (*Hylocichla mustelina*), most warblers, scarlet tanager (*Piranga olivacea*), and rose-breasted grosbeak (*Pheuticus ludovicianus*). There is growing concern by amateur and professional ornithologist alike that many of these species are suffering dramatic decreases in population. Although the magnitude of this decrease has not yet been demonstrated to everyone's satisfaction, scientists have identified two major factors that appear to be contributing to the decline—one factor is at work where these birds breed and the other where they winter. Less is known about how the perils of migration affect bird populations, but it does appear that these travelers are facing increasing hazards everywhere they go.

The blight here at home is forest fragmentation, whereby surviving tracts of woods become isolated and small and/or riddled by clearings and roads. In both instances the amount of forest edge increases and remoteness of the interior decreases. In discussing this issue, John Terborgh, an ornithologist who has been instrumental in drawing attention to the plight of Neotropical migrants, wrote: "Forest margins are brighter, warmer, drier, and windier than the interior and support more shrubs, vines, and weeds. Perhaps certain birds were averse to edges and rejected small tracts because none of the habitat was sufficiently far from edges." However, studies demonstrated that forest birds readily nested in edge areas. Something else, what Terborgh called "a mysterious pathology," was at work.[24]

Scientists eventually keyed in on nest predation and parasitism as the twin culprits. Chris Whalen, now at Midewin National Tallgrass Prairie, studied nesting wood thrushes and robins (*Turdus migratorius*) at the Morton Arboretum. He found that raccoons, opossums, domestic cats, blue jays (*Cyanocitta cristata*), and American crows (*Corvus brachyrhynchos*) are the most serious predators of bird nests in the region. These species thrive in urbanized and edge environments. And not only are they increasing in population, these predators have an easier time discovering nests placed in shrubs and open woods than they do in denser forest interiors. Scott Robinson and his colleagues have attempted to quantify this phenomenon using data compiled from across the Midwest. As the acreage of forest interior decreased from study site to study site, daily nest mortality increased: red-eyed vireo (*Vireo olivaceus*)— 7 percent; wood thrush—2 percent; ovenbird (*Seiurus aurocapillus*)—4 percent; and indigo bunting (*Passerina cyanea*)—7 percent. Over the course of a twenty-three-to-twenty-seven-day nesting cycle, these increases mean that some species have nest mortality rates in excess of 80 percent.[25]

Research on nest parasitism indicates that the single most important bird in the woods of the eastern United States and Canada is in fact a bird of the grasslands. The brown-headed cowbird (*Molothrus ater*) was originally a prairie species, deriving its living from the insect swarms that followed the great herds of bison. Because the bison were constantly on the move, cowbirds would have starved if anchored to one nesting spot. Consequently, they evolved the habit of laying their eggs in the nests of other birds. Female cowbirds lay from thirty to forty eggs a season (in captivity, up to seventy-seven) and can seek wooded nesting sites up to five miles from open-country food sources.[26]

In the period before European settlement, cowbirds routinely deposited eggs in the nests of about fifty different species. But as the timber fell and agriculture gushed across the land like water from a ruptured dam, the cowbird expanded its distribution and discovered a host of new foster parents. The number of species it now parasitizes has increased almost fivefold. This new group has been particularly hard hit because they lack any defenses against the cowbird. And among these, Neotropical migrants are most susceptible to parasitism because many, such as the red-eyed vireo, hooded warbler, and wood thrush (one nest held fifteen cowbird eggs) construct open-topped nests, easily violated by cowbirds. Just as reductions in the amount of forest interior increased predation, they also increased the percentage of parasitized nests, but at much higher levels: ovenbird—70 percent; indigo bunting—80 percent; red eyed vireo—90 percent; and wood thrush—100 percent.[27]

Edge species that have long been in contact with the cowbird have evolved protective strategies. Robins, brown thrashers (*Toxostoma rufum*), and Baltimore orioles (*Icterus galbula*) are big enough to remove the alien eggs from their nests. The yellow warbler (*Dendroica petechia*), the Chicago region's most common breeding warbler, and the prairie warbler (*Dendroica discolor*), now confined as a local nester to an isolated colony in the Indiana Dunes, are too small to remove the foreign eggs. If they were to puncture them, the nest would be unusable. The yellow warbler has developed the practice of burying cowbird eggs, usually along with their own, with nesting material, and then laying a replacement clutch. One nest was found with six stories, each containing cowbird eggs.[28]

Such behavior by prairie warblers, however, is extremely rare. Instead, they often abandon contaminated nests. Val Nolan, whose decades-long work on this one species is without rival, learned that nests established early in the breeding season were much more apt to be parasitized than those later in the season. But late season broods are usually smaller to compensate for uncertain food supplies. And because adults need to fatten up for fall migration, their own fitness could be jeopardized by the demands of feeding young.[29]

Which is worse—predation or parasitism? It may be an impossible question to answer. When a predator attacks a nest, it tends to destroy every egg and young that it can find. The presence of cowbird eggs, however, does not necessarily spell disaster for the host species because some number of young may successfully fledge. The chances of this happening are enhanced when the host lays eggs before the cowbird does, thereby reducing the advantage usually enjoyed by the cowbird, whose young hatch two or three days earlier than nest mates. On the other hand, when a pair loses its progeny through predation, it may nest again, perhaps with greater success. And in some areas cowbird densities are so high that certain hosts, most clearly the wood thrush, are parasitized at rates approaching 100 percent.

Much of the research on the effects of parasitism and predation on Neotropical migrants has been performed by Scott Robinson of the Illinois Natural History Survey. He has found that although reproduction for many of these species is extremely low, populations on his study sites in central and southern Illinois do not seem to be falling. (Chris Whalen's work on wood thrushes and robins in DuPage County also reveals poor reproduction success but steady populations.) Robinson explains this seeming anomaly by suggesting that the birds breeding in Illinois are being produced elsewhere, perhaps in the Missouri Ozarks, northern Wisconsin, or south-central Indiana, where large blocks of forests remain conducive to successful nesting.[30]

Arriving on their wintering grounds, Neotropical migrants also face habitat destruction. John Terborgh points out that half of the birds that nest in 6,230,000 square miles of Canada and the United States winter in 836,000 square miles distributed across five countries (Mexico, the Bahamas, Cuba, Haiti, and the Dominican Republic). Haiti and Cuba have already lost most of their forests, and the other countries seem to be in the process of following suit. Terborgh concludes "that the effects of tropical habitat destruction are amplified several times; clearing one hectare [2.5 acres] of forest in Mexico is equivalent to expanding urban sprawl by perhaps five to eight hectares [twelve to twenty acres] in the Northeast."[31]

What impact this has on bird populations isn't clear. Many species behave very differently in winter than they do in summer. For example, the eastern kingbird (*Tyrannus tyrannus*) is known to us in the north as an insectivore that guards its nesting territory so zealously it battles hawks and crows three times its size. In the tropics, however, it forms large flocks and feeds on fruit. Since most of what is known about the Neotropical migrants pertains to their time on the nesting ground, there are many unanswered questions about their winter requirements and how they are affected by the loss of forests. But a growing literature suggests that as lands once covered with trees become sugarcane fields and cattle ranches, a decline in many species will surely follow.[32]

Nesting Season: Birds of Grasslands and Marshes

The greatest loss of breeding birds has been among prairie and marsh species. Initial settlement wiped out a relatively small number of species, among them some of the most spectacular members of the local avifauna. While birds restricted to wet prairies and marshes have been hardest hit by changes in land use, many of the upland species adapted well to the Eurasian meadows that replaced the tallgrass prairie. Unfortunately, however, as agriculture becomes more intensive, or gives way to commercial and residential development, these birds too are beginning to decline at alarming rates.

Apparently requiring the admixture of habitats that characterized this ecotone, the American swallow-tailed kite (*Elanoides forficatus*) was one of the first birds to disappear from this area. It is a magnificent species that used to nest as far north as Minnesota, but has since retreated into the swamps of the southeastern United States. A. C. Barry, writing in 1854 about southeastern Wisconsin, said that "at one time [it was] quite numerous upon our prairies, and quite annoying to us in grouse shooting; now rarely met with in this vicinity." It nested in tall elm trees near Racine until 1849, and remained a rare migrant for another fifty years. That three were shot over Highland Park, Lake County (Ill.), in 1905 is a difficult thing to imagine.[33]

Another vision that strains the imagination is that of the two-foot-tall long-billed curlew (*Numenius americanus*) rising in noisy flocks from prairie swales. Edward Nelson said of its local status: "Formerly very abundant during the migrations, and a common summer resident." Unfortunately, "the curlew will not stay long on cultivated ground, but leaves with the disappearance of the original prairie sod." Last nesting at Lake Calumet in 1873, the species has totally vanished from the region, with only three reported sightings since 1900.[34]

The sharp-tailed grouse (*Tympanuchus phasianellus*) reached the southern edge of its range in Chicago. It seemed to prefer areas with some scattered trees over those of pure prairie. Writing in the 1850s, Kennicott said it was formerly "not uncommon" in Cook County. Hunters shot birds in Chicago during a few winters in the mid-1840s, and it had become rare in Racine by 1852. The last definite record for the area was in the fall of 1863 or 1864: "While two gentlemen were shooting prairie chickens near Waukegan, they found and secured a covey of these birds, numbering fourteen individuals."[35]

Whooping cranes (*Grus americana*) nested in the area, as did trumpeter swans (*Cygnus buccinator*). Apart from a 1710 report from the confluence of the Des Plaines and Illinois rivers, nesting swans were restricted to the Kankakee Marshes, where they were last recorded in 1872. Whooping cranes appeared most commonly in spring and fall and were once described as abundant. Now in the Smithsonian, a whooper was shot in Chicago in June 1858, a date suggesting that it bred locally. A few recent sightings, most notably the adult photographed by Bob Hughes as it migrated over Illinois Beach State Park on Veterans' Day 1998, indicate that the species still occasionally passes through the region.[36]

The stories of the common raven (*Corvus corax*) and the American crow illustrate the dynamics of bird populations over time. Kennicott stated that both the raven and the crow were common throughout the state. The raven thrived in the open prairies, while the crow was largely restricted to woods. But destruction of the prairies and huge increases in the human population put an end to the raven—it had become a rare wintering species by 1876 and disappeared thirty years later. Agriculture, however, had the opposite effect on the crow, which benefited greatly from both enhanced food supplies and the spread of trees. In the modern world, the crow continues to adapt and is common in cities and suburbs.[37]

One of the most elusive of North American birds, the black rail (*Laterallus jamaicensis*) migrates through the Chicago region and is even seen on very rare occasions. A bird showed up on Memorial Day 1994 at Montrose Harbor. By late afternoon, arriving bird-watchers had to literally wade through a throng of picnickers and sunbathers to reach the small copse that sheltered the rail. Six years later, a pair lingered into July at Springbrook Prairie Forest Preserve, DuPage County.

But before the desecration of the Calumet marshes, black rails bred within Chicago. In fact, the first nest of this species known to science was found here in 1875:

> On the 19th of June . . . while collecting with me near the Calumet River, Mr. Frank DeWitt, of Chicago, was fortunate enough to discover a nest of this species containing ten freshly laid eggs. The nest was placed in a deep cup-shaped depression in a perfectly open situation of the border of a marshy spot, and its only concealment was such as a few straggling carices

afforded. It is composed of soft grass blades loosely interwoven in a circular manner. The nest, in shape and construction, looks much like that of a
meadow lark. . . . Owing to the small diameter of the nest the eggs were in
two layers.[38]

Now known to local bird-watchers as uncommon migrants, the Nelson's
sharp-tailed sparrow (*Ammodramus nelsoni*) probably nested here, and the
Leconte's sparrow (*Ammodramus leconteii*) definitely nested. The sharp-tailed
sparrow summered at Lake Calumet in the 1870s, although no actual nests were
discovered. (The species was described from specimens collected at Calumet by
Nelson, for whom it is named.) LeConte's sparrows were "more or less abundant" during the summer of 1908, when they were found breeding on the border of the Skokie Marsh. Several nests have been located since then, including
one at Evergreen Park in 1932. A few of us enjoyed a singing male at Lake
Calumet in June 1968, when there was still some marsh left at 103rd and Doty.[39]

One marsh species with an unusual nesting history is the Forster's tern
(*Sterna forsteri*), common and widespread as a migrant. Historically, it bred at
Lake Delavan (Walworth) but was gone by 1919. It also nested once at Powderhorn Lake (Cook) and three times between 1957 and 1962 at a small marsh
in Gary that no longer exists. But apart from those records, Grass Lake (Lake
County, Ill.) harbors the region's only nesting colony, a colony that has been
active during most years since at least the 1870s. Nelson's description of that
discovery is worth quoting at length:

> While we were collecting eggs among the wild rice patches on Grass Lake,
> June 14, Mr. Douglas observed a pair of these terns hovering near a small
> patch of *Sagittaria* leaves growing in several feet of water, and rowing to the
> spot found the nest, which was a loosely built structure of coarse pieces of
> reeds resting upon a mass of floating plants and concealed from view by the
> surrounding leaves. Upon the side of the nest was a single young bird about
> to scramble into the water, but upon seeing Mr. Douglas it crouched to
> avoid being observed, and was captured. A thorough search at the time
> failed to reveal any other young ones, so the adults that had been darting
> and screaming about his head were secured with a second pair that had es-
> poused the cause of their companions. . . That evening we found and se-
> cured two more young upon the nest found in the morning. The next
> morning fortune favored me, and, while passing between several floating
> masses of decaying vegetable matter I observed four small heaps of wild
> rice stems, which were obviously brought from some distance, as the near-
> est patch of rice was several rods distant. The nests were quite bulky, the
> bases being two feet or more in diameter. Two the nests contained three

eggs, and two contained two eggs each. . . . [By] concealing myself in the rice, . . . I soon secured several of the parent birds as they flew about the nests, uttering angry cries at the spoliation of their treasures.[40]

Protecting the marshland species that still nest here has proven to be a major challenge because they vary in their requirements, particularly with respect to the ratio of vegetation and open water present at a given site. Wetlands represent a continuum from wetter to drier, each range providing habitat to a particular guild of birds:

Range 1. Open water: Waterfowl.

Range 2. Water-vegetation interspersion: pied-billed grebe (*Podilymbus podiceps*), least bittern (*Ixobrychus exilis*), common moorhen (*Gallinula chloropus*), black tern (*Chlidonias niger*), and yellow-headed blackbird (*Xanthocephalus xanthocephalus*).

Range 3. Thickly vegetated: American bittern (*Botaurus lentiginosus*), king rail (*Rallus elegans*), Virginia rail (*Rallus limicola*), sora rail (*Porzana carolina*), sedge wren (*Cistothorus platensis*).[41]

From year to year, any given site undergoes changes in response to precipitation levels. During droughts, range 2 can become 3, and 3 can cease being wetland. In a wet year, on the other hand, levels 2 and 3 can become flooded. As these transformations occur, some birds lose habitat while others gain. The key is that, in any given year, places of enough diversity are available to ensure adequate habitat regardless of ambient conditions.[42]

A large site like Deer Lake, Lake County (Ill.), has the diversity needed to provide different habitats at the same time. But even here, there are years when it supports yellow-headed blackbirds and black terns and other years when it does not. It is also important to maintain smaller sites that may ordinarily have too much open water or too little but that can offer essential habitat during a particular year when the usually more favorable spots are too wet or too dry. Palatine Road Marsh, Cook County, is a good example. It is a deep-water marsh that in many years lacks rare wetland birds but during the droughts of 1988 and 1989 attracted yellow-headed blackbirds and black terns. These areas of lesser size are also the most vulnerable to disturbances and when possible should be adequately buffered. Of course, marsh conditions can be managed to enhance their suitability. This could include manipulating water levels or instituting controlled burning.[43]

Red-winged blackbirds (*Agelaius phoeniceus*) and Canada geese (*Branta canadensis*) are two wetland species that have met the challenges thrown their way by human activity and have prevailed to an extraordinary degree. The best measure of how successfully redwings adapted to new situations is found in the Grabers' *A Comparative Study of Bird Populations in Illinois, 1906–1909 and 1956–1958.* This remarkable work compares data from a comprehensive survey of the state's birds at the turn of the century with the Grabers own similar survey fifty years later. At the time of the first study, 60 percent of the red-winged population resided in marshes. (By then the species had already begun to make adjustments, for writing twenty years earlier, Ridgway said redwings always nested in or near wet areas.) Over the next five decades marshland in Illinois decreased from six hundred thousand to sixty thousand acres. During the same period, redwings swarmed into newly created agricultural habitats. The most dramatic example is that the average of thirteen individuals summering on a hundred acres of hayfield increased to 130. The Grabers estimated that Illinois's breeding population of redwings grew from 5,100,000 birds to 11 million, of which only 3 percent still nested in marshes.[44]

The Canada goose has also undergone major population shifts since the Europeans first arrived. One of the earliest Canada goose accounts comes from Henry Thacker, who spent the winter of 1844–45 trapping muskrats in the marshes of Mud Lake, the low portage between the Chicago and Des Plaines Rivers:

> One day as I was pushing my little boat along through the tall reeds, I saw at a distance something unusual on the top of a muskrat house. As it was lying flat, almost hidden from view, I at first sight took it to be an otter. . . . As usual at the sight of game, my rifle was quick as thought brought to bear, and away sped the bullet, and over tumbled a large wild goose, making a great splashing as she fell into the water. On examination I found she had a nest of seven eggs, all fresh. The goose weighed 14½ pounds. The same day I found another nest with several eggs, and took them to a farmer who was anxious to get them to hatch. He placed the eggs under a hen, but a few days before they were ready to hatch . . . the skunk ate up hen, eggs, and all, to the great sorrow and indignation of the farmer. He said the young geese would have been worth five dollars a pair.[45]

In the 1850s, Canada goose "eggs were gathered by the bushel in a marsh north of Racine" and were described as being abundant in Cook County. But by the 1920s, hunting and habitat loss had probably eliminated it as a breeding species in Illinois and Indiana, where the Kankakee Marshes were its last refuge.[46] Kumlien and Hollister summarized the plight of the bird for southern Wisconsin: "Fifty years ago a common breeder in almost any swamp or large marsh, or on the 'prairie sloughs' (now a feature of the past). At the present time only scattered pairs nest as far south as the southern third of the state. The last nesting record we have for southern Wisconsin was in Jefferson County—from the years 1891–1899, inclusive, when a goose deposited her eggs on the edge of a tamarack swamp. . . . No mate was ever noticed to have visited her."[47]

Starting with two pairs of geese at Jasper-Pulaski in the mid 1930s, Canada geese were reintroduced throughout much of the area. Those original birds reproduced, and their numbers were further augmented by additional introductions so that the population grew to 150 pairs by 1978. During the 1940s, the largest local flock was kept at the Bright Land Farm in Barrington, Cook County, property now part of the Crabtree Lake Forest Preserve holdings. It consisted of about 250 individuals, "a fourth of which were free flying."[48] In 1950 the State of Illinois obtained birds from this and other flocks for a statewide restocking program. No one could have guessed how successful these efforts would prove to be. Indeed, if anyone had thought that the Canada goose population would climb to the levels that it did in the 1980s and 1990s, all such programs would probably have been terminated.

Since nobody censuses breeding Canada geese on a systematic basis, the use of Christmas bird count data is a good way to demonstrate the dramatic rise in goose numbers. Christmas bird counts are conducted under the auspices of the National Audubon Society and the U.S. Fish and Wildlife Service during a three-week period encompassing Christmas and New Years. Each count covers an area within a fifteen-mile diameter circle. The Evanston North Shore Christmas count is located in northeastern Cook and southeastern Lake Counties. Table 8 shows the number of Canada geese that were recorded on the count from 1963 to 1993.

Canada geese still inhabit marshes but have moved into the newest of "wetlands": neatly mowed lawns surrounding concrete retention ponds. Food, protection,

Table 8. Increase in Canada Geese on Evanston North Shore Christmas Bird Count, 1963–93

Year	Count
1963	0
1965	0
1967	9
1969	11
1971	41
1973	325
1975	322
1977	301
1979	331
1981	2,304
1983	1,193
1985	8,059
1987	2,274
1989	5,883
1991	6,448
1993	9,206

and year-round open water have transformed the Canada goose into an abundant permanent resident. A skein of geese honking across a dusky sky is now less likely to signify seasonal change than it is a simple movement from one corporate lakelet to another.

As the paths of people and geese cross with greater frequency, conflicts between the two have become common. Both state and federal agencies are involved with "goose problems." In northern Illinois, the U.S. Department of Agriculture takes the lead in handling citizen complaints. Between October 1994 and May 1995, they received seventy-six letters and fifty phone calls from people in Lake, Cook, Will, and DuPage Counties who were annoyed with their local geese.

Complainants have two major concerns. The first involves possible impacts of goose excrement. Apparently with respect to ponds and swimming pools, this can be a legitimate problem because the large nutrient load can create algal blooms detrimental to human use of the waters. But the other fear, that *Escherichia coli* bacteria in the droppings pose a disease threat, has never been documented or, for that matter, considered enough of a problem to warrant serious study. John Fischer of the Southeastern Cooperative Wildlife Disease Study at the University of Georgia says that people use this as an excuse for justifying ridding themselves of unwanted geese. He believes that common sense and rudimentary hygiene is enough to eliminate any hazard.[49] (Make sure that anything you put in your mouth is either well cleaned or well cooked.)

The second issue is the aggressive behavior of some geese, which becomes most serious when a goose nests near a doorway or trail heavily used by people. In their efforts to avoid goose attacks, people have suffered broken bones by tripping over curbs and other obstacles.

Fortunately, there exist a number of effective nonlethal techniques to ameliorate goose problems. These include the cessation of all feeding, the installation of barriers, and direct harassment of the geese using noisemakers, dogs, and other tactics. If there are still too many geese for human taste, open water and grazing space can be eliminated. Under the most extreme of circumstances, permission may be granted to sterilize eggs; currently, killing geese or destroying their nests is not legally sanctioned.

Another antigoose measure may prove to be more harmful than the geese themselves. A number of landscaping outfits have peddled mute swans (*Cygnus olor*—native to Europe) as a way to keep geese at bay. A pair of swans go for as high as $4,000, and many of the firms will collect the swans and board them during the winter for additional fees. Unfortunately, landowners who go this route usually wind up with more geese than they started with. There are several reasons for this: people tend to feed their swans, an activity which also attracts geese; if the swans are kept over the winter, they need open water, which also attracts geese; and since swans are pinioned and can't fly, they act as decoys for yet more geese.[50]

Only wild mute swans with young aggressively chase other waterfowl. Thus, for swans to be effective goose deterrents, they must be allowed to produce cygnets. But a large feral population of mute swans distributed throughout the few remaining marshes poses a threat to native waterfowl. Some biologists are predicting that mute swans may become the next nuisance species. Not only should the dissemination of mute swans be curtailed, feral birds should be destroyed before they harm native species that are already in low numbers. Fortunately, they seem susceptible to disease; for example, forty mute swans recently died on Wolf Lake (Indiana-Illinois border) from what was probably intestinal hemorrhaging.[51]

◄o► ◄o► ◄o►

As prairie was converted into Eurasian grassland, most of the upland (mesic to dry) prairie species were able to adapt to the new conditions. Some clearly did better than others.

As early as 1889, Robert Ridgway noted a decrease in upland sandpipers (*Bartramia longicauda*), which he attributed to hunting and the destruction of nests by cats and dogs. In southeast Wisconsin, Hoy called the species "abundant" in 1853, but Kumlien and Hollister wrote fifty years later of its imminent demise: "This once abundant species is disappearing at such a rate that, if the decrease in the next twenty years is as great as it has been since 1870, the bird will become extinct. Formerly every meadow, border of marsh, or grassy lake shore contained great numbers of this bird." By the beginning of the twentieth century, the sandpiper had been reduced in Indiana "to such a scattered few that it was believed to be in danger of extinction."[52]

Fortunately, before the dire predictions came true, hunting pressures were lifted, and the bird began to exploit the new grasslands. Upland sandpipers were particularly fond of pastures and airfields, two refuges that became important to the species' recovery. These birds show little aversion to urban areas, as long as they can find suitable habitat remnants. One birder spent the summer of 1948 studying a population of twelve sandpipers that bred "in a subdivision west of Evanston." She found that the birds confined their activities to three square blocks of degraded prairie at Main Street and Crawford Avenue.[53]

Unfortunately, upland sandpipers seem to be declining once again. Changing agricultural methods have reduced the acreage of pasture and hayfields, and in the more urbanized areas, few blocks of land remain free of concrete or structures. One large population still remains in the region, however. In May 1993 biologists counted fifty-five sandpipers on the 23,500-acre Joliet Army Arsenal in Will County, now part of Midewin National Tallgrass Prairie. Access to the property is restricted, and grazing is still permitted, thus affording the species large blocks of habitat and minimal disturbance.

The loggerhead shrike (*Lanius ludovicianus*), another once abundant grassland species, has become steadily rarer since the early 1900s. Since shrikes nest heavily in hedgerows, particularly Osage orange (*Maclura pomifera*), many writers attributed the decrease to the replacement of these vegetative fences with barbed wire. Ornithologists believe that the slow decline in northern and central Illinois began accelerating in about 1957 and continued until shrikes were virtually gone by 1962. During 1967 and 1968, Wisconsin conducted statewide surveys of the species and could locate only seven nesting locations per year within its borders. Locally, the one place where the bird is holding its own or even increasing is Midewin National Tallgrass Prairie, where eleven nests were found in 1993.[54]

There are two particularly disturbing aspects of the ongoing loggerhead shrike decline. First, no one knows what caused it (there are too many hedgerows left to account for it); and second, the shrike family (Laniidae) has in general been experiencing population decreases throughout the world.[55]

International concern over shrike decline spawned research that has already identified at least one limiting factor previously overlooked. In addition to adequate prey supplies and nesting sites, loggerhead shrikes require elevated perches from which they can hunt, the kinds of woody elements often removed through burning and other techniques common in prairie management. The quantity and placement of these perches determine the size of each shrike's territory. When there are few perches, individual shrikes exert energy defending larger areas, even though they cannot efficiently utilize the full extent of the territory. This means both that fewer shrikes can use otherwise adequate range and that the reproductive success of a given pair is compromised. In contrast, numerous perches mean more shrikes can establish smaller territories on the same acreage and with enhanced chances of fledging young.[56]

A bird of the Great Plains, the Swainson's hawk (*Buteo swainsoni*) presents an unusual case. There are few authenticated records of it for Indiana, and it is has never been found nesting in Wisconsin. But there is a small isolated colony in Kane County that has persisted for years. Two researchers from Wisconsin discovered five active nests in May 1973. Charley Clark saw the birds on May 13: "We saw one soaring above a small wooded area, watched it go into a very fast glide, right to the ground—but it wasn't the ground. He landed on the female and copulated." Subsequently, two of the nests were abandoned, but the remaining ones fledged five young. The number of nests reported varies from year to year, a function, in part, of the time spent looking for them. One pair has evidently moved a bit east, and during the summer of 2000 was found nesting for the first time in McHenry County, near Coral Woods Forest Preserve. It will be amazing if the Swainson's hawk survives the suburban sprawl that is engulfing Kane and McHenry counties.[57]

The bobolink (*Dolichonyx oryzivorus*) is one of the most distinctive and best known of the grassland birds. Its song is almost indescribable, and the breeding male's pattern of light above, dark below is shared with few other North American birds. Less pleasing, nineteenth-century diners valued it highly, as this 1889 account of the Chicago game market testifies: "Reedbirds [bobolinks] are one of the most popular varieties of game, and are probably called for in the restaurants more often than any other of the smaller varieties. The prevailing belief that the English sparrow frequently masquerades as a reedbird appears to have no deterring effect, and the verdict is: 'sparrow or no sparrow, he is mighty good eating.'"[58]

Around 1912, over 720,000 bobolinks were shipped from Georgetown, South Carolina, in one year alone.[59] Despite that carnage, the 1906–9 Illinois bird survey found the species to be the most common grassland bird. By the time the Grabers and Herkert did their surveys, the bird had dropped in ranking to three, but its percentage of the total decreased even more.

The U.S. Fish and Wildlife data are the most alarming of all because they show that, unlike some grassland species whose declining populations have recently leveled off, the bobolink's fall has spanned two decades. James Herkert, with the Illinois chapter of the Nature Conservancy, blames the crash on new strains of alfalfa that enable farmers to harvest earlier and more often, in intervals of thirty-five days rather than forty-five. This shorter cycle makes it impossible for bobolinks to nest and fledge young before the fields are cut. Under such cropping regimes, farmers produce shredded tweets, and bobolink nesting success shrinks by 90 percent.[60]

Table 9 is by Jim Herkert, and it summarizes the changing status of selected grassland birds. (The 1987–89 data are from Herkert's own study, conducted in central and northern Illinois, including six sites within the Chicago region.) He believes that many of "these species are in a sense victims of their own adaptability." As vesper sparrows (*Pooecetes gramineus*), Savannah sparrows (*Passerculus sandwichensis*), Eastern meadowlarks (*Sturnella magna*), and others moved into abandoned agricultural land, they became vulnerable to human indifference. There is nothing glamorous in saving an old field devoid of conservative plants. Even if efforts were made, the cost of such land would make it difficult to acquire sufficient quantities to maintain viable bird populations.

Another critical aspect to protecting these birds is that they vary from one another in their requirements. (See fig. 90.) Scott Kobal of the DuPage

Table 9. Relative Abundance of Prairie Birds within Illinois, 1850–1989

Species	Prior to 1900	1906–9 %	1906–9 Rank	1956–58 %	1956–58 Rank	1987–89 %	1987–89 Rank	USFWS % Change
Eastern meadowlark	Abundant	25.5	2*	20.0	2*	11.8	2	−67.0
Dickcissel	Abundant	13.1	3	8.7	4	7.7	5	−46.7
Grasshopper sparrow	Abundant	5.9	5	5.3	6	8.6	4	−56.0
Bobolink	Abundant	25.8	1	9.7	3	11.4	3	−90.4
Henslow's sparrow	Abundant	<1.0	15	<1.0	14	1.6	12	†
Red-winged blackbird	Very common	9.9	4	36.2	1	26.8	1	−18.8
Greater prairie chicken	Very common	<1.0	13	0.0	16	0.0	16	†
Upland sandpiper	Very common	2.3	9	<1.0	12	<1.0	13	−16.8
Vesper sparrow	Common	1.3	11	1.4	10	<1.0	15	+12.1
Horned lark	Common	4.9	6	4.8	7	<1.0	14	0.0
Field sparrow	Common	4.0	7	2.9	9	5.6	7	−52.6
Song sparrow	Common	2.6	8	1.0	11	3.3	10	−29.3
Savannah sparrow	Common	2.3	10	5.8	5	3.5	9	−58.9
American goldfinch	Common	1.2	12	3.1	8	4.7	8	−42.8
Common yellowthroat	Common	<1.0	14	<1.0	15	5.8	6	−8.8
Sedge wren	Common	<1.0	16	<1.0	13	2.8	11	−22.5

Source. Herkert 1991b; references omitted.

Note: USFWS— U.S. Fish and Wildlife Service. USFWS data are based on changes noted in their breeding bird surveys from 1967 to 1989.

*Relative abundance estimates are for eastern and western meadowlarks combined.

†Present on too few routes for accurate trend analysis.

County Forest Preserve District explored the issue to see how it pertains to the nonnative grasslands owned by the district. His findings emphasize the challenges in maintaining diverse grassland bird populations.

Species composition and density differed as to whether the field was in fescue (*Festuca*), mixed grass, or mixed grass/forbs; they differed according to variations in litter depth, vertical density of vegetation, and percent cover of grasses and forbs within habitats; and although they all need perches, each species prefers a particular height range. A good example of mutually exclusive conditions is the depth of plant litter: low suits grasshopper sparrows, intermediate bobolinks, and high Henslow's sparrows. Another tricky situation involves preventing the encroachment of woody vegetation, which degrades grassland bird habitats. Fire is the common tool to accomplish this, yet fire also eliminates perches and litter that a species may require.[61]

If nothing is done, succession turns a grassland parcel into one of shrubs

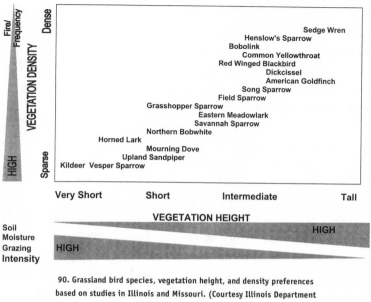

90. Grassland bird species, vegetation height, and density preferences based on studies in Illinois and Missouri. (Courtesy Illinois Department of Natural Resources, Division of Natural Heritage, Springfield.)

and trees. But it would also be a shame to sacrifice the bird population in the name of creating tallgrass prairie or favoring one bird over another simply because one management technique is easier to employ than another or because one is easier than several. Large tracts under carefully implemented and varying management regimens, including grazing and mowing, will be necessary to ensure that the full range of grassland birds are represented in the region.

In Passage: Migration and Vagrancy

Excluding human beings, the most mobile of all vertebrates are birds. One great manifestation of this mobility is migration—the regular seasonal movement from one place to another. (The Arctic tern (*Sterna paradisaea*), an accidental visitor to the Chicago region, is the only species on earth whose individual members breed in the Arctic and winter in the Antarctic.) Although at its minimum in January and early February, some bird migration is visible throughout the year in Chicago. These movements endow the region with an ongoing avian show that at times can be breathtaking. Not only does this display attain beauty at the most profound level, but it also reveals creatures struggling to obey the commands of their genetic heritage. Watch kettles of broadwinged hawks (*Buteo platypterus*) peel to the south across a cloud-flecked sky or warblers stream through the trees at the Lincoln Park Bird Sanctuary, and you witness firsthand the forces of nature.

Without doubt, the largest number of species passes through this region from mid-April to May. And although there are more individuals present in the fall, spring has produced some mind-boggling counts for particular species. Single day results from the lakefront of Berrien County include northern flicker (*Colaptes auratus*)—five to ten thousand; blue jay—twenty thousand; American robin—seven thousand; cedar waxwing (*Bombycilla cedrorum*)—five thousand; and meadowlark (probably Easterns)—two thousand.[62]

Not only is variety at its height during this period, but so is the brilliance of plumage and proclivity to sing. Possessing all three of these attributes, the wood warblers are synonymous with spring migration. Louis J. Halle calls these birds "the principal glory of the North American spring, quick and dainty in their movements, incessantly active, as bright and varied in color as the butterflies."[63] Their very names evoke kaleidoscopic variety: blue-winged (*Vermivora pinus*), golden-winged (*Vermivora chrysoptera*), orange-crowned (*Vermivora celata*), yellow (*Dendroica petechia*), black-throated blue (*Dendroica caerulescens*), bay-breasted (*Dendroica castanea*), cerulean (*Dendroica cerulea*), and prothonotary (*Protonotaria citrea*). During the second and third weeks in May, as many as thirty-four of the thirty-nine species of warblers breeding in the eastern United States have been found in one day at Jackson Park, Chicago, by a single observer.

Laurence C. Binford, one of the most astute of local ornithologists (now living in Louisiana), says that during typical springs, there are three major waves of passerine migrants. (The largest order of birds is the Passeriformes, the perching birds.) The first tends to occur at the end of April and usually brings with it several species of warblers, ruby-crowned kinglets (*Regulus calendula*), white-throated sparrows (*Zonotrichia albicollis*), and other birds. There is then a hiatus until the next wave arrives, usually around May 5 but later in a cold year. This is the first good flight, with more species and individuals. In years where these early pushes are strong, southern migrants such as white-eyed vireos, summer tanagers (*Piranga rubra*), worm-eating warblers (*Helmitheros vermivorus*), and Kentucky warblers appear in unusually large numbers.[64]

At this point, there is a steady movement of birds until May 15 or 16, when the last big flight arrives. Cuckoos, yellow-bellied flycatcher (*Empidonax flaviventris*), Philadelphia vireo (*Vireo philadelphicus*), and Canada warblers (*Wilsonia canadensis*) are among the new arrivals. Heavy migration continues for another ten days or so, but as a continuous flow rather than defined waves. More flycatchers, mourning warbler (*Oporornis philadelphia*), and Connecticut warbler (*Oporornis agilis*) appear during this period, after which migration tapers off.

With careful planning and lots of energy, it is possible for one group to find over 150 total species in a day. The Chicago region record for many years was 167, set by Charley Clark and two companions on May 18, 1963. But totals of over 170 have been set by several groups, both in Illinois and Indiana. The current high count is 188, established in May 1999 by a team who spent the day in northwestern Indiana. (With the exception of a brief foray into Benton County, they stayed within the Chicago region). The major impediment to maximizing a day's tally in this region is that habitats are so scattered there is not enough time to reach all the necessary sites. But cadres of birders continue to conduct big days, spurred on by the dream that the date they have selected will coincide with a major wave of migrants.

Something close to this dream became a reality on May 7, 1983, the day of the Illinois Department of Natural Resource's annual spring bird count.[65] Southerly winds had been blowing throughout May 6 and continued into May 7, creating ideal conditions for northward moving migrants. When rain began to fall late in the morning, and the winds had still not subsided, the prospects for decent birding seemed to be over. But then something amazing happened. Along with the precipitation, birds literally descended from the sky. In Chicago, thrushes, common yellowthroats (*Geothlypis trichas*), gray catbirds (*Dumetella carolinensis*), and white-throated sparrows were so numerous that nonbirders called newspapers in wonderment. I was in northwest Lake County, where front-yard lawns seethed with warblers: yellow-rumped (*Dendroica coronata*), yellow, cerulean, black-and-white (*Mniotilta varia*), and others. The sight of these usually arboreal warblers feeding on the ground was unforgettable. Lake County tallied 205 species and Cook 204, records that still stand. Statewide, 485,997 individual birds were logged on the count, shattering the old record by more than eighty thousand birds.[66]

The spring bird count of May 6, 1989 also proved to be unusual, but for a very different reason. Two days of warm air gave way to a major cold front that produced wind chills of 10°–20°F and an inch and a half of snow. Birdwatchers found themselves in the midst of what David Johnson called a "winter warbler wonderland." He tells what it was like to be birding that morning at Ryerson Conservation Area in Lake County:

> [When] visibility for observing birds was at its worst (about 9:30 A.M.) . . . we spotted a Red-eyed Vireo, heard both a Warbling and Solitary vireo, and saw a Great Blue Heron flying in the blizzard like an eerie 'Pterodactyl.'. . . The forest floor was blanketed with white, and all the tree limbs and trunks were covered too. . . . I saw a nice male Bay-breasted Warbler on the river bank at my feet in the snow storm; scads of Palms and Myrtles were kicked up as I walked along and Nashville, Ovenbirds, and Blackthroated Green warblers could be heard—all singing in the snow-covered

woods. . . . [In a field] even cowbirds and Red-winged blackbirds were noted . . . but the best birds there had to be . . . seven male Indigo Buntings—bobbing like little blue corks in and out of the snow-covered furrows.[67]

In two articles published in *Audubon Magazine*, J. P. Perkins provides a unique view of migration in this region. Perkins plied the waters of the western Great Lakes for more than thirty years as an officer in the U.S. Steel Corporation's fleet of ore boats. As chief officer, he created a floating forest by placing fourteen trees on his vessel to attract birds. Perkins believes that seventeen principal flyways exist across the lakes. One of these he calls the "South End Flyway," which covers the southern tip of Lake Michigan from Miller, Indiana, to Wind Point in Racine, Wisconsin. According to Perkins this is where "cross-lake migration reaches its greatest intensity," as migrants fly east to west in spring and west to east in fall.[68]

As his ship was heading south toward port in East Chicago, Lake County (Ind.), on May 15, 1960, Perkins encountered "an almost unbelievable" flight: "Shortly after daybreak migrating birds started swarming aboard, and they continued in waves until we entered the harbor at 4 P.M. . . . By mid-afternoon there were so many birds on board that they had to fly off to let crewmembers pass. Of 44 species listed, 15 were warblers."[69]

One seeming quirk of spring migration is the frequently observed and perplexing phenomenon of reverse migration. A striking example occurred on May 6, 1972, when four to five thousand birds were counted flying south at Waukegan. Common grackles (*Quiscalus quiscula*) and red-winged blackbirds made up the bulk, but blue jays, tree swallows (*Tachycineta bicolor*), barn swallows (*Hirundo rustica*), robins, bobolinks, and northern orioles were present as well. No one has apparently come up with the definitive explanation of reverse migration. Laury Binford finds merit in the view that when nocturnal migrants discover with the light of morning that they are over inhospitable terrain, they turn directly around and go back where they are more likely to encounter favorable habitat. Another explanation may be more germane to the reverse migration noted at lakefront sites like Waukegan. Most of the birds involved— blackbirds and swallows, for instance—are both diurnal migrants and flocking species. It is therefore possible that these birds are merely leaving a night roost located to the north.[70]

Fall land bird migration is more drawn out than spring. There is no two-week span when birds are as concentrated as they are in May. Young of the year swell the total numbers of individuals, but many birds become difficult to find and identify because their plumage has dulled and singing has stopped. Fall warblers are notoriously challenging. Species whose breeding males are identifiable at a glance become models of drabness whose diagnostic field marks involve leg or even foot color, the absence or presence of back streaking, and buff washes on undertail feathers. The highest one day species counts for the season are: August—113; September—121; October—113.[71]

Several land birds congregate in the fall in huge numbers. The common nighthawk (*Chordeiles minor*) is most often detected by the sound of its nasal "peent" as it hunts for insects on summer nights. But come late August, large circling flocks appear in the early evening sky. Seven thousand were counted in Kenosha on August 31, 1979.[72]

Purple martins also gather in immense concentrations. In September 1949, ten thousand birds were present on the Chicago lakefront from Foster to Addison, and similar numbers have been recorded at Waukegan.[73] Another aggregation roosted at Thatcher Woods, River Forest, in Cook County. In language reminiscent of passenger pigeon stories, Esther Craigmile described what she saw over several days in August 1938:

> August 22. By 7:30 I began to notice purple martins coming in large flocks from the northwest. My vision easily scanned 30 acres, which had a ceiling above the tree tops 100 feet deep dense with martin life. As I glanced toward the sunset glow, a ceaseless procession of our largest swallows continued. . . . It was the most spectacular migration of purple martins I had ever witnessed.
>
> August 25. Cloudy and rainy. Soon after 7:00 flocks of martins began to arrive, coming from all directions. By 7:20 the air was literally alive with them. Like clouds of black locusts they circled above. . . . Huge flocks quickly swooped down to their accustomed perches. By 7:30 not a bird was left in the air. . . . This was noticeably the largest martin population during the week. I estimated there were at least two million.[74]

In October and November when most of the passerines have left, migration is at its best on days blasted by cold northerly winds. A local adage claims that the more horrific the weather, the more terrific the birding. It is on such days that birders plunk themselves down on the pier at Gillson Park in Wilmette, Cook County (where the shoreline juts out into the lake), or, even better, at Miller Beach in Gary, Lake County (Ind.), to wait for jaegers. Just as warblers epitomize spring for many birders, jaegers, for very different reasons, define the fall.

The appeal of jaegers stems in part from the remoteness of their usual environs—these gull-like raptors are born in the Arctic and spend the rest of the year at sea. Some occur inland, where they are drawn to the Great Lakes or even to more modest reservoirs of human origin. But even here, they tend to stay far offshore, arcing against the sky to harass a gull or slicing low over the dark waves of the lake. They are relatively rare, usually seen at great distances through moisture-coated optical equipment, and the three species are difficult to separate from one another, particularly when in immature plumage. Finding them requires patience and often an insensitivity to physical discomfort.

The three species of jaegers are parasitic (*Stercorarius parasiticus*), pomerine (*S. pomarinus*), and long-tailed (*S. longicaudus*). Of the minority that are identified, the parasitic is by far the most common, although the other two are being seen with increasing regularity. One rainy October day in 1981, Phoebe Snetsinger and I saw three birds at Gillson Park in Wilmette over the course of nine hours. At least two could be identified as parasitic. But the highest numbers occur in Indiana, where seasonal totals often exceed forty birds.[75]

Ken Brock explains the jaeger presence as a product of Lake Michigan's "funnel effect": "During autumn the elongate north-south boundaries of the lake become airways along which thousands of migrants navigate towards wintering areas." As these birds proceed south, they eventually run out of lake and accumulate off the northern Indiana shore. Once they hit "the toe of the lake," some have thought that the jaegers fly overland all the way to the Gulf of Mexico, although no direct evidence of this exists. Another theory holds that most of the birds simply die for lack of food. Jaegers derive much of their living from robbing gulls (hence the name parasitic). This strategy works fine when the gulls are eating fish, but those on the Great Lakes subsist heavily on garbage, which provides less sustenance for the jaegers.[76]

Hawks (Falconiformes) also engage in conspicuous migrations through the region. The earliest report of a major hawk flight was made by Kennicott and is quite curious. Under red-shouldered hawk (*Buteo lineatus*), he wrote: "In October 1854, a flight of apparently several thousand of this hawk passed over Chicago from the lakes, moving towards the southwest." Nelson, writing of the red-shouldered, quotes Kennicott and goes on to say:

> The main fall migration of hawks in this vicinity takes place the last of September or first of October, and a statement of the numbers which pass in a single day, to one who has not observed them, would be received with incredulity. . . . The hawks commence moving south early in the day and continue flying the entire day, and so numerously that, taking a stand at a good point, one would have from one to fifty hawks in view, with but very few intermissions, throughout the day. Among these occur all the migrants, but by far the greater number consist of the smaller species.[77]

What is strange is that neither of these two naturalists mentions the occurrence of the broad-winged hawk, which based on current circumstances fits what they describe much better than the red-shouldered. Huge flocks of broad-wings do appear in spring and late September. On April 30, 1973, four thousand birds moved north along the Berrien County lakefront, but most of the biggest concentrations have been seen in September. Over the course of two days in September 1987, observers at Mount Hoy in DuPage County counted more than three thousand broad-wings.[78]

The largest flight on record, however, was observed early in the evening of September 18, 1992: "At 4:15 . . . while driving west on Route 22 in Highland Park in Lake County, I saw in the distance what first appeared to be a gigantic flock of starlings darkening the eastern sky. Upon reaching the intersection of Routes 41 and 22 the 'the starlings' turned into one of the largest flights of Broad-winged Hawks that I have ever seen." Before the day ended, fourteen thousand birds were counted, including three thousand that descended into trees at Heller Nature Center.[79]

I caught the tail end of the migration the next morning as I pulled into a Dominick's parking lot to procure my weekly groceries. Looking up, I saw kettles of broad-wings circling low over the store as they slowly drifted south. Straining my eyes, I counted a couple of hundred birds. I quickly decided that a day such as this should be spent on something more enduring than shopping, but unfortunately, I was wrong—several hours of looking failed to turn up any additional broad-wings.

Hawk watching is a special love that shares with certain infamous viruses the property of lodging in your blood indefinitely. For two wonderful autumns, I sat on the Johns Manville asbestos dump overlooking the south end of Illinois Beach State Park as part of a coordinated effort to monitor hawk migrations. From September to November, the changing procession of raptors would course southward in dribbles, spurts, and streams. There would be days of southeast winds, warm and flat, when the sky was empty, and days marked by fronts from the west or northwest that propelled the hawks forward. Numerous memories remain vivid: the season's first snowfall, so weak that only someone sitting outdoors in one place would have noticed (a secret shared by very few); a sharp-shinned hawk (*Accipiter striatus*) tearing through a flock of Lapland longspurs (*Calcarius lapponicus*) and flying off with one in its talons; the *Plegadis* ibis passing over as it headed north; and 1982's unprecedented flight of Northern goshawks (*Accipiter gentilis*).

In addition to Illinois Beach, organized hawk watches have been conducted in the fall at Mount Hoy in DuPage County and in the spring at various points in the Indiana Dunes, particularly a dune at Johnson Beach.[80] Success depends on people devoting hours of their weekdays to the project. The Illinois Beach effort collapsed after two years when the fanatics obtained employment or moved away to pursue graduate school; Mount Hoy was conscientiously manned from 1985 to 1988, but changing circumstances of the principals reduced the effort there too. Hawk migration records in the Indiana Dunes date to 1950, but for many of the years the total hours spent in a season were less then ten, though interest since 1983 has increased.

Spring hawks at the Indiana Dunes begin to appear in March, with about a quarter of all Northern harriers (*Circus cyaneus*) passing through. The highest single day for harriers was on March 29, 1960, when fifty were seen. Red-shouldered hawks peak in this month—a remarkable five-day flight in 1990 produced 116 individuals, including seventy-five on March 14 alone. That same day yielded another regional high count as well: ten bald eagles. But the heaviest migration is in April when the five most frequent species, making up well over 80 percent of all the hawks recorded, are on the move: red-tailed hawk (*Buteo jamaicensis*), sharp-shinned hawks, broad-winged hawks, turkey vultures (*Cathartes aura*), and ospreys (*Pandion haliaetus*). (In the most recent taxonomic revision, vultures have been removed from the raptor order and placed with storks and herons.)

Of these five birds, the turkey vulture is the only one whose abundance as a spring migrant through the dunes far exceeds that of its fall flights at Mount Hoy and Illinois Beach. In two years alone, 1989 and 1990, dune hawk watchers saw over four hundred. Turkey vultures have clearly been increasing over the years, in the dunes and throughout the region. One interesting aspect of its spring movements through the dunes is its penchant for feeding on dead fish, including alewives.[81]

Autumn hawk migration begins in mid-September with the broad-wings and falcons. The falcon flight is virtually confined to the Lake Michigan shore and is dominated by merlins (*Falco columbarius*) and peregrines (*F. peregrinus*).[82] Regardless of the wind, these powerful fliers barrel down the lakefront through mid-October. Thirty-six merlins, many engaging in dramatic displays of aerial wizardry, passed the watchers on September 27, 1981, from 11:30 A.M. to 6:00 P.M. The following year, thirty-three merlins were counted on October 14. (Although a thousand kestrels were seen along the Berrien County shore on September 20, 1972, neither of the Illinois stations have ever reported large numbers of the species.)

In medieval days, only kings could keep peregrine falcons, and it is no wonder. The maneuverings of this bird as it chases prey is flight at its most developed level. On September 27, 1981, observers at Illinois Beach listed twenty peregrines, almost half of the season's total of forty-seven. But the most remarkable tally of all was set at Evanston on windswept and rainy October 1, 1977: several birders counted forty-seven migrating peregrine falcons, thereby establishing the single-day inland record for the United States.[83]

Sharp-shinned hawks, red-tailed hawks, ospreys, and Northern harriers also contribute substantially to the volume of autumn hawk migration. Sharp-shins are at their greatest numbers from late September to mid-October; Mount Hoy yielded the highest one-day total—311 on September 28, 1986. Red-tails are seen throughout the fall, but peak from mid-October to mid-November. Two hundred and three were tallied at Illinois Beach on October 22, 1983. Most of the ospreys come through in September, but the single day record of twelve was established at Illinois Beach on October 1, 1981. Northern harriers, peaking from late October through the middle of November, cruise the Illinois Beach swales, slowly going back and forth in search of prey. This behavior made it difficult for us to obtain accurate counts because we didn't know whether a given bird was on its way south or merely hunting.

It was luck, sheer and magnificent, that my tenure as a full-time hawk watcher coincided with the greatest Northern goshawk flight ever witnessed in the Midwest. The Northern goshawk is a bird of the boreal forest and taiga. It is fast and powerful, with short wings and a long tail that give it the maneuverability to hunt ruffed grouse and snowshoe hares. When grouse and hare populations crash every ten or so years, goshawks descend southward in large numbers. Prior to 1972, incursions into the Chicago region were modest.

But in that year the largest incursion of goshawks ever known plowed into the Midwest. From September 30, 1972, to April 8, 1973, 243 goshawks were reported from Illinois. Cedar Grove, just north of Milwaukee, had a one-day total of 206 on October 14, 1972. The magnitude of the flight was so tremendous that Helmut Mueller and his colleagues at Cedar Grove "suggested that at least a considerable fraction of the entire goshawk population emigrated." They went on to say that the species suffered a population reduction of 70 percent and that "goshawks will require several 10-year cycles to regain population levels existing in 1971." Two other Wisconsin ornithologists, Thomas Erdman and David Brinker from Little Suamico Ornithological Station near Green Bay, disagreed, saying that because goshawk losses were only 40 percent, "populations will recover sufficiently by the early 1980s so that another 'invasion' should occur." [84]

Exactly ten years later, an even larger flight of goshawks poured into the region. Although the first bird of the 1982 season at Illinois Beach was seen on October 14, the incursion began in earnest on November 3, when I counted thirty-one birds after seven hours. The next three days produced totals of forty-two, ninety-six, and fifty-two goshawks, respectively, and on the heaviest day no one arrived to count until late in the morning. The last bird was seen on December 6, bringing the final tally up to 293. No goshawk influx has been noted since.

More than perhaps any other North American bird, the goshawk is unintimidated by human beings. Old accounts tell of goshawks pursuing chickens: one followed the fowl up the skirts of a woman while another continued the chase into a kitchen even though the hen was firmly clutched in the hand of the farmer. Two members of the now defunct Barrington Bird Club related their experiences with three immature goshawks in the winter of 1931–32: "It was probably one of these . . . which we saw pick up a large cat from the far side of our field on January 6. The bird rose heavily until about ten feet above the ground when the cat was dropped. The cat walked away as if not injured. On January 10 one of the these hawks was caught in a trap on a neighboring farm and was shot as it was attempting to fly away with the trap."[85]

In January 1983, I was birding in a tract of conifers at Orland Hills Forest Preserve, Cook County, when I came upon an immature goshawk with a shredded rabbit in its talons. It looked up at me, its amber eyes conveying total indifference. I approached to within three feet and it stood its ground, confident that in a confrontation it would prevail.

◄◦► ◄◦► ◄◦►

Most birders would say that migration isn't as good as it used to be. The work of Sidney Gauthreaux of Clemson University supports this view. Using radar data, he has presented strong documentation that from the 1960s to the 1980s migration across the Gulf of Mexico declined by half.[86]

In contrast, at least with respect to land birds, local ornithologists have yet to discern such a trend. David Willard and his colleagues at the Field Museum have gathered one to two thousand dead birds a year for fifteen years from McCormick Place on Chicago's lakefront. Although his analysis of the data is not complete, Willard speaks of what has been found so far: "We are not seeing any significant dips. . . . Our urban data is not showing a correlation with the declining bird numbers shown by breeding bird surveys."[87]

The meticulous field notes of Laury Binford and Ken Brock generally agree with Willard's results. Binford believes that except for decreases in red-eyed vireos and Swainson's thrushes (*Catharus ustulatus*) and increases in the southern species (white-eyed vireo, worm eating warbler, etc.), migrant populations have remained stable since at least the 1950s when his records begin. Brock studied fall warbler migration at a fourteen-acre wooded landfill in Hammond, Lake County (Ind.), known as the "Migrant Trap." Fourteen years of data based on 119 outings failed to show any declines. Brock then compared his results with those of a similar study done at Lincoln Park in Chicago from 1946 to 1950 and again could find no significant evidence of change.[88]

Unfortunately, very little research has been conducted on migrant birds—their requirements during this stressful stage of their lives are poorly known.[89] Watching thirty-five species of passerines sporting about the hedge at Chicago's Montrose Harbor could lead one to conclude that any bit of greenery provides sufficient habitat. But no one knows for sure. The Grabers and Kirk summarize the situation well: "While breeding populations distribute themselves more or less uniformly in the available habitat, migrant populations arrive in large numbers at a given area and must survive (or not) on the resources they find there. The problem is undoubtedly of great significance to the warblers. . . . The habitats which a flight of warblers reach after a night migration may be unknown to the birds except in the perspective that evolutionary history provides, and evolution cannot prepare a wild population for the elimination of habitats at the rates perpetrated by modern man."[90]

Mortality during migration is high. Adverse weather claims many birds, particularly when combined with such hazards as Lake Michigan and tall buildings. How much of an impact these impediments have on avian populations is yet another unknown. Presumably, for species enjoying large populations and a wide distribution, the effects of individual disasters are local in extent and are reversed over time. But given that the life of a migrating bird is becoming ever more dangerous, the cumulative damage of massive killings might impose profound and long-term harm. Such a scenario is even likely when the affected species is rare and with a limited range. In either case, human beings should take the necessary steps, often simple and cheap, to minimize the carnage.

Unseasonably cold weather, especially when accompanied by freezing rain and snow, can take a serious toll on insectivorous species. What few insects remain are concentrated on the ground, where even arboreal birds are forced to forage. This results in greater competition for high-quality animal food and the necessity of utilizing inferior vegetable matter such as grass seeds. In those circumstances, the birds burn more energy than is being replenished.[91]

The May snowfall described earlier by Dave Johnson fortunately proved to be of short duration, and no bird fatalities were noted. But that is not always the case. From May 11 to May 12, 1888, temperatures dropped from 70 to the midthirties, where they stayed until at least through May 13. The devastation of birds that followed was so dramatic two different writers published accounts. In the vicinity of Racine, Philo Hoy found over 645 dead birds of twenty-three species, mostly warblers: "On Saturday morning the 12th hundreds of birds . . . were found on the ground, they not being able to remain on the trees; they were suffering from cold and hunger, and many were caught with hands alone. They entered houses of every description, regardless of noise or confusion." And Joseph Hancock described what he saw in Chicago:

> While it is usual to see many of these birds passing from tree to tree in the
> city, this spring on May 12 they were observed in great numbers scattered
> over the ground in open lots, and on the larger prairies within the business
> part of the town where some were run down by passing vehicles, and

others met their death under the feet of pedestrians. They would permit a close approach, but when almost stepped on would make a spasmodic effort to mount into the air, only to find themselves dropping back to the ground again, helpless, weak, and benumbed by the cold. This strange effect of the weather extended over many miles of country and across Lake Michigan to the east. The shores between Lake Forest, Evanston, and Chicago were bestrewn with lifeless birds which had been washed up by the waves.[92]

Among the thirty-two species he encountered on the ground were spotted sandpiper (*Actitis macularia*), redheaded woodpecker (*Melanerpes erythrocephalus*), least flycatcher (*Empidonax minimus*), Eastern kingbird, house wren (*Troglodytes aedon*, golden-crowned kinglet (*Regulus satrapa*), Eastern bluebird, and ten species of warblers.

The Great Lakes are famous for their unpredictable weather. In the words of Stan Rogers's haunting ballad "White Squall": "I told that kid a hundred times, don't take the lakes for granted, They go from calm to a hundred knots so fast they seem enchanted."

Rapidly changing weather conditions may help explain why so many migrants perish in the waters of the Great Lakes, even though these same species routinely cross much greater expanses of ocean. The worst storm-induced bird kill recorded from the lakes in spring happened over the Memorial Day weekend of 1976, when the corpses of two hundred thousand warblers, thrushes, and blue jays were counted on a fifty-mile stretch of beach along Lake Huron. Ten thousand more birds were estimated to have drowned in Lake Michigan at the same time. But a letter published by the *Chicago Tribune* on September 3, 1881 vividly documents an even greater loss of avian life:

> Two years ago there was a heavy storm, lasting some twenty-four hours. It occurred during the first week in September, and the eastern shore of Lake Michigan was strewn with dead birds. I took some pains to count these on a certain number of yards, and estimated that if the eastern shore was alike through all its length over half a million of birds were lying dead on that side of the lake alone. It is more than likely that nearly as many more were on the west. Not all the birds could be counted, because many were immediately buried in the sand. . . .
>
> It was a strange and pitiful sight, some were so fresh and perfect, and their feathers so unruffled, that it seemed impossible that they had been drowned. There were multitudes of wrens, with narrow, gauzy wings spread out, so that the wind swept them up and down on the sand, like autumn leaves sere and brown. Tiny creepers, looking ghastly with only a

head and wing unburied, and moving as if alive; kinglets with their bright crowns defaced huddled into a group, where I counted a robin with fair unruffled breast, a kingbird, a summer yellowbird [goldfinch], and one orange-crowned warbler. The greatest number of any one species was the yellow-winged [grasshopper] sparrow, both young and old. The grass finch [vesper sparrow] and the song sparrow were abundant, as was also the familiar little pair bird.[93]

Even without storms, Lake Michigan is a formidable obstacle to many land birds. It is not uncommon to spot a tiny passerine over the lake, struggling to clear the swells as it heads for shore. On August 21, 1971, several of us watched a Blackburnian warbler (*Dendroica fusca*) come in low off the lake and collapse on the beach virtually at the water line. Any wave at all would have bowled it over. But it must have had some energy left, because as I bent down to pick it up, the bird flew into a nearby willow.

The Blackburnian was lucky there were no gulls around. Taking advantage of their prowess as both swimmers and flyers, gulls relentlessly hunt avian landlubbers caught over the lake. Chief Officer Perkins had extensive opportunities to watch these birds in action:

> After cruising the Great Lakes for 31 years, I am convinced that gulls are a formidable hazard to migrating birds. Few people realize how predaceous herring and ring-billed gulls are. Gulls seldom snatch birds from the air, but I've seen a flock of them annihilate a small flock of sparrows. Small birds put on some flying acrobatics to avoid this fate, but the gulls, with their greater endurance and number, usually win. I've seen gulls destroy various species from small warblers and sparrows to saw-whet owls, least and American bitterns, and coots. After these larger birds have fallen or been knocked into the water, the gulls gather around and tear them apart.[94]

At Gillson Park one September morning, I witnessed the misfortune of a cuckoo as it attempted to reach land. It made steady progress until several ring-billed gulls began to mob it. The larger birds would rise above the cuckoo and then dive at it, attempting to drive it into the water. Initially the cuckoo was able to foil these efforts by gaining altitude following the attack. But each time the gulls regained their advantage until finally the cuckoo rose no more.

Birds have been dying like this since they adopted migration as a way of life. But changes in human technology have created entirely new hazards. Tall buildings, floodlights, communication wires, and reflective windows are taking an ever-heavier toll. The worse single disaster happened near Macon, Georgia, and involved a ceilometer, a beacon designed to measure the height of cloud cover. On one overcast night, more than fifty thousand birds lost their lives, either through impact with the tower or from exhaustion.[95]

The earliest local incident that I have found of bird mortality due to a lighted building is over a century old. Late in 1885, the Chicago Board of Trade installed a ring of twenty electric arc lights, thirty feet in diameter around the dome of its building, three hundred feet above the ground. First lit on New Year's night of 1886, the marvel was burning brightly five months later:

> On the night of May 8, a terrific thunderstorm passed over the city be-
> tween the hours of 11 P.M. and midnight. During the storm, the attention
> of the few people who were on the street at the time was attracted to the
> spectacle of a great number of birds hovering about this ring of lights and
> dashing at them. In the morning it was discovered that hundreds of dead
> birds were scattered about the foot of the tower and hundreds more found
> on the roof of the building. When the workmen ascended the tower to re-
> new the carbon in the lights, they found many of the globes occupied by
> the bodies of birds, some containing as many as eight, and many of the car-
> bons had been broken off by the birds. Over 200 bodies were picked up by
> one of the workmen . . . which was but a small part of those carried away
> by the newsboys and others in the morning. A person who saw them be-
> fore any were taken away estimated that more than a thousand were killed.
> But even this was but a small portion of what were seen in the air about the
> tower. . . . From the testimony of those who saw them, [the victims] appear
> to have been the smaller song birds.[96]

In the modern era, the John Hancock building had been Chicago's most notorious of architectural bird killers. After years of effort, William Beecher finally succeeded in shaming management into dimming lights during periods of migration. (Extinguish lights, not birds!) The way Beecher won this battle— again demonstrating his unsurpassed effectiveness as a conservationist—was by displaying a single night's worth of Big John's avian casualties. The sight of a thousand dead birds had its intended effect.

If Hancock was the premier avian death trap of the 1970s, the current champion has been the building at 311 S. Wacker, nicknamed the "Wedding Cake" because of the gaudy lighting that adorns its top. Citizens made manage-ment aware of the problem, and there was a promise to cooperate, but on many a night the lights remained on.[97] Things changed, however, in March 2000, when Mayor Richard Daley issued the request that buildings turn off their lights during migration. Chicago's skyline is much darker now in spring and fall, and birds will have an easier time negotiating the former obstacle course. (How

91. Dr. William Beecher with birds that had flown into John Hancock
Building, Chicago. (Courtesy Chicago Academy of Sciences.)

conservation in all of its facets has grown over thirty years: from the days when
Bill Beecher was virtually a lone voice, to the present when Mayor Richard M.
Daley recently signed the "Treaty for Birds," which commits the city to a broad
program of bird conservation.)

Another feature of urban architecture that wreaks havoc with birds are
the sheets of glass that gird so many buildings. These plates reflect the images
of shrubs and other landscaping, thus presenting to migrants the deadly illu-
sion of refuge. The speech pathology building on Northwestern University's
lakefront campus in Evanston is decorated with mirror-like windows. I have
seen many birds trapped in the walkway, surrounded on three sides by the mys-
tifying mirrors. As people enter, the birds fly up to escape, only to smack into
the glass with painful thuds. As a small and fruitless protest, I once piled up all
the corpses in the doorway so any visitor would have to notice. The base of the
Hancock Building presents the same problem; twenty species of warblers were
picked up there over the fall of 1993.

Daniel Klehm, Jr., an ornithologist at Muhlenberg College in Pennsylvania, is probably the leading authority on window-induced bird mortality. He
estimates that within the United States alone a minimum of 1 billion birds a

year die by flying into glass windows. (Because of his conservative assumptions, the actual carnage may well be a hundred times greater.) Klehm believes that such collisions account for one-third of all avian mortality at the hands of humans and may be second only to habitat destruction as the greatest threat to birds. As intrinsically appalling as all of this is, even worse is that many of the deaths could be avoided by simply drawing shades and turning off lights.[98]

Humans indirectly cause bird deaths in other ways as well. I have already mentioned prairie chickens flying into telegraph wires near Chicago in the 1840s. One of the most remarkable things I have ever seen was a green heron (*Butorides virescens*) that flew over the road in front of me in April 1995. As it crossed a front yard, the bird literally disassembled: a wing went skittering one way and the rest of the body plummeted straight down like a rock. After a long double take, I realized it had flown into a telephone wire and severed its wing.

Oil spills have claimed loons, grebes, and other species on Lake Michigan. An oil spill of unknown origin befouled (and perhaps defowled) the waters off northwestern Indiana in November 1955 and killed hundreds of water birds, 95 percent of which were horned grebes (*Podiceps auritus*). It also disabled six red-necked grebes (*Podiceps grisegena*), an extremely rare bird in the state.[99]

◄o► ◄o► ◄o►

Migratory birds have a way of getting lost. Seeing, or ideally discovering, such waifs is one of the joys of birding; many of us have traveled thousands of miles in search of rarities. With its active cadres of experienced observers, Chicago has had its share of amazing sightings.

One of the most amazing of all was made on July 15, 1949. On that date, Albert and Lee Campbell decided to bird the Lake Calumet area. While scanning a sand pit south of 103rd Street, they spotted a tern "unconcernedly preening himself." When they saw the huge yellow bill and yellow legs, the Campbell's knew that they had found something extraordinary, a feeling that was confirmed when a quick check of Peterson's *A Field Guide to the Birds* failed to reveal anything remotely like it. After further research, they identified the bird as a large-billed tern (*Phaetusa simplex*), the continent's first record of this South American species. (This was the first and only time the Chicago area produced a bird not hitherto known to have occurred in North America.) It hung around for about ten days, long enough for numerous people to see it.[100]

While the lazuli bunting (*Passerina amoena*) has appeared from time to time in the Midwest, the Chicago region has a lone record: a male that took up residence at a feeder in Elgin, Kane County, from December 17–21, 1973. Birders learned of it on what proved to be its last day here, which also coincided with a sleet storm. Interstates 294 and 90 were almost impassable. I was fortunate that there weren't more drivers on the road, but then only those pursuing essential business would face such adverse conditions. The people whose feeder hosted the bunting were very pleasant, and the bird proved to be cooperative as well.

Six years later another call necessitated a quick change of plans. It was 7:30 A.M. on May 8, 1991, and I had just arrived at work, earlier than usual. The phone rang, and it was Andy Sigler informing me that he had just seen a brown pelican (*Pelecanus occidentalis*) at Montrose Harbor, about twenty-five minutes to the north. Very few records of the species existed for Illinois or the Chicago region. Dressed in my suit, I raced outside, hailed a cab, and headed toward Montrose. Upon arriving, I asked the driver to wait until my mission was completed. I spied Peg Walsh and Catherine Monday birding at the hedge and ran to them. Grabbing Peg's binoculars (with her permission of course; at least I think I asked first), I went to the beach, where I spotted the pelican amid the gulls. After watching it for a couple of minutes, I returned the binoculars and sped back to the office, a state-bird richer and $20 poorer. (What was presumably the same bird hung around all summer, with observations from just south of the Wisconsin line to Indiana.)

Every birder has had similar experiences. While the appearance of vagrants undoubtedly furnishes birding with some of its most exciting moments, does it tell us anything more profound? Although little research has been conducted on the subject (perhaps because most professional ornithologists are fearful that such an inquiry would smack too much of birding than of science), Laury Binford believes it does: "All migrant species throw off vagrants from the breeding population. There is a selective advantage to that, because if something happens to the core population or its habitat it is an advantage for birds to go somewhere else. In other words, it increases the chances that the species can survive a catastrophe to its core population. But many more vagrants are being found today than before. Is this simply a function of better coverage? Or is there something biological happening here? If the latter, we should know about it because it would seem to be an aberrant behavior."[101]

As examples of range changes that were foreshadowed by increasing vagrancy, Binford cites the northern parula warbler (*Parula americana*), an eastern species that now breeds in California, and the glaucous-winged gull (*Larus glaucescens*), a bird of the northwest coast that now breeds inland and has wintered as far east as Lake Calumet.

Species most likely to succeed as colonizers are those that are long-lived and philopatric (those that tend to return to the same spot year after year). These two factors increase the chances that a vagrant will encounter others of the same kind; over time, an area previously out of range will begin to support a regular population. There has to be, of course, suitable habitat to sustain this new population. For the glaucous-winged gull, dumps and reservoirs have enabled it to move east.

The little gull (*Larus minutus*) and cattle egret are cases in point. Nineteen thirty-eight was a significant year in the annals of local little gull history: on April 29 the first record for the region and Illinois was established when William Dreuth found one in Lincoln Park, Chicago, and on November 17 Ed Prins saw the region's second, and Wisconsin's first, in Racine. This European species increased over the years and has shown up in every month. A bird even hung around for a week at diminutive Crabtree Lake in Cook County. By 1972, little gulls attempted to nest at Green Bay, Wisconsin, where three years later they succeeded in fledging two young, the first such record in the United States.[102]

Cattle egrets are famous for their ability to colonize new territory. Originating in Africa and tropical Asia, the cattle egret managed to cross the Atlantic, reaching Surinam (South America) between 1877 and 1882. Birds have landed on ships at sea, a possible means of negotiating the long distances of open water. The first records for the United States were during the 1940s in southern Florida, where they began nesting in 1953.[103] (They have also spread to Australia and even isolated Bermuda.)

The first inland cattle egret record for the country was established when two birders sighted a breeding plumaged individual at Saganashkee Slough (Cook County) on August 10, 1952. The bird would not be found in Wisconsin until 1960 and Indiana until 1964. Today, however, it is widely seen during migration, and several pairs nest annually at Lake Renwick.

Thriving in the Cold: Wintering Birds

Christmas bird counts represent the principal effort to census wintering bird populations. As explained earlier, the goal is to count all the birds found in a day within a fifteen-mile diameter circle. The project was started at the turn of the century as an alternative to the Christmas hunt, and 1,650 counts are now conducted throughout the Western Hemisphere. These are compiled and published by the National Audubon Society for national distribution.

The Chicago region hosts as many as twenty-five counts; Christmas bird counts held between December 19, 1997, and January 4, 1998, for example, averaged sixty-three species, and many had higher than usual totals.[104] The ninety species tallied on the Evanston North Shore Count established a new regional record high.

The species encountered on the counts can be placed in four groups—

permanent residents, regular winter residents, winter visitants that are prone
to periodic invasions, and out-of-season lingerers (most of these usually disappear by January or February). Since I have already dealt with many of the year-
round residents, I will focus on the other three categories.

Approximately ten species fall into that group of birds that arrive in fall,
depart in spring, and can be expected to do so each year in reasonable numbers.
Their abundance from year to year is determined by such factors as snow
depth, seed crop, and rodent populations. American tree sparrows (*Spizella ar-
borea*) and dark-eyed juncos (*Junco hyemalis*) are the most common and widespread of this group, although development has eliminated many of the fallow
fields that support them. Dave Johnson experienced this firsthand. While participating on the Waukegan Christmas count on January 1, 1984, he saw more
than a thousand tree sparrows swarming in one field, now part of the Gurnee
Mills Shopping Center in Gurnee, Lake County.

Snow buntings (*Plectrophenax nivalis*) seem to put in their first fall appearance along the lakefront, then spread inland with the onset of winter.
While at the Skokie Marsh on the morning of November 29, 1927, a duck
hunter witnessed a flight of these birds that must have resembled a blizzard.
For three hours, "flocks estimated at from 200 to 1,000 were passing continuously." The birds "flew south, at about 100 feet elevation, in large flocks . . . and
the air was filled with their calls." The observer estimated that twenty-five
thousand buntings passed that morning.[105]

Less than a hundred years ago, snow buntings were deliberately slaugh-
tered for a number of purposes. A 1903 report tells of eighty thousand snow
buntings found in a single freezer, all to satisfy the "gourmet trade." Milliners
also highly coveted the species: "The beauty of the black, white and brown
plumage rendering it particularly attractive as a 'hat bird.'" Walter Barrows, in
his *Michigan Bird Life*, reported that when bounties were paid on house sparrows, "thousands of heads of snow buntings were palmed off on more or less
unsuspecting county clerks as those of sparrows." Despite these attacks, snow
buntings seem to have escaped noticeable reductions in population.[106]

Other species have experienced changes in status over the years. Although rough-legged hawks (*Buteo lagopus*) are said to peak in three-to-five-
year intervals, data from the Evanston North Shore Christmas count suggest
that high populations occur every nine to ten years. This may mean that overall population levels are so low that only extremely large influxes are discernible. Mumford and Keller write of its decrease in northwest Indiana: "Before
fall plowing became common in this section of the state, one might see as many
as six rough-legged hawks feeding in a single field. But fall plowing dramatically decreased the grain stubble that harbored mice and voles, eliminating

most of the hawk's good wintering forage habitat. They now must find odd patches of fallow fields, ditch banks, railroad and highway rights-of-ways, and the very few remaining brushy fencerows, to search for prey."[107]

The short-eared owl (*Asio flammeus*) has fared even worse. It is now a very rare breeder and uncommon winter resident that is most frequently seen migrating along the lake front, a far cry from Nelson's 1876 assessment: "The most abundant species of the family. . . . They are common everywhere, on prairies and marshes, during the winter."[108]

Lake Michigan has a lot to offer the birder in winter. Besides such expected species as long-tailed duck (*Clangula hyemalis*), common goldeneye (*Bucephala clangula*), and common merganser (*Mergus merganser*), rarities are frequently discovered. Birders routinely find Thayer's (*Larus thayeri*), glaucous (*Larus hyperboreus*), and other uncommon gulls by chumming stale bread.

Adverse weather can, of course, provide challenging conditions. On days when air temperature is low but the lake is unfrozen, an impenetrable layer of fog settles low over the water making it impossible to see anything less conspicuous than a pelican. At other times, strong winds, common in this season, drive great chunks of ice toward shore, often creating vistas of frozen bleakness extending beyond the limit of vision. Bird-watchers hope for open leads close enough to identify the ducks bobbing in the choppy water, for not many people are willing to follow the example of W. Nordenholt. On January 25, 1920, he hiked across two miles of ice in order to reach open water. His effort was rewarded by one female and three male harlequin ducks (*Histrionicus histrionicus*), a rare but increasingly regular winter visitant that is also stunning in appearance.[109]

⊰⊱ ⊰⊱ ⊰⊱

One or two snowy owls (*Nyctea scandiaca*) appear somewhere in the area most every year. In Berrien County alone, the species has been seen in twenty-nine out of thirty years. But the single most reliable place to see them is Meigs Field, Chicago, where a large tract of protected lakefront is the ideal place for an owl to dally. (One owl allegedly perched atop the scoreboard at Soldier Field, very close to Meigs Field, and managed to short it out. Chicago Park District personnel had to scramble to fix it before the commencement of the Bears-Cowboys playoff game.) But roughly every four years, when the lemmings, hares, and other prey species decline, snowy owls head south from their Arctic breeding grounds in unusually large numbers.[110] The invasions of 1980–81 and 1991–92 topped all previous ones in this region.

Helen Dancey spent six weeks in late 1981 studying the foraging of a snowy owl in the Michigan City area. Her observations, augmented by those of others, and analysis of pellets (owls and hawks regurgitate bones, feathers, and other undigested food items), demonstrate the wide-ranging tastes of this species. Prey included Norway rats, cottontail rabbits, herring gulls, black scoters (*Melanitta nigra*), common loon (*Gavia immer*), snakes, snow bunting, and a Northern saw-whet owl. On New Year's Eve 1963, two birders watched a snowy owl gnaw on a live mallard frozen in Belmont Harbor. Eventually, the owl flew off with the duck's top portion, leaving the remainder still encased in ice.[111]

The winter of 1967–68 was a flight year. On December 9, 1967, five owls were seen in Berrien County. It was also the year I saw my first one. My mother had received the call in the afternoon, so when I arrived home from school, the last day before Christmas break 1967, we immediately left for Northwestern University, where members of the Evanston North Shore Bird Club had located a snowy owl. As our search took us to the south end of the university's landfill, my mother stopped and yelled, "There it is!" I had already spotted the white mass and rejected it as obvious garbage. Moments after I started explaining the folly of my mom's identification, the object of my discourse took off in slow ponderous flight. (I know; I should have learned my lesson with the cranes.) It circled around and landed at the far end of the lagoon, where it was lost from sight.

Pine siskins (*Carduelis pinus*), pine grosbeaks (*Pinicola enucleator*), evening grosbeaks (*Coccothraustes vespertinus*), red crossbills (*Loxia curvirostra*), white-winged crossbills (*L. leucoptera*), common redpolls (*Carduelis flammea*), and hoary redpolls (*C. hornemanni*) are collectively known in bird-watching parlance as winter finches. They nest in the boreal forests or the tundra (redpolls) and feed on seeds of various types. (Red crossbills and siskins have even bred in this region on rare occasions.) When the crop is either poor or buried by snow, one or more of these species emigrate south in unusual numbers.

The largest single movement of pine siskins was seen on the Berrien County lakefront on October 29, 1971, when three thousand birds streamed by. Berrien County was also the scene for the largest evening grosbeak migration—two thousand on November 6, 1972. Other flights occurred in 1951–52 and 1968–69. Only one spectacular incursion of white-winged crossbills is preserved in writing: "In the year 1894, from the ninth to the twentieth of November, enormous flocks of these crossbills passed along the lake shore, and many were shot with slingshots by boys."[112]

Data from Wisconsin Christmas counts suggest that the ebb and flow of common redpolls is generally on an every-other-year or every-two-year basis.[113] Evanston North Shore Christmas count figures also reflect that pattern, except for a virtual absence of the species during a nine-year span from 1979 to 1987. The largest single flock of redpolls ever seen in this region remained for at least a week in a twenty-acre field south of Michigan City, La Porte County, in February 1972. Biologist David Easterla counted more than four thousand individuals feeding on rough pigweed (*Amaranthus retroflexus*) and lambs quarter (*Chenopodium album*). At dusk, the birds left the area and disappeared to the north, possibly to a wooded roost. In among the masses of common redpolls, Easterla discovered several hoary redpolls, the winter finch that appears in this latitude least frequently of all. Of the twelve hoaries estimated to be present, he shot five of them, one of which was destroyed by the blast and discarded.[114]

The Bohemian waxwing (*Bombycilla garrulus*) has a long way to travel from breeding grounds in northwestern Canada but visits the region periodically. In those years when it does appear, it is usually as a small single flock. The most recent exception was the winter of 1962 when it occurred throughout the area, including a group of seventy-five at the Morton Arboretum.[115] One year, however, was unlike any other:

> The present season, 1919–1920 will be long remembered for its great flight of Bohemian Waxwings, one of the most aristocratic and beautiful of birds. . . . An unusual flight of these birds was observed by Mr. Colin Sanborn and the writer on Nov. 30th, 1919, five miles north of Waukegan, Illinois. . . . The wind was blowing a gale from the northwest, with snow squalls, the first day of real winter weather, but our hopes ran high as waxwings had been reported a day or two before. . . . Soon after daylight they appeared, flock after flock of them, whirling southward before the wind, following the same general course, a couple of hundred yards from the Lake Michigan shoreline. Along toward ten o'clock some of the flocks would stop a few minutes to feed, swarming into some small dead tree till it was full to overflowing with feathered beauties, while hungry members of the flock fed on the berries of nearby junipers. . . . Altogether on this never-to-be-forgotten day, we saw at least twelve hundred waxwings, probably a good many more. The flocks contained from thirty to perhaps a hundred birds each, sometimes appearing every few minutes, at others an hour or so elapsing between arrivals. They were not wandering flocks, searching the countryside for food, but in full migration, the flocks following one another as if on a beaten path.[116]

During the first half of the 1980s, the North Shore Channel, an artificial waterway running between Wilmette Harbor and the North Branch of the Chicago River (near Foster Avenue on Chicago's north side) held an unprecedented number of Neotropical migrants well into the winter. This phenomenon was first detected by Richard Biss and Steven Mlodinow, and their early reports were met with skepticism in some circles. But as more bird-watchers confirmed their discovery, any doubts vanished.[117]

The most productive section of channel was the ten miles between Howard Street on the north (Evanston) and Berteau Street on the south (Chicago). This lies within the circle of the Chicago Urban Christmas count, compiled since its inception by Jeffrey Sanders. In 1979, the wintering birds of the channel made their first big splash when the count included the amazing combination of seventeen golden-crowned kinglets (a high number), two ruby crowned kinglets, sixty-nine yellow-rumped warblers (the one warbler that does frequently spend the winter, but this was a very high total), and particularly these three warblers: three palm (*Dendroica palmarum*), one Northern water-thrush (*Seiurus noveboracensis*), and one common yellowthroat. No Christmas count in the region ever had such a list before. Birders saw a Cape May warbler during the 1980 count period, but otherwise the next two years were quiet.

The hiatus was short lived, however, for 1982 and 1983 were absolutely amazing (see table 10) The regional Christmas count editor called the 1982 census "the weirdest count ever for Illinois." Fortunately, the number of birders participating on the count grew (after years of struggling to get helpers, Jeff Sanders was suddenly inundated by birders wanting to "do the canal"), and Dave Johnson was able to photograph most of the rarities. Since the channel has extremely steep vegetated slopes, four of us performed our 1982 count duties from canoes. The channel presents a locally unique paddling venue: rapids form where treated water is discharged at Touhy Avenue, and the lowest branches of the trees are festooned with condoms.

The outlandishness of some of these birds is easy to convey. The white-eyed vireos were the first of their family ever to be recorded on any Illinois Christmas count. Coot Bay, Florida, in Everglades National Park, was the only other count in the country to record prothonotary, Wilson's (*Wilsonia pusilla*), or three Cape Mays (*Dendroica tigrina*) in 1982. Besides Chicago Urban, the only counts in 1983 reporting bay-breasted warblers (one each) were San Diego and Sabine National Wildlife Refuge in Louisiana.

Although 1985 produced one palm warbler and one orange-crowned, the incredible abundance and variety of overwintering birds was never to be repeated. During the bountiful years, birders watched warblers feed on what they thought were newly hatched mosquitoes. The abrupt end of the insects corresponded with the disappearance of the birds, and observers surmised that the Metropolitan Water Reclamation District, the agency with jurisdiction over the channel, had added an insecticide to the water.

Actually, the birds vanished because the water had become cleaner. The

Table 10. Highlights of Chicago Urban Christmas Bird Count, 1982 and 1983

	1982	1983
White-eyed vireo	2	
Ruby-crowned kinglet	9	3
Yellow-rumped warbler	220	126
Yellow-throated warbler	Count period	...
Palm warbler	8	2
Northern yellowthroat	1	1
Cape May warbler	3	Count period
Orange-crowned warbler	2	2
Nashville warbler	2	2
Yellow warbler	...	1
Bay-breasted warbler	...	1
American redstart	...	1
Prothonotary warbler	1	...
Wilson's warbler	1	...

Note. Count period birds are those missed on the actual Christmas count but seen during the total period during which a count could take place. More recently this has been shortened to a period 3 days either side of count.

insects were midge flies (*Chironomus riparius*), a species that lives in the sediment at the bottom. However, when the water temperature reaches 52°–56°F, they emerge at the surface in their adult form. In April 1984 the Water Reclamation District discontinued chlorinating at its north-side plant, which discharges into the channel. At the same time, the deep tunnel project came on line, which meant that less storm water was entering the channel, another factor contributing to water quality. In response to the less polluted water, carp, goldfish, and other fish became more common and foraged heavily on the midges, a fact confirmed by district biologists. The growth of aquatic vegetation enabled snails and other organisms to thrive; with the more complex ecosystem, the midges had predators and thus were reduced in abundance.[118]

Figures in Fur: Mammals

This was the great North American faunal province, never so rich, so varied, as where the elk looked westward out of the woods across the prairies, and the little sleek pocket gophers of the steppe met the proud wall of the oaks. Here the marten from Canada paused in the tree-tops with the fox squirrel hanging in his jaws, and the cougar, out of the south, sneezed dubiously at the tang of the north upon the air. —Donald Culross Peattie (1938)

You get tired of
Hearing from
Coyote, right?

Well, he's long
Since tired of
Hearing from

You too,
You too,
Pilgrim. . . .
—"Gogisi" Caroll Arnett (in James Koller et al., *Coyote's Journal*, 1982)

Roughly sixty species of mammals were native to the Chicago region.[1] Of the fifty or so species currently present, most seem to be holding their own or increasing, although insufficient information on a number of these makes their true status impossible to know.[2] These surviving species are able to exist in one or more of the altered woodlands, edge, or meadows that comprise most of the persisting greenery. The largest are coyote (*Canis latrans*), beaver (*Castor canadensis*), and white-tailed deer (*Odocoileus virginianus*). They have done exceedingly well over the past two or three decades and, in the process, have generated more public interest than any other native mammals.

Mustelids, members of the weasel family (Mustelidae), occur throughout the region; their very presence makes the land seem less tame. But apart from the mink (I usually see at least a couple every year) and striped skunk, mustelids are masters at escaping detection. Even though the badger (*Taxidea taxus*) and long-tailed weasel (*Mustela frenata*) have been found in each of the nineteen counties, few people encounter them. More secretive still, the least weasel (*Mustela nivalis*) was virtually unknown in both Indiana and Illinois until the 1920s, when one individual died in the jaws of a dog and another had the misfortune of entering a house in Highland Park, Lake County (Ill.).

Even more retiring, bats, shrews, moles, eastern pocket gophers (*Geomys bursarius*), and native mice are all diminutive creatures that conduct their affairs at night or underground, beyond the ken of most people. In addition, some species can only be identified with certainty by counting teeth and measuring body parts. For these reasons, humanity largely ignores them (bats are an exception), and scientific studies are to thank for most of what is known about them.

Some mammals have spread from more traditional habitats into tracts dominated by lawns, houses, and concrete. Raccoons (*Procyon lotor*), opossums (*Didelphis virginiana*), and striped skunks may be more common now than they have ever been before and are quite comfortable living among their human neighbors, although the reverse is not as true. Conspicuous in neighborhoods throughout the area, eastern cottontail rabbits (*Sylvilagus floridanus*), eastern fox squirrels (*Sciurus niger*), and eastern gray squirrels (*S. carolinensis*) also fare well in the wake of the urban glacier.

This discussion of the mammals consists less of themes than portraits of the individual groups or species: what is most important is their very presence. The ones that disappeared signify what the region was like as wilderness, and the much larger set that persists represents the biodiversity still possible after three hundred years of Euro-American activity.

What a Time It Must Have Been: Extirpated Species

By the early years of the twentieth century, thirteen mammals had either virtually or entirely disappeared from the region: smoky shrew (*Sorex fumeus*), beaver, porcupine (*Erethizon dorsatum*), gray wolf (*Canis lupus*), black bear (*Ursus americanus*), river otter (*Lutra canadensis*), marten (*Martes americana*), fisher (*Martes pennanti*), mountain lion (*Puma concolor*), bobcat (*Lynx rufus*), white-tailed deer, wapiti (*Cervus elephus*), and bison (*Bison bison*). (Three of these species are treated elsewhere in this chapter: beaver and white-tailed deer have been reintroduced; and wolves are discussed with coyotes because of their similarity.) Various opinions have been expressed on the status of four other species: snowshoe hare (*Lepus americanus*), white-tailed jackrabbit (*Lepus townsendii*), lynx (*Lynx canadensis*), and pronghorn antelope (*Antilocapra americana*).

Among this group are the charismatic megafauna that help define the quality of an ecosystem. But these animals require vast amounts of space, cover, and food, elements generally incompatible with a large and demanding human population.

A number of these species vanished without leaving much of a record. All that can be said about the smoky shrew, which inhabits woodlands east and south of this region, is that Dr. Philo Hoy collected a single individual in Racine in 1853. He sent the specimen to the U.S. National Museum, where the faded skin and broken skull lay mislabeled for forty years.[3]

The marten and fisher, exquisite predators of northern forests, barely ranged this far south. At the turn of this century, Charles Cory wrote that a marten skeleton originating from Illinois was in the Chicago Academy of Sciences collection, but apparently the specimen is no longer there. The Northern Indiana Historical Society held the remains of another marten, found at Fort Saint Joseph in Berrien County. A portion of a fisher jaw has been recovered from the Indiana Dunes. Believed to be from a young male, it is more than 150 years old. The closest to circumstantial accounts of their presence are Robert Kennicott's 1855 comments that "the fisher used frequently to be seen in the heavy timber along Lake Michigan" and his even less definite 1859 remark that martens have "been seen, occasionally, in northern Illinois."[4]

Wapiti (commonly called elk) roamed into the 1830s, but few writers actually observed any. Joliet and Marquette saw them, and a Mr. Hamburgh found them plentiful outside Fort Saint Joseph in Berrien County in 1763. John Fonda, who delivered mail between Green Bay, Wisconsin, and Chicago in 1818, said wapiti lived along his route. Writing in 1855, Kennicott stated that several were known to have been shot in Cook County. Captain Levinge left Chicago to embark on a hunting excursion in the grasslands along the Fox River in 1838; he avers that "wapiti are to be found on these prairies, but the chance of getting at them appeared so uncertain, that we returned to Chicago without making the attempt."[5]

Although wapiti sightings have not survived, their antlers have shown up throughout the region. Indians placed antlers in trees or deposited them in lakes and rivers as offerings to the spirits. Elkhorn, Wisconsin, is said to have been named for two elk antlers found in a tree there in 1836. One Bert Dutton uncovered a very large pair in 1905 as he was installing drainage tiles in a marsh south of Whitewater, Walworth County. Lake Delavan (Walworth County) yielded a pair of antlers in 1937, as did the Kankakee River in Saint Joseph County, Indiana, in 1895. Several have also shown up in Berrien County bogs.[6]

The mountain lion is another sizable animal that was rarely encountered, which is not surprising given that the species is mostly nocturnal, tends to be retiring, and may have territories as large as 360 square miles. Traversing the prairies from southern Illinois to Chicago during the winter of 1815, the Callis family reported that they "frequently heard the cries of panthers during the night." August Conant, who established a homestead in Des Plaines in the 1830s, noted in his diary that on May 4, 1837, he hunted a panther. Another animal, nine feet long, is supposed to have been taken near Williams Bay, Walworth County, sometime during the early 1800s. Brennan quotes two old-timers as saying that when they first arrived in the Indiana Dunes in the 1830s, there were "large numbers of panthers in the Dunes, the beaches, and woods of the Valparaiso Moraine." The latest local record was of one shot in 1844 on the "Asa Turney farm [in the Blue Island area of southern Cook County] by one of the Crandalls."[7]

The following incident allegedly occurred in the late 1830s or early 1840s: "An amusing story is told of a hunter killing a panther on the Grand Calumet, near where is now the City of Hammond. The hunter fired at the big cat as it swam toward him, but becoming panic stricken, he threw away his rifle and fled, arriving home almost exhausted. His wife compelled him to return to the scene where the panther lay dead and the gun nearby. A boy on the opposite side of the river had witnessed the occurrence and the hunter never heard the last of it."[8]

Porcupines were almost exclusively restricted to the Indiana portion of the region. George Brennan, in his *The Wonders of the Dunes*, provides most of what is known about local porcupines: "The Porcupine, which was formerly common in the Dunes, was thought to have totally disappeared, but there may be some still in existence there, as in 1918 one was attacked by a dog near Furnessville and he filled the dog so full of quills that the dog almost died. . . . In 1915 [Fred Tharp] shot a porcupine . . . directly north of Cowles' tamarack swamp."[9]

Specimens taken in La Porte County in the late 1800s were deposited in the Indiana State Museum, and there are also reports from Lake County. The only other record is for Walworth County, that of a young animal caught in the Hollister Woods near Delavan in September 1918.[10] Apart from almost certain escapes, porcupines have eluded detection in Illinois. Given their presence in neighboring parts of Indiana and Wisconsin, this gap is curious.

◄◦► ◄◦► ◄◦►

The bobcat and river otter are animals among this group that still venture into the region from time to time. There may have always been an occasional bobcat, but the number of otter records has grown in recent years. With increasing prey for both species, large tracts of protected land, and freedom from hunters, these predators may once again become permanent members of the local fauna.

Bobcat pelts were traded at Fort Dearborn in the 1820s and brought a paltry twenty cents each. A bobcat was captured at Cedar Lake in Lake County, Indiana, in 1837 or 1838 in an alder thicket: "It was a fierce and formidable looking animal; the fur was taken east; and the thicket was long known as the Wild Cat Swamp." Southern Cook County harbored the species until the early 1850s; the last record is of one shot near Mount Greenwood in 1857. Harry Eenigenburg, in his history of the Calumet Region, said the animal was still present until the 1860s and 1870s but was scarce.[11] Bobcats are still sighted in the Chicago region on occasion, but most of these are difficult to confirm. John Whitaker, an authority on the mammals of Indiana, makes this comment: "That bobcats can be easily misidentified was made clear to me upon receipt of a 'definite bobcat' . . . , which turned out to be simply a house cat, *Felis domesticus*, complete with full-length tail."[12]

Some of these bobcat reports, however, are genuine. Kendall County's game warden knew of a "den with an old one and two young just outside Plano, Illinois," in 1967. In the winter of 1977–78, biologist Joe Sucheki was surveying 446-acre MacArthur Woods for the Lake County Forest Preserve District. On one occasion, he came upon a trail of prints that he believes was that of a bobcat. Although he never saw the animal, he did find scat and a rabbit kill neatly buried under the snow, both consistent with bobcat sign he had seen previously in the west. In the early 1980s, John Ball and I also found bobcat prints at MacArthur, and there were other sightings from Waterfall Glen Forest Preserve in DuPage County.[13]

Providing even more conclusive evidence, at least three specimens were killed in the region during the 1970s: one shot near Aurora, Kane County, in December 1971; a young adult found dead one mile west of Morris, Grundy County, on April 7, 1973; and a twenty-two-pound female hit by a car in Barrington, Cook County, in March 1976.[14]

Although probably never abundant, river otters were at one time found along rivers and in large marshes throughout the area. Mr. Hamburgh reported that otters were common along the Saint Joseph River in 1763. At two dollars each, otter pelts brought the highest prices of any fur being traded at Fort Dearborn in the 1820s. But after six weeks of trapping on the Des Plaines River in the winter of 1844–45, Henry Thacker obtained only one. In the

1850s, otters were still being caught in the Calumet area and on the Fox River in Kane County. The Indiana Dunes had its share of otters in the early years, and one small stream, Otter Creek, was named to memorialize that fact.[15]

Marcus Lyon recorded the circumstances of what would be the last otter in this region for many years: "Mr. Henry Duncker of South Bend, an old hunter and trapper of the Kankakee, tells me that he saw a dead Otter [*sic*] on the banks of the Kankakee in La Porte County in 1909, and a live one in the water which looked at him for some moments, while he cautiously reached for his gun, but dived out of sight before he had time to shoot it."[16]

The river otter's disappearance was driven by two principal factors. First, and most important, the price for otter pelts exceeded all others, and thus trappers went after it with zeal. Second, although it can travel overland, otters require rivers, lakes, or marshes rich and extensive enough to meet food requirements. As marshes disappeared, water quality decreased, and riparian areas shrunk, conditions were no longer conducive to their survival.

But as mentioned earlier, otters are making a comeback. During the winter of 1993–94, three otters and their sign appeared at the LaSalle Fish and Game Area on the border of Lake and Newton Counties.[17] Between 1971 and 1994, the Illinois Department of Natural Resources received fourteen otter reports from Lake, Kane, McHenry, DuPage, Will, Kankakee, and Kendall counties. Some are of animals purportedly seen; among these are five near Wilton Center, Will County, in 1981, "individuals sighted" at Waterfall Glen Forest Preserve in DuPage County in 1988, and two "playing on an ice floe" on the Fox River just below the South Elgin Dam in 1986.

Additional reports refer to tracks or other signs. One of the most recent reports was on April 2, 1994, at a small lake in McHenry County. The observer based his identification on two furrows leading into the pond and fifty catfish heads on the banks. While otters are famous for making narrow furrows as they slide into the water off embankments, it is not as well known that mink make similar (albeit smaller) slides as well. (Actually, so do beavers and muskrats.) Furthermore, a study of mink at Jasper-Pulaski Game Area in Jasper County found that mink feed heavily on bullhead (a type of catfish) when available.[18] I suspect very strongly that this observation, and many of the others including those purporting to be of living animals, is based on misidentified mink.

There has also been at least one instance in which an otter was mistaken for a mink. On September 23, 1999, a biologist with the Lake County (Ill.) Forest Preserve District saw a dead mustelid lying on the roadside near his office at the Almond Road Marsh Forest Preserve. It looked so large that if he had been in Wisconsin he would have called it an otter, but since the setting was northeastern Illinois he supposed it to be a mink. Fortunately, another district biologist also saw the animal and questioned the earlier identification.

The specimen was examined and discovered to be a forty-three-inch-long female river otter. Whether the animal originated from southern Illinois (where
the state is reintroducing them), the Mississippi River, or the Kankakee River
is unknown.[19]

◄O► ◄O► ◄O►

Bison were among the first mammals to fall victims to the European invasion.
Marquette and Joliet saw them on that famous trip in 1673, but the animal
would, with one possible exception, cease to exist by about 1810. The most detailed descriptions are from Father Louis Hennepin, a priest in the Recollect
Order, who observed them along the Kankakee River in 1679: "They are very
fat in autumn, because all the summer they are up to their necks in the grass.
These vast countries are so full of prairies, that it seems this is the element and
the country of the buffalo. There are at near intervals some woods where these
animals retire to ruminate, and to get out of the heat of the sun. . . . In the season you see herds of two and even of four hundred."[20]

Along the banks of the Saint Joseph River near Niles, Michigan, bison
gathered to graze in such numbers that the place was named "Parc aux vaches,"
or "park of the cows." As late as 1763, Hamburgh found "buffalos in abundance" in the Illinois River country and present even near the Chicago River.
In the ensuing years, however, people reported mostly remains, former wallows, or trails. Captain L. S. Hugunin stated that on a stagecoach trip from
Chicago to Galena, Illinois, in 1840, he observed "great fields or yards of
bleached bones" where herds of bison had perished in storms eighty years earlier. Skeletal remains have also been found in Berrien County and as recently
as 1978 in Kendall County.[21]

There is evidence, however, that bison persisted longer in the Kettle
Moraine area than anywhere else in the region. That evidence consists of a six-
foot-by-six-foot pelt that James Brom presented to the Wisconsin Department
of Natural Resources in 1980. Brom had kept the skin rolled up in his barn for
thirty-seven years. He had received it from the wife of John Mall, whose grandfather allegedly shot the animal in the early 1840s on his farm near Rome (in Jefferson County, just ten miles north of the Walworth County line).[22] If the record
is genuine, this would be the last bison ever taken east of the Mississippi River.

Three factors seem to account for the early demise of this conspicuous
animal. Bison were never all that common in this part of the country; the
image of millions of animals lolling in vast herds reflected the reality of the
western prairies rather than of the prairie peninsula. Frank G. Roe, in his
exhaustive (if not exhausting) study of the bison, believes that the species was
of "comparatively recent arrival on the eastern side of the Mississippi and in

92. James Brom with pelt of bison purportedly killed in the 1840s
in the Kettle Moraine area of Jefferson County, Wisconsin, ten
miles north of the Walworth County line. (Courtesy of Kettle
Moraine State Forest Archives, Eagle, Wis.)

relatively scanty numbers." As markets developed and firearms proliferated, hunting pressure accelerated to the point where the modest bison population could not sustain itself. Finally, some have claimed that the brutal winters of 1763–64 (when "throughout . . . Illinois the snow was from 10 to 12 feet deep"), 1779–80, and 1806–7 destroyed the last herds.[23]

Black bears were apparently both conspicuous and present in large numbers. Father Hennepin reported that while staying at the mouth of the Saint Joseph River in Berrien County in November 1679, the men became so tired of bear meat they threatened to mutiny. He attributed the high bear population to the abundance of grapes—a popular repast among bruins—that grew in the vicinity. In 1763, Hamburgh also found bears to be common along the Chicago River.[24]

Judge John Dean Caton, who served fourteen years on the Illinois Supreme Court and was a distinguished naturalist as well, committed to paper his recollection of one of the last bear hunts ever to take place within the Chicago city limits:

> While I lay sick . . . in December 1833, the town was thrown into a great commotion by a report that someone had seen a bear cross the prairie from the Oak Woods to the South Branch timber, which extended all along the east bank of the river as far north as Madison or Randolph streets and a little way up nearly as far east as Clark Street. The hunter's dogs and guns of the town were soon astir and the wood surrounded when the dogs were turned into the thick brush to hunt up the game. At last the motley pack gave tongue as near as I could understand near where the Rock Island Passenger Depot now stands and there on a good sized cottonwood tree bruin was found perched as he no doubt thought secure from his enemies, however, he was soon brought to grief and cut up into small pieces that all in the town who were fond of bear meat might have a taste.[25]

Six years later, a group of hunters mounted on ponies and armed with knives and clubs worked an area between the North Branch of the Chicago River and Lakeview. They were in the field for three days and returned with nineteen wolves and one bear. Erasmus Ketcham, a professional trapper who had lived in the Glen Ellyn area of DuPage County since 1825, told interviewers in 1904 that he had over the years taken "upward of a score of bears" from the roots of a single hollow tree that still stood.[26]

The most unusual bear encounter was undoubtedly the one recorded by passengers of a Lake Michigan steamer chugging north out of Chicago in the 1830s. Five miles northeast of Waukegan, the ship's captain spotted something swimming. Viewing it through a telescope, the captain announced that it was a bear. Not content with the remarkable sight, he decided it was imperative that the bear be caught and brought aboard, whatever the hazard:

> So the small boat was lowered . . . and started for poor Bruin, who, when he found they were after him, made most excellent time for the middle of the lake, and for a mile or two led them on a splendid race before they came up with him. After two or three attempts, the man at the bow threw the fatal noose over his head. Directly after the bear found he was caught, he turned and made for the boat, evidently intending to carry war into the enemy's camp; but they were too quick for him. . . . They turned and rowed for the steamer with all their might. This brought poor Bruin's nose under the water, and by the time they reached the steamboat, . . . he was almost drowned.

After being hauled into the bigger vessel, the bear proved to be seven or eight feet in length. Since no one could think of anything better to do with it, the animal was killed and skinned.[27]

In his meticulous studies of wildlife in early Wisconsin, Arlie Schorger found that in certain years when mast (acorns and other nuts) was low, black bears would engage in mass movements southward. One such year was 1844, when people saw nearly a hundred in Dane County (Madison) alone. In October a bear was caught in Lake Michigan as it swam off Long Point, Racine County. Fifteen years later, bears again emigrated southward; by October, two had reached Yorkville, Racine County, where one was killed.[28]

Fires engulfed both sides of Lake Michigan in October 1871, the consequence of a nearly rainless summer. Chicago was leveled, 1,152 people died at Peshtigo, Wisconsin, and a black bear wandered into the Indiana Dunes "where it was seen in the woods west of Waverly Beach, near what is now called Juniper Valley." It was the last time anyone was to see the species in this region, although such an event may happen again some day, for a black bear appeared in 1979 in Van Buren County, just north of Berrien County.[29]

◄O► ◄O► ◄O►

Of the four disputed species mentioned at the start of this section, the pronghorn antelope has the scantiest claim for inclusion on the list of local fauna. Evidence of its presence here relies primarily on several of the early French accounts, including those of Marquette and Hennepin. In addition to describing deer, bison, and wapiti, they used the term *chevreuil*, which is generally translated as "goat." Some nineteenth-century naturalists, including Dr. Hoy, believed that these "goats" were really antelope. The more commonly offered explanation is that *chevreuil* also refers to deer but individuals with small and unbranched antlers.[30]

I have uncovered another reference that places antelope in the region much later; so late, in fact, that I am not sure what to make of it. In 1904, Colonel William Cockrum wrote: "This is a very beautifully formed animal and probably the swiftest of all the deer family. . . . After the Americans came to Indiana, they were not often seen, as they inhabited the prairie sections around Terre Haute and in the north and northwestern part of the state. The soldiers on the Indian campaigns tell of seeing the antelope in small herds, which were always on the run. In the northwestern portion of the state the antelope was killed as late as 1840, but since that date there is no account of any having been seen in Indiana."[31] Biologists today tend to doubt that antelopes were once part of the local fauna, an opinion based in part on the lack of skeletal remains east of the Mississippi.

If the snowshoe hare (also called varying hare) once inhabited this region, it disappeared with little trace. There are intriguing, albeit very inconclusive, references to the species being in both the Indiana Dunes and the Kankakee marshes.[32] More definite are these words by Robert Kennicott: "It has been stated that a number were shot on the present site of the city of Chicago, in the winter of 1824. . . . In winter, the upper parts become nearly white in high latitudes, but in Northern Illinois retain a brownish tinge."[33]

White-tailed jackrabbits did formerly occur within the area's three Wisconsin counties, although they were apparently very rare and/or present for a brief period. In winter, the jackrabbits of Wisconsin are "pure white except for the black tips of the ears and the dark eyes, and sometimes a buffy tinge on upper parts, face, and feet."[34] These facts led Donald Hoffmeister to conclude that Kennicott's snowshoe hares were probably white-tailed jackrabbits.

But are Wisconsin's white-tailed jackrabbits native or the product of introductions? Aldo Leopold believed that while some jackrabbits had been released into Wisconsin, most of the state was inhabited by native populations moving eastward. Hartley Jackson, author of *Mammals of Wisconsin*, disagrees: "At one time, I too thought that the white-tailed jackrabbit was native to western Wisconsin, but my travels and inquiries . . . convince me that it is not indigenous to Wisconsin."[35]

I am inclined to believe that snowshoe hares may well have occurred in the region. The species can survive as isolated colonies (particularly in alder and tamarack swamps), but they quickly decline with human alteration of their habitat. Although the hare has never been found in this portion of Wisconsin or Michigan, there are substantiated records of it from adjacent counties (Wisconsin's Jefferson and Milwaukee counties).[36] Kennicott's report predates the spread of the white-tailed jackrabbit into eastern Wisconsin (or possibilities of their introduction), and, apart from Hoffmeister's suggestion, no one has ever claimed jackrabbits for northeastern Illinois. If any of those animals living in Walworth or Kenosha counties ever wandered south, the event apparently went unrecorded.

Another northern species at the edge of its range, the lynx also may have prowled the region in bygone times. In 1841 hunters supposedly killed a lynx in a tamarack bog on a tributary of the Root River in Racine. (By 1925, the site was a golf course in Racine's Washington Park.) Although no specimen seems to exist from any of the nineteen counties under study here, there is one in the University of Wisconsin collection from Jefferson County, just north of Walworth.[37]

Many early commentators failed to distinguish between bobcats and lynx, often using the terms "catamount" or "wildcat" to describe one or the other, or even mountain lion. Hoffmeister says the confusion is hopeless and that he doesn't believe lynx ever inhabited Illinois; all references to wildcat or lynx really pertain to the bobcat. Jackson, adopting a different view, wrote that "recognition of the differences of the three species seems to have been surprisingly common."[38]

Kennicott lists both the bobcat and the lynx as occurring in Cook County but does so without any comments. The only lynx records published in the state mammal books for this region are for the following Indiana counties: Lake, Porter, La Porte, and Starke. The Porter County sighting appears in *The Wonders of the Dunes*: "The Canadian Lynx, with its mottled grayish fur, tufted ears, and enormous paws, was one of the most vicious of predatory animals and was seen in this region until recent times. The last one seen in the Dunes was killed by Hunter Green in 1873 at Tremont on Beach Ridge, near the present Johnson house, which at that time was a thickly forested section with swampy woods on each side."[39]

They Fly by Night: Bats

Bats (Chiroptera) are among the most unusual of all mammals. They are unique in having the capacity to fly, and many utilize a highly developed method of sonar (echolocation) that enables them to perform intricate aerial maneuvers in complete darkness. Bats are also among the most maligned of all mammals. Victims of what naturalist Garyn Fyffe calls animal pornography, they are portrayed as vampires (usually in search of comely virgins) or carriers of rabies seeking long locks of human hair.[40]

Of the over 177 genera of bats in the world (totaling 925 species), only three bite sleeping animals and feed on the blood that trickles out of the incision. The risk they pose to larger victims is from disease and not anemia. Further, only one species of vampire bat, *Diphylla ecaudata*, has ever been recorded in the United States, and that was a single individual caught in a south Texas railroad tunnel in 1967. (This particular species, by the way, feeds exclusively on birds.)[41]

Extensive studies have looked at the incidence of rabid bats. Between 1965 and 1984, researchers in Indiana examined 3,564 individuals of nine species (the same nine species that make up the bat fauna of the Chicago region). A total of 154 individuals (or 4.3 percent) proved to be infected. The highest percentage of infection was among hoary bats (*Lasiurus cinereus*), followed by eastern pipistrelles (*Pipistrellus subflavus*), red bats (*Lasiurus borealis*), big brown bats (*Eptesicus fuscus*), silver-haired bats (*Lasionycteris noctivagans*), and little brown myotises (*Myotis lucifugus*). No rabies were found among the evening bats (*Nycticeius humeralis*), northern long-eared myotises (*Myotis septentrionalis*), or Indiana myotises (*Myotis sodalis*). Another study in Illinois looked at 990 bats collected between 1965 and 1981 and found that only seventy-seven (8 percent) were rabid.[42]

It is important to realize that these results actually reflect much higher rates of infection than occur randomly because usually only specimens manifesting illness were tested. Among the general population of bats, infection rates are probably 1 percent or less. Some species, such as northern myotis, have jaws too weak and teeth too small to even puncture the skin of a human hand.

The risk of contracting disease from bats is further reduced because they tend to get "dumb" rather than "furious" rabies. An animal with furious rabies is often aggressive, while one with dumb rabies can usually do little more than lie in near paralysis. Thus, in the unlikely event that a rabid bat is present, all one has to do to avoid infection is to forgo reaching out and touching it. (For a host of reasons, prudence dictates exercising caution before initiating physical contact with any strange animal, be it dog, cat, or human being.)

Most bat research in Illinois and Indiana has taken place in counties to the south, where there are caves supporting large populations of hibernating animals. But a few significant colonies have been discovered here, and the shoreline of Lake Michigan has proven to be an excellent place to study bat migration.

The largest local concentration of bats inhabits an old dairy barn at Volo Bog State Natural Area (Lake County, Ill.). Female little brown myotis gather here in spring to give birth and raise their young. Very few such nursery colonies have been found anywhere other than buildings. But for a structure to be an acceptable nursery, it should be "hot, dark, poorly ventilated, and must have several small access holes."[43] Within the space, there must be a temperature gradient that bats can exploit to buffer themselves from the thermal extremes of changing weather.

State biologists have been monitoring bat numbers at Volo since 1984. They conduct their census in July, when the young are on the wing. The first count yielded 805 individuals. In 1985, the bats returned as expected but didn't stay long; the barn had fallen into disrepair and no longer provided the right conditions. Swift action by the Department of Conservation (now Department of Natural Resources), however, fixed the roof and saved the colony. The 1986 total of 455 reflected the fiasco of the previous year, but by 1991 the colony had grown to more than a thousand. Four years later, the total exceeded fifteen hundred, a level that has been maintained ever since, with an all-time record count of more than seventeen hundred made in 1997.

Bear Cave, on the Saint Joseph River north of Buchanan in Berrien County, has not only yielded an interesting assemblage of bats but is also the region's only cave. Four to six feet wide and ten to fifteen feet high, it winds

150 feet into a massive deposit of tufa, lime solids that precipitated out of calcium-rich springs. Logs deposited during floods provided the framework for the narrow channel, although the wood has since decomposed and been replaced by the tufa. The bats concentrate in a small cavity at the eastern end of the cave. Over the course of one September week, the following species were found: eighty-seven northern myotis, 268 little brown bats, and two red bats.[44]

The Indiana myotis is the only federally endangered mammal in the region. For many years, its presence rested on a single specimen taken at the Field Museum (Chicago) on September 18, 1928. The local status of the species changed, however, when the Kankakee River Basin Commission proposed to remove snags and other blockages from the river's channel. As part of the environmental studies mandated by federal law, Virgil Brack and his research assistant Virgil Holmes spent July of 1982 searching for Indiana myotis along the river.[45]

Finding Indiana myotis in the summer is not easy. (Certain caves attract large concentrations in winter.) Indeed, it was not until 1974 that the first nursery colony of this species was discovered. The colonies are almost always situated under the peeling bark of trees that are either alive or dead and preferably along watercourses. They forage in the canopy and thus are difficult to net.

Brack and Holmes selected ten sites, each to be worked on a single night. The depth and width of the river made it impossible to place nets directly over the main channel, so they chose the points where feeder streams entered the river. They hung their mist nets from ropes secured to limbs high in the canopy. To do this, they climbed trees and used a fifty-five-pound bow with a three-foot steel rod arrow attached to a fine string.

Just before dawn, at two sites in Starke County and one in Porter County, they captured a total of fourteen Indiana myotis. All were females, of which eleven were adults. Ten of the bats, likely from one colony, were caught at a single location in Starke County.

Here was conclusive evidence that the Indiana myotis resides within the woods that fringe the Kankakee River. Removing dead and living trees would put the bat at risk. Even if some habitat were allowed to stand, the rapid changes inherent in floodplain forests could eliminate suitable nursery sites. The issue is well stated by Brack and Holmes in their conclusion: "Because a wild river's course is ephemeral, many riparian trees are fast growing and also ephemeral, the dead or dying remains of which provide a continual supply of roosts, although any single roost may last only two or three years. . . . Even if a few potential roost trees remain, they may not be attractive to the bats, or there may be insufficient numbers of such potential roost trees in the present or near future to provide alternate roosts as the need arises."

When the first light of an autumn's morning interrupts their migration, bats can often be seen flying off of Lake Michigan in search of resting places.[46] Almost all of these are red bats and silver-haired bats, two tree-roosting species whose summer range extends far to the north of this region. (Published data on red bats show that the peak migration period is during late August and early September.) They are apparently reluctant to fly over the lake and thus cling to the shoreline as they migrate south. This funnel effect may also help explain why the migration is virtually restricted to the fall: the extensive shoreline to the north concentrates the bats toward the lake's southern end.

Over the years, McCormick Place, Chicago's huge exposition center, has proven to be a deadly obstacle to many migrating bats along the lake. (As a "collector," the building has provided scientists with much of what is known about local bat migration.) During a storm in early November 1972, it claimed thirty-five silver-haired bats.[47] Over an eight-year span beginning in 1979, Field Museum staff retrieved forty-three red bats, twenty-seven silver-haired bats, and one little brown myotis from the grounds of the facility. In his study of that collection, Robert Timm surmised that the dark support beams, large windows, and murky interiors lure the bats with the false promise of a wooded refuge. This also suggests that the bats rely on sight to navigate during migration rather than echolocation.

Buildings aren't the only hazards facing migrating bats. Several red bats washed ashore at Michigan City, La Porte County, in the wake of an April thunderstorm.[48] And gulls will take bats when they have the opportunity. I was at Waukegan's beach one morning in September 1975 when I spotted a red bat heading for shore. Unfortunately for the bat, a flock of ring-billed gulls occupied the first point of land it was destined to reach. It made the flat beach, but a low foredune shielded the bat from my view. A brief commotion followed as the gulls converged on the spot where the intruder should have been. Confirming the obvious, I walked toward the gulls, they flushed, and there was no trace of the bat.

Burrowers, Tree Dwellers, and Engineers: Insectivores and Rodents

The Insectivore order is made up of the moles and shrews, of which there are only six species currently inhabiting the Chicago region. Rodents, in contrast, are a diverse group that number among its members more local species than any other mammalian order.[49]

Moles spend most of their lives underground and are most easily detected by the ridges of their burrows. The eastern mole (*Scalopus aquaticus*) is relatively common in dry soils throughout the region. The amazing-looking star-nosed mole (*Condylura cristata*), however, is rare and restricted to mucky soils in Berrien and La Porte Counties, where habitat loss is threatening its continued presence.

The short-tailed shrew (*Blarina brevicauda*) is found in all habitats (although to the south of this region it prefers woodland) and thus is said to be the most common mammal in each of the region's four states. In moist areas with heavy cover, the masked shrew (*Sorex cinereus*) is also very common. Few pigmy shrews (*Sorex hoyi*) have been located in the region. For many years, the only Illinois record was of a specimen taken in a Palatine (Cook County) garage during an ice storm in 1948.[50] The species has since been found at Elizabeth Lake (McHenry County) and at Poplar Creek Forest Preserve (Cook County).

Shrews are perhaps best known for being voracious feeders, although most of the data are from captive individuals that probably eat more than they do in the wild. A short-tailed shrew caught in Porter County consumed, on a daily basis, 1.7 times its own weight in food for the ten days it survived in captivity. Another account describes how an undersized short-tailed shrew relentlessly pursued a healthy and much larger white-footed mouse placed in the same cage. The mouse easily eluded the shrew for a half hour. Then the shrew managed to grip the tail of the rapidly tiring mouse. The mouse, newly energized, bounded around the cage, with the shrew hanging on tenaciously as it was dragged along. Eventually the shrew clamped its jaws on an ear, which it proceeded to devour. It continued to eat more of the mouse, until the larger animal finally succumbed within a half hour after being initially caught.[51]

There are nine species of mice and voles native to this region. In grasslands, the meadow vole (*Microtus pennsylvanicus*), deer mouse (*Peromyscus maniculatus*), and prairie vole (*Microtus ochrogaster*) predominate. All three of these species have expanded their ranges and numbers over the years as agriculture replaced woodlands; more recently, spreading suburbia has exerted negative shifts in population, particularly with respect to the prairie vole.

The best-documented instance of range expansion involves the western harvest mouse (*Reithrodontomys megalotis*). Unknown in Illinois until 1953, it has been steadily moving east and south from the prairies west of the Mississippi River. The animal reached Newton County by 1969 and Lake (Ill.) and Grundy Counties by the early 1970s and is now in Jasper County and points south.[52]

Also inhabiting tracts of grass and shrub, the less common meadow jumping mouse (*Zapus hudsonius*) prefers areas that are moist or near water. As it name suggests, this mouse has unusual leaping abilities: it can cover over six feet in a single bound. According to Hartley Jackson, individuals, for it is a solitary species, will jump about in areas of flattened grass as if dancing playfully upon a stage.[53]

The white-footed mouse (*Peromyscus leucopus*) is the most abundant mouse in woodlands. It is also quite resilient. Researchers studying isolated patches of woods in Evanston and northern Chicago found that the white-footed mouse was the only native mammal present.[54]

The largest and most conspicuous mouse is the muskrat (*Ondata zibethicus*). During the winter of 1844–45, Henry Thacker trapped them in the marshes of Mud Lake and neighboring lowlands. On the day he began his "campaign," the water had frozen hard enough to support his weight: "A sight was here presented that I had never seen before. I cannot describe the view better than by likening it to a large meadow covered with haycocks, so thickly was the marsh before me studded with muskrat houses." Six weeks later when his labors were completed, he had amassed a total of seven hundred muskrats.[55]

More impressive still were the Kankakee marshes that produced muskrats on a scale commensurate with their vastness. One trapper claimed to have taken ten thousand in one year, and another said "that when he came to the Kankakee country in 1865, muskrat houses were so closely spaced that it was possible to open three or four of them at a time from an anchored boat."[56]

Even with the dramatic decrease of marshland, muskrats are still numerous. They have taken readily to ponds, rivers, and ditches, where they nest in banks. I have even seen them in Lake Michigan. According to Colin Sanborn, in his *Mammals of the Chicago Area*, muskrats were particularly common in the Jackson Park Lagoons during the 1920s. The species prospers in the midst of people, he says, because "during the winter when the ponds are frozen, it can move about freely under the ice in search of food and yet cannot be seen. When there is space between the water and the ice, it can breathe there, and can always get air near the thin ice along the shore."[57]

But the classic muskrat habitat is the cattail marsh. Muskrats consume great quantities of cattails for food and to construct their conical houses, which can be as large as thirty-one feet in circumference and almost three and a half feet in height at water level. This use of cattails helps prevent the formation of the solid stands that are inimical to many birds and other marsh wildlife. Muskrat activity ensures the presence of the open water so important to the ecological health of marshes. But when muskrat numbers are too high, "eat-outs" may occur that can seriously diminish food supplies for years. Animals then disperse; they have been found as far away as a mile from water, or succumb to starvation and disease.[58]

◄◦► ◄◦► ◄◦►

Eight species of squirrels inhabit the region. The least squirrel-like is the woodchuck (*Marmota monax*). Early assessments of its status indicate that it was most common in heavily wooded areas. It has since adapted to open country and woodland edges, where it remains common. Because it has demonstrated a fondness for suburban produce, it ranks fourth as a nuisance animal: 2,298 were dealt with in the Illinois portion of this area in 1993.[59]

The eastern chipmunk (*Tamias striatus*) behaviorally, although not taxonomically, would appear to be the link between ground squirrels and tree squirrels. Kennicott wrote, "Though abundant in the prairie regions of Illinois, this species never leaves the woods."[60] And though a woodland animal, it spends most of its time on the ground. They are common in woods rich with logs and rocks that provide perching and nesting sites.

The thirteen-lined ground squirrel (*Spermophilus tridecemlineatus*) and the Franklin's ground squirrel (*S. franklinii*) are prairie species that have reacted differently to landscape changes. Kennicott wrote that the thirteen-lined inhabited open grasslands while the Franklin's preferred "thickets of low bushes, the edges of timber, . . . but does not occur in the woods." He observed further that the thirteen-lined ground squirrel "disappears before the plow, and, as it will never leave its burrow for any great distance, it does not generally invade well-cultivated fields, nor attack corn except by the sides of the field next to wild prairies or meadows inhabited by it." The Franklin's ground squirrel, in contrast, "is not so shy as the [thirteen-lined] and takes up its residence quite near dwellings. It is also less disturbed by the cultivation of land."

But in the 150 years that have since elapsed, the thirteen-lined has proven to be far more adaptable. It prefers dry land with short grass, and "rode the rails" into areas that would have been otherwise too wet. Its presence in the Kankakee River country, for example, was attributed to the high ground of railroad embankments.[61] Today, it is often common on golf courses, cemeteries, and other large expanses of closely cropped vegetation.

Even in Kennicott's day the Franklin's ground squirrel was much the rarer of the two. That is even truer now. Franklin's ground squirrels are very local and can be found in high-quality prairies such as Chiwaukee, Markham, and Goose Lake. But they can also select much less scenic environs, as did the pair that denned under a rusting car at Lake Calumet in 1987. (As far as anyone knows, the Franklin's ground squirrel has not yet ventured into Michigan, although it occurred in Michigan City only two miles from the state line.[62] A challenge for the enterprising naturalist.)

Strictly nocturnal, the southern flying squirrel (*Glaucomys volans*) is much more common than encounters with it might suggest. I have seen it twice. While visiting a friend in Skokie, Cook County, one summer evening, I heard what sounded like a chipmunk high in a tree. When we shined a light, we could see the squirrel for a few moments before it launched itself into a glide and disappeared. My other sighting occurred when one popped out of a hole in a hollow tree I had just whacked. Employing the same technique, biologists at

Willow Slough State Fish and Game Area, Newton County, found relatively high densities of the squirrel.[63] The species also shows up at bird feeders with some regularity.

Red squirrels (*Tamiasciurus hudsonicus*) have a complicated local history. Their early status in Illinois is unclear. Kennicott says of their distribution that they occurred "sparingly" in the forested parts of the state. Of four specific records before 1912, two were from Lake County, although no specimens seem to have survived. That was the last anyone heard about red squirrels in Illinois until the 1970s, when researchers working in Kankakee County discovered several populations estimated to total in the low hundreds. Whether they had always been there or were recent émigrés from Indiana is not known.[64]

The latter alternative is quite possible, for in Indiana red squirrels have increased over the years. They have long been known from the Kankakee River country, but within this area the species had a patchy distribution, as emphasized by Walter Hahn in 1907: "I was unable to hear of it in Roselawn in northern Newton County. In southern Porter County, 30 miles [to the] east, it was abundant in a country that does not differ in the character of soil, drainage, or timber."[65]

At Willow Slough, approximately fifteen miles southeast of Roselawn, red squirrels were unknown prior to 1971, but six years later they were found throughout the area. A question arises as to how this arboreal squirrel can reach sites surrounded largely by fields. Mumford and Whitaker suggest that the squirrels utilize trees along drainage ditches and scattered pine plantings to hopscotch their way into appropriate habitat. (Red squirrels are also found in the dunes region of both Indiana and Michigan.)

In the Wisconsin portion of the region, the story differs yet again. Jackson shows them as being present in Racine and Kenosha counties but absent from Walworth. Today they still inhabit Racine County, although they are restricted to conifer plantations and tamarack bogs. No one seems to know for sure whether they are in Kenosha County. There is less habitat for them there than in Racine, and Tom Becker, who worked the county for many years as a state game biologist, never saw one. But the species has spread into Walworth County where they can now be seen in evergreen plantings.[66]

Being almost ubiquitous in urban settings, the eastern gray squirrel (*Sciurus carolinensis*) may seem to epitomize the commonplace. But back before the human hand impoverished the living capital of the land, gray squirrels rode the primordial cycle of boom and bust in displays of grandeur. On a scale difficult to fathom, the species engaged in mass movements of tremendous proportions. These were not migrations but, rather, "wholesale outpourings of a huge population from one region to another." This phenomenon occurred in Racine in the years 1842, 1847, and 1852. Dr. Hoy recorded the emigrations and shared his findings with Kennicott, who published them. Ernest Thompson Seton, who made a thorough study of the early accounts, considered the descriptions by Kennicott and Hoy to be the best that have survived and "rejoice[s] that Kennicott and others of more exact mind were born in time to make a fairly satisfactory record."[67]

Kennicott wrote: "Near Racine, they were observed passing southward in very large numbers for about two weeks, at the end of September and the beginning of October; and it was a month before all had passed. They moved along rather leisurely, stopping to feed in the fields, and upon the abundant nuts and acorns of the forests. So far had they departed from their accustomed habits that they were seen on the prairie, four or five miles from any timber; but even there, as usual, they disliked to travel on the ground, and ran along the fences wherever it was possible."[68]

Seton calculated that such a horde would involve thirty thousand squirrels per square mile, "or 450,000 squirrels in the dimensions recorded." Once the teeming mass commenced to move, "they would not be turned aside by prairies, rivers, lakes of moderate size, or even villages." Kennicott believed that few of the squirrels survived the emigrations, for "no sudden increase in their numbers was heard of in northern Illinois after the several migrations from southern Wisconsin."[69]

No one knows for sure all the factors that triggered these crazed exoduses. A. W. Schorger found that the squirrel movements occurred in the same years that black bears emigrated. Since both fed on mast, primarily acorns, food shortages clearly played a part. Other suggested causes include overpopulation (which is of course related to food) and disease. Biologist Durward Allen saw it as "a device for clearing the land of a too-numerous population and converting a million animals back into the humus of the earth."[70]

Gray squirrels are forest animals, and thus the combination of hunting and clearing of timber severely depleted their population. In many places they disappeared, and zoologists attribute their current presence to reintroductions. The eastern fox squirrel, in contrast, was a denizen of savannas and woodland edges and apparently increased with settlement. By 1925, however, it was considered less common than the gray and was found in more remote areas.[71]

Today, both gray squirrels and fox squirrels frolic in the same neighborhoods and backyards, in city and suburb alike. These homogeneous environments seem to lack any mechanisms that would isolate one species from the other. Although I and others have seen specimens that seem to manifest characteristics of both species, no hybridization has yet been reported in the literature.[72]

John Koprowski, who studied interactions between fox and gray squirrels in Lawrence, Kansas, believes that the two species may be sexually receptive at slightly different times, thus inhibiting interbreeding. It is also possible that at close distances the animals smell noticeably different. Koprowski has seen male foxes pursue female grays but never any resulting copulations.

◄o► ◄o► ◄o►

No animal has been more important to the natural and social history of this region than the beaver (*Castor canadensis*).[73] Like all species, beavers have particular habitat requirements, but to a degree far surpassing any other native species, they have the ability to create those requirements. And what beavers need most is year-round water.

Where the availability of sufficient water is problematic, as on streams (even those up to fourth order) or marshes, beavers take matters into their own paws and construct dams. Although some huge dams have been reported—in Montana one was 2,140 feet long—they are generally less than two hundred feet across. The impoundments that result usually range from less than an acre to ten acres or more, with an average size of around six acres. A depth of six feet is usually enough to satisfy the beaver's needs.

Rollin Baker describes the process of dam building: "The beaver often selects as the dam site a narrow point in the stream bed where the flow is rapid and the banks are firm. The beaver then cuts branches and drags them into position, paralleling the current with the butt ends heading upstream. . . . The spreading branches, extending downstream, tend to become anchored in the steam bed. Stones, mud, and sod are also used to weigh down and position these branches."[74]

Beavers use various types of trees in dam making, particularly aspen, cottonwoods, and other early successional species commonly found in wet areas. When it is possible to do so, a tree may be downed so as to fall directly across the dam to strengthen further the structure. Beavers have also been known to incorporate more exotic materials such as cornstalks, bales of wire, and car doors. Reflecting its urban environment, one beaver dam on Farmer Creek in Des Plaines (Cook County) includes a sofa and plastic bags full of lawn waste.[75]

Once the base is set, additional layers of branches and mud are added until the proper height is reached. (The use of mud also benefits the beavers by deepening the pond.) But a single dam may not be enough. If high water volumes damage the principal dam, another structure might be constructed upstream as protection. And to maintain the pond at preferred levels, a dam might also be established downstream.

Where the river or lake provides ample water and no dam is needed or possible, as along the lower Des Plaines and Kankakee Rivers, beavers den in banks, which they excavate via openings beneath the water line. These commodious dens may have thin "ceilings," in part to facilitate ventilation, and so they are frequently fortified with branches placed upon the "roofs." Conflicts with humans commonly ensue when the bank is a levee, particularly one designed for use by heavy vehicles.

Where a dam and impoundment are necessary, beavers are apt to build lodges surrounded by water. These vary considerably in size, with large ones generally around six feet high and fifteen to twenty feet across at the waterline. Russell Mumford found an unusual lodge at Jasper-Pulaski Fish and Wildlife Area that enveloped a wooden viewing blind placed in four feet of water.[76] One of the largest lodges ever recorded was in Bayfield County, Wisconsin. It was sixteen feet high and forty feet wide, with a main room big enough to accommodate eight beavers or a six-foot person standing upright.

The pond should be deep enough to ensure that a water barrier to the lodge is maintained throughout the summer. It is equally important that there be enough open water under the ice for the beavers to swim about during the winter. Beavers also need adequate water to cache their winter food supply, mostly green branches.

There is yet one more manifestation of the engineering prowess possessed by beavers. As the supply of suitable trees near the lodge becomes depleted, beavers are forced to forage farther from home. Lugging trunks and branches overland would be an impossible burden, so beavers dig canals through which they transport their logs. These waterways can be "as long as a half mile, contain sufficient water in which to float and paddle a canoe, and may even contain 'locks' or small check dams designed to extend the canal at elevations higher than the beaver pond level."[77]

Over thousands of years, beaver activity can have a profound impact on the landscape. When beavers eventually leave an area, usually due to the exhaustion of accessible trees, the pond fills with silt. They move on to other sites along the stream, leaving behind their former ponds, which become a series of plains up and down the valley. This leads to the filling (or aggrading) of the valley, a process first described by two New York scientists: "[Beaver] work is characterized by complete aggrading of valley floors, originally in small descending steps, which disappear in time and leave a gently graded, even valley plane horizontal from bank to bank." Donald Hey, of the Des Plaines River Wetlands Demonstration Project at Wadsworth, Lake County, estimates that beaver have aggraded the upper Des Plaines Valley by as much as fifteen to twenty feet since the glacier left.[78]

Beavers were critical players in maintaining a healthy hydrologic balance. Their dams helped replenish water tables and held precipitation that would have otherwise swelled river flows. In their analysis of the great 1993 flood of the upper Mississippi River, Donald Hey and Anne Philippi write that the elimination of beavers through trapping was "the first and perhaps most dramatic alteration of the watershed's hydrologic cycle." They go on to estimate the extent of this alteration: "Forty million beavers in 1600 would have maintained 51 million acres of water surface, accounting for 11% of the 456 million acres of land in the upper Mississippi Basin. . . . At a depth of three feet, the original ponded area would have stored more than three floods the size of the 1993 event."[79]

The ecological effects of beaver activity are many. Standing water, marshes, and woods represented a diversity that might not otherwise have existed so close together. But as with all change, some species are helped, and some are harmed. When cold-running streams became ponds and warmer outflows, species composition was altered. Inundation created rich wetlands but killed trees and other terrestrial plants. The arboreal mortality, though, provided a boon to the many kinds of wildlife that favor snags. Even the lodges themselves provided roosting and nesting sites for waterfowl and raptors.

Even after beavers depart an area, their presence is felt, for the successional process they trigger runs its course. The barren flat that was once the pond begins supporting grasses and sedges, then shrubs, and finally the pioneering trees that were so important to the beavers in the first place. And so the cycle begins anew.

Despite what beavers accomplished on their own, it might be argued that their greatest impact on the region was to lure the early Europeans. Most of the whites who frequented the region during the 1700s did so in search of beaver pelts, either through trapping or trade with native people. Indeed, "the beaver was the most widely and intensively sought natural resource of the continent during the 1700s and 1800s."[80] The furs were used as currency and became known as "black gold." Their value was assured when the British Parliament in 1638 forbade the making of certain hats out of anything other than beaver. Eventually, conflicts between the French and British over access to the Great Lakes fur industry, largely based on beaver, escalated into the French and Indian War in 1754.

The early history of beavers in the Chicago region is short. Hamburgh found them to be abundant along the Saint Joseph River in 1763, but heavy trapping pressure decimated the population quickly. A fur trader in the same area handled only nine beaver pelts from 1800 to 1801. The last specimen known from southern Wisconsin died on Sugar Creek in Walworth County in 1819. Such precise dating is not available from other parts of the region, but that a list of fur prices offered to trappers at Fort Dearborn (Chicago) in the late 1820s has no mention of beaver suggests that the species was either already gone or at least extremely rare.[81]

So it was that for over a hundred years the beaver was absent from the waters of the Chicago region. Then in 1935, the Indiana Department of Natural Resources released a small number of beavers at the Jasper- Pulaski Fish and Wildlife Area and the Kankakee Fish and Wildlife Area (Starke County). These early releases proved successful, for three years later the species had spread up and down the Kankakee and had probably entered Illinois. Additional animals were liberated on Cook County Forest Preserve District land in the Palos area.[82]

Not long after beavers had become reestablished, they started interfering with the activities of humans. A study of complaints lodged against beavers in Illinois from 1946 to 1951 concluded "that 42 of the 53 beaver colonies examined . . . were incompatible or potentially incompatible with man's interests."[83] In the intervening years, beavers have become common and widespread, inhabiting most of the area's waterways. Beaver sign is even evident along Chicago's Bubbly Creek (a tributary of the South Branch of the Chicago River), so named because the slaughterhouses dumped so many carcasses into it that the subsequent decomposition created seemingly perpetual carbonation.

In 1993, nuisance animal handlers dealt with 899 beavers in the nine Illinois counties of this region. Owners of riparian land complain that beavers eat their landscaping or at least gird and sometimes bring down arboreal components of it. A civic-minded citizen of Chicago's Hyde Park raised the horrifying specter of a beaver gang that had invaded Jackson Park and chewed down crabapple trees. "How do we stop more from coming in?" she asked.[84]

We have already looked at the effects of beaver dams in the wilderness. Flooding in the urban setting, however, is generally neither appreciated nor long tolerated. Beaver activity has closed roads and damaged private property. Volo Bog State Natural Area was threatened with flooding when a dam created high water levels. To combat the flooding, dams are torn apart, although disappointed officials and landowners often find that a replacement has been erected within a few days. In many cases, the beavers are removed through lethal trapping or relocation. A more benign approach is a specially designed pipe-like instrument that allows water to pass through the dam without alerting the animals that there is a breach.

Even in an area teeming with millions of people, the marvels wrought by this amazing animal can still unfold. On forest preserve land in northern Cook County, beavers transformed what had been an ordinary field into a beautiful open water cattail marsh. In early April, hundreds of newly arrived tree swallows skimmed the smooth surface for insects. Painted turtles soaked in the spring sun, and chorus frogs filled the air with music. Yellow-headed blackbirds, pied-billed grebes, great-blue herons, and other water dependent birds nested or tarried during migration. On one occasion, a number of us watched an immature bald eagle perched high in a cottonwood overlooking the wetland. Then, after a few years, the beaver disappeared. There hasn't been as much water or wildlife since, but some day a young beaver looking for a home of its own will come upon the site, find it hospitable, and stay.

Adaptable Song Dog of City and Suburb: The Coyote

Separating gray (or timber) wolves from coyotes from coyote-dog hybrids (coydogs) can be accomplished if there are animals to weigh and measure. In the absence of specimens and specific knowledge, however, the matter can become confusing. Many early writers do distinguish between larger canids that they call timber wolves and smaller animals they call prairie wolves. Occasionally they recognize a third type called coyote; an early history of Kane County says that the prairie wolf should not be confused with the coyotes of the western states—in size the prairie wolf is between the timber wolf and the coyote.[85] While differences between prairie wolves and coyotes may have existed on some basis, imagined or real, there is no doubt that both names refer to *Canis latrans*, the coyote.

In recent times, the wolf having long been extirpated, the problem arises as to whether a given specimen refers to a coy-dog. These are apt to be bigger, more wolflike in appearance, perhaps bolder, and thus maybe more likely to prey on livestock.[86]

Although I have found no reference to a wolf specimen from this region, no one doubts that the species did occur in the early days.[87] Schapper, referring to southern Cook County, says that "timber wolves were very numerous especially in the woods near the present West Pullman. . . . I saw the last timber wolf in this vicinity in the woods on Vermont Street near Robinson Street in 1859." He saw his last "prairie wolf" in 1865 near Vincennes Road and 119th Street. According to contemporary newspaper articles "timber wolves were not uncommon" in southern Wisconsin (including Walworth County) as late as 1884, particularly during the harsh winters of 1880–81 and 1881–82. The last record for the southern half of the state is one killed in 1916 near Wautoma, substantially north of the Chicago region.[88]

Most wolves were gone from the region by the early 1800s. A few probably persisted until the 1880s in the most isolated locations. Wolf identifications made in the late nineteenth century warrant skepticism, and any more current reports can be considered no better than interesting. With that said, I offer some reports that suggest the author was at least distinguishing between different types of canids. In answer to a state survey, McHenry County's game warden wrote in 1912 that "a dozen years ago a timber wolf was killed occasionally here and west of here, but it is safe to say none are left." (He added that coyotes were gone from the region, hanging on only in western and central Illinois.) His counterparts from Kane, Kendall, and Grundy Counties responded to the same survey by saying that both timber wolves and coyotes were still present. While hunters might have taken two timber wolves in the Kankakee River swamps of Starke County in 1906, the last specific claim comes from Brennan: "The forests and deep glens at the [Indiana] Dunes have been splendid hiding-places for the wolves all these years. It is said that there were still a few of them left between Dune Park and Michigan City until 1919. Horace Greeley Green, the old hunter and trapper, said that in 1914, he trapped two big timber wolves in the dense woods some distance east of Dune Park near Oak Hill. . . . He assured me that the wolves among the Dunes were the genuine timber wolves and not the little coyotes or prairie wolves."[89]

Although they are called wolves in the accounts I am about to quote, these abundant animals that the local citizenry so delighted in torturing and hunting were mostly coyotes. Their brazenness, small size, and large numbers all point to this conclusion; just substitute "coyote(s)" for "wolf" or "wolves."

One early settler said that in the 1820s and 1830s "it was a poor day for wolves when the Chicago hunter couldn't kill a dozen within a few miles of the town," and on one particular hunt along the river, forty wolves were bagged in one day. Another resident of the same period, but living near Blue Island, Cook County, also reported that the animal was plentiful: "One not familiar with their howling might be led to believe that he was listening to a choir composed of a thousand voices with instrumental music included."[90]

Charles Cleaver related how he and his companions would break in their foxhounds. During his first winter in Chicago, in 1833, he lived at the corner of Kinzie and Rush Street. In the heavy woods that ran down to the river, they managed to trap a wolf by its hind leg that the animal had almost cut to the bone trying to escape. By putting a rope around the wolf's neck and then having someone at either end of the rope pull, the group rendered the animal compliant enough to place in a bag. The next morning, accompanied by one greyhound, one foxhound, and their captive, the boys canoed across the Chicago River for the prairie at the intersection of Wabash and Randolph. Upon releasing the wolf, the greyhound quickly caught it for the foxhound to finish off.[91]

Charles Hoffman describes how a wolf managed to elude five equestrians near the Des Plaines River, twelve miles west of Chicago, in January 1834. Having been flushed out of thick weeds, the wolf made for the river. "He had a bold rider behind him, however, in the gentleman who led the chase. The precipitous bank of the stream did not retard this hunter for a moment; but, dashing down to the bed of the river, he was hard upon the wolf before he could ascend the elevation on the other side. Four of us only reached the open prairie beyond in time to take part in the chase. Nothing could be more beautiful. There was not an obstacle to oppose us in the open plain; and all our dogs having long since given out, nothing remained but to drive the wolf to death on horseback."

The wolf, having a completely different agenda, suddenly stopped and passed through the ranks of the cavalry whose momentum carried them forward well beyond their quarry. But they managed to regain their advantage and prevent the wolf from escaping into the riparian vegetation. Finally, the wolf, appearing exhausted, allowed the hunters to converge upon him with the consequence that the speeding horsemen only narrowly avoided colliding with one another. The ensuing chaos enabled the wolf to reach the sanctuary of the river, as his closest pursuer became entangled in the branches of a tree.[92]

During the pioneering period, when the land under siege had not yet been vanquished (it never totally is), predators could pose a threat to the economic interests of people attempting to establish themselves. In the middle 1840s, one A. Y. Smith moved to southern Cook County from points east to start a sheep farm. His flocks grew to several thousand animals, but at the end of three years he threw in the towel, having been driven into bankruptcy by wolves. In Racine County, the presence of wolves made it "almost impossible for the settler to keep small stock of any kind, and those who tried to raise sheep suffered a most unhappy experience."[93]

Wolves also allegedly attacked people. These incidents usually involved lone travelers at night who discovered they were being trailed by the cowardly animals and were just able to reach shelter before the pack charged. One young man was allegedly treed and spent hours hanging on for dear life until his father rescued him. The most poignant story, though, is that of the unfortunate Mrs. Smith. She left the family farm near Blue Island late one afternoon on January 2, 1834, to deliver groceries to a neighbor. Before arriving at her destination, however, she was overcome by a blizzard. Becoming disoriented, she sat down to rest and started in on the groceries. Before the night was over, wolves had started in on her—all that was found the next day were bones and scraps of clothing. The press account said that wolves "suddenly pounced on her and devoured her." (But, of course, the only witness to the event had long been digested.) Far more likely, the wolves had come upon the fresh carcass with all the trimmings and simply scavenged. Mrs. Smith left behind a spouse and five children.[94]

What hunters did in the frenzy of wolf hunting was far more dangerous than the wolves themselves. As Cyrus Airey approached a wolf he had trapped in 1837, the animal broke the pin that fastened the trap to the ground and bounded off dragging the chain behind it. Airey, "a good runner and venturesome man," took off after the escapee, chasing it onto the Lake Michigan ice "that no one even for a moment thought was safe for a man to venture upon." After three miles, he finally caught the trap chain and made it back to shore with the wolf only three hours before the wind shifted and the ice disappeared. About the same time, in Naperville, DuPage County, Hiram Fowler waded into a fracas between his dog and a wolf and grabbed the wolf by its tail. Fowler swung "him around so violently he could not turn the biting end to defend himself." Still swinging the wolf with one arm, the man jumped on his horse and rode to the nearest dwelling where help awaited.[95]

To combat the wolf menace, governments offered bounties and citizens organized mass hunts. Fernando Jones, one of Chicago's earlier residents, did well in collecting the $1.25 bounty available in the 1830s, especially since he believed in recycling: "I am compelled to admit that I made the most of the scalps I take. In fact, the clerks in several counties grew suspicious before the scalps were worn out."[96]

During the 1840s, McHenry County gave $15.00 for the skin of every wolf over six months of age killed within the county. People from all over the region began bringing live wolves into the county so they could meet the bounty requirements and collect the money. One enterprising citizen of Nunda Township constructed cages in which he placed pups and raised them until they reached maturity and were redeemable for maximum value. A writer in 1885 said, "This came pretty near raising wolves for market."[97]

Will County citizens launched a major "wolf-control" effort in the summer of 1841 to render their homeland forevermore safe for sheep. Organizers recruited enough people to form a huge circle. Armed with "rifles and short guns," the participants slowly advanced inward, trapping many deer but apparently few wolves. The exercise proved so fruitless that few people admitted to having taken part. Some of these hunts were evidently more successful, however, with as many as sixty wolves being "riddled by rifle balls" by day's end.[98]

Despite the war against them, coyotes persisted, albeit in low numbers. A total of five of the region's Illinois counties reported coyotes in 1912. A similar questionnaire revealed that, by the first half of 1944, Kendall County paid one bounty (zero in all of 1943) and Will paid none (four in 1943). Indiana began experiencing an increase in coyotes as early as 1900; as woodlands were cleared, coyotes expanded into areas previously less suitable. For the hundred-year period ending in 1948, seventeen counties paid bounties on 1,325 coyotes. In 1946 alone, nine counties paid 102 bounties.[99]

How these animals managed to survive, and even increase, is amazing given that they were shot every time the opportunity arose. A coyote, which on close examination proved to be part domestic dog, was killed near Waukegan in December 1924. It "showed very plainly how it is received in a settled area, for it contained all sizes of shot, some of which it must have carried for nearly three years."[100]

In February 1930, two coyotes near Libertyville, Illinois, escaped "an army of 250 Lake County farmers and townsmen, armed with all manner of guns . . . who spent the day roaming hill and vale" looking for them. The following week, farmer Louis Mills spied what was presumably the same pair on his property. After failing to get within firing distance, Mills drove to Palwaukee Airport (Prospect Heights, Cook County) and chartered a pilot and plane. Spotted from the air, the animals proved no match for modern technology. "The farmer leaned far over the cockpit" and blasted away, killing one outright and wounding the second so that neighbors could follow its trail of blood on the snow.[101]

After this litany of coyote killings, I offer what I believe is one of most wonderful developments in the natural history of the region—coyotes have become common. According to Donald Hoffmeister this trend started in the 1950s and extended throughout the Midwest. In 1989, 932 coyotes were killed in Cook, Lake, Kane, DuPage, McHenry, and Boone Counties in Illinois, a 12 percent increase over the preceding year.[102] Recently, they have been observed feeding out of dumpsters, the ultimate adaptation to urban living.

One of the most noteworthy signs of coyote abundance is their appearance in the neighborhoods of Chicago, environments often challenging to the humans for whom they were designed and built, let alone for coyotes. Beginning in the early 1990s, coyotes were found on the northwest side in Riis Park (6100 West Fullerton) and Norwood Park, and on the far south side at 114th Street and Marshfield Avenue. But a major commotion followed the discovery of three coyotes caught within two months of each other in Lincoln Park and the Gold Coast areas. Yuppies were apparently uncomfortable with "yuckies," young urban coyotes. An intensive search for dens was conducted by "animal control officers, mounted police, police canine patrols, Park District security guards, and Anti-Cruelty Society personnel. Word is that [the effort] nearly emptied out the East Chicago Avenue police district station. Fliers were passed out in schools and grocery stores warning that a coyote may be lurking about."[103]

The hunt failed to locate the illicit den but succeeded in illuminating the groundless fear held by many of the local people. Animal control agents release captured coyotes into the Palos area forest preserves, a great advancement over the times when the unfortunate animals would be torn alive by dogs. But their presence still unleashes panic.

To be fair, some of the neighbors quoted in the various articles are

93. Coyote in backyard of home in the Norwood Park neighborhood of Chicago's Northwest side, April 1994. (Photo by C. Wagner, courtesy of *Chicago Tribune*.)

eminently reasonable. Tonilee Klueppel, identified as a lifelong resident in the neighborhood where the Norwood Park coyote appeared, said: "Four boys got out of the car with big sticks. . . . We think they were going to go over the fence and go try to go after the coyote. I wish everybody didn't have to know about it. . . . I don't consider it a threat. But if it's going to be harmed here, it probably should be moved."[104] She is right: the problem isn't the coyote, it's people.

Now that the novelty of local coyotes has subsided, reactions have probably tempered as well. A recent study of coyotes in DuPage County is full of positive comments by the numerous subjects interviewed. Several attributed decreases in the local goose flock to the arrival of coyotes, while a stable owner credited them with keeping her barn free of rodents.[105]

That a large carnivore can prosper in the heart of America's third largest metropolitan area is worthy of rejoicing. And not only is it here, but there is actually a decent chance you could see one. I have encountered them maybe fifteen times in recent years. Two particularly memorable sightings were the pups playing near the mouth of their den on an abandoned bunker at what was then the Joliet Army Arsenal and the female on the beach at Waukegan who, by the looks of her, had been recently nursing young. When the civil defense siren sounds every Tuesday morning, coyotes at the Wadsworth Prairie Nature Preserve in Lake County (Ill.) commence their wailings: an anthem celebrating the resilience of wildness.

Coyotes may be affecting another species besides human beings: the red fox (*Vulpes vulpes*), one of the loveliest mammals in the region. There has been concern that in the face of pressure from its larger cousin, red foxes have begun to suffer reductions in numbers and range. Studies from North Dakota and Ontario indicate that a red fox, which would lose a physical confrontation with a coyote, will minimize the potential for conflict by establishing its territory in an area not heavily frequented by the other species. But as coyotes increase, less space is available to foxes.[106]

The Illinois Natural History Survey is looking at coyote–red fox interactions in Champaign County, about fifty miles south of this region.[107] They have found that in urban areas mortality rates for young foxes are extremely high due to sarcoptic mange (*Sarcoptes scabiei* is the type of mite causing the mange). The foxes become infected due to their living in areas with high densities of dogs or other foxes. Rural fox pups do better, although 50 percent are killed by automobiles. (Eighty percent of young coyotes die, mostly by cars and hunters.) There was no recorded instance of coyote predation on foxes.[108]

Studies suggest that red foxes and coyotes prefer different types of areas. In Champaign County, foxes denned under suitable buildings while coyotes relied on the cover provided by drainage ditches and fencerows. Foraging locations also varied, with foxes favoring roadsides and coyotes using ditches and fencerows. DuPage County coyotes feed along waterways, most of which have some fringing vegetation, while red foxes are most often seen in the proximity of railroad tracks.

It seems likely that both species will continue to grace the region. The fox may benefit from its smaller size and more modest food requirements, thus being able to survive in environments unsuitable for the coyote. Indeed, the red fox may become increasingly urban as it colonizes small parks, empty lots, and other marginal sites incapable of maintaining high densities of coyotes.

Meet the Neighbors: Raccoons, Opossums, and Skunks

While their histories are not as dramatic as that of the coyote, several other species have successfully adapted to the ways of humankind. Preeminent among these is the raccoon (*Procyon lotor*), which was originally a woodland animal. Kennicott, writing in 1858, indicated that although "it may sometimes be found a few miles out on the prairie in summer, it does not live permanently far from forests." A mammal survey of Berrien County published in 1922 also found that the species was restricted to heavy woods. But predictions that raccoons would decline with the loss of timber proved to be wrong. They adapted to the Eurasian grasslands of agriculture, denning in haylofts and dining on corn and other feed left for livestock. And when the next wave of change hit in the 1950s, raccoons adjusted to life in middle-class suburbia.[109]

To thrive, raccoons need three things: permanent water supplies for foraging, denning locations, and food.[110] The first study of urban raccoons focused on Glendale, Ohio (suburban Cincinnati), and showed how effectively raccoons exploit this "new" environment. Besides streams and ponds, raccoons took advantage of birdbaths, fishponds, and twelve swimming pools. Sixty years ago, one scientist listed tree dens as an essential element of raccoon habitat. But the raccoon of today readily nests in sewers, holes in the ground, garages, houses (abandoned and occupied), and roofs of churches.

A review of published studies found that raccoons had consumed fifty-two different kinds of food items; the record for most diverse diet belonged to a group of raccoons living in the bottomland forests of the Illinois River, which subsisted on nineteen comestibles. But, befitting their new lifestyle, the urban raccoon has far more eclectic tastes, munching on forty-six different species of plants (including melons and grapes from garbage cans, millet from bird feeders, and oats from barns whose owners keep horses), insects, crayfish, eggshells, Norway rats, and eastern cottontail rabbits.

Given how unabashedly raccoons have helped themselves to the bounty of their new neighbors, it comes as no surprise that problems have arisen. Illinois deals with these problems by granting permits to individuals and governmental agencies that allow them to "control nuisance wildlife." In 1993, licensed wildlife control personnel handled 28,102 animals in the nine counties of Illinois that form the Chicago region. Of those, 8,923 were raccoons.[111]

For over eighteen years, Garyn Fyffe has operated a business designed to remove nuisance animals with the goal of rereleasing them into more hospitable environs. He summarizes the downside of homeowners trying to eradicate unwanted wildlife: "Everybody has all kinds of pet ways to get rid of animals. But if you start a fire in the chimney all that is going to do is cause lung damage to the baby raccoons or burn them alive. If you pour ammonia in all that's going to do is blind them or give them lung damage. And in the end, all you're going to end up with is 20 pounds of rotting meat in your fireplace."[112]

Fyffe's biggest challenge is not the lack of customers but finding landowners willing to let him release animals onto their property. County forest preserves own most of the open land in the region, and for a number of good reasons, such as those that follow, they are becoming increasingly reluctant to accept animals originating elsewhere. The state is also encouraging euthanasia over relocation. These agencies are concerned that moving animals to new sites can "(1) spread diseases to resident populations, (2) compound nuisance wildlife problems in nearby residential areas, (3) increase predation of Neotropical [bird] migrants and their eggs, and (4) disrupt social and behavioral mechanisms in resident populations."[113]

To investigate some of these issues, the Illinois Department of Natural Resources and the Kane County Forest Preserve District commissioned John Thompson of the Max McGraw Wildlife Foundation to study the movements and survival of thirty-one raccoons in 1993 and forty-five in 1994. Twenty-five of these animals were transplants from suburban areas to the rural Lone Grove Forest Preserve in Kane County, twenty-six were transplants from the rural Max McGraw Wildlife Foundation (Dundee, Kane County) to Lone Grove, and twenty-five were resident raccoons at Lone Grove. Each animal received a radio collar so that scientists could monitor its movements.[114]

The data revealed several interesting findings. The local raccoons stayed put, while those that had been translocated were gone from the preserve within a short period. Some began leaving Lone Grove within hours of release. Most of them wandered widely for the first two weeks, one winding up as a roadkill thirty-five miles away. After that they seemed to settle into territories, most of which were agricultural fields or on property used heavily by people, including barns, backyards, homes, and even a gas station. Overall, the survival rate for the three groups of raccoons was roughly the same.

While the study suggests that translocating a small number of raccoons probably has little impact on the raccoons themselves, many other questions remain. Given the great number of nuisance raccoons and the ever-diminishing areas into which they can be released, large-scale relocations might still prove to be problematic to both the releasees and the locals. And there are still the unresolved issues relating to the effects of newly arrived raccoons on other species, including humans.

No solution to the problems of wildlife interacting with people is imminent, but there is an approach that would surely help. People need to learn how they can avoid problems arising in the first place. If they are fortunate enough to reside in areas with large wildlife populations (near forest preserves, in recently developed areas, near waterways, etc.), homeowners should have their chimneys capped, window wells covered, and decks animal-proofed. Municipalities should consider requiring such alterations as part of their housing codes. Other, more simple, expedients include keeping pet food indoors, using animal-resistant trash bins (and making sure the lids are tightly fastened), and forgoing wildlife feeding, at least until the structural precautions just mentioned are completed.[115]

People who value wildlife neighbors should remember that once an animal becomes a problem and has to be live-trapped, its chances of survival are small. By law, because of rabies possibilities, skunks must be euthanized. For other species, landowners must give permission before someone can release an animal on their property. If no suitable site is found, the animal must be killed. If animals are transplanted to a new site, the negative impacts listed above may result. And from a conservation perspective, the new transplants may put additional pressure on prey species (i.e., ground nesting forest birds such as veery and wood thrush) that are often far more imperiled than the generalists that become problems.

━◦━ ━◦━ ━◦━

Because of the superficial resemblance, opossums (*Didelphis virginiana*) are often categorized by the unknowing as rats. In fact, they are marsupials, the order of pouched mammals that includes kangaroos and koalas. (On an evolutionary basis, rats and humans are much closer to each other than either is to opossums.) Two families live in the New World, and the Virginia opossum is the only species found north of Mexico. The Virginia opossum has a thin coat and a long unfurred tail, characteristics of a warm weather animal. During severe winters, many of them suffer frostbite and lose toes, fingers, and ears.[116] They have benefited from settlement, moving northward in the wake of agriculture, landscaping, and the construction of buildings, sewers and other warm enclaves. Today they rank number three as the subject of wildlife nuisances.

Human activities have helped opossums in another way as well. Although they often den underground, particularly during the winter, opossums are incapable of digging and thus must rely on woodchucks and skunks for the initial excavation. With fewer predators, these other species have increased and provided opossums with the dens they need. One burrow in Michigan offered simultaneous refuge to a skunk and opossum.[117]

The earliest report of opossums in this region is by Father Hennepin in 1683. At the portage between the rivers Kankakee and Saint Joseph, he awaited with other members of his party for the return of La Salle, "who had gone exploring on land": "The next day . . . we perceived him at a distance. . . . He had two animals of the size of muskrats, hanging at his belt, which had a very beautiful skin, like a kind of ermine, which he killed with blows of a stick, without these little animals taking flight, and which often let themselves hang by the tail from branches of trees, and as they were very fat, our canoeman feasted on them."[118]

While always present in southern Wisconsin, opossums were apparently rare enough to prompt the following headlines when one was found in a cemetery in Green County (the second county west of Walworth): "Unknown Grave Digger Captured" and "Cemetery Ghost Caught." Jackson gives 1920 as the year their population began to rocket in Wisconsin. The status of the species in northern Indiana has been described as "one of periodic fluctuation," whereby its growing presence would collapse in the face of a harsh winter, then build again during intervening mild winters.[119]

Opossums possess some unusual anatomical and behavioral peculiarities that have long made them subjects of human interest. The most unusual of these is their habit of "playing possum." When an animal is confronted and cannot otherwise escape, it frequently feigns death: "When in this condition an opossum will endure almost any abuse and torture, and limp and motionless, without showing any indication of suffering or concern, may be kicked and tumbled around, lifted by the tail, mauled, pummeled, and bitten by dogs, sometimes to the point of death."[120]

One of the strangest bits of folklore associated with any local mammal is (hopefully was) the widely held notion that the male opossum deposits his semen into the nose of the female. She then impregnates herself through sneezing. This odd belief sprung from the observation that the male has a forked penis and that the only double outlet on the female is her nose.[121] In reality, of course, they reproduce in the same familiar way as other mammals.

◄◦► ◄◦► ◄◦►

The striped skunk is by far the most common member of the weasel clan. Its unique capacity to offend the olfactories garnered unusual attention among the early explorers, just as it does today. The French called it *Enfant du Diable* (child of the devil) or, less poetically, *Bete Puante* (stinking beast). Jonathon Carver, who encountered it on his travels through the Midwest in the 1790s, said it is "the most extraordinary animal that the American woods produce."[122]

Henry Thacker, during his winter of muskrat trapping, ran afoul of skunks on many occasions. "The country at the time abounded with these animals," which he would frequently catch in his traps. His challenge was to kill the captives so they would refrain from discharging their scent and ruining the trap. After a fair amount of experimentation, he loaded his rifle with extra powder and crept within three feet of a captured skunk. The force of the bullet blew the animal's head off before it could retaliate. After congratulating himself on solving his vexing problem, Thacker went to release the trap when the skunk convulsed and "oh horror!, such a discharge of the genuine article, no man ever saw or smelt!"[123]

During Kennicott's time, skunks were "as abundant on the prairies as in the woods." The situation hasn't changed much over the intervening century and a half, except that they are now also well represented in urban areas. In addition to living in a wide range of habitats, skunks have been successful because humans have never seriously coveted their pelt (despite its striking beauty) or their flesh, which, as unlikely as it seems, is said to be tender and flavorful, like chicken.[124]

Skunks rank fourth among species handled by animal control personnel; in 1993, 2,195 skunks became problems in the region's nine Illinois counties. Skunks emerge from these encounters worse off than most species. First, their odoriferous emanations, which provide excellent protection against most predators, backfire with respect to people who would rather use lethal means than risk being sprayed. One example of this lethal behavior was that of an acquaintance who live-caught a skunk and decided that the safest thing to do was starve it to death in the trap. Such barbarism is unnecessary, however. Covering the cage with a lightproof material relaxes the skunk, which can then usually be moved with safety. And the prisoner can be released through the use of a long stick.

Second, and more important, skunks are notorious carriers of rabies and other diseases. Of all the mammals in the United States, both domestic and wild, they have the highest incidence of rabies.[125] As a result, by law, all trapped skunks must be euthanized. It is important to remember, though, that most skunks are not rabid and that a person can only become infected if he is bitten by an infected animal. Avoiding that kind of close contact is usually easy.

Are skunks in your neighborhood? The answer, my friend, is blowing in the wind, or lying dead along the road. But every so often you will be fortunate enough to see one, or maybe even a female leading her small procession of kits, shambling in its jaunty way, nose to the ground as it searches for subterranean prey. Lost in their pursuits, skunks have been known to pass within inches of a quiet observer who can follow closely behind without being noticed. This is an animal secure in its defenses, knowing that few predators will risk the consequences of an altercation.

The Metamorphosis of Bambi: White-Tailed Deer

White-tailed deer are animals neither of the open prairie nor the deep woods. They prefer savanna and edge and, thus, were probably quite common in the ecotonal landscape. One estimate of pre-1800 deer populations placed the density in southern Wisconsin at twenty to fifty animals per square mile. Abundance and their desirability as food make deer second only to wolves/coyotes in the attention paid them by early authors. Jean-François Buisson de Saint-

Cosme, on his journey of 1698, described the scenery along the Des Plaines River near Mount Joliet: "It is prairies skirted by hills and very fine woods, where there are numbers of deer as well as on the river."[126]

They were still common in the 1830s, when an early resident of Chicago said that "deer were so plentiful and so tame that I have known them to come and browse off the end of a log on my wagon." Another writer related how easy it was to drive deer into Lake Michigan and either kill them from boats or wait until they swam back to shore exhausted. Settlers in Delavan, Walworth County, preferred hunting deer in the winter from sleds. One guest on such an excursion in February 1842 said that soon after embarking the group came upon a large gathering of deer that she figured numbered in the hundreds. Two years later the surplus of deer meat was so great in Racine that whole carcasses brought only seventy-five cents apiece.[127]

The most disturbing single incident involving deer was the great hunt that occurred in the winter of 1838 on Bogus Island, in the Kankakee River swamps of Newton County. For some reason deer, wolves, and foxes concentrated on the island during the dry season when the water was shallow enough to wade. The severity of this particular season resulted in formation of ice that was "slick and glaring." The old hunters realized that the deer would have poor footing on the frozen lake surface and sought to take advantage of the situation:

> Notice was sent out to all the hunters. One participant said, "I will never forget it as . . . we got so many deer that we could not take care of them or get them home as we had no means of conveyance in those days." The island was alive with deer. . . . The old cap and ball rifle was used. With dogs, clubs, tomahawks, pitchforks, and corn-knives the massacre commenced at early morning and at sundown the battle closed. The crowd consisted of 25 men and boys and two women. One of the women killed a deer with a pitchfork. The party in all killed 65 deer, seven wolves, and two or three foxes. There were so many they could not kill them all at once, consequently that gave many a chance to escape. [One] buck was killed with a corn knife.[128]

In the face of slaughter and habitat loss, deer populations dwindled rapidly. State legislatures attempted to stem the trend by enacting various protective statutes. Wisconsin, in 1851, banned the hunting of deer between February 1 and July 1. Nine years later, it expanded the prohibition to the months of January and August. Illinois adopted similar legislation in 1873, establishing a closed season from January 1 to August 15. By 1901, the downward spiral had reached such a depth that the state proclaimed a total moratorium on deer hunting for five years. Unfortunately, these restrictions were too late in coming to rescue the deer of this region.[129]

According to his son, William Cox, twice-elected alderman of the first ward, holds the distinction of having killed the last deer within the city limits of Chicago. The event occurred in 1865 where "a forest of cottonwoods and oaks contested with a reluctant prairie," land that was to become the great stockyards. The Skokie Marsh lost its final deer in 1870 when a doe and its fawn were shot in Winnetka, Cook County, the latter selling for three dollars. Aldo Leopold, in his comprehensive survey of game animals in the north-central states, concluded that deer ceased to exist in northern Illinois after 1874. The last record for Racine County was in the form of tracks seen near the Fox River in December 1887; the animal itself was killed later in Burlington.[130]

Deer hung on in the Indiana Dunes until the early 1870s. One of the last deer in the region was killed in Michigan City, La Porte County, in 1880. But the final refuge for this species was the Indiana portion of the Kankakee River basin, where "even as late as 1878, sixty-five of these animals were bagged in a single day." Indiana's last deer was seen in 1893 in Knox County, far south of this region.[131]

Although deer had been eradicated by their hand, people seemed to miss this large and graceful animal. It wasn't long before deer were being reintroduced into the region. C. M. Eldredge, the McHenry County game warden, reported to the 1912 game survey that deer had been turned loose from enclosures in his county. An account of the Palatine area states that in 1918 "twenty-five deer will be put in Deer Grove Forest Preserve."[132]

Systematic restocking began in Indiana in 1934 when game biologists reintroduced thirty-five animals into seven counties. By 1955, they had released more than four hundred deer into twenty-two counties. In Illinois, escapees from a captive herd near Rockford, Winnebago County, began to repopulate the Rock River region. The Illinois Department of Conservation live-trapped some of those deer and released them in Cook County in 1950. The county received two more in 1952 and "a small herd" was liberated into the Zanders Woods holdings of the Cook County Forest Preserve District in 1960. Additional releases occurred in the Palos area of Cook County during the same decade. By the mid- to late 1980s, deer densities had reached alarming levels, in terms of number of deer per square kilometer, on protected land throughout northeastern Illinois: Waterfall Glen (DuPage County): 7–22; Ryerson Woods (Lake): 23; Wright and Lloyd Woods (Lake): 22; Ned Brown (Cook): 7–37; Des Plaines River from Central to Lake (Cook): 18–45; and Des Plaines River from Dundee to Lake/Cook (Cook): 26–40.[133]

The Bambi bomb had been ticking for a long time. And when the explosion finally occurred, it would create one of the most bitter controversies to plague local conservation forces.

Woven throughout the story is the Chicago Urban Deer Study (UDS). Aware of a growing problem, the Illinois Department of Conservation commissioned the Illinois Natural History Survey to investigate all aspects of deer biology in northeastern Illinois. (The Cook County Forest Preserve District, Illinois Nature Preserves Commission, and Lake County Forest Preserve District supplied additional funding.) Conducted from 1983 to 1989 by Dr. James Witham and Marty Jones, this project produced the information that helped local agencies in formulating sound deer management plans. Everyone who cares about maintaining the region's living diversity should applaud the contributions of these two scientists, who often found themselves at court proceedings and public hearings remote from deer habitat.

There are several reasons why the deer population metastasized in northeastern Illinois. Wolves and mountain lions had been gone for well over a century; coyotes will take the occasional fawn or sick adult but rely on much smaller prey and, thus, are not effective deer predators. State law bans the hunting of deer with firearms in Cook, Lake, DuPage, and Kendall Counties, and of course forest preserve districts prohibit all hunting. The nature of local land use has also led to deer increases. Looking at four counties (Cook, Lake, DuPage, and Kane), the UDS determined that over half the area provided some deer habitat, ranging from primary (wooded forest preserves) to secondary (wooded subdivisions, cropland, etc.) to tertiary (golf courses, cemeteries, etc.). But it also found that this deer habitat has been decreasing, particularly in the less urbanized portions of Lake and Kane counties. This results in "higher rates of mortality, dispersal or wandering, and/or increased deer densities on suitable remaining habitat."[134]

Three major problems are associated with an overabundance of deer in an urban environment. The first of these is the growing number of instances where deer intersect with their primary local predator—motor vehicles. This takes on special significance at O'Hare Airport, where aircraft have collided with deer at least twice. The jet involved in the second accident incurred over $100,000 in damages. Far more common, of course, are collisions between deer and land vehicles. From 1989 to 1992, the Illinois Department of Transportation reported 13,029 such accidents in seven counties of northeastern Illinois. Injuries were incurred by 670 people, and in 1992 there were four fatalities. The UDS determined that the average cost per accident per year from 1984 to 1988 ranged from $1,226.78 to $1,622.77. The highest cost for a single incident was $14,050.[135]

The second major ill effect of overpopulation is on the deer themselves. Of the herds examined by the UDS, the deer at Ned Brown Forest Preserve and along the Des Plaines River (both in Cook County) were the least healthy. Animals in these sites manifested smaller size, lower weight, and reduced fecundity. These populations were most at risk of a major die-off in the event of disease, harsh winters, or chronic malnutrition created by overbrowsing. A primary reason that these particular herds were doing poorly was that development had surrounded their habitat—deer were constricted in their movements, and thus pressure on the forest preserve properties was intensified.[136]

Although also at dangerously elevated numbers, deer at other locations were in surprisingly good health. At Ryerson Woods in Lake County, for example, the deer herd was characterized in 1988 as being "in excellent condition, there was no evidence of winter starvation, at least one doe produced triplets in 1988, and annual aerial counts suggest continued increase in population size." Three factors contributed to this anomaly. First, the deer had access to habitat offsite and, thus, could disperse. Second, although conditions were getting rapidly worse, the deer had not yet denuded ground vegetation to the same extent as they had at the two Cook County preserves. The third factor contributing to healthy deer, although ultimately exacerbating the overpopulation problem, was that some adjacent landowners were offering supplemental feeding.[137]

The final, and I think overriding, problem of an oversized deer population is that it leaves in ruin the ecosystems of which it is but one component. Busse Forest Nature Preserve, part of Cook County's Ned Brown Forest Preserve, was one of the first nature preserves in the entire system. It has long been known for its spring flower displays and has provided sanctuary to the state-endangered purple fringed orchid (*Habenaria psycodes*). Unfortunately, prior to the devastation, no one thought to accumulate the base line data necessary to quantify the damage being wrought, but by the mid-1980s the ground cover was virtually gone.

Even more profound, a well-defined browse line had developed at Busse Forest where the deer had consumed everything palatable, from the forest floor to tree foliage four to five feet above the ground, the maximum height they can reach. All the plants, mammals, birds, insects, and other organisms that over the millennia have come to rely on that layer of forest vegetation were decimated. And it was only a matter of time before the rest of Busse Forest would come under assault by the ravenous deer: an inventory of trees conducted in 1986 found that deer had stripped the bark of 256 American (*Ulmus americana*) and slippery elms (*U. rubra*). Of these, 163 later died and sixteen suffered reduced foliage production.[138]

Ryerson Woods was in better shape, but the warning signs had appeared. From 1984 to 1987 there was a gradual dawning on the part of the Ryerson staff and visitors that deer were increasing and the once spectacular display of spring ephemerals, particularly the large white trillium (*Trillium grandiflorum*), was diminishing. In addition, a browse line was becoming discernible. To demonstrate the severity of the deer damage, district personnel in the fall of 1987 constructed a deer exclosure measuring a thousand square meters. In just one growing season, there was a dramatic difference in density and cover of vegetation between protected and unprotected plots.[139]

Densities of such conservative species as large white trillium, smooth yellow violet (*Viola pensylvanica*), and white trout lily (*Erythronium albidum*) were greater within the exclosure by 83 percent, 61 percent, and 55 percent respectively. The disturbance-tolerant false Solomon's seal (*Smilacina racemosa*) grew 63 percent more densely outside the exclosure where it didn't have to compete with other plants more palatable to deer. In just one year, positive changes within the exclosure were striking: ground cover increased by 38 percent and overall plant density increased by 30 percent. The study is ongoing; the implementation of deer control has ameliorated the differences inside and outside the exclosures, but as of spring 1994 the plants protected from deer were both more numerous and vigorous.[140]

As an important part of their work, the UDS began removing deer from Busse Forest Preserve and O'Hare Airport during the winter of 1983–84. At that time, the deer herd at Busse was a minimum of 293. Thirty-five animals were taken for research purposes to determine survival rates of translocated animals and for evaluation of physical conditions. Beyond these, carefully supervised sharpshooters armed with high-powered rifles killed 334 deer from 1985 to 1988. This method was efficient, humane, and effective.[141]

The figure of 334 deer that needed to be culled represented the number necessary to reach the target goal of twenty-one deer per square mile (eight deer per square kilometer). Optimal deer population varies with the quality of the habitat, availability of habitat accessible offsite, and other factors. Other agencies at other places have selected different figures. Thus, Lake County has aimed for a limit of twelve or thirteen deer per square mile and DuPage about twenty per square mile. O'Hare represented a different situation, where human safety rather than habitat integrity was of paramount concern. Therefore, all but two of the sixty-six deer counted on airport property in January 1988 were either shot or relocated. These deer removal activities proceeded without a great deal of fanfare. Private not-for-profit landowning organizations were also ridding themselves of deer through lethal means, although doing so quietly.

After carefully evaluating the UDS results, the Lake County Forest Preserve District staff recommended adopting the same deer control methods at Ryerson Woods that proved so effective at O'Hare Airport and Busse Woods

94. Contrast in ground cover between area with deer exclosure and area
outside, Lloyd's Woods Forest Preserve, Lake County (Ill.), 1993.
(Courtesy Lake County Forest Preserve District, Libertyville, Ill.)

Forest Preserve. To reach the desired total of thirteen deer for Ryerson (which is roughly one square mile), sixty-four animals would have to be removed. This touched off a maelstrom, the effects of which are still being felt. A small but extremely vocal group of citizens organized opposition, raised funds, and set up pickets at Ryerson.

Their protest culminated in a lawsuit filed in January 1989 to enjoin the district, Lake County Board of Commissioners, Illinois Department of Conservation, and Illinois Nature Preserve Commission from approving or carrying out the deer control plan. After hearings a month later, the plaintiffs withdrew their action as part of an agreement with the defendants. Under the agreement, the agencies would delay the start of deer removal from February 1 to March 7 and, in the meantime, "make all reasonable efforts to translocate as many deer as possible." Expenses stemming from the relocation operation would be split between the district and the plaintiffs.[142]

As well intentioned as the opponents claimed to have been, their understanding of the problem was distressingly poor. They attempted to couch the issue as deer versus trillium: a leader of the group said of the forest preserve district that "the only reason they want to do this is because the deer have been eating the trillium this spring." Another of their principals sent a letter to the *Chicago Tribune* in which she was blissfully contemptuous of those who believe that organisms "must be checked and kept in balance in order to maintain the natural ecosystem."[143]

For me, the moment that best illustrated the plantiffs' grasp of conservation and natural history occurred during the court hearing when their counsel asked Jerry Soesbe, then Director of the Lake County Forest Preserve District, if he ever considered putting up fences around all the trilliums at Ryerson. Soesbe pointed out that "the preserve is laced with different plant species . . . and different habitats" and so the suggested action would mean "you'd have a whole preserve with pockets of exclosures."[144] Imagine the sight of thousands of fences scattered throughout the woods. The poor deer and every other wingless creature would have gone crazy trying to avoid them, assuming anything remained after the installation.

During this period, the one person who more than anyone else became the target of the opponents was Dan Brouillard, then director of conservation for the Lake County Forest Preserve District. He was vilified in letters to the editor and even received death threats. (So, by the way, did other district staff members, although as far as I know neither district property nor personnel was actually harmed.) For the health of public land throughout the region, it was imperative that the district move forward with its plans, and Brouillard's courage during this difficult period should be remembered. Director Soesbe and the county board itself also felt considerable political heat. Although it is not a popular thing to point out, most of the not- for-profit conservation groups let the public agencies under attack twist in the wind without providing any meaningful public support. And this assistance was requested. (During subsequent controversies, these groups have vigorously supported deer control.)

Under the terms of the court settlement, the district committed to translocating as many deer as possible. All along this had been a backup position of the opponents: if the status quo could not be maintained, then deer removal should be accomplished through live-trapping and removal to another site. Unfortunately, this approach has several serious drawbacks. First, it is expensive. Agencies must procure traps, cannon nets, tranquilizer guns, or other devices and train staff in their use. Once caught, the animals need to be tested for disease and then transported to their new locations. The minimum average cost of translocating each deer was $1,183, in this instance shared by the district and the opponents. The cost per animal killed was $288.[145]

Second, deer are not easy to live-trap. One of the first attempts at Ryerson was a roundup organized by the opponents, at least one of whom showed up in a full-length fur coat and high heels. They endeavored to drive the deer in front of them into burlap funnels leading into nets, but since white-tailed deer do not form tight herds like bison and antelope not a single animal was caught. Even when proven techniques are employed, deer become trap shy and increasingly difficult to catch. Eventually, however, twenty-seven deer were captured using box traps: eighteen were translocated, seven were equipped with radio collars and released on site, one tested positive for Lyme's disease antibodies (although not necessarily found to have the disease) and was euthanized, and one died during handling.[146]

The third difficulty with translocation arises from the presence of problematic deer numbers throughout the Midwest: few places are willing to accept transplants. In fact, despite a major effort to find more, only one suitable facility would accept Ryerson deer. Wildlife Prairie Park near Peoria agreed to receive eighteen deer in the winter of 1988–89 and eleven in 1989–90. In a letter written on October 9, 1990, the facility concluded that it was unable to take any more, but by February 1991 changed its mind and found room for six additional deer. This was still twelve less than the total awaiting removal.[147]

The fourth issue is one that ought to be particularly important to those motivated by a desire to see the deer treated humanely. Mortality rates for translocated deer are very high. Eight studies conducted from Texas to Florida revealed that death rates of translocated white-tailed deer ranged from 25 percent to 68 percent. Results depend on the condition of the deer, quality of receiving habitat, and presence at the new site of such decimating factors as hunting. Deer are also highly susceptible to capture myopathy, death brought on by the stress created during capture and handling. A deer appearing to be perfectly healthy in its new home may die up to a month after the event. Of the eighteen deer arriving at Wildlife Prairie Park in 1989, two escaped the park and were shot by hunters, three died within a month of relocation, and one died within four months.[148]

Eventually, thirty-nine deer were shot, and with the live captures, approximately fifteen of the seventy-six animals counted from aircraft were left on the property. (Much of the meat derived from culled deer was donated to charitable organizations providing food to needy citizens.) In most years since then, the district has succeeded in keeping the number around twelve or thirteen. Forest Preserve District staff have also removed deer from other high-quality preserves and carefully monitor conditions on holdings throughout the county. The forest preserve districts of Cook and DuPage Counties have implemented major deer control programs, too. Because of concern over damage to private property, the Village of Glencoe (Cook County) voted for lethal deer control by a 58–42 percent margin. It was probably the first referendum of its kind in the country. Other municipalities have since supported similar measures.[149]

By now you might think that the need to reduce deer populations by killing surplus animals would no longer be contested but, rather, accepted by all reasonable parties as a regrettable but necessary exigency of preserving biological diversity in an urban setting. Unfortunately, the opponents are still actively trying to thwart deer control, and despite their losses in court and at the ballot box, they succeed in intimidating the agencies. That is one reason I have detailed the events of 1988 and 1989 so thoroughly. It is not merely history I wish to recount but also facts that may prove helpful to those currently in the trenches and fighting for what is in the best interest of our natural heritage.

Raymond Schwarz, formerly superintendent of conservation of the Cook County Forest Preserve District, has eloquently summarized the reality of the deer problem, a reality not yet grasped by the opponents: "Unless something is done to increase the carrying capacity of a species' habitat, the yearly surplus of that species, whether it be made up of old or young animals, must die. There is unequivocally no biological argument about that incontestable fact; the surplus must die."[150] And in this instance, if the forest preserve officials didn't act, the entire ecosystem would be at risk. We might lose not only Bambi but Thumper, Flower, Mother Opossum, and Friend Owl as well.

Entering the New Century: Prospects for the Future

To preserve and enhance nature right here in the city— that is the commitment we make as adults for another generation. —Richard M. Daley (2000)

Nature does not seem to be obedient either to the learned theories and elaborate models of the day or to the wishful thinking of well-meaning land managers. —Gerould Wilhelm and Linda Masters (1994)

Those who plan and manage natural areas should learn that their systems are never static and that the present conditions are merely stages in a continually changing mosaic. They cannot be frozen in time. —Emily Russell (1997)

Do Go Gentle into That Good Fight: Ecological Restoration and Construction

Some years ago, I heard Ron Panzer say that he wouldn't be surprised if as many as 90 percent of all the organisms that ever inhabited the region still survived here. Given all the habitat that has been lost, such a claim seemed counter-intuitive. But now, having completed this project, I believe that Panzer's assessment is justified. The plants and animals with which we share this area tend to be more resilient than we might first imagine. This is not to say, however, that either Panzer or I am sanguine about the continued existence of many of these organisms. It is obvious that many species are represented by very small numbers; ours might be the last generation with the opportunity to save many of them.

Although the region has retained most of its species, two elements essential to healthy populations have been lost: time and space. Human actions are measured according to fiscal years, terms in office, or careers. Thus we tend to assess things and processes in increments of time that may be trivial when considering such natural events as forest maturation, dune formation, changes in the levels of Lake Michigan, or climatic cycles.

The loss of space is probably more devastating and is felt in so many ways. Acquiring extensive and diverse blocks of land is the goal of every conservation agency, for there is a substantial literature documenting the pernicious effects of habitat fragmentation.[1] Organisms must have territories large enough to contain adequate food sources, perches, denning sites, display areas, nursery ponds, and/or other elements needed for their survival. And, of course, there must be multiple territories to ensure successful reproduction into the future. It is also true that many of the more conservative species fare best in the interiors of woods or grasslands, isolated from the perils of the purlieus. These perils may include cars, road deicers, domestic cats, and brown-headed cowbirds, to name just four.

Fragmentation also hinders, if not outright prevents, the ability of a species to disperse and colonize. This is especially true in urban settings, where miles of concrete and innumerable risks separate populations. Over time this results in genetic isolation. Further, in an unbroken landscape, although a group might disappear, either gradually or suddenly as the result of some catastrophe, individuals from a nearby population may be able to recolonize the former territory if the habitat remains or becomes suitable in the future. Without the possibility of free movement across the landscape, however, local extirpations become permanent and ultimately the maintenance of any population becomes problematic.

Small tracts preclude the dynamism that marked so many of the region's ecosystems. Succession is resisted as managers attempt to lock in place a high-quality example of one seral state. A modestly sized preserve can hardly shift along a grassland woods continuum, for at its borders there is an impenetrable desert of concrete or farm fields. Employing management techniques that favor one community type over another (or that emphasizes plants over animals) will likely reduce the diversity of the given site. Controlled burns on small sites, for example, are different than burns on large sites and may well produce such unintended consequences as the loss of bird nesting habitat, decrease in certain invertebrates, and even the spread of alien species.[2]

To counteract fragmentation, agencies continue to increase their holdings, often concentrating on enlarging existing preserves. Cooperation between neighboring agencies can create functionally larger blocks of habitat whereby each of the participants improves the quality of its property. And where possible, as with states and the federal government, the eye is toward acquiring macrosites comprising thousands of acres.

Those areas of highest botanical quality are now mostly either protected (to a greater or lesser extent) or destroyed. Thus, most of the land now being bought has experienced significant disturbance; habitat restoration and re-creation will improve many of these parcels. But it is critical that these efforts take into account the important biota that are already on the site. A rare species should not be sacrificed merely because it is absent from an approved list for that particular community type. That the species is there is meaningful. As Steve Packard and Laurel Ross remind, land "managers need to heed a central principle of the healing arts, 'First do no harm.'"[3] By treading with a light step, we can go a long way toward preserving the full range of natural communities that contribute to the glory of this unique region.

I have said this before about birds, but it pertains to virtually all terrestrial vertebrates and probably most invertebrates as well: any species that requires high-quality plant communities is locally extinct because there aren't enough acres of high-quality plant communities to sustain it. In most cases, the species that are here have adapted to the environments that remain. Thus even a sizable tract of Eurasian weeds may support large populations of rodents, fox, snakes, insects, breeding birds, and wintering raptors. The Forest Preserve District of DuPage County discovered this when it planted large portions of its Springbrook Prairie Forest Preserve in fescue as ground cover while it prepared development plans. The preserve soon attracted such a variety of grassland birds, including summering northern harriers and short-eared owls, that it became the premier area for such species among the agency's twenty-three thousand acres. (As a result, a proposed reservoir was abandoned.)

◄o► ◄o► ◄o►

Perhaps because so little of the Midwest landscape has retained its original character, the region has been in the forefront of ecological construction efforts. (By construction, I mean creating community types where none are present.) Most of these projects, at least in recent years, have focused on wetlands, savannas, and prairies.

Reconstructed wetlands have popped up everywhere. Many of these represent mitigation projects, mandated by the U.S. Army Corps of Engineers as replacements for wetlands destroyed elsewhere. (This has spawned an industry, and an abundance of consultants are now available.) Others have been created by conservation agencies, which in many cases have only to remove drain tiles before hydric plants begin to reemerge from the once again saturated ground. In other instances, beaver have provided the labor that enables water to spread across the land.

Perhaps the best known of the new wetlands is the Des Plaines River Wetlands Demonstration Project.[4] Directed and conceived by Donald Hey, the project is a collaboration between the Lake County Forest Preserve District (which owns the property) and the Openlands Project, with substantial support from the federal government.

Hey and his associates wanted to establish an outdoor laboratory where they could investigate a host of issues relating to habitat restoration, water quality, and hydrology. They examined numerous sites before settling on 450 acres along a 2.8-mile stretch of the Des Plaines River, in Wadsworth, Lake County (Ill.). Although the tract was probably wet prairie at the time of the first surveyors, by the 1970s the area consisted mostly of abandoned farmland with some second growth woods and three water-filled gravel pits. The most important natural feature was a fairly high-quality woods at the southern end.

The project required extensive earth moving. The floodway of the river was widened so that as the water spilled across the newly formed plain it curled into backwaters. In effect the river was braided, reuniting it with the land that was once part of the same living system. West of the floodway, workers constructed four marshes. Fed by pumps, they receive roughly 15 percent of the river's flow. This water returns to the river via control structures and vegetated channels.

Researchers in many disciplines have availed themselves of the unique opportunities available at the project. The Illinois Geological Survey installed eighty wells to monitor water movement through the site, while the state Water Survey examined the changes in quality as water moved from one marsh to another. Climatologists studied soil moisture, solar radiation, temperature, wind, and precipitation.

For most people with an interest in natural history, the project's most conspicuous success has been the number of birds that now frequent the wetlands. The mudflats and open water attract migrant ducks, herons, and sandpipers of many species. A survey of the site for migrant waterfowl in the spring of 1985, prior to the wetland construction, found a total of thirteen individuals of three species. A similar study conducted five years later, after the wetland installation, yielded 617 individuals of fifteen species. Breeding birds also increased, from thirty-five species in 1985 to fifty species in 1991.[5] At least three of the additions are wetland species on Illinois's threatened and endangered list. (The white-eyed vireo [*Vireo griseus*], an uncommon and local nester, may have been a casualty of the project, as it bred there in 1985 but not since.)

Scott Hickman concluded his study of the demonstration project by paraphrasing the movie *Field of Dreams:* "If we build wetlands, birds will come."[6] Since a very few number of plant species dominate most constructed wetlands, this is further evidence that vegetational structure is more important to birds than floristics. Unfortunately, it is exceedingly difficult to replicate the rich assemblage of plants associated with high-quality marshes. And some natural communities, such as bogs and fens, depend on specific hydrologic and edaphic conditions that are probably impossible to duplicate.[7]

Perhaps because so few survived, the most overlooked of plant communities have been deep-soil shrublands and savannas. Recently, however, this has now changed, most particularly with respect to savannas. Many people are now devoting substantial energy to researching, restoring, and constructing these landscape types. The best of the restorations and constructions try to integrate the data from historical records with soil types, topography, fire frequency, and other factors that determine larger landscape patterns.

The techniques for savanna construction vary according to the site and attitude of the participants. The most aggressive involves the extensive clearing of brush and trees, including native species in the subcanopy and even canopy, in order to achieve the orchard-like appearance mentioned by some of the early travelers and land surveyors. These are burned regularly and often seeded with a variety of understory species.

The Forest Preserve District of DuPage County closely monitored the succession of species that appeared at their Bluff Savanna project at Waterfall Glen Forest Preserve. After one burn, woody species such as poison ivy and Virginia creeper decreased, as did garlic mustard and bluegrass. The only new plant noted was white snakeroot. But after two successful burns, marked changes began:

> The second year witnesses a virtual explosion of white snakeroot, black snakeroot, enchanter's nightshade, stickseed and false pennyroyal, which seems to come from nowhere. The third year, stickseed, enchanter's nightshade and false pennyroyal all but disappear while white and black snakeroot form a dense cover. The third year also begins an invasion of the agrimonies, bedstraws, and sedges. Venus looking glass (*Specularia perfoliata*) also puts in a brief appearance at this time. Starting with the fourth year, many of the other savanna plants, including the grasses, begin to move into the area. . . . After the grasses and sedges have provided for a good matrix, the more conservative plants begin to increase.[8]

Another approach, utilized by the Will County Forest Preserve at Raccoon Grove, is to let fires from surrounding grasslands penetrate as far as they can into wooded tracts. This represents a gradual process whereby the wooded edges are thinned, replicating the transitional aspect of natural savanna communities. The effort here is to emphasize the dynamic nature of the grass-land/woods interface.[9]

The first constructed prairie in this region, and the second anywhere, was started by Ray Schulenberg in 1962 at the Morton Arboretum, DuPage County. The project covers a hundred acres and now contains 350 species of native plants.[10] Many other artificial prairies have been undertaken since. Most of these lack the size and the long-term commitment of managers necessary to achieve optimal results. It is also unfortunate that few data have been collected from many of these efforts, thus minimizing any scientific value they may have.[11] But these projects do serve important educational purposes, by intro-ducing prairie to many people who would otherwise receive no exposure to it at all. This also protects the remnant prairies from traffic by those whose curi-osity is sated by the imitations.

In the Chicago region, the most celebrated large prairie conversion lies in western DuPage County.[12] Under the direction of Robert Betz, 640 acres of the Fermi National Accelerator Laboratory near Batavia are being trans-formed into prairie. The site had been cultivated for more than a century, and the few prairie species present inhabited fencerows and wet areas. Mesic species included big bluestem, prairie milkweed, prairie dock, and Culver's root. The more extensive wet areas still held such native plants as swamp milk-weed, porcupine sedge (*Carex hystericina*), water horehound, monkey flower, and ironweed.

Prairie construction began in June of 1975 when workers planted four hundred pounds of seed into soil disked the preceding fall. The seeds were a carefully chosen mix of species that could successfully compete with the weedy and mostly nonnative plants that constituted the vegetation on the site. Betz explained his strategy: "The prairie is established in waves with the more ag-gressive species of wider ecological tolerances entering first and preparing the way for others of narrower tolerances to follow. As the first wave of these ag-gressive prairie plants consolidate their position in association with fire and chemical microbiological changes that occur in the soil, a 'second wave' of species with more restricted requirements can slowly move in. These are fol-lowed by a 'third wave', then a 'fourth wave' and so on."

The first wave, called the prairie matrix, consisted of twenty-three species from seven families, including grasses, composites, and legumes. You can hear the joy in Betz's voice as he describes how over time blazingstars, lead plants, prairie clover and other conservative species have taken hold. Even though these wonderful changes have occurred, he knows that a quarter-century's worth of work represents a tiny step in trying to recreate a system that took thousands of years to evolve. But he is an optimist and estimates that their goal of replicating prairie should be reached in about two hundred years.

Sharing Space: Institutional Trends

In January 1999, the Openlands Project published the results of their study on land consumption in thirteen of the region's counties, an area totaling 4,409,757 acres. They found that in addition to the 25.7 percent of this land that was already developed, just over 28 percent was at high or medium risk of development. Over 20 percent of three counties—Kane, Kendall, and Lake (Ind.)—were considered to be at high risk.[13]

Every new subdivision, golf course, shopping center, or office complex gobbles up habitat and puts severe strains on existing roads and other infrastructure. This in turn puts pressures on conservation agencies to allow incursions across their holdings for such things as utility alignments, roads, game fields, and new multiuse trails. These agencies, in essence, are being asked to alleviate the problems caused by decisions made elsewhere.

Flooding is another serious problem that continues to worsen as more land becomes waterproofed. In 1996, the U.S. Army Corps of Engineers released a major study of flooding in the upper Des Plaines River basin. They estimated that annual flood damage averages more than $21 million. Even more telling, the corps determined that if all of the possible flood storage capacity was constructed, flooding along the river would still increase substantially.[14]

These problems have spurred the growing realization, more strongly felt in some places than others, that uncontrolled growth jeopardizes the quality of life that drew many people to the area in the first place.[15] Elected officials are being forced to deal with the issue, but they are hampered by several factors including the lack of coordination between different units of local government. In the six most populated counties of northeastern Illinois, for example, there are 1,246 local jurisdictions. This leads not only to inefficiencies but also to governments vying with each other for development projects and the concomitant taxes.

Within the past few years there have been a number of efforts inaugurated to help provide the coordination that has been lacking in land-use planning. Some of these have originated from the three regional planning commissions, while others have sprung from the nongovernmental sector.[16] One broad-based initiative is Chicago Wilderness, a consortium of federal, state, local, and private organizations. It seeks to preserve and protect the natural heritage of the Chicago metropolitan area by creating the world's first urban bioreserve. Chicago Wilderness has fostered increased cooperation between its members and is in the process of promoting a regional action plan.

At present, the most effective strategy in the face of sprawl is for agencies to continue to acquire open space. This requires taxpayer support, of course, but voters have shown a willingness to endorse well-conceived bond referenda. Three recent examples of this support occurred in the elections of April 1999, when citizens in Will, Lake, and Kane Counties approved by wide margins a total of $195 million for the purchase and management of open land. F. T. "Mike" Graham, Libertyville (Lake County, Ill.) Township supervisor and a stalwart of the open space movement, says that such expenditures constitute a bargain: "It costs more in taxes to pay for improvements for new homes than to buy the land."[17]

Although restricting growth in Chicago's collar counties remains an elusive goal, models of development exist that are far more environmentally benign than traditional approaches. A recent *Chicago Tribune* article lists three innovative types of residential plans: "Conservation development, with homes clustered on one part of the property and open space on the other; transit-oriented development built beside rail lines, perhaps with residences built over stores; [and] pedestrian friendly development, a neo-traditional style that encourages front porches and eliminates cul-de-sacs and marks a return to the grid pattern of streets."[18]

The conservation development model is particularly well suited for furthering another positive trend. An increasing number of developers and corporations are using native vegetation in the design of their properties. Ideally, this means that as much habitat on site will be left intact as possible, natural communities that are present will be restored, and/or natural communities will be constructed. At small sites, it means using indigenous plants in landscaping. This approach offers many benefits, including environmental, educational, and aesthetic. The most compelling reason to use native plants, however, may well be economic. The Northeastern Illinois Planning Commission says that landowners who use native vegetation instead of traditional landscaping materials can save up to 80 percent in installation and maintenance costs over ten years.[19]

The use of native vegetation is also an excellent method for controlling stormwater runoff. The various regional planning commissions within the Chicago area have produced model stormwater management ordinances adopted by many counties. Some of these are among the best in the nation, yet, as we have seen, flooding continues to plague the region.

A key element of the regulatory schemes is the rate of stormwater that leaves a developed site. But in these urbanized watersheds, the volume of water entering streams and rivers increases even if the rates are within acceptable limits. Planting native species increases the capacity of land surfaces to absorb precipitation, thereby reducing the amount of water that leaves the site. At least one organization, the Des Plaines River Watershed Team, is specifically promoting the use of native plants as a way to ameliorate the flooding that has been an insoluble problem for those within the upper Des Plaines watershed.[20]

Examples of conservation developments exist across the region. One of the oldest is a subdivision in Highland Park that was designed to preserve a significant prairie harboring the federally threatened eastern prairie fringed orchid. The natural area became so central to the entire project, and an important amenity for potential buyers, that the developers called the community Hybernia, a name based on the orchid's genus *Habenaria* (or *Platanthera*).

Both more ambitious and recent are the much larger Coffee Creek Center Development in Chesterton, Porter County; Prairie Crossing in Grayslake, Lake County (Ill.); and Mill Creek near Geneva, Kane County. Each of these developments will retain at least 40 percent of their area as open space, and each treats and retains stormwater runoff on site to minimize flows into nearby waterways. Much of Mill Creek's open space is in the form of a golf course and parks (127 acres will be maintained as wetlands), while Coffee Creek and Prairie Crossing emphasize preservation and restoration of native ecosystems.[21]

Nonresidential properties are also utilizing conservation principles. Abbot Laboratories in North Chicago (Lake County, Ill.) has adopted the new techniques to their corporate headquarters. Abbot has a natural prairie on its property and has worked with biologists in allowing regular burning and other management. In addition, it turned thirty acres of lawn into constructed prairie. This action has reduced the stormwater and sedimentation loads on the company's detention basin. The most desired reduction, however, has been in the cost of maintenance: from $1,200 an acre per year to less than $100. And as icing on the cake, employees enjoy the tract as a tranquil setting for walks.[22]

Lakeview Industrial Park is situated on a biologically diverse tract of fifteen hundred acres that straddles the Des Plaines River west of Pleasant Prairie, Kenosha County. In consultation with local authorities and the Wisconsin chapter of the Nature Conservancy, the developers agreed to use native landscaping on built areas and to dedicate a third of the land as a state natural area. This cooperative attitude not only resulted in a model project but undoubtedly facilitated regulatory approval as well, a result that might otherwise have been expensive and arduous.[23]

With acres of closely cropped sod and a heavy dependence on chemicals, golf courses are often little more than green wastelands. To improve matters, the Audubon Cooperative Sanctuary System (a division of Audubon International) initiated a program whereby golf courses are recognized for sound practices in six categories: environmental planning, wildlife and habitat management, public and member involvement, integrated pest management, water conservation and management, and water quality. JoEllen Zeh, an Audubon ecologist, says that the courses of the Chicago region are among the most active in the country. One hundred and two local courses currently participate in the program, twelve of which are certified in all six categories.[24] At last, the game that has adopted avian terms to describe the success of players has now taken measures that contribute to the success of birds (and other organisms).

A Place for All: Midewin National Tallgrass Prairie and Prairie Parklands

A fitting end to these pages is the story of Midewin National Tallgrass Prairie and Prairie Parklands.[25] It is a story still unfolding, and only the future will tell how much of the great potential will be realized. But in the telling, we return to some of the critical themes that define what has happened in the region since that first group of Europeans approached the headwaters of the Illinois over three centuries ago: exploitation of the land, nature's endurance, and the need for coordinated action to secure and manage the land so that biological diversity can flourish.

In 1993 an extraordinary opportunity to engage in landscape-scale restoration presented itself when the Department of Defense decided to decommission the 23,500-acre Joliet Army Arsenal. Built in the early years of World War II, the arsenal produced, at its peak, 5.5 million tons of TNT a week. (An accident in 1942 caused an explosion that killed forty-eight workers and was felt as far away as Aurora.) Over the ensuing decades, activities at the facility ebbed and flowed in accord with the nation's overseas conflicts. Operations finally ceased in 1977, when a private contractor began maintaining the site in a "standby" condition.

Although the arsenal had been a busy place for much of its existence, most of its area was used for row crops or grazing. Six thousand acres of pasture, plus woodlands, marshes, streams (including virtually the entire watershed of Grant Creek), and a five hundred–acre mosaic of high-quality and heavily disturbed prairie, made the site hospitable to an exceptionally diverse array of plants and animals. Field surveys were to discover such rare species as slender sandwort, leafy prairie clover, eastern prairie fringed orchid, red-veined leafhopper (*Aflexia rubranura*), the moth *Papaipema eryngii*, ellipse mussel, and Blanding's turtle. The area was best known, however, as a mecca for birds, particularly large populations of state-endangered upland sandpipers and loggerhead shrikes. Beginning in 1983, the Illinois Department of Natural Resources received special permission to conduct annual censuses of the arsenal's grassland birds.

While there was no question that the arsenal needed to be preserved, an even more ambitious vision soon emerged. Conservationists realized that with the arsenal as the centerpiece, Goose Lake Prairie State Natural Area, Des Plaines Conservation Area, Grant Creek Nature Preserve, Will County Forest Preserve land, and large tracts of fallow corporate holdings formed forty thousand acres of nearly contiguous habitat. This concentration of open land was named Prairie Parklands, and it represented a unique opportunity to preserve, enhance, and re-create the matrix of ecosystems that used to thrive here.

The effort to secure the arsenal for conservation purposes was an arduous one that took two years. Local interests had to be placated and Congress had to approve the plan that emerged. As one example of how difficult the process was, a powerful senator from another Midwestern state almost killed the project because he was angry at an Illinois senator for supporting a balanced budget amendment.

In the end, the land was transferred to the U.S. Forest Service to become the first National Tallgrass Prairie. Renamed Midewin National Tallgrass Prairie, the reserve currently holds fifteen thousand acres but has the potential of growing to 19,165 acres. ("Midewin" is a Potawatomi word for healing.) Other portions of the original site would become a veteran's cemetery, a landfill, and an industrial park.

A detailed account of the events that led to Midewin's creation could easily fill the pages of a substantial book and, thus, is beyond the scope of this work. Many public officials at all levels of government guided the plan through a myriad of obstacles. Not-for-profit organizations (particularly the Openlands Project) also provided vital support. But there are three individuals whose behind-the-scenes work was so crucial they deserve mention. Francis Harty of the Illinois Department of Natural Resources toiled full time on making Midewin a reality and was a principal architect of the strategy that eventually ensured preservation. Harty, in turn, has credited Benjamin Tuggle of the U.S. Fish and Wildlife Service as one of the participants most responsible for making the project happen. Tuggle's commitment was so strong, in fact, that he took positions that were controversial within his own agency when such action was necessary. And finally, Larry Stritch of the U.S. Forest Service was pivotal in guiding his own agency to make the proper choices once they acquired the land.

With Midewin's difficult but auspicious birth, a new chapter began. Not only do the interests of the many constituent groups need to be balanced, so must the differing needs of the plants and animals that spurred preservation in the first place. The issue is best illustrated with birds. The conversion of grazed meadows to tallgrass prairie would be inimical to upland sandpipers and loggerhead shrikes, which need large expanses of short grass. For optimal shrike habitat, there must also be perches for hunting and brush for nesting. Bobolinks do best in almost pure stands of tallgrass, while Henslow's sparrows require a mixture of dense grass and herbaceous vegetation. Henslow's sparrows also vacate recently burned tracts. Bell's vireos (*Vireo bellii*), whose continental populations are declining, survive in shrublands within a ten-year period of succession. Grazing benefits northern harriers and short-eared owls when it occurs in foraging areas and harms them when it involves potential breeding habitat. Add to the birds all of the other organisms that require management consideration, and it is clear that land managers must proceed carefully, lest they eliminate members of the ecosystems.

This is where the full import of Midewin and its adjacent parklands asserts itself. It will be possible to employ management regimes that replicate the multitude of niches that can develop in an environment shaped by the vicissitudes of nature, rather than the deliberate hand of modern humans. No species need be managed to extirpation. Because the acreage is so wonderfully vast, there should be room for all.

Appendix

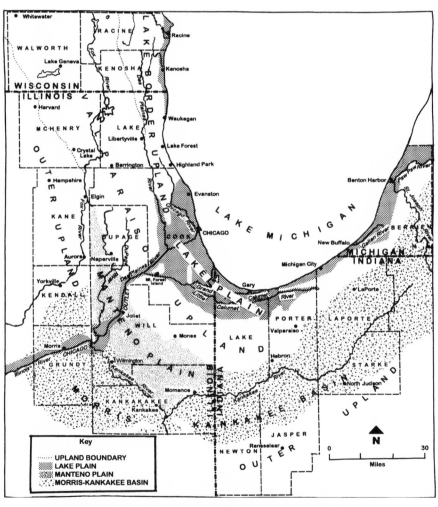

A1. Natural divisions of the region of Chicago by F. M. Fryxell (1927).
(Courtesy University of Chicago Press.)

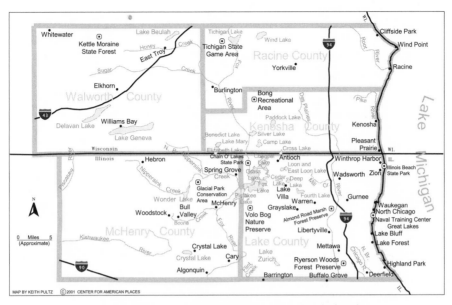

A2. Walworth, Racine, and Kenosha Counties in Wisconsin and Lake and McHenry Counties in Illinois, depicting place names mentioned throughout the text.

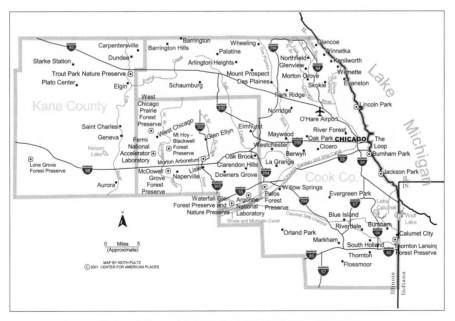

A3. Kane, DuPage, and Cook Counties in Illinois, depicting place names mentioned throughout the text.

A4. City of Chicago, depicting place names mentioned throughout the text.

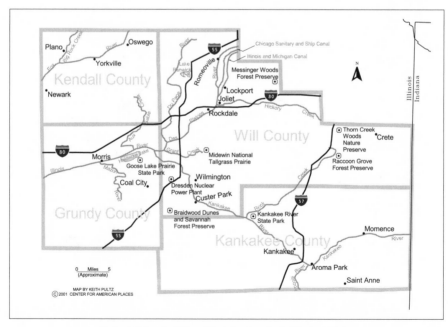

A5. Kendall, Grundy, Will, and Kankakee Counties in Illinois, depicting place names mentioned throughout the text.

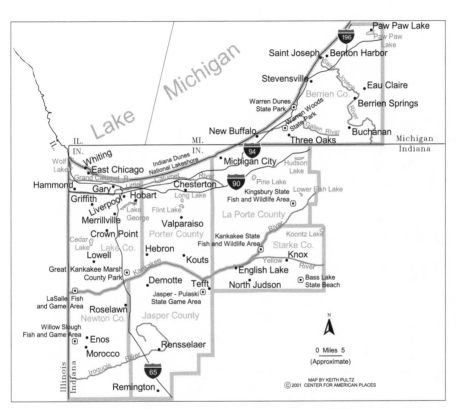

A6. Lake, Newton, Porter, Jasper, La Porte, and Starke Counties in
Indiana and Berrien County in Michigan, depicting place names
mentioned throughout the text.

Notes

Chapter One: *The Great Forces*

1. Kenton 1925, 366. A league is about 2.5 miles.
2. Thwaites 1900, 58:109. The cattle, oxen, and cows referred to in these passages were bison (*Bison bison*).
3. Fryxell 1927, 3.
4. Paulding 1849, 23. See Knight and Zeuch 1930, 1–8.
5. Schapper 1917, 14.
6. Dolomite is similar to limestone but differs in that it is made largely of magnesium carbonate rather than calcium carbonate.
7. Henry Cowles, quoted in Fryxell 1927, 34.
8. The older references on which this section on glaciation is primarily based include Bretz (1955), Goldthwait (1909), Willman (1971), and Willman and Fry (1970). However, work conducted over the past decade or so has supplanted much of the nomenclature and many of the conclusions that had been widely accepted for many years. The following publications are reflective of current thinking: Chrzastowski and Thompson (1994), Hansel and Johnson (1993), Hansel and Mickelson (1988), Killey (1998), and Wiggers (1997). But even current thinking is in flux, as the following examples attest. (1) For a very long time experts have considered the flat area along the lakefront that extends from Waukegan through most of Racine County to be part of the Chicago Lake Plain. (As is apparent, I have followed their lead in this work.) Mike Chrzastowski has determined, however, that the Zion Beach–Ridge Plain, as he calls this area, is much more recent and was created when wave action deposited eroded sediment that was once the delta at the mouth of the Root River in Racine County (see Chrzastowski and Frankie 2000). (2) The levels generally given for various lake stages are now believed to be 3.3–14.8 feet too high, but there is still not unanimity as to the exact figures. (3) Until recently, a Tolleston phase of Lake Chicago (the least extensive and most recent) was part of the standard discussion on lake levels. Today, geologists doubt whether such a phase existed, and the term is now obsolete. However, as a relic of the time when Tolleston was part of the accepted lexicon, there are dunes referred to as being of Tolleston age. These were formed during the Alonquin phase, which was the last phase of Lake Chicago.

9. For my treatment of soil, I relied on the assistance of John Losey, plus the writings of Fehrenbacher et al. (1984), Madson (1982, 114, 117), Paschke and Alexander (1970), and Simonson (1957).

10. Origin of soil: Atwater (1818, 116–28); composition of soil: Lesquereux (1865, 238–54); bison: E. T. Seton, quoted in Roe (1970, 842); fire and drought: Caton (1869, 1–30); and fire: Wells (1818, 331–37).

11. Sampson 1921, 523; Downing 1922, 95–96.

12. Henry Gleason, quoted in Curtis 1959, 301. See Transeau 1935, 434.

13. Anderson 1990, 14.

14. A number of sources were helpful on climate and weather: Anderson (1990, 12), Critchfield (1974), Eichenlaub (1979), Grazulis (1993), King (1982, 1) and McPherson et al. (1993).

15. Partridge 1902, 637–38.

16. McPherson et al. 1993, 11.

17. Cutler 1976, 13.

18. Eichenlaub 1979, 300–301.

19. Grazulis 1993, 1303.

20. Curtis 1959, 37.

21. Frey 1966, 309.

22. Woods 1861, 304.

23. Burley 1919, 16.

24. Kingman 1842, 38.

25. Trotter 1859, 231.

26. Sears 1969, 28. See the excellent discussion of prairie and forest fires in McClain and Elzinga (1994).

27. At the time of European arrival, the Illinois and the Miami tribes shared the region. But through slaughter and intimidation, the Potawatomi had replaced them by the 1770s. At the end of another sixty years, a series of treaties ended Indian presence in the region when the Potamatomies moved west of the Mississippi.

28. Anderson 1990, 9.

Chapter Two: *In Quality Unexcelled*

1. Clark 1842, 117.

2. Sears 1969, 7.

3. Weaver 1954, 23. There are two additional items to note here. First, vegetation refers to the total number of individual plants; flora refers to the number of species. And second, I have followed Swink and Wilhelm (1994, 105) in their use of *Andropogon scoparius* as the scientific name of little bluestem, although many authors call the plant *Schizachyrium scoparium*.

4. Sears 1969, 66.

5. Peattie 1938, 10.

6. Watts 1975, 125.

7. This discussion of grass adaptations is based on Weaver (1954).

8. It is important to note that although these ordinations reflect realities, anomalies abound

and differences fade at the edges: the finer the distinctions (dry mesic and wet mesic), the more blurred they become. Topography and ever-increasing habitat loss can also contribute to the blending of community types. In one study, Philip Whitford compared the species composition of prairie remnants in Racine and Kenosha Counties with the classification system developed by John Curtis for all of Wisconsin. He discovered a "high degree of mingling, with high or mesic prairie species occurring frequently on low sites and vice versa" (1958, 729).

9. The Illinois Natural Areas Inventory, a state-sponsored project to identify and categorize all the natural areas still extant in Illinois, distinguished another type of gravel prairie called "mesic gravel prairie." These occur where black-soil loam has developed over gravel deposited by glacial outwash. The limestone gravel has raised the calcium level of the soil sufficiently to support such calcium-dependent plants as common valerian (*Valeriana ciliata*), stiff aster (*Aster ptarmicoides*), and low calamint (*Satureja arkansana*). Only three such prairies were found in the entire state (all in this region): one is now destroyed, but happily the other two (Santa Fe Prairie and Chicago Ridge Prairie, both in Cook County) have been dedicated as Illinois Nature Preserves, although not before they were both significantly reduced in size.

10. Schennum n.d., 11.

11. Under the U.S. Endangered Species Act, "an *endangered species* is in danger of extinction throughout the area in which they are usually found" and "a *threatened species* is one that could become endangered in the near future." State endangered species acts use similar language except that endangered refers to species in danger of disappearing from the state.

12. Herkert 1991a, 1:8; Betz and Lamp 1990, 28.

13. Bill Wingate, interview by author, February 1994.

14. Curtis 1959, 270.

15. Pepoon 1927, 54.

16. Curtis 1959, 558; Bliss and Cox 1964, 115–28; and Hanson 1975a.

17. Short 1845, 188.

18. Leopold 1970, 52.

19. Short 1845, 190, 193.

20. Curtis 1959, 416; Swink and Wilhelm 1994, 132.

21. Weaver and Fitzpatrick 1934, 239.

22. Betz and Lamp 1990, 25.

23. This discussion of Mead's milkweed, including Rommel's discovery of the plant in Palatine, is based on Betz (1989 and interview by author, fall 1993).

24. See Cronon (1991, 393–94) and Swenson (1990) for discussions on the origin of Chicago's name.

25. Hill 1892a, 412.

26. Pepoon 1927, 47.

27. Calkins 1906–7, paper no. 1.

28. Woods 1861, 2980.

29. Swink and Wilhelm 1979, 851.

30. Sheviak 1974, 29.

31. Homoya 1993, 108–9.

32. Ibid., 174–75.

33. On eastern prairie orchids in early twentieth-century Chicago, see Pepoon 1927, 237.

34. Bowles et al. 1992, 29–31. The following two paragraphs on the two prairie orchids rely on Bowles (1983) and Bowles et al. (1992).

35. Hanson 1977, 16.

36. DeMauro 1986, 16–17.

37. Ibid., 16.

38. There are differing opinions with respect to the taxonomic status of the plant. (See Swink and Wilhelm 1994, 80.) Swink and Wilhelm refer to it as a species, *Actinea herbacea*, but Marcy DeMauro, an authority on the plant, believes that the cited differences between *Hymenoxys acaulis* and variety *glabra* are not consistent enough to warrant consideration as a full species (telephone conversation, spring 1994).

39. Pepoon 1927, 514.

40. The account of the plant's rediscovery and extirpation is from Betz (interview by author, fall 1993).

41. Marcy DeMauro (telephone conversation, spring 1994).

42. Hill 1879, 239–40.

43. Boltwood 1879, 219.

44. Baskin and Baskin 1973, 132; Pepoon 1927, 362.

45. Baskin and Baskin 1973, 139.

46. Jerry Wilhlem, interview by author, summer 1994.

47. Back in Vicksburg, Wilhelm reported his findings that there were two tiers of sites: C-2, which should not be disturbed, and the remaining forty-nine, which were equally suitable as dumps. Wilhelm's commanding officer still demanded that all the sites be rated from one to fifty. This led Wilhelm to the realization that many institutions prefer numerical values in making decisions, and thus the experience was a major prompt for his devising, along with Floyd Swink, the natural areas rating index that is so widely used in the Chicago region (Wilhelm, personal communication).

48. DeMauro, telephone conversation, spring 1994.

49. Baskin et al. 1972, 168, 179.

50. *Conservator* 1980, 2.

51. Clute 1931, 10. This entire section is based on Clute's volume. The quotes are from pages 9–10, 14, 22, 46, 51–54, and i.

52. Floyd Swink informs me that the plants responsible for turning the sand country roadsides rosy are fall witchgrass (*Leptoloma cognatum*) and purple love grass (*Eragrostis spectabilis*), not old witchgrass as claimed by Clute.

53. Bryant 1979.

Chapter Three: *In Quality Diminished*

1. City of Chicago 1976, 4.

2. De Gannes, quoted in Angle 1968, 22.

3. Sauer 1918, 50.

4. Dondore 1961, 39.

5. Wingate, interview by author, February 1994.

6. Battey 1883, 445–46.

7. Bryant 1851, 261.

8. On Monroe, see Poggi (1934, 97), and on Jasper County, see Battey (1883, 460).

9. Schafer 1927, 460.

10. Leach, newspaper column (June 9, 1925, in Leach Collection).

11. McManis 1964, 94.

12. Woodruff et al. 1878, 255.

13. Other parts of the Chicago region also suffered from malaria. Whitewater [Walworth] was hard hit in 1846 (Cravath 1906, 76), and as late as 1885, Racine was still reporting cases (Ackernecht [1945] 1977, 45–46).

14. Latrobe 1835, letter 12.

15. Levinge 1846, 212.

16. Ackernacht (1945) 1977, 30, 130.

17. Bryant 1846, 276.

18. Hamilton and Darroch 1916, 4. See McManis 1964, 39–40.

19. Hamilton and Darroch 1916, 4.

20. Least Heat-Moon 1991, 79.

21. For 1836, see Poggi (1934, 98), and for 1848, Cronon (1991, 67).

22. The three hundred thousand figure comes from Poggi (1934, 98); on settlement of Indiana and Michigan, see Smith (1992, 195).

23. Information on pioneer settlements in 1838–41 can be found in Manogaran (1977, 141); for development in 1843, see H. S. Durand to Elisha Cowles, 1843 (in Leach Collection).

24. A. C. Berry 1843 (in Leach Collection).

25. Watkin 1852, 64.

26. Bremer 1853, 209–10, 213.

27. Poggi 1934, 105.

28. Nichols 1965, 189.

29. Kemp 1927, 60–61.

30. Kohring 1981, 150–51. See also Thompson 1972.

31. Bowles et al. 1989, 32.

32. Weaver 1954, 286.

33. Curtis 1959, 426.

34. Wingate, interview by author, February 1994.

35. Kerr and White 1981, 182.

36. Indiana Division of Nature Preserves 1991, no page number.

37. Kemp 1927, 39; Ambrose n.d., 7.

38. Gleason 1910, quotes from 30 and 23.

39. Victor Shelford, quoted in Beecher 1969, 11.

40. Vestal 1914, 351–57. See Hanson 1975b, 7.

41. Sampson 1921, quotes from 528 and 534.

42. Pepoon 1927, 45.

43. Beecher 1969, 11; 1973, 170.

44. Peattie, August 28 (1925, 18).

45. Beecher 1969, 11.

46. Kummey 1942, 16.

47. Paul Strand, quoting former colleague (personal communication).

48. This discussion of Goose Lake Prairie is based on an interview with Bob Betz (fall 1993), two articles by Bill Beecher (1969, 1973), and an article by Bill Rutherford (1972).
49. White and Madany 1978, 132.
50. Alan Haney, letter to George Fell (July 23, 1976). The letters and news clippings that document this phase of the Buffalo Grove Prairie story are from the files of the Natural Land Institute in Rockford, Illinois.
51. Hurley 1976a.
52. September 1976 *Daily Herald* clipping.
53. Bev Hansen has kept me up to date on the status of the prairie.
54. Paintin 1929, quote from 152.
55. Al Rouffa, several conversations, 1994 and 1995.
56. Rouffa 1990.
57. Betz and Cole 1969, 51.
58. The discussion on Markham Prairie is based on interviews with Bob Betz (fall 1993) and Ron Panzer (fall 1993), as well as the works by Bartel (n.d.) and Hanson (1975a).
59. Wilhelm 1990, 299, 301, 305.
60. Herlocker 1976, 213 and 215. Bob Betz (interview by author, fall 1993) also contributed to my Hoosier Prairie account.
61. The account of Wolf Road Prairie is based on Hanson (1975b), personal knowledge, and Valery Spale (several telephone conversations, 1994).
62. Ferguson 1856, 372.
63. Vestal 1914, 361.
64. Sampson 1921, 538–539.
65. Betz, interview by author, fall 1993; Weaver 1954, 271. Indeed, except for one paper critical of burning that was published in 1934, "fire was simply not studied as an ecological factor until the construction of the Curtis Prairie in Wisconsin" during the late 1940s (Collins and Wallace 1990, 99). This lack of interest in and negativity toward fire may have stemmed, in part at least, from the time and place Weaver and his contemporaries performed their research. They worked during the drought years of the 1930s and in Nebraska and Kansas, where prairie was not threatened by woody vegetation. Under those circumstances, the deleterious effects of fire might have been amplified and the benefits less apparent (Collins and Wallace 1990, 81).
66. Cole et al. 1992, 177.
67. Kaufman, quoted in Collins and Wallace 1990, 78–79.
68. Wolff 1990, 122–23.
69. Park et al. 1953, 2–3.
70. Panzer 1988 and interview by author, fall 1993.
71. Williams 1993, 72–75. See also Swengel 1993a, 1993b; Fralish et al. 1994.
72. Shelford and Winterringer 1959, 85–95.
73. Figg 1988, 11.04.

Chapter Four: *The Nearly Vanished Transitions*
1. Thwaites 1900, 58:108–9.
2. Comment on Allouez and quote are both in Shea (1852, 67–73).

3. Parker 1835, 28.

4. Kirkland 1858, 480.

5. This section on the deep-soil shrublands and savannas relies heavily on the following papers, which appear in Fralish et al. (1994): Nuzzo (this widely reprinted article is especially recommended); White; and Bowles and McBride. Other particularly helpful writings about the transition lands include Anderson and Bowles (1997), Curtis (1959), Madany (1981), Packard (1986), and Taft (in Schwartz 1997).

6. Curtis 1959, 300.

7. Ibid., 177–81; White and Madany 1978, 337; Packard 1986, 01.14; and Chicago Wilderness 1999, 165.

8. Bowles and McBride in Fralish et al. 1994, 78. The oak listed here as scarlet (*Quercus coccinea*) is widely known as Hill's (*Q. ellipsoidalis*), but I am following Swink and Wilhelm (1994, 620), who merge the two under scarlet. There is strong local resistance to lumping these together, however, in some measure because Hill's oak is named for Reverend Hill based on specimens he collected in Cook County.

9. Bowles and McBride in Fralish et al. 1994, 79.

10. Curtis 1959, 330.

11. Ibid., 568.

12. Madany 1981, 177–81.

13. Bowles and McBride in Fralish et al. 1994, 77.

14. Anderson and Bowles 1998, 15.

15. This account of Middlefork Savanna is mainly from Al Westerman (interview by author, fall 1995) and Schennum (1993).

16. Swink and Wilhlem (1994) refer to local populations of beaked sedge (*Carex rostrata*) as *Carex utriculata*, common yellow sedge.

17. The Middlefork research appears in Bowles et al. (1997) and the Wolf Road Prairie research in Bowles and McBride (1998, 14–27).

18. Bowles et al. 1997, 10.

19. White and Madany 1978, 336–37.

20. Glass 1989.

21. This account of Thornton-Lansing is based mostly on Madany (1974) and Armstrong (1963).

22. From an interview of Paul Strand by the author (fall 1993).

23. Case 1964, 54.

24. Sheviak 1974, 35–36.

25. From ongoing conversations with Marlin Bowles and Paul Strand.

26. From an interview of Floyd Swink by the author (fall 1993).

27. This discussion of the Kankakee mallow relies mostly on Schwegman (1991, 1–8) and Sherff (1946), as well as personal communications with Bob Betz, Bill Glass, and John Schwegman.

28. Sherff 1946, 95.

29. Fernald 1950, 1003. See Swink and Wilhelm 1994, 416.

Chapter Five: *Witnesses to History*

1. Braun 1964, 188–89.

2. The reaction of three different reviewers to the discussion on the changing oak forests

provides a good example: one felt there was no issue because oaks are thriving; another that there was no issue because there is unanimity that intense management is necessary to save the oaks; and a third liked the controversy.

3. Curtis 1959, 103–68; White and Madany 1978, 322–28. Two comments are necessary regarding the forest categories that I am using. (1) The biggest difference between the *Illinois Natural Areas Inventory* (White and Madany 1978) and Curtis is that the flatwoods community is recognized by the former but not the latter. (2) The *Illinois Natural Areas Inventory* also makes subtler distinctions and identifies such additional forest types as the wet-mesic upland, wet floodplain, and mesic floodplain. However, these occur in small stands, are not very common, and do not differ significantly in their composition from the categories I discuss.

4. When I use the word "woodland," I mean it in a general sense of forested land and not as a specific community type.

5. Bowles, ongoing conversations.

6. Noel Pavlovic, interview by author, spring 1995; Lorimer 1987, 61.

7. Mendelson, interview by author; Westerman, interview by author, fall 1995.

8. Hill 1894, 413.

9. Bowles has addressed this issue in a letter to me: "I agree that oak forests may have had a layered understory of small trees and shrubs. . . . We have limited evidence (except for the fact that these shrubs had to occur somewhere) finding a shrub layer on more than half of the timbered section lines in Du Page County" (October 11, 1999). Additional information on the shrub layer is provided by Major L. H. Long (1817, 193–98) in his description of the forests he encountered in northern Illinois: "The undergrowth consists of sassafras, dogwood, haw, crabapple, hazel, elder, thorn, and bramble."

10. Solecki and Taft 1987, 24; Curtis 1959, 143.

11. Swink 1986, 12.

12. "One of the conspicuous herbaceous plants of the woodland" (Sheviak 1974, 28), and it often grows on east- and west-facing slopes (Homoya 1993, 100).

13. Wingate, interview by author, February 1994. Some of these yellow lady's slippers could also be of the small variety (*C. calceolus* var. *parviflorum*), which is most often found in bogs, seeps, and low prairies.

14. On the Morton Arboretum, see Wilhelm (1987, 1991a); the recent study of twenty-eight high-quality forests is Bowles et al. (1998b).

15. Ebinger 1986, 25; Fishbein n.d., 19–22.

16. Curtis 1959, 148.

17. Westerman, interview by author, fall 1995; Mendelson, personal communication.

18. Leitner 1987, 1–11.

19. Bowles et al. (1998b) did a similar study, looking at the changes in woody vegetation that took place in twenty-eight high-quality upland forests in northeastern Illinois from 1976 to 1996. They "found the maple invasion decreases along a gradient extending from maple > red oak > white oak forests" (personal communication).

20. Abrams 1992, 346.

21. Mendelson 1998, 138.

22. Ibid., 139–40.

23. On species not fruiting at all, see Waterman (1920, 240). For information on white oaks

seeding at intervals, see Fowells (1965, 633). The material on Thorn Creek Woods came from Mendelson (personal communication), and the study that found deer at the density of one per thirty acres is Downs (1949, 571).

24. Westerman, interview by author, fall 1995.

25. Donnelly, interview by author.

26. Solecki and Taft 1987, 25–27.

27. Westerman, interview by author, fall 1995.

28. Ibid.

29. Elton 1970, 41–54.

30. Jensen 1928, 69–71.

31. Curtis 1959, 104.

32. Cain 1935, 510.

33. Donnelly, interview by author; Poulson, interview by the author.

34. Poulson, interview by the author. See also Poulson and Platt 1996, 1234–53.

35. Apparently, however, humans have been writing on beech since Sanskrit was a living language. There is, in fact, an etymological connection between the words "book" and "beech."

36. Peattie 1966, 454.

37. Every species of local maple, including box elder, produces a sweet sap, but that of the sugar maple is superior in both quality and quantity. It is important to note that the early accounts do not specify which species of maple is being utilized. Some authors believe that the black maple (*A. nigrum*), once considered a type of sugar maple, was "the principal 'sugar tree' in our prairie provinces prior to settlement" (Swink and Wilhelm 1994, 77).

38. Joutel 1905, 227.

39. Betsey Mendelsohn (telephone conversation).

40. Burgh 1939, 91–93.

41. Curtis 1959, 113.

42. Ibid., 116–17.

43. Hill 1895, 412.

44. U.S. Fish and Wildlife Service 1993, 53,904. The small population in Berrien County is documented by Case and Schwab (1971, 39–43); the recent information on pogonias came directly from Case (telephone conversation).

45. Donnelly, interview by author.

46. DeMauro 1994, 4–5.

47. Tierra 1983, 127.

48. Coffey 1993, 19.

49. Ibid.

50. Pepoon 1927, 51.

51. Hu quoted in Coffey 1993, 153–54.

52. Hou 1978, 94–95, including quote.

53. The price for wild plants was told to me by Michael Penskar (telephone conversation); the U.S. Fish and Wildlife Service mandate is reported in Martin (1989, 8–9).

54. Martin 1989, 8–9.

55. Moseley 1941, 4.

56. W. E. Walsh quoted in ibid.

57. Thompson (quoted in Moseley 1941, 89–94).

58. On snakeroot containing tremetol, see Muenscher (1941, 225); Dr.Walsh is quoted in Rawlings (1994 [1927], 69).

59. Racine Historical Society.

60. Peattie 1966, 238.

61. Schmid 1975, 71.

62. Campbell and Schlarbaum 1994, 2.

63. Schmid 1975, 72–74.

64. Large cottonwood in Morris: Swink and Wilhelm (1994, 597); "Sentinel of Wind Point": Racine Historical Society.

65. This account of the "Big Tree," including Kotz quote, is from Harpel (ser. A, 23:348). Also see Ernst (1976, 7–8), who says the tree was 165 feet high with a circumference of forty-five feet, and Scheidenhelm (1926–29, 501).

66. Calkins 1896, 7.

67. Wilhelm 1993, 1.

68. Wilhelm and Lampa 1987, 43.

69. Miller 1980, 299.

70. Graham 1927, 72–73.

71. Benjamin 1995, 154.

72. Ibid., 217–18.

73. Sanders n.d.

74. Spencer 1995; Wiggers 1999, 6.

75. Information on studies in Lake County, Illinois, is from Westerman (interview by author, fall 1995) and on those at Thorn Creek comes from Mendelson, in Fralish et al. (1994, 103–6). Bowles's comment is from ongoing conversations.

76. This account on Lake County is largely from Westerman (interview by author, fall 1995).

77. "Allelopathy" refers to any "harmful effect by one plant on another through the production of chemical compounds" (Rice 1974, 1).

78. Schmid 1975, 19–22, 63.

79. Bill Wingate, interview by author, February 1994; Westerman, interview by author, fall 1995.

80. From a regional perspective, buckthorn is a serious problem in most of the Illinois and Wisconsin portion of the region under study here but remains uncommon in Indiana and Berrien County (Swink and Wilhelm 1994, 631).

81. This paragraph and next taken from Nuzzo (1993a, 30, 31; 1993b).

82. Higley and Raddin 1891, xvii.

83. Atwell 1910.

84. Simmons 1920, including quote 233.

85. Currey 1920.

86. Reeling 1928, 164–65.

87. Hemenway 1903.

88. Hill 1992, 9–11.

89. Located not far to the south, just west of McCormick Boulevard and between Church and

Dempster, an even larger forest remnant still survived in 1920. Covering a hundred acres, half of which had never been cut, it was eventually cleared with apparently little fanfare.

90. Curtis 1959, 156.

91. Hill 1992, 21.

92. Burgh 1939, 77 and 80.

93. Paddock 1917, 1.

94. Quotes this paragraph and next three from Chamberlain (n.d., 8–13).

95. Paddock 1917, 1.

96. Donnelly and Murphy 1987, 17.

97. Warren and Ruthven 1919, 12–19.

98. Cain 1935, 500–501.

99. Paddock 1917, 1.

100. See Hayes 1949.

101. Quotes this paragraph and next from Applied Ecological Services (1996, 43, 9).

102. Mendelson 1998, 144.

Chapter Six: *Of Two Worlds*

1. Peter Fritzell in Greeson et al. 1979, 526.

2. Mitsch and Gosselink 1986, 416.

3. Berwyn Historical Society 1983, 8.

4. Bingham et al. 1990, 2.

5. Apfelbaum 1993, 6.

6. Bingham et al. 1990, 23–26.

7. Mitsch and Gosselink 1986, 10.

8. The *Illinois Natural Areas Inventory* (White and Madany 1978, 325–26, 342–45) says that true swamps, wooded areas that are perpetually wet, do not occur in northern Illinois because the only local tree that can survive in permanent water bodies is the tamarack. Sites containing tamaracks are classified as bogs or wooded fens. The inventory does recognize the wet flood plain forest, characteristic of riverine areas that are wet much of the growing season. Curtis (1959, 156) refers to a lake border variant of the southern lowland forest that the inventory omits. He says it is usually referred to as a hardwood swamp. (For a discussion of what I believe to be a local example, see chap. 5.) Swink and Wilhelm (1994, 44), in contrast, do use the term "swamp" to describe "wetlands characterized by trees growing in large flats or basins that are poorly drained, with most of the water leaving through evapotranspiration." These can occur along rivers, in morainal depressions, or on sandy flats as in the Indiana Dunes. (See also Wilhelm 1990, 36; and discussion in chap. 10.) These authors are using different terms to describe roughly the same things, and I have chosen to discuss these wet woods in other chapters.

9. White and Madany 1978, 171.

10. Costello 1936, 640.

11. Stout 1914, 421.

12. Ibid., 418–19.

13. Costello 1936, 631–34; Schennum 1988, app. G.

14. Costello 1936, 631–34; Schennum 1988, app. G.

15. Curtis 1959, 580–81.
16. Costello 1936, 623.
17. Apfelbaum and Sams 1986, 71.
18. In the vicinity of East Troy, marsh haying continues to be a commercial enterprise to this day.
19. Meyer 1936, 371.
20. Stout 1914, 405.
21. Schennum 1988, app. G.
22. Curtis 1959, 388–89.
23. Sherff 1912, 488.
24. Hubbard 1969, 41.
25. Swink and Wilhelm 1994, 802.
26. Meyer 1936, map.
27. Niering 1985, 476.
28. Hill 1993, 3.
29. Weller 1981, 19–20.
30. Ibid., 65.
31. Apfelbaum 1985, 10; Wilhelm 1990, 31.
32. Stuckey and Salamon 1987, 4.
33. Swink and Wilhelm 1994, 758.
34. Apfelbaum 1985, 9, 13; see Beule 1979, 25–26.
35. Marsh 1955, 115; Morton 1975, 20.
36. Marsh 1955, 128–29. In order to find out whether the cattails used in these experiments came from a local source, I made unsuccessful attempts to identify the firm. If any reader can assist me, please contact me through the publisher.
37. Hough 1873, 366.
38. Ryder 1994, C-9–C-10.
39. E. J. Hill quoted in Halsey 1912, 338.
40. *Audubon Bulletin* 1922, 27.
41. Pepoon 1927, 304.
42. *Chicago Daily News* 1935, 9.
43. Ryder 1994, C-9–C-11.
44. In addition to the two authors quoted, this discussion of purple loosestrife relied on Lach (1996, 1, 2), Schennum (interview by author), Skinner et al. (1994, 14, 21), and Wiedenmann and Voegtlin (1995, 4).
45. As recently as 1985 the gardening magazine *Southern Living* published an article "Loosestrife Is a Sure Thing," in which the author states: "Loosestrife is a perennial every garden needs. It's stunning in leaf and flower, and grows just about everywhere" (quoted in Skinner et al. 1994, 3).
46. Heidorn 1990, 2.
47. Malecki et al. 1993, 685.
48. White and Madany 1978, 343.
49. Swink and Wilhelm 1994, 44; Waterman 1926, 266.
50. This discussion of Volo Bog's structure relies heavily on the excellent paper by Sheviak and Haney (1973).

51. Pepoon 1927, 376. The bog he attacked was in the Indiana Dunes.

52. Peattie 1966, 34.

53. Sheviak and Haney 1973, 109. Also see Waterman 1921, 83.

54. Sheviak and Haney 1973, 105.

55. Ibid., 100; Waterman 1923, 219.

56. My treatment of the carniverous plants is based on Higley (1885, 53–55), Juniper et al. (1989, 251–58), Lloyd (1942, 20–28), and Watts (1975, 79–83).

57. The fight to save Volo Bog is chronicled in Beecher (1970, 2).

58. Waterman 1926, 266.

59. Waterman 1921, 81.

60. General information on fens is from Curtis (1959, 362), Moran (1981, 164–68), and White and Madany (1978, 344–45). Information on Bluff Spring Fen is from Packard and Ridell (1986), Stoynoff (1993, 103), and Stoynoff and Hess (1986). Wagner Fen information is from Schennum and Byers (1994, 2–3).

61. The most complete account of Trout Park appears in the master plan by Bowles (1988). To enable me to expand on the park's history, Marlin Bowles allowed me to copy the following writings: Benke (1932a, 1932b), Neumann (n.d.), and Perry (1969). Wilhelm has also written about the flora of Trout Park (1978, 169–76).

62. Fowells 1965, 682; Bowles 1988, 8.

63. Herkert 1991a, 1:30.

64. Sheviak 1974, 64.

65. Perry 1969, pts. 2 and 3.

66. Perry 1969, pt. 1.

67. Benke 1932a; Neumann (n.d., 1, 2, 6, 7), including quotes.

68. The City of Elgin dedicated its portion of the fen as a nature preserve in 1972. The Chicago Junior School owns the remainder and designated it as an Illinois Natural Heritage Landmark, which, although nonbinding, demonstrates the owner's intent to preserve the land.

Chapter Seven: *The Last Wilderness*

1. Kuchenberg 1978, 34.

2. Goodyear et al. 1982, 98–99; J. Ellen Marsden, interview by author.

3. Eshenroder et al. 1995, 2.

4. Marsden, interview by author.

5. Milner 1874. The assertion that Milner's study was the first to look at pollution is in Wells and McLain (1973, 18).

6. Milner 1874, 6. On the use of three pound nets at the mouth of the Chicago River, see Nelson (1878, 785).

7. Kuchenberg 1978, 162.

8. Murphy in Furnwegger 1992, 34; U.S. Environmental Protection Agency 1992, 18.

9. Eshenroder et al. 1995, 3.

10. Ibid.

11. This two-paragraph discussion on phytoplankton is based on a lengthy interview of Nancy Tuchman by the author.

12. This paragraph is based on Ping Jiang (personal communication), Makarewicz et al. (1994, 44), Pennak (1953, 181), and S. A. Forbes quoted on *Leptodora* in Shelford (1937, 77).

13. The first effort to study the benthic fauna of Lake Michigan was undertaken by Dr. Philo Hoy of Racine, who became interested in the food of whitefish. From their stomachs, he found the opossum shrimp *Myses relicta*, then thought to be exclusively marine. This seeming anomaly prompted a joint expedition by the Chicago Academy of Sciences and the Wisconsin Academy of Arts and Letters in 1871 to obtain more specimens. Nothing more than a short note was ever published on the extensive collections that were made, however, because the great Chicago fire of that year consumed, as one of its final acts before expiring, the academy's building and all that was housed within (Cook and Johnson 1974, 771; Henson 1966, 37).

14. Beeton 1960, 517–39; Carpenter et al. 1973, 320.

15. See Savitz et al. 1990, 115.

16. Material in this and next paragraph is from Tuchman (interview by author).

17. Eddy 1927, 204.

18. Wells and McLain 1973, 20–22.

19. Garfinkel in Furnweger 1992, 16; Makarewicz et al. 1994, iii.

20. Wells 1970, 556–65; Makarewicz et al. 1994, 21.

21. This discussion on zebra mussels is largely based on Marsden in Furnwegger (1992, 19–27) and personal communication.

22. Material in this and next paragraph is from Nelson in Furnwegger (1992, 28–29).

23. Bogue 2000, 29–30. Although only tangential to our main story, the fishermen themselves are worthy of mention. Apparently they were held in low repute, for John Milner (1874, 3) was compelled to defend them: "Nor is there any truth to the aspersion on the class of men, who are industrious, hard-working citizens, and, considering the hardships and exposures incident to their calling, singularly free from the habit of hard drinking." Then there are the poignant references to the fisherman who "danced with the lady of the lake" and stumbled. These include the four Oemmich brothers, "lost in a squall in 1874" off South Chicago while tending their pound nets. Off Kenosha a year later, a northwest gale claimed two boats and their combined crews of eight: "The accident seriously disheartened those remaining, and many ceased fishing entirely." But the worst incident, which also happened in 1875, occurred when a "sudden and violent squall" struck eleven vessels working out of Saint Joseph. Four ships and eleven men were lost, while the remainder of the fleet sustained extensive damage (Earll et al. 1887, 649, 652).

24. Earll et al. 1887, 651; Rathbun et al. 1887, 125.

25. Kuchenberg 1978, 39.

26. Milner 1874, 17.

27. Kuchenberg 1978, 19, 91.

28. Milner 1874, 18.

29. Kuchenberg 1978, 22; Atkinson, personal communication.

30. Smith 1968, 671.

31. Emery 1985, 9; Hubbs and Lagler 1958, 57.

32. Baldwin et al. 1979, 138.

33. Ibid.; Wells and McLain 1973.

34. Wells and McLain 1973.

35. Sharks and rays form a third class (Chondrichthyes), no member of which has been found in this region.

36. Alen Feldman, interview by author.

37. Information in this paragraph and the next is taken from Becker 1983, 213.

38. Christie 1974, 833–36; Emery 1985, 5.

39. Kuchenberg 1978, 53; Christie 1974, 835.

40. Kuchenberg 1978, 54; Mills et al. 1993, 6–7.

41. Becker (1983, 211) documents the first lamprey found in Lake Michigan. The estimate of forty pounds of lake trout per adult lamprey is from Feldman (interview by author). Statistics about the collapse of lake trout are from Baldwin et al. (1979, 137).

42. Smith 1968, 683.

43. Smith 1971, 224–25, including quote.

44. Kuchenberg 1978, 66–67.

45. Page and Laird 1996, 9. The cost of lamprey control comes from Gavin Christie of the Great Lakes Fishery Commission (telephone conversation).

46. Feldman, interview by author.

47. Emery 1985, 4; Christie 1974, 840–41.

48. Christie 1974, 842.

49. Wells and McLain 1973, 15.

50. The quote is from Smith (1968, 684–85); the 85 percent figure was provided by Feldman in Furnweger (1992, 10).

51. Smith 1968, 688. See Wells 1968, 3–5.

52. Baldwin et al. 1979, 126; Becker 1983, 269.

53. Becker 1983, 268; the U.S. Fish and Wildlife Service data can be found in Brown (1968, 1).

54. Brown 1968, 1. Survival temperatures for alewives are found in Becker (1983, 266); information on winter survival comes from Smith (1968, 688); and the effects of getting trapped in shallow water were described by Marsden (interview by author).

55. Kuchenberg 1978, 73.

56. Ibid., 15.

57. Eshenroder et al. 1995, 10.

58. Kuchenberg 1978, 80–82; Mills et al. 1993, 10.

59. The quote is from Becker (1983, 310); the cost of processing a single salmon comes from Marsden (personal communication); and the amount of money spent by states to maintain their salmon fisheries is from Botts (1993, 28).

60. Eshenroder et. al. 1995, 14.

61. Feldman, personal communication. See also Stewart et al. 1981, 751–763.

62. Eshenroder et al. 1995, 13; Botts 1993, 31.

63. Botts 1993, 31.

64. Bailey and Smith in Eshenroder et al. (1995, 5).

65. Donald Stewart, personal communication.

66. Information on the longnose dace comes from Greg Seegert (interview by author) and on lake chub from Becker (1983, 464) and Lawrence Page (interview by author).

67. On the decline of sculpin, see Deason (1939, 106) and Wells and McLain (1973, 47). The quote is from Marsden (interview by author).

68. Marsden, interview by author.

69. Becker 1983, 508; Wells and McLain 1973, 46; Stewart et al. 1981, 753.

70. Nelson 1878, 789–93.

71. On Indiana's walleyes, see Baldwin et al. (1979, 151–52); on the current status of drum, see Greenfield and Rogner (1984, 82).

72. Savitz et al. 1990, 115.

73. Koelz 1929, 522.

74. Baldwin et al. 1979, 143.

75. Walden 1964, 275.

76. Harkness and Dymond 1961, 7.

77. Becker 1983, 223; Harkness and Dymond 1961, 8–9.

78. Harpel, ser. A, 1:156.

79. Harkness and Dymond 1961, 3–4.

80. Milner 1874, 72–73.

81. Ibid.; Nelson 1878, 793–94.

82. Milner 1874, 74.

83. Becker 1983, 223; Harkness and Dymond 1961, 77.

84. Smith and Snell 1891, 167.

85. Hough 1889c, 173.

86. Information on Illinois and Indiana is from, respectively, Brofka and Marsden (1995, 32) and Francis (1994, 3).

87. Becker 1983, 888.

88. Nelson 1878, 792. Commercial fishing figures are from Wells and McLain (1973, 37).

89. Material in this paragraph and the next two is from Francis et al. (1996, 18–19).

90. Marsden, personal communication. The theory of alewife predation was suggested by Francis (personal communication).

91. Rich Hess, Illinois Department of Natural Resources, personal communication

92. Milner 1874, 19.

93. Koelz 1926, 564; Wells and McLain 1973, 26; and Smith 1968, 674.

94. Smith 1968, 674. See also Coble et al. 1990, 989, 985.

95. Wells and McLain 1973, 28; Eshenroder et al. 1995, 10.

96. This account of the effort to establish breeding lake trout is from Marsden (personal communication).

97. Ono et al. 1983, 33.

98. Becker 1983, 334.

99. Robert Todd, the authority on the group, told me over the telphone that the taxonomic status of these fish remains far from settled. Two conflicting trends seem to be developing: populations within supposed species are becoming less similar to one another while there is "continued introgression of characters among broader species groups" (Todd and Smith 1992, 265). And to confuse things even more, some of the early taxonomy was none too careful.

100. Unfortunately, *C. johannae* received the common name "deepwater cisco," the same phrase used to describe collectively the seven species of ciscoes that live at greater depths. To avoid confusion, I will use *johannae* when discussing this species.

101. Koelz 1926, 564–565.

102. Smith 1964, 155.
103. The material from this and next two paragraphs is from Moffett (1956, 397–403).
104. Wells and McLain 1973, 31; Smith 1964, 162.
105. Living in several Canadian lakes are populations of ciscoes that have traditionally been identified as blackfin. Experts now believe that these fish are more likely to be a form of lake herring (Todd, personal communication).
106. Material in the remainder of the chapter is from Todd (1985 and personal communication).

Chapter Eight: *Approaching the Way*

1. Holden in Harpel, ser. B, 2:62–63.
2. Stephen Long quoted in Andreas 1884, 148.
3. Sources for the material in this paragraph are as follows: Father Charlevoix—Quaife (1913, 14–15); Hubbard (1969, 117); and on La Salle County—Quaife (1913, 1–20).
4. Darby 1819, Add. No. 2.
5. Smith 1940, 12. Sometime after looking at the voluminous documents associated with the case (housed at the Federal Archives Depository in Chicago), I told Steve Apfelbaum about it. He, too, examined the material, and mined it far more profitably than I was able to. He generously supplied me with a summary of the hundreds of pages he copied, as well as a copy of the paper he wrote based on the gauge data.
6. The Apfelbaum discussion on the changing watershed of the Des Plaines River is from his 1993 paper. Quotes are from pages 2–4.
7. Thwaites 1900, vol. 58.
8. Hubbard in Harpel, ser. A, 2:79–83.
9. Various sources were consulted for information on the Illinois and Michigan Canal (Andreas 1884, 147–53; Goldthwait 1909, 8; Cronon 1991, 65).
10. Nelson 1878, 798. In addition to providing this description, Nelson lists almost twenty species of fish that used to be caught in the Des Plaines, Kankakee, and Du Page Rivers but disappeared following the rerouting of the Chicago River. All but one have been found again, at least in the Kankakee. That exception is the paddlefish (*Polyodon spathula*), a primitive species whose presence in these rivers is otherwise unrecorded.
11. I relied on Sanitary District of Chicago (1928, 8, 13–15) for the material in this paragraph and next.
12. The name was later changed to the Metropolitan Sanitary District of Greater Chicago and, more recently, to the Metropolitan Water Reclamation District.
13. My sources for this paragraph and the one following were Forbes and Richardson (1913, 510–11, 516–17), Thompson (1928, 301), and Mills et al. (1966, 15).
14. Sanitary District of Chicago 1928, 27, 31.
15. Lanyon and Lue-Hing (1987, 105, 108) is the source for this and the following paragraph.
16. Polls et al. 1994, 12, 29.
17. Kevin Cummings, interview by the author.
18. Lopinot 1972, 2, 8, 24, 25, 31.
19. Kwak 1993, 136.
20. Cummins 1972, 33.
21. My sources for the preceding paragraph were as follows: Rock River watershed, Becker

(1983, 30); new attitudes about nuisance fish, Joe Ferencak (interview by the author); and the rotenone poisonings of Lake Delavan, Don Fago (telephone conversation).

22. For a good summary of impacts on aquatic organisms, see Page et al. in Schwartz (1997, 189–12).

23. This section relies heavily on the excellent works by Becker (1983), Hynes (1970), and Shelford (1937).

24. Eddy and Underhill 1974, 99.

25. Maitland, quoted by Hynes 1970, 396–97.

26. For data on Wisconsin streams, see Smith (1979, 70).

27. Miller, quoted by Becker 1983, 438–39.

28. The crayfish discussion here is based on Page (1985, 412), Taylor and Redmer (1995, 9–10), and Taylor (personal communication).

29. Burr and Page 1986, 303.

30. Seeburger 1975, 8.

31. Pennak 1953, 14; Ross 1944, 183; and Vinikour and Anderson 1984, 95.

32. Hynes 1970, 15.

33. Polls, interview by author.

34. Hynes 1970, 139.

35. Forbes and Richardson 1920, 278; Forbes, quoted by Eddy and Underhill (1974, 373).

36. Becker 1983, 487.

37. The material in this paragraph is from Greg Seegert (interview by author), Becker (1983, 583), and Seeburger (1975, 6).

38. Sule and Skelly 1985.

39. Brigham et al. 1978, 94.

40. Seegert, interview by author.

41. Information on the status of the pallid shiner in Wisconsin is from Fago (telephone conversation), in Missouri from Becker (1983, 503), in Indiana from Robertson (1971–172, n.p.), and in Illinois from Skelly and Sule (1983, 131–38).

42. Eycleshymer 1901, 915.

43. Information on the early carp introductions can be found in Emery (1985, 7), Laird and Page (1996, 14), Forbes and Richardson (1920, 105), and Becker (1983, 420).

44. The quote from the Colorado Fish Commissioner is from Kuchenberg (1978, 18) and the one from Lapham is from Becker (1983, 425).

45. Forbes and Richardson 1920, 108, 106.

46. Laird and Page 1996, 13–14.

47. Becker 1983, 427.

48. Williams et al. 1993, 6. Material on mussel biology and status that is not otherwise referenced is based on information generously provided by Kevin Cummings.

49. Hynes 1970, 394.

50. Parmalee 1967, 10–13.

51. Neves 1993, 4.

52. Williams et al. 1992, 7.

53. Neves 1993, 3.

54. The source for the data in this paragraph is Moy and Sparks (1991, 110–11).

55. Page et al. 1990–91.

56. Howard 1951, 1–6.
57. Wilson and Clark 1912, 15–16.
58. Cummings and Mayer 1991; Starrett 1971.
59. Havera 1987, 155.
60. Lewis and Brice 1980; Suloway 1981.
61. Wilson and Clark 1912, 36.
62. Danglede 1914, 31.
63. Eldridge 1914, 4. My source on the pearl at McHenry Dam was Ryder (1999, 14).
64. Wilson and Clark 1912, 51, 11.
65. Peattie, September 11 (1925, 6).
66. In an article he did for the *Reader*, Peter Friederici (1992, 15) wrote that to recite the common names of mussels "is to speak a sort of vernacular poetry." He goes on to list, among others, elktoes, pistolgrips, round hickorynut, heelsplitters, and ring pinks. But in addition to the pretty names he provides, there were those based on racial slurs (*Fusconaia ebena*) and phallic euphemisms (*Elliptio dilitata*). *Ligumia recta* had a colloquial name that incorporated both elements. (All three of these are found in the Chicago region.) Robert Coker (1919, 15) made an allusion to these sobriquets in his study of the mussel industry: "With the development of the fishery the shellers on the several streams applied the common names which have suggested themselves as appropriate to the appearance of the shell or those which seem to have originated in a spirit of facetiousness." Most of these species had alternate names that were benign, but not so *F. ebena*. I have not made an exhaustive study of the subject, but it is interesting to see how modern writers have dealt with what is a patently offensive common name. It clearly has proven a challenge for those who are interested in popularizing mussels. Of the materials in front of me, the species is still referred to by its traditional common name in a 1951 article published by the Chicago Academy of Sciences. In his 1967 *Freshwater Mussels of Illinois*, Paul Parmalee deals with the issue by omitting any common name at all. But by the time Kevin Cummings and Christine Mayer published their work on Midwest mussels in 1992, the species is called the ebony shell, and under "other common names" appears the word "none."
67. Parmalee 1967, 2.
68. It seems that the residents of Cedar Lake, Lake County (Ind.) used to gather giant floaters (*Pyganodon grandis*) for culinary purposes, but otherwise people have shown little interest in such indulgence (Wilson and Clark 1912, 27; Friederici 1992, 16). During its heyday, the button industry produced ten thousand tons a year of mussel meat. Some of this was fed to pigs and some was used as fish bait, but much of it was simply dumped into the river from which it came, a practice that proved problematic when the stuff rose "to the surface in a state of decomposition and . . . washed ashore to cause an offensive stench" (Coker 1919, 61).
69. Danglade 1914, 32.
70. Coker 1919, 15. On species in the Illinois River, see Danglade (1914, 37–40).
71. Friederici 1992, 17.
72. Sources for the data in this paragraph are as follows: on the twenty states with button factories, Coker (1919, 89); button factories on the Illinois River, Cummings and Mayer (1991, 21); the role of the Fox River, Eldridge (1914, 7); and shells collected from the Kankakee River, Jasper-Newton Counties Genealogical Societies (1985a, 14).

73. The quote is from Danglede (1914, 8). On the tonnage of shells in 1913 in the Illinois River, see Cummings and Mayer (1991, 21).
74. Eldridge 1914, 6–7.
75. For profiles of Lake County, Illinois, lakes, see Tichacek and Wight (1972).
76. Benton 1957, 90–1.
77. Ryder 1994, C-5; 1999, 5. See also Harper 1950.
78. Ferencak, personal communication.
79. For this and the next paragraph, I relied on Southeast Wisconsin Regional Planning Commission (1985b, 72–76).
80. Forbes 1925, 542 (this quote and the one that follows).
81. Snearly 1977, 109.
82. Swink and Wilhelm 1994, 598–603.
83. Shelford 1937, 65, 131.
84. McCurdy 1914–15, 12–13.
85. Wisconsin Department of Natural Resources 1969, 7.
86. The lake chubsucker is also known from a single site in Du Page County. It is an abandoned quarry, filled with cold clear water and an abundance of submerged vegetation, a manmade analogue of a glacial lake (Ludwig et al. 1987, 160.).
87. Don Fago and his staff at the Wisconsin Department of Natural Resources maintain an up-to-date master fish file of more than twenty-two thousand collections going back to 1890. All these records can be accessed at ftp://webout.dnr.state.wi.us/Research/.
88. Becker 1983, 559.
89. Seegert 1990, 3–5.
90. Seegert, personal communication.
91. Tichacek and Wight 1972, 23.
92. Snearly 1977, 166; Ferencak, personal communication.
93. Forbes and Richardson 1920, 32, 41.
94. Becker 1983, 248.
95. Eddy and Underhill 1974, 132.

Chapter Nine: *Casualties of a Modern World*

1. Mitsch et al. 1979, 10; SEG Engineers 1989, 2–3; and Weeks 1931, 11.
2. Authors vary greatly in the acreages they give for the Kankakee marshes: 400,000 (Indiana Department of Natural Resources 1990, 61; Ivens et al. 1981, 2; Weeks 1931, 9); 425,000 (Frazier and Sapirie 1934, 2); 500,000 (Cannon 1927, 187; SEG Engineers 1989, 2; State of Indiana et al. 1976, IV-1), 600,000 (Schorger 1964, 334), or 1,000,000 (Bartlett 1907, 1).
3. The winter of 1830–31 was known as "the winter of deep snows," and when a warm spring rain melted the forty-eight inches of snow, "the bottomlands flooded from bluff to bluff" (Weeks 1931, 32).
4. Bartlett 1907, 1–2.
5. The quotes are from Meyer 1936, map.
6. Deam 1940, 737.
7. Ling 1935, 199.
8. Bartlett 1907, 24–25.

9. The quote and the material in the next paragraph are from Meyer (1936, 368–74).

10. The quotes and other information in this paragraph and the next are from Nichols (1965, 180, 183–85).

11. The note about huckleberries originates with Nichols (1965, 58) and that about the store owner traveling to New York with Bartlett (1907, 18–21).

12. Meyer 1936, map.

13. Ling 1935, 198.

14. Hough 1875.

15. This and the quote that follows in the next paragraph are from Burroughs (1925, 110, 112–13).

16. Schorger 1964, 334–36.

17. Ling 1935, 203.

18. Meyer 1936, 368.

19. Ball 1900, 439; Isaacs n.d., 83–84.

20. On the drying up of the funds, see Battey (1883, 621–3) for documentation of the improprieties, see Isaacs (n.d., 83–84); and on the new legislation and the introduction of the steam dredge, see Indiana Department of Natural Resources (1990, 63), Ivens et al. (1981, 4), and Nichols (1965, 188).

21. Ivens et al. 1981, 4.

22. Frazier and Sapirie 1934, 3.

23. Cannon 1927, 191; Indiana Department of Natural Resources 1990, 63); Gordon Graves (interview by author).

24. Burroughs 1925, 129–31. Graves told me that his grandfather recalled being able to smell the stench forty miles away.

25. This paragraph and the next two are based on information from Graves (interview by author) and Jody Melton (interview by author).

26. Melton 1987, 30.

27. Fryxell 1927, 15. Later, natural forces and the human hand would turn the single river into three. The northern channel became the Grand Calumet and the southern channel the Little Calumet. They both flow west, the Little Calumet doubling back at Riverdale until it joins the Grand Calumet at Hegewisch to form the Calumet, which flows north through an artificially widened channel to Lake Michigan near South Chicago. Today, as will be discussed later, the Cal-Sag Canal takes the water away from Lake Michigan.

28. Eenigenburg 1935, 8.

29. Dr. Meyer (1950, 177) defines the Calumet Region as the area at "the head of Lake Michigan" and drained by the Little Calumet and Grand Calumet rivers. He further says that it "is divisible into two districts: (1) the earliest settled Indiana section, dominantly timbered, with the district trading in pioneer days centered on Michigan City; (2) the Illinois section, dominantly prairie, with its pioneer trade focused on Chicago. The state line coincidentally conforms to the zone of transition of the two districts" (1956, 312). To include the four lakes in this discussion, I have moved the boundary line between the two districts a little east to be roughly that of Routes 12 and 20. The region east of there is covered in detail in the Indiana Dunes portion of chap. 10.

30. Landing 1986, 4.

31. The quotes in this paragraph are from Clarke (1889, n.p.; 1887, n.p.).

32. Hough 1889b, 44.

33. Pepoon 1927, 83–86.

34. Peattie, September 18 (1925).

35. This discussion of *Thismia* is based on the following sources: Jonker (1938, 12, 228), Maas et al. (1986, 31, 144, 166–72), Masters (1995), Mohlenbrock (1985, 31–39), Pfeiffer (1914, 124; 1952, 1), and Rodkin (1994).

36. Thorne in Maas et al. (1986, 31).

37. The quote is from Eenigenburg (1935, 9). On Roches Woods, see Schapper 1917, 274).

38. These paragraphs on fish are all from Nelson (1878, 793–96).

39. During 1981 and 1982, faunal surveys of Lake Calumet and the areas immediately adjacent to it were conducted. The fish study revealed that Lake Calumet still supported twenty-six species, a mix that was considered "good" under one standard index (Greenfield 1982, sec. 3, 16–22). This might seem surprising given how much fill and pollution have gone into the lake.

40. Webb in Harpel, ser. A, 2 : 16–17.

41. Eenigenburg 1935, 12; Stephen Douglas cited in City of Chicago 1916, 14.

42. Bluewing 1884, 322.

43. Fetter 1963, 3; Beecher 1981, 3.

44. Clark notebooks, Field Museum, Chicago.

45. Much of this discussion relies on Dr. Craig E. Colten's marvelous *Industrial Wastes in the Calumet Area, 1869–1970: An Historical Geography* (1985), one of the best environmental histories I have seen on any portion of the Chicago region.

46. Meyer 1956, 356; Landing 1986, 7.

47. Eenigenburg 1935, 8–9.

48. The quotes and other material in this paragraph and next two are from Colten (1985, 14, 18–20).

49. Buder 1967, 81; Doty 1893, 29–30.

50. Quoted and other material in this paragraph and the next nine are from Colten (1985, 23, 20, 23–25, 35–39, 76, 78, 60, and 75).

51. Chicago Department of Aviation 1990, sec. 2, 23–27.

52. Landing 1986, 49–50.

53. *Chicago Tribune* 1925, 6.

54. Chicago Department of Aviation 1990, sec. 1, 5.

55. Perkins 1904, 71–72. As proconservation as Perkins was, he could still write in the same report: "In the Calumet District, these marshes are too much the controlling feature. They demand some modification. Water and land represent almost one dead level. . . . The vegetation found in these swamps varies very little. . . . A retrenchment of this swamp vegetation must necessarily become one of the important steps in reclaiming such lands for park purposes" (96).

56. Colten 1985, 81.

Chapter Ten: *Lake Michigan's Rim*

1. Chrzastowski and Thompson 1994, 13.

2. Bowles et al. n.d., 3.

3. Michael Chrzastowski, ongoing conversations.

4. Lakefront consists of manmade fill (Willman 1971, surficial geology map) and unprotected beach plants (Greenberg and Milde 1994, 113–15).

5. Pepoon 1927, 103; Watts 1975, 67.

6. Pratt 1935, 13, 19.

7. Calkins 1906–7, paper no. 6.

8. Wille 1972, 54.

9. This discussion of the Indiana Dunes focuses on the area between Michigan City on the east and Routes 12 and 20 in Whiting on the west. All portions of the Indiana Dunes National Lakeshore are included except for Hoosier Prairie, which is treated in chap. 3.

10. The Nature Conservancy Great Lakes Program 1994, 3.

11. Cowles 1899, 95.

12. Ibid., 114.

13. Shelford 1937, 219.

14. Cowles 1899, 116.

15. Greenberg and Milde 1994, 113–15.

16. The three paragraphs on early succession are based on an interview with Tom Poulson. Since then he has published his findings (Poulson 1999, 172–76;Poulson and McClung 1999, 177–79).

17. Poulson, interview by author.

18. Hill 1893, 51.

19. Krekeler 1981, 3-77.

20. Pepoon 1927, 123.

21. Pavlovic 1994, 161, 165.

22. Chapin 1907, 177.

23. Data in this and the following paragraph are from Cole and Taylor (1995, 4, 5).

24. Cole and Pavlovic n.d., 13, 17.

25. Cockrell 1988, 17.

26. Watts 1975, 61.

27. Pepoon 1927, 117.

28. Poulson, personal communication.

29. The only exceptions to this statement are the two Pitcher's thistles collected by Cowles in 1896 and 1906 at Thornton, Cook County, fifteen miles inland from Lake Michigan and in sand deposited during the Glenwood Stage. These specimens are unique in the annals of the species. This discussion of Pitcher's thistle draws extensively from U.S. Fish and Wildlife Service (1992b).

30. This treatment of the two wet woods relies on Wilhelm (1990, 253) and Barbara Plampin (interview by author).

31. Krekeler 1981, 3-135 to 3-141.

32. Discussion of the Heron Rookery based on Wilhelm (1990, 295) and Plampin (interview by author).

33. Hiebert et al. 1986, 279.

34. Swink and Wilhelm 1994, 48.

35. Peattie 1922, 57–85.

36. Swink, interview by author.

37. Pepoon 1927, 123.

38. Swink 1966, 706.

39. On the abundance of lady's slippers, see Hill (1895, 413) and Swink (1966, 707). Information on their harvest by the florist trade comes from Pavlovic (personal communication) and on overcollecting by botanists from Homoya (1993, 112).

40. Chapin 1907, 192.

41. The story of Tolleston Bog and Swamp is from Swink (personal communication); the quote later this paragraph is from Swink and Wilhelm (1994, 365).

42. Ken Klick, interview by author.

43. Dolak 1985, IV-12.

44. Cockrell 1988, 15; Krekeler 1981, 3-245 to 3-250.

45. Pavlovic, personal communication.

46. Wilhelm 1990, 135.

47. Pavlovic (personal communication), including "decent shape" quote.

48. Wilhelm 1990, 315 and 322, including discovery of bog bladderwort.

49. Pepoon 1927, 131.

50. Krekeler 1981, 3-31.

51. Engel 1983, 83.

52. Franklin and Schaeffer 1983, 6.

53. Latrobe 1835, 190.

54. This paragraph and the next are based on Cook and Jackson (1978, 34, 36–37).

55. Keating 1824, 158; Ball 1900, 455.

56. The forest scientist is quoted in Lorenz (1944, 51); on the current status of white pine, see Menges and Armantano (1985, 270).

57. Ball 1900, 515; Pepoon 1927, 80–81.

58. E. T. Cox quoted in Ball 1900, 510.

59. E. T. Cox quoted in Ball (1900, 511); my source for the cranberry marsh near Dune Acres was Cook and Jackson (1978, 52).

60. Cook and Jackson 1978, 48.

61. Peyton 1869, 341.

62. Cook and Jackson 1978, 61, 63.

63. Cockrell 1988, 16.

64. The quoted and other material in this paragraph are from Franklin and Schaeffer (1983, 16, 20).

65. Rutherford Platt quoted in Engel 1983, 5.

66. Franklin and Schaeffer 1983, 32.

67. Cockrell 1988, 18.

68. The account of Mather's contribution and the hearing he sponsored is principally from Franklin and Schaeffer (1983, 40–43) and Cockrell (1988, 19–23).

69. Franklin and Schaeffer 1983, 74–78.

70. Richard Leiber's desire to preserve Indiana's scenic features apparently stems from a trip to Brown County in 1910: "This whole county ought to be bought up by the state and then made into a State Park so that all the people of Indiana could enjoy this beautiful spot" (quoted in ibid., 77). Contemplating macro-sites in 1910, he was obviously ahead of his time.

71. Sources for this paragraph and the next were Cockrell (1988, 28–29) and Franklin and Schaeffer (1983, 93–94).

72. Dustin 1973, 35.

73. Franklin and Schaeffer 1983, 130.

74. Engel 1983, 129.

75. This paragraph and the next are based on Franklin and Schaeffer (1983, 159, 155–56).

76. Herb Read, personal communication.

77. Franklin and Schaeffer (1983, 134–37, 173) provide the biographical details on Douglas in this and the next paragraph.

78. Read, personal communication.

79. Cockrell 1988, 85.

80. Engel 1983, 283–84.

81. Pavlovic, personal communication.

82. Brown 1982, 2.

83. E. K. Warren quoted in "Historical Information, Warren Dunes" [1970], 2.

84. Grand Mere Association 1973, 49, 50.

85. Fowells 1965, 704.

86. On extensive system of large dunes, see Wells and Thompson (1982, 14); and particulars about the Johnson Dune are from Grand Mere Association (1973, 44).

87. Wells and Thompson (1983, 24, 16) are the source for this paragraph and the next.

88. Grand Mere Association 1973, 64–65.

89. This paragraph and the next are based on Henderson (1988, 9, 20).

90. Gates 1912, 261.

91. Lyon 1937, 29.

92. Gates (1912, 261) is responsible for pointing out the impression created by the pine groves. Douglas's tree planting is documented in Ferry (1907, 122).

93. Gates 1912, 261–62.

94. Swink and Wilhelm 1994, 119. The quote about the ridges is from Horton (1936, 1).

95. Sources for this paragraph are Pepoon (1927, 11); Gates (1912, 306–7), who defines heath "as an area of low evergreen vegetation"; and Swink and Wilhelm (1994, 432).

96. Gates 1912, 307; Ross 1963, 20, 22.

97. Halsey 1912, 330.

98. According to Bowles et al. (1998a, 166), "Gates found only four thistles and apparently collected three of them!"

99. J. L. Smith in Halsey (1912, 330) writes about fringed gentian pastures; Horton (1936, 2).

100. As far as I have been able to determine, these paragraphs represent the first written attempt to document the history of Illinois Beach State Park. Fortunately, Jeanette Aiken Black and other members of the Dunesland Preservation Society saw fit to create scrapbooks filled with newspaper clippings. The publication names and dates are often missing, but the story survives in materials these conservationists carefully collected and that are now housed at the state park office. Robert Grosso and Susan Wright of the park graciously allowed me access to these records.

101. Prominent in press reports of the efforts to make the Waukegan Flats into a state park are Douglas's pines. They became the symbol of the area's scenic attributes and enjoyed wide appeal. While naturalists obviously appreciated the richness of the native flora and fauna, the trees provided a bridge to politicians and the larger public. This has been a recurring

theme in the Illinois Beach story. In the 1960s, when the City of Waukegan proposed that the state give them the south end of the park for a marina and golf course, the request was in part justified by saying the acreage desired contained no trees. Thus not only did the nurseryman sow the seeds of this artificial forest but preservation efforts as well.

102. Sander 1995, 22; Gasiorkiewicz 1986.

103. *Chicago Tribune* clipping without attribution of authorship in Dunesland Preservation Society files. Handwritten notation says "probably 1942."

104. This history of the effort to preserve Chiwaukee Prairie is largely from Sander (1995) and Krampert (1972).

105. Swink, interview by author.

106. Moran 1978b, 128.

107. Owen Ayres & Associates n.d., 18–23.

108. For this paragraph and the next, see Cowles (1901b, 164, 166–67).

109. These slumps were characterized as very treacherous for botanizing by Pepoon (1927, 24). See Swink and Wilhelm (1994, 596) on balsam poplar, Moran (1978b, 128) on red pine, and Pepoon (1927, 24) on the other various prairie species.

110. Moran 1978b, 126.

111. Schmoll 1919, 223; Fryxell 1927, 17.

112. Cowles 1901a, 87.

113. Moran 1978b, 124–25; Swink and Wilhelm 1994, 328, 309.

114. Chapin 1907, 177–96.

Chapter Eleven: *Many More Than We Know*

1. James Lloyd, in a written review of this chapter, placed the world total of species at more than 40 million, while Post (1991, 466) indicates that seventeen thousand occur in Illinois alone. The quip from Eisner was passed on to me by Donald Young (interview by author).

2. Williams 1995, 2.

3. See Opler 1992; Pyle et al. 1992.

4. Hahn 1910, 179–84.

5. Suter and Park 1962, 1.

6. Panzer et al. 1995, 101–2.

7. Young 1995 and interview by author; A. Williams, interview by author.

8. Stannard 1968, 519–20.

9. Lloyd, personal communication. Information on *P. lupalus* is from Panzer (personal communication).

10. Donald Webb, personal communication.

11. Newton 1973, 120–21, and personal communication. The discovery that the beetle was decreasing was largely a matter of chance. While mapping specimens of species from the genus *Platydracus*, on which Dr. Newton is an expert, he came across the decline of *vulpinus*. Otherwise, this animal's seeming path to oblivion would have probably gone unnoticed.

12. Lomolino et al. 1995, 605.

13. The field museum's holdings were detailed by Alfred Newton (personal communication). The decline of the burying beetle was termed the most dramatic population collapse of any

insect by Kriska and Young (1995, 3); suggestions about the factors contributing to its decline are from Young (personal communication).

14. This account of the *Papaipema* moths is based largely on interviews generously provided by Ron Panzer.

15. Ibid.

16. Cashatt and Vogt 1990, 1–2.

17. Cashatt et al. 1992, 2, 6.

18. U.S. Fish and Wildlife Service 1999, 15, 40.

19. Cashatt et al. 1992, 11.

20. John Shuey, personal communication.

21. U.S. Fish and Wildlife Service 1992a, 21,566.

22. Shuey, personal communication.

23. U.S. Fish and Wildlife Service 1996, 8–10.

24. Ibid., 22–25.

25. U.S. Fish and Wildlife Service 1992a, 21,566.

26. Panzer, personal communication.

27. U.S. Fish and Wildlife Service 1992a, 21,567.

28. Marler 1994, 1–32.

29. Much of this discussion on Karner blues is based on interviews with Ralph Grundel and Noel Pavlovic.

30. Savignano 1994, n.p.

31. Irwin Leeuw, interview by author. The previous state record is recorded in Irwin and Downey (1973, 23).

32. Spencer 1993.

33. Grundel, personal communication; Henderson 1996, 22–23.

34. This discussion relies heavily on an interview with Bernard Greenberg.

35. Greenberg 1991, 565.

36. Another ephemeral ecosystem is the log, also manifesting discrete phases of decomposition: (1) from death of tree until bark begins to detach, (2) sapwood decays but heartwood remains hard, (3) wood is soft but still retains shape, and (4) log loses all structure and becomes at one with the forest floor. Each phase is marked by a distinctive guild of insects, including beetle larvae (Daggy 1946, 6–10) and ants (Talbot 1934, 427).

37. Greenberg 1991, 567.

38. Borror and White (1970, 367) define "instar" as the "stage of an insect between successive molts."

39. Greenberg 1991, 568.

40. Park 1948, 4 and 7.

41. Sightings in Racine and Chicago are documented in Williams (1930, 142, 147).

42. Hinchman 1990, 56.

43. Alan Stokie, personal communication.

44. Reports on green darners come from Cashatt (telephone conversation) and Stokie (personal communication).

45. This paragraph and the beginning of the next rely on Park (1949, 7–9).

46. Mutt 1978, 236.

47. This discussion on fireflies relies largely on Teale (1960, 76–79); Lloyd (1966, 23–24;

1984, 2; and personal communication), Pyle et al. (1992, 241 [conservation]), and Reitman (n.d., 1–2 [Firefly Scientists Club]).

48. Spieth 1941, 233–37.

49. The lack of documentation of local mayfly decline was noted by Irwin Polls (interview by author). Lake Michigan's support of huge hatches of the mayfly has been observed by Richard Merritt (telephone conversation), Bernard Greenberg (interview by author), and Robert Behrstock (ongoing conversations).

50. A few periodic cicadas emerge most every year, but in such negligible quantities that they garner little attention. These are very different animals than the annual cicada or harvester fly (*Tibicen*) that is common every summer. Then, finally, there is a third species of periodic cicada, the relatively rare *M. septendecula*, which occurs south of this area.

51. Quoted material is from *Chicago Tribune* (1888a, 6; 1888b, 1) . Forbes's statement appeared in (*Chicago Tribune* (1888c, 2).

52. Ridgway 1922, 16.

53. On the sale of cicadas, see Hepler (1990, 2). The description of the flavor of cicadas comes from Dybas (1973, 7).

54. Simon 1979, 42–44; Lloyd et al. 1983, 1162–69.

55. Dybas 1973, 3; Simon 1979, 40.

56. The theory of hypothetical predators can be found in Dybas (1973, 7); details of actual predators are in Hepler (1990, 1–2).

57. The "chorusing centers" quote is from Lloyd and Karban (1983, 299); the second quote is from Gorner (1990, 18). The noise level is documented in Dybas (1973, 5).

58. Dunning quoted in Lloyd and Karban, 303.

59. Dybas and Davis (1962, 443) attribute the differential between the two habitats to fewer predators in the floodplain. The eastern mole preys on larval cicadas in the uplands but is scarce in areas of frequent flooding. There is also less ground cover on the lowlands due to rapid decomposition and flooding; this means fewer beetles and other invertebrate predators.

60. Monte Lloyd (personal communication) provided information on *Massopora cicadina* and Lynn Hepler (personal communication) on Ryerson Woods. (On the fungus in ruderal environments, see White et al. (1979, 307).

61. Gorner 1990, 23.

Chapter Twelve: *Survivors in Trouble*

1. Champion Turtle Catcher 1881, 242.

2. Cahn 1937, 198.

3. Clark and Southall 1920, 4, 6.

4. Saloons had long "dealt extensively in turtle soup" as an inexpensive something that needed to be washed down with more commercially significant libations (ibid., 5). Prohibition closed this outlet, but repeal spawned a resurgence of both the purveyors and purveyed that helps explain the difference in demand for turtle between the two decades.

5. Cahn 1937, 45.

6. Lagler 1943, 267.

7. Information based on interviews with Gary Casper, Tom Anton, and Michael Redmer.

8. Casper, interview by author.

9. Cahn (1937, 80), including paraphrase of Garman.

10. Ludwig, ongoing conversations; and Redmer, interview by author.

11. Casper, interview by author; and Redmer, interview by author.

12. Cahn 1937, 72.

13. Moll 1988, 4–5.

14. David Mauger, interview by author.

15. Grant 1934, 244.

16. This and the next four paragraphs are based on Salzberg (1994, 3, 27–28,4, 12; and telephone conversation). Material also comes from Steve Swanson (interview by author).

17. Salzberg 1994, 4.

18. A most bizarre incident occurred on November 4, 1930, when five hundred ornate box turtles were released on Michigan Avenue in Chicago. The origin of these turtles was apparently never ascertained, but Cahn, no doubt relying on the opinion of Karl Schmidt of the Field Museum who retrieved the animals, surmises that "they were the chief performers in the thrilling sport of turtle racing, probably belonging to a 'stable' the owner of which went broke." Schmidt released the specimens "in the sandy area around Waukegan"; few survived the winter, and his doubts that the "species would take" proved well founded (Cahn 1937, 101).

19. Timothy Sickmeyer, chief of investigations, Illinois Department of Natural Resources (personal communication).

20. Although not otherwise discussed in the text, the following turtle species are known from the Chicago Region: stinkpot (*Sternotherus odoratus*), Illinois mud turtle (*Kinosternon flavescens*), false map turtle (*Graptemys pseudogeographica*), Ouachita map turtle (*G. ouachitensis*), and map turtle (*G. geographica*).

21. McNeely and Wachtel 1990, 71–74.

22. Eenigenburg 1935, 15.

23. Ibid., 11.

24. Tom Anton, interview by author. The account of the blue racers is from Alan Resetar (interview by author).

25. Resetar, interview by author.

26. "Control the Watersnake" is cited in Lagler and Salyer (1947, 179), which is also the source for feeding habits of water snake (176–79) along with Vogt (1981, 164). Casper, personal communication.

27. Seibert and Hagen 1947, 6–7; the fact concerning density is from Mierzwa (1989, 21).

28. Ed Lace, interview by author.

29. Sources for this paragraph are as follows: Seibart and Hagen (1947, 6 [smooth green snakes]); Minton (1972, 298); and Casper (interview by author [lack of toxicological studies]).

30. Redmer, interview by author.

31. Casper, interview by author.

32. This species is near and dear to the hearts of Chicago herpetologists because Robert Kennicott published the first scientific description of it in 1856 based on a specimen he collected near Glenview, Cook County.

33. Bavetz 1993, 29. Redmer (personal communication) is the source of the assertion about the

most reliable local spot for Kirtland's snake and Conant (1943, 331–32) for the fact about its notority for dying in captivity.

34. Garman, quoted in Bavetz 1993, 28.

35. Vogt 1981, 131.

36. Mierzwa 1988.

37. The observation about the glass lizard's eyelids and ear openings is from Conant (1975, 131) and about its ability easily to discard its tail is from Coe (1944, 40).

38. Although not discussed elsewhere in the text, the following snakes occur in the Chicago region: ringneck snake (*Diadophis punctatus*), black snake (*Elaphe obsoleta*), western ribbon snake (*Thamnophis proximus*), eastern ribbon snake (*T. sauritus*), and northern red-bellied snake (*Storeria occipitomaculata*).

39. Anton, personal communication.

40. A. A. Parker (1835, 52), who traveled through the Chicago region in 1834, offers a rare dissent on the question of the snake's abundance. He stated that near the Fox River in Kane County the animals "are not plenty": "Men told me that they had passed a whole year without seeing one."

41. Barker 1955, 15.

42. Tinkham [1831]; Levinge 1846, 219.

43. Pearce n.d., n.p.

44. Hoy 1883, 424.

45. That the last rattlesnake was seen in the Calumet area about 1860 is recorded by Schapper (1917, 102); and the founding of Baileytown in 1822 is documented by Brennan (1923, 315). The recent abundance of rattlers in the Indiana Dunes was recounted by Resetar (interview by author).

46. Bushey 1976, 101.

47. Schorger 1967–68, 35; Wright 1941, 671.

48. Lyon and Bishop 1936, 255–56.

49. The rattlesnake bite of the farmer is recorded in ibid. and that of the snake collector in LaPointe (1953, 128–9). Joe LaPointe, the snake collector just referred to, wrote a short article describing his medical adventure. There is evidently a tradition among wounded herpetologists to publish and perish. The great Karl Schmidt of the Field Museum wrote a detailed account of the hours it took for him to die by the fangs of an African boomslang. Even more impressive, the final article by German herpetologist Robert Mertens described the effects of being bitten by his longtime pet twig snake. Eighteen excruciating days elapsed before the author was finished.

50. Schorger 1967–68, 37.

51. Will County account from Mauger (interview by author).

52. Much of this account is from Ed Lace (interview by author) and Steve Swanson (interview by author).

53. Anton, interview by author.

54. Ibid.

55. Casper, interview by author.

56. Milner 1874, 62.

57. The Jasper County record of the water siren is from Lannoo (1998, 125–36) and Resetar (interview by author). Since Lace's report is so unusual and not based on the taking of a

specimen, I asked Alan Resetar, the authority on northwestern Indiana's reptiles and amphibians, whether I should include the record. Having earlier discussed the sighting with Lace, he felt the sighting merited inclusion.

58. Mierzwa 1986, 1988; Mauger, interview by author.

59. Information on Saint Charles is from Babwin (1993, 3).

60. This discussion, including Brandon quote, from Redmer (interview by author) and Val Beasley (telephone conversation). The six local salamanders not discussed further are Tremblay's (*Ambystoma tremblayi*)/silvery (*A. platineum*) (some consider these to be species of hybrid origin while others see them as simply hybrids not meriting specific status), marbled (*A. opacum*), small-mouthed (*A. texanum*), central newt (*Notophthalmus viridescens*), and southern two-lined (*Eurycea cirrigera*). All but the newt have very restricted ranges within this region.

61. This paragraph and the next rely on Chamberlain (1900, 252–53).

62. The account on Sphung is from McCormick (1915, 596), including quotes.

63. Chamberlain 1900, 253.

64. Kennicott 1855, 76. Hoy (1883, 425), active during the same period as Kennicott and based in Racine, said that it was common in Wisconsin.

65. Resetar, personal communication.

66. Pope 1947, 95.

67. Redmer and Mierzwa 1994, 22–24.

68. Necker 1939, 4.

69. Stille 1952, 154–55; Breden 1988, 14–15.

70. Smith 1961, 79; Minton 1972, 99; Vogt 1981, 64.

71. Beasley, personal communication.

72. Lannoo 1998, 337.

73. The following local frogs are not discussed in the text: eastern gray treefrog (*Hyla versicolor*), Cope's gray treefrog (*H. chrysoscelis*), and plains leopard frog (*H. blairi*).

Chapter Thirteen: *Of Extinction and Resurrection*

1. Schorger 1955, viii. Where not otherwise cited, the information in this section can be found in Schorger's book.

2. Brennan 1923, 277. The comments on the nesting near Racine are those of Atticus (Eugene W. Leach Collection, July 2, 1925).

3. Quoted and other material in this paragraph and the next three are from Schorger (1955, 120, 141, 143).

4. Coale 1922b, 255.

5. Lawson 1974, 8; Charles Douglas cited in Coale 1922b, 254.

6. Mumford and Keller 1984, 145.

7. Both accounts from Stone (1916, 488).

8. Schapper 1917, 102.

9. Ibid.; Lucien Yoe quoted in Arpee 1991, 46–47.

10. The quote appears in *American Field* (1883).

11. Clark 1894, 44.

12. Schorger 1955, 287, 292.

13. The September 30, 1891, date is given in Woodruff (1907, 89) and September 30, 1901, in Coale (1922a, 137). Coale published his article fifteen years after Woodruff's book and made no mention of the discrepancy. This strikes me as curious, given that Coale, Woodruff, and Clingman all knew each other.

14. Schorger 1955, 290.

15. Robert Feldt, personal communication

16. Madson 1982, 143.

17. Thwaites 1900, 59:173.

18. Fonda 1868–69, 232; Daniel Tasker in Harpel (ser. A. 2:236); and Pearse n.d., n.p.

19. Schorger 1944, 7.

20. Kennicott 1855, 536. The quote is from Merritt 1904, 258–61.

21. Landwehr n.d., n.p. The note about residents setting fires to facilitate egg collection was made by Schorger (1944, 14).

22. Schorger 1944, 15.

23. Harpel, ser. A, 16:205.

24. "Four-horse prairie schooner" is from ibid. The shipments from Lake and La Porte counties are documented in Schorger (1944, 21), and the six hundred thousand figure is Westemeier's (1985, 20).

25. Cunynghame 1851.

26. The three records can be found in, respectively, Schorger (1944, 8); FJF (1873, 100); and Amateur (1873, 99).

27. Schorger 1944, 42–43.

28. Ibid., 54; Robbins 1991, 234.

29. Ridgway 1889–95, 2:12.

30. Gault 1937, 20.

31. Klingenberg n.d., n.p.; Westcott, interview by author.

32. Howard Christian, letter to author; Paul Spittel, letter to author. The state survey in question was documented in Yeatter (1944).

33. Roland Eisenbeis, telephone conversation; Robert Morris, personal communication. The prairie chicken sighting at McGinnis Slough is recorded in Coursen (1947, 15).

34. The discussion of the effort to reintroduce prairie chickens is from Westcott (interview by author).

35. Jones 1992, 44.

36. The yearly decline is reported in Whitaker and Gammon (1988, 51, 52) and the bird shot by the old-time hunter in Jones (1992, 44).

37. Jones 1992, 47.

38. Leopold 1970, 102.

39. Kennicott 1855, 587; Hoy in Hunt et al. 1976, 5.

40. Burroughs 1925, 127–28.

41. Sources for this paragraph are as follows: Kennicott 1855, 587; Hoy in Hunt et al. (1976, 5); Bohlen (1989, 63); Hunt et al. (1976); Mumford and Keller (1984); and Walkinshaw (1949, 178–79).

42. This paragraph relies on various authors in Hunt et al. (1976, 9–10).

43. Mumford and Keller 1984, 108; Walkinshaw in Hunt et al. (1976, 9). The quote is from Byrne (1884, 592–93).

44. Harpel, ser. B, 13:58–59.

45. Kennicott quoted in Henderson (1970, 104); Landwehr n.d., n.p. Sandhill cranes as pets, as well as the story of the crane killed in California in 1881, are discussed in Hunt et al. (1976, 10).

46. The benefits of cranberry marshes to sandhill cranes are discussed in Hunt et al. (1976, 10). Their ability to make do with small marshes is described in Walkinshaw (1949, 132).

47. Walkinshaw 1949, 133.

48. This paragraph is from Mumford and Mumford (1982, 108–9).

49. Shroufe 1975, 28; Indiana Department of Natural Resources 1994.

50. Mlodinow 1984, 104. Based on observations from northern Indiana, Ken Brock, of Indiana University–Northwest, believes that most of the cranes travel over Crown Point, Lake County (Ind.). This is well to the north of Willow Slough.

51. Indiana's first recent nesting is discussed in Mumford and Keller (1984, 108).

52. Leopold 1970, 103.

53. Matthiessen 1959, 168.

54. Robbins 1991, 302.

55. Laurence Binford, personal communication.

56. Marcisz 1994; Brock 1991.

57. Milosevich 1994, 7–9.

58. Mlodinow 1984, 73.

59. The Wisconsin heron surveys are in Robbins (1991, 133); the Illinois herons are considered in Graber et al. (1978, 13–14).

60. Butler 1897, 657–59.

61. Ling 1935, 100.

62. Marcisz 1994, 135.

63. This account of Baker's Lake's history is largely from Greenberg (1987, 1–2).

64. This account of Lake Renwick's history is largely from Milosevich (1990). Also see Sullivan (1986).

65. Discussion of management of Lake Renwick by Will County Forest Preserve is from DeMauro (1993).

Chapter Fourteen: *For Everything There Is a Season*

1. This is consistent with the conclusion reached by Richard Brewer with respect to Michigan. He says that about two hundred species of birds nested in the state around 1800, and the *Atlas of Breeding Birds* (based on data collected from 1983 to 1988) found 233 species definitely or probably nesting (Brewer et al. 1991).

2. Blockstein 1990, 849.

3. The Father Marquette quote is in Thwaites (1900, 59:174–76). On wild turkeys in the Calumet area, see Brennan (1923, 274), and their final years in Illinois and northwest Indiana, see Ford (1956, 33).

4. The note about ruffed grouse foraging with chickens is from Brennan (1923, 274). The

sightings in LaGrange and Park Ridge are recorded in, respectively, Hulsberg (1917, 48) and Duncan (1936, 8).

5. Robbins 1991, 233.

6. Clark 1931–71. On grouse being more numerous than usual in the Dunes, see Stoddard (1920, 38). The latest observations in the Indiana Dunes are found in Brock (1986, 58; 1997, 76).

7. Brewer et al. 1991, 185.

8. Ball 1900, 454.

9. Woodruff 1907, 99.

10. Information about Paul Downing was provided by Jim Neal (telephone conversation). Bent (1940, 274) chronicles the chimney swift nesting in the outhouse.

11. Deane 1908, 317.

12. Mumford and Keller 1984, 199. The description of Fort Dearborn is by Hurlburt in Harpel (ser. A, 2:244).

13. An account of the shift in nesting sites can be found in Graber et al. 1971, 34); the network, in northeastern Illinois, of people monitoring bluebird houses was described by Libby Hill (personal communication).

14. On weather-related impacts on bluebirds and martins, see Robbins (1991, 432) and Mumford and Keller (1984, 231).

15. McKinley 1980.

16. McKinley 1978, 57.

17. The two Illinois specimens are discussed in ibid. (59–61); Eliot Downing is quoted in Bent (1940, 12).

18. Brewer et al. 1991, 47.

19. Robbins 1991, 527.

20. Clark 1931–1971. The various works on the Indiana Dunes are Eifrig (1918), Brennan (1923), and Brock (1986, 100).

21. See, generally, Richard Brewer et al. (1991, 38). On the red-bellied woodpecker in southern Wisconsin, see Robbins (1991, 365) and on the impact of Dutch elm disease, see Brewer et al. (1991, 38). Their preference for heavy woody understory has been suggested by Robert Russell (telephone conversation).

22. Hoy is cited in Robbins (1991, 448). On the capture and sale of mockingbirds, see Hall (1938, 94).

23. Bohlen (1989, 142) and Mumford and Keller (1984, 240) talk about the changing status of the mocking bird. Their current status (Mlodinow 1984, 157).

24. Terborgh 1992, 99–100.

25. Chris Whelan, telephone conversation; Robinson et al. 1995, 189.

26. Robinson 1987, 16–17; Robinson et al. 1993, 94. A rare sympathetic view of the cowbird appears in an early history of Kane County: "Their habit of familiar attendance upon the cattle was pleasant and interesting. They would follow the grazing or working animals closely and constantly, almost alighting upon them, and when the tired creatures lay down to rest, their little attendants never left them. The companionship seemed mutually agreeable, and children used to think the birds protected the cattle from the tormenting flies" (Bateman, et al. 1904, 627). Then there was the statement by Henry Coale (in Halsey 1912,

362) in his "Birds of Lake County": "On April 24, 1909, I saw a flock of over 500 roosting at dusk in a huge elm; a very unusual sight. One shot at long range brought down a shower of them."

27. The number of species parasitized can be found in Robinson et al. (1993, 94) and the percentage of parasitized nests in Robinson et al. (1995, 1989).

28. Morse 1989, 139.

29. Nolan 1978, 141–42.

30. Robinson 1992, 415–16.

31. Wilcove 1990, 10.

32. Ibid.

33. A. C. Barry is quoted in Robbins (1991, 202); the information on the swallow-tailed kite in Racine is from Hoy (1853, 306) and on the three shot in Higland Park is from Coale in Halsey (1912, 358).

34. Nelson (1876, 130). On the curlew's unwillingness to stay long on cultivated ground, see Kumlien and Hollister (1903, 42) and on its last nesting in the area, see Nelson (1876, 130).

35. Kennicott (1855, 586). On the sharp-tailed grouse's apparent preference for areas with some scattered trees, see Brewer et al. (1991, 50), and sightings in Racine and Waukegan, see, respectively, Schorger (1944, 27) and Nelson (1876, 121).

36. Schorger (1964, 333) provided information on swans nesting in this region. Material on whooping cranes as migrants is from Nelson (1876, 133) and on the one shot in Chicago is from Bohlen (1989, 63).

37. Kennicott 1855, 74. The remainder of the paragraph is based on Schorger (1941, 105).

38. Nelson 1876, 134.

39. Nelson (1876) was the source for information on Nelson's sharp-tailed sparrow summering at Lake Calumet; on LeConte's sparrows in Skokie Marsh, see Baker (1910) and on additional nests located in the region recently, see Ford (1956, 88).

40. Sources on terns nesting at various locations in the area are as follows: for Lake Delavan, Robbins (1991, 317); for Powderhorn Lake, Mlodinow (1984, 126); for Gary, Brock (1997, 122); and for Grass Lake, including quote, Nelson (1876, 147–49).

41. Dudek 1988, 36.

42. Heidorn et al. 1991, 8.

43. Ibid., 10.

44. Graber and Graber 1963; Ridgway in Herkert (1991b, 394).

45. Thacker 1867, 146–58.

46. On the abundance of goose eggs near Racine, see Hanson (1965, 73) and in Cook County, Kennicott (1855, 588). The likelihood of Canada geese no longer breeding in Illinois and in Indiana is posited by, respectively, Bohlen (1989, 23) and Mumford and Keller (1984, 26).

47. Kumlien and Hollister 1903, 22.

48. Hanson 1965, 74.

49. John Fischer, telephone conversation.

50. Andrew Montony, telephone conversation.

51. Scott Garrow, telephone conversation.

52. Ridgway in Herkert 1991b, 394; Hoy cited in Robbins 1991, 263; Kumlein and Hollister 1903, 41. The quote on sandpipers in Indiana is from Keller (1958, 7).

53. Herkert (1994, 465) reports on the upland sandpiper's lack of aversion to urban areas; Helmer (1949, 1) describes her study of sandpipers breeding in the Evanston area in 1948.

54. Kennicott 1855, 582; Graber et al. 1973, 5–8. The statewide surveys done in Wisconsin are discussed in Robbins (1991, 457).

55. Yosef 1994, 228.

56. Yosef and Grubb 1994, 467.

57. Clark 1931–71. The absence of Swainson's hawk nests in Wisconsin is documented by Robbins (1991, 216); the Kane County nests were discovered by Keir and Wilde (1976, 658–59).

58. Harpel, ser. A, 16:178.

59. Bent 1958, 42.

60. The data in this paragraph and the next are from Jim Herkert (personal communication).

61. Kobal 1990, iii–iv.

62. Mlodinow 1984.

63. Halle 1947, 59. Their small size and constant movement prompted another response from writer Frances Lee Jacques (in Peterson 1957, 58): "The difference between a warbler and no warbler is very little."

64. Laurence Binford (personal communication)

65. Participants in the spring bird count confine their efforts to one county; they count individuals as well as species. Full-blown big days are limited only by the distances profitable to cover within twenty-four hours, and the only goal is to record species.

66. Kleen 1983, 11–20.

67. Johnson 1989, 62.

68. Perkins 1964, 299.

69. Perkins 1965, 44.

70. Clark 1931–71; Binford, personal communication.

71. Brock 1992, 156; Clark 1931–71.

72. Mlodinow 1984, 134.

73. Clark 1931–71; Jim Neal cited in Mlodinow 1984, 144.

74. Craigmile 1939, 13.

75. Brock 1997, 109.

76. Ibid., 4; Landing 1966, 34.

77. Kennicott 1855, 581; Nelson 1876, 119.

78. The 1973 Berrien County sighting is noted in Mlodinow (1984, 95) and the 1987 sighting in Mount Hoy by Dick Young (personal communication).

79. Siegle 1994, 61–62.

80. Information on Mount Hoy is from Dick Young (personal communication); Indiana Dunes from Ken Brock (1990, 165–75); and Illinois Beach from David Johnson (personal communication) and my own records.

81. Tureky vultures feeding on alewives is recorded by Baxter (1967, 117).

82. Prior to their introduction in the 1980s, there were no definite records of the peregrine falcon breeding in northeastern Illinois. Hoy (1853, 305), however, did write of one pair which "nested for several years within ten miles of this city [Racine]; constructing their nest on the top of a large red beech-tree." In the same paper, he noted that a few merlins also nested in the vicinity.

83. The record forty-seven peregrines is recounted by Mlodinow (1984, 98).

84. Mueller et al. 1977, 660; Erdman and Brinker 1980. The large incursion of goshawks is discussed in Burr and Current (1974, 175).

85. Work 1933, 41.

86. Terborgh 1992, 102–4.

87. Philips 1994, 126.

88. Brock 1992, 154–62.

89. Morse 1989, 189.

90. Graber et al. 1983, 2.

91. Morse 1989, 211.

92. Philo Hoy quoted in Deane 1888, 385; Hancock 1883, 433.

93. Henshaw 1881, 195–96. I have no idea to what species the "little pair bird" refers.

94. Perkins 1965, 42–43.

95. Weir 1976, 14.

96. Beal 1886, 270.

97. This two-paragraph discussion on bird mortality caused by Chicago buildings is based in part on Philips (1994).

98. Klehm 1992, 80–90.

99. Brock 1986, 28.

100. Zimmermann 1949, 4–5.

101. Binford, personal communication.

102. The first record of little gulls in Illinois is recorded in Clark and Nice (1950, 30) and the first in Wisconsin in Robbins (1991, 297).

103. Reilly 1968, 41.

104. Lebaron 1998.

105. Grasett 1928, 221.

106. The 1903 report is documented in Bent (1968, 1671); information on milliners use of snow buntings and on bounties on house sparrows can be found in Barrows (1912, 486).

107. Mumford and Keller 1984, 82.

108. Nelson 1876, 117.

109. Nordenholt 1920, 43.

110. Tom Erdmann cited in Robbins 1991, 339.

111. Dancey 1983, 143; the Belmont Harbor incident is described in Brechlin and Brechlin (1964, 5).

112. A record of the pine siskin flights is in Mlodinow (1984, 197) and of white-winged crossbills in Woodruff (1907, 130).

113. Data on the Wisconsin bird counts can be found in Robbins 1991, 598–99).

114. Easterla 1978, 51–52.

115. Mlodinow 1984, 159.

116. Stoddard 1920, 37.

117. The Christmas bird count records used in this discussion can be found in Heilbrun (1980, 525; 1983, 611) and Rubega (1984, 642). The quote from Bohlen is in Heilbrun (1983, 394). Also see Johnson (1984, 17–23).

118. Erwin Polls, personal communication.

Chapter Fifteen: *Figures in Fur*

1. In addition to the indigenous species present, three nonnative mammals have become established in the region. The house mouse (*Mus musculus*) and brown rat (*Rattus norvegicus*) are almost ubiquitous, while the stone marten (*Martes foina*), native to Eurasia, is restricted to Kettle Moraine State Forest and other woodlands in Walworth and Racine counties.

2. It is interesting to compare the fate of local mammals with those of reptiles and amphibians. While sixty species of native reptiles and amphibians also inhabited the region, all but one or two are still present. However, virtually all of these have undergone serious population decreases.

3. Jackson 1961, 33.

4. Cory 1912, 385; Kennicott 1855, 578; 1859, 243. On the Northern Indiana Historical Society, see Baker (1899, 7); on the fisher jaw at Indiana Dunes, see Rand and Rand (1951, 655).

5. Hamburgh 1916, 359; Fonda 1867–69, 24; Kennicott 1855, 580; Levinge 1846, 218.

6. Sources for elk antler discoveries are as follows: Whitewater, Korowski (personal communication); Kankakee River, Lyon (1936, 304); and Berrien County, Baker (1983, 569).

7. The Callis family is quoted in Harpel, ser. A, 2:112–13; August Conant is cited in Collyer (1868, 46); the old-timers are quoted by Brennan (1923, 247; and the latest local record can be found in Schapper (1917, 1:102–3).

8. Schapper 1917, 1:247.

9. Brennan 1923, 255, 257.

10. Lyon 1936, 285–86; Jackson 1961, 273.

11. The price of bobcat pelts at Fort Dearborn was documented by Gale (in Harpel, ser. A, 2:257); the quote about the bobcat captured at Cedar Lake can be found in Ball (1873, 247); sightings in southern Cook County are recorded in Schapper (1917, 1:102). See also Eenigenburg 1935, 10.

12. Whitaker and Gammon 1988, 20.

13. Joe Sucheki, personal communication. On a bobcat den just outside of Plano, see Calhoun (1971, 68); other sightings in Du Page County are documented by Dan Ludwig (personal communication).

14. Illinois Nature Preserves Commission 1976.

15. Hamburgh 1916; Thacker 1867, 146–58. Sources detailing the presence of otters at various locations are as follows: Fort Dearborn, Gale (in Harpel, ser. A, 2:257); Calumet region, Schapper (1917, 1:102); Fox River in Kane County, Bateman et al. (1904, 625); and Indiana Dunes, Brennan (1923, 256).

16. Lyon 1936, 117.

17. John O. Whitaker, personal communication.

18. Mink slides are discussed in Birkenholz (1973, 5); the mink study at Jasper-Pulaski is documented in Mumford and Whitaker (1982, 462).

19. Frank Drummond, telephone conversation; Ken Klick, telephone conversation.

20. Hennepin 1880, 143–49.

21. I relied on the following sources for information on bison: along the banks of the Saint Joseph River, Baker (1899, 6); in Illinois River country, Hamburgh (1916, 362–63); the quote

by L. S. Hugunin, Bond (1884, 57); and skeletal remains found in Berrien County, Baker (1983, 622).

22. Wisconsin Department of Natural Resources biologist Ron Kurowski has studied the matter closely, interviewing members of the Mall family and consulting with a variety of experts from across the state. Although he can't verify the story with certainty, Kurowski believes that the facts all point to its authenticity.

23. Roe 1970, 228. The quote about tough winters is from Bond (1884, 57). See Hoffmeister 1989, 28.

24. Hamburgh 1916, 362. Black bears in Berrien County are discussed in Baker (1899, 5).

25. Pratt 1935, 21.

26. Harpel, ser. B, 54:183.

27. Cleaver in Harpel, ser, A, 2:65–67.

28. Schorger 1949a, 32.

29. The black bear sighting in Indiana Dunes is recorded in Brennan (1923, 246); in Berrien County, in Baker (1983, 433).

30. For good discussions of the question, see Cory (1912, 92) and Henderson (1881, 299).

31. Cockrum 1907, 436.

32. Lyon 1936; Elliot Downing cited in Fryxell 36, 1927.

33. Kennicott 1857, 84.

34. Jackson 1961, 105. Ron Kurowski has spent many years searching for accounts of wildlife in the historical literature of Walworth County and other parts of the Kettle Moraine country. He has never encountered a single reference to jackrabbits.

35. Jackson 1961, 106.

36. Snowshoe hares surviving as isolated colonies are discussed in Baker 1983, 149) and their presence in nearby Wisconsin counties in Jackson (1961, 110).

37. The lynx killed in a tamarack bog near Root River is documented in the Leach Collection (box 3); and on the lynx specimen in Jefferson County, see Jackson (1961, 398).

38. Hoffmeister 1989, 35; Jackson 1961, 398.

39. Kennicott 1855, 579.The lynx records in Indiana counties can be found in Lyon (1936, 163); *The Wonders of the Dunes* is by Brennan (1923, quote on 249).

40. Garyn Fyffe, personal communication.

41. Wilson and Ruff 1999, 80–81.

42. The Indiana rabies study can be found in Whitaker and Douglas (1986, 571–84) and the Illinois rabies study in Hoffmeister (1989, 87–88).

43. The discussion on bats at Volo Bog is from Miller (1996, 4,5); acceptable nursery conditions are detailed by Chapman and Feldhamer (1982, 58).

44. Bear Cave is described by Winkler and Van Besien (1963, 80) and by Kurta (1980, 69).

45. The material on Indiana myotis in the following five paragraphs builds on Brack and Holmes (1982, 1–28). Quote from page 22.

46. This discussion is largely based on Timm (1989, 2–6).

47. Hoffmeister 1989, 108.

48. Mumford and Whitaker 1982, 193.

49. The least shrew (*Cryptotis parva*), woodland vole (*Microtus pinetorum*), and southern bog lemming (*Synaptomys cooperi*) also occur within the Chicago region but are not discussed in the text.

50. Sanborn and Tibbitts 1949, 1–2.
51. The account of the shrew in captivity in Porter County is from Edgren 1948, 1–2) and of the shrew chasing the mouse from Jackson (1961, 52).
52. The spread of the western harvest mouse into Illinois is chronicled by Hoffmeister (1989, 200–202) and into Indiana by Mumford and Whitaker (1982, 304–5). See also Becker 1975, 14–15; Pigage and Pigage 1994, 47–49.
53. Jackson 1961, 265.
54. David Fox, personal communication.
55. Thacker 1867, 147.
56. Mumford and Whitaker 1982, 371.
57. Sanborn 1925, 13.
58. The size of muskrat houses is specified in Jackson (1961, 249); information on "eat-outs" is from Chapman and Feldhamer (1982, 296).
59. Kennicott 1857, 652; Bluett 1994, 4.
60. The discussion of chipmunks and the two ground squirrels are mostly from Kennicott (1857, 638, 645–50).
61. Walter Hahn cited in Mumford and Whitaker 1982, 243.
62. Baker 1983, 190–91.
63. Mumford and Whitaker 1982, 287.
64. Kennicott 1857, 68; Hoffmeister 1989, 177–78.
65. This paragraph and the next rely on Mumford and Whitaker (1982, 278–79).
66. Jackson 1961, 171. My information on red squirrels was provided by John Bielfeldt for Racine County (telephone conversation), Tom Becker for Kenosha County (telephone conversation), and Ron Kurowski for Walworth County (telephone conversation).
67. The two quotes in this paragraph are from Seton (1929, 23, 21).
68. Kennicott 1857, 65.
69. Seton 1929, 23; Kennicott 1857, 64. On the movement of the "teeming mass," see Schorger (1949b, 215).
70. Allen 1969, 465.
71. Sanborn 1925, 5.
72. Koprowski 1991, 117.
73. The information on beaver is mostly from Jackson (1961), Edward Hill in Chapman and Feldhammer (1982), Baker (1983), and Mumford and Whitaker (1982).
74. Baker 1983, 256.
75. Bill Eyring, personal communication.
76. Mumford and Whitaker 1982, 301.
77. Baker 1983, 256.
78. Donald L. Hey, personal communication. The two New York scientists are Ruedemann and Schoonmaker (1938, 525).
79. The two quotes are from Hey and Philippi (1995, 9, 14).
80. Hill in Chapman and Feldhammer 1982, 265.
81. Hamburgh 1916, 362. Engels (1933, 9) is the source for numbers on pelts from 1800 to 1801, Jackson (1961, 194) for the last beaver Sugar Creek, and Gale in Harpel (ser. A, 2:257) for fur prices at Fort Dearborn.
82. The likelihood of the beaver entering Illinois is conjectured by Pietsch (1956, 195);

information about the release of beavers in Cook County comes from Peter Dring (personal communication).

83. Pietsch 1956, 197.

84. Drell 1994.

85. Bateman et al. 1904, 624.

86. Mumford and Whitaker 1982, 415.

87. Gray wolves now inhabit portions of Wisconsin as far south as Juneau County, which is only about 125 miles from Walworth County. While most of that distance is farm country poorly suited to wolves, it seems to me possible that a wandering animal might some day cross into this region. When, or if, the big feet first pad across that invisible boundary, a deep wound more than a century old will have closed just a bit, if only briefly.

88. Schapper 1917, 102; Jackson 1961, 293–94.

89. Brennan 1923, 253. The survey of game wardens can be found in Forbes (1912). See also Lyon 1936, 154.

90. The quotes are from Beubien (in Harpel, ser. A, 2:51) and from Rexford, the resident living near Blue Island (in Schapper 1917, 232).

91. Charles Cleaver in Harpel, ser. A, 2:65–67.

92. Hoffman 1882, 24–28.

93. A. Y. Smith cited in Schapper 1917, 202. The quote about Racine County is from Stone (1916, 484).

94. Harpel, ser. A, 2:153.

95. Cyrus Airey in Harpel, ser. A, 16:57; Blanchard 1882, 53–54.

96. Jones in Harpel, ser. A, vol. 2, 249.

97. *History of McHenry County* 1885, 831.

98. The hunt of 1841 is described by Holden in Harpel, ser. A, 2:62–63) the hunt in which sixty wolves were killed is written about in Richmond and Vallette (1857, 181).

99. The two surveys were Forbes (1912) and Yeatter (1944). On increasing numbers of coyotes in Indiana, see Mumford and Whitaker (1982, 415–16).

100. Sanborn 1925, 28. The capacity of coyotes to overcome what are seemingly debilitating wounds strains the imagination. François Leydet, in his *The Coyote: Defiant Song Dog of the West* (1988, 47), relates the following two examples: (1) A coyote was found "whose lower jaw had been completely shot away"—by the time it was finally killed, "the original wound had completely healed, so it managed to survive quite some time without a lower jaw"; and (2) "during a helicopter hunt, . . . two adult coyotes were spotted running from a den. One of them had a gait that was not quite normal. 'No gross limp,' [Dr. Frederick] Knowlton said, 'just a little odd.' The coyotes were shot, and when the men landed they discovered that the animal whose run had been a little peculiar had lost both right legs."

101. *Crystal Lake Herald* 1930, 1.

102. Dawes 1991, 42.

103. Sightings of coyotes in Chicago in various neighborhoods are documented by, on the northwest side, Kendall (1994, 3); on the south side, Rechtenwald (n.d.); and in Lincoln Park/the Gold Coast, Papajohn (1991, sec. 2, 1) and Byrne (1992, 25).

104. Kendall 1994, 3.

105. Malo 1998, 4.

106. The North Dakota study is analyzed in Sargeant et al. (1987, 285–93) and the Ontario study in Voight and Earle (1983, 852–57).
107. Gosselink and Van Deelen 1998, 1, 8.
108. The third canid in the region is the gray fox (*Urocyon cinereoargenteus*). Inhabiting wooded areas across the region, this animal climbs trees and thus can easily escape a coyote. It can also get along well in urban areas, as evidenced by the individual who for several years spent its days lying on an exposed branch in Saint Boniface Cemetery, at the corner of Lawrence Avenue and Clark Street in Chicago.
109. Kennicott 1858, 254; Wood 1922, 3.
110. The discussion in this paragraph and the next relies on Hoffman and Gottschang (1977).
111. This paragraph is based on Bluett (1994, 1–5).
112. Gores 1980, 3; Fyffe, personal communication.
113. Bluett 1994, 4.
114. Thompson 1994, 1–4.
115. For more information about dealing with problem wildlife contact the Illinois Department of Natural Resources, 524 S. Second Street, Springfield, IL 62706 (217-782-6384); Wisconsin Department of Natural Resources, Box 7921, Madison, WI 53707 (800-433-0688); or Indiana Department of Natural Resources, 402 W. Washington Street, #C256, Indianapolis, IN 46204 (317-232-4020).
116. Fyffe, personal communication.
117. Baker 1983, 521.
118. Hennepin 1880, 137.
119. The material on opossums in Wisconsin is from Jackson (1961, 19) and in Indiana from Mumford and Whitaker (1982, 88).
120. Jackson 1961, 20.
121. Jackson 1961, 21; Randolph 1964, 240.
122. Carver (1797, 165–68), including the French terms.
123. Thacker 1867, 155–56.
124. Kennicott 1858, 248. Mumford and Whitaker (1982, 128) provide the description of the skunk as food.
125. Mumford and Whitaker 1982, 474.
126. The density figures for Wisconsin are from Jackson 1961, 416); Saint-Cosme is quoted in Angle (1968, 31).
127. I made use of the following sources for the material in this paragraph: the early resident of Chicago is Daniel Tasker (in Harpel, ser. A, 2:236); driving deer into Lake Michigan, Wilson (in Harpel, ser. A, 2:67); settlers in Delavan, Schorger (1953, 204); and price of deer meat in Racine, Schorger (1953, 204).
128. Werich 1920, 46.
129. Hunting restrictions on deer in Wisconsin are noted in Schorger (1953, 213) and in Illinois in Pietsch (1954, 5).
130. The anecdote about William Cox appears in City of Chicago (1916, 14–15); details about the last deer in Skokie Swamp are recorded in Harnsberger (1977, 164); Aldo Leopold is quoted by Pietsch (1954, 5); and the last deer in Racine County is documented by Schorger (1953, 236–37).

131. Brennan (1923, 251) discusses deer in the Indiana Dunes; Mumford and Whitaker (1982, 481) make note of the last deer in Michigan City and in Indiana generally; and the quote about deer in Kankakee River country is by Barnes in Pietsch (1954, 5).

132. The reintroduction of deer into McHenry County is chronicled by Forbes (1912) and in Deer Grove by Paddock et al. (1955).

133. Data on the restocking of deer originates with the following: in Indiana, Mumford and Whitaker (1982, 481); in Illinois, Pietsch (1954, 9); in Zanders Woods, Madany (1974, 5); and in the Palos area Peter Dring (personal communication). Deer density figures for the late 1980s are from Witham and Jones (1992, tables 5–8).

134. Witham and Jones 1992, app. F.

135. Ibid., 34–35, table 41.

136. Ibid., 82.

137. The quote and other details in this paragraph are from Lake County Forest Preserve District (1988, 1, 2).

138. Witham and Jones 1992, 59.

139. Lake County Forest Preserve District 1992, app. B.

140. Lake County Forest Preserve District 1993, app. A; Frank Drummond, personal communication.

141. This paragraph and the next relied on Witham and Jones (1992, 64, 68–69).

142. *Concerned Veterinarians and Citizens to Save the Ryerson Deer v. Lake County Board of Commissioners*, No. 89, chancery 57 (19th Cir. 1989). The agreement is discussed in Witham and Jones (1992, 39).

143. Quotes from opponents are from, respectively, Carney (1988, 2) and Terry (1989).

144. Transcript, February 2, 1989, Lake County Courthouse, Waukegan, Ill.

145. Witham and Jones 1990, 72

146. Dan Brouillard, interview by author.

147. Rosemann 1991, 20.

148. Jones and Witham 1990, 438–39; Brouillard, personal communication

149. Lynn Hepler, personal communication.

150. Schwarz n.d.

Conclusion: *Entering the New Century*

1. See Harris 1984; Primack 1993; and Soulé 1986.

2. See chap. 3. See also Bowles et al. 1998a, 17; and J. Taft in Schwartz 1997, 34, 42–45.

3. Packard and Mutel 1997, 73.

4. U.S. EPA 1993, 164–72.

5. Hickman 1992b, 10; 1992a, 12.

6. Hickman 1992a, 12. If proponents of wetland constructions point to birds as evidence of success, those who advocate creating prairies and, particularly, savannas tend to emphasize plants.

7. Wilhelm 1991b, 5.

8. Forest Preserve District of Du Page County 1994, 26.

9. Marcy DeMauro, telephone conversation.

10. Morton Arboretum 1997, 1.

11.   Anderson et al. 1993, 14–15.

12.   This discussion of Fermi Lab is based on an interview with Robert F. Betz and on his 1984 article (179–85).

13.   Openlands Project 1999, 18.

14.   U.S. Army Corps of Engineers 1996, 85.

15.   Data from Cook, Du Page, Will, Lake, McHenry, and Kane Counties demonstrate that the problem is less population growth than how the land is being developed: from 1970 to 1990 population increased by 4 percent while the number of households grew by 40 percent.

16.   The three principal planning agencies responsible for most of this region are the Southeastern Wisconsin Regional Planning Commission, Northwestern Indiana Regional Planning Commission, and Northeastern Illinois Planning Commission. (In northeastern Illinois there is also the Chicago Areas Transportation Study, a permanent agency specializing in transportation issues.) Among the other efforts to promote planned growth are the Commercial Club of Chicago's Chicago 2020 Project, Openlands Project's Strategic Openlands at Risk, Metropolitan Planning Council's Campaign for Sensible Growth, and Illinois House of Representatives' Smart Growth Task Force.

17.   Handley 1998, 8.

18.   Ibid.

19.   Northeastern Illinois Planning Commission 1997b, 9.

20.   It is important to understand that what is suggested here is but one piece in an overall strategy to combat flooding. A detailed discussion of storm-water management is too lengthy for inclusion here but for more information, see Lake County Stormwater Management Commission (1994), Watershed Management Institute (1997), Northeastern Illinois Planning Commission (1997a), Potter (1997), and Eyring and Greenberg (1998).

21.   Details about these projects are mostly from promotional materials prepared by the developers.

22.   Gene Fuller, grounds manager of Abbot Labs, personal communication.

23.   Northeastern Illinois Planning Commission 1997b, 43.

24.   JoEllen Zeh, personal communication. The twelve fully certified golf courses are (1) Flossmoor Country Club (Cook County), (2) Olympia Fields Country Club (Cook), (3) Silver Lake Country Club (Orland Park, Cook), (4) Naperville Country Club (Du Page), (5) Village Links of Glen Ellyn (Du Page), (6) Cantigny Golf Club (Wheaton, Du Page), (7) Saint Charles Country Club (Kane), (8) Aurora Country Club (Kane), (9) Potawatomi Golf Course (Saint Charles, Kane), (10) Ivanhoe Club (Lake, Ill.), (11) Countryside Golf Course (Mundelein, Lake, Ill.), and (12) Sand Creek Country Club (Chesterton, Porter).

25.   The written sources that I relied most heavily on in this discussion of Midewin are Illinois Department of Natural Resources (1994, 1996) and Glass (1994).

Bibliography

NOTE: *For the ease of future researchers I have identified the locations of some of the older references:* CHS—*Chicago Historical Society;* NLI—*Natural Lands Institute; and* MAL—*Morton Arboretum Library.*

Abrams, Marc D. 1992. Fire and the Development of Oak Forests. *BioScience*, vol. 42, no. 5 (May).

Ackerknecht, Erwin H. (1945) 1977. Malaria in the Upper Mississippi Valley: 1760–1900. Supplements to the *Bulletin of the History of Medicine*, no. 4. Baltimore: Johns Hopkins University Press. Reprinted, New York: Arno Press, 1977 (page references are to the reprint edition).

Allen, Durward. 1969. Boom and Bust. In *Our Natural World*, edited by Hal Borland. Philadelphia and New York: J. B. Lippincott.

Amateur. 1873. Grouse Shooting in Indiana. *Forest and Stream.*

Ambrose, Dave. n.d. Life on the Sand Prairie. *Outdoor Highlights.*

American Field. 1883. Letter on passenger pigeons from Morgan Park, Chicago. *American Field.* October 6.

Anderson, Roger C. 1978. The Use of Fire as a Management Tool on the Curtis Prairie. In *Proceedings of Third Northern Illinois Prairie Workshop*, edited by Russell Kirt. Batavia, Ill.: Fermi National Accelerator Laboratory.

———. 1982. The Eastern Prairie-Forest Transition—an Overview. In *Proceedings of the Eighth North American Prairie Conference*, edited by Richard Brewer. Kalamazoo: Western Michigan University.

———. 1990. The Historic Role of Fire in the North American Grassland. In *Fire in North American Tallgrass Prairies*, edited by S. Collins and L. Wallace. Norman: University of Oklahoma Press.

Anderson, Roger C., et al. 1993. Science and Restoration. *Science*, vol. 262 (October 1).

Anderson, Roger C., and Marlin Bowles. 1999. Deep-Soil Savannas and Barrens of the Midwestern United States. In *Savannas, Barrens, and Rock Outcrop Communities of North America*, edited by Roger C. Anderson, James S. Fralish, and Jerry M. Baskin. New York: Cambridge University Press.

Andreas, A. T. 1884. *History of Cook County, Illinois.* Chicago: A. T. Andreas.

Angle, Paul. 1968. *Prairie State: Impressions of Illinois, 1673-1867.* Chicago: University of Chicago Press.

Apfelbaum, Steven I. 1985. Cattail (*Typha* sp.) Management. *Natural Areas Journal*, vol. 5, no. 3 (July).

———. 1993. The Role of Landscapes in Stormwater Management. In *National Conference on Urban Runoff Management: Enhancing Urban Watershed Management at the Local, County, and State Levels.* Cincinnati, Ohio: U.S. Environmental Protection Agency.

Apfelbaum, Steven I., and Charles Sams. 1986. Ecology and Control of Reed Canary Grass (*Phalaris arundiniacea* L.). *Natural Areas Journal*, vol. 7, no. 2 (April).

Applied Ecological Services, Inc. 1996. Program Summary: An Overview of the Findings . . . of the DuPage County Natural Areas (NAMP) Investigations on the Ecological Conditions of Natural Areas. Report submitted to the Forest Preserve District of Du Page County, Glen Ellyn, Ill.

Armstrong, Alvah C. 1963. The Vegetation of Zanders Woods with Emphasis on the Sand Pits. Master's thesis, Chicago Teachers College (now Northeastern Illinois University).

Arpee, Edward. 1991. *Lake Forest, Illinois: History and Reminiscences, 1861–1961.* Lake Forest, Ill.: Lake Forest–Lake Bluff Historical Society.

Atwater, Caleb. 1818. On the Prairies and Barrens of the West. *American Journal of Science*, vol. 1, no. 2.

Atwell, C. B. 1910. Native Forests Are a Surprise. *Evanston Index*, April 2.

Audubon Bulletin. 1922. Destruction of lotus beds. *Audubon Bulletin* (Spring).

Babwin, Don. 1993. Leapin' Lizards! Slithery, Uninvited Guests Inundate Subdivision in St. Charles Area. *Chicago Tribune*, September 12, sec. 2.

Bacone, John, and Ronald K. Campbell. 1980. Presettlement Vegetation of Lake County, Indiana. In *Proceedings of Seventh North American Prairie Conference*, edited by Clair L. Kucera. Springfield: Southwest Missouri State University.

Baker, Frank. 1910. Ecology of the Skokie Marsh Area, with Special Reference to the Mollusca. *Bulletin of the Illinois State Laboratory of Natural History*, vol. 7, article 4 (February).

Baker, George A. 1899. *The St. Joseph–Kankakee Portage.* Northern Indiana Historical Society Publication no. 1. South Bend: Northern Indiana Historical Society.

Baker, Rollin H. 1983. *Michigan Mammals.* East Lansing: Michigan State University Press.

Balcer, Mary, et al. 1983. *Zooplankton of the Great Lakes.* Madison: University of Wisconsin Press.

Baldwin, Norman S., et al. 1979. *Commercial Fish Production in the Great Lakes: 1867–1977.* Technical Report no. 3. Ann Arbor, Mich.: Great Lakes Fishery Commission.

Ball, Timothy H. 1873. *Lake County, Indiana from 1834 to 1872.* Chicago: J. W. Goodspeed.

———. 1900. *Northwestern Indiana from 1800 to 1900.* Chicago: Donohue & Henneberry.

Barker, Francis. 1955. *From the Green Mountains to the Prairies.* Great Barrington, Mass.: Berkshire Courier Press.

Barrows, Walter. 1912. *Michigan Bird Life.* Lansing: Michigan Agricultural College Press.

Bartel, Karl. n.d. Audio cassette history of Markham Prairie. In author's possession.

Bartlett, Charles H. 1907. *Tales of Kankakee Land.* New York: Charles Scribner's.

Baskin, Carol C., et al. 1972. Observations on the Ecology of *Astragalus tennesseensis. American Midland Naturalist*, vol. 88, no. 1.

Baskin, Jerry M., and Carol C. Baskin. 1973. The Past and Present Geographical Distribution of *Petalostemon foliosus* and Notes on Its Ecology. *Rhodora*, vol. 75.

Bateman, Newton, et al. 1904. *Historical Encyclopedia of Illinois and History of Kane County.* Chicago: Munsell.

Battey, F. A. 1883. *Counties of Warren, Benton, Jasper, and Newton, Indiana: Historical and Biographical.* Chicago: F. A. Battey & Co.

Bavetz, Mark. 1993. Geographic Variation, Distribution, and Status of Kirtland's Snake, *Clonophis kirtlandii* (Kennicott), in Illinois. 1993. Master's thesis, Southern Illinois University, Carbondale.

Baxter, Ralph C. 1967. Dead Alewives Attract Migrating Turkey Vultures to Southern Lake Michigan Beach. *Indiana Audubon Quarterly*, vol. 45, no. 4 (November).

Beal, F. 1886. Bird Migrations. *American Field* (September 18).

Becker, Carl N. 1975. First Record of *Reithrodontomys megalotus* North of the Kankakee River in Illinois. *Transactions of the Illinois State Academy of Science*, vol. 68, no. 1.

Becker, George C. 1983. *Fishes of Wisconsin.* Madison: University of Wisconsin Press.

Beecher, William J. 1969. Lost prairies. *Inland: Magazine of the Midwest* (Summer). (MAL)

———. 1970. The Battle to Save Volo Bog. In Volo Bog State Natural Area files, Brandenburg, Ill.

———. 1973. The Lost Illinois Prairie. *Chicago History*, vol. 11, no. 3 (Spring–Summer).

———. 1981. Chicago's Lost Marsh. *Chicago Academy of Sciences Newsletter*, vol. 5, no. 1 (April).

Beeton, A. M. 1960. The Vertical Migration of *Mysis relicta* in Lakes Huron and Michigan. *Journal Fisheries Research Board of Canada*, vol. 17.

———. 1969. Changes in the Environment and Biota of the Great Lakes. In *Eutrophication: Causes, Consequences, Correctives.* Washington, D.C.: National Academy of Sciences.

Benjamin, Denis R. 1995. *Mushrooms: Poisons and Panaceas.* New York: Freeman & Co.

Benke, H. C. 1932a. Trout Park Wonderland Is Revealed. *Elgin Courier News*, March 29.

———. 1932b. More Trout Park Flora Is Listed. *Elgin Courier News*, March 30.

Bent, Arthur Cleveland. 1940. Life Histories of North American Cuckoos, Goatsuckers, Hummingbirds and Their Allies. *U.S. National Museum Bulletin*, no. 176. Reprinted, New York: Dover Publications, 1964.

———. 1958. Life Histories of North American Blackbirds, Orioles, Tanagers, and Allies. *U.S. National Museum Bulletin*, no. 211. Reprinted, New York: Dover Publications, 1965.

———. 1968. Life Histories of North American Cardinals, Grosbeaks, Buntings, Towhees, Finches, Sparrows, and Allies. *U.S. National Museum Bulletin*, no. 237. Reprinted, New York: Dover Publications, 1968.

Benton, Colbee. 1957. *A Visitor to Chicago in Indian Days.* Chicago: Caxton Club.

Berwyn Historical Society. 1983. *Stories of an Earlier Berwyn.* Berwyn: Berwyn Historical Society.

Betz, Robert F. 1976. The Prairies of Indiana. In *Proceedings of Fifth Midwest Prairie Conference*, edited by D. C. Glenn-Lewin and R. Q. Landers. Ames: Iowa State University Press.

———. 1984. One Decade of Research in Prairie Restoration at the Fermi National Accelerator Laboratory (Fermilab), Batavia, Illinois. In *Proceedings of the Ninth North American Prairie Conference*, edited by G. K. Clambey and R. H. Pemble. Fargo, N.D.: Tri-College University Center for Environmental Studies.

———. 1989. Ecology of Mead's Milkweed (*Asclepias meadii* Torrey). In *Proceedings of the*

Eleventh North American Prairie Conference, edited by T. B. Bragg and J. Stubbendieck. Lincoln: University of Nebraska Printing.

Betz, Robert F., and Marion Cole. 1969. The Peacock Prairie—a Study of a Virgin Illinois Mesic Black-Soil Prairie Forty Years after Initial Study. *Transactions of the Illinois Academy of Sciences*, vol. 62, no. 1.

Betz, Robert F., and Herbert F. Lamp. 1990. Flower, Pod, and Seed Production in Eighteen Species of Milkweeds (*Asclepias*). In *Proceedings of the Twelfth North American Prairie Conference*, edited by Daryl Smith and Carol Jacobs. Cedar Falls: University of Northern Iowa Press.

Beule, John D. 1979. *Control and Management of Cattails in Southeastern Wisconsin Wetlands.* Technical Bulletin 112. Madison: Wisconsin Department of Natural Resources.

Bingham, Gail, et al. eds. 1990. *Issues in Wetlands Protection.* Washington D.C.: Conservation Foundation.

Birkenholz, Dale E. 1973. Mammals of Goose Lake Prairie Nature Preserve. *Natural History Miscellanea*, no. 191 (July 5).

Blanchard, Rufus. 1882. *History of DuPage County.* Chicago: D. L. Baskin.

Blatchley, Willis S. 1910. *An Illustrative and Descriptive Catalogue of the Coleoptera or Beetles (Exclusive of the Rhynchophora) Known to Occur in Indiana.* Indianapolis: Nature Publishing Co.

Bliss, L. C., and George W. Cox. 1964. Plant Community and Soil Variation within a Northern Indiana Prairie. *American Midland Naturalist*, vol. 72, no. 1.

Blockstein, David E. 1990. Disappearing Birds: A Review of John Terborgh's *Where Have All the Birds Gone? BioScience*, vol. 40, no. 11 (December).

Bluett, Bob. 1994. Nuisance Wildlife Control in Illinois—1993 Summary. Springfield: Division of Wildlife Resources, Illinois Department of Natural Resources.

Bluewing. 1884. Recollections of Calumet. *American Field* (April 5).

Bogue, Margaret B. 2000. *Fishing the Great Lakes: An Environmental History, 1783–1933.* Madison: University of Wisconsin Press.

Bohlen, H. David. 1989. *The Birds of Illinois.* Bloomington: Indiana University Press.

Boltwood, H. L. 1879. Notes from Ottawa, Illinois. *Botanical Gazette*, vol. 4.

Bond, E. S. 1884. How Long the Buffalo Remained in Illinois. *American Field* (July 19).

Borror, Donald J., and Richard E. White. 1970. *A Field Guide to the Insects.* Boston: Houghton Mifflin.

Botts, Paul. 1993. Unnatural Selection. *Chicago Reader*, vol. 22, no. 45 (August 13).

Bowles, Marlin. 1983. The Tallgrass Prairie Orchids *Platanthera leucophaea* (Nutt.) Lindl. and *Cypripedium candidum* Muhl. ex Willd.: Some Aspects of Their Status, Biology, and Ecology, and Implications toward Management. *Natural Areas Journal*, vol. 3.

———. 1988. Master Plan for Trout Park Nature Preserve. Presented to Illinois Nature Preserves Commission, Springfield.

———. 1989. Evaluation of Clarke and Pine, Tolleston Ridges, and Gibson Woods, Lake County, Indiana as Potential National Natural Landmarks. Report prepared for Division of Natural Landmarks, National Park Service, by Morton Arboretum, Lisle, Ill.

Bowles, Marlin, et al. 1989. Master Plan for the West Chicago Prairie Nature Preserve. Prepared for Forest Preserve District of Du Page County, City of West Chicago, and Illinois Nature Preserves Commission, Springfield, Ill. (Never approved.)

————. 1992. Status and Population Fluctuations of the Eastern Prairie Fringed Orchid (*Platanthera leucophaea* [Nutt.] Lindl.) in Illinois. *Erigenia*, vol. 12 (November).

————. 1993. Recovery Planning and Reintroduction of the Federally Threatened Pitcher's Thistle (*Cirsium pitcheri*) in Illinois. *Natural Areas Journal*, vol. 13, no. 3.

————. 1997. Vegetation Composition, Structure, and Temporal Change in a Midwestern Silt-Loam Mesic Savanna. Report for the Morton Arboretum, Lisle, Ill.

————. 1998a. *Twenty-Year Woody Vegetation Changes and Groundlayer Species Richness in Northeastern Illinois Upland Forests.* Lisle, Ill.: Morton Arboretum.

————. 1998b. *Landscape Vegetation Pattern, Composition, and Structure of DuPage County, Illinois, as Recorded by the U.S. Public Land Survey (1821–1840).* Lisle, Ill.: Morton Arboretum.

————. n.d. Potential for Reintroduction of Lupine to Spring Bluff Nature Preserve. Report prepared for Morton Arboretum and Forest Preserve District of Lake County, Lisle, Ill.

Bowles, Marlin, and Jenny McBride. 1995. *High Quality Savanna and Woodland Natural Areas in Northern Illinois.* Report to the Illinois Department of Natural Resources. Lisle, Ill.: Morton Arboretum.

————. 1998. Vegetation Composition, Structure, and Chronological Change in a Decadent Midwestern North American Savanna Remnant. *Natural Areas Journal*, vol. 18, no. 1.

Brack, Virgil, and Virgil Holmes. 1982. Determination of Presence and Habitat Suitability for the Indiana Bat (*Myotis sodalis*) along Portions of the Kankakee River, Indiana. Report to the U.S. Army Corps of Engineers, no. DACW 23-82-M-0629, Chicago.

Braun, E. Lucy. 1964. *Deciduous Forests of Eastern North America.* New York: Hafner Publishing Co.

Brechlin, Mr. and Mrs. Fred. 1964. Snowy owl observation. *Audubon Bulletin* (June).

Breden, Felix. 1988. Natural History and Ecology of Fowler's Toad, *Bufo woodhousei fowleri* (Amphibia: Bufonidae), in the Indiana Dunes National Lakeshore. *Fieldiana: Zoology*, n.s., no. 49 (September 30).

Bremer, Frederika. 1853. *The Homes of the New World.* Vol. 2. London: Arthur Hall Virtue & Co. (CHS)

Brennan, George A. 1923. *The Wonders of the Dunes.* Indianapolis: Bobbs-Merrill Co.

Bretz, J. Harlan. 1955. *Geology of the Chicago Region.* Pts. 1 and 2. Urbana: Illinois State Geological Survey.

Brewer, Lawrence G., et al. 1984. Presettlement Vegetation of Southwestern Michigan. *Michigan Botanist*, vol. 23 (October).

Brewer, Richard, et al. 1991. *The Atlas of Breeding Birds of Michigan.* East Lansing: Michigan State University Press.

Brigham, Warren U., et al. 1978. The Watersheds of Northeastern Illinois: Quality of the Aquatic Environment Based upon Water Quality and Fishery Data. Illinois Natural History Survey Staff Paper no. 31. Northeastern Illinois Planning Commission, Chicago.

Brock, Kenneth. 1979. Birdlife of the Michigan City Area, Indiana. *Indiana Audubon Quarterly*, vol. 57, no. 2 (May).

————. 1986. *Birds of the Indiana Dunes.* Bloomington: Indiana University Press.

————. 1990. Indiana Dunes Spring Hawk Flights: 1950–1990. *Indiana Audubon Quarterly*, vol. 68, no. 4 (November).

————. 1991. Confirmed Ring-Billed Gull Nesting in Indiana. *Indiana Audubon Quarterly*, vol. 69, no. 4 (November).

———. 1992. Fall Warblers at the Migrant Trap, Hammond, Indiana. *Indiana Audubon Quarterly*, vol. 70, no. 3 (August).

———. 1997. *Birds of the Indiana Dunes*. 2d ed. Michigan City, Ind.: Shirley Heinze Environmental Fund.

Brofka, Wayne A., and J. Ellen Marsden. 1995. A Survey of Sport Fishing in the Illinois Portion of Lake Michigan. Aquatic Ecology Technical Report 95/6. Illinois Natural History Survey, Champaign.

Brown, Dave. 1982. Should the Dunes Be Mined? *Lake Country Chronicle* (Buchanan, Mich.), vol. 1, no. 2 (August 17).

Brown, Edward H. 1968. Population Characteristics and Physical Condition of Alewives, Alosus pseudoharengus, in a Massive Dieoff in Lake Michigan, 1967. Technical Report 13. Great Lakes Fisheries Commission, Ann Arbor, Mich.

Bryant, David. 1979. The Braidwood Preserve. *Conservator* (Spring).

Bryant, William Cullen. 1851. Letters of a Traveller, or Notes of Things Seen in Europe and America. New York: Putnam. (CHS)

Buck, Solon. 1914. *Travel and Description: 1765–1865*. Springfield: Illinois Historical Society.

Buckingham, J. S. 1842. *The Eastern and Western States of America*. Vol. 3. London: Fisher, Son & Co. (CHS)

Buder, Stanley. 1967. *Pullman*. New York: Oxford University Press.

Burgh, R. 1939. *The Region of Three Oaks*. Norwood, Mass.: Plimpton Press.

Burley, Augustus. 1919. A Pioneer Couple: Letters of Mr. and Mrs. Augustus Burley. In *Chicago's Yesterdays: A Sheaf of Reminiscences*, edited by Caroline Kirkland. Chicago: Daughaday & Co.

Burr, Brooks M., and David Current. 1974. The 1972–1973 Goshawk Invasion in Illinois. *Transactions of the Illinois Academy of Science*, vol. 67, no. 2 (June).

Burr, Brooks M., and Lawrence M. Page. 1986. Zoogeography of Fishes of Lower Ohio–Upper Mississippi Basin. In *The Zoogeography of North American Freshwater Fishes*, edited by C. Hocutt and E. Wiley. New York: John Wiley.

Burroughs, Burt. 1925. *Tales of an Old Border Town and along the Kankakee*. Fowler, Ind.: Benton Review.

Burt, William H. 1946. *The Mammals of Michigan*. Ann Arbor: University of Michigan Press.

Bushey, Charles L. 1976. Man's Effect upon a Colony of *Sistrurus catenatus* (Raf.) in Northeastern Illinois. In *Proceedings of Fifth Midwest Prairie Conference*, edited by D. C. Glenn-Lewin and R. Q. Landers. Ames: Iowa State University Press.

Butler, Amos. 1897. *The Birds of Indiana*. Indianapolis: Indiana Department of Geology and Natural Resources.

Byrne. 1884. Colonel Brackett on the Cranes. *American Field* (June 12).

Byrne, Dennis. 1992. Coyotes Lead a Dog's Life in Chicago. *Chicago Sun-Times*, January 21.

Cahn, Alvin R. 1937. Turtles of Illinois. *Illinois Biological Monographs*, vol. 16.

Cain, Stanley A. 1935. Studies on Virgin Hardwood Forest: Warren Woods, a Beech-Maple Climax Forest in Berrien County, Michigan. *Ecology*, vol. 16, no. 3 (July).

Calhoun, S. R. 1971. The Wild Mammals of Kendall County, Illinois. Master's thesis, Western Illinois University.

Calkins, W. W. 1896. The Lichen Flora of Chicago and Vicinity. *Bulletin of the Geological and Natural History Survey*, no. 1.

———. 1906–7. Flora Round about Berwyn. *Berwyn Current*. (Seven articles appearing between fall 1906 and March 15, 1907; clippings in files of Trailside Nature Center, Cook County Forest Preserve District, River Forest, Ill.)

Campbell, Faith T., and Scott E. Schlarbaum. 1994. *Fading Forests*. Washington, D.C.: Natural Resources Defense Council.

Cannon, Thomas H., ed. 1927. *History of the Lake and Calumet Region of Indiana*. Indianapolis: Historian's Association.

Carney, Diana. 1988. Ryerson Deer Harvest Plan Stirs Angry Protesters. *Waukegan News Sun*, July 9–10.

Carpenter, G. F., et al. 1974. Abundance and Life History of *Mysis relicta* in the St. Lawrence Great Lakes. *Journal Fisheries Research Board of Canada*, vol. 31, no. 3.

Carver, Jonothan. 1797. *Travels throughout the Interior Parts of North America*. Boston: John Russell.

Case, Frederick W. 1964. Orchids of the Western Great Lakes Region. *Cranbrook Institute of Science Bulletin*, no. 48.

Case, Frederick W., and William Schwab. 1971. *Isotria medeoloides*, the Smaller Whorled Pogonia, in Michigan. *Michigan Botanist*, vol. 10.

Cashatt, Everett D., et al. 1992. Illinois 1992 Critical Habitat and Recovery Investigations for the Hine's Emerald Dragonfly (*Somatochlora hineana* Williamson). Report submitted to the U.S. Fish and Wildlife Service, Chicago Metro Wetlands Office, Barrington, Ill.

Cashatt, Everett D., and Brad G. Simms. 1993. Illinois 1993 Critical Habitat and Recovery Investigations for the Hine's Emerald Dragonfly (*Somatochlora hineana* Williamson). Report submitted to the U.S. Fish and Wildlife Service, Chicago Metro Wetlands Office, Barrington, Ill.

Cashatt, Everett D., and Timothy E. Vogt. 1990. The Illinois 1990 Status Survey for the Ohio Emerald Dragonfly (*Somatochlora hineana*) Williamson. Report submitted to U.S. Fish and Wildlife Service, Office of Endangered Species. Cooperative agreement no. 14-16-0003-89-931. Barrington, Ill.

Caton, John D. 1869. Origins of the Prairies. *Transactions of the Ottawa Academy of Natural Sciences* (December 30).

Chamberlain, F. M. 1900. *Notes on the Edible Frogs of the United States and Their Artificial Propagation*. Pages 249–61 of the Report of the Commissioner of Fisheries for 1896/87. U.S. Commission of Fish and Fisheries. Washington: Government Printing Office.

Chamberlain, Henry. n.d. Mills. Copy of Chamberlain manuscript in possession of Dr. Gerard Donnelly, Morton Arboretum (Lisle, Ill.).

Champion Turtle Catcher. 1881. *American Field* (October 15).

Chapin, Louella. 1907. *Round about Chicago*. Chicago: Unity Publishing Co.

Chapman, Joseph A., and George A. Feldhamer, eds. 1982. *Wild Mammals of North America*. Baltimore: Johns Hopkins University Press.

Chase, Agnes. 1917. Rev. E. J. Hill. *Rhodora*, vol. 19, no. 220 (April).

Chicago Daily News. 1935. Lotus Beds of Grass Lake Draw Thousands Each Year. *Chicago Daily News*. June 15.

Chicago Department of Aviation. 1990. *Lake Calumet Airport Feasibility Study*. Chicago: Chicago Department of Aviation.

Chicago Tribune. 1888a. Unfamiliar Bugs and Birds. *Chicago Tribune*. May 17.

———. 1888b. Locusts Have Come Again. *Chicago Tribune*. June 12.

———. 1888c. The Threatened Locust Pest. *Chicago Tribune*. June 13.

———. 1925. Harbor Bill Signed; Huge Project Ready. *Chicago Tribune*. June 8.

Chicago Wilderness. 1999. *Biodiversity Recovery Plan*. (First Draft for Public Review). Chicago: Chicago Wilderness.

Christie, W. J. 1974. Changes in the Fish Species Composition of the Great Lakes. *Journal of the Fisheries Research Board of Canada*, vol. 31, no. 5.

Chrzastowski, Michael J. 1991. The Building, Deterioration and Proposed Rebuilding of the Chicago Lakefront. *Shore and Beach* (April).

Chrzastowski, Michael J., and Wayne Frankie. 2000. *Guide to the Geology of Illinois Beach State Park and the Zion Beach–Ridge Plain, Lake County, Illinois*. Champaign: Illinois State Geological Survey.

Chrzastowski, Michael J., and Todd A. Thompson. 1994. Late Wisconsinan and Holocene Geologic History of the Illinois-Indiana Coast of Lake Michigan. *Journal of Great Lakes Research*, vol. 20, no. 1.

City of Chicago. 1916. *Chicago City Manual*. Chicago: Bureau of Statistics, City of Chicago. (CHS)

———. 1976. *Historic City: The Settlement of Chicago*. Chicago: City of Chicago.

Clark, Charles T. 1931–71. Bird Records. Field Museum, Chicago.

Clark, Charles T., and Margaret M. Nice. 1950. *William Dreuth's Study of Bird Migration in Lincoln Park, Chicago*. Special Publication no. 8. Chicago: Chicago Academy of Sciences.

Clark, E. B. 1894. Last of His Race? *Chicago Tribune*, November 25.

Clark, H. Walton, and John B. Southall. 1920. *Fresh-Water Turtles: A Source of Meat Supply*. App. 7 to the *Report of the U.S. Commissioner of Fisheries for 1919*. Bureau of Fisheries Document no. 889. Washington, D.C.: Government Printing Office.

Clark, John A. 1842. *Gleanings by the Way*. Philadelphia: Simon. (CHS)

Clarke, S. C. 1887. Lakes Calumet and Gogebic. *Forest and Stream*.

———. 1889. Old Times about Chicago. *Forest and Stream*.

Clute, Willard N. 1931. *Swamp and Dune: A Study in Plant Distribution*. Indianapolis: Willard Clute & Co.

Coale, Henry K. 1922a. On the Nesting of *Ectopistes migratorius*. *Auk*, vol. 39 (April).

———. 1922b. Notes on *Ectopistes migratorius*. *Auk*, vol. 39 (April).

Coble, Daniel W., et al. 1990. Lake Trout, Sea Lampreys, and Overfishing in the Upper Great Lakes: A Review and Reanalysis. *Transactions of the American Fisheries Society*, vol. 119.

Cockrell, Ron. 1988. *A Signature of Time and Eternity: The Administrative History of Indiana Dunes National Lakeshore, Indiana*. Omaha, Nebr.: National Park Service's Midwest Regional Office.

Cockrum, William M. 1907. *Pioneer History of Indiana*. Oakland City, Ind.: Press of Oakland City Journal.

Coe, J.E. 1944. The glass snake. *Chicago Naturalist*, vol. 7, no. 2 (June).

Coffey, Timothy. 1993. *The History and Folklore of North American Wildflowers*. New York: Facts on File.

Coker, Robert E. 1919. Freshwater Mussels and Mussel Industries of the United States. *Bulletin of the United States Bureau of Fisheries*, vol. 32.

Cole, Kenneth, et al. 1992. Fire Temperature Monitoring during Experimental Burns at Indiana Dunes National Lakeshore. *Natural Areas Journal*, vol. 12, no. 4 (October).

Cole, Kenneth L., and Noel B. Pavlovic. n.d. Howes Prairie: A Remnant of the Indiana Dune Prairie Preserved by Periodic Flooding. Report prepared for Indiana Dunes National Lakeshore, Porter.

Cole, Kenneth L., and Robert S. Taylor. 1995. Past and Current Trends of Change in a Dune Prairie/Oak Savanna Reconstructed through a Multiple-Scale History. *Journal of Vegetation Science*, vol. 6.

Collins, Scott L., and Linda Wallace, eds. 1990. *Fire in North American Tallgrass Prairies*. Norman: University of Oklahoma Press.

Collyer, Robert. 1868. *A. H. Conant: A Man in Earnest*. Chicago: J. R. Walsh.

Colten, Craig E. 1985. *Industrial Wastes in the Calumet Area, 1869–1970: An Historical Geography*. Champaign, Ill.: State Water Survey Division, Illinois Department of Energy and Natural Resources.

Conant, Roger. 1943. Studies on North American Water Snakes. 1. *Natrix kirtlandii* (Kennicott). *American Midland Naturalist*, vol. 29, no. 2.

———. 1975. *A Field Guide to Reptiles and Amphibians of Eastern and Central North America*. Boston: Houghton Mifflin Co.

Conservator. 1980. Site of Rare Vetch: Last-Minute Action Saves Shoop Prairie. *Conservator* (Spring).

Cook, David G., and Murray G. Johnson. 1974. Benthic Macroinvertabrates of the St. Lawrence Great Lakes. *Journal Fisheries Research Board of Canada*, vol. 31, no. 5.

Cook, Sarah G., and Robert S. Jackson. 1978. *The Bailly Area of Porter County, Indiana*. Report to Indiana Dunes National Lakeshore. Evanston, Ill.: Robert Jackson & Associates.

Cory, Charles B. 1912. *The Mammals of Illinois and Wisconsin*. Publications of the Field Museum of Natural History, no. 153. Chicago: Field Museum.

Costello, David F. 1936. Tussock Meadows in Southeastern Wisconsin. *Botanical Gazette*, vol. 97 (March).

Coursen, C. Blair. 1947. Birds of the Orland Wildlife Refuge. Supplement of *Turtox News*. Chicago: General Biological Supply House.

Cowles, Henry C. 1899. The Ecological Relations of the Vegetation on the Sand Dunes of Lake Michigan. *Botanical Gazette*, vol. 28, no. 2 (February).

———. 1901a. The Physiographic Ecology of Chicago and Vicinity: A Study of the Origin, Development, and Classification of Plant Societies. *Botanical Gazette*, vol. 31, no. 2 (February).

———. 1901b. The Physiographic Ecology of Chicago and Vicinity: A Study of the Origin, Development, and Classification of Plant Societies (Concluded). *Botanical Gazette*, vol. 31, no. 3 (March).

———. 1901c. *The Plant Societies of Chicago and Vicinity*. Chicago: Geographic Society of Chicago.

Craigmile, Esther A. 1939. A Popular Bird Roost. *Audubon Bulletin*, no. 30 (June).

Cravath, Prosper. 1906. *Early Annals of Whitewater*. Whitewater, Wis.: Whitewater Federation of Women's Clubs.

Critchfield, Howard J. 1974. *General Climatology*. Englewood Cliffs, N.J.: Prentice-Hall, Inc.

Cronon, William. 1991. *Nature's Metropolis: Chicago and the Great West*. New York: W. W. Norton & Co.

Crystal Lake Herald. 1930. Kills Coyotes from His Seat in Plane. *Crystal Lake Herald*, February 6.

Cummings, Kevin S., and Christine A. Mayer. 1991. Freshwater Mussels of the Illinois River: Past, Present, and Future. In *Proceedings of the Governor's Conference on the Management of the Illinois River System*, comp. Holly Korab. Report no. 20. Urbana: Water Resources Center, University of Illinois.

———. 1992. *Field Guide to Freshwater Mussels of the Midwest.* Champaign: Illinois Natural History Survey.

Cummins, Kenneth W. 1972. What Is a River?—a Zoological Description. In *River Ecology and Man*, edited by Ray T. Oglesby, Clarence A. Carlson, and James A. McCann. New York: Academic Press.

Cunynghame, Arthur. 1851. *A Glimpse at the Great Western Republic.* London: Beurley.

Currey, J. S. 1920. Currey Writes Forest History of North Shore. *Evanston News Index*, August 2.

Curtis, John. 1959. *The Vegetation of Wisconsin.* Madison: University of Wisconsin Press.

Cutler, Irving. 1976. *Chicago: Metropolis of the Mid-Continent.* Dubuque, Iowa: Kendall/Hunt.

Daggy, Tom. 1946. The Ecology and Taxonomy of Certain Wood-Inhabiting Coleoptera of the Chicago Region. Ph. D. diss., Northwestern University

Dancey, Helen. 1983. Winter Foraging Habits of a Snowy Owl. *Indiana Audubon Quarterly*, vol. 61, no. 4 (November).

Danglede, Ernest. 1914. *The Mussel Resources of the Illinois River.* App. 6 to the *Report of the U.S. Commissioner of Fisheries for 1913.* Bureau of Fisheries Document no. 804. Washington D.C.: Government Printing Office.

Darby, William. 1819. *A Tour from the City of New York to Detroit.* New York: Kirk & Mercein. (CHS)

Davis, Anthony M. 1977. The Prairie-Deciduous Forest Ecotone in the Upper Middle West. *Annals of the Association of American Geographers*, vol. 67, no. 2 (June).

Dawes, K. O. 1991. Coyote's Call Increasingly Common Here. *Chicago Sun-Times.* March 3.

Deam, Charles. 1940. *Flora of Indiana.* Indianapolis: Department of Conservation.

Deane, Ruthven. 1888. Destruction in Migration. *Forest and Stream*, vol. 31, no. 20 (December 6).

———. 1895. Additional Records of the Passenger Pigeon in Illinois and Indiana. *Auk*, vol. 12 (July).

———. 1908. Curious Fatality among Chimney Swifts. *Auk*, vol. 25 (July).

Deason, H. J. 1939. The Distribution of Cottid Fishes in Lake Michigan. *Michigan Academy of Sciences, Arts, and Letters*, vol. 24, no. 2.

DeMauro, Marcella. 1986. A Vegetational and Plant Community Survey of the Lockport Prairie Nature Preserve and the Romeoville Prairie Nature Preserve. Report to Forest Preserve District of Will County, Joliet, Ill.

———. 1993. Colonial Nesting Bird Response to Visitor Use at Lake Renwick Heron Rookery, Illinois. *Natural Areas Journal*, vol. 13, no. 1 (January).

———. 1994. A Proposal to Dedicate Messenger Woods as an Illinois Nature Preserve. Report from Will County Forest Preserve District to Illinois Nature Preserves Commission, Springfield.

Dempsey, Dave. 1993. A Rare Butterfly Faces Four Lanes of Traffic. *Detroit Free Press*, December 26.

Dolak, David. 1985. *Water Resources Management at the Indiana Dunes National Lakeshore: A Baseline Inventory, 1985*. Prepared with cooperation of the School of Public and Environmental Affairs, Indiana University and the National Park Service. Porter: Indiana Dunes National Lakeshore.

Dondore, Dorothy Anne. 1961. *The Prairie and the Making of Middle America*. New York: Antiquarian Press.

Donnelly, Gerard T., and Peter G. Murphy. 1987. Warren Woods as Forest Primeval: A Comparison of Forest Composition with Presettlement Beech-Sugar Maple Forests of Berrien County, Michigan. *Michigan Botanist*, vol. 26, no. 1 (January).

Doty, Mrs. Duane. 1893. *The Town of Pullman*. Pullman, Ill.: T. P. Struhsacker. Reprinted, [Pullman, Ill.]: Historic Pullman Foundation, 1991.

Downing, Elliot. 1922. *A Naturalist in the Great Lakes Region*. Chicago: University of Chicago Press.

Downs, Albert A. 1949. Trees and Food from Acorns. In *Trees: The Yearbook of Agriculture*, edited by Alfred Stefferud. Washington D.C.: U.S. Department of Agriculture.

Drell, Adrienne. 1994. Lesson from Park's Past: Don't Leave It to Beavers. *Chicago Sun-Times*, April 26.

Dudek, Terese. 1988. Avian Community Composition in Relation to Wetland Habitat Characteristics. Master's thesis, Northern Illinois University.

Duncan, Donald. 1936. Interesting Records Obtained Near Park Ridge, Illinois. *Audubon Bulletin*, no. 26.

Dustin, Thomas E. 1973. The Battle of the Indiana Dunes. In *Citizens Make the Difference*. Washington D.C.: Citizens Advisory Committee on Environmental Quality.

Dybas, Henry. 1973. It's the Year of the Cicada. *Field Museum Bulletin*, vol. 44, no. 6 (May).

Dybas, Henry, and D. Dwight Davis. 1962. A Population Census of Seventeen-Year Periodical Cicadas (Homoptera: Cicadidae: *Magicicada*). *Ecology*, vol. 43, no. 3.

Earll, R. E., et al. 1887. A Geographical Review of the Fisheries Industries and Fishing Communities for the Year 1880. Sec. 2 of *The Fisheries and Fishery Industries of the United States*, by G. Brown Goode et al. Washington, D.C.: Government Printing Office.

Easterla, David A. 1978. Mixed Flocks of Common and Hoary Redpolls in Northern Indiana. *Indiana Audubon Quarterly*, vol. 56, no. 2 (May).

Ebinger, John. 1986. Sugar Maple, a Management Problem in Illinois forests. *Transactions of the Illinois Academy of Science*, vol. 79, nos. 1–2.

Eckert, Allan W. 1965. *Silent Sky*. Boston: Little, Brown & Co.

Eddy, Samuel. 1927. The Plankton of Lake Michigan. *Illinois Natural History Bulletin*, vol. 17, article 4.

Eddy, Samuel, and James C. Underhill. 1974. *Northern Fishes*. Minneapolis: University of Minnesota Press.

Edgren, R. A. 1948. Notes on a Northern Short-Tailed Shrew. *Natural History Miscellanea*, vol. 25 (September 25).

Eenigenburg, Henry. 1935. *The Calumet Region and Its Early Settlers*. Chicago: Arrow Printers.

Eichenlaub, Val L. 1979. *Weather and Climate of the Great Lakes Region*. Notre Dame, Ind.: University of Notre Dame Press.

Eifrig, C. W. G. 1918. The Birds of the Sand Dunes of Northwestern Indiana. *Proceedings of Indiana Academy of Science*, vol. 28.

———. 1921. Notes from the Field. *Audubon Bulletin* (Spring).

Eldridge, John A. 1914. *The Mussel Fishery of the Fox River.* App. 7 to the *Report of the U.S. Commissioner of Fisheries for 1913.* Bureau of Fisheries Document no. 804. Washington D.C.: Government Printing Office.

Elton, Wallace M. 1970. Forest Distribution and Soil Texture along the Valparaiso Moraine in Northwestern Indiana. *Geographical Bulletin*, vol. 1.

Emery, Lee. 1985. *Review of Fish Species Introduced into the Great Lakes, 1819–1974.* Technical Report no. 5. Ann Arbor, Mich.: Great Lakes Fishery Commission.

Engel, J. Ronald. 1983. *Sacred Sands: The Struggle for Community in the Indiana Dunes.* Middletown, Conn.: Wesleyan University Press.

Engels, William L. Notes on the Mammals of St. Joseph County, Indiana. 1933. *American Midland Naturalist*, vol. 14, no. 1.

Erdman, Thomas C., and David Brinker. 1980. Goshawk Population Cycles and the 1972–73 "Invasion." In *Proceedings of the Ninety-eighth Stated Meeting of the American Ornithologists' Union: 11–15 August 1980, Fort Collins, Colorado.* n.p.: American Ornithologists' Union.

Ernst, Isabel, ed. 1976. *Roots: A Glenview Story.* Glenview, Ill.: Glenview Bicentennial Commission.

Eshenroder, Randy L., et al. 1995. *Fish-Community Objectives for Lake Michigan.* Special Publication 95-3. Ann Arbor, Mich.: Great Lakes Fishery Commission.

Eycleshymer, Albert C. 1901. Observations on the Breeding Habits of *Ameirus nebulosus. American Naturalist*, vol. 35, no. 419.

Eyring, Bill, and Joel Greenberg. 1998. Managing Stormwater in Lake County to Reduce Flood Hazards. Prepared for Liberty Prairie Foundation, Grayslake, Ill.

Farb, Peter. 1963. *Face of North America.* New York: Harper & Row.

Fehrenbacher, J. B., et al. 1984. *Soils of Illinois.* Bulletin 778. Champaign-Urbana: University of Illinois College of Agriculture Agricultural Experiment Station.

Ferguson, William. 1856. *America by River and Rail; Or, Notes by the Way on the New World and Its People.* London: Nisbit. (CHS)

Fernald, Merritt L. 1950. *Gray's Manual of Botany.* 8th ed. New York: American Book Co.

Ferry, John F. 1907. Ornithological Conditions in Northeastern Illinois, with Some Notes on Winter Birds. *Auk*, vol. 24, no. 2 (April).

Fetter, Harold. 1963. Nesting Report on Wilson's Phalaropes. *Audubon Bulletin* (March).

Figg, Dennis. 1988. Prairie Invertebrate Conservation. [Also titled "The prairie mole cricket and other insects that go unnoticed."] In *Proceedings of the Tenth North American Prairie Conference*, edited by Arnold Davis and Geoffrey Stanford. Dallas: Native Prairie Association of Texas.

Finley, Dean, and J. E. Potzger. 1952. Characteristics of the Original Vegetation in Some Prairie Counties of Indiana. *Butler University Botanical Studies*, vol. 10, Paper 13 (August).

Fishbein, Mark. n.d. Forest Dynamics at Ryerson Conservation Area, Lake County, Illinois. Report to the Ryerson Fellowship Committee, Deerfield, Ill.

FJF. 1873. Letter. *Forest and Stream.*

Fonda, John. 1867–69. Early Reminiscences of Wisconsin. In *Report and Collections of the State Historical Society of Wisconsin, for the years 1867, 1868 and 1869.* Vol. 5. Madison: Atwood & Rublee. (CHS)

Forbes, Stephen A. 1912. Results of Statewide Game Survey. Unpublished responses housed at Illinois Natural History Survey, Champaign.

———. 1925. The Lake as a Microcosm. *Illinois Natural History Survey Bulletin*, vol. 15, article 4 (November).

Forbes, Stephen A., and R. E. Richardson. 1913. Studies on the Biology of the Upper Illinois River. *Bulletin of the Illinois State Laboratory of Natural History*, vol. 9, article 10 (June).

———. 1920. *The Fishes of Illinois*. Urbana: Natural History Survey of Illinois.

Ford, Edward. 1956. *Birds of the Chicago Region*. Chicago: Chicago Academy of Sciences.

Forest Preserve District of DuPage County. 1994. Report on the Restoration and Management in the Bluff Savanna, Waterfall Glen. Forest Preserve District of DuPage County, Wheaton, Ill.

Fowells, H. A. 1965. *Silvics of Forest Trees of the United States*. Agriculture Handbook no. 271. Washington, D.C.: U.S. Department of Agriculture, Forest Service.

Fralish, James, et al. 1994. *Proceedings of the North American Conference on Barrens and Savannas*. Chicago: Great Lakes National Program Office, Region Five, U.S. Environmental Protection Agency.

Francis, James T. 1994. Indiana's Lake Michigan Creel Survey Results. Indiana Division of Fish and Wildlife, Indianapolis.

Francis, James T., et al. 1996. Yellow Perch Management in Lake Michigan: A Multi-Jurisdictional Challenge. *Fisheries*, vol. 21, no. 2 (February).

Franklin, Kay, and Norma Schaeffer. 1983. *Duel for the Dunes*. Urbana and Chicago: University of Illinois Press.

Frazier, W. H., and S. R. Sapirie. 1934. *Report on Kankakee River Survey to Determine Areas for Restoration*. Indianapolis: Indiana Department of Conservation.

Friederici, Peter. 1992. Lonely at the Bottom. *Chicago Reader*, vol. 22, no. 6 (November 6).

Frey, David. 1966. Limnology. In *Natural Features of Indiana*, edited by Alton Lindsey. Indianapolis: Indiana Academy of Science and Indiana State Library.

Fryxell, F. M. 1927. *The Physiography of the Region of Chicago*. Chicago: University of Chicago Press.

Furnweger, Karen, ed. 1992. Our Lake—What's in It? *Aquaticus*, vol. 23, no. 2.

Gasiorkiewicz, E. C. 1986. *Chiwaukee Prairie Plant Checklist*. Kenosha: University of Wisconsin—Parkside.

Gates, Frank C. 1912. The Vegetation of the Beach Area in Northeastern Illinois and Southeastern Wisconsin. *Bulletin of the Illinois State Laboratory of Natural History*, vol. 9, article 5 (March).

Gault, Benj. T. 1937. Reminiscences of Early Experiences in the Chicago area. *Audubon Bulletin*, no. 27.

Gerking, Shelby D. 1945. Distribution of the Fishes of Indiana. *Investigations of Indiana Lakes and Streams*, vol. 3.

Gilmore, Melvin R. 1922. *Prairie Smoke*. Bismarck, N.D.: M. R. Gilmore.

Ginn, William E. 1954. American Egret Nesting in Indiana. *Indiana Audubon Quarterly*, vol. 32, no. 1 (January).

Glass, William D. 1989. Proposal for the Dedication of Wilmington Shrub Prairie, Will County, Illinois. Report from Natural Heritage Division, Illinois Department of Conservation, to Illinois Nature Preserve Commission, 121 Meeting, Item 20, Springfield.

———. 1994. *A Survey of the Endangered and Threatened Plant and Animal Species of the Joliet Army Ammunition Plant and Joliet Training Area Will County, Illinois.* Springfield: Illinois Department of Conservation (now Illinois Department of Natural Resources).

Gleason, Henry A. 1910. The Vegetation of the Inland Sand Deposits of Illinois. *Bulletin of the Illinois State Laboratory of Natural History,* vol. 9, article 5 (October).

Goder, Harold. 1956. Pre-settlement Vegetation of Racine County. *Wisconsin Academy of Sciences, Arts and Letters,* vol. 45.

Goldthwait, James W. 1909. Physical Features of the Des Plaines Valley. *Bulletin of Illinois State Geological Survey,* no. 11.

Goodyear, Carole D., et al. 1982. *Atlas of the Spawning and Nursery Areas of Great Lakes Fishes,* vol. 4, *Lake Michigan.* FWS/OBS-82/52. Washington D.C.: U.S. Fish and Wildlife Service.

Gores, Paul. 1980. Noah's Helper. *Panorama Magazine* in *The Sunday Herald,* vol. 3, no. 28 (July 13).

Gorman, Owen T. 1987. Fishes and Aquatic Insects of Nippersink Creek, McHenry County, Illinois. *Transactions of the Illinois State Academy of Science,* vol. 80, nos. 3–4.

Gorner, Peter. 1990. The Day of the Cicadas. *Chicago Tribune Magazine,* May 6.

Gosselink, Todd E., and Tim Van Deelen. 1998. Coyotes and Foxes in the Town and Country. *Illinois Natural History Survey Reports,* no. 350 (March–April).

Graber, Jean, Richard Graber, and E. L. Kirk. 1971. Illinois Birds: Turdidae. *Illinois Natural History Survey Notes,* no. 75.

———. 1973. Illinois Birds: Laniidae. *Illinois Natural History Survey Notes,* no. 83.

———. 1977. Illinois Birds: Picidae. *Illinois Natural History Survey Notes,* no. 102.

———. 1978. Illinois Birds: Ciconiformes. *Illinois Natural History Survey Notes,* no. 109.

———. 1979. Illinois Birds: Sylviidae. *Illinois Natural History Survey Notes,* no. 110.

———. 1983. Illinois Birds: Wood Warblers. *Illinois Natural History Survey Notes,* no. 118.

Graber, Richard, and Jean Graber. 1963. A Comparative Study of Bird Populations in Illinois, 1906–1909 and 1956–1958. *Illinois Natural History Survey Bulletin,* vol. 28.

Graham, V. O. 1927. Communities of Mushrooms. *Transactions of the Illinois State Academy of Science,* vol. 20.

Grand Mere Association. 1973. *Grand Mere: A Very Special Place.* Kalamazoo, Mich.: Kalamazoo Nature Center, Inc.

Grant, Chapman. 1934. Notes on the Spotted Turtle in Northern Indiana. *Proceedings of Indiana Academy of Science,* vol. 44.

Grasett, Frank. 1928. A Flight of Snow Buntings at Glencoe, Illinois. *Auk,* vol. 45 (April).

Grazulis, Thomas P. 1993. *Significant Tornadoes, 1680–1991.* Saint Johnsbury, Vt.: Environmental Films.

Greenberg, Bernard. 1991. Flies as Forensic Indicators. *Journal of Medical Entomology,* vol. 28, no. 5 (September).

Greenberg, Joel. 1987. Baker's Lake: The Tale of a Suburban Heronry. *Chicago Academy of Sciences NewsCast* (May–June).

Greenberg, Joel, and Margo Milde. 1994. The Occurrence of Four Rare Plants in Cook County. *Transactions of the Illinois State Academy of Science,* vol. 87.

Greenfield, David W. 1982. Habitat Evaluation Based on the Project Area's Fish Fauna. In *Final Report: Habitat Evaluation of Lake Calumet Harbor Area Road and Site Development,* edited by W. E. Southern. Contract no. 54-379. Prepared for City of Chicago. DeKalb, Ill.: ENCAP, Inc.

Greenfield, David W., and John D. Rogner. 1984. An Assessment of the Fish fauna of Lake Calumet and Its Adjacent Wetlands, Chicago, Illinois: Past, Present, and Future. *Transactions of Illinois Academy of Science*, vol. 77, nos. 1–2.

Greeson, Philip E., et al., eds. 1979. *Wetland Functions and Values: The State of Our Understanding.* Minneapolis: American Water Resources Association.

Gross, David, and Richard Berg. 1981. *Geology of the Kankakee River System in Kankakee County, Illinois.* Environmental Geology Notes 92. Champaign: Illinois State Geological Survey.

Hahn, Walter L. 1910. An Analytic Study of Faunal Changes in Indiana. *American Midland Naturalist*, vol. 1, no. 6 (February).

Hall, Fred. 1938. Eastern Mockingbird: Newton County. *Indiana Audubon Society Year Book*, vol. 16.

Halle, Louis J. 1947. *Spring in Washington.* New York: William Sloane.

Halsey, John, ed. 1912. *A History of Lake County, Illinois.* Chicago: Harmegnies & Howell.

Hamburgh, Mister. 1916. Minutes of Mr. Hamburgh's Journal. In *Travels in the American Colonies,* edited by Newton Mereness. New York: MacMillan. (CHS)

Hamilton, Louis, and Darroch, William, eds. 1916. *A Standard History of Jasper and Newton Counties, Indiana.* Chicago: Lewis Publishing Co.

Hancock, Joseph L. 1883. Impeded Migration and Destruction of Birds at Chicago. *Auk*, vol. 5 (October).

Handley, John. 1998. A Growing Dilemma. *Chicago Tribune*, November 22, sec. C, p. 1.

Haney, Alan. 1976. Letter to George Fell [Buffalo Grove Prairie], July 23. Files of Natural Land Institute, Rockford, Ill.

Hansel, Ardith, and W. H. Johnson. 1993. *Fluctuations of the Lake Michigan Lobe during the Late Wisconsin Subepisode.* ISGS Publications, reprint 1993F. Champaign: State Geological Survey Division, Illinois Department of Natural Resources.

Hansel, Ardith K., and David M. Mickelson. 1988. A Reevaluation of the Timing and Causes of High Lake Phases in the Lake Michigan Basin. *Quaternary Research*, vol. 29.

Hanson, Harold C. 1965. *The Giant Canada Goose.* Carbondale: Southern Illinois University Press.

Hanson, Philip. 1975a. Wolf Road Prairie. *Field Museum of Natural History Bulletin* (February).

———. 1975b. A Vegetational Study of the Gensburg-Markham Prairie. Master's thesis, Northeastern Illinois University.

———. 1977. Treasures of the Des Plaines. *Field Museum of Natural History Bulletin*, vol. 48, no. 7 (July–August).

———. 1981. The Presettlement Vegetation of the Plain of Glacial Lake Chicago in Cook County, Illinois. In *Proceedings of the Sixth North American Prairie Conference,* edited by Ronald Stuckey and Karen Reese. Columbus: Ohio Biological Survey Notes.

Harkness, W. J. K., and J. R. Dymond. 1961. *The Lake Sturgeon.* Toronto: Ontario Department of Lands and Forests.

Harnsberger, Caroline T. 1977. *Winnetka: The Biography of a Village.* Evanston, Ill.: Schori Press.

Harpel, Charles. Scrapbooks on "Chicago Men and Events," 1880s and 1890s—ser. A;

Scrapbooks of "Clippings Relating to Chicago," 1880s and 1890s—ser. B. Chicago Historical Society.

Harper, Robert A. 1950. Recreational Occupance of the Moraine Lake Region of Northeastern Illinois and Southeastern Wisconsin. Ph. D. diss., University of Chicago.

Harper, Samuel. 1928. *A Hoosier Tramp*. Chicago: Prairie Club.

Harris, Larry. 1984. *The Fragmented Forest*. Chicago: University of Chicago Press.

Havera, Stephen P. 1987. The Historic Illinois—Once Changed, Always Changed? In *Management of the Illinois River System: The 1990s and Beyond*. Special Report 16. Urbana: University of Illinois Water Resources Center.

Hay, O. P. 1887. The Massasauga and Its Habits. *American Naturalist*, vol. 21, no. 3 (March).

Hayes, William P. 1949. Development of the Forest Preserve District of Cook County, Illinois. Master's thesis, DePaul University.

Heidorn, Randy. 1990. Purple Loosestrife (*Lythrum salicaria* L.). *Vegetation Management Guidelines*, vol. 1, no. 17. Springfield: Illinois Nature Preserves Commission.

Heidorn, Randy, et al. 1991. *Northeastern Illinois Wetland Survey for Endangered and Threatened Birds*. Technical Report no. 1. Springfield: Illinois Department of Conservation, Division of Natural Heritage.

Heilbrun, Lois, ed. 1980. Eightieth Christmas Bird Count (1979–1980). *American Birds*, vol. 34, no. 4 (July).

———. 1983. Eighty-third Christmas Bird Count (1982–1983). *American Birds*, vol. 37, no. 4 (July–August).

Helmer, Dorothy. 1949. The Upland Sandpiper. *Audubon Bulletin*, no. 69 (March).

Hemenway, Henry B. 1903. Oaks Are Old Residents. *The Evanston Index*, September 5.

Henderson, Harold. 1988. Saved from the Sandsuckers. *Chicago Reader*, October 7.

———. 1996. A Wing and a Prayer. *Chicago Reader*, June 28.

Henderson, John. 1881. Was the Antelope Hunted by the Indians on the Prairies of Illinois? *American Field*, vol. 16–17 (November 5).

Hendrickson, Walter. 1970. Robert Kennicott, an Early Professional Naturalist in Illinois. *Transactions Illinois State Academy of Science*, vol. 63, no. 1.

Hennepin, Louis. 1880. *Description of Louisiana*. Translated by John Gilmary Shea. New York: John G. Shea. Reprinted, March of America Facsimile Series no. 30, Ann Arbor, Mich.: University Microfilms, 1966.

Henshaw, H. W. 1881. On Some of the Causes Affecting the Decrease of Birds. *Bulletin of the Nuttall Ornithological Club*, vol. 6, no. 4 (October).

Henson, E. Bennette. 1966. *A Review of Great Lakes Benthos Research*. Great Lakes Research Division Publication no. 14. Ann Arbor: Great Lakes Research Division, University of Michigan.

Hepler, Lynn. 1990. Notes to the Naturalists of 2007 from Those of 1990: Periodic Cicadas at Ryerson. Manuscript. Ryerson Conservation Area, Riverwoods, Ill.

Herkert, James, ed. 1991a. *Endangered and Threatened Species of Illinois: Status and Distribution*. Vol. 1, *Plants*. Vol. 2, *Animals*. Springfield: Illinois Endangered Species Protection Board.

———. 1991b. Prairie Birds of Illinois: Population Response to Two Centuries of Habitat Change. In *Our Living Heritage: The Biological Resources of Illinois*, edited by Lawrence M. Page and Michael R. Jeffords. Illinois Natural History Survey Bulletin, vol. 34. Champaign, Ill.: Illinois Natural History Survey.

———. 1994. The Effects of Habitat Fragmentation on Midwestern Grassland Bird Communities. *Ecological Applications*, vol. 4, no. 3.

Herlocker, Irene S. 1976. The Hoosier Prairie Story—a Political Odyssey. In *Proceedings of Fifth
Midwest Prairie Conference*, edited by D. C. Glenn-Lewin and R. Q. Sanders. Ames: Iowa
State University.

Hey, Donald L., and Nancy S. Philippi. 1995. Flood Reduction through Wetland Restoration:
The Upper Mississippi River Basin as a Case History. *Restoration Ecology*, vol. 3, no. 1
(March).

Hickman, Scott. 1990. Evidence of Edge Species Attraction to Nature Trails within Deciduous
Forest. *Natural Areas Journal*, vol. 10, no.1.

———. 1992a. The Des Plaines River Wetlands Demonstration Project. Pt. 1. *Meadowlark*,
vol. 1, no. 1 (Summer).

———. 1992b. The Des Plaines River Wetlands Demonstrtion Project. Pt. 2. *Meadowlark*, vol. 1,
no. 2 (Fall).

Hiebert, Ronald D., et al. 1986. Vegetation Patterns in and among Pannes (Calcareous In-
tradunal Ponds) at the Indiana Dunes National Lakeshore, Indiana. *American Midland
Naturalist*, vol. 116, no. 2 (October).

Hight, Stephen D. 1993. Control of the Ornamental Purple Loosestrife (*Lythrum salicaria*) by
Exotic Organisms. In *Biological Pollution: The Control and Impact of Invasive Exotic Species*,
edited by Bill McKnight. Indianapolis: Indiana Academy of Science.

Higley, William K. 1885. A Paper on the Northern Pitcher-Plant or the Sidesaddle Flower,
Sarracenia purpurea L. *Bulletin of the Chicago Academy of Sciences*, vol. 1, no. 5.

Higley, William K., and Charles S. Raddin. 1891. The Flora of Cook County, Illinois, and a
Part of Lake County, Indiana. *Bulletin of the Chicago Academy of Sciences*, vol. 2, no. 11.

Hill, E. J. 1879. The Geographical Range of *Petalostemum foliosum* Gray, in Illinois. *Botanical
Gazette*, vol. 4.

———. 1892a. Late Summer Flowers on the Prairie. *Garden and Forest*, vol. 5, no. 236 (August 31).

———. 1892b. Notes on the Flora of Chicago and Vicinity. *Botanical Gazette*, vol. 17, no. 8
(August).

———. 1893. Coast Dune Flora of Lake Michigan. *Garden and Forest*, vol. 6, nos. 255 and 258
(January 11 and February 1).

———. 1894. Prairie Woodlands. *Garden and Forest*, vol. 7, no. 347 (October 17).

———. 1895. A Season with the Native Orchids. *Garden and Forest*, vol. 8, no. 399 (October 16).

———. 1896. Sand Dunes of Northern Indiana and Their Flora. *Garden and Forest*, vol. 9, nos.
445, 447, 448, and 449 (September 2, 16, 23, and 30).

Hill, Libby. 1991. Oaks versus Maples: An Inquiry into Ecological Restoration in Northeastern
Illinois. Paper prepared for the graduate course "Natural Environment in Winter."
Northeastern Illinois University, Chicago.

———. 1992. A Management Proposal for Dwight Perkins Woods. Report to Cook County
Forest Preserve District, River Forest, Ill.

———. 1993. Cattail Physiology and Ecology, and Implications for Management. Paper prepared for "Seminar in Wetlands and Streams." Northeastern Illinois University, Chicago.

Hinchman, Lynea. 1990. Massive Monarch Migration. *Indiana Audubon Quarterly*, vol. 68, no. 1
(February).

Historical Information, Warren Dunes. [1970]. Current and Historical Information, Warren Dunes State Park and Warren Woods (E. K. Warren and Family.) Five-page fact sheet in files of Gerard Donnelly, Morton Arboretum, Lisle, Ill.

History of McHenry County, Illinois. 1885. Chicago: Inter-State Publishing Co.

Hoffman, Charles. 1882. *A Winter in the West.* Chicago: Fergus Printing Co. (CHS)

Hoffman, Cliff O., and Jack L. Gottschang. 1977. Numbers, Distribution, and Movements of a Raccoon Population in a Suburban Residential Community. *Journal of Mammalogy,* vol. 58, no. 4 (November).

Hoffmeister, Donald F. 1989. *Mammals of Illinois.* Urbana and Chicago: University of Illinois Press.

Holden, Charles. 1882. Good Old Times: The Old Settlers' Recollections of the Way Things Were Done in 1836. *Chicago Times,* June 6. In Harpel Scrapbook, ser. A, 2:62–63. (CHS)

Homoya, Michael A. 1993. *Orchids of Indiana.* Bloomington and Indianapolis: Indiana Academy of Sciences.

Homoya, Michael A., et al. 1985. The Natural Regions of Indiana. *Transactions of the Indiana Academy of Science,* vol. 94.

Horton, Minnie G. 1936. A Desert That Blooms—the Waukegan Moors. *Garden Glories.* In Dunesland Preservation Society Archives, Illinois Beach State Park, Zion.

Hou, Joseph. 1978. *The Myth and Truth about Ginseng.* South Brunswick and New York: A. S. Barnes & Co.

Hough, Emerson. 1873. Chicago and the West. *Forest and Stream.*

———. 1875. Chicago and the West. *Forest and Stream.*

———. 1889a. Shooting Clubs of Chicago—no.1: The Fox Lake District. *Forest and Stream.*

———. 1889b. Shooting Clubs of Chicago—no. 5: The Tolleston Club. *Forest and Stream* (February 7).

———. 1889c. Shooting Clubs of Chicago—no.11: The Grand Calumet Heights Club. *Forest and Stream* (March 21).

Howard, Arthur D. 1951. A River Mussel Parasitic on a Salamander. *Natural History Miscellanea,* no. 77 (January 19).

Hoy, Philo P. 1853. Notes on the Ornithology of Wisconsin. *Proceedings of the Philadelphia Academy of Sciences* (March 2).

———. 1879. Fauna of Wisconsin. In *The History of Racine and Kenosha Counties, Wisconsin.* Chicago: Western Historical Co.

———. 1883. Catalogue of the Cold-Blooded Vertebrates of Wisconsin. In *Atlas of the Geological Survey of Wisconsin, 1873–1879,* by Thomas C. Chamberlin et al. Vol. 1. [Milwaukee, Wis.] : Milwaukee Lithographic & Engraving Co.

Hubbard, Gurdon S. 1969. *The Autobiography of Gurdon Saltonstall Hubbard.* New York: Citadel Press.

Hubbs, Carl L., and Karl F. Lagler. 1958. *Fishes of the Great Lakes Region.* Ann Arbor: University of Michigan Press.

Hulsberg, Edmund. 1917. Spring Census and Migration Data: LaGrange. *Audubon Bulletin* (Spring).

Hunt, Richard A., et al. 1976. *The Sandhill Crane in Wisconsin.* Research Report 86. Madison: Wisconsin Department of Natural Resources.

Hurley, Bill. 1976a. Bulldozers vs. Conservationists over Roadwork. *Buffalo Grove Herald*, [August?]. (NLI)

———. 1976b. Ecologists Fight to Save Virgin Land. *Buffalo Grove Herald*, September 3. (NLI)

Hynes, H. B. N. 1970. *The Ecology of Running Waters.* Toronto: University of Toronto Press.

Illinois Department of Conservation. 1994. *Aquatic Plants: Their Identification and Management.* Fishery Bulletin no. 4. Springfield, Ill.: Department of Conservation, Division of Fisheries.

Illinois Department of Natural Resources. 1994. Background Qs and As for the Joliet Army Ammunition Plant, Will County, Ill. Photocopy obtained from Illinois Department of Natural Resources, Midewin National Tallgrass Prairie, Wilmington, Ill.

———. 1996. Background Information on the History of the [Joliet Army] Arsenal. Photocopy obtained from Illinois Department of Natural Resources, Midewin National Tallgrass Prairie, Wilmington, Ill.

Illinois Nature Preserves Commission. 1976. Registry of Endangered, Threatened, Vulnerable, and Rare Species of Illinois: Bobcat. Illinois Nature Preserves Commission, Springfield.

Indiana Department of Natural Resources. 1990. *Water Resource Availability in the Kankakee River Basin, Indiana.* Indianapolis: Indiana Department of Natural Resources.

———. 1994. Peak Fall Counts of Sandhill Cranes at Jasper-Pulaski Fish and Wildlife Area. Indianapolis: Division of Fish and Wildlife, Indiana Department of Natural Resources, Indianapolis.

Indiana Division of Nature Preserves. 1991. *Directory of Indiana's Dedicated Nature Preserves.* Indianapolis: Indiana Department of Natural Resources.

Injerd, Daniel. 1987. Illinois' Lake Michigan Water Diversion. In *Management of the Illinois River System: The 1990s and Beyond.* Special Report 16. Urbana: University of Illinois Water Resources Center.

Irwin, Roderick R., and John C. Downey. 1973. *Annotated Checklist of the Butterflies of Illinois.* Biological Notes no. 81. Urbana: Illinois Natural History Survey.

Isaacs, Marion. n.d. *The Kankakee: River of History.* N.p. In collections of DeMotte, Ind., and Rensselaer, Ind., Public Libraries.

Ivens, J. Loreena, et al. 1981. *The Kankakee River Yesterday and Today.* Champaign: Illinois Department of Energy and Natural Resources.

Jackson, Hartley H. T. 1961. *Mammals of Wisconsin.* Madison: University of Wisconsin Press.

Jasper-Newton Counties Genealogical Societies. 1985a. *History of Jasper County, Indiana.* Rensselaer, Ind.: Jasper-Newton Counties Genealogical Societies.

———. 1985b. *History of Newton County, Indiana.* Rensselaer, Ind.: Jasper-Newton Counties Genealogical Societies.

Jensen, Jens. 1928. Native Beeches in the Chicago Region. *Transactions of the Illinois Academy of Science*, vol. 21.

Johnson, Charles. 1896. *Angling in the Lakes of Northern Illinois.* Chicago: American Field Publishing Co.

Johnson, David B. 1984. Illinois' Winter Warbler Wonderland. *Illinois Audubon Bulletin*, no. 209 (Summer).

———. 1989. Spring Bird Count or Winter Warbler Wonderland. Pt. 2. *Illinois Birds and Birding*, vol. 5, no. 3 (July–September).

Johnson, Elmer W. 1998. *Executive Summary: Chicago Metropolis 2020.* Chicago: Commercial Club of Chicago.

Jones, A. D. 1838. *Illinois and the West.* Boston: Weeks, Jordan, & Co. (CHS)

Jones, Jon M., and James H. Witham. 1990. Post-translocation Survival and Movements of Metropolitan White-Tailed Deer. *Wildlife Society Bulletin,* vol. 18, no. 4.

Jones, Steve. 1992. After the Boom: The Demise of the Indiana Prairie Chicken. *Traces* (Spring).

Jonker, Fredrik P. 1938. *A Monograph of the Burmanniaceae.* Utrecht: Kemink en Zoon N. V. (MAL)

Joutel, Henri. 1905. Account of Joutel. In *The Journey of Rene Robert Cavelier Sieur de La Salle As Related by . . . His Trusted Subordinate, Henri Joutel,* edited and translated by Isaac Joslin Cox. Vol. 2. New York: A. S. Barnes & Co.

Juniper, B. E., et al. 1989. *The Carnivorous Plants.* London: Academic Press.

Keating, William. 1824. *Narrative of an Expedition to the Source of St. Peters River. . . .* Vol. 1. Philadelphia: Carey & Lea. (CHS)

Keibler, June D., and Steven Byers. 1993. Proposal for Dedication of Chicago Ridge Prairie as an Illinois Nature Preserve. Prepared for the Illinois Nature Preserves Commission, Springfield.

Keir, James R., and Deann D. Wilde. 1976. Observation of Swainson's Hawk Nesting in Northeastern Illinois. *Wilson Bulletin,* vol. 88, no. 4 (December).

Keller, Charles E. 1958. The Shorebird Families: Charadriidae, Scolopacidae, Recurvirostridae, and Phalaropidae of Indiana. Pt. 4. *Indiana Audubon Quarterly,* vol. 36, no. 1 (January).

Kemp, Harold. 1927. Observation of Geographic Minutiae as Exemplified by a Survey in Bloom Township, Cook County. Master's thesis, University of Chicago.

Kendall, Peter. 1994. Long in Exile from City, coyotes Set up Den, Make Selves at Home. *Chicago Tribune,* April 20.

Kendeigh, S. Charles. 1982. Bird Populations in East Central Illinois: Fluctuations, Variations, and Development over a Half-Century. *Illinois Biological Monographs,* no. 52.

Kennicott, Robert. 1855. Catalogue of Animals Observed in Cook County, Illinois. *Transactions of Illinois State Agricultural Society.*

———. 1857. The Quadrupeds of Illinois, Injurious and Beneficial to the Farmer. *Transactions of Illinois State Agricultural Society.*

———. 1858. *The Quadrupeds of Illinois, Injurious and Beneficial to the Farmer.* Agriculture Report, 1857. U.S. Patent Office Report.

———. 1859. *The Quadrupeds of Illinois, Injurious and Beneficial to the Farmer.* Agriculture Report, 1858. U.S. Patent Office Report.

Kenton, Edna, ed. 1925. *The Jesuit Relations and Allied Documents.* New York: Albert and Charles Boni.

Kerr, Kathryn, and John White. 1981. A Volunteer-Supported Effort to Find and Preserve Prairie and Savanna Remnants in Illinois Cemeteries. In *Proceedings of the Sixth North American Prairie Conference,* edited by Ronald Stuckey and Karen Reese. Columbus: Ohio Biological Survey.

Kilburn, Paul D. 1959. The Forest-Prairie Ecotone in Northeastern Illinois. *American Midland Naturalist,* vol. 62, no. 1 (July).

Killey, Myrna M. 1998. *Illinois' Ice Age Legacy.* GeoScience Education Series 14. Champaign: Illinois State Geological Survey.

Kindscher, Kelly. 1987. *Edible Wild Plants of the Prairie: An Ethnobotanical Guide.* Lawrence: University Press of Kansas.

King, James L. 1982. *The Prairies of Illinois.* Information Sheet no. 14. Prairie Preservation Society of Ogle County. March.

Kingman, John. 1842. *Letters Written by John Kingman While on a Tour to Illinois and Wisconsin in the Summer of 1838.* Hingham, Mass.: J. Farmer.

Kirkland, Caroline. 1858. Illinois in Springtime with a Look at Chicago. *Atlantic Monthly,* vol. 11 (September). (CHS)

Kleen, Vernon M. 1983. Report and Results: '83 Statewide Spring Bird Count. *Illinois Audubon Bulletin,* no. 206 (Fall).

Klehm, Daniel. 1992. The Invisible Killer. *Bird Watcher's Digest,* vol. 14, no. 4 (March–April).

Klingenberg, William. n.d. Anecdotes and Personal Experiences in Early History of Barrington. Manuscript, Barrington Historical Museum, Barrington, Ill.

Knight, Robert, and Lucius Zeuch. 1930. Mount Joliet: Its Place in Illinois History and Its Location. *Journal of the Illinois State Historical Society,* vol. 23, no. 1 (April).

Kobal, Scott. 1990. Abundance, Habitat Selection, and Food Habits of Grassland Birds in Three Non-native Grasslands in Northern Illinois. Master's thesis, University of Wisconsin—Stevens Point.

Koelz, Walter. 1926. *Fishing Industry of the Great Lakes.* U.S. Bureau of Fisheries Document no. 1001. Washington D.C.: Government Printing Office.

———. 1929. Corregonid Fishes of the Great Lakes. *Bulletin of the U.S. Bureau of Fisheries,* vol. 43, pt. 2.

Kohring, Margaret. 1981. Saving Michigan's Railroad Strip Prairies. In *Proceedings of the Sixth North American Prairie Conference,* edited by R. Stuckey and K. Reese. Columbus: Ohio Biological Survey.

Koprowski, John L. 1991. Mixed Species Mating Chases of Fox Squirrels, *Sciurus niger,* and Eastern Gray Squirrels, *S. carolinensis. Canadian Field Naturalist,* vol. 105.

Krampert, Alfred P. 1972. The Chiwaukee Story. In *Proceedings of the Second Midwest Prairie Conference,* edited by J. Zimmerman. Madison and Parkside: University of Wisconsin.

Krekeler, Carl H. 1981. Ecosystem Study of the Indiana Dunes National Lakeshore. Vol. 2, The Biota. Report 81-01. Indiana Dunes National Lakeshore Research Program, Porter.

Kriska, Nadine, and Daniel Young. 1995. A Survey to Determine the Occurrence of the American Burying Beetle, *Nicrophorus americanus* Olivier, in Northern and Central Wisconsin. A joint proposal to the 1995–96 Wisconsin/Hilldale Undergraduate/Faculty Research Fellowships, Madison.

Kuchenberg, Tom. 1978. *Reflections in a Tarnished Mirror: The Use and Abuse of the Great Lakes.* Sturgeon Bay, Wis.: Golden Glow Publishing.

Kumlien, L., and N. Hollister. 1903. The Birds of Wisconsin. *Wisconsin Natural History Society Bulletin,* vol. 3. Reprinted, Madison: Wisconsin Society for Ornithology, 1951, with revisions by A. W. Schorger.

Kummey, Anna P. 1942. Forbs of a Relict Prairie within the City Limits of Chicago. *Chicago Naturalist,* vol. 5.

Kurowski, Ronald C. n.d. *Kettle Moraine—Prairie Country.* Milwaukee: Wisconsin Department of Natural Resources, Southeast District Headquarters.

Kurta, Allen. 1980. Notes on Summer Bat Activity at Michigan Caves. *National Speleological Society Bulletin*, vol. 42, no. 4 (October).

Kwak, Thomas. 1993. The Kankakee River: A Case Study and Management Recommendations for a Stream Diverse in Habitat, Fauna, and Human Values. In *Proceedings of the Symposium on Restoration Planning for the Rivers of the Mississippi River Ecosystem*, edited by Larry Hesse et al. Biological Report 19. Washington, D.C.: National Biological Survey.

Lach, Jeanette. 1996. MCCD Battles Wetland Weed with Bugs. *Crystal Lake (Ill.) Northwest Herald*, July 24.

Lagler, Karl F. 1943. Food Habits and Economic Relations of the Turtles of Michigan with Special Reference to Fish Management. *American Midland Naturalist*, vol. 29, no. 2 (March).

Lagler, Karl F., and J. Clark Salyer. 1947. Food and Habits of the Common Watersnake, *Natrix s. sipedon*, in Michigan. *Papers of the Michigan Academy of Science, Arts and Letters*, vol. 31.

Laird, Christopher A., and Lawrence M. Page. 1996. Non-native Fishes Inhabiting the Streams and Lakes of Illinois. *Illinois Natural History Bulletin*, vol. 35, article 1 (March).

Lake County Stormwater Management Commission. 1994. *Lake County Watershed Development Ordinance of Lake County, Illinois: Draft: Recommended Federal/State Changes: Voluntary SMC Changes*. Libertyville, Ill.: The Commission.

Lake County Forest Preserve District. 1988. Control of White-Tailed Deer in Ryerson Conservation Area. Proposal to Illinois Department of Conservation, Springfield.

———. 1992. Deer Management Application to the Illinois Department of Conservation and Illinois Nature Preserves Commission: Control of White-Tailed Deer in the Lake County Forest Preserves. In the files of the Illinois Nature Preserves Commission, Springfield, and the Lake Country Forest Preserve District, Libertyville, Ill.

———. 1993. Deer Management Application to the Illinois Department of Conservation and Illinois Nature Preserves Commission: Control of White-Tailed Deer in the Lake County Forest Preserves. In the files of the Illinois Nature Preserves Commission, Springfield, and the Lake Country Forest Preserve District, Libertyville, Ill.

Landing, James. 1966. Jaeger Migration in Northwestern Indiana. *Indiana Audubon Quarterly*, vol. 44, no. 2 (May).

———. 1986. *Conceptual Plan for the Lake Calumet Ecological Park: Chicago*. Chicago: Lake Calumet Study Committee.

Landwehr, William. n.d. Anecdotes and Personal Experiences in Early History of Barrington. Manuscript. Barrington Historical Museum, Barrington, Ill.

Lannoo, Michael J., ed. 1998. *Status and Conservation of Midwestern Amphibians*. Iowa City: University of Iowa Press.

Lanyon, Richard, and Cecil Lui-Hing. 1987. MSDGC Activities in the Upper Illinois Basin. In *Management of the Illinois River System: The 1990s and Beyond*. Special Report 16. Urbana: University of Illinois Water Resources Center.

LaPointe, Joe. 1953. Case Report of a Bite from the Massasauga, *Sistrurus catenatus catenatus. Copeia*, no. 2.

Latrobe, Charles. 1835. *The Rambler in North America*. Vol. 2. London: Seely & Burnside. (CHS)

Lawson, Edward S. 1974. *A History of Warren Township*. Gurnee, Ill.: Warren Newport Public Library.

Leach, Eugene W., Collection. Newspaper Columns and Notes. University of Wisconsin—Parkside, Kenosha.

Least Heat-Moon, William. 1991. *PrairyErth*. Boston: Houghton-Mifflin.

Lebaron, Geoffrey, ed. 1998. Ninety-eighth Christmas Bird Count (1997–1998). *American Birds*.

Leitner, Lawrence A. 1987. Three Decades of Change in Three Southeastern Wisconsin Woodlots. *University of Wisconsin—Milwaukee Field Station Bulletin*, vol. 20, no. 2.

Leopold, Aldo. 1970. *A Sand County Almanac*. San Francisco and New York: Sierra Club/Ballantine Book.

Lesquereux, L. 1865. On the Origin and Formation of Prairies. *American Journal of Science and Arts*, vol. 39, no. 117.

Levinge, R. G. A. 1846. *Echoes from the Backwoods, Or, Sketches of Transatlantic Life*. Vol. 2. London: Henry Colburn. (CHS)

Lewis, Randall B., and James R. Brice. 1980. A Comparison of the Past and Present Freshwater Mussel Fauna of the Kankakee River in Illinois. *Natural History Miscellanea*, no. 211 (October 15).

Leydet, François. 1988. *The Coyote: Defiant Song Dog of the West*. Norman: University of Oklahoma Press.

Lindsey, Alton A., ed. 1966. *Natural Features of Indiana*. Indianapolis: Indiana Academy of Science.

Ling, F. E. 1935. The Kankakee in the Old Days. *Bulletin of New York Zoological Society*, vol. 38, no. 6 (November–December).

Lloyd, Francis E. 1942. *The Carnivorous Plants*. Waltham, Mass.: Chronica Botanica Co.

Lloyd, James E. 1966. *Studies on the Flash Communication System in Photinus Fireflies*. Museum of Zoology Miscellaneous Publications no. 130. Ann Arbor: University of Michigan Press.

———. 1984. Lights in the Summer Darkness. In *1985 Yearbook of Science and the Future*. Chicago: Encyclopaedia Britannica.

Lloyd, Monte, et al. 1983. A Simple Mendelian Model for 13 and 17 Year Life Cycles of Periodical Cicadas, with Historical Evidence of Hybridization between Them. *Evolution*, vol. 37, no. 6.

Lloyd, Monte, and Richard Karban. 1983. Chorusing Centers of Periodical Cicadas. *Journal of the Kansas Entomological Society*, vol. 56, no. 3 (August 11).

Logan, James. 1838. *Notes of a Journey through Canada, the United States of America, and the West Indies*. Edinburgh: Fraser & Co. (CHS)

Lomolino, Mark V., et al. 1995. Ecology and Conservation of the Endangered American Burying Beetle (*Nicrophorus americanus*). *Conservation Biology*, vol. 9, no. 3 (June).

Long, Charles A. 1995. Stone Marten in Southeast Wisconsin, U.S.A. *Small Carnivore Conservation: The Newsletter and Journal of the IUCN/SSC Mustelid, Viverrid and Procynid Specialist Group*, no. 13 (October).

Long, L. H. 1817. Letter to George Graham, Acting Secretary of War. *National Register*, vol. 3, no. 13 (March 29).

Lopinot, A. C. 1972. *Channelized Streams and Ditches of Illinois*. Special Fisheries Report no. 35. Springfield: Illinois Department of Conservation.

Lorenz, Ralph. 1944. Eastern White Pine as a Timber Tree in Illinois. *Transactions of Illinois Academy of Science*, vol. 37.

Lorimer, Craig G. 1987. The Role of Fire in the Perpetuation of Oak Forests. In *Eighth Northern Illinois Prairie Workshop*. Sponsored by Forest Preserve District of Will County, Joliet, Ill.

Lowther. 1883. Then and Now—the Extermination of Game. *American Field* (September 22).

Ludwig, Daniel R., et al. 1987. *A Survey of the Fish Populations within the Forest Preserve District of Du Page County.* Wheaton, Ill.: Forest Preserve District of DuPage County.

Lunn, Elizabeth T. 1982. *Plants of the Illinois Dunesland.* [Waukegan, Ill.]: Illinois Dunesland Preservation Society.

Lyon, Marcus W. 1923. Notes on the Mammals of the Dune Region of Porter County, Indiana. *Proceedings of the Indiana Academy of Science*, vol. 31.

———. 1936. Mammals of Indiana. *American Midland Naturalist*, vol. 17.

Lyon, Marcus W., and Charles A. Bishop. 1936. Bite of the Prairie Rattlesnake. *Proceedings of the Indiana Academy of Science*, vol. 45

Lyon, William. 1937. First Record of Common Terns Nesting in Illinois. *Audubon Bulletin*, no. 27.

Maas, P. J. M., et al. 1986. *Flora Neotropica.* Monograph no. 42: Burmanniaceae. New York: New York Botanical Garden.

Madany, Michael. 1974. An Ecological History of Thornton-Lansing Road and Jurgensen's Woods Nature Preserve[s]. Independent study, Illiana Christian High School, Lansing, Ill.

———. 1981. A Floristic Survey of Savannas in Illinois. In *Proceedings of the Sixth North American Prairie Conference*, edited by R. Stuckey and K. Reese. Columbus: Ohio Biological Survey.

Madson, John. 1982. *Where the Sky Begins.* San Francisco: Sierra Club Books.

Makarewicz, Joseph C., et al. 1994. Epilimnetic Phytoplankton and Zooplankton Biomass and Species Composition in Lake Michigan, 1983 to 1992. U.S. Environmental Protection Agency, Great Lakes National Program Office, Chicago.

Malecki, Richard A., et al. 1993. Biological Control of Purple Loosestrife. *BioScience*, vol. 43, no. 10 (November).

Malo, Marie G. 1998. Public Sightings of Coyotes and Red Foxes in DuPage County, Illinois. Report to Willowbrook Wildlife Center, Forest Preserve District of DuPage County, Wheaton, Ill.

Manogaran, Chelvadurai. 1977. Geography and Agriculture. In *Racine: Growth and Change in a Wisconsin County*, edited by Nicholas Burckel. Racine: Racine County Board of Supervisors.

Marcisz, Walter. 1994. Lake Calumet: Birders in Paradox. *Meadowlark*, vol. 3, no. 4.

Marler, Sam. 1994. Biological Opinion to Federal Highway Administration of Effects on Mitchell's Satyr Created by US-31 Freeway Bypass in Berrien County, Michigan. Log no. 94-R3-ELFO-1. U.S. Fish and Wildlife Service, Fort Snelling, Minn.

Marsh, Frank. 1978. *Prairie Tree: Early Days on the Northern Illinois Prairie.* New York: Vantage Press.

Marsh, Leland C. 1955. The Cattail Story. *Garden Journal* (July–August).

Martin, Nancy. 1989. Ginseng Renaissance. *Outdoor Highlights*, vol. 17, no. 16 (August).

Masters, Linda A. 1995. *Thismia americana* N. E. Pfeiffer, a History. *Erigenia*, no. 14 (November).

Matthiessen, Peter. 1959. *Wildlife in America.* New York: Viking Press.

McClain, William E., and Sherrie L. Elzinga. 1994. The Occurrence of Prairie and Forest Fires in Illinois and Other Midwestern States, 1679 to 1854. *Erigenia*, vol. 13 (June).

McCormick, Joseph. 1915. *A Standard History of Starke County, Indiana.* New York: Lewis Publishing Co.

McCurdy, G. E., ed. 1914–15. *Report of the Survey and Proposed Improvement of the Fox River.* Springfield: State of Illinois Rivers and Lakes Commission.

McKinley, Daniel. 1978. The Carolina Parakeet in Illinois: A Recapitulation. *Indiana Audubon Quarterly*, vol. 56, no. 2.

———. 1980. The Balance of Decimating Factors and Recruitment in the Extinction of the Carolina Parakeet. *Indiana Audubon Quarterly*, vol. 58, nos. 1–3.

McManis, Douglas R. 1964. *The Initial Evaluation and Utilization of the Illinois Prairies, 1815–1840.* Chicago: University of Chicago, Department of Geography.

McNeely, Jeffrey A., and Paul S. Wachtel. 1990. *Soul of the Tiger.* New York: Paragon House.

McPherson, E. Gregory, et al. 1993. *Chicago's Evolving Urban Forest: Initial Report of the Chicago Urban Forest Climate Project.* Report NE-169. Radnor, Pa.: U.S. Forest Service, Northeastern Forest Experiment Station.

Melton, Jody. 1987. Setbacks Spell Progress. *Outdoor Indiana*, vol. 52, no. 10 (November).

Mendelson, Jon. 1998. Restoration from the Perspective of Recent Forest History. *Transactions of the Wisconsin Academy of Science, Arts and Letters*, vol. 86.

Menges, Eric S., and Thomas V. Armentano. 1985. Successional Relationships of Pine Stands at Indiana Dunes. *Transactions of Indiana Academy of Science*, vol. 94.

Merritt, H. Clay. 1904. *The Shadow of a Gun.* Chicago: F. T. Peterson Co.

Meyer, Alfred H. 1936. The Kankakee "Marsh" of Northern Indiana and Illinois. *Papers of the Michigan Academy of Science, Arts and Letters*, vol. 21.

———. 1950. Fundament Vegetation of the Calumet Region, Northwest Indiana–Northeast Illinois. *Papers of the Michigan Academy of Science, Arts and Letters*, vol. 36.

———. 1956. Circulation and Settlement Patterns of the Calumet Region of Northwest Indiana and Northeast Illinois. Pt. 2. *Annals of the Association of American Geographers*, vol. 46.

Mierzwa, Kenneth S. 1986. A Preliminary Report on the Spring Breeding Ecology of the Blue-Spotted Salamander, *Ambystoma laterale*, Ryerson Conservation Area, Lake County, Illinois. Report to the Forest Preserve District of Lake County, Libertyville, Ill.

———. 1988. Amphibians and Reptiles in Will County, Illinois. Prepared for the Forest Preserve District of Will County, Joliet, Ill.

———. 1989. Results of the 1989 Herpetofauna Survey in McHenry County, Illinois with Notes on Other Vertebrates. Report to McHenry County Conservation District, Woodstock, Ill.

Miller, Orson K. 1980. *Mushrooms of North America.* New York: E. P. Dutton.

Miller, Stacy. 1996. Little Brown Bats of Volo Bog. *Bog Log*, vol. 13, no. 2 (Summer).

Mills, Edward L., et al. 1993. Exotic Species in the Great Lakes: A History of Biotic Crises and Anthropogenic Introductions. *Journal of Great Lakes Research*, vol. 19, no. 1.

Mills, Harlow, et al. 1966. *Man's Effect on the Fish and Wildlife of the Illinois River.* Illinois Natural History Survey Biological Notes, no. 57. Champaign, Ill.: Illinois Natural History Survey.

Milner, John W. 1874. Report of the Fisheries of the Great Lakes: The Result of Inquiries Prosecuted in 1871 and 1872. In *Report of the U.S. Commissioner of Fisheries for 1871 and 1872.* Washington D.C.: Government Printing Office.

Milosevich, Joe B. 1990. Lake Renwick: From Gravel Quarry to Nature Preserve. *Illinois Audubon*, no. 233 (Summer).

———. 1994. A Tale of Two Colonies. *Meadowlark*, vol. 3, no. 1.

Minton, Sherman A. 1972. *Amphibians and Reptiles of Indiana.* Indianapolis: Indiana Academy of Science.

Mitchell, J. K. 1968. Indecision. In *Come Fly to the Prairie* by Leone Schmidt. Mendota, Ill.: Wayside Press.

Mitchell, S. A. 1837. *Illinois in 1837.* Philadelphia: Mitchell. (CHS)

Mitsch, William J., et al. 1979. *The Momence Wetlands of the Kankakee River in Illinois—an Assessment of Their Value.* Document no. 79/17. Chicago: Illinois Institute of Natural Resources.

Mitsch, William J., and James G. Gosselink. 1986. *Wetlands.* New York: Van Nostrand Reinhold Co.

Mlodinow, Steven. 1984. *Chicago Area Birds.* Chicago: Chicago Review Press.

Moffett, James W. 1956. Recent Changes in the Deepwater Fish Populations of Lake Michigan. *Transactions of the American Fisheries Society.*

Mohlenbrock, Robert H. 1975. *Guide to the Vascular Flora of Illinois.* Carbondale: Southern Illinois University Press.

———. 1985. Recent Developments in *Thismia americana* N. E. Pfeiffer. *Erigenia*, no. 5.

Moll, Edward O. 1988. Status Survey of Three Rare and Endangered Turtles in Illinois. Report to the Illinois Endangered Species Protection Board, Springfield.

Moran, Robbin C. 1978a. Presettlement Vegetation of Lake County, Illinois. In *Proceedings of Fifth Midwest Prairie Conference*, edited by D. C. Glenn-Lewin and R. Q. Landers. Ames: Iowa State University.

———. 1978b. Vascular Flora of the Ravines along Lake Michigan in Lake County, Illinois. *Michigan Botanist*, vol. 17.

———. 1981. Prairie Fens in Northeastern Illinois. In *Proceedings of the Sixth North American Prairie Conference*, edited by R. Stuckey and K. Reese. Columbus: Ohio Biological Survey.

Morleigh. 1842. *Life in the West: Back-Wood Leaves and Prairie Flowers . . .* London: Saunders & Otley. (CHS)

Morse, Douglass H. 1989. *American Warblers: An Ecological and Behavioral Perspective.* Cambridge, Mass.: Harvard University Press.

Morton, Julia F. 1975. Cattails (*Typha* spp.)—Weed Problem or Potential Crop? *Economic Botany*, vol. 29 (January–March).

Morton Arboretum. 1997. The Schulenberg Prairie. Morton Arboretum, Lisle, Ill.

Moseley, Edwin Lincoln. 1941. *Milk Sickness Caused by White Snakeroot.* Bowling Green: Ohio Academy of Science.

Moses, John, and Joseph Kirkland. 1895. *History of Chicago, Illinois.* Vol. 1. Chicago and New York: Munsell & Co.

Moy, Philip, and Richard Sparks. 1991. Value of Mussel Beds to Sport Fishing. Center for Aquatic Ecology Technical Report 91/17. Illinois Natural History Survey, Urbana.

Mueller, Helmut C., et al. 1977. The Periodic Invasions of Goshawks. *Auk*, vol. 94 (October).

Muenscher, Walter C. 1941. *Poisonous Plants of the United States.* New York: Macmillan.

Mumford, Russell E., and Charles E. Keller. 1984 *The Birds of Indiana.* Bloomington: Indiana University Press.

Mumford, Russell E., and Vivian Mumford. 1982. Preliminary Annotated List of the Birds of Jasper-Pulaski Fish and Wildlife Area, Indiana. *Indiana Audubon Quarterly*, vol. 60, no. 3 (August).

Mumford, Russell, and John O. Whitaker. 1982. *Mammals of Indiana*. Bloomington: Indiana University Press.

Mutt, Jose A. M. 1978. Swarming of *Entomobrya unostrigata* (Insecta: Collembola) in South Holland, Cook County, Illinois. *Transactions of the Illinois State Academy of Science*, vol. 71, no. 2.

Nature Conservancy Great Lakes Program. 1994. *The Conservation of Biological Diversity in the Great Lakes Ecosystem: Issues and Opportunities*. Chicago: Nature Conservancy Great Lakes Program.

Nearing, Helen, and Scott Nearing. 1970. *The Maple Sugar Book*. New York: Schocken Books.

Necker, Walter L. 1939. Records of Amphibians and Reptiles of the Chicago Region, 1935–1938. *Bulletin of the Chicago Academy of Sciences*, vol. 6, no. 1.

Nelson, Edward W. 1876. Birds of Northeastern Illinois. *Bulletin of the Essex Institute*, vol. 8. (CHS)

———. 1878. Fisheries of Chicago and Vicinity. In *Report of the Commissioner of Fish and Fisheries*. Washington D.C.: Government Printing Office.

Neumann, Robert. n.d. The History of Botanical Gardens, Formerly Trout Park. Handwritten notebook copied by Virginia Umberger in October 1960. Copy in possession of Marlin Bowles, myself, and probably others.

Neves, Richard J. 1993. A State-of-the-Unionids Address. In *Conservation and Management of Freshwater Mussels*, edited by K. S. Cummings et al. Rock Island, Ill.: Upper Mississippi River Conservation Committee.

Newton, Alfred F. 1973. A Systematic Revision of the Rove Beetle Genus *Platydracus* in North America. Ph.D. diss., Harvard University.

Nichols, Faye F. 1965. *The Kankakee*. New York: Theo. Gaus & Sons.

Niering, William A. 1985. *Wetlands*. New York: Alfred Knopf.

Nolan, Val. 1978. *Ecology and Behavior of the Prairie Warbler* Dendroica discolor. Ornithological Monograph no. 26. Washington D.C.: American Ornithologists Union.

Nordenholt, W. 1920. Oak Park. *Audubon Bulletin* (Spring).

Northeastern Illinois Planning Commission (NIPC). 1997a. *Reducing the Impacts of Urban Runoff: The Advantages of Alternative Site Design Approaches*. Chicago: NIPC.

———. 1997b. Source Book for Natural Landscaping for Local Officials. Chicago: NIPC.

Nuzzo, Victoria A. 1993a. Current and Historic Distribution of Garlic Mustard (*Alliaria petiolata*) in Illinois. *Michigan Botanist*, vol. 32.

———. 1993b. Distribution and Spread of the Invasive Biennial Garlic Mustard (*Alliaria petiolata*) in North America. In *Biological Pollution: The Control and Impact of Invasive Exotic Species*, edited by B. McKnight. Indianapolis: Indiana Academy of Science.

Ono, R. Dana, et al. 1983. *Vanishing Fishes of North America*. Washington, D.C.: Stone Wall Press.

Openlands Project. 1999. *Under Pressure: Land Consumption in the Chicago Region, 1998–2028*. Chicago: Openlands Project.

Opler, Paul. 1992. Management of Prairie Habitats for Insect Conservation. In Karner Blue Butterfly: Population and Habitat Viability Assessment Workshop (Briefing Book). WIll.DS and IUCN/SSC Captive Breeding Specialist Group, Zanesville, Ohio.

Owen Ayres & Associates. n.d. Ecological Study: Racine County, Wisconsin. Racine County Coastal Management Program, Geographic Area of Management Concern 16, Racine.

Packard, Stephen. 1986. Rediscovering the Tallgrass Savanna of Illinois. In *Proceedings of the Tenth North American Prairie Conference*, edited by A. Davis and G. Stanford. Dallas: Native Prairie Association of Texas.

Packard, Stephen, and Cornelia Mutel, eds. 1997. *The Tallgrass Restoration Handbook*. Washington D.C.: Island Press.

Packard, Stephen, and Jill Riddell. 1986. A Proposal for Preservation of Bluff Spring Fen by Dedication as an Illinois Nature Preserve. Presented to Illinois Nature Preserves Commission, Springfield.

Paddock, Stuart, et al. 1955. *Palatine Centennial Book*. Palatine, Ill.: Palatine Chamber of Commerce.

Paddock, Wendell. 1917. Impressions of the Warren Woods. *The Acorn*, vol. 26 (October 25).

Page, Lawrence M. 1985. The Crayfishes and Shrimps (Decapoda) of Illinois. *Illinois Natural History Survey Bulletin*, vol. 33, article 4 (September).

Page, Lawrence M., et al. 1990–91. Biologically Important Streams in Illinois. Center for Biodiversity Technical Report 1992. Illinois Natural History Survey, Champaign.

Paintin, Ruth Davis. 1929. The Morphology and Nature of a Prairie in Cook County, Illinois. *Transactions of the Illinois Academy of Science*, vol. 21.

Panzer, Ron. 1988. Management of Prairie Remnants for Insect Conservation. *Natural Areas Journal*, vol. 8, no. 2 (April).

Panzer, Ron, et al. 1995. Prevalence of Remnant Dependence among the Prairie- and Savanna-Inhabiting Insects of the Chicago Region. *Natural Areas Journal*, vol. 15, no. 2 (April).

Papajohn, George. 1991. City Coyote Returns to True Nature. *Chicago Tribune*, November 5.

Park, Orlando. 1948. Observations on the Migration of Monarch Butterflies through Evanston, Illinois, in September, 1948. *Natural History Miscellanea*, no. 30 (October 21).

———. 1949. A Notable Aggregation of Collembola. *Annals of the Entomological Society*, vol. 42.

Park, Orlando, et al. 1953. Pselaphid Beetles of an Illinois Prairie: The Population. *Ecological Monographs*, vol. 23, no. 1 (January).

Parker, A. A. 1835. *Trip to the West and Texas*. Concord, N.H.: White & Fisher. (CHS)

Parmalee, Paul W. 1967. *The Fresh-Water Mussels of Illinois*. Popular Science Series, vol. 8. Springfield: Illinois State Museum.

Partridge, Charles A. 1902. *History of Lake County* [Illinois]. Chicago: Munsell.

Paschke, John E., and John D. Alexander. 1970. *Soil Survey of Lake County, Illinois*. Washington D.C.: U.S. Department of Agriculture, Soil Conservation Service.

Paulding, James K. 1849. Illinois and the Prairies. *Graham's American Monthly*, vol. 18 (February).

Pavlovic, Noel B. 1994. Disturbance-Dependent Persistence of Rare Plants: Anthropogenic Impacts and Restoration Implications. In *Restoration of Endangered Species*, edited by M. L. Bowles and C. J. Whelan. London: Cambridge University Press.

Pearse, William. n.d. *Autobiography of William Samuel Pearse: 1824–1909*. n.p. [CHS].

Peattie, Donald Culross. 1922. The Atlantic Coastal Element in the Flora of the Great Lakes. *Rhodora*, vol. 24, nos. 280–81 (April–May).

———. 1925. Hikes around Chicago: no. 3, Beverly Hills; no. 4, Aetna to Hobart; no. 5, Wolf Lake; no. 8, Blue Island to Harvey. *Chicago Daily News*, August 28, September 11, September 18, October 9 (respectively).

———. 1938. *A Prairie Grove*. New York: Literary Guild of America.

————. 1966. *A Natural History of Trees of Eastern and Central North America*. Boston: Houghton-Mifflin.

Pennak, Robert W. 1953. *Fresh-water Invertebrates of the United States*. New York: Ronald Press.

Pepoon, Herman S. 1927. *An Annotated Flora of the Chicago Area*. Chicago: Chicago Academy of Sciences.

Perkins, Dwight, comp. 1904. *Report of the Special Park Commission to the City Council of Chicago on the Subject of a Metropolitan Park System*. Chicago: W. J. Hartman Co.

Perkins, J. P. 1964. Seventeen Flyways over the Great Lakes. Pt. 1. *Audubon Magazine* (September–October).

————. 1965. Seventeen Flyways over the Great Lakes. Pt. 2. *Audubon Magazine* (January–February).

Perry, Hazel Belle. 1969. Old Elgin Tales: pt. 1, Early Owners and Promoters of Trout Park; pt. 2, Trout Park and the Botanical Gardens; pt. 3, Last of the Trout Park Stories. *Elgin Free Press*, May 14, 21, and 28 (respectively).

Peterson, Roger Tory, ed. 1957. *The Bird Watcher's Anthology*. New York: Harcourt, Brace & Co.

Peyton, John. 1869. *Over the Alleghanies and across the Prairies*. London: Simpkin, Marshall, & Co. (CHS)

Pfeiffer, Norma E. 1914. Morphology of *Thismia americana*. *Botanical Gazette*, vol. 57 (February).

————. 1952. Letter to Dr. Theodore Just. Archives of the Botany Department of the Field Museum.

Philips, Christine. 1994. Death Traps: Birds and Urban Mortality. *Meadowlark*, vol. 3, no. 4.

Pianka, Eric. 1974. *Evolutionary Ecology*. New York: Harper & Row.

Pierce, Bessie Louise, ed. 1933. *As Others See Chicago*. Chicago: University of Chicago Press.

Pietsch, Lyle R. 1954. White-Tailed Deer Populations in Illinois. [*Illinois Natural History Survey*] *Biological Notes*, no. 34.

————. 1956. The Beaver in Illinois. *Transactions of Illinois State Academy of Science*, vol. 49.

Pigage, Jon C., and Helen K. Pigage. 1994. The Western Harvest Mouse (*Reithrodontomys megalotis*) Moves to Northeastern Illinois. *Transactions of the Illinois State Academy of Science*, vol. 87, nos. 1–2.

Poggi, Edith Muriel. 1934. *The Prairie Province of Illinois*. Urbana: University of Illinois Press.

Polls, Irwin, et al. 1994. *Fact or Fiction: Has the Water Quality Improved in Chicago Area Waterways?* Report no. 94-23. Chicago: Metropolitan Water Reclamation District of Greater Chicago, Research and Development Department.

Pope, Clifford. 1947. *Amphibians and Reptiles of the Chicago Area*. Chicago: Chicago Natural History Museum.

Post, Susan L. 1991. Native Illinois Species and Related Bibliography. In *Our Living Heritage: The Biological Resources of Illinois*, edited by Lawrence M. Page and Michael R. Jeffords. Illinois Natural History Survey Bulletin, vol. 34. Champaign, Ill.: Illinois Natural History Survey.

Potter, Kenneth. 1997. Augmentation of Groundwater Recharge by Purposeful Infiltration of Runoff from Impervious Surfaces. Research proposal from University of Wisconsin—Madison, Department of Civil and Environmental Engineering, Madison.

Poulson, Thomas L. 1999. Autogenic, Allogenic, and Individualistic Mechanisms of Dune Succession at Miller, Indiana. *Natural Areas Journal*, vol. 19, no. 2.

Poulson, Thomas, and Charles McClung. 1999. Anthropogenic Effects on Early Dune Succession at Miller, Indiana. *Natural Areas Journal*, vol. 19, no. 2.

Poulson, Thomas L., and William J. Platt. 1996. Replacement Patterns of Beech and Sugar Maple in Warren Woods, Michigan. *Ecology*, vol. 77, no. 4 (June).

Pratt, Harry E., ed. 1935. John Dean Caton's Reminiscences of Chicago in 1833 and 1834. *Illinois State Historical Society Journal*, vol. 28 (April).

Primack, Richard. 1993. *Essentials of Conservation Biology*. Sunderland, Mass.: Sinauer Assoc.

Pyle, R., et al. 1992. Insect Conservation. In Karner Blue Butterfly: Population and Habitat Viability Assessment Workshop (Briefing Book). WIll.DS and IUCN/SSC Captive Breeding Specialist Group, Zanesville, Ohio.

Quaife, Milo. 1913. *Chicago and the Old Northwest: 1673–1835*. Chicago: University of Chicago Press.

———. ed. 1918. *Pictures of Illinois One Hundred Years Ago*. Chicago: Lakeside Press.

Quinn, Bowden. 1993. Literary Butterfly Makes Room for a Landfill. *Chicago Environment*, vol. 2, no. 4 (Summer).

Racine Historical Society. Notes on Elm and "Huge Cottonwood Landmark Trees"; Based on 1954 Newspaper Clipping. Racine Historical Society, Racine, Wis.

Rand, Austin, and A. S. Rand. 1951. Mammal Bones from Dunes South of Lake Michigan. *American Midland Naturalist*, vol. 46, no. 3 (November).

Randolph, Vance. 1964. *Ozark Magic and Folklore*. New York: Dover Press.

Rathbun, R., et al. 1887. The Fishing Grounds of North American. Sec. 3 of *The Fisheries and Fishery Industries of the United States*, by G. Brown Goode et al. Washington, D.C.: Government Printing Office.

Rawlings, Isaac D. 1994 [1927]. *The Rise and Fall of Disease in Illinois*. Springfield: Illinois Department of Public Health.

Recktenwald, William. n.d. South Side Coyote Hit, Destroyed. *Chicago Tribune*.

Redmer, Michael, and Kenneth S. Mierzwa. 1994. A Review of the Distribution and Zoogeography of the Pickerel Frog, *Rana palustris*, in Northern Illinois. *Bulletin of the Chicago Herpetological Society*, vol. 29, no. 2.

Reed, Earl. 1920. *Tales of a Vanishing River*. New York: John Lane.

Reeling, Viola C. 1928. *Evanston—Its Land and Its People*. Evanston: Fort Dearborn Chapter of Daughters of American Revolution.

Reilly, Edgar M. 1968. *The Audubon Illustrated Handbook of American Birds*. New York: McGraw-Hill Book Co.

Reitman, Valerie. n.d. Scientists Are Abuzz over the Decline of the Gentle Firefly. *Wall Street Journal*.

Reshkin, Mark, et al. 1981. *Basic Ecosystem Studies of the Indiana Dunes National Lakeshore*. Volume One. Report 81-01. Porter: Indiana Dunes National Lakeshore Research Program.

Rice, Elroy L. 1974. *Allelopathy*. New York: Academic Press.

Richmond, C. W., and H. F. Vallette. 1857. *A History of the County of DuPage, Illinois*. Chicago: Scripps, Bross, & Spears.

Ridgway, Frank. 1922. Cicada Swarms Play Symphony along Fox River. *Chicago Tribune*, June 9.

Ridgway, Robert. 1889–95. *The Ornithology of Illinois*. Vols. 1–2. Springfield: Illinois Natural History Survey.

Robertson, Robert. 1971–72. *Kankakee River Basin Stream Survey Report*. Indianapolis: Indiana Department of Natural Resources.

Robbins, Samuel D. 1991. *Wisconsin Birdlife*. Madison: University of Wisconsin Press.

Robinson, Scott K. 1987. Woodland Birds of Illinois. *Field Museum of Natural History Bulletin* (September).

———. 1992. Population Dynamics of Breeding Neotropical Migrants in a Fragmented Illinois Landscape. In *Ecology and Conservation of Neotropical Migrant Landbirds*, ed. J. M. Hagan and D. W. Johnston. Washington, D.C.: Smithsonian Institution Press.

Robinson, Scott, et al. 1993. Management Implications of Cowbird Parasitism on Neotropical Migrant Songbirds. In *Status and Management of Neotropical Migrant Birds*, ed. D. Finch and P. Stangel.. Technical Report RM-229. Fort Collins, Colo.: Rocky Mountain Forest and Range Experiment Station, U.S. Forest Service.

———. 1995. Regional Forest Fragmentation and the Nesting Success of Migratory Birds. *Science*, vol. 267 (March 31).

Rock, Harold W. 1981. *Prairie Propagation Handbook.* Milwaukee: Wehr Nature Center.

Rodkin, Dennis. 1994. Searching for *Thismia*. *Chicago Reader*, vol. 23, no. 51 (September 23).

Roe, Frank G. 1970. *The North American Buffalo.* Toronto: University of Toronto Press.

Rohr, Fred W., and J. E. Potzger. 1951. Forest and Prairie in Three Northwestern Indiana Counties. *Butler University Botanical Studies*, vol. 10.

Rosemann, Kathy. 1991. Deer Relocation Problems Rise. *Lake County Pioneer Press*, February 28.

Ross, Herbert H. 1944. Caddis Flies of Illinois. *Illinois Natural History Bulletin*, vol. 23 (August).

———1963. *The Dunesland Heritage of Illinois.* Circular 49. Urbana: Illinois Natural History Survey.

Rouffa, Albert. n.d. James Woodworth Prairie Preserve: Checklist of Plants by Families. Available at Woodworth Prairie Preserve, Glenview, Ill.

———. 1990. James Woodworth Prairie Preserve. University of Illinois, Chicago. Available at Woodworth Prairie Preserve, Glenview, Ill.

Rubega, Margaret, ed. 1984. Eighty-fourth Christmas Bird Count. *American Birds*, vol. 38, no. 4 (July–August).

Ruedemann, Rudolph, and W. J. Schoonmaker. 1938. Beaver-dams as geologic agents. *Science*, n.s., 88 (December 2): 523–25.

Russell, Emily. 1997. *People and the Land through Time: Linking Ecology and History.* New Haven, Conn.: Yale University Press.

Rutherford, William L. 1972. The Story of Goose Lake Prairie. In *Proceedings of the Second Midwest Prairie Conference*, edited by James Zimmerman. Madison and Parkside: University of Wisconsin.

Ryder, Keith. 1994. Recreation and Changing Environment of the Chain O' Lakes–Fox River, 1875–1992. App. C in *Final Environmental Impact Statement: Fox River–Chain O' Lakes.* Chicago: U.S. Army Corps of Engineers.

———. 1999. Recreation and Changing Environment of the Chain-O'-Lakes and Upper Fox River, 1875–1996. Unpublished report for U.S. Army Corps of Engineers, Chicago.

Salamun, Peter, and Forest Stearns. 1978. *The Vegetation of the Lake Michigan Shoreline in Wisconsin.* Advisory Report no. WIS-SG-78-420. Milwaukee: University of Wisconsin Sea Grant College Program.

Salzberg, Allen. 1994. *Preliminary Report: Live Freshwater Turtle and Tortoise Trade in the United States.* Washington D.C.: Humane Society of the United States and Humane Society International.

Sampson, Homer C. 1921. An Ecological Survey of the Prairie Vegetation of Illinois. *Bulletin of Illinois Natural History Survey*, vol. 13, article 16 (August).

Samson, Fred, and Fritz Knopf. 1994. Prairie Conservation in North America. *BioScience*, vol. 44, no. 6 (June).

Sanborn, Colin. 1922. *Chicago Winter Birds.* Zoology Leaflet no. 2. Chicago: Field Museum of Natural History.

———. 1925. *Mammals of the Chicago Area.* Zoology Leaflet no. 8. Chicago: Field Museum of Natural History.

Sanborn, Colin, and Douglas Tibbitts. 1949. Hoy's Pygmy Shrew in Illinois. *Natural History Miscellanea*, vol. 36.

Sander, Phil. 1995. *Chiwaukee Prairie Memories.* Kenosha: Chiwaukee Prairie Preservation Fund.

Sanders, Edwin F. n.d. My Mushroom Story. Racine Historical Society, Racine, Wis.

Sanitary District of Chicago. 1928. *Engineering Works.* Chicago: Sanitary District of Chicago.

Sargeant, Alan B., et al. 1987. Spatial Relations between Sympatric Coyotes and Red Foxes in North Dakota. *Journal of Wildlife Management*, vol. 51, no. 2.

Sauer, Carl O., et al. 1918. *Starved Rock State Park and Its Environs.* Bulletin no. 6. Chicago: Geographic Society of Chicago and University of Chicago Press.

Savignano, Dolores A. 1994. Benefits to Karner Blue Butterfly Larvae from Association with Ants. In *Karner Blue Butterfly: A Symbol of a Vanishing Landscape*, edited by David Andow et al. Saint Paul: Minnesota Agricultural Experiment Station.

Savitz, J., et al. 1990. The First Records of Three Fish Species in Illinois Waters of Lake Michigan: Longear Sunfish (*Lepomis megalotis peltastes*), Black Crappie (*Pomoxis nigromaculatus*), and the Channel Catfish (*Ictaluris punctatus*). *Transactions of the Illinois State Academy of Science*, vol. 83, nos. 1–2.

———. n.d. Inshore Area Surveys and Species Introduction, 1 July 1988 through 30 June 1990. Final report to Illinois Department of Conservation, Springfield.

Sawyer, Amos. 1946. How the Forest Encroached upon the Prairies of Illinois. *Chicago Naturalist*, vol. 9, no. 1 (May).

Schafer, Joseph. 1927. *Four Wisconsin Counties: Prairie and Forest.* Madison: State Historical Society of Wisconsin.

Schantz, Orpheus M. 1919. Indiana's Unrivaled Sand Dunes. *National Geographic*, vol. 35, no. 5 (May).

Schapper, Ferdinand. 1917. Southern Cook County and History of Blue Island before the Civil War. Vol. 1. Typed manuscript. Chicago Historical Society.

Scharrer, Edward M. 1972. Relict Prairie Flora of Southwestern Michigan. In *Proceedings of the Second Midwest Prairie Conference*, edited by J. Zimmerman. Madison and Parkside: University of Wisconsin.

Scheidenhelm, Mrs. Edward. 1926–29. Early History of Skokie Valley and Its Neighbors. Historical Manuscripts of Chicago Women's Club. Chicago Historical Society.

Schennum, Wayne E. n.d. Master Plan: Cary Prairie Nature Preserve. Prepared for Illinois Nature Preserves Commission, Springfield.

———. 1988. Lyons Prairie and Marsh Nature Preserve: Master Plan. Prepared by the McHenry County Conservation District for the Illinois Nature Preserves Commission, Springfield.

———. 1993. A Proposal to Dedicate Middlefork Savanna, Lake County, as an Illinois Nature Preserve. Illinois Nature Preserve Commission, Springfield.

Schennum, Wayne E., and Steven Byers. 1994. A Proposal to Dedicate Tower Lakes Fen and Wagner Fen as Illinois Nature Preserves. Prepared for the Tower Lakes Improvement Association, Citizens for Conservation, and the Illinois Nature Preserves Commission, Springfield.

Schmid, James A. 1975. *Urban Vegetation: A Review and Chicago Case Study*. Department of Geography, Research Paper no. 161. Chicago: University of Chicago, Department of Geography.

Schmoll, Hazel M. 1919. Ecological Survey of Forests in the Vicinity of Glencoe, Illinois. *Transactions of Illinois State Academy of Science*, vol. 12.

Schorger, A. W. 1941. The Crow and the Raven in Early Wisconsin. *Wilson Bulletin*, vol. 53, no.2 (June).

———. 1944. The Prairie Chicken and Sharp-Tailed Grouse in Early Wisconsin. *Transactions of Wisconsin Academy of Science, Arts and Letters*, vol. 35.

———. 1949a The Black Bear in Early Wisconsin. *Transactions of Wisconsin Academy of Science, Arts and Letters*, vol. 39.

———. 1949b. Squirrels in Early Wisconsin. *Transactions of Wisconsin Academy of Science, Arts and Letters*, vol. 39.

———. 1953. The White-Tailed Deer in Early Wisconsin. *Transactions of Wisconsin Academy of Science, Arts and Letters*, vol. 42.

———. 1954. The Elk in Early Wisconsin. *Transactions of Wisconsin Academy of Science, Arts and Letters*, vol. 43.

———. 1955. *The Passenger Pigeon: Its Natural History and Extinction*. Madison: University of Wisconsin Press.

———. 1964. Trumpeter Swan as a Breeding Bird in Wisconsin, Minnesota, Illinois, and Indiana. *Wilson Bulletin*, vol. 76, no. 4 (December).

———1967–68. Rattlesnakes in Early Wisconsin. *Transactions of Wisconsin Academy of Science, Arts and Letters*, vol. 56.

Schwartz, M. W., ed. 1997. *Conservation in Highly Fragmented Landscapes*. New York: Chapman & Hall.

Schwarz, Raymond. n.d. White-Tailed Deer Management. Clipping from unidentified publication of Forest Preserve District of Cook County. In author's possession.

Schwegman, John. 1983. Illinois Prairie: Then and Now. *Outdoor Highlights* (January 17).

———. 1991. The Vascular Flora of Langham Island, Kankakee County, Illinois. *Erigenia*, vol. 11 (March).

Scott, James L. 1843. *A Journal of a Missionary Tour through Pennsylvania, Ohio, Indiana, Illinois, Iowa, Wiskonsin [sic] and Michigan*. Providence, R.I.: James L. Scott. (N)

Sears, Paul. 1969. *Lands beyond the Forest*. Englewood Cliffs, N.J.: Prentice-Hall.

Seeburger, George. 1975. Fishes of Walworth County. In *Contributions to Ichthyology*, edited by George C. Becker, Henry E. Booke, and Charles A. Long. Reports on the Fauna and Flora of Wisconsin no. 10. Stevens Point: Museum of Natural History.

Seegert, Greg. 1990. The Status of the Pugnose Shiner, *Notropis anogenus*, in Lake County, Illinois. Prepared for Endangered Species Office, Illinois Department of Conservation, Springfield.

SEG Engineers and Consultants. 1989. Kankakee River Master Plan. Prepared for Kankakee River Basin Commission, Highland, Ind.

Seibert, Henri C., and Charles W. Hagen. 1947. Studies on a Population of Snakes in Illinois. *Copeia*, no. 1 (April 20).

Seton, Ernest Thompson. 1929. *Lives of Game Animals*. Vol. 4. New York: Doubleday, Doran, & Co.

Shea, John G. 1852. *Discovery and Exploration of the Mississippi Valley with the Original Narratives of Marquette, Allouez, Membre, Hennepin, and Anastase Douay*. Clinton Hall, N.Y.: Redfield.

Shelford, Victor. 1937. *Animal Communities in Temperate America*. Chicago: University of Chicago Press.

Shelford, Victor, and Glen Winterringer. 1959. The Disappearance of an Area of Prairie in the Cook County, Illinois Forest Preserve District. *American Midland Naturalist*, vol. 61, no. 1.

Sherff, Earl. 1912. The Vegetation of Skokie Marsh, with Special Reference to Subterranean Organs and Their interrelationships. *Botanical Gazette*, vol. 53 (May).

———. 1913. Vegetation of Skokie Marsh. *Bulletin of Illinois State Laboratory of Natural History*, vol. 9, no. 11.

———. 1946. Notes on Certain Plants in the Gray's Manual Range. *Rhodora*, vol. 48, no. 569 (May).

Sheviak, Charles. 1974. *An Introduction to the Ecology of the Illinois Orchidaceae*. Paper 14. Springfield: Illinois State Museum.

Sheviak, Charles, and Alan Haney. 1973. Ecological Interpretations of the Vegetation Patterns of Volo Bog, Lake County, Illinois. *Transactions of the Illinois State Academy of Science*, vol. 66, nos. 1–2.

Short, E. W. 1845. Observations on the Botany of Illinois, More Especially in Reference to the Autumnal Flora of the Prairies. *Western Journal of Medicine and Surgery*, n.s., vol. 3.

Shroufe, Duane L. 1976. Seasonal Migrations of the Greater Sandhill Crane through Northwest Indiana. In *Proceedings of the International Crane Workshop: 3-6 September, 1975, International Crane Foundation, Baraboo, Wisconsin*, edited by James C. Lewis. Stillwater: Oklahoma State University.

Shull, Ernest M. 1987. *The Butterflies of Indiana*. Bloomington and Indianapolis: Indiana Academy of Science.

Siegle, Allen H. 1994. Fourteen Thousand Broad-Winged Hawks in Lake County. *Meadowlark*, vol. 2, no. 2.

Simmons, Lillian M. 1920. Forest Distribution at the Ends of the Lake Chicago Beaches. *Transactions of the Illinois Academy of Science*, vol. 13.

Simon, Chris. 1979. Debut of the Seventeen-Year-Old Cicada. *Natural History* (May).

Simonson, Roy W. 1957. What Soils are. In *Soils: The 1957 Yearbook of Agriculture*, edited by Alfred Stefferud. Washington, D.C.: U.S. Department of Agriculture.

Skelly, Thomas M., and Michael J. Sule. 1983. The Pallid Shiner, *Notropis amnis* Hubbs and Greene, a Fare Illinois Fish. *Transactions of the Illinois State Academy of Science*, vol. 76, nos. 1–2.

Skinner, Luke C., et al. 1994. *Minnesota's Purple Loosestrife Program: History, Findings and Management Recommendations*. Special Pub. no. 145. Saint Paul: Minnesota Department of Natural Resources.

Smith, Bernard M. 1971. Sea Lampreys in the Great Lakes of North America. In *Biology of Lampreys*, edited by M. W. Hardesty and I. C. Potter. Vol. 1. New York: Academic Press.

Smith, Daryl. 1988. Mystique of the Prairie. In *Proceedings of the Tenth North American Prairie Conference*, edited by A. Davis and G. Stanford. Dallas: Native Prairie Association of Texas.

———. 1992. Tallgrass Prairie Settlement: Prelude to the Demise of the Tallgrass Ecosystem. In *Proceedings of the Twelfth North American Prairie Conference*, edited by Daryl Smith and Carol Jacobs. Cedar Falls: University of Northern Iowa.

Smith, Herman D. 1940. *The Des Plaines River, 1673–1940: A Brief Consideration of Its Names and History*. Lake Forest, Ill.: privately printed [by Wisconsin Cuneo Press].

Smith, H. M., and M. Snell. 1891. Review of the Fisheries of the Great Lakes in 1885, with Introduction and Description of Fishing Vessels and Boats. In *Report of the U.S. Commissioner of Fish and Fisheries*. Washington D.C.: Government Printing Office.

Smith, Philip W. 1961. The Amphibians and Reptiles of Illinois. *Illinois Natural History Survey Bulletin*, vol. 28, article 1 (November).

———. 1979. *The Fishes of Illinois*. Urbana: University of Illinois Press.

Smith, Stanford H. 1964. Status of the Deepwater Cisco Population of Lake Michigan. *Transactions of the American Fisheries Society*, vol. 93.

———. 1968. Species Succession and Fishery Exploitation in the Great Lakes. *Journal Fisheries Research Board of Canada*, vol. 25, no. 4.

Snearly, K. E. 1977. Environmental Inventory of the Chain of Lakes and Fox River Region of Illinois. Chain of Lakes–Fox River Commission, Fox Lake, Ill.

Snowy Owl Committee. 1947. Snowy Owl Migration of 1945–46. *Wilson Bulletin*, vol. 59, no. 1 (June).

Solecki, Mary Kay, and John Taft. 1987. Thorn Creek Woods Master Plan. Prepared for the Illinois Nature Preserves Commission and the Thorn Creek Nature Preserve Management Commission, Springfield, Ill.

Soulé, Michael, ed. 1986. *Conservation Biology: The Science of Scarcity*. Sunderland, Mass.: Sinauer Assoc.

Southeast Wisconsin Regional Planning Commission. 1985a. *A Land Use Management Plan for the Chiwaukee Prairie–Carol Beach Area of the Town of Pleasant Prairie*. Waukesha: Southeast Wisconsin Regional Planning Commission.

———. 1985b. *A Water Quality Management Plan for Geneva Lake, Walworth County, Wisconsin*. Waukesha: Southeast Wisconsin Regional Planning Commission.

Sparks, Richard, and William Starrett. 1975, An Electrofishing Survey of the Illinois River, 1959–1974. *Illinois Natural History Survey Bulletin*, vol. 31, article 8 (August).

Spencer, LeAnn. 1993. Ethics of the Butterfly Hunt. *Chicago Tribune*, September 16.

———. 1995. Mushrooms: A Sign of Life for Ecosystem? *Chicago Tribune*, September 19.

Spieth, Herman T. 1941. Taxonomic Studies on the Ephemeroptera. II. The Genus *Hexagenia*. *American Midland Naturalist*, vol. 26, no. 2 (September).

Stannard, Lewis J. 1968. The Thrips, or Thysanoptera, of Illinois. *Illinois Natural History Bulletin*, vol. 29, article 4.

Starrett, William C. 1971. A Survey of the Mussels (Unionacea) of the Illinois River: A Polluted Stream. *Illinois Natural History Bulletin*, vol. 30, article 5 (February).

State of Indiana, U.S. Department of Agriculture, and U.S. Department of Interior. 1976. *Kankakee River Basin Indiana: Report on the Water and Related Land Resources*. Washington, D.C.: U.S. Soil Conservation Service.

Steele, Emma. 1841. *A Summer Journey in the West*. New York: John Taylor & Co. (CHS)

Stewart, Donald, et al. 1981. Forage Fish and Salmonid Predators in Lake Michigan. *Transactions of the American Fisheries Society.*

Stille, W. T. 1952. The Nocturnal Amphibian Fauna of the Southern Lake Michigan Beach. *Ecology*, vol. 33, no. 2 (April).

Stoddard, Herbert. 1920. Chicago Area. *Audubon Bulletin* (Spring).

Stolzenburg, William. 1992. The Mussels' Message. *Nature Conservancy* (November–December).

Stone, Fanny S., ed. 1916. *Racine and Racine County Wisconsin.* Vol. 1. Chicago: S. J. Clark Publishing Co.

Stout, A. B. 1914. A Biological and Statistical Analysis of the Vegetation of a Typical Wild Hay Meadow. *Transactions of the Wisconsin Academy of Science, Arts, and Letters*, vol. 17.

Stoynoff, Nick. 1993. A Quantitative Analysis of the Vegetation of Bluff Spring Fen Nature Preserve. *Transactions of the Illinois State Academy of Science*, vol. 86, nos. 3–4.

Stoynoff, Nick A., and W. J. Hess. 1986. Bluff City Fen: Communities, Vegetation History, and Management. *Transactions of the Illinois State Academy of Science*, vol. 79, nos. 1–2.

Stuckey, Ronald, and Douglas Salamon. 1987. *Typha angustifolia* in North America: A Foreigner Masquerading as a Native. *Ohio Journal of Science*, vol. 87, no. 4.

Sule, Michael J. and Thomas M. Skelly. 1985. The Life History of the Shorthead Redhorse, *Moxostoma macrolepidotum*, in the Kankakee River Drainage, Illinois. *Illinois Natural History Survey Biological Notes*, no. 123.

Sullivan, Jerry. 1986. Lake Renwick: Unlikely Haven for the Endangered. *Field Museum of Natural History Bulletin*, vol. 57, no. 5 (May).

Suloway, Liane. 1981. The Unionid (Mollusca: Bivalvia) Fauna of the Kankakee River in Illinois. *American Midland Naturalist*, vol. 105, no. 2 (April).

Suter, Walter R., and Orlando Park. 1962. *Some Relatively Undisturbed Areas in the Chicago Region: A Microcoleopterological Ordination of Natural Communities.* Chicago: Chicago Academy of Sciences.

Swengel, Anne B. 1993a. Observations of Karner Blues and the Barrens Complex in Wisconsin, 1987–1993. Report to National Biological Survey and U.S. Fish and Wildlife Service, Baraboo, Wis.

———. 1993b. Research on the Community of Tallgrass Prairie Butterflies. Report to National Biological Survey, Nature Conservancy, and U.S. Fish and Wildlife Service.

Swenson, John. 1990. Chicagou/Chicago: The Herbal Origins of a Place Name. *The Herbalist.*

Swink, Floyd. 1966. Orchids of the Indiana Dune Region. *American Orchid Society Bulletin* (September).

———. 1986. Spring Wildflowers of the Chicago Area. *Field Museum of Natural History Bulletin*, vol. 57, no. 4 (April).

Swink, Floyd, and Gerould Wilhelm. 1979. *Plants of the Chicago Region.* 3d ed. Lisle, Ill.: Morton Arboretum.

———. 1994. *Plants of the Chicago Region.* 4th ed. Indianapolis: Indiana Academy of Sciences.

Taft, John, and Mary Kay Solecki. 1990. Vascular Flora of the Wetland and Prairie Communities of Gavin Bog and Prairie Nature Preserve, Lake County, Illinois. *Rhodora*, vol. 92, no. 871.

Talbot, Mary. 1934. Distribution of Ant Species in the Chicago Region with Reference to Ecological Factors and Physiological Toleration. *Ecology*, vol. 15, no. 4 (October).

Taylor, Christopher A., and Michael Redmer. 1995. Status and Distribution of the Rusty Crayfish, Orconectes rusticus, in Illinois. Center for Biodiversity Technical Report no. 15.
Illinois Natural History Survey, Champaign.

Taylor, J. Wolford, ed. 1986. *The Kettle Moraine State Forest Turns Gold: A 50 Year Celebration of
the Great Glacier.* Madison: Wisconsin Department of Natural Resources.

Teale, Edwin Way. 1960. *Journey into Summer.* New York: Dodd, Mead, & Co.

Terborgh, John. 1992. Why American Songbirds Are Vanishing. *Scientific American,* vol. 266,
no. 5 (May).

Terry, Davida. 1989. Letter. *Chicago Tribune,* September 10.

Thacker, Henry. 1867. Muskrat Hunting. In *The Trappers Guide* by Sewell Newhouse. Walling-
ford, Conn.: Oneida Community.

Thompson, David H. 1928. The "Knothead" Carp of the Illinois River. *Illinois Natural History
Survey Bulletin,* vol. 17, article 8.

Thompson, John D. 1994. Movements and Survival of Raccoons Translocated from the Suburban Environment. Quarterly Report: September 1, 1994–November 30, 1994, Max
McGraw Wildlife Foundation, Dundee, Ill.

Thompson, Paul W. 1972. The Preservation of Prairie Stands in Michigan. In *Proceedings of the
Second Midwest Prairie Conference,* edited by J. Zimmerman. Madison and Parkside: University of Wisconsin.

Thorp, James H., and Alan P. Covich. 2001. *Ecology and Classification of North American Freshwater Invertebrates.* 2d ed. San Diego, Calif.: Academic Press.

Thwaites, Reuben G. ed. 1900. *The Jesuit Relations and Allied Documents.* 73 vols. Cleveland:
Burrows Brothers.

Tichacek, Gregg, and Harry Wight. 1972. *Lake County Surface Water Resources.* Springfield: Illinois Department of Conservation, Division of Fisheries.

Tierra, Michael. 1983. *The Way of Herbs.* New York: Pocket Books.

Timm, Robert M. 1989. Migration and Molt Patterns of Red Bats, *Lasiurus borealis* (Chiroptera:
Vespertilionidae) in Illinois. *Bulletin of the Chicago Academy of Sciences,* vol. 14, no. 3.

Tinkham, R. Letters. Chicago Historical Society.

Todd, Thomas N. 1985. Status of Great Lakes Coregonines. Ann Arbor, Mich.: National Fisheries Research Center- Great Lakes.

Todd, Thomas N., and Gerald R. Smith. 1992. A Review of Differentiation in Great Lakes Ciscoes. *Polish Archives of Hydrobiology,* vol. 34, nos. 3–4.

Transeau, Edgar N. 1935. The Prairie Peninsula. *Ecology,* vol. 16, no. 3.

Trotter, Isabella. 1859. *First Impressions of the New World on Two Travellers from the Old in the Autumn of 1858.* London: Longmans. (CHS)

Turnbull, Olive. 1950. Notes on Passenger Pigeons and Prairie Chickens Prior to 1865. Racine
Historical Society, Racine, Wis.

U.S. Army Corps of Engineers. 1996. *Upper Des Plaines River, Illinois, Flood Damage Reduction
Study Feasibility Report and Environmental Impact Statement, Draft.* Chicago: Chicago District, North Central Division.

U.S. Environmental Protection Agency. 1992. *Lake Michigan Lakewide Management Plan: Draft.*
Chicago: U.S. Environmental Protection Agency, Region V.

———. 1993. The Des Plaines River Wetlands Project. *Constructed Wetlands for Wastewater*

Treatment and Wildlife Habitat: 17 Case Studies. EPA832-R-93-005. Chicago: U.S. Environmental Protection Agency.

U.S. Fish and Wildlife Service. 1992a. Determination of Endangered Status for Mitchell's Satyr Butterfly. *Federal Register.* Rules and Regulations, vol. 57, no. 98 (May 20).

———. 1992b. *Pitcher's Thistle (Cirsium pitcheri) Recovery Plan.* Twin Cities, Minn.: U.S. Fish and Wildlife Service.

———. 1993. Proposed Rule to Reclassify the Plant *Isotria medeoloides* (Small Whorled Pogonia) from Endangered to Threatened. *Federal Register.* Rules and Regulations, vol. 58, no. 200 (October 19).

———. 1996. Recovery Plan for Mitchell's Satyr Butterfly (*Neonympha mitchellii mitchellii* French). Technical/Agency Draft. U.S. Fish and Wildlife Service, Fort Snelling, Minn.

———. 1999. *Hine's Emerald Dragonfly (Somatochlora hineana) Draft Recovery Plan.* Technical/Agency Draft. Fort Snelling, Minn.

Van Denack, Julia. 1961. An Ecological Analysis of the Sand Dune Complex in Point Beach State Forest, Two Rivers, Wisconsin. *Botanical Gazette*, vol. 122, no. 3.

Vestal, Arthur G. 1914. A Black-Soil Prairie Station in Northeastern Illinois. *Bulletin of the Torrey Botanical Club*, vol. 41, no. 7 (July).

Vick, Timothy. 1993. Water, Water. *Chicago Daily Southtown Economist*, special ed., Sunday magazine, April 25.

Vinikour, William S., and Richard V. Anderson. 1984. Macroinvertebrates and Fishes of Trout Park Nature Preserve, Elgin, Illinois. *Transactions of Illinois Academy of Science*, vol. 77, nos. 1–2.

Vogt, Richard C. 1981. *Natural History of Amphibians and Reptiles in Wisconsin.* Milwaukee: Milwaukee Public Museum.

Voigt, Dennis R., and Barry D. Earle. 1983. Avoidance of Coyotes by Red Fox Families. *Journal of Wildlife Management*, vol. 47, no. 3.

Walden, Howard. 1964. *Familiar Freshwater Fishes of America.* New York: Harper.

Walkinshaw, Lawrence H. 1949. The Sandhill Cranes. *Cranbrook Institute of Science Bulletin*, no. 29.

Warren, Paul C., and Alexander Grant Ruthven. 1919. Edward Kirk Warren, April 7th 1847–January 16th, 1919. *The Acorn* 28, no. 10 (February 6).

Waterman, Warren G. 1919. A Preliminary Report on the North Two Tiers of Sections in Niles Township, Cook County, Illinois. *Transactions of Illinois Academy of Science*, vol. 12.

———. 1920. Distribution of Oaks on the Lake Chicago Bars in Evanston and New Trier Townships. *Transactions of Illinois Academy of Science*, vol. 13.

———. 1921. Preliminary Report on the Bogs of Northern Illinois. *Transactions of the Illinois State Academy of Science*, vol. 14.

———. 1923. Bogs of Northern Illinois. *Transactions of the Illinois State Academy of Science*, vol. 16.

———. 1926. Ecological Problems from the Sphagnum Bogs of Northern Illinois. *Ecology*, vol. 7, no. 3 (July).

Watershed Management Institute. 1997. *Institutional Aspects of Urban Runoff Management: A Guide for Program Development and Implementation.* Washington D.C.: Watershed Management Institute.

Watkin, Edward. 1852. *Trip to the United States and Canada*. London: Smith & Sons. (N)

Watts, May T. 1975. *Reading the Landscape of America*. New York: Macmillan.

Weaver, John. 1954. *North American Prairie*. Lincoln, Nebr.: Johnson Press.

Weaver, John E., and T. J. Fitzpatrick. 1934. The Prairie. *Ecological Monographs*, vol. 4. Reprinted, Aurora: Prairie-Plains Resource Institute of Nebraska, 1980.

Weeks, W. C. 1931. *Report from the Chief of Engineers on the Kankakee River, Ill. and Ind., Covering Navigation, Flood Control, Power Development, and Irrigation*. 71st Cong., 3d sess., H. Doc. 784.

Weir, R. D. 1976. *Annotated Bibliography of Bird Kills at Man-Made Obstacles: A Review of the State of the Art and Solutions*. Ottawa: Environment Canada—Canadian Wildlife Service.

Weller, Milton W. 1981. *Freshwater Marshes: Ecology and Wildlife Management*. Minneapolis: University of Minnesota Press.

Wells, James R., and Paul W. Thompson. 1982. Plant Communities of the Sand Dunes Region of Berrien County, Michigan. *Michigan Botanist*, vol. 21.

Wells, LaRue. 1968. Seasonal Depth Distribution of Fish in Southeastern Lake Michigan. *Fishery Bulletin*, vol. 67, no. 1.

———. 1970. Effects of Alewife Predation on Zooplankton Populations. *Limnology and Oceanography*, vol. 15.

Wells, LaRue, and Alberton L. McLain. 1973. *Lake Michigan: Man's Effects on Native Fish Stocks and Other Biota*. Technical Report 20. Ann Arbor, Mich.: Great Lakes Fishery Commission.

Wells, R. W. 1818. On the Origin of the Prairies. *American Journal of Science*, vol. 1, no. 4.

Werich, J. Lorenzo. 1920. *Pioneer Hunters of the Kankakee*. [Logansport, Ind.: Chronicle Printing Co.].

Westemeir, Ronald L. 1985. The History of Prairie Chickens and Their Management in Illinois. In *Selected Papers in Illinois History*, edited by R. W. McCluggage. Fourth Annual Illinois History Symposium. Springfield: Illinois State Historical Society.

Whitaker, John O., et al. 1994. *Mammals of Indiana Dunes National Lakeshore*. Scientific Monograph NPS/NRInd.DU/NRSM-94/24. Denver: U.S. Department of Interior, National Park Service.

Whitaker, John O., and Louis R. Douglas. 1986. Bat Rabies in Indiana. *Transactions of the Indiana Academy of Science*, vol. 95.

Whitaker, John O., and James R. Gammon. 1988. *Endangered and Threatened Vertebrate Animals of Indiana: Their Distribution and Abundance*. Monograph no. 5. Indianapolis: Indiana Academy of Science.

White, JoAnn, et al. 1979. Faulty Eclosion in Crowded Suburban Periodical Cicadas: Populations out of Control. *Ecology*, vol. 60, no. 2 (April).

White, John, and Michael Madany. 1978. *Illinois Natural Areas Inventory Technical Report*. Vol. 1, *Survey Methods and Results*. Urbana: Illinois Department of Conservation, Illinois Natural Areas Inventory.

Whitford, Philip B. 1958. A Study of Prairie Remnants in Southeastern Wisconsin. *Ecology*, vol. 39, no. 4 (October).

Wiedenmann, Rob, and Dave Voegtlin. 1995. Memorandum to State and County Land Managers Regarding 1995 Releases of *Galerucella* and *Hylobius*. Illinois Natural History Survey, Champaign.

Wiggers, Raymond. 1997. *Geology Underfoot in Illinois.* Missoula, Mt.: Mountain Press Publishing Co.

———. 1999. Mushrooms: Exploring Chicagoland's Middle Kingdom. *Chicago Wilderness,* vol. 3, no. 1 (fall).

Wilcove, David. 1990. Empty Skies. *Nature Conservancy Magazine* (January–February).

Wilhelm, Gerould. 1978. *Kane County Natural Area Survey.* Geneva: Kane County Urban Development Division.

———. 1987. The Arboretum's East Woods: Are They Forever? *Morton Arboretum Quarterly,* vol. 23, no. 4 (winter): 54–62.

———. 1990. *Special Vegetation of the Indiana Dunes National Lakeshore.* Porter, Ind.: Indiana Dunes National Lakeshore, Research Division.

———. 1991a. Implications of Changes in Floristic Composition of the Morton Arboretum's East Woods. In *Proceedings of Oak Woods Management Workshop,* edited by George V. Burger, John E. Ebinger, and Gerould S. Wilhelm. Charleston, Ill.: Eastern Illinois University.

———. 1991b. Vascular Vegetation of Lake County, Illinois, with Special Reference to Its Use in Wetland Mitigation. No other data.

———. 1993. *Lichens of the Chicago Region.* Lisle, Ill.: Morton Arboretum.

Wilhelm, Gerould, and Wayne Lampa. 1987. Macrolichens of DuPage County, Illinois. *Transactions of the Illinois Academy of Sciences,* vol. 80, nos. 1–2.

Wilhelm, Gerould, and Linda Masters. 1994. Floristic Quality Assessment and Application Computer Programs for the 22-County Chicago Region. Lisle, Ill.: Morton Arboretum.

Wille, Lois. 1972. *Forever Open, Clear and Free: The Struggle for Chicago's Lakefront.* Chicago: Henry Regnery Co.

Williams, Andrew. 1993. Letter. *Natural Areas Journal,* vol. 13, no. 2.

———. 1995. Letter dated July 1. *Natural Areas Journal,* vol. 15.

Williams, C. B. 1930. *The Migration of Butterflies.* Edinburgh and London: Oliver & Boyd.

Williams, James D., et al. 1992. Conservation Status of Freshwater Mussels of the United States and Canada. *Fisheries,* vol. 18, no. 9 (September).

Willman, H. B. 1971. *Summary of the Geology of the Chicago Area.* Circular 460. Urbana: Illinois State Geological Survey.

Willman, H. B., and John C. Frye. 1970. Pleistocene Stratigraphy of Illinois. *Illinois State Geological Survey Bulletin,* vol. 94.

Wilson, Charles B., and H. Walton Clark. 1912. *The Mussel Fauna of the Kankakee Basin.* U.S. Bureau of Fisheries Document 758. Washington, D.C.: Government Printing Office.

Wilson, Don E., and Sue Ruff, eds. 1999. *The Smithsonian Book of North American Mammals.* Washington D.C.: Smithsonian Institution Press.

Winkler, E. M., and A. C. Van Besien. 1963. Bear Cave, a Tufa Cave in Glacial Drift near Buchanan, Michigan. *National Speliological Society Bulletin,* vol. 25.

Wisconsin Department of Natural Resources. 1969. Lake Geneva. Lake Use Report no. FX-1. Prepared for Southeastern Wisconsin Regional Planning Commission. Wisconsin Department of Natural Resources, Madison.

———. 1987. *Environmental Impact Statement on the Acquisition, Management, and Development of the Lulu Lake State Natural Area, Walworth County, Wisconsin.* Madison: Wisconsin Department of Natural Resources.

Witham, James H., et al. 1990. White-Tailed Deer Habitat Change in Metropolitan Northeastern Illinois. Paper in my possession prior to publication.

Witham, James H., and Jon M. Jones. 1992. Biology, Ecology, and Management of Deer in the
Chicago Metropolitan Area. Project no. W-87-R. Final report submitted to Illinois Department of Conservation, Division of Wildlife Resources, Champaign.

Wolff, Robert J. 1990. Spiders in Prairies: What Do We Know? In *Proceedings of the Ninth
Northern Illinois Prairie Workshop.* Chicago: Northeastern Illinois University.

Wood, Norman A. 1922. Notes on the Mammals of Berrien County, Michigan. *Occasional Papers of the Museum of Zoology,* no. 124 (July).

Woodruff, Frank. 1907. Birds of the Chicago Area. *Bulletin of the Natural History Survey,* no. 6.

Woodruff, George, et al. 1878. *The History of Will County, Illinois.* Chicago: Le Baron & Co.
(CHS)

Woods, Nicholas A. 1861. *Prince of Wales in Canada and the United States.* London: Bradbury &
Evans. (N)

Work, Ruth. 1933. Field Notes: Barrington Bird Club. *Audubon Bulletin,* no. 23.

Wright, Bernard A. 1941. Habit and Habitat Studies of the Massasauga Rattlesnake (*Sistrurus
catenatus catenatus* Raf.) in Northeastern Illinois. *American Midland Naturalist,* vol.25,
no. 3.

Yeatter, Ralph E. 1943. The Prairie Chicken in Illinois. *Illinois Natural History Survey Bulletin,*
vol. 22 (May).

———. 1944. Responses to Statewide County Game and Fur Animal Survey. Housed at Illinois
Natural History Survey, Champaign.

Yosef, Reuven. 1994. Evaluation of the Global Decline in the True Shrikes (Family Laniidae).
Auk, vol. 111, no. 1 (January).

Yosef, Reuven, and Thomas C. Grubb. 1994. Resource Dependence and Territory Size in Loggerhead Shrikes (*Lanius ludovicianus*). *Auk,* vol. 111, no. 2 (April).

Young, Daniel. 1995. Letter to Editor. *Natural Areas Journal,* July 20.

Zimmermann, Janet. 1949. Rare Birds Visit Chicago Area. *The Audubon Bulletin* (September).

References to figures are printed in boldface type; those to tables in italic.

Blatchley, Willis S., 291

blazing stars, 22, 36, 57, 251, 279, 465

Blenz, David, 56

bloater cisco, 175–76

bloodroot, 78, 262

blowflies, 307

blowout, 251

blue aster, 48

blue beech, 88

blue-eyed grass, 250–51, 278

blue-eyed Marys, 91

blue flag iris, 122–23, 284

bluegill, 193, 199, 210

bluegrass, 45, 47, 61, 130

blue-green algae, 144, 208

blue-hearts, 250

Blue Island, 9

blue jays, 248, 377, 392

blue racers, 327

blue-spotted salamander, 337, 338, 339

blue-stemmed goldenrod, 253

blue violet, 89

blue-wing teals, 233

bluffs and ravines, 287–89, **289**

    plants of, 288

Bluff Spring Fen, 135–36, **136**

bluntnose minnow, 210

bobcat, 416, 419

bobolink, 389

bobwhite, 12

Boepple, John, 202–3

Bogardus, Adam, 350

bog arrow grass, 254

bog bladderwort, 259

bog lobelia, 136

bogs, 118, 129–35, 257

    and carnivorous plants, 132–33

    formation of, 129

    and low shrubs, 131

    and mat, 131–32

    and Pinhook Bog, 259

    plant communities around, 129–32

    and short-shrub zone, 131, 135

    and tall-shrub bog, 130–31, 135

    and tamaracks, 131

    and Volo Bog, 129–34

    See also fens

"Bogus Island," 115–16, 451

bog valerian, 136

bog willow, 131

Bohemian waxwings, 412

boreal blueberry, 244

Bowen, Otis, 58

bowfins, 166, 213–14, 220

Bowles, Marlin, 28, 66, 68, 76, 101

box elder, 94

box huckleberry, 135, 253–54

box turtles, 324

Brack, Virgil, 428

bracken fern, 72

bracted orchid, 36

Braidwood Dune and Savanna Nature Preserve, 34–35

Braidwood Nuclear Power Plant, 193

Brandon, Ron, 340

brassy minnow, 192

Braun, E. Lucy, 75

Bremer, Fredrika, 44

Brennan, George, 349, 418

Brinker, David, 399

bristly blackberry, 70

bristly green brier, 106

broad-leaved cattail, 123, 130, 132

broad-wing dragonfly, 298

broad-winged hawk, 391–92, 396–97

Brock, Ken, 376, 396, 400

Brom, James, 421, **422**

brook amphipod, 186

Brothers, Manley, 274–75

Brouillard, Dan, 457

Brown, Edward, 161

Brown, Ralph, 69

brown fox sedge, 120

brown-headed cowbird, 378, 509–10n. 26

brown thrashers, 378

Bryant, William Cullen, 42

bryophyte (*Marchantia polymorpha*), 120

buckbean, 132, 134

buckthorn, 61, 70, 83, 104, 336, 485n. 80

Buell, Dorothy, 266